Process
of Aging

Process of Aging

Social and Psychological Perspectives
Volume 1

Richard H. Williams,
Clark Tibbits,
Wilma Donohue, editors

AldineTransaction
A Division of Transaction Publishers
New Brunswick (U.S.A.) and London (U.K.)

First paperback printing 2009
Copyright © 1963 by Transaction Publishers, New Brunswick, NJ.

This book is printed on acid-free paper that meets the American National Standard for Permanence of Paper for Printed Library Materials.

Library of Congress Catalog Number: 2008027926
ISBN: 978-0-202-36303-5
Printed in the United States of America

Library of Congress Cataloging-in-Publication Data

Process of aging : social and psychological perspectives / Richard H. Williams, Clark Tibbits, and Wilma Donohue.
    p. cm.
  Reprint of the 1963 ed. published by Atherton Press, New York, in series: The Atherton Press behavioral science series.
  Previous ed. entered under Richard H. Williams.
  Includes bibliographical references and index.
  ISBN 978-0-202-36303-5 (alk. paper)
    1. Older people. 2. Aging. 3. Older people--Psychology. I. Williams, Richard Hays, 1912- II. Tibbitts, Clark, 1903- III. Donahue, Wilma T. (Wilma Thompson), 1900-

HQ1061.P75 2008
305.26--dc22

2008027926

PREFACE

Processes of Aging: Social and Psychological Perspectives is based on studies prepared for an international seminar on the psychological and social aspects of aging in relation to mental health. The seminar was convened to give scientists from North America, Western Europe, and other countries an opportunity to explore together the concepts, methodological problems, and conclusions of their researches in the rapidly growing field of gerontology. Much editorial work has been done in an attempt to present this material in sequential and systematic fashion. Original work of sixty-six research workers from twelve countries is represented in these volumes. They are an inventory of the principal fields of gerontological research, except in the purely biological and medical areas, in the countries where most of the work is currently being done.

Human aging, in its many ramifications, is becoming one of the major areas of research interest among an increasing number of students in the biological, behavioral, and social sciences. Although the phenomena of aging were largely overlooked as subject matter for research during the early stages in the development of all the basic sciences, it was inevitable that students would eventually become curious about the final processes of maturation. What are the causes of decline in the organism? What are the characteristics of psychological capacities, personality, and social adjustment over the life span? What influences do older people exert in creating social norms and expectations? What societal adjustments are being adapted to the increasing number of old people?

Events of recent years have hastened the need for social action on behalf of older people and, consequently, the need for scientific knowledge about their characteristics, circumstances, and requirements. The first half of the century witnessed a great increase in the number and proportion of older people in all highly developed societies of the world and in almost all other countries. Simultaneously, economic changes, stemming largely from the exponential growth in the use of inanimate energy and machines in the production of commodities and services, and changes in culture patterns have altered the status and roles of older people and created many new personal and social problems.

Thus, over the past twenty or more years, all Western nations have shown increased concern over the changes in the age structure of their populations and in the dislocations, problems, and accommodations associated therewith. All affected countries have developed or are developing programs of income maintenance, medical facilities and services, institutional care and housing, and social services designed to enable older people to live as healthy, secure, and satisfied members of society. At the same time, knowledge about the processes of aging, about older people and their needs, and about the impact of older people on social institutions and practices has become a necessity. Research has, in fact, been initiated in virtually every country of the Western world and in the more developed countries elsewhere. The scientific literature on aging has grown enormously, particularly over the past ten to fifteen years. There is increasing evidence of the willingness of public agencies to support research and teaching in gerontology in order to increase understanding of the processes of aging and to provide a firm basis for social planning. It was against this background that the seminar and the two meetings that preceded it took place.

The seminar was a joint undertaking of the Social Research Committee of the International Association of Gerontology, represented by Drs. E.W. Burgess and Clark Tibbitts; of the Professional Services Branch of the National Institute of Mental Health, represented by Dr. Richard H. Williams; and of the Division of Gerontology of The University of Michigan, represented by Dr. Wilma Donahue. The seminar had its origin in a meeting of social and psychological scientists held in Sheffield, England, under the auspices of the Nuffield Foundation, just prior to the Third International Congress of Gerontology (1954). The Foundation's guess that researchers would have common interests was borne out in the enthusiastic response to the conference and in the subsequent establishment of the Social Research Committee with European and American branches in the framework of the International Association of Gerontology. The first seminar organized by the committee took place in Merano, Italy, in 1957.

The first two seminars produced positive results in the form of international acquaintances which led to discussion of mutual research interests, international visits and exchanges, and development of parallel or cross-national studies. The seminar for which the materials in the present volumes were prepared was an extension of the enthusiasm engendered at the first two meetings. The National Institute of Mental Health became involved because it had been cooperating in and supporting several important American studies in some of the areas proposed for consideration in the third seminar. The Professional Services Branch of the National Institute of Mental Health collaborated with the Division of Gerontology at The University of Michigan because of the Division's long experience in organizing conferences, symposia, and seminars on aging and because of its chairman's knowledge of research and research personnel in Europe as well as in her own country.

The National Institute of Mental Health financial support (Grant MHO1962-02) made it possible to bring four Europeans to the United States almost a year before the seminar in order to plan with the American branch of the Social Research Committee. From Europe came Henning Friis of Denmark, Martin Roth and Alan T. Welford of England, and Jean-René Tréanton of France; from the United States the planners were E. Everett Ashley, III, Walter M. Beattie, Jr., James E. Birren, Leonard Z. Breen, Ernest W. Burgess, Ewald W. Busse, Wilbur J. Cohen, Wilma Donahue, Margaret S. Gordon, Robert J.Havighurst, Robert W. Kleemeier, Bernice L. Neugarten, Harold L. Orbach, Klaus F. Riegel, Leo W. Simmons, Alexander Simon, Clark

Tibbitts, Richard H. Williams, Seymour L. Wolfbein, and Marian
Radke Yarrow. Maria Pfister attended as a representative of the World
Health Organization.

The planning group selected four general topics for the discussions and appointed leaders for each one, as follows: psychological
capacities, Alan T. Welford and James E. Birren; personality, life
styles, and social roles, Jean-René Tréanton and Robert J. Havighurst;
mental health and rehabilitation, Martin Roth and Wilma Donahue;
and income, employment, and retirement, Henning Friis and Seymour
L. Wolfbein. The seminar was held in Berkeley, California, over a
five-day period during August, 1960. The National Institute of Mental
Health support, along with National Institute of Health travel grants
for the Congress itself, made it possible to defray the travel and sub-
sistence costs of the Europeans. These, with sixty-three American and
Canadian contributors and discussants, brought the number of participants to ninety.

Invited papers were prepared in advance of the seminar and
made available to all participants. Seminar sessions were conducted as
four simultaneous roundtables on specific research problems in each of
the areas mentioned above. A final general session gave rise to repeated
expressions of the continuing need for interdisciplinary conferences of
an international character.

Alan T. Welford, James E. Birren, Marian Radke Yarrow,
and Harold L. Orbach participated in the early phases of the editorial
work. Final editorial responsibility was taken by Richard H. Williams
for Volume I, Parts I and II, and Volume II, Part V; by Wilma
Donahue for Volume I, Part III, and Volume II, Part VI; and by Clark
Tibbitts for Volume II, Part VII. In Volume I, the focus is largely on
individual aging processes. Volume II is concerned largely with social
factors and influences on the individual and with the effects of aging
on family and social relationships and the larger institutions and norms
of society.

Processes of Aging: Social and Psychological Perspectives
will be of interest to research workers, teachers, and advanced students
concerned with the psychological, psychiatric, psychosocial, and socioeconomic aspects of aging. Many of the theoretical and analytical discussions and the specific studies offer guidance for top-level planners
and administrators in public agencies and voluntary organizations.

—Richard H. Williams
—Clark Tibbitts
—Wilma Donahue

CONTENTS

Volume I

CONTRIBUTORS

Volume I

John E. Anderson, professor emeritus of psychology, University of Minnesota, Minneapolis

Seymour Axelrod, assistant professor of medical psychology, Duke University Medical Center, Durham, North Carolina

Louise S. Barker, University of Kansas Midwest Psychological Field Station, Oskaloosa, Kansas

Roger G. Barker, professor of psychology, University of Kansas, Lawrence, Kansas

James E. Birren, chief, Section on Aging, National Institute of Mental Health, Bethesda, Maryland

François Bourlière, M.D., professor, Faculty of Medicine, University of Paris; director, Claude-Bernard Center of Gerontology, Paris

Dennis B. Bromley, lecturer, Department of Psychology, University of Liverpool, England

Ewald W. Busse, M.D., director, Regional Center for the Study of Aging; chairman, Department of Psychiatry, Duke University Medical Center, Durham, North Carolina

Sheila M. Chown, psychologist, Medical Research Council, Unit for Research on Occupational Aspects of Ageing, University of Liverpool, England

Wilma Donahue, chairman, Division of Gerontology, Institute for Human Adjustment, and lecturer in psychology, The University of Michigan, Ann Arbor

Stephen Griew, research associate, Department of Psychology, University of Bristol, England

Ward C. Halstead, director of medical psychology, Department of Medicine, Medical School, The University of Chicago, Illinois

Robert J. Havighurst, professor of education, The University of Chicago, Illinois

Alastair Heron, deputy director, Unit for Research on Occupational Aspects of Ageing, University of Liverpool, England

James Inglis, assistant professor of clinical psychology, Department of Psychiatry, Queen's College, Kingston, Ontario, Canada

Werner Janzarik, M.D., lecturer in psychiatry and neurology; chief physician, Neurology Clinic, University of Mainz, Germany

D.W.K. Kay, M.D., Department of Psychological Medicine, King's College Medical School, Newcastle upon Tyne, England

Bertha Klien, M.D., Section of Ophthalmology, Department of Surgery, Medical School, The University of Chicago, Illinois

Martin Lakin, assistant professor of psychology, Departments of Psychology and Psychiatry, Duke University, Durham, North Carolina

Morton A. Lieberman, psychologist, Department of Psychiatry, The University of Chicago, Illinois

Pat Merryman, Medical School, The University of Chicago, Illinois

Donald F. Morrison, Section on Biometrics, National Institute of Mental Health, Bethesda, Maryland

Christian Muller, Psychiatric Clinic, University of Zurich, Switzerland

Miron W. Neal (deceased), psychologist, Geriatric Research Project, Langley Porter Neuropsychiatric Institute, San Francisco, California

Bernice L. Neugarten, associate professor, Committee on Human Development, The University of Chicago, Illinois

Suzanne Pacaud, research associate, National Center of Scientific Research; assistant director, School of Advanced Studies, Sorbonne, Paris

Felix Post, M.D., physician, The Maudsley Hospital, London

Klaus F. Riegel, assistant professor of psychology, The University of Michigan, Ann Arbor

Martin Roth, M.D., professor of psychological medicine, King's College Medical School, University of Durham, Newcastle upon Tyne, England

Peter Sainsbury, Medical Research Council, Clinical Psychiatry Research Unit, Graylingwell Hospital, Chichester, England

Barry M. Shmavonian, chief psychologist, Psychological Laboratory, Duke University, Durham, North Carolina

Alexander Simon, M.D., medical director, Langley Porter Neuropsychiatric Institute, San Francisco, California

Jean-René Tréanton, research associate, Faculty of Letters and Humane Sciences, University of Lille, France

Alan T. Welford, lecturer in experimental psychology, Cambridge University; fellow, St. John's College, Cambridge, England

Richard H. Williams, chief, Professional Services Branch, National Institute of Mental Health, Bethesda, Maryland

Marian Radke Yarrow, chief, Section on Social Development and Family Studies, National Institute of Mental Health, Bethesda, Maryland

PROCESSES

OF AGING

VOLUME I

PART ONE

Psychological
Capacities

INTRODUCTION

JAMES E. BIRREN

As an adult moves forward in age, there are changes in his thinking, in the way he feels about himself and the world, and in the way he behaves in relation to others. There are also simultaneous physiological changes. These changes may not all be related, and yet most people who have worked in psychology have the clear impression that, to some unknown extent, aging should be considered as the joint product of physiological, psychological, and social factors.

The intention of the seminar on psychological capacity was to follow the relations among these factors in a series of papers and discussions embracing all three. Such a seminar was thought to be especially suitable as an activity of the Gerontological Association, an organization which includes representatives of many sciences and professions.

The planning committee—J.E. Birren, E.W. Busse, A.T. Welford, and Marian R. Yarrow—regarded the seminar as both an inductive and a deductive exercise aimed, on one hand, at making inferences about the likely consequences of physiological factors for health and psychological characteristics and, through these, for social behavior; and attempting, on the other hand, to analyze the factors of environment and individual performance and capacity which affect behavior during later life. The plan was realized by having the seminar participants discuss current research findings and from them to outline likely relationships with other sets of data.

In Part One of this book, the papers have been divided into three sections: (1) those mainly concerned with the analysis of individual behavior in psychological terms, as these were felt to be central to the whole theme; (2) those on the physiological side; and (3) the environmental.

Taking the three sections in turn, Section I deals mainly with problems of cognition ranging from simple perceptuomotor skills, through more complex performances and memory functions, to thinking and problem-solving. The emphasis in these papers is on individual performance, although the authors have been aware of physiological background and possible social influences at work.

Section II contains papers more especially concerned with the attempt to tie behavior to physiological models and to relate age changes in behavior to known physiological changes. Our ability to do this is still rudimentary, but here is a field which is attracting considerable thought and research. The studies range from those which, as far as physiology is concerned, are avowedly speculative, to those dealing with assessments of health in old age using both physiological and behavioral criteria.

Section III attempts to discuss and define the nature of psychological environment in relation to aging. The contented older person who behaves productively and adequately in relation to others and is free from psychopathological symptoms does so not only as the result of sound constitutional and psychological capacities, but also because of a facilitative social environment. This environment has not often been explored, and it was the particular desire of the seminar to examine the ways in which the psychological environment of the older person can be conceptualized as a prelude to effective research in this area.

The form and coverage of the seminar reflect the belief of the planning committee that, although research in psychology, physiology, and sociology inevitably proceeds separately, each has much to gain by keeping in touch with the others and, on occasion, working closely with them. Research on aging has developed in a way that fosters this kind of cooperation, and it is hoped that the present seminar will indicate some of its potential advantages in a practical form.

SECTION I

Studies of
Cognition

CHAPTER 1

Intellectual Capacities,
Aging, and
Man's Environment

JAMES E. BIRREN,
KLAUS F. RIEGEL, and
DONALD F. MORRISON

Whereas we have made significant advance in summarizing what we know about aging, the field is still backward in the sense that it does not have a detailed, articulated map on which one can go from facts about the nervous system to consequences for behavior or from psychological capacities to personality. Since few disciplines in the past have considered extensively the principles which might elucidate the phenomenon of aging, our discussions must still be conducted in a mixture of common-sense language and borrowed terms and concepts.

Generally we tend to be cautious in speculating about the psychology of aging because of the danger that the implications of speculation can become unmanageable in so vast a topic, and obfusca-

9

tion, rather than clarification, results. My present intent is to steer a middle course between speculation about the subject matter and adherence to results of two recent studies.[1] A usual, though not necessarily stated, intent of speculation is to secure a better understanding of the context of the subject under discussion and of how it might be "articulated." Cornfield (1959) has used the term "articulation" in describing the extent of organization of fields of research: "The degree of articulation of a field is measured by the extent to which the phenomena with which the field is concerned are potentially capable of being explained and predicted in terms of a small number of fundamental concepts and constants" (p. 240). It would seem that the principal function of psychological research on aging is to reduce the great variety of changes in behavior associated with age to a smaller number of concepts.

The word "important" is so often used to describe problems of aging that we might examine a few of its implications. "Important" may connote implied action—do something about important problems, but not about unimportant ones. Another meaning of "important" is frequency; an important problem is characteristic of many people in the population. Severity of consequences is also an aspect of importance. Rare, but severe, diseases may be regarded as important because of the consequences for an affected individual. The meaning of "important" in the sense of pervasiveness lies close to that often found in scientific discussions in which an important problem is one which is central or antecedent to a great variety of related problems and one whose solution would facilitate solution of related problems —it leads to articulation. The psychologist tends to use the word "important" in relation to aging in a mixture of meanings, since he is not frequently in a position of knowing exhaustively the importance of frequency, severity, or pervasiveness.

ENVIRONMENTAL CHANGE FOR PSYCHOLOGY

Although the dramatic changes in man's environment in the past century are subjects for historians, sociologists, and anthropologists, the trends in man's relation to his environment have some

[1] Parts of this paper have been previously published in Birren, J.E., & Morrison, D.F. *J. Geront.*, 1961, **16**, 363-369, and Birren, J.E., Riegel, K.F., & Morrison, D.F. Age differences in response speed as a function of controlled variations of stimulus conditions: Evidence of a general speed factor. *Gerontologia*, 1962, **6**, 1-18 (Basel and New York: S. Karger).

fundamental implications for psychological research. Fewer than one hundred years ago, muscle power of men and animals was the main source of energy in transforming the environment and performing the essential activities of life; motors now do the heavy work. Next, after strength and endurance were made obsolete, man's fine handicrafts began to be replaced by machines. Many fine serial movements requiring precision and careful timing can now, for the most part, be better done by machines. Most of the essential psychomotor skills of our great-grandfathers and grandfathers are irrelevant to the requirements of contemporary life, and only nostalgia keeps some skills alive. Man's role has become that of a long range administrator of his environment in the sense that he programs long range decisions, but no longer carries out these decisions. There are special sensing devices to keep track of events and either inform him or, within limits, directly effect a response.

The question may be raised as to what implications this trend has for psychology and our concepts of intelligence. If we pursue a description of man's emerging role as a decision-maker, we soon find ourselves discussing topics like thinking and consciousness, phenomena of suspicious repute in past psychological research. As a decision-maker and long-term programmer, man must make choices among a variety of possible actions. Reasoning and decision-making about alternatives seems to take place in a period of aroused, but deferred, action, in a state of maximum focused attention or awareness. Few psychologists have found it attractive to study the crucial interval between input and output. Experimental psychologists in general, and particularly those concerned with phenomena of aging, should seriously consider recovering the discarded concept of consciousness and trying to develop methods for studying more closely the associated phenomena. Decision-making in the light of experience and circumstances implies a conscious individual who can tell you what he is doing. If the evolution of our environment is placing us more in the position of decision-makers and programmers and less in the role of effectors, it seems desirable that more attention be given to what goes on between input and output—unless, of course, we wish to assume that the consciousness has no function as an independent variable in determining behavior. The authors prefer to believe that some transformations of information take place in and are fostered by the conscious mind and that these transformations are the antecedents of new behavior.

It would be convenient if we had a measure of reasoning

capacity independent of or uninfluenced by that which is reasoned about. The history of psychology, however, shows limited success in obtaining absolute measures of intellectual capacity. In order to estimate the mind's capacities, we seemed to require samples of the mind doing characteristic operations. Perhaps the information theorists may help by suggesting ways in which absolute information-handling capacity of the organism can be measured, but one suspects they are faced with the same limitations in that the content of what is being processed affects the size of the unit being measured. In complex skills the transition from early to advanced levels is often brought about by simplification of the process so that the individual can attend to increasingly large units, as in reading; the highly skilled person attends only to certain critical parts of the task by learning essential cues.

ENVIRONMENT AND MEASUREMENT

It is difficult to maintain that man's capacities as a receiving, processing, and effecting system can be characterized independently of some environment in which he functions. In practice, we have to infer potential capacities from some sample of observed behavior in a particular environmental context; it is most difficult to divorce a description of function from the context in which the function is to be employed. Issues long present in mental measurement are currently being emphasized because of concern about interpretations of data from older adults who are functioning in a constantly changing environment. As long ago as 1906, a committee of the American Psychological Association was appointed to standardize testing methods. In 1954, a subsequent committee made some statements which are relevant here although not specifically pointed at aging (American Psychological Association, 1954):

> Validity information indicates to the· test user the degree to which the test is capable of achieving certain aims. Tests are used for several types of judgment, and for each type of judgment, a somewhat different type of validation is involved. We may distinguish four aims of testing:
>
> 1. The test user wishes to determine how an individual would perform at present in a given universe of situations of which the test situation constitutes a sample.
>
> 2. The test user wishes to predict an individual's future performance (on the test or on some external variable).
>
> 3. The test user wishes to estimate an individual's present status on some variable external to the test.

4. The test user wishes to infer the degree to which the individual possesses some trait or quality (construct) presumed to be reflected in the test performance.

The article continues, "To determine how suitable a test is for each of these uses, it is necessary to gather the appropriate sort of validity information" (p. 213). Much emphasis is given to the question of how well the test samples the situation to which reference is being made. One may be impressed, if not depressed, with the lack of evidence about validity of tests for older adults.

FACTOR ANALYSIS

Accounting for age changes in mental abilities in elementary processes is a highly analytical task. One is faced with an array of age changes in mental test scores, and the task is to explain these changes in a minimum of elementary processes. An early task consists of grouping the age-related behaviors according to their common antecedent. One way of proceeding would be to sample a large range of behaviors in a wide range and then to subject the total correlation matrix to a factor analysis which would indicate the clusters of age-related variance. Such an approach allows for the identification of incremental age factors that might result from increased experience and simultaneously allows for the identification of decremental age factors that might result from sensory limitations. The analysis of data from large samples of subjects and measurements is now feasible with machine methods, although gathering data in such a scheme is not so feasible, for it requires that the same subjects be measured on all variables.

A longitudinal study could be analyzed in a similar manner, but the basic datum now becomes a difference value. Correlations would be determined for the differences among measurements separated in time. The factor analysis would identify the common variance among the changes which occur in individuals. A convenient assumption might be that the changes are linear with age. Although not necessarily valid, the assumption is an expedient one for initiating analysis. The day is still distant when fitted individual curves on a variety of measurements will be available so one can analyze the dependencies among the parameters of fitted complex functions which correspond to our verbal statements about aging.

Statistical analysis of individual differences is not usually appealing to the experimental scientist, who prefers to explain relationships he can manipulate, yet the results of factor analyses can be used to point out the cluster of measurements of greatest change with age for more detailed experimental analysis. These clusters can also be examined in order to generate hypotheses which can lead to experiments in which the antecedents can be manipulated.

The results of two studies which were designed to help isolate the nature of age changes in a limited sample of intellectual abilities follow.

PART A: FACTORS IN THE ORGANIZATION OF MENTAL ABILITIES WITH ADVANCING AGE

James E. Birren and Donald F. Morrison

The primary purpose of this study was to apply a statistical method, principal component analysis, to help clarify aging of mental abilities. The subject matter partially resists clarification, because probably there is not one phenomenon, but a group of processes, of aging, and methodologically the separation of these processes is not simple. The recent comprehensive review by Jones (1959) identifies most of the unresolved issues, some of which are under investigation here. The present analysis was based on data obtained with the WAIS (Wechsler Adult Intelligence Scale). Previous studies have been concerned with age changes in scores on the WAIS or the Wechsler-Bellevue (Balinsky, 1941; Birren, 1952; Cohen, 1957a; Cohen, 1957b; Doppelt & Wallace, 1955; Eisdorfer, Busse, & Cohen, 1959; Kallmann & Jarvik, 1959; Wechsler, 1955a; Wechsler, 1955b). The important difference between previous studies and the present one is that this one includes both age and educational attainment as continuous variables in an analysis of intercorrelations of mental test scores.

With advancing age, the cumulative effect of experience presumably leads to increased scores on tests which have a large component of achievement like vocabulary and general information. In contrast, negative correlations are found between chronological age and certain sensory and perceptual functions. To the extent that a test involves a mixture of achievement and perception, the scores should correlate to varying degrees positively or negatively with age. There is also an effect produced by the lower educational attainment of older generations; in the present adult population, educational level is somewhat negatively correlated with age. Other issues remain to be elucidated, like the effect of change in content of education. Is a year of schooling today equivalent to that of thirty years ago?

To discuss the effects of aging, it is useful to have a system of description independent of any particular measurements. The concept of structure of mental abilities embodies the idea of an invariant system of description. Guilford (1960) used the title "A Morphological Model for Human Intelligence" for a paper in which he described a set of logically related factors which may be used to account for individual differences in performance of intellectual tasks. The choice of the term "morphological" is, to our mind, a good one, for it emphasizes the conceptual scheme used in descriptions of the intellect independent of any particular data. If we are required to shift our frame of reference for intellectual abilities every time we change our study population, we are precluded from drawing some of the most important inferences, such as what the major changes with advancing age are in the organization of intellectual function.

For simplicity we might pose an initial hypothesis that an analysis of age and mental test data should show at least one incremental factor reflecting increased experience and one decremental factor reflecting changed functioning of the nervous system. Although suitable for testing, such a simple hypothesis, the principal component analysis of the present study, does not preclude the possibility of identifying larger numbers of mutually independent incremental and decremental age factors in intellectual performance.

The data on which the present analysis is based are part of the standardization data of the Wechsler Adult Intelligence Scale (Wechsler, 1955a). These data were used because they were, perhaps,

TABLE 1
DISTRIBUTION BY AGE AND EDUCATION

	Years of schooling			
Age	0-8	9-12	13+	Total
25-34	58	118	37	213
35-44	151	52	99	302
45-54	54	133	40	227
55-64	85	87	19	191
Total	348	390	195	933

the most adequate available from a population of a wide age span and known characteristics of educational and occupational background. Their use is made possible through the kindness of David Wechsler and the Psychological Corporation. To avoid the problems of language and educational equivalence and opportunity, only data from male and female native-born white subjects were used. Nine hundred thirty-three male and female subjects from twenty-five to sixty-four were used in the analysis (Table 1).

Product moment correlations were computed for thirteen variables—the eleven WAIS subtests, age, and education (Table 2). Correlations were initially determined for men and women separately, but the sex differences were judged to be of impractical significance, so the data were combined. From the data in Table 2 it is possible to compute partial correlation matrices with the subtests intercorrelated with the separate or joint effect of age and education held constant. Table 3 shows the results of removing the effects of education by partial correlation. The correlation and partial correlation matrices were subjected to principal component analyses by Hotelling's method. To conserve space, only the results of the two most pertinent analyses are reported here, that of the original matrix and that with the effect of education held constant.

As might be expected from the size of the correlation coefficients in Table 2, the variance attributable to the first component was rather large (Table 4). Component I accounted for 51 per cent of the total variance in the correlation matrix. This component was identical with the first factor extracted by a centroid factor analysis and can be regarded as the common factor (G) measured to some extent by all subtests of the WAIS. Of interest is the relatively small coefficient associated with age, –.13, in contrast to the higher coefficient for education, .29. In fact, the relation between the first component and education is about as high as that between the first component and any other single subtest; thus, as a single variable, educational attainment is about as good as any other single subtest in estimating the level of ability as measured by the common variance of the WAIS.

When the principal components were extracted from the partial correlation matrix of Table 3, which holds education constant, the first component accounted for only about 37 per cent of the total variance (Table 5). In this analysis the relation of age to the first component becomes trivial in comparison with the WAIS subtests.

In contrast to the first component where age was of little importance, the second component was intimately associated with age.

TABLE 2
WAIS CORRELATION MATRIX
(Decimal points omitted)

	1	2	3	4	5	6	7	8	9	10	11	12
1. Information												
2. Comprehension	67											
3. Arithmetic	62	54										
4. Similarities	66	60	51									
5. Digit span	47	39	51	41								
6. Vocabulary	81	72	58	68	45							
7. Digit symbol	47	40	41	49	45	49						
8. Picture completion	60	54	46	56	42	57	50					
9. Block design	49	45	48	50	39	46	50	61				
10. Picture arrangement	51	49	43	50	42	52	52	59	54			
11. Object assembly	41	38	37	41	31	40	46	51	59	46		
12. Age	-07	-08	-08	-19	-19	-02	-46	-28	-32	-37	-28	
13. Education	66	52	49	55	43	62	57	48	44	49	40	-29

Note — In tables 2-3 *N* is 933 native-born white males and females from twenty-five to sixty-four.

TABLE 3
WAIS PARTIAL CORRELATION MATRIX:
EDUCATION CONSTANT
(Decimal points omitted)

	1	2	3	4	5	6	7	8	9	10	11
1. Inf.											
2. Com.	50										
3. Arth.	46	38									
4. Sim.	48	43	32								
5. D.S.	28	21	38	22							
6. Voc.	68	60	40	52	26						
7. D. Sy.	15	15	18	25	27	21					
8. P.C.	44	39	30	40	27	39	31				
9. B.D.	29	29	33	34	25	26	34	50			
10. P.A.	29	32	25	31	27	32	34	46	41		
11. O.A.	21	22	22	25	17	21	31	40	51	33	
12. Age	17	08	08	−04	−.08	22	−38	−.16	−22	−27	−19

In fact, chronological age was the largest single contributor to the common variance identified in Component II for the analyses reported in tables 4 and 5. In contrast with Component I, Component II accounts for a much smaller proportion of the variance and is narrower in scope in that it involves few subtests. Components III and IV are too small in proportion of variance and relation to age to be discussed here.

If we call Component I the "general ability component" and Component II the "aging component," we would be correct in a descriptive sense, yet the term "aging component" does not imply much in an analytical sense, for we find that the tests are positively or negatively related to the component. The largest negative value was associated with the digit symbol test, known to lower with advancing age; apart from chronological age, the largest positive value was associated with the vocabulary test, known to rise with age in some populations. Thus, in Component II both aspects of the original simple hypothesis—incremental and decremental processes—are demonstrated.

One might choose to look on the age component as bipolar.

However, if one were to interpret Component II literally as a bipolar factor, then high vocabulary scores would necessarily be associated with low digit symbol scores, and conversely. It is difficult to see why low digit symbol scores should necessarily be associated with high vocabulary scores. About the only plausible bipolar factor which could exist in aging would be a use-disuse dimension, in which the degree of use determines the extent to which a function improves, remains unchanged, or atrophies. If selecting the functions we exercise precludes use of other functions, a negative relation would necessarily develop. In this manner, if a high verbal comprehension factor was gained through speaking or reading at the expense of increasing a spatial perception factor, then we would indeed have correlations resulting from the fact that an adult is time-limited—if he does some things, he cannot do others. Because of what we know about changes in sensation and perception with age, the major consideration is not likely to be such a simple, bipolar, use-disuse dimension. Rather, it seems that there are at least two essentially independent processes simultanously operating in opposite directions.

TABLE 4
WAIS CORRELATION MATRIX: PRINCIPAL COMPONENTS
(Decimal points omitted)

	I	II	III	IV	$\Sigma\, l_i^2$
1. Inf.	32	28	−04	−12	.199
2. Com.	29	26	08	−20	200
3. Arth.	28	21	−09	42	305
4. Sim.	30	12	00	−25	170
5. D.S.	24	00	−42	69	713
6. Voc.	32	32	−03	−19	242
7. D. Sy.	28	−30	−29	−09	254
8. P.C.	30	−08	−28	−01	173
9. B.D.	28	−22	40	21	336
10. P.A.	28	−19	05	−06	123
11. O.A.	25	−25	53	15	428
12. Age	−13	67	29	21	591
13. Ed.	29	01	−33	−27	266
Latent roots	6.69	1.42	.80	.71	
Variance	51.47%	10.90%	6.15%	5.48%	
Σ variance	51.47%	62.37%	68.52%	74.01%	

TABLE 5
PRINCIPAL COMPONENTS WAIS PARTIAL
CORRELATION MATRIX: EDUCATION CONSTANT
(Decimal points omitted)

	I	II	III	IV	$\Sigma\, 1_i^2$
1. Inf.	34	32	−03	−07	220
2. Com.	32	25	−16	−16	212
3. Arth.	29	17	41	33	387
4. Sim.	32	11	−15	−32	238
5. D.S.	23	−04	76	11	645
6. Voc.	34	34	−08	−21	285
7. D. Sy.	23	−36	21	−36	357
8. P.C.	34	−12	−20	05	174
9. B.D.	31	−25	−16	41	354
10. P.A.	30	−23	−06	−17	172
11. O.A.	26	−27	−30	51	492
12. Age	−.06	59	−05	34	464
Latent roots	4.39	1.83	.95	.83	
Variance	36.57	15.27	7.90	6.94	
Σ variance	36.57	51.85	59.75	66.69	

To compute component scores for a subject, one cross multiplies scores, coefficients, and sums for each component, thus the individual's standard scores on the subtests are multiplied by the normalized coefficients in columns I, II, III, and IV of tables 4 and 5. These coefficients differentially weight the subtest according to its contribution to the common variance of the components. In a more general manner, one could devise an age index for adults by differentially weighting all subtests according to their correlation with chronological age. This is a less analytical way of proceeding, since the inferences one could draw from a single age index would be less precise than those drawn from component scores. For example, a multiple correlation between age and the eleven subtests can be computed as was done for this sample, yielding the multiple correlation 0.60. If education is held constant, the multiple R between all subtests and age is 0.57. Since this is for the age range twenty-five to sixty-four, the multiple R is somewhat lower than it would be if subjects over sixty-five were included. The opposite trend of digit symbol and vocabulary scores is seen in the multiple regression weights of Table 6. These two tests are weighted about the same in extent, but opposite in sign. This result we had already seen in the principal component analysis, so it seems clear that the two tests are different in their relation to age.

TABLE 6
MULTIPLE REGRESSION OF AGE ON WAIS SUBTESTS:
WEIGHTS BASED ON STANDARD SCORES

Subtest	Weight	Weight, education held constant
1. Inf.	.08	.12
2. Com.	.00	.01
3. Arth.	.10	.09
4. Sim.	−.11	−.09
5. D.S.	−.04	−.02
6. Voc.	.40	.35
7. D. Sy.	−.43	−.32
8. P.C.	−.08	−.08
9. B.D.	−.09	−.08
10. P.A.	−.25	−.21
11. O.A.	−.04	−.04

Multiple correlation coefficient R = .60   R = .57

One could proceed with the analysis in a different manner by computing the canonical correlations of age and education and the eleven WAIS subtests. This analysis would answer the question: Given two sets of variables (education and age and the eleven subtests), what is the linear combination of the scores in the first set which will have maximum correlation with some linear compound of the other set's variables? The results of the canonical correlations are presented in Table 7. Of the larger values, positive weights with age are seen for vocabulary, information, and arithmetic subtests; negative weights for digit symbol, picture arrangement, picture completion, block design, and similarities.

These findings support the impression one gains from an examination of the graphs of each subtest plotted against age. In Fig. 1 it is seen that educational level makes a difference for all sub-tests for all age groups. The age trends are less marked, and, for

TABLE 7
CANONICAL CORRELATIONS AND VECTORS FOR AGE AND EDUCATION AND THE ELEVEN SUBTESTS OF THE WAIS

I.

Variable		Canonical vectors
	1	2
1. Education	1.000	.452
2. Age	−.187	1.000
Canonical correlation	.737	.564

II.

Variable		Canonical vectors
	1	2
1. Information	.908	.505
2. Comprehension	.115	.036
3. Arithmetic	.014	.244
4. Similarities	.239	−.185
5. Digit span	.138	−.039
6. Vocabulary	.073	1.000
7. Digit symbol	1.000	−.686
8. Picture completion	−.109	−.227
9. Block design	.036	−.192
10. Picture arrangement	.332	−.477
11. Object assembly	.135	−.096

most tests, the age effect is much lower than educational level. Even in the digit symbol test, the effect of educational level is maintained despite the manifest age decline; the educational effect is also seen in vocabulary scores concomitant with the rise in score with age.

DISCUSSION

The fact that education was found to be much more significant for the first component (the G factor of the WAIS) than chronological age in the age range from twenty-five to sixty-four is encouraging for improving the intellectual performance of future

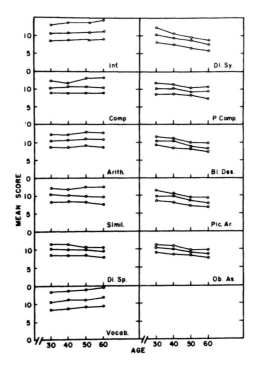

Fig. 1. Mean scores on the WAIS subtests as a function of age and education. Upper curves for education thirteen years and above, middle curves for eight to twelve years, and lower curves for fewer than eight years. Age intervals are twenty-five to thirty-four, thirty-five to forty-four, forty-five to fifty-four, and fifty-five to sixty-four years.

generations of older adults. It is not likely, however, that all the variance removed in the analyses of this study by holding education constant could be attributed to years of education alone. An unknown part is related to educability since, to some extent, the people most likely to profit by further education are selected, or decide to receive more of it. A partial correlation, therefore, removes a mixture of the effects of education and an ability to profit from education. The effect of education may, therefore, be somewhat exaggerated, just as the effect of aging is exaggerated in an opposite direction if the covariance of differing educational attainments of the generations is left uncorrected.

One of the most intriguing aspects of the results is the

opposite effects seen in the vocabulary and digit symbol tests. Although these two measures go in opposite directions over the adult years, in childhood they show a concurrent advance. Some hints about such opposite age effects may come from the nature of the tests.

The vocabulary test of the WAIS requires the subject to define an unambiguously presented word. Neither the stimulus, the word, nor the operation of searching for the response seems particularly important. For the most part the subject either can or cannot identify the word. This view does not deny the effects of aging on language functions, but merely indicates that the WAIS vocabulary test is largely a test of stored verbal information which may be increased by living in an advantageous environment. In contrast to the vocabulary test, the digit symbol test consists of an unfamiliar task, translating symbols according to a numbered system. Although the task is timed, the timing seems less important than other features. In a sample of forty-seven elderly men previously studied (Birren, Botwinick, Weiss, & Morrison, 1958), the correlation between the digit symbol test and simple auditory reaction time was .53, whereas its correlations with the block design and the object assembly subtests in the same population were .65 and .72 respectively; thus it is doubtful that inability to record answers quickly is the pertinent variable. Performance on the digit symbol test seems to involve remembering a perceived unfamiliar symbol while performing a decoding operation. Since the digit span test of the WAIS does not show appreciable change with age, it is not likely that the digit symbol performance is low because of inability to retain simple perceptions. It may be, however, that the limiting variable is the ability to keep the symbol in mind while searching to decode it; this would be somewhat analogous to memory through distraction or to task set. Equally plausible, however, is the notion that the decoding operation itself is the critical factor. Beyond this we cannot go at present; future experiment will have to reveal whether the critical element is the operation of transforming symbols or retaining information while the relevant operation is developed.

The principal component method of analysis seems to have had considerable value in this study, for it helped identify the larger sources of variance as well as the effects of age and education. As a consequence of the analysis, the decremental aspects of aging now appear to be more specific in their consequences. We will not attempt to decide whether the principal component method is the only or best method of procedure. The same data were also analyzed by centroid factor analysis with subsequent rotation of axes. The two analyses were comparable in major results; the interpretation of components which involve slight variance was not attempted in either instance, since the reliability of several subtests would not lend itself to having more than a 50 per-cent common variance at the most.

PART B: AGE DIFFERENCES IN
RESPONSE SPEED

James E. Birren and Klaus F. Riegel

Previous work has shown that with age there are both incremental and decremental changes in intellectual performance. In language functions older adults perform better, whereas measures involving psychomotor speed and perception frequently favor young adults. The problem is determining the extent to which the incremental or decremental changes associated with age are large or small and whether they are general. The present study compares the performance of young and old adults on tasks in which the symbolic content was varied while the manner of presenting stimuli and registering responses was held constant. Most responses show some increase in latency of response with age, although it is not known what implications extended latencies of a possible neurophysiological basis have for intellectual activity. Slowing down may primarily affect processes of specific response, although, on the contrary, the change in latency of response may represent such a general alteration in the nervous system that no behavior could be expected to be independent of its influence. In this connection, the quality of and capacity for thinking might be limited by the speed of the mediating processes which simultaneously manipulate and synthesize information for appropriate response; slowing down here would reduce the information which can be received. This might be illustrated in listening to a conversation in which a grasp of the issues depends on adequate speed in perceiving and integrating the words.

In addition to assumed biological antecedents, another group of determinants are those of experience. Thus, with age, word associations may differ in strength of habit as a consequence of selective use of certain word combinations. Different response speeds may presumably arise from experience of a special sort. These two general determinants probably overlap; thus, avoiding certain classes of words would not necessarily reflect an experiential determinant since it could also compensate for increased cognitive strain incurred by attempts to grasp certain abstractions. A preference for certain words can arise, and with age there is very likely a unique pattern of word habits typical of a given individual. The individual may also share some general tendency in word usage common to most persons of his age group. Such phenomena may be largely limited to social relations, but they might also have consequences for thinking. Word choices represent not only patterns of expression, but also of thought.

The apparatus used in this study was the psychomet. Its general features were patterned after the apparatus previously developed by Dr. Harry Kay in the psychological laboratory of Oxford University. The present apparatus was designed by Dr. Michael Davis in consultation with Dr. Conan Kornetsky and J. Birren. It consists of a subject's panel on which the light and key associations are programmed and the speed and accuracy of the responses are registered. Fig. 2 shows the physical arrangement of the subject's and experimenter's panels. The experimenter can pair any light with any response button and also present the stimulus lights in any predetermined order. The time the subject takes to respond to the onset of each light by pressing the appropriate button is recorded on 1/100 second electric timers. A total of twenty-two stimulus-response conditions were studied; each condition consisted of ten light-button pairings, and each series was presented twice.

All subjects went through the experimental conditions in the order given below. Each condition was repeated as soon as the data were recorded from the experimenter's panel; the two successive series are designated *A* and *B*. The specific instructions given the subjects are found in Appendix A.

1. *Simple movement time.* The subject presses the buttons as fast as he can from left to right, turning off the lights in the same order.

Lights (L): 1 2 3 4 5 6 7 8 9 0
Buttons (B): 1 2 3 4 5 6 7 8 9 0

2. *Serial simple movement time.* Subject presses the buttons and turns off the lights as above, but begins a new cycle after completing the last response. Each trial consisted of three cycles (thirty responses).

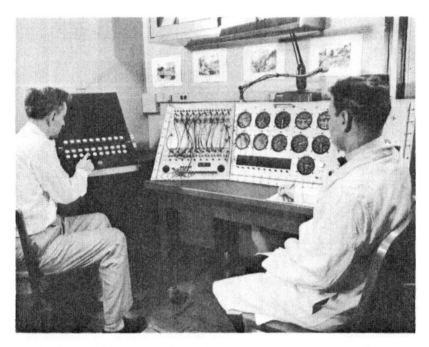

Fɪɢ. 2. The psychomet apparatus with the subject's panel on the left and the experimenter's control panel on the right. The subject has been photographed in an askew position in order to show the arrangement of the lights (upper row) and buttons (lower row). Above each button is its coded designation. Start button is placed in the lower center of the subject's panel.

3. *Choice reaction time.* Lights and buttons were regularly paired, but presented in a random order: Light 5 was first, 4 was second, and so on.

L: 5 4 8 9 6 7 2 0 3 1
B: 5 4 8 9 6 7 2 0 3 1

4. *Choice reaction time.* Same as Test 3, but with a different random order.

L: 9 1 8 5 7 4 3 6 0 2
B: 9 1 8 5 7 4 3 6 0 2

5. *Numbers.* The lights and buttons were numbered from 1 to 0. Buttons turn off lights with corresponding numbers. Lights are presented regularly from left to right, but designated with random numbers from 1 through 0; buttons are ordered regularly from left to right.

L: 2 5 7 1 6 0 9 4 3 8
B: 1 2 3 4 5 6 7 8 9 0

6. *Numbers.* Both lights and buttons were numbered from 1 through 0 as in Test 5. Button designations as well as lights were randomized.

L: 0 5 6 9 3 1 8 2 7 4
B: 2 4 7 0 9 3 8 6 5 1

7. *Letters.* Lights and buttons were designated with letters of the alphabet: A through K except J, an ambiguous letter in the style used. Lights were presented regularly from left to right, but designations were randomized; buttons were in alphabetical order from left to right.

L: I D G A F H E K C B
B: A B C D E F G H I K

8. *Letters.* Both light and button designations were randomized.

L: A I G D B K E C F H
B: H F I K B D A C E G

9. *Colors.* Lights and buttons were designated with colors, five with single colors, five with two colors each. Lights were presented in

random order. Y = yellow, G = green, R = red, B = blue, O = orange.

Order:	7	10	2	3	9	6	8	1	4	5
L:	Y	OG	B	GR	O	YR	G	BO	R	YB
B:	R	GR	O	B	BO	G	Y	YR	YB	OG

10. *Colors and symbols.* Lights and buttons were designated with one of two symbols, X or O, and with one of five colors. A correct response consisted of the proper selection of both color and symbol.

Order:	5	8	9	4	6	10	1	7	3	2
L:	YO	RX	GO	OX	RO	YX	BX	GX	BO	OO
B:	RO	GX	BO	OX	YX	OO	YO	BX	GO	RX

11. *Digit symbol.* Lights were designated with numbers 1 through 10; buttons were designated with symbols which had to be decoded by reference to a card placed on the subject's panel; lights were presented regularly from left to right.

L:	5	2	10	3	6	1	7	9	8	4
B:	D	S	P	V	C	U	Y	T	L	H

Decoding card:

1	2	3	4	5	6	7	8	9	10
P	L	S	H	U	V	C	Y	D	T

All the verbal relations stimuli (lights) were presented from left to right in regular sequence. See Appendix A for instruction details.

12. *Syllable matching.*

L:	be	cor	ex	tab	ans	gard	den	sold	morn	im
B:	ex	gard	tab	morn	im	den	be	ans	sold	cor

13. *Word matching.*

L:	short	cold	foot	girl	light	blue	head	joy	bed	salt
B:	bed	blue	foot	salt	cold	girl	short	joy	head	light

14. *Word association.* Button with the word which goes best with the stimulus is pressed.

L	B
table	flower
man	woman
slow	bird
hard	soft
eagle	short
bread	butter
long	fast
hammer	chair
king	queen
blossom	nail

15. *Word association.*

L	B
hand	fear
whistle	mind
wish	stop
earth	grass
memory	foot
bath	tiger
child	baby
lion	clean
green	want
afraid	round

16, 17, 18. *Word relations.* The same stimulus words are used for response words of three kinds—coordinates, superordinates, and parts.

L	B coordinates	B superordinates	B parts
scissors	adult	animal	page
fruit	ant	tool	tone
baby	beer	edifice	blade
house	Koran	liquid	feeler
whiskey	earth	art	angle
moon	tongs	person	orbit
music	hotel	planet	arm
square	meat	figure	peel
spider	poetry	scriptum	alcohol
Bible	rhombus	food	walls

19. *Word completion: adjectives and adverbs.*

L	B
al	haps
hap	py
rath	ant
pleas	ten
pret	deed
sud	el
in	er
of	most
per	ty
cru	den

20. *Word completion: concrete nouns.*

L	B
val	en
win	tain
mon	ley
kitch	nal
moun	ion
farm	ey
jour	dow
bu	ny
po	reau
on	er

21. *Word completion: verbs.*

L	B
ap	ter
fol	pear
ad	fer
ar	get
ex	mit
for	turb
suf	rive
dis	low
flat	tain
main	pect

22. *Word completion: abstract nouns.*

L	B
pow	ner
sys	ces
af	er
ef	fair
man	lem
meth	tion
na	od
prob	it
spir	tem
suc	fort

Thirty young and twenty-three elderly adults were studied. The young group consisted of fifteen men and fifteen women between eighteen and thirty-three years. Their mean education was 14.0 years. Thirteen were religious volunteers for research in the Clinical Center of the National Institutes of Health; the remainder were volunteer employees. The elderly group consisted of women and men in the age range of sixty to eighty. Their mean education was 12.9 years. These subjects were all volunteers and either retired government employees or spouses of retired employees.

Under all experimental conditions the elderly subjects were slower in their responses than the young subjects. In Table 8 the mean values of the two groups are shown; the means of the older group were, in almost all instances, more than one standard deviation greater than those of the younger group. The differences in response time can be considered in both absolute and relative terms. The smallest absolute age difference in the mean values for the two age groups was in simple movement time, about .14 seconds, and choice reaction time. The differences in choice reaction times were .18 and .16 seconds. The largest differences were in work relationships; superordinate, part, and coordinate association times differed by 1.75, 1.99, and 1.86 seconds respectively. Several of the word association measures did not show such large relative age differences as some of the simpler tasks.

The experimental conditions showing a large absolute and a large relative difference in mean response time were color matching; color and symbol matching; digit symbol; superordinate, coordinate and part word associations; and word completion using verbs. Those showing least absolute and relative age difference were the choice

TABLE 8
INTERCORRELATIONS OF PSYCHOMET VARIABLES:
YOUNG SUBJECTS (N = 30), MEDIAN VALUES, FIRST TRIAL
(Decimal points omitted)

	1	2	3	4	5	6	7	8	9	10	11	12	13	14	15	16	17	18	19	20	21	22
1.		53	15	23	-01	-18	-07	05	-23	-17	-26	04	-05	-44	-16	-12	-32	-10	-26	-33	-10	-08
2.			41	45	16	-04	10	30	-05	09	-05	13	10	-19	-03	08	-25	19	-15	-02	-04	-04
3.				77	52	07	41	04	-12	30	20	12	30	02	-13	-07	-16	17	17	18	22	33
4.					60	09	57	13	-12	44	39	27	35	-13	03	02	-15	26	12	08	20	30
5.						14	55	30	29	58	33	56	49	22	30	10	02	30	23	04	15	29
6.							16	42	08	37	28	23	10	-02	33	34	39	34	12	42	14	42
7.								34	29	53	20	52	40	07	33	20	24	12	05	30	36	34
8.									26	37	-10	36	36	16	35	52	30	25	03	19	07	16
9.										47	-07	34	25	23	22	39	11	25	08	31	11	05
10.											10	37	37	23	43	34	12	42	12	41	12	21
11.												11	02	23	25	-11	05	38	35	06	27	40
12.													44	13	42	31	43	25	22	16	37	47
13.														31	22	42	17	27	45	12	16	35
14.															58	33	27	38	65	28	34	30
15.																43	30	44	41	30	33	35
16.																	52	48	40	42	38	41
17.																		26	26	30	37	31
18.																			54	47	44	46
19.																				38	53	56
20.																					62	45
21.																						79

TABLE 9
PRINCIPAL COMPONENT ANALYSIS
OF CORRELATIONS IN TABLE 8
PSYCHOMET RESULTS: YOUNG GROUP, MEDIAN VALUES,
FIRST TRIAL

Variable	Component*				
	I	II	III	IV	V
1	−.33	.71	−.23	1.00	−.48
2	.13	80	−.24	.89	−.45
3	.49	88	.56	−.01	.24
4	.60	1.00	39	−.05	.16
5	.84	.63	−.08	−.85	−.07
6	.66	−.17	−.22	.52	1.00
7	.85	.48	−.26	−.43	.45
8	.67	.10	−.99	.43	−.04
9	.55	−.21	−.81	−.64	−.10
10	.90	.28	−.53	−.61	29
11	.51	.08	1.00	−.43	.47
12	.88	19	−.43	−.04	.04
13	.81	25	−.26	−.33	−67
14	.72	−.55	.31	−.61	−76
15	.88	−33	−19	−16	−19
16	87	−.38	−58	64	−35
17	65	−58	−29	36	39
18	94	−11	.26	37	−.23
19	85	−38	.76	−.02	−.69
20	83	−.33	.11	.45	39
21	89	−.21	.66	65	3
22	1.00	−.04	.63	.62	11
Latent roots	6.47	3.16	2.13	1.60	1.39
Proportion of variance in component	29.4	14.4	9.7	7.3	6.3
Cumulative proportion of variance		43.8	53.5	60.8	67.1

*Largest variable set equal to 1.00; others adjusted proportionately.

reaction time measurements. In view of the work that has established
the fact that reaction times show significant differences with age, it is
surprising that reaction time is not necessarily the task in which the
largest difference in speed appears, either absolutely or relatively. In
a general way, the difference in speed appears to increase as the task

requires more manipulation of the stimulus before a response is given.

The effects of randomizing the numbers or letters on response buttons can be examined by comparing the performance of the subjects on experimental conditions 5 and 6 (numbers) with 7 and 8 (letters). In both instances the essential difference between succeeding experimental conditions is between a regular order and a scrambled order of response buttons. In both instances the elderly subjects showed a greater difference in response time than did the young when responses were randomized in position (number .38 versus .56 seconds; letters .46 versus .68 seconds, respectively). In percentage terms, however, both groups increased their response time to approximately the same extent in the scrambled response order. This suggests that for both age groups the time required with increased complexity is in proportion to the time required in the more regular stimulus response associations.

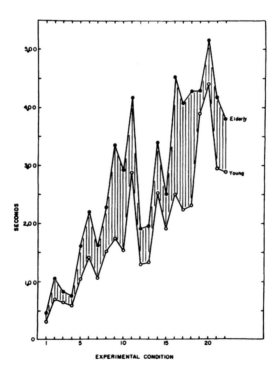

FIG. 3. Performance time for elderly and young subjects on twenty-two experimental conditions.

TABLE 10
MEAN TIME OF CORRECT PERFORMANCE OF YOUNG AND ELDERLY SUBJECTS ON THE PSYCHOMET: INDIVIDUALS, MEDIAN VALUES, FIRST TRIAL
(In hundredths of seconds; decimal points omitted)

										Experimental condition												
		1	2	3	4	5	6	7	8	9	10	11	12	13	14	15	16S	17P	18C	19	20	21	22
Young	Mean	32	70	64	58	104	142	105	151	174	153	288	129	133	252	181	250	223	230	389	442	294	279
	σ	9	12	8	6	12	27	11	27	40	21	49	22	22	80	53	82	65	52	23	251	124	122
	N	30	30	30	30	30	30	30	30	30	30	30	30	30	30	30	29	30	29	29	25	28	29
Elderly	Mean	46	105	82	74	161	220	162	228	336	292	418	190	195	340	250	453	408	428	428	516	418	380
	σ	18	34	10	10	29	51	31	47	160	96	65	41	38	89	59	136	124	104	205	256	159	97
	N	21	21	21	21	21	21	21	20	21	20	21	21	21	21	21	21	21	21	21	20	21	20
Old-young		14	35	18	16	57	78	57	77	162	139	130	61	62	88	69	203	185	198	39	74	124	101
Per-cent difference		144	150	128	128	155	155	154	151	193	191	145	147	147	135	138	181	183	186	110	117	142	136

The median response times of the subjects were all inter-correlated for the twenty-two experimental conditions. This yielded two correlation matrices, one for the young and one for the old. Each matrix was analyzed by the principal component method.

The analysis suggests two differences between the age groups. The young group has a smaller first component which is not so consistent as that of the elderly. The first component for the elderly accounted for 46 per cent of the total variance, whereas in the young it accounted for 29 per cent (tables 9 and 10). Furthermore, in the young group the simple movement time measurements showed little relation to the first component. Thus, how quickly the young make simple movements has little relation to the time they require in making responses when various symbolic manipulations are involved. By contrast, the results on the older subjects show both simple and complex speed measurements to be related.

Of particular interest is the fact that the digit symbol condition correlated very highly with the first component in the elderly group, as high as that for choice reaction time. The digit symbol test, when given as a part of an adult intelligence test, has been found closely related to chronological age. The present findings suggest that it shares an important common process with speed measurements, which grow in pervasiveness with advancing age.

SUMMARY

1. The purpose of this study was to compare the speed of performance of young and elderly subjects in a standardized experimental context, varying the nature of selected stimulus and response associations. The subject's task was to respond to one of ten signal lights by pressing one of ten buttons. There was always a predetermined association between lights and buttons. The subject turned off the ten lights serially by pressing the correct buttons as rapidly as possible. A total of twenty-two experimental conditions were used, ranging from simple movement and reaction times through numbers, letters, colors, symbols, and word associations of a predetermined nature.

2. Thirty young subjects, between eighteen and thirty, and twenty-three elderly subjects, between sixty and eighty, were studied. Under all experimental conditions the elderly subjects were slower than the young. The largest relative and absolute differences appeared for the superordinate, coordinate, and part word associations, and the

color and color symbol associations. The smallest differences were found for reaction time and adjective word associations.

3. It is apparent from these results that differences between young and old in speed of response are not limited to the simple motor aspects of tasks, but involve, to a greater extent, the associative processes. Even if one were to dissociate the time required for simple reaction time from the response times for complex associations, only about 10 to 15 per cent of the differences between age groups would be removed. Furthermore, it is not obvious that this is a justifiable computation, since the difference may involve processes common to any stimulus-response association, including relatively simple choice reactions and complex verbal associations.

4. The increased common variance with differences in speed of association requires further analysis, since some generality of process is implied.

APPENDIX A

Psychomet Instructions

1, 2. This we call a psychomet. You notice here that there are lights and keys. You may press one of these buttons or keys. You see it depresses and clicks. Now what I am going to do is to have these lights light up, and your task is to turn them out as fast as you can by depressing the key beneath each light. Just like this. You see? Every time you press a key, a light will go out, and another light will come on. When you are ready, press the green button. That will turn on the first light, and then do the task as fast as you can. Press the keys just as fast as you can. Are there any questions? Try to make no errors. If there are no further questions, sit there comfortably, and, as soon as you are ready, press the green button and go. Ready?

3, 4. *Reaction time.* Instead of the lights coming on in a regular order, this time they will come on in a somewhat random order. However, the key beneath each light is a key which turns the light off. Understand? When you are ready to go again, press the green button. As soon as you press the green button, the first light will come on. Turn that light off by pressing the key beneath it. The lights will come on in a random order. Just like before, I want you to do this as fast as you can without making errors. Any questions? As soon as you are comfortable, press the green button and go. Ready? Now I am going to have you do another series, but this time the lights will come on in different order. The task is the same. As soon as the light comes on, turn it off by pressing the key beneath it. Ready?

5. *Numbers.* This time it's going to be a little different. When the lights come on you will see a number there, and each key is also numbered. You see there is a number above each key. The number

above each key will tell you which light it turns off. That is, suppose this first light had a number 2 on it. Key number 2 would turn that light off. In some of these procedures the lights will not be numbered in order from 1, 2, 3, 4, 5, up to 0, but may be randomized; always remember the key with the same number as the light, turns off that light. No matter how they come on, you press the key with the corresponding number, and that will turn off the light. Are there questions?

6. This time the task is just about the same for you. The difference this time is that the numbers in the lower set, or the key numbers, are not in regular order but are scrambled. Would you read aloud for me the numbers above the keys? I want to impress upon you the fact that the numbers are scrambled. Read. If there are no further questions, get comfortable and press the green button when you are ready to go. Ready?

7. *Letters.* This time instead of having numbers for the lights and keys, there will be letters, but the same principle holds. That is, if the light has a letter A, Key A turns off that light. Light B is turned off by Key B and so on. In the first case you will see that the lights will come on in regular order from left to right except the letters do not come in any particular order but are scrambled. You will notice that the keys are lettered regularly A, B, C, D, and so on. Are there any questions? Remember the key with the same letter as the lights turns off that light. When you are comfortable and ready to go, press the green button. Ready?

8. This time the task is almost the same except that the letters above the keys are now scrambled. I would like to have you read to me the letters above the keys to show how they are scrambled. Please read.

9. This time, instead of having numbers or letters, the lights will come on showing different colors. The principle, though, is still the same. The key with the same color as a light turns off that light. For example, a light with red will be turned off by a key with red. To be sure you see the colors the same way I do, I would like to have you name the colors in the lower row or the key colors from left to right. This is what? Please read. That's right. As before, when you are ready to go, press the green button, and the first light will come on showing a color. Turn that light off by pressing the key with the same color. All right? Ready; go.

10. This time the task is almost the same except that we have added a symbol over a color. That is, you will see the symbol X or O placed over a color. The principle is the same, however. The key which has the same color and symbol as the light turns off that light. For example, Symbol O on top of the color green would be turned off by the key with Symbol O on green above it. This time then you have to use two facts to decide which key to press, the color and the symbol—whether it is a cross or a circle. When you are ready to go, press the green button and the first light will come on. Match the color and the symbol with the proper key. Ready? Go. Please read the lower row or the key colors and symbols from left to right.

11. *Symbols.* This time the task remains the same but has an additional feature in it which I will explain to you. Each light will turn on a number. On the card above the lights row you will see a row of numbers. For example, if the light came on lighting up Number 1, below Number 1 you will see a symbol. This is the symbol which you look for in the lower row, or the key row. This symbol will turn off that light. The task thus consists of looking at the light which has come on, reading the number, looking for the number in the top row of the symbol key, finding the symbol below it, and then looking for that symbol in the key row and turning off the light. Let me show you an example. Suppose the light came on lighting up Number 9. What key would you press to turn off Light 9? That's correct. Suppose the light came on illuminating Number 2. What symbol key would you press to turn off Light 2? That's correct. As soon as you are comfortable, press the green button and go. Ready?

VERBAL RELATIONS

Controls

12. This time we will have a syllable in every window or circle. The syllables above the keys tell you which light they turn off. That is, suppose the first light had the syllable "tab" on it, then *this* key would turn off the light. The lights will come on one after the other in a regular order. The left light will come on first after you have pressed the green button. Before we begin, please read all syllables on the lower row aloud to me.

13. This time we will have a word in every window or circle. The word above each key tells you which light it turns off. That is, sup-

pose the first light had the word "girl" on it, then *this* key would turn off the light. The lights will come on one after the other in a regular order. The left light will come on first after you have pressed the green button. Before we begin, please read all words on the lower row aloud to me.

Word Association

14, 15. This time there will be words again on the circles which may help you to find the correct button. *Select always that word on the lower row which seems to go best with that on the upper row.* Before we begin, read all the words in the lower row aloud to me.

Word Relations

16, 17, 18. The next task needs a short explanation. If you take any word, there are always a number of others which belong to it which are coordinates to the word. For instance, coordinates to the word "chair" are table, bed, cabinet, desk, couch, bookshelf, bench.

All these coordinates have something in common; all denote parts of the household—products, furniture, equipment. One calls such a word as "furniture" a superordinate to the word "chair." It includes more or embraces more. Finally, all the things named above consist of many parts. Thus parts of a chair are the legs, the wood, the seat, the back.

Altogether we have three groups of words: coordinates, superordinates, and those which denote parts. (The instruction may be repeated.)

Now, in the first (second, third) problem it will be your task *to select always that word in the lower row which is a coordinate to the word which will appear in the upper row.* Make as few errors as possible, and work as fast as you can. Before we begin, read all the words in the lower row aloud to me.

In the second (first, third) problem, it will be your task *to select always that word in the lower row which is a superordinate to the word which will appear in the upper row.* Make as few errors as possible and work as fast as you can. Before we begin, read all the words in the lower row aloud to me.

In the third (first, second) problem, it will be your task *to select always that word in the lower row which denotes a part of that thing which will be named in the upper row.* Make as few errors as possible and work as fast as you can. Before we begin, read all the words in the lower row aloud to me.

Word Completion

19. In the last task, only syllables will be presented in the circles. *One syllable in the upper row and one syllable in the lower row will make up a word.* The first syllable will be always in the upper row. In the first problem these words will be adjectives or adverbs like clev-er, ex-tra, ear-ly, charm-ing. Before we begin, read all the syllables in the lower row aloud to me.

20. In the second problem, the words will be concrete nouns; that is, they will denote something which you can touch, see, smell, or hear, like brid-ge, fin-ger, la-ke, bro-ther. Before we begin, read all the syllables in the lower row aloud to me.

21. In the third problem, the words will be verbs like re-main, pretend, pun-ish, en-ter. Before we begin, read all the syllables in the lower row aloud to me.

22. In the fourth problem, the words will be abstract nouns; that is, they will denote something which one can just think of, which are mere ideas like beau-ty, de-gree, ac-tion, mo-ment. Before we begin, read all the syllables in the lower row aloud to me.

REFERENCES

American Psychological Association. Technical recommendations for psychological tests and diagnostic techniques. *Psychol. Bull. Suppl.*, 1954, **51,** 1-38.

Balinsky, B. An analysis of the mental factors of various age groups from nine to sixty. *Genet. Psychol. Monogr.*, 1941, **23,** 191-234.

Birren, J.E. A factorial analysis of the Wechsler-Bellevue scale given to an elderly population. *J. consult. Psychol.*, 1952, **16,** 399-405.

Birren, J.E., Botwinick, J., Weiss, A.D., & Morrison, D.F. An analysis of perceptual and mental tests given to healthy elderly men. *J. Geront.*, 1958, **13,** 444. (Abstract)

Cohen, J. A factor-analytically based rationale for the Wechsler adult intelligence scale. *J. consult. Psychol.*, 1957, **21,** 451-457. (a)

Cohen, J. The factorial structure of the WAIS between early adulthood and old age. *J. consult. Psychol.*, 1957, **21,** 283-290. (b)

Cornfield, J. Principles of research. *Amer. J. ment. Defic.*, 1959, **64,** 240-252.

Doppelt, J.E., & Wallace, W.L. Standardization of the Wechsler adult intelligence scale for older persons. *J. abnorm. soc. Psychol.*, 1955, **51,** 312-330.

Eisdorfer, C., Busse, E.W., & Cohen, L.D. The WAIS performance of an aged sample: The relationship between verbal and performance IQ's. *J. Geront.*, 1959, **14,** 197-201.

Guilford, J.P. A morphological model for human intelligence. Paper read at the National Academy of Sciences, Washington, D.C., April 25, 1960.

Jones, H. Intelligence and problem solving. In J.E. Birren (Ed.), *Handbook of aging and the individual: Psychological and biological aspects.* Chicago: The University of Chicago Press, 1959. Pp. 700-738.

Kallmann, F.J., & Jarvik, Lissy F. Individual differences in constitution and genetic background. In J.E. Birren (Ed.), *Handbook of aging and the individual: Psychological and biological aspects.* Chicago: The University of Chicago Press, 1959. Pp. 216-263.

Wechsler, D. *Manual for the Wechsler adult intelligence scale.* New York: Psychological Corporation, 1955. (a)

Wechsler, D. The measurement and evaluation of intelligence of older persons. In *Old age in the modern world,* Edinburgh: E. &. S. Livingstone, 1955. Pp. 275-279. (b)

CHAPTER 2

Psychological and Psychomotor
Functions in Aging

SUZANNE PACAUD

To the present, research in biometrical and psychological gerontology has tended to be separate from research in general or comparative psychology and biometrics. This is to be deplored. None of the problems raised by the latter investigations has yet found its place in any gerontological research except A. T. Welford's works on age and skill (Welford, 1951; Welford, 1958). This is easy to understand considering the lack of data which would lead gerontological research in that direction, but it seems that it is a particular turn of mind, rather than lack of data, which has prevented researchers in gerontology, whose scope was exclusively observation of the aged, to use their investigations on senescence to clarify the fundamental problems of biometrics and psychology. So doing, they deprived gerontological research of the possibilities of formulating its own theoretical foundations. I wished to contribute to another way of thinking in gerontology by studying whether intellectual and psychomotor functions underwent changes in aging. For this purpose I chose the method of factor analysis.

The fundamental object of all the sciences is unique; the form of expression, nevertheless, changes with the methodology of the disciplines. In this research we shall apply only the techniques in Thurstone's *Multiple Factor Analysis* (Thurstone, 1947). I believe it necessary to recall, at the start, the definition which Thurstone (1955) proposed at the Factor Analysis Colloquium in Paris. The fundamental object of each science, according to Thurstone, is the accumulation of data and the determination of principles which enable one to draw precise predictions in a particular discipline. The factor analysis contributes to the realization of this aim in two ways: (1) directly, by condensing and identifying the sources of variance, thus attempting a conceptual frame which could make possible the understanding of behavior; (2) indirectly, by isolating factors, making it possible to suggest variables and patterns of variables which might be studied more intensively by other methods. It seems to me this study finds its justification in this definition.

For a long time studies using factor analysis have shown that psychological and psychophysiological functions tend to group into constellations though the structure of such groupings is still under discussion. These discussions, however, are usually concerned with the superiority of one or another technique—the naming of factors, their independence or hierarchical order, or, in the latter case, the primacy of one factor. The factorial structure of the functions has never been questioned. Its study, in connection with age, has given rise to numerous works, mostly related to children, where the G factor has been identified many times with the factor of intellectual maturation. Besides, whatever the significance given it, the G factor does not seem to vary in the course of development, even in children from ten to fourteen years old, who have outgrown the stage when tests in which the G factor does not predominate may be used almost exclusively.

Thus I decided to reconsider the problem which is essential for elaborating in psychology a valid theory of the structure of psychological functions. We believe gerontological research can shed new light on the problem, which we phrased this way: Whatever the factorial structure observed in a group of young adults, is it modified in older groups and, if it is modified, in which direction?

TABLE 1
CLUSTERS AROUND CENTERS OF GRAVITY

Number of test	Name of test	Designation of the function corresponding to the cluster
1	Instructions	Function A: Cluster of in-
2	Apprehensive memory	tellectual tests
3	Associated words evoking memory	
4	Oral text evoking memory	
8	Logical intelligence test	
5	Speed of sign-barring in the con- centrated-attention test (free rhythm)	Function B: Cluster of speed tests at free rhythm or un- der stress
9	Speed in adjusting simple motions in the pointing test (rhythm un- der stress)	
12	Speed in coordinating motions in the turning test (free rhythm)	
6	Accuracy in sign-barring in the concentrated-attention test	Function C:* Concentrated at- tention (isolated test)
7	Recognition of preliminary heard auditory images	Function D: Mnemonic (iso- lated test)
	Precision in coordinating motions in the turning test:	Function E: Cluster of tests setting in action precision in coordinating motions (free rhythm)
10	Number of errors	
11	Duration of errors	
13	Learning psychomotor choice re- actions (number of errors in the diffused-attention test)	Function F: Learning (iso- lated test)
	Precision of psychomotor choice reactions in the diffused-attention test:	Function H: Cluster of tests setting in action precision of psychomotor choice re- actions at rhythm under stress
14	Visual stimuli	
15	Audiovisual stimuli	

*Later eliminated from the study.

We carried out a multiple-factor analysis of fifteen tests
(Table 1). The subjects formed two samples of the same social and
professional group. The only difference, a very small one, was the
level of education. All the subjects in the first sample had an elementary school certificate; all the subjects from the second had only a few
years' schooling and no examination certificate. All applicants for
S.N.C.F. (French National Railway) jobs, however, have to pass an
examination corresponding to three years of schooling so the samples
were homogeneous.

Each sample contained a large number of subjects. The least
numerous group had about one hundred subjects for each test, the
most numerous nearly one thousand. The subjects ranged from
twenty to fifty-five years of age, and we fixed an interval of five years
to divide the groups. The whole study included about four thousand
subjects. All of them were examined at the S.N.C.F. Laboratory of
Applied Psychology under strictly controlled conditions to eliminate,
as far as possible, experimental errors. To carry out the factor analysis,
we chose a pilot group—the youngest adults—who ranged from nineteen years and six months to twenty-four years and five months in age
and who had elementary school certificates. It is on this group that all
rotations of the axes were performed.

I started from the following hypothesis: If the constellations
of the studied functions remain constant with aging, the axial rotations performed on the pilot group, when automatically carried to the
other groups, must show constellations consistent with those observed
in the pilot group. If, on the contrary, modifications in the functional
constellations take place in aging and if these modifications obey certain rules, I should be able to discern a certain regularity in the
variations, in either the saturation of the functions by the factors or
the displacing of the functions from one factor to another. Lastly, if
in aging the constellations obey only the law of disorderly fluctuations,
I should not find the pattern of the pilot group's constellations in any
group that had been submitted to the automatic rotations.

The five first rotations performed on the pilot group showed
many clusters. The first cluster was composed of the instructions (also
called immediate memory of digits), apprehensive memory, associated
words evoking memory, oral text evoking memory, and logical intelligence test (Table 1, tests 1, 2, 3, 4, and 8). The second cluster was
composed of speed of sign-barring in the concentrated-attention test,
speed in adjusting simple motions in the pointing test (rhythm under

stress), speed in coordinating motions (free rhythm) in the turning test [1] (Table 1, tests 5, 9, and 12).

Although it appeared isolated, the accuracy of sign-barring in the concentrated-attention test showed disorderly placement and hindered the choice of axes, which should lead to a distinct separation among the other clusters, so I decided to eliminate this test after many fruitless attempts at rotations (Table 1, Test 6). In contrast, the form of memory explored by the test of recognition in preliminarily heard auditory images appeared isolated, but was regular in its relations with the other clusters (Table 1, Test 7). Another cluster was composed of the number and duration of errors in the turning test, precision in coordinating motions in the turning test (Table 1, tests 10-11). Learning psychomotor choice reactions (number of mistakes in the diffused-attention test) still appeared isolated, with a noticeable distance from the other clusters (Table 1, Test 13). Lastly, another cluster emerged, composed of the precision of psychomotor choice reactions to visual and audiovisual stimuli in the diffused-attention test, the stimuli appearing rhythmically under stress (Table 1, tests 14-15).

So it appeared, with evident clarity, that it was not necessary to continue isolated tests for the research, but that, on the contrary, it was of great interest to constitute clusters according to the psychological functions the observed clusters measured. Guided by these considerations, I composed six new elements—four clusters and two isolated tests—for the objects of further axial rotations. The third column of Table 1 indicates each of the seven elements, which are designated by the functions they seem to concern. Each function is designated by a letter, and hereafter I shall call it by that letter. Let me mention again that Function C was eliminated from the investigation.

We studied the six functions in Table 1, and, when a cluster was involved, the subsequent rotations were carried out on the mean calculated from the coordinates of the tests composing it. For instance, regarding Function E, Axis I has been chosen to pass by the intersection of the abscissa and ordinate respectively, representing the mean of abscissas and ordinates in tests 10 and 11. I proceeded in the same way for the other functions.

I must insist on the following: my first concern is not to discuss the particular configuration of the functions; whatever the

---

[1] In France this is a well-known test devised by Professor J.M. Lahy to assess complex coordination of hand movements.

TABLE 2
FUNCTION A: DEFINITIVE COORDINATES

Educational level	Age groups*	Factors				
		I 4	II 4	III 6	IV 5	V 5
I.P. (Little school- ing, no certi- ficate)	19-6 to 24-5	.20	.28	−.03	.21	.48
	24-6 to 29-5	.08	.33	.05	.30	.40
	29-6 to 34-5	.20	.39	.01	.31	.41
	34-6 to 39-5	.05	.32	.16	.30	.40
	39-6 to 44-5	.14	.46	.14	.32	.41
	44-6 and over	.20	.28	−.04	.29	.43
C. E. P. (Elementary school certi- ficate)	19-6 to 24-5	.15	.30	−.02	.17	.51
	24-6 to 29-5	.15	.31	−.13	.32	.44
	29-6 to 34-5	.23	.18	−.08	.33	.36
	34-6 to 39-5	.20	.36	−.03	.16	.42
	39-6 to 44-5	.20	.32	−.09	.21	.35
	44-6 and over	.16	.47	.07	.23	.44

*In tables 2-7, age groups are by years and months (19-6 to 24-5 signifies nineteen years, six months, to twenty-four years, five months).

TABLE 3
FUNCTION B: DEFINITIVE COORDINATES

Educational level	Age groups	Factors				
		I 4	II 4	III 6	IV 5	V 5
I.P.	19-6 to 24-5	.12	.41	.17	.27	.05
	24-6 to 29-5	.34	.27	.17	.12	.29
	29-6 to 34-5	.17	.19	.34	.04	.32
	34-6 to 39-5	.34	.35	−.24	.05	.18
	39-6 to 44-5	.27	−.01	−.14	.29	.49
	44-6 and over	.46	.22	.21	−.10	.14
C.E.P.	19-6 to 24-5	.05	.40	.26	.45	.01
	24-6 to 29-5	−.03	.11	.21	.25	.44
	29-6 to 34-5	−.06	.43	.20	.13	.28
	34-6 to 39-5	−.09	.09	.25	.35	.20
	39-6 to 44-5	.11	.14	.25	.29	.32
	44-6 and over	.29	−.03	−.02	.13	.54

TABLE 4
FUNCTION D: DEFINITIVE COORDINATES

Educational level	Age groups	Factors				
		I 4	II 4	III 6	IV 5	V 5
I.P.	19-6 to 24-5	.21	.32	−.06	.69	.29
	24-6 to 29-5	−.15	.13	.23	.71	.08
	29-6 to 34-5	.40	.18	−.25	.44	.29
	34-6 to 39-5	.08	.29	.12	.55	.41
	39-6 to 44-5	.22	.62	.05	.17	.18
	44-6 and over	.18	.43	−.28	.44	.20
C.E.P.	19-6 to 24-5	.08	.72	.12	.48	−.03
	24-6 to 29-5	.37	.36	−.28	.17	.28
	29-6 to 34-5	.22	.28	−.32	.21	.10
	34-6 to 39-5	.28	.35	−.39	.37	.10
	39-6 to 44-5	.10	.48	.19	.48	.07
	44-6 and over	−.10	.40	.04	.31	.32

TABLE 5
FUNCTION E: DEFINITIVE COORDINATES

Educational level	Age groups	Factors				
		I 4	II 4	III 6	IV 5	V 5
I.P.	19-6 to 24-5	.92	.21	.12	−.02	−.19
	24-6 to 29-5	.77	−.32	.24	.03	.41
	29-6 to 34-5	.83	.18	.08	−.15	−.04
	34-6 to 39-5	.79	−.36	.32	.19	.25
	39-6 to 44-5	.95	.16	.16	−.08	.05
	44-6 and over	.75	−.26	.36	.35	.35
C.E.P.	19-6 to 24-5	.97	0	.41	0	0
	24-6 to 29-5	.83	.56	.71	−.06	−.20
	29-6 to 34-5	.78	−.09	.50	−.26	.24
	34-6 to 39-5	.86	.63	.53	.06	−.20
	39-6 to 44-5	.76	.39	.77	.16	.08
	44-6 and over	.93	.22	.63	−.07	.02

TABLE 6
FUNCTION F: DEFINITIVE COORDINATES

Educational level	Age groups	Factors				
		I 4	II 4	III 6	IV 5	V 5
I.P.	19-6 to 24-5	.29	.24	.63	.13	.45
	24-6 to 29-5	.55	.56	.49	.04	.36
	29-6 to 34-5	.32	.32	.55	.30	.01
	34-6 to 39-5	.44	.56	.39	.34	−.12
	39-6 to 44-5	.30	.23	.60	.18	.54
	44-6 and over	.35	.55	.44	.30	.15
C.E.P.	19-6 to 24-5	.27	.29	.44	.10	.17
	24-6 to 29-5	.55	.05	.32	.25	.30
	29-6 to 34-5	.25	.24	.66	.42	.04
	34-6 to 39-5	.55	.01	.36	.13	.31
	39-6 to 44-5	.61	.01	.22	.25	.21
	44-6 and over	.49	.10	.71	.30	−.06

TABLE 7
FUNCTION H: DEFINITIVE COORDINATES

Educational level	Age groups	Factors				
		I 4	II 4	III 6	IV 5	V 5
I.P.	19-6 to 24-5	.20	.18	.57	.14	.27
	24-6 to 29-5	.41	.30	.39	.21	.41
	29-6 to 34-5	.23	.05	.59	.43	.02
	34-6 to 39-5	.48	.40	.27	.15	−.32
	39-6 to 44-5	.37	.07	.61	.33	.30
	44-6 and over	.29	.45	.45	.40	−.12
C.E.P.	19-6 to 24-5	.25	.28	.50	0	0
	24-6 to 29-5	.50	−.06	.39	.04	.30
	29-6 to 34-5	.30	.44	.36	.27	−.17
	34-6 to 39-5	.56	−.16	.31	.30	.07
	39-6 to 44-5	.73	−.02	.57	.35	−.04
	44-6 and over	.33	.07	.69	.35	.06

observed configuration, I want to know only how it may be influenced by aging. From that point of view, two phenomena which are central in any factorial analysis were examined: (1) the contribution of each factor to each function (the degree of saturation of each function in each factor); and (2) the constellation of functions in relation to each factor. From the gerontological point of view, the two phenomena interested me not so much in their essence as in their evolution with age. The second interested me more.

THE CONSTELLATION OF FUNCTIONS IN CONSIDERATION OF EACH FACTOR

We isolated five factors for the six functions mentioned above. The value of the definitive coordinates for the six age groups and the two samples characterized by level of education will be found in tables 2-7. Thus we have a table of twelve groups of subjects for each function.

In certain functions it can immediately be seen which factor holds each of them. For instance, Factor V controls Function A (the intellectual) and is maintained whatever the age and education of the sample. Similarly, Factor I controls Function E (coordinating motions), and this also holds whatever the age and education of the sample.

For the other functions the patterns are not so clear so synoptical tables (tables 8-13) were formed to show, for each function and group of subjects, the factors in decreasing order of saturation. I decided to take twenty-five as the significant limit of saturation, thus the factors which did not reach that limit for a given function are not in the tables.

Function A

In Table 8 Factor V has primacy in ten out of twelve groups concerning Function A. As for the two other groups, although Factor II is in first place, it is immediately followed by Factor V, and the differences in saturation are very slight. It is to be noticed that Factor IV concerns Function A to a significant degree, though much less than Factor II. Factors I and III are not on Table 8 since they did not reach the limit of significance. Thus Factor V is the chief "controller" of Function A, and the position of Function A is maintained despite age and education.

In relation to aging, the second statement is important. Another phenomenon is also worth discussion here. It seems normal that a factor which is saturated to a high degree should show constancy of saturation in all age groups, but factors which have low, or, practically speaking, no saturation should show disorderly fluctuations at different ages and levels of education. But for Function A, a remarkable phenomenon appears—whatever degree of saturation a factor has, the degree shows surprising constancy for all age groups and either level of education.

Function B

The regularity found in Function A does not appear in Function B (Table 9). Five factors take first place in the twelve groups here, and the positions of the other factors offer no suggestion about this change. Speed does not seem to concern one factor more than it does any other. In regard to gerontology, it is difficult to assign a constant constellation to this function.

Function D

As for Function D (Table 10), a remarkable regularity appears again. Factors II and IV are very clearly involved in this func-

TABLE 8
FUNCTION A

Age group	Educational level	Factor saturations					
1	I.P.	V	.48	II	.28		
	C.E.P.	V	.51	II	.30		
2	I.P.	V	.40	II	.33	IV	.30
	C.E.P.	V	.44	IV	.32	II	.31
3	I.P.	V	.41	II	.39	IV	.31
	C.E.P.	V	.36	IV	.33		
4	I.P.	V	.40	II	.32	IV	.30
	C.E.P.	V	.42	II	.36		
5	I.P.	II	.46	V	.41	IV	.32
	C.E.P.	V	.35	II	.32		
6	I.P.	V	.43	IV	.29	II	.28
	C.E.P.	II	.47	V	.44		

TABLE 9
FUNCTION B

Age group	Educational level	Factor saturations						
1	I.P.	II	.41	IV	.27			
	C.E.P.	IV	.45	II	.40			
2	I.P.	I	.34	V	.29	II	.27	
	C.E.P.	V	.44	IV	.25			
3	I.P.	III	.34	V	.32			
	C.E.P.	II	.43	V	.28			
4	I.P.	II	.35	I	.34			
	C.E.P.	IV	.35	III	.25			
5	I.P.	V	.49	IV	.29	I	.27	
	C.E.P.	V	.32	IV	.29	III	.25	
6	I.P.	I	.46					
	C.E.P.	V	.54	I	.29			

TABLE 10
FUNCTION D

Age group	Educational level	Factor saturations						
1	I.P.	IV	.69	II	.32	V	.29	
	C.E.P.	II	.72	IV	.48			
2	I.P.	IV	.71					
	C.E.P.	I	.37	II	.36	V	.28	
3	I.P.	IV	.44	I	.40	V	.29	
	C.E.P.	II	.28					
4	I.P.	IV	.55	V	.41	II	.29	
	C.E.P.	IV	.37	II	.35	I	.28	
5	I.P.	II	.62					
	C.E.P.	II	.44	IV	.48			
6	I.P.	IV	.44	II	.43			
	C.E.P.	II	.40	V	.32	IV	.31	

TABLE 11
FUNCTION E

Age group	Educational level	Factor saturations			
1	I.P.	I .92			
	C.E.P.	I .97	III .41		
2	I.P.	I .77	V .41		
	C.E.P.	I .83	III .71	II .56	
3	I.P.	I .83			
	C.E.P.	I .78	III .50		
4	I.P.	I .79	III .32	V .25	
	C.E.P.	I .86	II .63	III .53	
5	I.P.	I .95			
	C.E.P.	III .77	I .76	II .39	
6	I.P.	I .75	IV .35	V .35	III .30
	C.E.P.	I .93	III .63		

TABLE 12
FUNCTION F

Age group	Educational level	Factor saturations			
1	I.P.	III .63	V −.45	I .29	
	C.E.P.	III .44	II .29	I .27	
2	I.P.	II .56	I .55	III .49	V .36
	C.E.P.	I .55	III .32	V .30	IV .25
3	I.P.	III .55	I .32	II .32	IV .30
	C.E.P.	III .66	IV .42	I .25	
4	I.P.	II .56	I .44	III .39	IV .34
	C.E.P.	I .55	III .36		
5	I.P.	III .60	V .54	I .30	
	C.E.P.	I .61	IV .25		
6	I.P.	II .55	III .44	I .35	IV .35
	C.E.P.	III .71	I .49	IV .30	

tion. They alternate for primacy, and, when they do not appear in first place, they are, in most cases, in second. Factor I appears three times for the twelve groups, and only once is it in first place. We can conclude that factors II and IV are mnemonic factors and that of these two Factor II is more general since it is closely related to Function A which represents a cluster where other forms of memory are present (the memory of an oral text, digits, and associated words). Factor IV, consequently, might be more a specific mnemonic form of recognition. Finding it associated with Function A is not surprising, since one of the tests in Cluster A employs some of the words that are used in the recognition test concerning Function D. From the gerontological point of view, there is a remarkable constancy regarding factors II and IV.

Function E

Constancy despite age and education appears strong for Function E, which concerns precision in coordinating motions (Table 11). This function, explored by the number and duration of errors in the test of turning, is undoubtedly general. It seems to be the equivalent on the psychomotor plane of the logical intelligence test on the intellectual plane. In fact, in my experience with job selection, I have seldom found a subject who got a very good result in another psychomotor test when he had not achieved a fairly significant level in the test of turning. Moreover, in all the studies done for selection in occupations requiring manual dexterity, the test of turning is always extremely valid.

Not only does Function E almost always involve Factor I, but also the saturation of this factor reaches values seldom found in factorial analysis. In the only group where Factor I does not have primacy, it appears in second place, and the difference of saturation is negligible. It is Factor III which appears most often in second place. The other factors are very rarely represented. In relation to aging, once again there is remarkable constancy in this function's constellation.

Function F

Function F involves several factors, but Factor III predominates, occupying first place six, and second place three, out of twelve times (Table 12).

Knowing that the only test figuring under Function F concerns learning psychomotor choice reactions, I understood why Factor III came second in Function E, for the test of turning, which involves Function E, is repeated three times for each subject, and it is the mean of these three trials which is the final result. It is obvious that, in the last analysis, the factor of psychomotor learning is important, and this holds true for all subjects. Thus, Factor III held an important place for Function E. For Function F, on the contrary, we shall find Factor I, involving coordinating motions, in first place three times and in second place four times, since learning here involves the coordination of psychomotor choice reactions to visual and audiovisual stimuli. Again we find the two mnemonic factors; this is not surprising, since learning enters here. Factor II, which is more general, figures three times in first place, and twice in second, for the twelve groups.

In relation to aging, the pattern of the constellation is constant enough, although this constancy is less clear than that of functions A and E. It is generally Factor III or Factor I which predominates at any age and level of education.

Function H

For Function H, Factor III always dominates (Table 13). It might be thought that, as 'the tests progress, improved precision of psychomotor choice reactions would persist as the saturating characteristic, though mastery of it is practically accomplished in the preparatory phase where, in the rotations of the axes, it was separated under the name of Function F.

Again, from a gerontological point of view, there is constancy in the constellation of Function H, but factorial analysis shows that this function ought to be interpreted in terms of improvement rather than attention, as is generally done. One might be equally tempted to interpret Factor III in terms of attention rather than improvement, for concentration plays an effective part in the test of turning as well as in the acquisition and automatization of psychomotor reactions to visual and audiovisual stimuli appearing in rapid rhythm. This interpretation, however, does not seem to hold true, for the complete absence of Factor III for Function A, which concerns intellectual tests, could not be explained if it did.

I would like to insist that the constellation's (of Function H) constancy in aging has all the more significance, since it proved to be independent of education. (I shall speak of the four exceptions below.) This statement is important in considering the phenomenon demonstrated by previous research: the difference between the two levels of education is significant throughout aging for results from the same tests taken by subjects belonging to the same samples.

I would like to draw attention to another interesting phenomenon. In very few cases—only four—did the power of saturation by a factor regularly separate the two samples of unequal educational level. The first case concerns the factor of coordinating motions (Factor I) in speed (Function B). It is the only factor showing some stability in the constellation for Function B. For the less educated (I.P.) the speed function is more strongly saturated in the factor of coordinating motions than it is for the more educated (C.E.P.) for whom saturation in Factor I is nonexistent before forty; beyond that age, saturation by Factor I increases for both samples. One might be tempted to think that work speed will mean different ways of organizing work and that for the more educated subjects motor coordination is not important. From a gerontological point of view, the constant separation between the two samples until forty is to be noticed.

The second case is related to factors II and IV in Function D. Factor IV, the more specific of the mnemonic forms, is utilized in the auditory images recognition test and saturates this function to a much

TABLE 13
FUNCTION H

Age group	Educational level	Factor saturations			
1	I.P.	III .57	V .27		
	C.E.P.	III .50	II .28	I .25	
2	I.P.	I .41	V .41	III .39	II .30
	C.E.P.	I .50	III .39	V .30	
3	I.P.	III .59	IV .43	I .23	
	C.E.P.	II .44	III .36	I .30	IV .27
4	I.P.	I .48	II .40	III .27	
	C.E.P.	I .56	III .31	IV .30	
5	I.P.	III .61	I .37	IV .33	V .30
	C.E.P.	III .69	IV .35	I .33	
6	I.P.	III .45	II .45	IV .40	I .29
	C.E.P.	III .69	IV .35	I .33	

greater extent for the less educated subjects. This phenomenon becomes still more interesting when, on examining Factor II, one
observes the reverse situation—the saturations are higher for the more
educated subjects. It has already been seen that Factor II is a more
general mnemonic factor since it involves Cluster A. One might think
that more educated subjects call forth a general memorization mechanism even when a very particular form of memory is concerned,
whereas less educated subjects remain, in their memorization, dependent on the particular form and are limited because they do not
try other associative supports. From a gerontological point of view, the
constancy of separation to forty years of age is to be pointed out, but
the fact that at this age the phenomenon vanishes, even reverses
slightly, for Factor II, as well as for Factor IV, is interesting.

The third case is the most accentuated. It involves Factor III,
which is interpreted in terms of improvement, in Function E (coordinating motions). The saturation in the improvement factor is far
higher in the more educated sample. Moreover—and this is important
for gerontology—this separation is constant and very distinct for all
age groups.

Comparing the saturations of Function E by Factor I, which
is a psychomotor factor, and by Factor III, which concerns improvement, I can conclude that education induces no difference in saturation when an organic phenomenon, such as an aptitude to general
motor coordination, is in question. Education does make a noticeable
difference, however, when the point is improving this coordination by
learning from the errors in a course of successive experiences. This,
moreover, is true for all age groups.

SUMMARY AND CONCLUSIONS

In accordance with the initial hypothesis, I may conclude the
following.

The constellations of the psychological and psychomotor
functions studied here remain constant despite aging, since the axial
rotations performed on a pilot group and automatically carried to
eleven other groups reveal in the latter groups patterns of constellations similar to those observed in the pilot group. Evidently this
constancy persists with some latitude of fluctuation. (This latitude
ought to be admitted with even more tolerance since the rotations
were carried out automatically.) An exception must be made, how-

ever, for the cluster of speed tests (Function B). No constancy of constellation appears for any factor in this function except Factor I, which saturates the function more for the less educated subjects.

The difference in saturation between the education samples remains distinctly constant in all age groups. This difference can be explained by saying that the performance in speed initiates different forms of work organization and that with less educated subjects the factor of psychomotor organization must have primacy over all other forms of organization.

The same phenomenon of regular separation of saturation despite aging appears in two other cases. The two mnemonic factors, II and IV, saturate Function D in reverse for both education samples. The more general factor (II) has greater saturation in the less educated subjects, whereas the more specific mnemonic factor (recognition of auditory images, Factor IV) saturates Function D less in the less educated sample. After the age of forty, the separation vanishes, and the phenomenon even reverses slightly. I think we can interpret this in light of the fact that more education trains subjects to use higher, more general techniques of memorization even when a very specialized form of memory is in question, whereas the less educated subjects remain concerned with the specific form and do not try other associative supports for memorization. The most distinct separation is manifested for the improvement factor (Factor III) in coordinating motions (Function E). This function is more saturated by the improvement factor at the higher education level.

Besides, if the identity of saturations for the two samples by Factor I is taken into consideration, the psychomotricity factor and these two phenomena are brought close, one can say that when purely organic aptitudes are in question, education causes no difference of saturation whatever the age group; in contrast, for drawing consequences from errors, education modifies the saturation power of the involved factor and modifies it in the same way for each age group.

In the twenty-six other cases, the constancy of the constellation is independent of education. This phenomenon is worthy of emphasis, as our other research has shown how much education influences the decline of psychological functions. This leads me to say that, whatever the level of these functions or aptitudes, the constellations of the functions remain similar.

How can one interpret the fact that, in this whole set of regularities and constancies, the sole speed function (B) is alien to the laws? All the studies in gerontology, particularly those of A.T. Welford (1951; 1958) and J.E. Birren (1955; 1959), have proven that speed is much altered by aging. To my mind, the rational explanation would be that maintaining speed—whether perceptive or psychomotor—throughout life depends on diverse factors whose influences can completely modify the normal organic ones. Occupation, athletics, driving a car, family environment, or, on the contrary, yielding to the slowness of old age by assimilating an environment of old people—all greatly modify the speed mechanism and its possible decline with age. These influences, moreover, specifically touch the individual and the speed function among the other psychological, psychomotor, and motor functions. The observed laws of decline are either caused by organic factors which provoke aging in the individual or by ecological factors which cause the senescence of the individual. These laws are altered by everybody's personal way of life. This is why speed does not inevitably decline with other functions. Besides, under such influences, the assumed links between speed and the other functions may deteriorate at any given age, and new links will be established. This could explain why one finds no constancy in the speed constellation although its decline has been demonstrated by all gerontologists.

REFERENCES

Birren, J.E. Age changes in speed of simple responses and perception and their significance for complex behavior. In *Old age in the modern world*. Edinburgh: E. & S. Livingstone, 1955. Pp. 235-247.

Birren, J.E. Sensation, perception and modification of behavior in relation to the process of aging. In J.E. Birren, H.A. Imus, & W.F. Windle (Eds.), *The process of aging in the various systems*. Springfield, Ill.: Charles C Thomas, 1959. Pp. 143-165.

Thurstone, L.L. *Multiple factor analysis*. Chicago: The University of Chicago Press, 1947.

Thurstone, L.L. Problèmes actuels et méthodes nouvelles en analyse factorielle. In *L'analyse factorielle et ses applications*. Paris: Centre National de la Recherche Scientifique, 1955. Pp. 31-41.

Welford, A.T. *Skill and age*. London: Oxford University Press, 1951.

Welford, A.T. *Ageing and human skill*. London: Oxford University Press, 1958.

CHAPTER 3

*Information Transmission
and Age*

STEPHEN GRIEW

The theme of this paper is the aging individual's changing ability to receive and transmit information and the implications of this change for the maintenance of complex skills. The paper will consist of an attempt to put into perspective a section of the experimental work undertaken since 1955 by the Bristol University Unit for Research on Employment of Older Workers. Since the work of the unit formally ended in 1960 and since most of its experimental work has been concerned with information transmission, it seems appropriate at this time to attempt to summarize this part of its efforts and try to draw them together within a single framework.

63

BACKGROUND AND STUDIES

The history of research in aging and skill has been profoundly influenced in Great Britain by the ideas of Craik (1947; 1948), as the first report (Welford, 1951) of the Nuffield Unit for Research into Problems of Ageing at Cambridge University demonstrates. The basis of Craik's approach was that the exponent of skills may be regarded as a link in a communication network, receiving, processing, and transmitting information from devices designed to present data to him (displays) to others designed to receive data from him (controls). In acting this way, the operator is conceived rather like a self-regulating servomechanism, maintaining by his own intervention a state of equilibrium in the system he controls and of which he is a part.

Although it has been customary to fragment research on human performance into studies of sensory efficiency on one hand and motor performance on the other, the true significance of what takes place between the reception of signals at the sense organs and the initiation of responses by muscle groups has probably been properly appreciated only recently. Craik's early work led to a great deal of research into central limitations on performance. The introduction of concepts of cybernetics into psychology (Wiener, 1948) and the statistical procedures of modern communications theory (Shannon & Weaver, 1949) have done much to place the early analogical thinking on an empirical, quantitative basis. Numerous studies serve to reinforce the view of the human operator as a single channel of communication (for discussions see Broadbent, 1958; Welford, 1952; Welford, 1959c) of limited capacity (see especially Crossman, 1953; Fitts, 1954; Hick, 1952; Hyman, 1953; Quastler, 1955).

It has long been known that aging is associated with a marked slowing of responses and an increase in what is frequently termed "caution," and it was not unreasonable that early work on the effects of aging on skilled performance was concerned with whether this slowing down was caused mainly by peripheral or central factors. The literature on this topic has been reviewed by Birren (1955; 1956) and Welford (1958; 1959b), and it is apparent that the central mechanisms which classify, process, and decide about incoming signals are among those on which aging has its greatest effects. One of the hypotheses set up to account for this slowing, originally made by Crossman and Szafran (1956), is that the rate at which information can be transmitted from display to control declines with age. Direct experimental tests of this hypothesis were not attempted until recently. A study by Goldfarb (1941), however, of multiple-choice reaction time lends itself to information analysis. His data, when plotted as a function of log choice—the conventional measure of information conveyed by a signal (Bricker, 1955)—give more-or-less linear relations at all ages studied. These curves, however, are roughly parallel at different ages, and so the hypothesis that information transmission becomes slower with age is not well supported. This finding is corroborated by a card-sorting experiment by Crossman and Szafran (1956), which was undertaken to test the hypothesis directly. Despite the fact that both these experiments took intervals of time which included muscular movements as dependent variables and thus were not strictly measures of central efficiency, they must still be regarded as important objections to the generalization that the rate of information transmission declines with age.

Later studies did much to reaffirm the usefulness of the hypothesis. One of the first of these, conducted and reported by A.T. Welford (1958), essentially repeated an experiment of Fitts (1954) which investigated the information capacity of the motor system in controlling amplitude of movement. It was found that the rate of information transmission decreased very markedly with age. Recent experiments by Suci, Davidoff, and Surwillo (1960) and Griew (1958d) employing more formal choice reaction time tasks and excluding movement time in the measures of response latency used as dependent variables report linear relationships between reaction time and log choice at all ages studied and add that the slopes of the regression lines increase with age. These studies may be taken as direct support of the hypothesis that aging is accompanied by a decrease in the rate of transmission of information.

It is clear from this discussion that the concept of a reduced capacity for dealing with information is very useful in providing a framework for research into aging and skilled performance. At the same time, it is also clear that in very similar tasks a decrease with age may or may not be found. In order to elucidate the issues raised by this approach, it is necessary to know something about the effect of other variables which might influence the rate at which information can be transmitted by subjects of different ages. In addition to providing information which might be valuable in demonstrating the limits within which this approach is useful, a knowledge of these effects might also help clarify other issues concerned with the relation of age to different aspects of task complexity. This knowledge seems to be needed in view of the inescapable inference from research on aging and skilled performance that complex tasks might militate more severely against the old than the young (Clay, 1957; Kay, 1951; Welford, 1958). The research reported in this paper represents an attempt to clarify some of these issues.

The studies of information transmission outlined here were concerned with the relations of the speed and accuracy of the central processes, age, and a number of independent variables which were thought likely to be important aspects of task complexity. The grounds on which a decision to study any particular aspect of task complexity was made included the purely a priori, findings of previous experiments in related fields, and observation of the performance of older people. Although the conceptual framework of information theory was employed in all these studies, the quantitative analysis of information transmission was attempted in only a few. In most cases it was thought sufficient for the present to relate the speed and accuracy with which decisions are made to changes in task complexity.

A direct test was made of the hypothesis that rate of information transmission decreases with age, and other aspects of task complexity were studied, including the effects of stimulus-response incompatibility, of varying response complexity, of interrupting signals and enforced short-term storage of information in continuous controlling tasks, and of unbalanced signal frequencies.

CONDITIONS OF OPTIMAL CODING

The first experiment attempted to derive relationships between reaction time and log choice in a task which involved moving a stylus from a central position to one of a number of targets which bore a direct relationship with a signal light appearing in a semicircular array of signals. The apparatus used in this experiment has been described in detail by Griew (1959a). Sixteen subjects in two age groups (twenty to thirty and forty-six to sixty) took part in this experiment; all subjects were matched for intelligence, education, and occupation. Signal choice was varied at four levels (1/1, 1/2, 1/4, 1/8), and subjects attempted the four conditions in balanced orders. Suitable practice was given before they performed for experimental purposes. The regression equations which were calculated from the mean reaction time data (each mean was derived from 128 individual reaction times) were

R.T.=0.073 log² n + 0.288 (younger subjects)
R.T.=0.094 log² n + 0.307 (older subjects), where
n=the number of alternative signals which might be presented and
R.T.=mean reaction time (seconds).

From the constants of these equations (Bricker, 1955), rates of information transmission of 13.70 and 10.60 bits/second were calculated for younger and older subjects respectively.

These data provide support for the hypothesis that rate of information transmission decreases with age. The result is in line with that reported by Suci et al. (1960), but is in conflict with those of Crossman and Szafran (1956) and Goldfarb (1941).

CONDITIONS OF SUBOPTIMAL CODING

When the relation between stimulus and response is indirect, or incompatible (Fitts & Seeger, 1953), response latency appears to increase (Crossman, 1956; Fitts & Seeger, 1953; Morin & Grant, 1955). It has been suggested by Taylor (1960) that this increase might be caused by the complication of the stimulus coding involved. Crossman (1956), employing a multiple-choice reaction time task involving stimulus-response incompatibility, has shown consistently lower rates of information transmission than are found in tasks involving stimulus-response compatibility. An increase in complexity of this nature might be expected to affect the performance of older subjects more than that of younger and might be characterized by a greater proportional decrease in rate of information transmission.

In order to test this suggestion, this first experiment was repeated, but in this case the subject's task was to move the stylus to the target directly opposite that indicated by the signal light. In all other ways this experiment was identical with the first. The regression equations derived from the results of this study were

R.T.=0.127 log² n + 0.296 (younger subjects)
R.T.=0.171 log² n + 0.301 (older subjects).

The relation between mean reaction time and log choice remains linear, the slope constant increases in both cases, and the indication is that rate of information transmission has decreased in both groups (Griew, 1958d). These data suggest that a greater proportional decrease in information transmission may have occurred in older than in younger subjects. Calculation of rates of information transmission from the constants in the equations derived from this experiment, however, are 7.90 and 5.80 bits/second for younger and older subjects, respectively. Close examination of these rates of transmission in relation to those derived from the results of the first experiment suggest that the proportional decrease with age caused by the introduction of an incompatible stimulus-response relation is very small. If the rates in the optimally coded task are expressed as a fraction of the rates in the second task, figures of the order of 1.80 may be calculated for both younger and older subjects; the effect of increased complexity of task in the second experiment appears to be proportionate as a function of age. In both cases the important consideration appears to be how the information is handled by the central processes once it has been decoded, not the complexity of decoding. Although no firm conclusions may be drawn from so limited a study, the data suggest that stimulus-response incompatibility as such may not be an important obstacle to the efficiency with which older subjects process and transmit information.

CONDITIONS OF
VARYING RESPONSE COMPLEXITY

Another variable which may have to be employed in defining the complexity of a task concerns the level of complexity of the response which has to be made at the appearance of a signal. Although Woodworth (1938) claims that, as the motor complexity of responses increases, their latencies rise, evidence presented by Brown and Slater-Hammel (1949) and Searle and Taylor (1948) fails to support this view. The question remains, however, whether a differential effect exists according to age in the relation between response complexity and response latency. If such an effect is found, it would be interesting to see whether it is associated with a reduced rate of information transmission or an increased response latency which is the same at all levels of signal choice.

The third experiment concerned this issue. It has been reported in full by Griew (1959a). The apparatus employed was the same as that used in the preceding experiments with the single modification that the motor complexity of the responses could vary slightly by demanding, in one set of conditions, a response which included not only moving the stylus to the target disc, but also, on arrival, thrusting the point of the stylus into a small hole in the middle of the disc. This increased the manipulative complexity of the response. Twenty-four younger and twenty-four older subjects took part, half of each group responding to signals presented at intervals of six seconds, half to signals presented continuously (each signal occurred as the response to the preceding signal was concluded). Each subject responded at both levels of complexity. Experimental conditions were attempted in balanced orders, and a compatible stimulus-response relation was used.

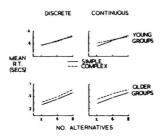

FIG. 1. Reaction time as a function of age, choice, and response complexity. (Griew, 1959a, p. 86. Reprinted with permission.)

The mean reaction times derived from this experiment are plotted in Fig. 1. They demonstrate a clear increase in reaction time of the older subjects when more complex responses are involved. This difference is not observable in the younger subjects' performance. The response latencies in this case, as in all cases reported in this series of experiments, included *only* the time elapsing between the appearance of the signals and the moment at which the response began. It is interesting that the time spent in actually moving the stylus to the target disc varied only slightly under the differing situations.

The data presented in Fig. 1 suggest that there is no decrease in the rate at which information is transmitted by older subjects when the response becomes more complex, but rather that increasing response complexity is accompanied by a constant addition to response latency which is the same at all choice levels. Therefore, despite the fact that in the strict communications-theory sense of the term rate of gain of information is unaffected by increasing response complexity, the speed of the older subjects' central decision-making processes is clearly reduced under these circumstances.

The interpretation of this finding most favored by the writer is that the manipulative part of the response, which at the more complex level follows the initial movement to the target, probably cannot be prepared by older subjects while the initial movement is being guided and monitored. This may be because of their visual and kinesthetic inability to process the information presented about the course of the initial movement at the same time that they are making decisions about what has to be done when the movement has been completed. If this is so, the preparation of the detailed, manipulative part of the response might occur before the response begins, during the latent period. Younger subjects, on the other hand, may be able to process this extra information while making decisions about the end part of responses, and so their response latencies would not be affected. Such an interpretation brings us back once more to the notion that older subjects' efficiency is generally reduced when coping with incoming information—in this case information derived from a feedback system on which successful monitoring of movement is probably based. This interpretation is consistent with, and might be thought to clarify, Welford's conclusion (1958) that ". . . there seems to be an added source of slowness due to difficulty in making decisions while executing movements, and this may be the cause of an inability to integrate series of actions into 'flowing' rhythmic wholes" (p. 107).

To elucidate further, Murrell and Entwisle (1960) have conducted a series of tests involving very high-speed chronocyclographic recordings of the patterns of response movements of varying complexity. These studies are not yet completed, but it seems clear that the patterns of movement are determined in some measure by the complexity of the responses of which they are a part. Plotting acceleration against time, a less regular pattern is observable in older subjects, especially in more complex responses.

CONTINUOUS TASKS

Until now our discussion has been of tasks in which series of discretely presented signals have been involved. Crossman (1960) has demonstrated that the quantitative methods of communication theory may be valuably applied to the analysis of continuous controlling tasks of the tracking variety. Tracking performance has been shown to deteriorate with age, and Welford (1958) has argued that this deterioration is caused by older subjects' compensating for their slower reaction time to signals derived from the track by reducing their accuracy in reproducing swings of the track, thus decreasing choice. This accounts for an increased amplitude error, which is particularly characteristic of tracking performances of older subjects.

Two studies involving continuous tracking performance have been included in the program. In both experiments the same basic apparatus was used. It was originally built by A.E. Earle and used by Welford (1958) and Crossman (1960). Its modifications for the present experiment have been described in Griew (1958a).

Short-Term Storage of Information

The experiment on short-term storage was designed to test the hypothesis that information loss would be relatively greater in older than in younger subjects in situations where data have to be stored for short periods of time prior to use. Six younger and six older subjects were presented with a pursuit tracking task in which a substantial preview of the course was given, but in which the course was obscured for a brief interval just prior to the time when matching took place. In this way, subjects were forced to use data a short time after they had been presented. The results of this experiment demonstrate a substantial increase in amplitude error by older and younger subjects when storage is required. The increase is relatively larger in the case of older subjects (Griew, 1958a). This finding is not entirely unexpected and is in line with other demonstrations that short-term retention deteriorates with age (Kirchner, 1958).

Two other points which deserve mention arise from the results. First, an analysis of the rates of information transmission from display to control in this experiment showed that older subjects transmit information more slowly than younger at all tracking speeds and degrees of obscurity. As obscurity increased, rate of information transmission decreased, and this decrease was more marked in older than in younger subjects. Enforced storage appeared, in fact, to result in a reduced rate of information transmission which was relatively greater in older subjects. Second, an analysis of tracking error clearly suggests that within the limits of duration—up to one second in this case—the main determinant of amplitude errors when storage is required was the amount of information to be stored irrespective of the duration of storage.

Effects of Interrupting Signals

The second experiment in this group concerned interfering signals to which rapid response has to be made during tracking performance. Ten younger and ten older subjects tracked with their left hands, keeping their right hands above a response key which had to be pressed whenever an auditory signal appeared. Again, double tasks of this sort may be regarded as more complex than either of the component tasks taken singly and merit consideration in any study of task complexity.

The results showed that tracking performance was worse and reaction time to the interrupting auditory signals was higher while tracking was taking place, but to the same extent in both age groups (Griew, 1958b; Griew, 1959b). The results suggest, rather surprisingly, that the efficiency of the central processes handling information is no more impaired in older than in younger subjects when two tasks are undertaken simultaneously. Such a conclusion is, perhaps, consistent with the idea of the human operator as a single channel of communication. Signals from the two tasks are treated as a single series of signals, and the efficiency with which they are handled depends on the capacity of the channel. An over-all decline with age in this efficiency might be expected to result in a corresponding decline in the speed and accuracy of response to both types of signals, but the decline of the older group is not relatively greater than that of the younger. It is only fair to add, however, that none of the subjects in this experiment was over fifty and that the results might have differed with subjects in their sixties and seventies.

Unbalanced Signal Frequency

Crossman (1953) and Hyman (1953) have shown that loss of information caused by frequency unbalance is reflected in reduced reaction times, and Hyman has shown that responses to frequent signals are faster than those to infrequent. In information-theory terms, the more probable signals convey less information than the less probable ones and hence occupy the central processes for a shorter time. This will not occur, however, until the subject has had some opportunity to learn the frequencies, which, it has been shown, he does fairly quickly (Hake & Hyman, 1953; Skinner, 1942).

Starting from a hypothesis based, perhaps, on an a priori assessment of the situation, subjects appear to modify their expectations about the occurrence of signals on the basis of experience with the series to which they are submitted. However, their expectations of receiving a certain signal at any point may not be closely related to a mathematically determined probability of this signal's occurrence, although their expectations will come closer to what actually occurs as their learning progresses. This topic and the closely related topic of the effect of sequential dependencies on behavior have recently been submitted to extensive examination (Collier & Verplanck, 1958; McGill, 1954; Senders & Sowards, 1952; Verplanck, 1955; Weiss, Coleman, & Green, 1955) and provide an intriguing field for further experimentation.

Although there seems to be no reason to expect age differences in handling frequency unbalance once it has been recognized, the process of achieving an accurate assessment of the probable occurrence of possible signals is one which might be expected to show variations with age. Assuming that the subject is left to formulate his own hypothesis about the frequency of signals at the outset and that learning will take the form of modifying his initial hypothesis on the basis of experience during the experiment, it might be predicted that older subjects will modify their initial hypotheses less readily. Kay (1951) found that errors made early in learning tended to persist among older subjects, and Korchin and Basowitz (1956) and O'Doherty, reported by Welford (1958), found that perceptual flexibility, as measured by the ability to revise interpretations of drawings which gradually changed, decreased with age. These studies point to the rigidity which is frequently discussed in relation to aging and which might be expected to influence the recognition of probabilities.

The prediction that older subjects would learn the nature of frequency unbalance more slowly than younger subjects was tested by taking readings of reaction times to different signals having unbalanced frequencies of occurrence. In view of the reduced amount of information conveyed by the more frequent signals and the increased amount conveyed by the less frequent ones, reaction times to the former should become shorter once the nature of unbalance was recognized, whereas those to the latter should lengthen. Two signals were employed, the first (A) occurring three times and the second (B) occurring nine times in every series of twelve. The signals in each series were in random order in those proportions, and ten series were presented without a break. Before dealing with the signals, all subjects responded to a series of twelve signals randomly drawn so that A and B each occurred six times. This series directly preceded the longer, unbalanced series. It was given to assist subjects in forming a hypothesis which was inadequate for the main task. The point at which the inadequate hypothesis was relinquished was that at which reaction time to Signal A differed significantly from reaction time to Signal B.

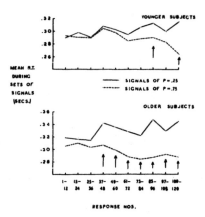

Fig. 2. The modification of reaction time during learning the statistical structure of series of signals. (Arrows indicate sets of signals in which differences between mean R.T.'s to signals of P=.75 and P=.25 are significant at the 5 per-cent level.) (Griew, 1962, p. 767.)

The results of the performances of ten younger and ten older subjects matched for intelligence, education, and occupation are shown in Fig. 2. They fail to support the hypothesis. They suggest, in fact, that the inadequate hypothesis was relinquished earlier by the older subjects. Certainly the type of inflexibility reported by Korchin and Basowitz (1956) in their perceptual study is not evident in the present results.

The implications of this finding are not yet fully understood. A number of explanations are possible, not the least important of which is that this finding may be an artifact of quicker and more efficient learning by younger subjects of the inadequate initial hypothesis. Some of these possible explanations are being explored in Bristol by G.S. Tune and this writer. A fuller account of this experiment and the work to which it is hoped it will lead is given elsewhere.

DISCUSSION AND CONCLUSIONS

These studies form part of a program which is to be continued. In the opinion of the writer, no realistic attempt to present these findings in a common theoretical framework is possible until further studies have been undertaken and the results of other current research are available. Tentative conclusions may be drawn, however, and suggestions made which might assist in framing appropriate hypotheses for further empirical testing.

With the exception of the last experiment, in all the experiments reported here the slopes of comparable curves relating reaction time to log choice are steeper and the amplitude errors in tracking performance greater in the older subjects' results. These results suggest very clearly that the basic rate of information transmission of older subjects is slower than that of younger ones. This supports the argument that aging is accompanied by a reduced capacity for transmitting information from display to control. Why should this be so? Why are there sometimes unexpected effects on the rates of information transmission when task complexity is introduced?

Crossman and Szafran (1956) suggest that random neural activity in the central nervous system increases with age so that older subjects require more time to accumulate data and distinguish them from noise. Gregory (1959) has already demonstrated the usefulness of this hypothesis in accounting for sensory decrements with age, and Welford (1958; 1959a) has also discussed it. If one accepts the idea that random noise may be evenly distributed through the tissue involved in a central activity and that the number of nerve cells involved in decision-making is proportional to the logarithm of the alternative decisions which might be made, it is easy to see how the extra time taken by older subjects in decision-making may also be related to the logarithm of the choice involved. The random activity of each extra ensemble of neural elements involved will contribute proportionally, and the measured rate of information transmission will decrease with age. This seems, in the light of present knowledge, the most profitable way of looking at possible behavioral and neurophysiological bases of what is otherwise a convenient, mathematically oriented description. Information theory, as the present writer understands it, was never meant to replace traditional methods of explanation in psychology (Quastler, 1955). As a statistical technique, it is valuable; as a system of concepts which assist in establishing a framework in which experimental work may progress, it is probably even more valuable. To imagine, however, that a description of behavior in terms of information transmission may pass as sufficient explanation of behavior is surely erroneous. What is required of the experimental psychologist interested in aging and performance is an explanation of the fact that the rate of information transmission appears to decline with age.

The second and, from some points of view, more interesting result of these experiments has been to demonstrate that the introduction of task complexity does not inevitably widen the gulf between the rates of information transmission of older and younger subjects. When stimuli are suboptimally coded, for example, we find that rates of information transmission are reduced to the same extent in both age groups. This suggests that the total capacity of the system may remain constant despite the added task complexity and that the decoding operation—which reappears at a speed proportional to the logarithm of the choice involved—is linked in some way to the process of handling information once it is decoded. The writer has suggested (Griew, 1958d) that it might be useful to view this simply as a way in which the amount of information conveyed by an event may vary with its means of presentation.

The findings in short-term storage require more elucidation than it has been possible to give them until now. The results of this study suggest that the interdependence of this and other forms of limitation may be considerable, especially in view of the subsidiary finding that information loss in this area is determined mainly by the amount of information to be stored.

Finally two comments may be hazarded about the general program of future research in this field. First, it seems fairly clear that there will be no sudden breakthrough in this area. The problems which remain are numerous, and the temptation to overindulge in theorizing should be resisted. The most suitable research at present involves long-term programs to obtain more information about the parameters of information transmission and a continual search for models. Looking to neurophysiology for these models seems, at present, premature, since, as someone recently described it, looking for something in the brain is like looking for a needle in a haystack thirty yards away.

The second program which might be extended is combined laboratory and field studies to test in the field predictions made from laboratory studies. A good example of this work is that of Belbin (1953). Early studies along these lines in Bristol have involved investigation of the accident behavior of workers of different ages in jobs of differing complexity (Griew, 1958c), the age structure of jobs of differing complexity (Murrell & Griew, 1958; Murrell, Griew, & Tucker, 1957) and the identification of behavioral elements of jobs of differing age structure (Griew & Tucker, 1958; Murrell & Tucker, 1960). K.F.H. Murrell and D.G. Entwisle are now conducting work in which the elements of specific machine operations in relation to age are being studied in an experimental setting and in which timing of the responses which form work cycles is being examined. Further work in this area seems to be desirable and should not only clarify certain basic problems concerning the adaptability of older subjects to their increasing limitations, but should also improve the quality of industrial field research in aging by serving as a valuable check on laboratory findings.

REFERENCES

Belbin, R.M. Difficulties of older people in industry. *Occup. Psychol.*, 1953, **27,** 177-190.

Birren, J.E. Age changes in speed of simple responses and perception and their significance for complex behaviour. In *Old age in the modern world.* Edinburgh: E. & S. Livingstone, 1955. Pp. 235-247.

Birren, J.E. The significance of age changes in speed of perception and psychomotor skills. In J.E. Anderson (Ed.), *Psychological aspects of aging.* Washington, D.C.: American Psychological Association, 1956. Pp. 97-104.

Bricker, P.D. Information measurement and reaction time. In H. Quastler (Ed.), *Information theory in psychology.* Glencoe, Ill.: The Free Press, 1955. Pp. 350-359.

Broadbent, D.E. *Perception and communication.* London: Pergamon Press, 1958.

Brown, J.S., & Slater-Hammel, H.T. Discrete movements in the horizontal plane as a function of their length and direction. *J. exp. Psychol.*, 1949, **39,** 84-95.

Clay, Hilary M. The relationship between time, accuracy and age on similar tasks of varying complexity. *Gerontologia*, 1957, **1,** 41-49.

Collier, G., & Verplanck, W.S. Non-independence of successive responses at the visual threshold as a function of interpolated stimuli. *J. exp. Psychol.*, 1958, **55,** 429-437.

Craik, K.J.W. Theory of the human operator in control systems: I. The operator as an engineering system. *Brit. J. Psychol.*, 1947, **38,** 56-61.

Craik, K.J.W. Theory of the human operator in control systems: II. Man as an element in a control system. *Brit. J. Psychol.*, 1948, **38,** 142-148.

Crossman, E.R.F.W. Entropy and choice time: The effect of frequency unbalance on choice response. *Quart. J. exp. Psychol.*, 1953, **5,** 41-51.

Crossman, E.R.F.W. The information capacity of the human operator in symbolic and non-symbolic control processes. In *Information theory and the human operator.* Ministry of Supply Publication, 1956, WR/D 2/56. (Ministry of Supply, London)

Crossman, E.R.F.W. The information capacity of the human motor system in pursuit tracking. *Quart. J. exp. Psychol.*, 1960, **12,** 1-16.

Crossman, E.R.F.W., & Szafran, J. Changes with age in the speed of information intake and discrimination. *Experientia Supplementum*, 1956, **4,** 128-135.

Fitts, P.M. The information capacity of the human motor system in controlling the amplitude of movement. *J. exp. Psychol.*, 1954, **47,** 381-391.

Fitts, P.M., & Seeger, C.M. S-R compatibility: Spatial characteristics of stimulus and response codes. *J. exp. Psychol.*, 1953, **46,** 199-210.

Goldfarb, W. An investigation of reaction time in older adults. *Teach. Coll. Contr. Educ.*, 1941, No. 831. (Columbia University, New York)

Gregory, R.L. Increase in "neurological noise" as a factor in ageing. In *Proceedings of the 4th congress, international association of gerontology, Merano, Italy.* Vol. 1. Florence: Tipographica Tito Mattioli [1959]. Pp. 314-324.

Griew, S. Age changes and information loss in performance of a pursuit tracking task involving interrupted preview. *J. exp. Psychol.*, 1958, **55,** 486-489. (a)

Griew, S. A note on the effect of interrupting auditory signals on the performance of younger and older subjects. *Gerontologia*, 1958, **2,** 136-139. (b)

Griew, S. A study of accidents in relation to occupation and age. *Ergonomics,* 1958, **2,** 17-23. (c)

Griew, S. Information gain in tasks involving different stimulus-response relationships. *Nature*, 1958, **182,** 1819. (d)

Griew, S. Complexity of response and time of initiating responses in relation to age. *Amer. J. Psychol.*, 1959, **72,** 83-88. (a)

Griew, S. Set to respond and the effect of interrupting signals upon tracking performance. *J. exp. Psychol.*, 1959, **57,** 333-337. (b)

Griew, S. The learning of statistical structure: A preliminary study in relation to age. In C. Tibbitts & Wilma Donahue (Eds.), *Social and psychological aspects of aging.* New York: Columbia University Press, 1962. Pp. 763-769.

Griew, S., & Tucker, W.A. The identification of job activities associated with age differences in the engineering industry. *J. appl. Psychol.*, 1958, **42,** 278-282.

Hake, H.W., & Hyman, R. Perception of the statistical structure of a random series of binary symbols. *J. exp. Psychol.*, 1953, **45,** 64-74.

Hick, W.E. On the rate of gain of information. *Quart. J. exp. Psychol.*, 1952, **4,** 11-26.

Hyman, R. Stimulus information as a determinant of reaction time. *J. exp. Psychol.*, 1953, **45,** 188-196.

Kay, H. Learning of a serial task by different age groups. *Quart. J. exp. Psychol.*, 1951, **3,** 166-183.

Kay, H. The effects of position in a display upon problem solving. *Quart. J. exp. Psychol.*, 1954, **6,** 155-169.

Kirchner, W.R. Age differences in short-term retention for rapidly changing information. *J. exp. Psychol.*, 1958, **55,** 352-358.

Korchin, S.J., & Basowitz, H. The judgment of ambiguous stimuli as an index of cognitive functioning in aging. *J. Pers.*, 1956, **25,** 81-95.

McGill, W.J. Multivariate information transmission. *Psychometrika*, 1954, **19,** 97-116.

Morin, R.E., & Grant, D.A. Learning and performance on a key-pressing task as a function of the degree of spatial stimulus-response correspondence. *J. exp. Psychol.*, 1955, **49,** 39-47.

Murrell, K.F.H., & Entwisle, D.G. Age differences in movement pattern. *Nature*, 1960, **185**, 948-949.

Murrell, K.F.H., & Griew, S. Age structure in the engineering industry: A study of regional effects. *Occup. Psychol.*, 1958, **32**, 86-88.

Murrell, K.F.H., Griew, S., & Tucker, W.A. Age structure in the engineering industry: A preliminary study. *Occup. Psychol.*, 1957, **31**, 150-168.

Murrell, K.F.H., & Tucker, W.A. A pilot job study of age related causes of difficulty in light engineering. *Ergonomics*, 1960, **3**, 74-79.

Quastler, H. (Ed.) *Information theory in psychology*. Glencoe, Ill.: The Free Press, 1955.

Searle, L.V., & Taylor, F.V. Studies of tracking behavior: I. Rate and time characteristics of simple corrective movements. *J. exp. Psychol.*, 1948, **38**, 615-631.

Senders, V.L., & Sowards, A. Analysis of response sequences in the setting of a psychophysical experiment. *Amer. J. Psychol.*, 1952, **65**, 358-374.

Shannon, C.E., & Weaver, W. *The mathematical theory of communication*. Urbana: University of Illinois Press, 1949.

Skinner, B.F. The processes involved in the repeated guessing of alternatives. *J. exp. Psychol.*, 1942, **30**, 495-503.

Suci, G.J., Davidoff, M.D., & Surwillo, W.W. Reaction time as a function of stimulus information and age. *J. exp. Psychol.*, 1960, **60**, 242-244.

Taylor, F.V. Human engineering. In S. Koch (Ed.), *Psychology: A study of science*. Vol. 5. New York: McGraw-Hill, 1960.

Verplanck, W.S. Non-independence of successive responses in coin guessing. In Response mechanisms at the visual threshold: A methodological study. (O.N.R., U.S. Navy Contract NSori-07639, Project NR140-015, Final Report.) Washington, D.C.: Office of Naval Research, 1955.

Weiss, B., Coleman, P.D., & Green, R.F. A stochastic model for time ordered dependencies in continuous scale repetitive judgements. *J. exp. Psychol.*, 1955, **50**, 237-244.

Welford, A.T. *Skill and age*. London: Oxford University Press, 1951.

Welford, A.T. The psychological refractory period and the timing of high speed performance—a review and a theory. *Brit. J. Psychol.*, 1952, **43**, 2-19.

Welford, A.T. *Ageing and human skill*. London: Oxford University Press, 1958.

Welford, A.T. Channel capacity and slowness in sensorimotor performance. In *Proceedings of the 4th congress, international association of gerontology, Merano, Italy*. Vol. 1. Florence: Tipographia Tito Mattioli [1959]. Pp. 334-337. (a)

Welford, A.T. Evidence of a single-channel decision mechanism limiting performance in a serial reaction task. *Quart. J. exp. Psychol.*, 1959, **11**, 193-210. (b)

Welford, A.T. Psychomotor performance. In J.E. Birren (Ed.), *Handbook of aging and the individual: Psychological and biological aspects*. Chicago: The University of Chicago Press, 1959. Pp. 562-613. (c)

Wiener, N. *Cybernetics*. New York: John Wiley & Sons, 1948.

Woodworth, R.S. *Experimental psychology*. New York: Henry Holt, 1938.

CHAPTER 4

Experimental-Clinical
Method and
the Cognitive Disorders
of the Senium

JAMES INGLIS

Much effort has been devoted to the study of cognitive disturbances in elderly psychiatric patients (Dörken, 1954; Eysenck, 1946; Granick, 1950; Grewel, 1953; Inglis, 1958; Jones & Kaplan, 1956). Many, if not all, of these studies have been based on the prior selection of psychiatric groups, usually in terms of some such diagnosis as senile dementia. This study will examine and illustrate the difficulties and dangers inherent in this kind of research and will propose an alternative method for use in this field. This method is one which has been recommended mainly by Shapiro (1951) and Payne (1953) and employed by them in the study of overinclusive thought disorder (Payne, Matussek, & George, 1959) and delusional thinking (Shapiro & Ravenette, 1959).

Some of the difficulties and dangers involved in basing the investigation of abnormal behavior on psychiatric diagnosis are, in a sense, practical ones, for example, the dependability with which these nosological categories can be determined (Ash, 1949; Foulds, 1955; Mehlman, 1952; Schmidt & Fonda, 1956). For the purposes of the present discussion it seems more important to look at what may be called the difficulties in principle in using diagnosis as a basis for research.[1] These difficulties have been ably dscussed by Payne (1958), who has pointed out that diagnosis in psychiatry is almost entirely a matter of label. Few investigators, however, are interested in the label for its own sake. It is only useful insofar as it carries certain fairly specific implications, commonly four in number.

1. Descriptive implications: the parts of the labeling system that give a short picture of the presenting abnormalities, symptoms, or signs to which the psychiatrist accords importance.

2. Prognostic implications: the references to the natural history, likely course, and outcome of the disorder.

3. Etiological implications: the indications of the likely cause or precipitants of the disturbance.

4. Therapeutic implications: the indications inherent in the label as to what may be done about the disorder.

When the psychologist comes to investigate behavioral disorders and build a study on psychiatric labels, it is usually one or all of these implications that he has in mind, not the label itself. Still the dangers of fallacious inference in this process are great and deserve detailed consideration.

DESCRIPTIVE IMPLICATIONS

The relations which can exist among the label, its descriptive implications, and the results of any psychological investigation of performance variables may be considered first.

The criterion groups (which may be labeled "organic," "functional," "demented," "depressed," or the like) are usually chosen because the individuals comprising them show certain supposedly char-

[1] This paper was prepared for the International Research Seminar on Social and Psychological Aspects of Aging with the assistance of a summer research associateship from the Faculty of Arts and Science, Queen's University, Kingston, Ontario, in the summer of 1960.

acteristic behavioral abnormalities. An attempt to secure performance variables which will also be characteristic of such groups, however, must be built on the knowledge that a psychiatric label can correlate with the abnormalities which draw the attention of the psychiatrist and the selected performance measures even if there is no correlation between the abnormalities and the measures. This may be simply illustrated geometrically, since the size of the correlation between variables is equivalent to the cosine of the angle between the vectors represent-

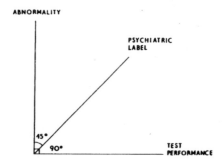

FIG. 1. Geometrical illustration of the size of the correlation between variables. (Cosine 45° = 0.7; cosine 90° = 0.)

ing them. It can be seen from Fig. 1 that, unless the correlation of each of two variables with a third is greater than .70, these two variables need not correlate with each other. Probably the reliability of psychiatric diagnosis seldom exceeds .70, thus it cannot correlate to a greater degree than that with any other variable, and psychological measures validated against diagnosis need never necessarily relate to any descriptive implications the label may suggest.

It is feared that the apparent success of some attempts to relate such labels, their descriptive implications, and performance variables is spurious and frequently the result of "criterion contamination" of some kind.

Direct criterion contamination results, of course, when the performance under investigation is used as one of the criteria for sorting the groups against whose behavior the relevance of the performance variables is being evaluated. This contamination can be seen in the study of Ames, Learned, Métraux, & Walker (1954) on Rorschach responses in old age. These investigators sought to discover what effect chronological age might have on performance on this test by examining decade groups of elderly people from sixty to one hundred years of age. Thus grouped, their test protocols did not show marked differences among the age groups. The authors then sorted the groups in terms of their test results and discovered that this method produced more significant differences among the group. (It would indeed have been surprising if they had failed to find significant differences then.)

More often, however, contamination enters such studies more subtly, as indirect contamination. Suppose a test is to determine whether the presence of Characteristic X (memory disorder) has any relation to the existence of Condition Y (organic brain lesions). To study this problem, it would first be necessary to secure at least two groups, one (Group Y+) with, one (Group Y−) without, Condition Y. Even if direct contamination were excluded, should the tester establishing the groups use his own judgment on the presence of X as a criterion for putting a person into Group Y+ and the absence of X for putting another into group Y−, and, if his judgment were good, it would then follow that any objective measure of X subsequently given to these individuals would inevitably show that Characteristic X was more frequent in the members of Group Y+ than in the members of Group Y−. It can be seen, however, that the original question about the association of Characteristic X with State Y remains unanswered and can be satisfactorily answered only when groups Y+ and Y− are initially sorted without any reference to X.

One study by Shapiro, Post, Löfving, and Inglis (1956) was specifically concerned with the possible effects of such indirect contamination. This study was initially intended to examine the efficiency of certain popular clinical tests to discriminate among functional, doubtful, and organic groups of elderly psychiatric patients. When the psychiatrist first formed the groups on the bases of examination, histories, and clinical judgment, analysis of variance revealed that no fewer than twenty-four of the twenty-eight subtests used discriminated among the groups at a 5 per-cent or higher level of significance.

The psychiatrist who classified the patients in this study had no knowledge of the results of the psychological tests, so that direct contamination could not have taken place; nevertheless, he could not fail to have formed impressions of general cognitive efficiency and memory functioning from the patients' histories and his clinical examination. These impressions might influence his criteria for sorting the patients. The purpose of the test items, however, was to objectify such impressions so that their diagnostic value could be empirically determined. If these impressions formed part of the criteria for classification, any agreement between the psychiatrist's sorting and the test results would mean that his impressions of cognitive status could be confirmed by objective tests. Indirect contamination might, therefore, have taken place, since the aim was to investigate the nature of the relation of cognitive and memory functions to illness, not merely to measure a relation already assumed to exist.

In order to eliminate the possibility of such contamination, it was necessary, therefore, for the psychiatrist to reclassify the same patients into the functional, doubtful, and organic categories, this time using only the most objective possible criteria which were entirely unrelated to cognitive or memory function. To achieve this, the psychiatrist provided a check list of signs (avoiding as far as possible any which might be related to cognitive function) that he considered useful in deciding whether a patient could be classified organic. He provided eight signs, four from the histories and four from the examination of the patients, and then reclassified according to these signs alone. The presence or absence of these signs was determined by the psychologist independently of the patients' case histories.

Three main questions could be answered by the second analysis.

1. Was there any other than a chance relation between the psychiatrist's first and second groupings?

2. If the two groupings were not completely independent, would it be possible to discover whether any significant change had taken place in the classification?

3. What effect had any changes in the grouping had on the discriminating power of the tests, and were such effects consistent with the hypothesis of indirect contamination?

Seventy-five of the 102 subjects remained in the same category on the first and second analyses. The results are shown in Table 1.

The relation of the two groupings was tested in the manner described by Garrett (1948) for a χ^2 test of independence in contingency tables. The χ^2 value was 76.45, which, with four degrees of freedom, is significant beyond the 1 per-cent level. These results answered the first question stated above, confirming the reliability (which was about 75 per cent) of the psychiatrist's diagnosis in these three groups after one year.

Since it had been shown that the two sets of data were related, it was necessary to determine whether any systematic change had taken place in the grouping on the second occasion compared with

TABLE 1
CHANGES IN DIAGNOSIS AFTER REDUCTION
OF THE INFLUENCE OF INDIRECT CONTAMINATION

Those diagnosed on second occasion as	Those diagnosed on first occasion as			
	Functional	Doubtful	Organic	Total
Functional	47	14	6	67
Doubtful	5	10	2	17
Organic	–	–	18	18
Total	52	24	26	102

the first. Unsystematic variation alone would have been expected to cause approximately as many individuals to be displaced in one direction as in another—the number of diagnoses changed, for example, from doubtful to functional should have been the same as the number changed from doubtful to organic. An alternative hypothesis was formulated which predicted that the flow of change would be significantly greater in the direction of functional diagnosis away from the doubtful and the organic groups. This change seemed caused by the fact that if the patient had, on the first occasion, presented enough objective evidence of brain lesions (such as abnormal neurological findings strongly indicative of pathology), he was placed in the organic group. Any impression of apparent preservation of cognitive efficiency did not seem to influence the diagnosis toward doubtful or functional. The fact that an individual showed few or none of the objective signs, although his mental functioning seemed impaired, did appear to influence the diagnosis, more likely making it doubtful or organic. It follows that reclassification when impressions of cognitive and memory functions were excluded would change the flow mainly in one direction, away from organic toward doubtful and functional and away from doubtful toward functional. This hypothesis was tested in the manner described by McNemar (1949) for a test of change in correlated proportions. This technique gave a critical ratio of 2.46, which is significant beyond the 1 per-cent level on a one-tailed test of significance (the direction of change having been predicted). This result permitted confident rejection of the null hypothesis and confirmed the alternative notion that the influence of the clinician's impression of cognitive and memory function had biased the first classification in favor of organic diagnosis. This result was also consistent with the hypothesis that the first phase of the study had produced a classification involving some contamination of the data.

Variance of the group results on each of the subtests was again analyzed to see what effect the changes in classification had on the discriminating efficiency of the tests. It was shown that now only eleven of the twenty-eight subtests discriminated at the 5 per-cent or higher level and that the general levels of significance were much lower. It is worth while to emphasize that one test which successfully discriminated between the groups on both occasions was a version of the Bender-Gestalt drawing test (Bender, 1946).

This study thus showed that spuriously positive relations between psychiatric labels and performance variables may be caused by inadequate control over the factors contributing to selection of criterion groups. Having recognized this difficulty, however, another possible difficulty must be remembered. Suppose that for the purpose of defining groups Y+ and Y– Characteristic X had been one of the most important criteria. To deny the person sorting the groups his judgment on this variable might deprive him of crucial information and weaken the criterion groups eventually chosen. How, then, can we determine the relation between the aspects of disturbed behavior which psychiatric labels apparently describe and objective estimates of performance? One answer is, of course, that the investigation of such relations may be determined directly.

In this way Inglis (1957) chose to examine, as directly as possible, one descriptive aspect of behavior commonly held important in senile cognitive impairment. The initial problem chosen for examination was to discover what, in objective psychological terms, could be shown to characterize patients said to be suffering from memory disorder. Here, it should be emphasized, the behavioral pursuit of the characteristic disorder was not mediated by any diagnostic label, but was undertaken directly in terms of the symptomatic disturbance.

Two major findings emerged from this study. First, patients said to be suffering from memory disorder had a marked disability in the acquisition phase of learning paired associates. Although this finding may hardly seem surprising, the approach used permitted at least the operational analysis of descriptive clinical impressions and also provided a method for examining memory deficit in an objective, quantifiable way relatively independent of the subject's past experience. Incidentally, these results illustrate the force of Hull's (1917) early insistence that neither the common nor clinical use of the term "memory" differentiates specifically enough between the acquisition and retention phases in the learning process, phases which may properly be held relatively distinct.

The second finding was that elderly patients with memory disorders showed a larger mean discrepancy between the verbal and performance scales (VS > PS) of the Wechsler-Bellevue Scale (Wechsler, 1944) and that this difference, at least in the memory-disorder group, seemed to be related to the amount of difficulty experienced in the acquisition of new knowledge. The connection between learning and some aspects of intelligence in these subjects seemed to be related to Cattell's (1943) and Margaret Davies Eysenck's (1945) use of "fluid" and "crystallized" ability.

This investigation showed that certain descriptive elements commonly held important in some of the psychiatric disorders of the elderly could be related to objectively defined performance variables, which, in turn, may also be relevant to both etiological and therapeutic implications. Thus, the relative usefulness of the prognostic implications of diagnostic categories and their relation to performance variables was demonstrated.

PROGNOSTIC IMPLICATIONS

Often enough the psychologist is concerned not merely with those contemporaneous descriptive elements which may or may not be implied by the use of a psychiatric label; frequently he is concerned with some prognostic indicator of the likely course of behavioral changes, such as deterioration, in the disordered.

It can be argued that the attempt to relate performance variables to psychiatric labels cannot ensure the existence of such a relation. Payne (1958) has argued this point. He supposes that the psychiatrist who originally labeled the criterion groups had been able to provide a fairly accurate prognosis for these groups and that each group member was labeled in terms of the presence or absence of ten symptoms and/or signs. It is possible that only four of these symptoms might be relevant to prognosis. The label would then have a significant, but imperfect, correlation with prognosis. Even a performance variable with a proven relation to the descriptive implications of the label might be related to a different set of four of these ten symptoms; thus, although the test would also have an imperfect, but perhaps significant, correlation with the label, it need not be related to any of the elements which are related to prognosis.

As has been noted above, the Bender-Gestalt Test has been shown to discriminate between functional and organic elderly patients (Inglis, Shapiro, & Post, 1956) even when the most stringent measures have been taken to rule out the possibility of any criterion contamination. Furthermore, Shapiro, Field, and Post (1957) have been able to show that a more objective measure derived from the same test also differentiated the criterion groups at a high level of significance. Another investigation was undertaken by Inglis, Colwell, and Post (1960) to study the prognostic power of such test results. In this study, fifty-nine elderly psychiatric patients whose results on this test were available were individually followed up approximately two years after they had been tested. The follow-up data were collected by psychiatric social workers and evaluated by the psychiatrist and psychologist. Information was collected about each patient's day-to-day activities; changes in symptomatology, cognitive status, and personality; hospitalization record; and the like. It emerged, upon analysis, that there was little or no relation between the test score and the estimates made of the patients' conditions during the follow-up period, even though it was confirmed that the original psychiatric labels did have some predictive power (Norris & Post, 1954).

This investigation demonstrated what Payne (1958) had contended: even a test which has been validated and cross-validated in terms of its classification power does not necessarily have the prognostic power of the classification system against which it was initially standardized. It seems likely that failure in this case is caused by the indirect (label-mediated) way in which the relation between the functions involved in test performance and behavioral disturbance was determined.

It has to be suggested again that a more profitable approach to determining psychological variables which carry some valid implications for psychiatric diagnosis may be made through the direct study of the principal descriptive characteristics of psychiatric disturbances. Inglis has made an attempt to use this method in a second analysis (1959c) of some data originally collected by Walton (1958), who had been concerned with assessing the predictive utility of a learning test for psychiatric disorders of the senium simply in terms of changes in diagnosis over a two-year period. However, of the forty-eight cases described by Walton, enough data were provided on nineteen to permit a further, perhaps more valid, direct prognostic evaluation in terms of the outcome of illness. Two outcomes could be discerned: favorable (for example, recovery and/or discharge) and unfavorable (for example, death). When the patients were also classified in terms of their test scores (scores of thirty-one or more trials indicated poor learning and were called "high," scores of below thirty-one, "low"), a fourfold table relating outcome to test score could be constructed (Table 2).

TABLE 2
PREDICTION OF OUTCOME OF ILLNESS
FROM LEARNING TEST SCORES

Test score	*Outcome*	
	Favorable	Unfavorable
Low	10	3
High	0	6

A value of 9.47 was obtained for a X^2 measure of association between these categories (Garrett, 1948) which is significant beyond the 1 per-cent level.

It is of interest to compare this direct prognostic (or, as Zubin [1952] might insist, at least, "hysterognostic") estimate provided by the test with the predictive efficiency of the original diagnoses. Thus, outcome in these cases could also be related to initial diagnosis in terms of another fourfold table, as shown in Table 3.

TABLE 3
PREDICTION OF OUTCOME OF ILLNESS
FROM INITIAL DIAGNOSIS

Initial diagnosis	*Outcome*	
	Favorable	Unfavorable
Functional	4	4
Organic	6	5

This association yielded a nonsignificant X^2 value of .025, showing that in some instances, at least, a direct objective estimate of a crucial element in abnormality may be a more satisfactory prediction than a label-mediated prognosis. In the case of prognosis, as in the case of description, therefore, available data support the contention that a direct attack on the implications of a given diagnostic label may be as profitable in the case of cognitive disturbances of the elderly as Payne (1958) has argued it may be in the psychological approach to general behavioral disorder.

ETIOLOGICAL IMPLICATIONS

It is possible to show that etiological implications may be related to psychiatric labels and psychiatric labels related to performance variables without the postulated etiology and observed performances being related themselves.

So little is certain about the etiology of the disorders indicated by psychiatric labels that it might be imagined this kind of mistaken inference would be rare. One common danger, however, in the case of the cognitive disorders of the aged is that using diagnostic labels as criteria may tie the investigator to psychiatric hypotheses which, in this area, are often organic in content and despairing in nature. Too often such implicit hypotheses as those lying behind the term "senile dementia" suggest causes at once inaccessible and irreversible. If these causes are accepted too readily, society may feel absolved from any responsibility other than custody.

A study by Bartlet and Shapiro (1956) illustrates the different activities which may be stimulated or suppressed merely by different ways of talking about a disorder. They cite the case of a boy of about average intelligence who was apparently unable to read. This child was said to be suffering from congenital word blindness, which, as Payne (1957) has pointed out, is a tenable hypothesis insofar as it accounted for most of the facts, but a sterile one insofar as it suggested few ways of controlling and discovering new facts about the disorder. Bartlet and Shapiro defined the child's difficulties as a defect of specific learning mechanisms and, with this new definition, were eventually able to effect some improvement in his condition.

In the case of cognitive and other behavioral abnormalities of the aged, analogous arguments may be put forward. What the psychologist must aim to produce are hypotheses which allow the usual scientific processes of description, prediction, and control. As Shapiro (1957) has argued, unless and until we can point to failure after long and stubborn attempts to erect and evaluate such hypotheses, we, as psychologists, have no right to fall back on psychiatric notions which are often simply hypotheses of despair.

A principal virtue of psychological hypotheses is that their interest is, or should be, focused directly on regularities or irregularities in the observed behavior. These hypotheses may be couched in language which involves neurophysiological elements, but can also be expressed in terms which do not involve any reference to such processes. Whatever the choice of language, however, interest remains directed at behavior as such and is not diverted to the vicissitudes of the machine—or, for that matter, the ghost—as is all too frequently the case with many psychiatric hypotheses.

Another attempt has been made (Inglis, 1958) to comprehend some data gathered in the psychological investigations of cognitive deficit of elderly psychiatric patients in the framework provided by Hebb's (1949) neuropsychological theory. It is possible to demonstrate experimentally (Inglis, 1959a) that Hebb's hypothesis can be used to relate impairment shown on learning tasks by some elderly psychiatric patients to particular defects in general intellectual ability, especially disturbances of conceptual usage.

It is also possible, and sometimes more convenient, to express relations between behavioral observations in language that is not committed to any neurophysiological frame of reference. Broadbent (1958) has suggested that some terms used to describe processes in information transmission may be used in a neutral fashion. An attempt has been made to conceive of learning disorder in elderly persons in these terms by Inglis (1960) in the suggestion that the failure in learning that is evinced by some elderly patients may be caused by a breakdown of the short-term storage system which Broadbent (1956) has used to account for the ability of normal subjects to respond sequentially to information delivered simultaneously through two channels. The results of a similar experiment with elderly patients are in accord with this hypothesis.

The direct study of abnormal behavior, then, can lead not only to greater clarity of description and more valid prediction, but might also formulate more fruitful, less stereotyped descriptive and explanatory hypotheses.

THERAPEUTIC IMPLICATIONS

The same possibilities of false inference exist in using psychiatric labels to mediate connections between control elements and performance variables. If these elements may be tackled directly, however, there are at least two functions which the psychologist may have in relation to them. First, the psychologist's function can be only evaluative, since he commonly lacks the qualifications which would permit him to play an executive role in treatment. Even if this argument is accepted, distinctive functions remain for him to fulfill directly in relation to evaluation processes.

The principal function here brings us back to the primary task of description. Most attempts which have been made to assess the effects of treatment on any kind of psychiatric disorders have been bedeviled by the almost complete lack of satisfactory means to measure changes in behavior. Attempts to carry out such assessment have commonly relied on changes in diagnosis or admittedly unsatisfactory rating scales. It cannot, however, too often be repeated that, unless we can estimate with a known degree of precision what is wrong with a person's behavior or how wrong it is, we cannot make a valid estimate of improvement or deterioration.

Even the best studies which have tried to assess the effects of various treatments (oxygen intake, hormone and vitamin administration, and so on) on cognitive disturbances of the elderly (Inglis, 1958; Post, 1959) have produced inconclusive results, either because no systematic, objective evaluation of the relevant cognitive functions had been made or because such assessment had been made by inappropriate techniques. An unpublished study by Inglis, Kendrick, and Post on the psychological effects of vitamin treatment for elderly psychiatric patients with memory disorders has attempted to circumvent some of these problems by using tests (Inglis, 1959b) which have been validated at least for the groups on which they were used.

The psychologist who is concerned with cognitive and other disorders of behavior in the elderly must attempt to assess directly the relevant aspects of such disorders through precise description, not indirectly through the mediating agency of psychiatric labels. One need not concede, however, that the psychologist should be concerned only with evaluating treatment devised by others. If the psychologist can describe behavior precisely enough, make hypotheses convincingly enough, and, as a consequence, provide controls efficient enough, the mechanics of the control procedures could, if necessary, be turned over to people with different qualifications, who would certainly be willing to apply them.

DISCUSSION

It has been advanced that the principal implications of psychiatric labeling procedures may—indeed, must—be explored directly by the psychologist and not, as is commonly the case, indirectly through the investigation of performance characteristics of pre-selected diagnostic groups. This recommendation may be expanded to include the suggestion that the psychologist should abstain altogether from using such loaded words as "diagnosis," "prognosis," "etiology," and "treatment."

What is the behavioral scientist interested in when he is faced with the problems of disordered behavior? Broadly, these are the questions he usually would like to answer.

1. Of what does this abnormality precisely consist? This question demands that investigation try first to describe the disorder as closely as possible.

2. How can we conceive of it in relation to other observations? To satisfy ourselves as scientists, we should be able to construct a working model which will comprehend our description of the abnormal phenomena and other apparently related observations.

3. How useful is our model? The way of talking about such observations must not only fit them together as neatly as possible, but, ideally, should also be manipulable in that it can produce further testable expectations. Since expectations, to be testable, must usually be related to change and since we are concerned primarily with abnormalities and their distressing consequences, we do our best to arrange for changes in the direction of amelioration.

To discuss what the psychologist does in terms of observation, hypothesis-making, and hypothesis-testing is simply to suggest that the psychologist whose concern is abnormal behavior should try to do in his area what other behavioral scientists do in theirs. The approach outlined here has proved, and will prove, fruitful in investigating general disorders of behavior and in understanding particular cognitive disorders of the elderly.

94

REFERENCES

Ames, Louise B., Learned, Janet, Métraux, Ruth W., & Walker, R.N. *Rorschach responses in old age.* New York: Hoeber, 1954.

Ash, P. The reliability of psychiatric diagnosis. *J. abnorm. soc. Psychol.*, 1949, **44**, 272-276.

Bartlet, Deone, & Shapiro, M.B. Investigation and treatment of a reading disability in a dull child with severe psychiatric disturbances. *Brit. J. educ. Psychol.*, 1956, **26**, 180-190.

Bender, Lauretta. *Instructions for the use of the visual-motor Gestalt test.* New York: American Orthopsychiatric Association, 1946.

Broadbent, D.E. Successive responses to simultaneous stimuli. *Quart. J. exp. Psychol.*, 1956, **8**, 145-152.

Broadbent, D.E. *Perception and communication.* London: Pergamon Press, 1958.

Cattell, R.B. The measurement of adult intelligence. *Psychol. Bull.*, 1943, **40**, 153-193.

Dörken, H. Psychometric differences between senile dementia and normal senescent decline. *Canad. J. Psychol.*, 1954, **8**, 187-194.

Eysenck, Margaret D. An exploratory study of mental organization in senility. *J. neurol. neurosurg. Psychiat.*, 1945, **8**, 15-22.

Eysenck, Margaret D. The psychological aspects of aging and senility. *J. ment. Sci.*, 1946, **92**, 171-181.

Foulds, G.A. The reliability of psychiatric, and the validity of psychological, diagnosis. *J. ment. Sci.*, 1955, **101**, 851-862.

Garrett, H.E. *Statistics in psychology and education.* (3rd ed.) New York: Longmans Green, 1948.

Granick, S. Studies in the psychology of senility: A survey. *J. Geront.*, 1950, **5**, 44-58.

Grewel, F. Testing psychology of dementias. *Folia Psychiat. Neerl.*, 1953, **56**, 305-339.

Hebb, D.O. *The organization of behavior: A neuropsychological theory.* New York: John Wiley & Sons, 1949.

Hull, C.L. The formation and retention of associations among the insane. *Amer. J. Psychol.*, 1917, **28**, 419-435.

Inglis, J. An experimental study of learning and "memory function" in elderly psychiatric patients. *J. ment. Sci.*, 1957, **103**, 796-803.

Inglis, J. Psychological investigations of cognitive deficit in elderly psychiatric patients. *Psychol. Bull.*, 1958, **55**, 197-214.

Inglis, J. A paired-associate learning test for use with elderly psychiatric patients. *J. ment. Sci.*, 1959, **105**, 440-443. (a)

Inglis, J. Learning, retention and conceptual usage in elderly patients with memory disorder. *J. abnorm. soc. Psychol.*, 1959, **59**, 210-215. (b)

Inglis, J. On the prognostic value of the modified word learning test in psychiatric patients over 65. *J. ment. Sci.*, 1959, **105**, 1100-1101. (c)

Inglis, J. Dichotic stimulation and memory disorder. *Nature*, 1960, **186**, 181-182.

Inglis, J., Colwell, Catherine, & Post, F. An evaluation of the predictive power of a test known to differentiate between elderly "functional" and "organic" psychiatric patients. *J. ment. Sci.*, 1960, **106**, 1486-1492.

Inglis, J., Shapiro, M.B., & Post, F. Memory function in psychiatric patients over sixty: The role of memory in tests discriminating between "functional" and "organic" groups. *J. ment. Sci.*, 1956, **102**, 589-598.

Jones, H.E., & Kaplan, O.J. Psychological aspects of mental disorders in later life. In O.J. Kaplan (Ed.), *Mental disorders in later life.* (2nd ed.) Stanford: Stanford University Press, 1956. Pp. 98-156.

McNemar, Q. *Psychological statistics.* London: Chapman Hall, 1949.

Mehlman, B. The reliability of psychiatric diagnosis. *J. abnorm. soc. Psychol.*, 1952, **47**, 577-578.

Norris, Vera, & Post, F. Treatment of elderly psychiatric patients: Use of a diagnostic classification. *Brit. med. J.*, 1954, **1**, 675-679.

Payne, R.W. The role of the clinical psychologist at the institute of psychiatry. *Rev. Psychol. appl.*, 1953, **3**, 150-160.

Payne, R.W. Experimental method in clinical psychological practice. *J. ment. Sci.*, 1957, **103**, 189-196.

Payne, R.W. Diagnostic and personality testing in clinical psychology. *Amer. J. Psychiat.*, 1958, **115**, 25-29.

Payne, R.W., Matussek, P., & George, E.I. An experimental study of schizophrenic thought disorder. *J. ment. Sci.*, 1959, **105**, 627-652.

Post, F. Early treatment of persistent senile confusion. *Geront. clin.*, 1959, **1**, 114-121.

Schmidt, H.O., & Fonda, C.P. Reliability of psychiatric diagnosis: A new look. *J. abnorm. soc. Psychol.*, 1956, **52**, 262-267.

Shapiro, M.B. An experimental approach to diagnostic psychological testing. *J. ment. Sci.*, 1951, **97**, 748-764.

Shapiro, M.B. Experimental method in the psychological description of the individual psychiatric patient. *Int. J. soc. Psychiat.*, 1957, **3**, 89-102.

Shapiro, M.B., Field, J., & Post, F. An enquiry into the determinants of a differentiation between elderly "organic" and "non-organic" psychiatric patients on the Bender Gestalt tests. *J. ment. Sci.*, 1957, **103**, 364-374.

Shapiro, M.B., Post, F., Löfving, Barbro, & Inglis, J. Memory function in psychiatric patients over 60: Some methodological and diagnostic implications. *J. ment. Sci.*, 1956, **102**, 233-246.

Shapiro, M.B., & Ravenette, A.T. A preliminary experiment on paranoid delusions. *J. ment. Sci.*, 1959, **105**, 295-312.

Walton, D. The diagnostic and predictive accuracy of the modified word learning test in psychiatric patients over 65. *J. ment. Sci.*, 1958, **104**, 1119-1122.

Wechsler, D. *The measurement of adult intelligence.* (3rd ed.) Baltimore: Williams and Wilkins, 1944.

Zubin, J. Discussion of contributions dealing with diagnosis and prognosis of mental disorder. In P.H. Hoch & J. Zubin (Eds.), *Relation of psychological tests to psychiatry.* New York: Grune and Stratton, 1952.

CHAPTER 5

Age Differences in
Conceptual Abilities

DENNIS B. BROMLEY

The term "conceptual thought" refers to the proc-
esses of abstraction and generalization, especially if they involve sym-
bolism. Humphrey (1951) has defined concept formation as follows:
"The activity whereby an organism comes to effect a constant modification towards an invariable feature or set of features occurring in a
variable context" (p. 256). It is not yet clear whether conceptual ability is a relatively distinct process like memory span or verbal fluency
or simply an aspect of high-grade intelligence, since the process of
forming concepts in both everyday life and the laboratory appears to
involve the intellect as a whole.

Methods of assessing conceptual thought take various forms,
but in general they require the subject to apply some principle or set

of principles which will enable him to either sort or order a number of otherwise diverse items or account for an existing arrangement. He may be required to order or sort blocks or cards according to shape, color, or number; he may be asked to continue a series of terms such as "apple, bun, cake, . . ." or to find the odd member in a group of otherwise similar items. One common method is to ask the subject to state the meaning (give the abstract and general principle) of a proverb. At the University of Liverpool, Hearnshaw (1956) devised a novel form of testing which stresses the element of temporal integration in the formation of concepts by presenting the stimulus material over time and by introducing abstract principles of organization which involve temporal progression.

Considerable interest has been shown in the effects of mental disease and brain injury on conceptual thought processes (Goldstein & Scheerer, 1941; Halstead, 1947; Rapaport, Gill, & Schafer, 1944), but relatively few investigations have been made on the normal effects of aging. It is not intended to review these investigations here, but rather to outline some recent findings arising from some work, which is still incomplete, at the University of Liverpool.

METHODS AND RESULTS

This study is designed to give data on age differences in conceptual abilities compared with age differences in general intellectual abilities. The underlying assumption is that, because conceptual thought processes appear to be easily, often seriously, impaired in mental disease and brain injury, one can expect the normal processes of aging to have deleterious effects on them, too. These effects should reveal themselves in two sorts of age difference: (1) quantitative differences which should show significant, perhaps substantial, systematic decrements with age in conceptual test scores, and (2) qualitative differences which should show systematic alterations with age in the kinds of response made.

Observed age differences on conceptual tests can be compared with observed age differences on the various subtests of the Wechsler-Bellevue Scale (Wechsler, 1944) in order to see whether abstraction and generalization are processes which decline relatively quickly or slowly with age. (Wechsler speaks of "hold" and "don't hold" abilities, Cattell [1943] of "crystallized" and "fluid" abilities in connection with this differential decline.)

The author has published several studies in the *Journal of*

Gerontology (Bromley, 1956; Bromley, 1957), but not all of them are concerned with conceptual thought processes. They are based on a cross-sectional design using parametric methods of statistical inference. For various reasons a change was recently made to nonparametric methods, and the results and matching procedures have been reworked without departing from the basic cross-section design.

From a pool of 256 volunteer subjects, eighty men and eighty women were selected to secure comparability of Wechsler-Bellevue I.Q. (intelligence quotient), Wechsler-Bellevue vocabulary, and social background rating at all age levels. Sex differences in these variables and in chronological age were eliminated. This group of 160 subjects constitutes the middle (main) sample with an age range of seventeen to seventy-eight (median=48) and an I.Q. range of 110 to 132 (median=122). According to Wechsler (1944), intelligence quotients of this order are characteristic of the top 25 per cent of the population. In addition, a group of forty-eight superior subjects, mostly men, were selected for the upper sample with an age range of twenty-three to seventy-seven (median=51) and an I.Q. range of 128 to 145 (median=133). Finally, a group of forty-eight average subjects, mostly older women, were selected for the lower sample with an age range of seventeen to eighty-two (median=63) and an I.Q. range of 88 to 112 (median=103).

The use of three samples makes it possible to cross-validate observations, because reliable age differences should be observable in all three samples. It must be pointed out, however, that the subjects in the upper and lower samples are not so well matched as the subjects in the middle sample. Nevertheless, when inferences are being drawn, it should prove possible to make some allowance for this lack of comparability, especially since our interest lies in relative rather than absolute age differences and not, for the moment at least, in sex or ability differences in normal intellectual decline with age.

Many nonparametric statistics can be used to establish matched groups and examine age differences in intellectual abilities, but it is also possible to use graphs to illustrate some points which might otherwise receive less attention. The relation between scores on the Wechsler-Bellevue subtests and chronological age can be summarized in terms of Spearman's rank order correlation (r_s). Table 1 shows the r_s of each subtest with age and ranks of these correlations within samples. If the r_s can be regarded as an indication of the rate at which an ability is declining with age—and the graphs suggest that this is so—then, provided we can demonstrate a measure of agreement among the three samples, we have not only cross-validated our observations, but we have also made it possible to get a more exact estimate of the differential decline with age in the Wechsler-Bellevue subtests. The Kendall coefficient of concordance (W) expresses the degree of association between k ranked variables; in this case, $k = 3$ and $W = 0.89$. It is clear that there is considerable agreement among the three samples in the way in which the subtest scores are associated with age.

Several features of Table 1 call for comment. In the middle sample, the difference in correlation between the least and most declining subtests is very large ($+ 0.11$ and -0.71). The least declining performance subtest, object assembly, declines more than the most declining verbal subtest, arithmetic. This confirms Wechsler's opinion that performance tests seem to be more sensitive than verbal tests to the deleterious effects of aging. The similarities subtest, which is generally considered to involve conceptual thought, can be regarded as a declining verbal subtest, especially since it is untimed. Vocabulary, of course, has been experimentally held constant in the middle sample and is not strongly associated with age in either of the other two samples. Vocabulary is a base line of sorts in the examination of the differential effects of age in other subtests; that is, other scores change with age relative to vocabulary. The separation of verbal and performance subtests into hold and don't hold categories does not exactly coincide with that of Wechsler, but this does not concern us at the moment.

The graphs which illustrate the age relationships need a few words of explanation. They are intended to show the general trend of age differences in a sample when the test scores have been transformed to ranks. The graphs have been constructed by plotting the mean chronological age of a subgroup against the mean rank of that subgroup on a given variable. For instance, taking the middle sample with $N = 160$, we can select the twenty youngest subjects as the first subgroup and find their mean chronological age and rank on the Wechsler-Bellevue vocabulary, enabling us to plot the first point. We then take the twenty next youngest subjects, find their mean chronological age and rank for vocabulary, and plot the second point, and so on until we have plotted the mean Wechsler-Bellevue vocabulary ranks for eight age groups of twenty subjects each. If adjacent points are connected by straight lines, a general age trend will be shown. The size of the subgroups will determine the upper and lower limits of discrimination, and these limits are stated. As usual, a slope from upper left to lower right indicates a decreasing score with increasing age. In summary, the graphs show the mean rank of successive age groups on a test variable; the left ordinate shows the scale of ranks.

The first line in figs. 1, 2, and 3 and the fifteenth line in figs. 4, 5, and 6 show the relations between chronological age and Wechsler-Bellevue vocabulary and I.Q. respectively. For the middle sample (figs. 2 and 5), there is no consistent age trend, and the trend lines fluctuate about the midpoint (80.5) of the scale of ranks; the subgroups are matched in very narrow limits as far as raw scores on the matching variables—vocabulary, I.Q., and social background rating

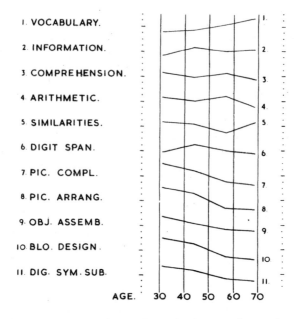

FIG. 1. Upper sample. (Applies to figs. 1-6.) See text for explanation of age differences in terms of ranks. In figs. 1, 3, 4, and 6, where $N = 48$, each interval on the vertical scale equals six ranks, the dash marks the median rank, and the limits of each graph lie eighteen ranks above and below the median. In figs. 2 and 5, where $N = 160$, each interval on the vertical scale equals ten ranks, the dash marks the median rank, and the limits of each graph lie seventy ranks above and below the median.

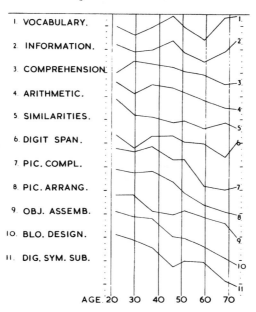

1. VOCABULARY.
2. INFORMATION.
3. COMPREHENSION.
4. ARITHMETIC.
5. SIMILARITIES.
6. DIGIT SPAN.
7. PIC. COMPL.
8. PIC. ARRANG.
9. OBJ. ASSEMB.
10. BLO. DESIGN.
11. DIG. SYM. SUB.

AGE. 20 30 40 50 60 70

Fig. 2. Middle sample.

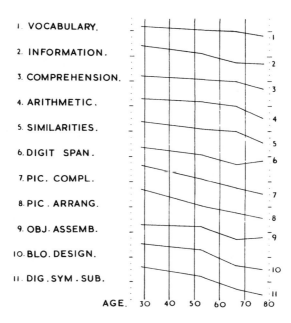

1. VOCABULARY.
2. INFORMATION.
3. COMPREHENSION.
4. ARITHMETIC.
5. SIMILARITIES.
6. DIGIT SPAN.
7. PIC. COMPL.
8. PIC. ARRANG.
9. OBJ. ASSEMB.
10. BLO. DESIGN.
11. DIG. SYM. SUB.

AGE. 30 40 50 60 70 80

Fig. 3. Lower sample.

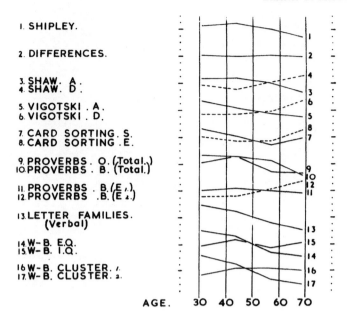

FIG. 4. Upper sample.

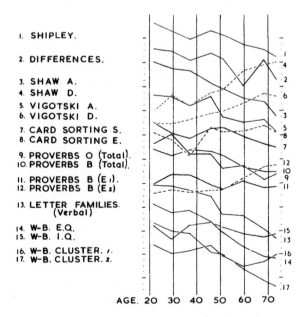

FIG. 5. Middle sample.

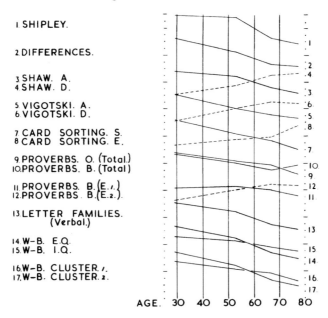

1 SHIPLEY.

2 DIFFERENCES.

3 SHAW. A.
4 SHAW. D.

5 VIGOTSKI. A.
6 VIGOTSKI. D.

7 CARD SORTING. S.
8 CARD SORTING. E.

9 PROVERBS. O. (Total.)
10 PROVERBS. B. (Total)

11 PROVERBS. B. (E.1.)
12 PROVERBS. B. (E.2.)

13 LETTER FAMILIES.
   (Verbal.)

14 W-B. E.Q.
15 W-B. I.Q.

16 W-B. CLUSTER. 1.
17 W-B. CLUSTER. 2.

AGE. 30 40 50 60 70 80

FIG. 6. Lower sample.

(not shown)—are concerned. Tables of equivalent raw scores have been omitted for reasons of economy. In the upper sample (figs. 1 and 4), there are slight increments with age in vocabulary, which can be attributed to inadequate matching, although Wechsler-Bellevue I.Q. shows no change with age. In the lower sample (figs. 3 and 6), there are very slight decrements with age in vocabulary and I.Q. By contrast, the fourteenth line on figs. 4, 5, and 6 shows age differences in Wechsler-Bellevue efficiency quotient (E.Q.) for the three samples. It is obvious that, as would be expected, age decrements in average intellectual efficiency are consistent and substantial.

It will be easier to judge the normal effects of aging on conceptual abilities if we first establish a frame of reference by studying the normal effects of aging on the abilities measured by the eleven subtests of the Wechsler-Bellevue Scale. Lines 1 to 11 on figs. 1, 2, and 3 show, for each sample, the normal effects of aging on vocabulary, information, comprehension, digit span, similarities, arithmetic, digit symbol substitution, block design, object assembly, picture arrangement, and picture completion. The figures illustrate and confirm the age differences already catalogued in Table 1. But in addition, it is possible to see that the age profiles are more similar between certain

TABLE 1
RANK ORDER CORRELATIONS BETWEEN AGE
AND WECHSLER-BELLEVUE SUBTESTS RANKED FROM
LARGEST POSITIVE TO LARGEST NEGATIVE R$_S$
IN THREE SAMPLES

(Decimal points omitted)

Wechsler-Bellevue subtest	*Sample*					
	Upper		Middle		Lower	
	r$_S$	rank	r$_S$	rank	r$_S$	rank
Vocabulary	+384	1	+110	1	−224	1
Information	+127	2	−022	2	−514	7
Comprehension	−064	3	−222	4	−308	2
Similarities	−166	5	−272	5	−498	5
Digit span	−109	4	−123	3	−325	3
Arithmetic	−248	6	−341	6	−500	6
Block design	−684	10	−706	11	−746	10
Picture arrangement	−723	11	−644	10	−728	9
Object assembly	−517	8	−473	7	−389	4
Picture completion	−620	9	−603	8	−814	11
Digit symbol substitution	−418	7	−636	9	−724	8

Note—In tables 1 and 2, if N is larger than 25, then $z = r_s \sqrt{N-1}$ may be referred to tables of normal probability:

N	z	r_s
48	1.960	.286
	2.576	.376
160	1.960	.155
	2.576	.204

tests than between others. (Vocabulary and information are very similar in this respect.) The similarity between digits backward and digit span compared with digits forward is not shown in these graphs. Object assembly seems to be different from the other Wechsler-Bellevue performance subtests in its relation to age.

CONCEPTUAL ABILITIES

Having seen something of the method and results achieved when the method is applied to familiar material, let us turn to

TABLE 2
RANK ORDER CORRELATIONS BETWEEN AGE AND CONCEPTUAL ABILITIES RANKED FROM LARGEST POSITIVE TO LARGEST NEGATIVE R$_s$ IN THREE SAMPLES
(Decimal points omitted)

Test	Response category	*Sample*					
		Upper		Middle		Lower	
		r$_s$	rank	r$_s$	rank	r$_s$	rank
Shaw test	A (abstract)	−377	14	−634	17	−621	13
Shaw test	D (deteriorated)	+306	5	+612	1	+597	1
Proverbs 0	2 (abstract)	−499	17	−463	15	−533	11
Proverbs 0	1 (functional)	+495	2	+406	2	+535	2
Proverbs 0	0 (concrete)	+236	6	+401	3	+364	5
Proverbs B	2 (right)	−296	11	−289	11	−273	10
Proverbs B	1 (half right)	+235	7	+077	8	−105	8
Proverbs B	0 (wrong)	+336	3	+243	6	+232	7
Proverbs B	E$_1$ (normal errors)	−156	10	−124	9	−241	9
Proverbs B	E$_2$ (deteriorated errors)	+521	1	+381	4	+336	6
Vigotski	A (abstract)	−416	15	−443	14	−595	12
Vigotski	D (deteriorated)	+317	4	+374	5	+496	3
Card sorting	No. exposures required	+100	8	+130	7	+380	4
Card sorting	No. sortings made	−324	13	−256	10	−654	14
Shipley		−301	12	−390	13	−679	16
Differences		−023	9	−333	12	−671	15
Letter families	Performance	−476	16	−599	16	−756	18
Letter families	Verbal	−623	18	−693	18	−746	17

conceptual abilities. Rather than present in detail the results for one test, I have presented the results for several in outline.

The Shaw Test

The Shaw test consists of four wooden blocks which can be arranged in at least fifteen different series, according to height, weight, position of notch, and so on. In addition to the fifteen normal, frequent, abstract, and clearly defined sequences (Grade A responses), there are at least five Grade D responses, usually failures of comprehension and inane responses (building towers with the blocks or describing them). No time limit was imposed, and the subjects were, in a sense, tested to the limit of their capacity for producing ideas.

The figures show the effects of age on performance in the Shaw test. There are substantial decrements in the high-grade intellectual processes concerned with abstracting and ordering according to principles and, at the same time, substantial increments in symptoms of intellectual deterioration.

Proverb Interpretation

The creative response test in proverb interpretation consists of fourteen proverbs of the type, "You must not cast pearls before swine," in which the subjects are asked to explain the meaning. No time limit was imposed, and answers were scored according to their conceptual level. The multiple-choice section consists of ten proverbs printed on separate cards; underneath each proverb are three explanations of its meaning at different conceptual levels. No time limit was imposed, and subjects were asked to rank the explanations in order of merit, receiving credit according to the accuracy of their judgment.

On the creative response part of the test, errors were scored 0 and classified as normal errors (E_1) consisting of abstract misinterpretations and "don't know" responses, and abnormal errors (E_2), consisting of literal explanations, anecdotes, and confused or irrelevant associations.

The figures show the normal effects of aging on the two tests of proverb interpretation, substantial decrements in the high-grade intellectual processes concerned with abstract thought, shifts in the level of understanding, and increments in symptoms of intellectual deterioration.

Sorting Tests

The Vigotski test is a sorting test that consists of twenty-two wooden blocks varying in shape, color, and the like. In the present inquiry, subjects were asked to sort the blocks one way and then another until they could think of no further sortings. No time limit was imposed. Responses, as for the Shaw test, fell into two main types: abstract, logical, and clearly defined; and concrete, disorganized, rigid, constricted, inappropriate, global, arbitrary, inaccurate, confused, and repetitive.

Another sorting test, the card test, consists of thirty-two cards featuring either bottle or glass shapes, which are large or small in size, two or three in number, vertically or horizontally arranged, and outlined or filled in. Subjects were instructed to sort the cards into two packs as soon as they could devise a way while the experimenter placed the cards face up one by one. One score is the number of exposures required before the first sorting; the other score is the number of different sortings the subjects devised spontaneously. No time limit was imposed.

The figures show the normal effects of aging on performance in the two sorting tests. Substantial decrements in the ability to categorize, substantial increments in abnormalities of conceptual thought, and a slight increment in the amount of time or information needed before the first response result.

Verbal Tests

The Shipley conceptual test is a well-known paper and pencil test consisting of twenty series of mixed numerical, alphabetical, and verbal material, which subjects are required to continue. The differences test is a paper and pencil test consisting of seventy verbal items. In each the subjects have to draw a line under the one word which is different from the other three.

No time limits were imposed for these verbal tests. The graphs show that the normal effects of aging appear greater for the Shipley test although it has fewer items and a narrower range of scores.

Temporal Integration Test

The letter families test is one of a number of tests of temporal integration devised by Prof. L.S. Hearnshaw at the University of Liverpool. The idea behind the tests is that conceptual cognition involves abstracting relevant data from the mass of experience and formulating an ordered system of thought which will consistently adjust to the constant features among the complex, variable, and random stimuli of environment. The essential feature in a temporal test of conceptual cognition is a family of instances: Xi, Xii, Xiii, and so on, each containing the invariable feature X. The subject's task is to make a consistent response to the common feature by either choosing additional instances of X or describing the invariant feature X. Form A of Hearnshaw's letter families test was specially constructed for exploratory studies with children, old people, and psychiatric patients.

It consists of ten subtests preceded by an explanation and two examples. Each subtest is a separate family, and the first six cards in each pack show the subject what the members of the family have in common. (All the letters on a card may be the same; the letters may be arranged in two rows of four in an ABAB arrangement which is reversed in the bottom line.) The exposure time for each of the first six cards is limited. Next, ten test cards are shown to the subject who must decide whether each one belongs to the family. Finally, he has to explain in what ways the members of the family are alike. This gives a performance score (number of items correctly identified) and a verbal score (the number of family characteristics correctly described). One can expect the verbal and performance scores to be closely correlated.

Time limits were imposed. The figures show the normal effects of aging on performance on the test of temporal integration. The performance and verbal scores are not independent; with increasing age, they both substantially decline in similar ways.

The amount of qualitative information gathered in the letter families test is much less than might be expected. The nature of the test excludes altogether the very deteriorated person and confines the abnormal intellectual symptoms of aged persons in very narrow limits, leaving the intellect no such freedom of expression as one finds in the data of the sorting tests, which reveal significant facts about thinking and intelligence. Nevertheless, a few examples of abnormal intellectual processes were observed among older subjects—tendencies to look for relations found in earlier families, especially the demonstration families; to recall the individual members of a family rather than look for the common principle; to remain content after having discovered one superficial principle and not look for more complex characteristics; to fail to notice shifts in the kinds of relations exhibited by the families; to explain by giving examples or making gestures rather than by explaining a principle; to claim understanding without the ability to explain. The letter families test proved to be a hard one for older subjects, and it seemed likely that qualities of personality as well as intellect were important in determining success or failure on it.

No qualitative data are available for the Shipley, differences, or card sorting tests. On the remaining tests, data which are normally thought qualitative have been quantified (D responses on the Shaw and Vigotski tests; E_2 responses on the creative response part of proverb interpretation). The detailed information about these different *kinds* of responses is too large for inclusion in this report.

Qualitative data in the form of abnormal intellectual processes are not difficult to elicit, especially from very old people and psychiatric patients suffering from mental disease or brain injury. What is required is a situation allowing the experimenter to do more than merely mark a response right or wrong; he must be able to record and later classify the many abnormal sorts of responses which deteriorated subjects make even to the most standard type of intellectual test. In an earlier pilot study in this field, Bromley (1953) showed that when deteriorated psychiatric patients verbalized their solutions to Raven's progressive matrices test (Raven, 1938), they were not only less intelligent than normal subjects; the whole organization of their cognitive and perceptual processes was different.

Table 2 shows the degree of association in terms of Spearman's rank order correlation coefficient between chronological age and various tests of conceptual ability and the rank order of these correlations in each sample. The procedure is the same as that of the Wechsler-Bellevue subtests shown in Table 1. In the case of Table 2, Kendall's coefficient of concordance is 0.92, which means that there is a substantial agreement among the three samples in the way that the eighteen conceptual test scores are associated with age.

To some extent the results of Table 2 confirm the impression that performance test scores are more adversely affected than verbal test scores by the normal effects of aging, but perhaps the most interesting fact is the demonstration confirmed by the graphs that the normal effects of aging include not only a decline in the capacity for abstraction and generalization, but also an increase in pathological forms of thought previously ascribed to conditions of brain injury and mental disease.

If the middle sample, with $N = 160$, can be regarded as giving the most reliable data on age differences, it seems that the creative response test of proverb interpretation (B on the figures) is similar in its association with age to the similarities subtest of the Wechsler-Bellevue Scale, also a verbal test of conceptual ability. On the other hand, the Shaw test (A on the figures) and the letter families test are similar to the picture arrangement subtest, which may have some connection with the process of temporal integration.

On the whole, the verbal tests of conceptual ability seem to be more closely associated with age than the verbal subtests of the Wechsler-Bellevue Scale are, whereas the performance tests of conceptual ability seem to be associated with age to about the same extent as the Wechsler-Bellevue performance subtests. It should be noted that of the conceptual tests only the letter families involves time limits, and one could expect that, if time limits were imposed on the other tests, the correlations would increase in size.

One limitation of this study is a lack of sufficient spread in some of the score distributions; ties have been taken into account, of course, in the calculation of r_s, but in some cases the failure of a test to differentiate sufficiently, especially among high-grade subjects, has meant that the real associations between intellectual abilities and age have been blurred. Two further limitations are that some of the tests have low reliabilities, although this only makes it more difficult to demonstrate any relation between such tests and age, and that the conceptual tests are assumed to be valid measures of the capacity for abstraction and generalization although this cannot be demonstrated.

A study of the graphs showing the relations between conceptual abilities and age indicates that the age trends are similar for the Vigotski A test and the differences test and for the card sorting and Shipley tests and that age trends are, with few exceptions, fairly consistent. Although not shown, the score responses for the multiple-choice proverbs test labeled "half right" (1) and "wrong" (0) have similar age trends; this suggests that the shift from an abstract to a concrete attitude does not go through an intermediate functional stage, but this finding is not supported by the results of the creative response proverbs test.

With the exception of the letter families test and Shaw test A categories, none of the conceptual tests approaches the limit of discrimination against age; the r_s values do not approach unity, and the trend lines do not approach the upper and lower boundaries of the graphs. In this respect the conceptual tests are not dissimilar to the subtests of the Wechsler-Bellevue Scale. In the scores of the letter families and Shaw test A, the discrimination against age is not far short of that achieved by the combined Wechsler-Bellevue subtests represented by the trend line of the Wechsler-Bellevue E.Q. (efficiency quotient) against age and the rank order correlations of −0.713, −0.715, and −0.817 in the upper, middle, and lower samples.

Lines 16 and 17 on figs. 4, 5, and 6 illustrate the effects of age on two cluster factors extracted from the matrices of rank order intercorrelations between the eleven subtests of the Wechsler-Bellevue Scale by a nonparametric analogue of factor analysis developed by the author (Bromley, 1959) and called rank order cluster analysis. The findings relating to this method cannot be described in detail in this report. All that can be said here is that Cluster 2 represents a verbal cluster and Cluster 1 a performance cluster. Work is in progress to apply the method to larger matrices which will include the tests of conceptual thought referred to in this report.

SUMMARY

An investigation was carried out to determine the effects of age on abstraction and generalization. Three samples were used to provide some measure of cross-validation, and a variety of verbal and performance tests of conceptual thought were administered with the Wechsler-Bellevue Scale. Tables of rank order correlations and graphs of age trends showed that the Wechsler-Bellevue subtest scores tend to be associated with age in much the same way as previous workers had found and provided a frame of reference for assessing the effects of age on conceptual abilities.

The Shaw test and the Hearnshaw letter families test of temporal integration proved to be very susceptible to the normal effects of aging, and discriminated against age almost as well as an E.Q. based on the eleven subtests of the Wechsler-Bellevue Scale. The verbal tests of conceptual ability were less closely associated with age than performance tests of conceptual ability.

Further research work in this area will use a consistently nonparametric approach including a method of rank order cluster analysis to cope with the problem of classifying intellectual processes and simplifying the general picture of the differential decline with age of mental abilities.

The data appear to be accounted for by the hypothesis that high-grade intellectual potentialities, such as seem to be involved in abstraction and generalization, are adversely affected in some way by age. But an additional hypothesis, such as that normal aging brings about regression to a more primitive cognitive level, or that normal aging brings about cognitive deterioration similar to that found in conditions of mental disease and brain injury, is needed to account for the fact that a normal increase in age is associated with an increase in abnormal and deteriorated forms of response.

REFERENCES

Bromley, D.B. Primitive forms of response to the matrices test. *J. ment. Sci.,* 1953, **99**, 374-393.
Bromley, D.B. Some experimental tests of the effect of age on creative intellectual output. *J. Geront.,* 1956, **11**, 74-82.

Bromley, D.B. Some effects of age on the quality of intellectual output. *J. Geront.*, 1957, **12**, 318-323.

Bromley, D.B. Rank order cluster analysis. Unpublished manuscript, University of Liverpool, 1959.

Cattell, R.B. The measurement of adult intelligence. *Psychol. Bull.*, 1943, **40**, 153-193.

Goldstein, K., & Scheerer, M. Abstract and concrete behaviour: An experimental study with special tests. *Psychol. Monogr.*, 1941, **53**, No. 239.

Halstead, W.C. *Brain and intelligence: A quantitative study of the frontal lobes.* Chicago: The University of Chicago Press, 1947.

Hearnshaw, L.S. Temporal integration and behaviour. *Bull. Brit. Psychol. Soc.*, 1953, **30**, 1-20.

Humphrey, C. *Thinking.* London: Methuen, 1951.

Rapaport, D., Gill, M., & Schafer, R. Manual of diagnostic and psychological testing. Vol. 1. Diagnostic testing of intelligence and concept formation, *Menninger Clin. Monogr.*, 1945, Series No. 3. (Chicago: Year Book Publishers)

Raven, J.C. *Progressive matrices, sets A, B, C, D, and E.* London: H.K. Lewis, 1938.

Wechsler, D. *The measurement of adult intelligence.* (3rd ed.) Baltimore: Williams and Wilkins, 1944.

SECTION II

Psychophysiological
Problems

CHAPTER 6

Social, Psychological, and
Physiological Gerontology—
An Experimental
Psychologist's Approach

ALAN T. WELFORD

It is no exaggeration to say that the majority of studies on aging are undertaken with a social aim. In particular, studies on those who have not yet retired are aimed at specifying work suitable for older people and minimizing the strains that result from changing capacity with age. After retirement, the problems divide into two classes: (1) how to enable older people to cope with the business of living and thus remain substantially independent, and (2) how to care for them either at home or in institutions when this is no longer possible. These questions are almost certainly the driving force behind most biological, clinical, and immediately social research.

The direct approach to these problems is fact-finding, assessing the adequacy of conditions and of people, describing attitudes and opinions, and recognizing such difficulties and needs as loneliness or squalor brings. Attempts may be made to go behind the surface data and identify changes with age in clusters of attitudes by factor analyzing attitude-scale data. These attempts are, however, still fundamentally descriptive and often suffer because they depend on statements made by subjects. Verbal reports of this kind can be seriously inaccurate either because of genuine inability to report correctly or deliberate falsification in statements of income, for instance, when there is a suspicion that too high a level may increase tax liability or lower pension or welfare payments.

The fundamental approach, of course, is to study the changes with age in the anatomy and physiology of the organism on which these other changes must depend, including the submicroscopic changes in the nervous system that would inevitably underlie the preservation and mediation of experience.

The experimental psychologist occupies an intermediate position between the social scientist and the physiologist, a position which can be of key importance. Sociological studies of aging often are not explanatory and thus are unlikely to lead to the formulation of valid general principles. The fundamental biological studies, on the other hand, are still at a stage at which their use in explaining behavior is very restricted. The situation of studies on aging is, in short, similar to that of psychology generally. The social psychologist is coming to recognize that he must explain social phenomena in terms of individual behavior. The experimental psychologist, aiming to understand behavior, recognizes social phenomena as a challenge, but also acknowledges that he must sooner or later relate behavior to physiological processes. The physiological psychologist and those who work near him in physiology and neurology know their important position, but find that their pace is set by the experimental psychologist's study of behavior.

This paper will explore the possibilities of applying to sociology certain behavioral and physiological principles of human function that recent studies have proven to change with age and to be significant in performance at the laboratory level. Two problems, especially, which between them seem capable of directly or indirectly explaining a number of observed age changes in individual behavior will be discussed. They are the speed of decision and the capacity of short-term memory. Consideration of these functions and the neural mechanisms behind them leads to a discussion of some aspects of the relation between brain and personality.

DECISION TIME

Since the early days of experimental psychology, it has been known that, if a subject has to choose one of several possible actions or identify which of several possible signals appeared, he takes more time as the alternatives increase. The relation between choice time and number of alternative choices has been formulated by Hick (1952) in a way which can be represented as Equation 1,

$$\text{choice time} = a + b \log N$$

where N is the equivalent of equally probable alternatives between which the subject has to discriminate and where a and b are constants, the former being close to zero if all experimental errors and artifacts are eliminated. Hick's formula opens a new quantitative approach in this field and also ties speed and accuracy together in a common framework. Errors can be conceived as part of the process of not carrying choice far enough—to the subject's behaving as if N were smaller than it is. Doing so saves time but results in misidentifications and wrong choices. The constant b varies according to the task, being less when the relation between perception and action is straightforward than when some symbolic translation from perception to action is required. Fairly constant values have been found, however, for certain broad classes of tasks.

The same approach seems to apply to other decision processes, such as control of movement and discrimination between objects of different magnitudes. In the former, the subject making an accurate movement can be thought of as choosing movements which will fall within prescribed limits out of a larger class which may fall anywhere from the starting point to the farthest limit allowed. In the latter case, the subject can be conceived as choosing the greater between two different magnitudes (Welford, 1960b).

Some recent results (Leonard, 1959; Mowbray & Rhoades, 1959) suggesting that Hick's formula may break down because all choice times become equal with very long practice must be regarded with caution pending more complete evidence. In any case, equality would probably be attained only when the number of alternatives was fairly small.

Different studies show some conflict over the effect of age on choice time. Crossman and Szafran (1956) found that the age effect increased the constant a in Equation 1. On the other hand, results from

Griew (1959) showed age effect to increase b. The same conflict runs through studies of discrimination and control of movement (Welford, 1960a) and must be recognized to pose a question in urgent need of answer. Whatever the form of the age effect, however, there is agreement that some progressive slowing occurs from the twenties on.

The main studies in this field have used laboratory tasks, but a few tentative attempts to extend the principle to behavior outside the laboratory have been promising (Crossman, 1956; Crossman, 1960), and it seems reasonable to suppose that the age effect applies at all levels from simple manual tasks to high-grade administrative thinking. If it does, it can be argued that, as the range of possible decisions increases, the average time at all levels will rise, and the number of decisions that can be made in a given time will fall. Any attempt to circumvent this limitation of human capacity will lead to strain or over hasty decision and thus to errors.

To study the individual's ability to cope with his environment as he grows older, environmental demands must be related to individual capacities. This requires a job analysis of both in the same terms. In the present case, environmental demands must be specified not only in number and type of decision, but also in time available for making the required decisions and in the complexity of the decisions. At once, a far more quantitative approach than usual is apparent.

Pacing

When the subject can determine his own time, any such slowness as that coming from increasing age will result merely in his taking a little longer. There are, however, many situations in which the pace of decision is determined by outside events or environmental circumstances. A well-known example in industry is the assembly line, where objects pass along a conveyor and the operators have to do their work on each article as it passes; if they do not complete their operation in time, the fault cannot be redeemed later. Other examples occur when automatic or semi-automatic machines have to be adjusted for incorrect operation; the times at which adjustments have to be made are usually determined by the process, and the operator must comply. At the executive level the same conditions often occur in the sense that decisions are occasioned by external events not under the executive's control.

In all these cases slowness means that decisions may not be completed in time unless they are hurried, at the risk of increasing errors. Even though the average time may be adequate, the events requiring decision occur at irregular intervals; thus sometimes several will come close together and cause a temporary overload. These overloads can be minimized by designing systems so that signals for action are unlikely to collect or demand such immediate attention that they cannot wait.

Apart from the question of temporary overloads, pacing, in relation to age, illustrates an important general point about the relation between environmental demand and individual capacity. If the pace is slow enough, the effects of age, or any other factor which slows performance, will make little or no difference at first; all the necessary decisions will be made in the available time, although there will be less spare time. Some confirmation of this in age trends is observed in industrial jobs where older men equal the achievement of, but work more steadily than, younger men. When this happens, any change in performance caused by age will be masked unless measures of over-all achievement are supplemented by measures of how achievement has been attained.

If performance slows to the extent that all spare time is absorbed, the subject will be chronically overloaded, and from this point on his achievement will show a functional relation to the degree of slowing down—either fewer decisions or more errors will be made. If, therefore, slowing down progresses with age, achievement will remain stable until the point of inflection is reached, and slowing down begins to show a functional relation to age. The inflection would ideally be a sharp one, although it would be smoothed in any actual case because the point would change slightly on different occasions. Such changes would result from moment-to-moment variability, day-to-day speed of performance, and the fact that temporary overloads would begin to affect achievement before chronic overloading occurred. If a group of subjects were studied, the smoothing would be still greater because speed of performance and degree of slowing with age are likely to vary among individuals and thus produce different points of inflection for different subjects.

This model has implications beyond paced tasks. Some of the clearest examples are the homeostatic mechanisms. In addition, a number of environmental demands seem to be within the capacity of young adults, but to exceed that of older people. In these cases, achievement is likely to remain stable up to a given age and, beyond that point, to show a functional relation with age (Welford, 1958). Although this model would show an average drop in achievement with age, this would be caused by only some individuals who were severely enough changed by age to fall below the level of adequate performance; the drop would increase as more individuals ceased to achieve adequate performance. In this case, there would be not only an increase in variability among individuals as they grew older, but also an increase in the coefficient of variation among their performances.

Load-shedding

General experimental studies have suggested that subjects may spontaneously and unconsciously shed overloads by reducing the range of signals or actions they consider. The classic example is the pilot in an artificial cockpit who, in times of stress, neglects to reset his fuel indicator and concentrates on the instruments in continuous use (Davis, 1948). One can, perhaps, see a parallel to this in the actions of an industrial manager, especially one in later middle age, who simplifies his work by neglecting departments whose activities do not continuously impinge upon his notice.

Similarly Verville and Cameron (1946) and Wallace (1956) have shown that under difficult conditions experimental subjects viewing pictures attempt to reduce their field of search by placing each object in the same class as the previous one. Having identified one picture as an animal, they try several animal names for the next picture before broadening their range of search to inanimate objects. Both sets of results found this tendency to increase with age. The phenomenon should probably be linked with the greater rigidity in problem-solving observed among older people.

The implication of this tendency for the employment and care of old people is that tasks may be brought into their range not only by reducing the number of decisions they are required to make, but also by reducing the range. At the shop, work might be arranged so that the variety of jobs and problems became less as a man grew older. At the executive level, effective delegation would achieve the desired result if it meant that substantial classes of decision were left to others by the senior man. Simplifying layout and standardizing equipment in the design of old people's living accommodations would achieve the same ends and be a worthwhile object of study.

Coding and Sequencing

A spontaneous tendency in human perception and action to recognize ways in which objects, signals, or actions hang together is illustrated in many experimental studies. This coherence is used to code patterns or sequences so that they can be treated as single units. This procedure reduces the subject's load because separate decisions about individual items are no longer needed. Instead, a single decision can be made to turn on the whole pattern or sequence. Thus, an object can often be recognized by observing only part of it, and a whole sequence of actions can be run automatically once it has been decided which sequence is required.

Much coding of incoming data and planning of everyday routines seem to be done spontaneously and unconsciously in ways that maximize economy of decision and minimize missing of important details. In some cases, however, for example, establishing work routines and administrative systems, optimum coding and sequencing require sustained analytical thought. It seems likely that suitable analysis and coding or sequencing of such work could often bring jobs now too difficult for older people into their range.

The price paid for this economy of decision is that of missing some details. Identifying an object as one of a class means that individual features are neglected, and a standard sequence of actions may not work well for the precise circumstances of a particular event. There is the risk of becoming rigid when dealing with problems, especially if conditions change so rapidly that routines and codes quickly become outmoded. It is tempting to see this as at least a partial explanation of the rigidity shown by some older people, especially those in administrative positions. They have, perhaps, reacted to a reduced speed in decision-making by increasing their reliance on standard solutions and standard routines. Changing circumstances could render these solutions and routines obsolete. On the other hand, it is only by coding and sequencing that the highest levels of thought can be attained. Dealing in larger units of data and action makes possible a wider grasp and broader scale of conceptualization. Coding and sequencing are essentially the products of experience, and the breadth of vision and depth of understanding they make possible are among the benefits of the increased experience that comes with age.

SHORT-TERM RETENTION

In addition to the data stored in the memory over long periods, still larger amounts are stored for a few seconds and then completely forgotten. Some short-term retention of this kind is necessary for integrating data that arrive serially, so that a melody can be heard in its entirety. Such retention is a fundamental requirement for maintaining orientation in space and time.

Recently published research on short-term retention, with some unpublished observations of the author, suggests a model somewhat like this: (1) data from the sense organs are fed into a short-term store (Store 1); (2) Store 1 feeds the data into the decision mechanism, which, in turn, feeds them into two other mechanisms, (3) an effector mechanism, which organizes and coordinates responses, and (4) a second store (Store 2), which retains data for varying lengths of time and feeds them back to the input of the decision mechanism. This model is similar in form to one tentatively proposed by Broadbent (1958, p. 299), although the present writer sees it operating somewhat differently.

Data which arrive while the decision mechanism is occupied with other data can be held in Store 1 for a few seconds until the decision mechanism is free. Broadbent (1954; 1956) has provided evidence that Store 1 is really a group of stores with separate storage for each ear, hearing, and vision; there are probably other stores in the group for other senses. These stores are limited in the number of items they can retain and the time for which they can retain them. It is probably their capacity which limits the forward digit span: the first two or three digits in a list pass straight to the decision mechanism, the rest collect in Store 1 until it is full. Any digits that arrive before the store has been emptied into the decision mechanism will interfere with those in the store, distorting or displacing them. It should be noted that Store 1 seems to store items (words, syllables, letters, digits) rather than information (in the information-theory sense), so that, in information-theory terms, its capacity varies greatly, according to the way the information is coded.

When the decision mechanism feeds Store 2, some trace is laid down. At first, this trace is fragile and liable to be disrupted by other data arriving from the decision mechanism, but, if it is left undisturbed long enough or is sufficiently reinforced by repetition, it lays down a long-term trace.

It seems necessary, therefore, to distinguish three forms of retention: (1) immediate memory in Store 1, (2) short-term memory by the traces initially formed in Store 2, and (3) long-term memory dependent on traces built over a period of time in Store 2.

Although age seems to have little effect on Store 1, it has a profound effect on the viability of the short-term traces in Store 2. Thus, the forward digit span, which probably depends on Store 1, changes little after young adulthood (Gilbert, 1941; Wechsler, 1944), whereas the ability to retain data a short period while other things are done falls greatly (Cameron, 1943; Kirchner, 1958; Suci, Davidoff, & Braun, 1960). Presumably, in the latter case, the extra data fed into Store 2 as a result of the intervening activity disrupt the short-term traces.

Losses of short-term memory are marked in clinical senility; patients may forget what they have seen, heard, said, or done a short time before and may, in severe cases, become disoriented. Less marked, but nevertheless significant, losses appear during middle age. Because of these losses, it is important to consider ways of lightening the load on short-term memory for people in middle and old age.

The value of building retention devices into industrial machinery so that operators do not have to remember data from one moment to another is being recognized and increasingly practiced on an empirical basis. The equipment in railway signal boxes, for example, used to rely on bell codes to describe trains offered from one rail to the next, and signalmen were expected to remember what trains had been offered. Modern equipment displays the descriptions of trains on panels with a light code which remains in view until the train has passed.

As far as the writer is aware, no systematic work has been done on the value of diaries, aids to memory, or self-reminding routines for office and administrative work. It is likely, however, that means of relieving the "mental in-box" would be worth study, especially for older office workers and executives. Without such devices, the person responsible for remembering to take some future action must prime his memory constantly to the exclusion of other mental activities. It is tempting to see the failure to shed loads as a potent cause of breakdown among responsible executives who are approaching later middle age.

Loss of short-term memory has, perhaps, fewer definite implications for the care of old people than it has for the design of work, but it would seem worthwhile to ensure that old people's accommodations are arranged to indicate how to find their way about their surroundings and where to find the things they need.

Some Ramifications

Short-term memory seems a key factor in many problem-solving tasks and processes of abstraction in which the subject has to absorb and retain data while seeking other data to combine with them.

One of the main sources of limitation on performance in these tasks seems to be that the first data are forgotten while the second are being gathered. This difficulty and its increase among older people have been illustrated in experiments by Clay (Clay, 1954; Clay, 1956; Clay, 1957; Welford, 1958) in which subjects were required to place numbered counters on checker boards to add up to given marginal totals. The main difficulty appeared in the correction of errors; subjects, having identified the row or column which was incorrect, would look for another with an opposite error so that exchanging these two counters would make both correct. Having found the second, however, they could not remember the first. Many subjects found it helpful to mark the first row or column in some way and thus obviate the need to retain information in short-term memory. There seems little doubt that such devices as this and systematic procedures for breaking complex problems into simple jobs which can be tackled one at a time would greatly increase the tasks that older people could master.

Hebb (1949) has suggested that short-term memory traces are essential in forming long-term traces. If they are, short-term memory must occupy a key place in learning and training (Welford, 1956; Welford, 1958). When learning or designing training procedures, it would be especially important to ensure that short-term traces are left undisturbed long enough for long-term traces to be established. Any material subsequently passing through the decision mechanism is likely to enter Store 2 and disrupt short-term memory there. This interference has been proven greater if the new material is similar to that already retained than if it is different from it (Sanders, 1961). Thus, interference can be minimized by limiting the material presented for learning on any one occasion and spacing the presentations with periods of inactivity. The first recommendation coincides with a method which has been found successful in training operators for semiskilled industrial work (Seymour, 1954), and the latter follows a principle which has been recognized since the early days of experimental psychology.

PHYSIOLOGICAL MECHANISMS

It is becoming possible to discuss both decision and short-term retention as fundamentals in the sense that physiological causes can be tentatively assigned to the ways decision and short-term retention change with age.

Decision-making must stimulate some cells in the brain more than others to distinguish one particular identification or action among many other similar possibilities. Presumably this implies intensifying activity until a threshold difference is reached between the desired activity and the others from which it must be distinguished. The time required for such an intensification most likely depends partly on the strength of the signals from the sense organs and from one part of the brain to another. It will also depend on the level of random background neural activity going on in the brain and the pathways concerned with it (Crossman & Szafran, 1956; Gregory, 1956; Gregory, 1959; Welford, 1956; Welford, 1958). Random "neural-noise" impulses, when added to signals, tend to blur them and thus lengthen the period necessary to secure discrimination.

As for the physiological mechanisms of retention, long-term memory must presumably depend on some submicroscopic synaptic growth or enduring biochemical change in the cells of the cortex. Immediate and short-term memory may, perhaps, be caused by reverberant neural circuits forming dynamic traces (Hebb, 1949) or stimulation of a synaptic pathway, which, in turn, lowers the threshold for re-stimulation of the same pathway within a few seconds or minutes (Eccles, 1953; Russell, 1959).

Decision-making and short-term memory are interdependent. On one hand, the intensified activity required for decision-making implies cumulating, and, therefore, the storing, data over brief periods; on the other hand, accurate short-term memory implies getting clear, unambiguous signals from the memory traces. Achieving such signals is probably akin to making decisions.

Both decision-making and short-term memory are, therefore, dependent on the ratio of signal to noise in the brain and on neural pathways, and anything, like age, which changes this ratio is likely to lead to both slower decision-making and poorer short-term memory. The decrease with age in the number of active brain cells or their malfunction because of factors such as mild anoxia from poor circulation would almost certainly lower the signal level. At the same time, any additional activity in the remaining cells to compensate for loss of signal and the fact that fewer cells are operating would tend to increase randomness. Some evidence for increased randomness appears to be provided by E.E.G. (electroencephalogram) records. Although several investigations have shown that slower basic rhythms are not associated with age changes in performance, there are indications that the records of older people are less regular than the average (Obrist, 1954).

Capacity and Personality

Looking from physiology back to behavior, one can perhaps see some reasons for the marked narrowing of interests often found in old people. Some narrowing is likely the result of bodily changes which discourage physical activity and make strenuous exercise less attractive with advancing age. More important, a lower ratio of signal to noise, reducing the capacity of brain mechanisms, is likely to increase load-shedding and decrease differentiation among brain processes. Both tendencies would be likely to narrow the range of decisions made, the first by conscious or unconscious exclusion of all but the most pressing signals, the second because only the strongest signals, for the most dominant interests and needs, would be likely to lead to definite action. Interests, thus, would narrow with age until, in extreme cases, only the signals for such basic matters as food and bowels remained. Undoubtedly the cause of narrowing can be identified: if it were caused by load-shedding, other interests could be aroused by effort and stimulation, whereas if it were caused by sheer loss of capacity, all other possible interests would also have disappeared.

Any loss of capacity with age is likely to have indirect as well as direct effects on behavior. This is especially so if—and this often seems the case—older people spontaneously and unconsciously make the best use of their remaining capacities to compensate for losses. They seek an environment which will support them while making minimum demands on them. Thus, many old people, especially those who are seriously incapacitated, cling to their families. Some do this to the extent that a daughter and son-in-law (or son and daughter-in-law) are prevented from going out or taking holidays together. Illness is sometimes feigned or magnified if someone proposes leaving the older person alone even for a few hours. Such behavior is an understandable, if unfortunate, reaction to the knowledge that one cannot do without help and prefers the help of his family to that of strangers in an institution, but there is no absolute contract binding the younger generation to continue care indefinitely. The argument for regarding this behavior as an attempt to ensure continued care is strengthened by the change often shown when the move to an institution is finally made. Many old people who were extremely difficult when living at their child's home become entirely tractable in a hospital where help and care are permanently ensured.

Neurological Impairment and Age Changes

It seems fair to say that changes in behavior and personality with age mimic a wide range of known neurological impairments. Two examples may be mentioned.

First, the changes of memory in senile states appear similar in certain ways to such organic syndromes as the Korsakow: immediate and long-term memory are hardly affected, whereas short-term memory is strikingly impaired. Second, the tendency for deterioration to be most severe in the frontal lobes of the old brain (Bondareff, 1959) may be related to the tendency of some old people's behavior to mirror that found in frontal syndromes. With both mild degrees of senility and frontal injury, a mechanism seems to get lost. This mechanism acts, in relation to the rest of the brain, as a condenser in an electrical circuit, blunting the immediacy of momentary impulses and providing self-control and firm purpose. In both cases, the underlying personality seems to be revealed. A pleasant person may scarcely change, but a person who has controlled his unpleasant personality traits in earlier life may become disagreeable, demanding, greedy, lustful, and thoughtless. At the same time, with all personality types, ambition and sustained purpose may diminish so that, just as the young patient with frontal injury cannot hold a job or pursue a course of study, the senile patient becomes a slave to immediate needs.

On theoretical grounds, it is tempting to attribute most important changes in behavior with age to deterioration in particular areas of the brain. The main argument against this view is that attempts to correlate performance in old age with brain condition at post-mortem examination have met with little success. If, however, the model of limiting factors described earlier is correct, this objection is invalid. The relation between capacity and demand is likely to apply to neural mechanisms as much as it applies to the performance of the whole organism. The question is not, therefore, merely whether a given brain mechanism is impaired, but whether the impairment is serious enough to pull the brain's functioning below the level that is required. To put it another way, not only the degree of impairment must be considered, but also the degree of stress to which the particular brain mechanism is subjected. Severe deterioration in one part of the brain may have little effect on performance, whereas slight deterioration in another part would have a great effect. This is not to say that correlating neurological and behavioral conditions with age is hopeless, but that it is more complex than often assumed.

ORGANIC CHANGE AND THE
EFFECTS OF EXPERIENCE

The main discussion in this paper has deliberately concentrated on physical changes and their effects on behavior. Better coding of data and sequence of action—benefits which the experience of age causes—have also been mentioned. Two other points deserve special mention because they might lead to results that, at first sight, appear to be organic in nature.

First, prejudices or inhibitions caused by training or a few unfortunate experiences may restrict the range of what is attempted and parallel the effects of a true loss of capacity—indeed, they may lead to a genuine loss through disuse. Second, an individual is likely, during his life, to experience a number of vivid successes and striking failures. The probability of experiencing a success or failure more extreme than any previous ones will diminish as each year passes. In the same way, the likelihood of any radically new experience will lessen. Together these may lead to an emotional flatness, because nothing really exciting happens any more. This could resemble the lack of drive shown in some organic syndromes.

Separating environmental from organic factors in relation to age is not always easy, or, indeed, possible, since experience depends on capacity to gain experience and since this, in turn, depends on organic capacities and past experience. As far as a separation can be made, the apparently organic factors are so directly and indirectly fundamental and widespread in their effects that they, not experience, seem the main determinants of age changes in behavior. Support for this view can, perhaps, be seen in the research of Chown (1960) who found, by a factor analysis of performances on rigidity tests, that two types of rigidity could be distinguished—that caused by fixed attitudes and unwillingness to change and that caused by inability to master what was new. She found that only the latter type was associated with age: older subjects appeared to be inflexible not from lack of trying, but from impaired capacity.

THE COORDINATION OF RESEARCH

Experimental psychology has benefited greatly in the study of aging from close contact with the environmental problems of work, and both experimental psychology and physiology have, in general, found it of the greatest value to keep close track of one another. This paper has attempted to show that cooperation, all the way from social problems through individual behavior to physiology and anatomy and back again, has an important part to play in the development of aging studies.

At first sight, the ideal method of securing this cooperation would be to encourage general training in all aspects of gerontology for those intending to do research in the field. Such training would, however, demand a considerable number of well-established research centers where the trained worker could make a career. Present opportunities hardly seem sufficient to justify training young men in this way. The realistic course for the time being appears, thus, to be to encourage research from people whose training and interests are centered in one of the established social or biological human disciplines. Doing so has the advantage of joining disciplines, so that a broader background of knowledge and insight are brought to bear on gerontological problems.

On the other hand, there is the risk that the disciplines will develop their own problems, interests, and methods in ignorance of the contributions they might receive from others. Help in keeping them together may come from a few individuals who have sufficiently broad understanding and sympathy to comprehend more than one of the traditional disciplines. Most of the coordination, however, seems likely to result from deliberate attempts to keep workers in different fields informed of each other's work and from the determined efforts of the research workers to understand each other's problems and methods.

REFERENCES

Bondareff, W. Morphology of the aging nervous system. In J.E. Birren (Ed.), *Handbook of aging and the individual: Psychological and biological aspects.* Chicago: The University of Chicago Press, 1959. Pp. 136-172.

Broadbent, D.E. The role of auditory localization in attention and memory span. *J. exp. Psychol.,* 1954, **47,** 191-196.

Broadbent, D.E. Successive responses to simultaneous stimuli. *Quart. J. exp. Psychol.,* 1956, **8,** 145-152.

Broadbent, D.E. *Perception and communication.* London: Pergamon Press, 1958.

Cameron, D.E. Impairment of the retention phase of remembering. *Psychiatric Quart.,* 1943, **17,** 395-404.

Chown, Sheila M. The Wesley rigidity inventory: A factor analytic approach. *J. abnorm. soc. Psychol.*, 1960, **61**, 491-494.

Clay, Hilary M. Changes of performance with age on similar tasks of varying complexity. *Brit. J. Psychol.*, 1954, **45**, 7-13.

Clay, Hilary M. An age difficulty in separating spatially contiguous data. *J. Geront.*, 1956, **11**, 318-322.

Clay, Hilary M. The relationship between time, accuracy and age on similar tasks of varying complexity. *Gerontologia*, 1957, **1**, 41-49.

Crossman, E.R.F.W. Perception study—a complement to motion study. *Manager*, 1956, **24** (2), 141-145.

Crossman, E.R.F.W. *Automation and skill.* London: H.M. Stationery Office, 1960.

Crossman, E.R.F.W., & Szafran, J. Changes with age in the speed of information intake and discrimination. *Experientia Supplementum*, 1956, **4**, 128-135.

Davis, D.R. *Pilot error.* Air Ministry Publication, 1948, A.P. 3139A. (London: H.M. Stationery Office)

Eccles, J.D. *The neurophysiological basis of mind.* London: Oxford University Press, 1953.

Gilbert, Jeanne G. Memory loss in senescence. *J. abnorm. soc. Psychol.*, 1941, **36**, 73-86.

Gregory, R.L. An experimental treatment of vision as an information source and noisy channel. In C. Cherry (Ed.), *Information theory: 3rd London Symposium 1955.* London: Methuen, 1956.

Gregory, R.L. "Neurological noise" as a factor in aging. In *Proceedings of the 4th congress, international association of gerontology, Merano, Italy.* Vol. 1. Florence: Tipographica Tito Mattioli [1959]. Pp. 314-324.

Griew, S. Complexity of response and time of initiating responses in relation to age. *Amer. J. Psychol.*, 1959, **72**, 83-88.

Hebb, D.O. *Organization of behavior.* New York: John Wiley & Sons, 1949.

Hick, W.E. On the rate of gain of information. *Quart. J. exp. Psychol.*, 1952, **4**, 11-26.

Kirchner, W.R. Age differences in short-term retention of rapidly changing information. *J. exp. Psychol.*, 1958, **55**, 352-358.

Leonard, J.A. Tactual choice reactions, I. *Quart. J. exp. Psychol.*, 1959, **11**, 76-83.

Mowbray, G.H., & Rhoades, M.V. On the reduction of choice reaction times with practice. *Quart. J. exp. Psychol.*, 1959, **11**, 16-23.

Obrist, W.D. The electroencephalogram of normal aged adults. *EEG clin. Neurophysiol.*, 1954, **6**, 235-244.

Russell, W.R. *Brain, memory, learning.* London: Oxford University Press, 1959.

Sanders, A.F. Rehearsal and recall in immediate memory. *Ergonomics*, 1961, **4**, 25-34.

Seymour, W.D. *Industrial training for manual operations.* London: Pitman, 1954.

Suci, G.J., Davidoff, M.D., & Braun, J.C. Interference in short-term retention as a function of age. Paper presented at the 5th Congress, International Association of Gerontology, San Francisco, 1960.

Verville, E., & Cameron, N. Age and sex differences in the perception of incomplete pictures by adults. *J. genet. Psychol.*, 1946, **68,** 149-157.

Wallace, Jean G. Some studies of perception in relation to age. *Brit. J. Psychol.*, 1956, **47,** 283-297.

Wechsler, D. *The measurement of adult intelligence.* (3rd ed.) Baltimore: Williams and Wilkins, 1944.

Welford, A.T. Age and learning: Theory and needed research. *Experientia Supplementum,* 1956, **4,** 136-143.

Welford, A.T. *Ageing and human skill.* London: Oxford University Press, 1958.

Welford, A.T. Age changes in the times taken by choice, discrimination and the control of movement. Paper presented at the 5th Congress, International Association of Gerontology, San Francisco, 1960. (a)

Welford, A.T. The measurement of sensory-motor performance: Survey and reappraisal of twelve years' progress. *Ergonomics,* 1960, **3,** 189-230. (b)

CHAPTER 7

Cognitive Tasks in Several Modalities

SEYMOUR AXELROD

For the past two years, we have been concerned with certain broadly defined aspects of nonpsychometric cognitive functioning.[1] Our specific interests have been in selected sensory and perceptual functions. Wherever possible, our approach has been to investigate the performance of a small young-adult group and a small senescent group on analogous tasks in two or more sensory modalities and to follow promising leads. The inclusion of analogous tasks in

[1] This work was supported by U.S. Public Health Service grants H 3582, M 900 C, and M 2109. Various aspects of it were conceived and executed in collaboration with Dr. Louis D. Cohen, Dr. Carl Eisdorfer, and Mr. Robert Canestrari, who have agreed to the inclusion of some of our joint efforts in this report. Some of the suggestions for investigating neural correlates of performance have arisen from conversations with Dr. W.D. Obrist, who is developing refined techniques for analyzing electroencephalographic responses to stimulation. Dr. David Arenberg gave us valuable advice and assistance in some phases of this work.

132

more than one modality represents one approach to the definition of psychological function. To use an example with which we have been working (Cohen & Axelrod, 1960), it has been demonstrated in well-controlled studies (Basowitz & Korchin, 1957; Crook, Alexander, Anderson, Coules, Hanson, & Jeffries, 1958) that senescence reduces the ability to recognize a simple figure when it is embedded in a complex, figured background, as in the traditional Gottschaldt (1926) task. It is as though the "visual noise" of the complex background is too distracting (Crook et al., 1958). These are interesting findings, but it appears to us that the next question might be, "Is the ability to recognize a figure reduced because the figure is embedded or because the task is visual?" The answer, if there is one, will obviously influence our thinking about the performance in behavioral or physiological terms. If a complex task of this type is poorly performed by the aging only when it is presented to the visual modality, then a disorder like agnosia, in which modality-specificity is required by definition, may be considered, with the further provisions that dementia and elementary sensory deficits can be ruled out. If, on the other hand, reduced ability to perform a visual Gottschaldt-type task is associated with a similar decrease in ability to extract a tactual figure from a tactual ground or an auditory figure from an auditory ground, it becomes reasonable to consider the possibility that the embedding per se, rather than the modality, causes the decrease. The area of complex perceptual performances is not the only one in which generalization on single-modality studies has been questioned. In a review, Inglis (1958) has called attention to the dearth of multiple-modality work in investigations of the effects of senescence on memory and learning functions.

ABSOLUTE AND DIFFERENTIAL SENSITIVITY

One of our first cross-modality efforts was an exploratory one, with small groups, designed to investigate possible modality interrelations among thresholds in vision, audition, and somesthesia. Visual thresholds were determined, after forty-five minutes of dark adaptation, by a simple instrument in which stimulus intensity was varied by changing the distance between a standard source and a screen of frosted glass. Auditory thresholds were measured with pure tones at 250, 1,000, and 5,000 cycles per second (cps). Absolute and differential light-touch thresholds on thumbs and palms were determined with a graded series of pressure esthesiometers, which Drs. Josephine Semmes and Sidney Weinstein constructed of nylon monofilaments along the classic lines described by von Frey. A vernier caliper with jaws machined down to blunt points was used to get two-point thresholds on thumbs and palms.

Our results for absolute thresholds in these modalities were consonant with those reported by others (Weiss, 1959): the aging had higher limens than the young adults. Correlations in the group were negligible, however, suggesting that the lowered sensitivities in the three modalities had separate determinants. Curiously, we were unable to confirm our expectation that differential thresholds would be significantly larger for our older subjects. Our samples were small (eleven in each group), and the variability was great. It is possible that larger samples might have brought our results into line with our expectation and others' results.

As far as observable central nervous system (c.n.s.) correlates of thresholds are concerned, the electroencephalogram appears to be an extremely likely tool, especially in view of recent advances in recording and analysis. Two kinds of electroencephalographic response offer possibilities for correlative work. First, it is clear that where alpha waves characterize the resting record, sensory stimulation often disturbs the synchronized spontaneous rhythms—thus the familiar "alpha blocking." Second, evoked potentials can be recorded through the intact scalp, although the technical problems are considerable, especially in distinguishing between evoked and background activity (Walter, 1950). In reference to the difficulties of recording and interpreting evoked activity, it should be remembered that these difficulties do not limit work with animals from which electrocorticograms may be obtained. There seems to be no reason why correlative studies of the type suggested here cannot be done on infrahuman organisms. As far as the age variable is concerned, cross-sectional investigations with animals are clearly possible; with the current advances in techniques of chronic electrode implantations, longitudinal studies may also become feasible. Such investigations would help to fill the gap noted by Magladery (1959), who, reviewing the literature on the neurophysiology of aging, could find "no serious investigations of alterations due to aging . . . carried out on central physiological mechanisms in experimental animals of reasonable size and degree of organization" (p. 183).

In animal or man, then, it might be fruitful to attempt to relate absolute sensory thresholds to the characteristics of blocking and evoked activity—to the latency or duration of blocking, for example, or the latency, magnitude, or wave form of the evoked potential.

Thus, blocking latency to photic stimulation appears to be systematically related to frequency of resting alpha (Bernhard & Skoglund, 1943), and alpha frequency, after rising from ages six months to twenty-five years, drops markedly in senescence (Bernhard & Skoglund, 1943; Obrist, 1954). Similarly, a direct study attempting to correlate resting frequency with sensory acuity suggests itself.

Similarly, one might look for correspondence between perceptual differential thresholds and the just noticeable difference (jnd) of the cortical response. Here is implied the possibility that the difference between the electrical responses to two stimuli most likely has to have critical magnitude in order for the stimuli to evoke the verbal response, "different."

Absence of correlations among modalities in the group means that both young and elderly subjects have high acuity in some modalities and low acuity in others. Especially useful would be studies relating differences in thresholds to differences in electrographic responses to stimulation of the modalities.

Responses to Rapidly Repeated Stimuli

Using the same eleven subjects, we obtained a nonsignificant difference in the anticipated direction (elderly worse) in an auditory shortest-noticeable-off-time task (SNO), in which ability to discriminate between one click and two clicks was measured. Weiss and Birren (1957) had earlier obtained similar results. On a visual shortest-noticeable-off-time task, we also did not obtain a significant group difference. Lindsley and Lansing (1956) have demonstrated that this variety of temporal resolution involves processes different from those involved in traditional measures of critical flicker frequency (CFF), in which elderly individuals suffer a well-documented decline (Coppinger, 1955). There is no significant correlation between SNO and CFF, they go on to report; one does not seem to limit the other.

The failure to obtain deficits in auditory and visual SNO's in our elderly group is especially interesting in view of an apparent dissociation between these tasks and a somesthetic analogue we have used. Pairs of moderately intense condenser shocks were delivered to either one hand at a time or both hands at once, and the subject was asked to judge whether they were simultaneous or successive. Here our older group showed considerable, statistically significant deficits. Correlations in the group among the three tasks were negligible; again, the determinants of performance do not appear to be common to the three modalities.

Deficits in tasks which demand discrimination among successively presented stimuli suggest an increased refractoriness of the receptive or neural elements involved in the transmission of impulses or, at least, an inability to follow the stimulation rate. The residual effects of a stimulus (S_1) appear to persist, so that a second stimulus (S_2), following S_1 by a fraction of a second, arrives before the processes initiated by S_1 are over, and "smearing" occurs. It is worth considering a possible association between a subject's ability to resolve successively presented stimuli and electroencephalographic indicators of the persistence of stimulus effects. One measure which it might be fruitful to correlate with CFF's or SNO's is duration of alpha-blocking after offset of the blocking stimulus. The data of Travis and Knott (1937) suggest that this is a highly reliable index, at least in an experimental session, even when relatively crude manual measurements are used. Another more direct approach might well be taken to the problem of the neural correlates of temporal resolution and the effects of age thereon. Lindsley (1958) has pointed out that the cat's or monkey's cortical shortest-noticeable-off-time in vision (the minimum interflash time which gives two evoked potentials from the exposed cortex rather than one) is about the same as the human observer's perceptual shortest-noticeable-off-time. It seems reasonable to expect a systematic relation between the characteristics of such potentials to paired stimuli and the subject's perceptual resolving power.

A third possibility suggests itself, the correlation of the following rate to continuously repetitive (flickering) stimulation with perceptual fusion frequency. Halstead (1947) considers it "very probable that the higher the rate at which the brain waves of an individual can be organized or reactivated from the periphery . . . the higher will be the critical-fusion frequency . . ." (p. 72). Early workers obtained conflicting results. Adrian and Matthews (1934) and Durup and Fessard (1935) could not drive cerebral rhythms anywhere near CFF, but Jasper (1937) reported correspondence between the upper limit for synchronization and CFF. Differences in instrumentation may be involved in this conflict, and much remains to be done. More recently, Rutschmann (1955) has been unable to get systematic E.E.G. counterparts of flicker and fusion, but it is possible that recording and analyzing techniques different from the ones he used may be more successful in revealing the assumed relationship. It may be noted that in audition repetitive clicks in the cortex of a cat are reported to evoke responses which follow up to 100 per second (H. Davis, cited by Jasper, 1937), so that cross-modality work in this area seems possible.

What has all this to do with aging? Is there any reason for believing that the aged nervous system is more susceptible than the younger to stimulus persistence? A positive answer is suggested by a provocative report of Mundy-Castle (1953) that electroencephalographic afterdischarges following the cessation of photic stimulation were more frequent in older than in younger persons. It is an intriguing question, and a testable one, whether such cortical persistence as Mundy-Castle reports is associated with the longer term perseveration noted in the perceptual performances of aging subjects, their tendency to hold to a percept in the face of changed characteristics of the stimulus (Korchin & Basowitz, 1956) or instructions to organize an alternative percept (Botwinick, Brinley, & Birren, 1959). Although the times are of different magnitudes and the symbolic significance of the stimuli radically different (photic stimulation being relatively meaningless compared with the animal and human figures presented in the perceptual experiments), it would be reasonable to look for systematic relationships between the two types of perseveration.

The most striking difference between the resting E.E.G. of the senescent and young adult is the decline in the former of the alpha frequency (Obrist, 1954). This provides another possible tie-in among senescence, temporal resolution, and the electrical activity of the brain. It has been proposed (Bishop, 1933; Lindsley, 1952) that alpha activity represents an alternating excitability cycle of cells or cell aggregates and that small aggregates can be independently active with random phase relations at alpha frequencies, but do not give recordable alpha rhythms unless they become synchronized; impulses initiated by stimulation gain access to cerebral centers more easily if they arrive at a time when one or another aggregate is in an excitable phase. This implies more frequent excitable periods and thus more frequent access to the centers as alpha frequency increases. Temporal resolution might then be expected to be worse the lower the alpha frequency is. This would coincide with what is known about CFF and alpha frequency in sensescence, although it is unclear whether CFF and alpha frequency are, in fact, systematically correlated. Lindsley and Lansing (1956) were unable to find such a relationship, thus conflicting with the results of Reuning (1955) and Shoul and Reuning (1957).

Smearing and "Arousal"

Two lines of recent research suggest a mechanism which may be useful in explaining—or at least exploring—the deficits in temporal resolution which aging subjects exhibit on some tasks. First, Lindsley

(1958) has studied the temporal resolving power of various points along the visual transmission route from optic tract to cortex in animals. Like Halstead (1947) and his colleagues, Lindsley reports that following repetitive photic stimulation, as indexed by evoked potentials, is much better at precortical levels than at the cortex; the implication is that the cortex is the limiting structure in resolving power. Working also with pairs of flashes, a shortest-noticeable-off-time situation, Lindsley found that he could get the cortex of a cat to follow higher than normal stimulation rates if he first stimulated the ascending reticular activating system, the brain stem of the diffusely projecting, relatively nonspecific "second sensory system" which has been implicated in arousal processes by Lindsley, Magoun, and others (Ellingson, 1956; Lindsley, 1951; Lindsley, 1958).

Second, recent evidence that neural arousal mechanisms may, under certain conditions, be less activating in aging people dovetails neatly with Lindsley's report. Botwinick and Kornetsky (1960) report that electrodermal responses (EDR) to auditory stimuli adapt more quickly in elderly than in young subjects, and that the former group acquires conditioned EDR more slowly. These results can be interpreted to imply less arousability in senescent subjects. Results that can be similarly interpreted are reported by Shmavonian, Silverman, and Cohen (1958) and Silverman, Cohen, and Shmavonian (1958), also working with electrodermal measures. These investigators found that senescent subjects were less responsive than young adults in terms of both amplitude of "specific" EDR's to presented stimuli (tones and adjectival phrases) and nonspecific, spontaneous fluctuations in skin resistance during interstimulus intervals. The implication of these two findings would appear to be that in senescence the neural mechanisms underlying both arousal and the kind of perceptual efficiency involved in resolving repetitive stimuli may be chronically functioning at a low level.

It is possible, but not necessary, to think of the senescent subject's reticular system as intrinsically hypofunctional; the elderly subject simply may not view the experimental situation as especially important. Everyday experience indicates that individuals can voluntarily inhibit or facilitate their levels of arousal, and everyday laboratory experience indicates that subjects can be aroused by anxiety-provoking instructions ("You're doing very poorly on this test.") and calmed down by reassurance. These effects, involving symbolic processes (language), are presumably of cortical origin and may, as Lindsley (1958) suggests, be mediated by corticofugal pathways to the reticular formation (French, Hernandez-Peon, & Livingston, 1955). This arousal-by-instruction has been employed in an unpublished experiment on visual critical flicker frequency in general medical patients by L.D. Cohen.[2] Cohen found it possible to raise the flicker thresholds of his subjects by implying that they could do better and signaling bad trials. (It is, of course, conceivable that subjects simply avoided the negative signals by reporting "flicker" when they actually experienced "steady." A control study is now being run in our laboratory in which a presumptive state of arousal is being maintained by randomly presented electric shocks.) The senescent subject performing a relatively dull psychophysical task just may not be particularly interested in it. Cortical facilitation of the activating system is low; CFF falls. If he does become ego-involved, the indications are that he can be aroused. Silverman et al. (1958) found that in spite of a generally lowered reactive level, as indexed by electrodermal activity, arousal is possible if the stimuli are ego-involving like the phrase, "an old failing body."

Time Errors

Another way to examine responses to timed inputs is to attend to the errors of judgment when a subject is asked to compare successively presented stimuli. Variable errors give rise to estimates of his precision and differential thresholds. Constant errors may tell something about processes during the interstimulus interval. Köhler (1923) has suggested that time errors, over- or underestimates of S_2 relative to S_1, can be used to index the fate of the trace of S_1.

Whether conceived as an electrochemical process, as the Gestaltists do; a reverberating circuit phenomenon, as Hebb does (1949); or a process whose neurology is of no concern to the psychologist; the trace seems a necessary assumption. Broadly defined, it is indexed by the effects of perceptions on subsequent ones. The decreased ability to discriminate stimuli presented in rapid succession is one such effect. Are there other effects that differentiate older and younger subjects?

Fig. 1 presents data on intensive auditory time errors for half-second tones (750 cps) at one, two, four, and six seconds, obtained by constant stimulus differences (Axelrod & Eisdorfer, 1960). The curve of the senescent group is monotonic, time error becoming more negative as the interstimulus interval is extended, whereas the curve

---

[2] This finding was reported in a personal communication.

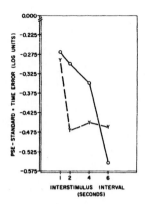

Fig. 1. Auditory time errors for tones (750 cps, 0.5 second) as a function of interstimulus interval.

Source—Tibbitts, C., & Donahue, Wilma. (Eds.) *Social and psychological aspects of aging*. New York: Columbia University Press, 1962. P. 778.

of the young group levels at about two seconds. The interaction is statistically significant. It looks as though some process supervened at around two seconds in the younger, but not in the older, group. We have speculated that the trace of S_1 remained salient for the senescent subjects over the six seconds, but that, for the younger group, it began to be replaced as a magnitude against which to judge S_2 by some central tendency of all the stimuli heard in the experiment. Bruner (1957) points out, "It is still something of a moot point how the nervous system estimates the first moment of magnitude or quality of the distribution of objects that are arranged in a class" (p. 343), but there is certainly good evidence from so-called context experiments in psychophysics (Needham, 1935) that such averaging occurs, and the work by Helson (1947) on adaptation level provides an approach to its quantification. In any case, the implication of our conjecture is that context is less effective for older than for younger subjects. We are now following this by collecting data in an experiment in which the context effects are directly assessable.

Insofar as the context effects may be considered similar to those of mental set, this interpretation conflicts with studies of set in complex perceptual and problem-solving situations which clearly show greater effects in older than in younger adults (Heglin, 1956; Korchin & Basowitz, 1956). More critically, this interpretation runs counter to those of Botwinick et al. (1957), whose data are open to the interpretation that elderly adults were more susceptible than young ones to context effects in an auditory reaction time task.

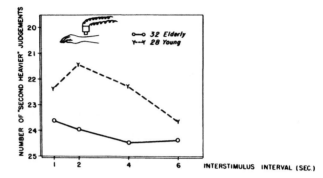

Fig. 2. Time errors in weight judgment as a function of interstimulus interval. Note—Ordinates greater than 20 signify negative time error (Axelrod & Eisdorfer, 1960).

Before the possibility of the effects of context occurred to us, we collected the data on time errors in weight judgments summarized in Fig. 2. A single weight was dropped on the forearm for one half-second, lifted for one, two, four, or six seconds, and then dropped again for one half-second. The subject was not told that the weight was the same both times and was instructed to judge whether the second weight was lighter or heavier than the first. (This design does not allow for the operation of context effects.) Like Weinstein (1955), who used a similar technique to investigate tactile time errors after brain injury, we did not obtain a significant interval effect; like Weinstein's brain-injured subjects, our senescent group had more negative time errors than their controls, although this difference was not significant. Unfortunately, the two time error situations were not analogous. The question of modality-specificity or -generality awaits at least two cross-modality experiments: one in which context effects can show themselves and another in which they cannot.

A Complex Task

The final cross-modality study tests the ability to extract a figure from a complex ground (Cohen & Axelrod, 1960). We gave nineteen young and thirty senescent adults a traditional visual embedded figures task (Fig. 3). The subject was to trace the simple figure (sample figure) embedded in the complex one (test figure). Fourteen of the sample test pairs were projected on plywood boards, and balsa replicas of the visual figures were mounted on the boards. These wooden figures were screened from the subject's view, and he was required to touch the sample and then trace its counterpart in the complex figure. No time limit was placed on either task; the subjects were told they could take as long as they wished, because accuracy was the important consideration.

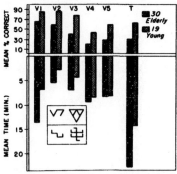

FIG. 3. Performances on five parts of a visual embedded figures task (V) and on a tactile analogue (T). Inset shows two items from the tasks (Thurstone, 1944, after Gottschaldt, 1926; cited by Cohen & Axelrod, 1960).

The senescent group performed more slowly and less accurately than the younger group (Fig. 3). The groups did not differ on the Wechsler vocabulary scale score, which we used as an approximate index of psychometric functioning. The group differences on the tactile task remained significant after covariance analysis to eliminate the effect which two-point threshold might have had on the performance.

Performances on the visual and tactile analogues were positively correlated to a significant degree; this is a situation in which modality-specificity does not apear to have an effect. It is possible, of course, that the subjects tended to visualize the tactile forms or "tactualize" the visual ones, thus making the generality across modalities more apparent than real. In an attempt to shed some light on this question, we have begun to recall our subjects and ask them to identify visually forms which they feel. The data are not yet in. All we can say at this point is that these embedded figures tasks have central common processes. Here again, Grey Walter's ideas suggest the possibility of correlative studies.

CONCLUSION

We have emphasized the importance of cross-modality work because we are convinced that whether one operates exclusively with psychological variables or relates these to the substrate, the definition of behavioral functions must take both the specific and the general into account. Knowledge of both obviously provides clues about what to look for in behavior and the nervous system.

The same consideration applies to the use of advanced age as a variable. Study of "experiments of nature," people in whom deficit-producing processes are at work, provides an important tool in the analysis of normal function. This has been the rationale, for example, of investigations of brain damage (cf. Head, 1920; Teuber, 1959), where the situation is, perhaps, clearest. But other types of derangement have been employed. In 1709, Berkeley (1948) observed blind people to support his account of the genesis of visual space and cases of congenital cataract-removal to confirm his prediction that, without prior visual experience, tactually familiar objects cannot be visually recognized. (Hebb [1949] has, of course, had similar recourse more than two hundred and fifty years later.)

So it is with normal aging, which has the advantage to the researcher seeking subjects of being a universal experiment of nature. The questions are similar to those asked in studies of brain-injured individuals. What performances decline? What associations indicate a more-or-less general function and substrate? What dissociations suggest absence of a general factor? What might be the neural mechanisms underlying the deficit behaviors? The answers are bound to elucidate not only our understanding of the deficits, but also our knowledge of optimum functions.

REFERENCES

Adrian, E.D., & Matthews, B.H.C. The Berger rhythm: Potential changes from the occipital lobes of man. *Brain,* 1934, **57,** 355-384.

Axelrod, S., & Eisdorfer, C. Aging and the stimulus trace: Auditory time error in younger and older persons. Paper presented at the 5th International Congress of Gerontology, San Francisco, 1960.

Basowitz, H., & Korchin, S.J. Age differences in the perception of closure. *J. abnorm. soc. Psychol.,* 1957, **54,** 93-97.

Berkeley, G. *An essay todard a new theory of vision.* Vol. 1. A.A. Luce & T.E. Jessop (Eds.), *The works of George Berkeley.* London: Thomas Nelson, 1948.

Bernhard, C.G., & Skoglund, C.R. On the blocking of the cortical alpha rhythm in children. *Acta Psychiat. Neurol.,* 1943, **18,** 159-170.

Bishop, G.H. Cyclic changes in excitability of the optic pathway of the rabbit. *Amer. J. Physiol.,* 1933, **103,** 213-224.

Botwinick, J., Brinley, J.F., & Birren, J.E. Set in relation to age. *J. Geront.*, 1957, **12**, 300-305.

Botwinick, J., & Kornetsky, C. Age differences in the acquisition and extinction of the GSR. *J. Geront.*, 1960, **15**, 83-84.

Botwinick, J., Robbin, J.S., & Brinley, J.F. Reorganization of perceptions with age. *J. Geront.*, 1959, **14**, 85-88.

Bruner, J. Neural mechanisms in behavior. *Psychol. Rev.*, 1957, **64**, 340-358.

Cohen, L.D., & Axelrod, S. The performance of young and elderly persons on embedded-figure tasks in two sensory modalities. Paper presented at the 5th International Congress of Gerontology, San Francisco, 1960.

Coppinger, N.W. The relationship between critical flicker frequency and chronologic age for varying levels of stimulus brightness. *J. Geront.*, 1955, **10**, 48-52.

Crook, M.N., Alexander, Edith A., Anderson, Edythe, Coules, J., Hanson, J.A., & Jeffries, N.T. *Age and form perception.* (Report No. 57-124.) Randolph Air Force Base, Texas: U.S. Air Force School of Aviation Medicine, 1958.

Durup, G., & Fessard, A. L'électroencéphalogramme de l'homme. *Année psychol.*, 1935, **36**, 1-34. Cited by E. Simonson & J. Brozek, Flicker fusion frequency: Background and applications. *Physiol. Rev.*, 1952, **32**, 349-378.

Ellingson, R.J. Brain waves and problems of psychology. *Psychol. Bull.*, 1956, **53**, 1-34.

French, J.D., Hernandez-Peon, R., & Livingston, R.B. Projections from cortex to cephalic brain stem (reticular formation) in monkey. *J. Neurophysiol.*, 1955, **18**, 74-95.

Gottschaldt, K. Über den einfluss der erfahrung auf die wahrnehmung von figuren. I. *Psychol. Forsch.*, 1926, **8**, 261-317.

Halstead, W.C. *Brain and intelligence.* Chicago: The University of Chicago Press, 1947.

Head, H. *Studies in neurology.* London: Oxford Medical Publications, 1920.

Hebb, D.O. *The organization of behavior.* New York: John Wiley & Sons, 1949.

Heglin, H.J. Problem-solving set in different age groups. *J. Geront.*, 1956, **11**, 310-317.

Helson, H. Adaptation-level as a frame of reference for prediction of psychophysical data. *Amer. J. Psychol.*, 1947, **60**, 1-29.

Inglis, J. Psychological investigations of cognitive deficit in elderly psychiatric patients. *Psychol. Rev.*, 1958, **55**, 197-214.

Jasper, H.H. Electrical signs of cortical activity. *Psychol. Bull.*, 1937, **34**, 411-481.

Köhler, W. Zur theorie des sukzessivvergleichs unde der zeitfehler. *Psychol. Forsch.*, 1923, **4**, 115-175.

Korchin, S.J., & Basowitz, H. The judgment of ambiguous stimuli as an index of cognitive functioning in aging. *J. Pers.*, 1956, **25**, 81-95.

Lindsley, D.B. Emotion. In S.S. Stevens (Ed.), *Handbook of experimental psychology.* New York: John Wiley & Sons, 1951. Pp. 473-516.

Lindsley, D.B. Psychological phenomena and the electroencephalogram. *EEG clin. Neurophysiol.*, 1952, **4**, 443-456.

Lindsley, D.B. Psychophysiology and perception. In R. Glaser & others (Eds.), *Current trends in the description and analysis of behavior*. Pittsburgh: University of Pittsburgh Press, 1958. Pp. 48-91.

Lindsley, D.B., & Lansing, R.W. Flicker and two-flash fusional thresholds and the EEG. *Amer. Psychologist*, 1956, **11**, 433. (Abstract)

Magladery, J.W. Neurophysiology of aging. In J.E. Birren (Ed.), *Handbook of aging and the individual: Psychological and biological aspects*. Chicago: The University of Chicago Press, 1959. Pp. 173-186.

Mundy-Castle, A.C. An analysis of central responses to photic stimulation in normal adults. *EEG clin. Neurophysiol.*, 1953, **5**, 1-22.

Needham, J.G. The effect of the time interval upon the time-error at different intensive levels. *J. exper. Psychol.*, 1935, **18**, 530-543.

Obrist, W.D. The electroencephalogram of normal aged adults. *EEG clin. Neurophysiol.*, 1954, **6**, 235-244.

Reuning, H. A new flicker apparatus and its application to the measurement of temperament. *J. Nat. Inst. Personnel Res.*, 1955, **6**, 44-54.

Rutschmann, J. Recherches sur les concomitants électroencéphalographiques éventuels du papillotement et de la fusion en lumière intermittente. *Arch. Psychol., Genève*, 1955, **35**, 93-192.

Shmavonian, B.M., Silverman, A.J., & Cohen, S.I. Assessment of central nervous system arousal in the elderly. Paper presented at the annual meeting of the Gerontological Society, Philadelphia, 1958.

Shoul, Shirley M., & Reuning, H. Speed and variability components in Pauli test, CFF and alpha rhythm. *J. Nat. Inst. Personnel Res.*, 1957, **7**, 28-44.

Silverman, A.J., Cohen, S.I., & Shmavonian, B.M. Psychophysiological response specificity in the elderly. Paper presented at the annual meeting of the Gerontological Society, Philadelphia, 1958.

Teuber, H.L. Some alterations in behavior after cerebral lesions in man. In A.D. Bass (Ed.), *Evolution of nervous control from primitive organisms to man*. Washington, D.C.: American Association for the Advancement of Science, 1959. Pp. 157-194.

Thurstone, L.L. *A factorial study of perception*. Chicago: The University of Chicago Press, 1944.

Travis, L.E., & Knott, J.R. Brain potential studies of perseveration: I. Perseveration time to light. *J. Psychol.*, 1937, **3**, 97-100.

Walter, W.G. Normal rhythms—their development, distribution, and significance. In D. Hill & G. Parr (Eds.), *Electroencephalography*. London: Macdonald, 1950. Pp. 203-227.

Weinstein, S. Time error in weight judgment after brain injury. *J. comp. physiol. Psychol.*, 1955, **48**, 203-207.

Weiss, A.D. Sensory functions. In J.E. Birren (Ed.), *Handbook of aging and the individual: Psychological and biological aspects*. Chicago: The University of Chicago Press, 1959. Pp. 503-542.

Weiss, A.D., & Birren, J.E. Age changes in click perception. *Amer. Psychologist*, 1957, **12**, 385. (Abstract)

CHAPTER 8

The Halstead Index and Differential Aging

WARD C. HALSTEAD,
PAT MERRYMAN, and
BERTHA KLIEN

Death, taxes, and aging are among the expectations of modern man. About the first two, there is little argument, but is the term "aging" more than a metaphor? Is aging a clearly definable series of biological and social events, or is it a process so subtle that it can be discussed only metaphorically? We believe that the literature of geriatrics, ably reviewed by James Birren (1959), indicates that aging is still discussed as a metaphor. There are no mechanical, electrical, or chemical processes that parallel aging; senility (chronic neurological impairment) is, perhaps, the most similar process.

Whether the undesirable changes denoted in the term "aging" are causally related directly to the brain is a moot question. If it is, to which brain? Man's brain is fourfold, consisting of the neuronal brain, the glial brain, the biochemical brain, and the vascular brain.

146

Each of these brains has its own genetic history and is vulnerable to specific processes. Which one most directly controls the life span of the individual is unknown. At present, there are no means of analyzing these four sources of variance to evaluate aging. From an objective study of behavior, is it possible to construct for these four brains acting in unison a global indicator which would be useful in evaluating the relative aging of individuals? It is the purpose of this chapter to raise the possibility of such an indicator and to explain the lines of analysis that we are presently pursuing.

Nonpatient populations, primarily production workers and business executives, have been under study at the University of Chicago clinics since 1952. Objective and quantitative neuropsychological tests developed in the Laboratory of Medical Psychology for measuring higher-brain functioning have been applied in conjunction with standard medical indicators of general mental and physical health. A collateral purpose of these studies is to elucidate the incidence and nature of possible changes in higher-brain functioning which are associated with aging. The psychological indicators constitute the Halstead battery of neuropsychological tests. These tests, developed during the past twenty-five years, have proven reliable and valid in defining the state of higher-brain functioning independently of calendar age, sex, formal schooling, ethnic origin, occupational history, and psychometric intelligence (I.Q.). As far as we know, this is the first "culture-free" battery of psychological instruments for measuring adaptive brain power which has been directly validated, with appropriate controls, on neurosurgical and neurological patients. Essentially, the tests are nonverbal and attempt to determine the brain's ability to integrate in time and space information supplied to it through vision, hearing, and touch. More detailed descriptions of the ten tests in the battery have already been published (Chapman, Thetford, Guthrie, Berlin, & Wolff, 1958; Halstead, 1947; Kløve, 1959; Reitan, 1955).

In applying these instruments to the problem of aging, several considerations must be kept clearly in mind. One of these is the motivation factor. Are the tests interesting or dull, fun or boring to take? Does repetition induce substantial increase in score through learning? Are the tests too intellectual for the general population? Is the meaning of each test so evident that willful distortion or malingering is likely? We believe that our combined experience—which now includes work in several laboratories—and the data for several thousand people show that the test battery is novel and diversified in content and normally elicits a high level of cooperation. Many subjects describe taking the tests as "fun." The test-retest reliability is very high. The nonverbal content of the tests requires special norms and objective scoring keys for evaluating performance, so the subject does not know at the end of testing whether he has performed well. His cooperative attitude and serious approach to the test are reinforced throughout by the attitudes of the personnel and by the maintenance of an appropriate environment.

EXPERIMENTAL DESIGN

Experimental behavioral studies of aging in man are either cross-sectional or longitudinal. A cross-sectional study is usually a single measurement of a sample of the general population in which the experimental variables are related to the chronological age of the subjects. Longitudinal studies measure the same individuals at different times. Each design has its strengths and weaknesses. In the longitudinal study the individual is his own control. The cross-sectional approach is particularly vulnerable to the cryptic, or hidden, variable. An example of this is cited in the study of Jones and Conrad (1933), who applied a modification of the Army Alpha examination from World War I to all the adults between the ages of twenty and sixty in a New England community. The decrement in psychometric intelligence after thirty was attributed by the authors to aging, but Lorge (1956) has cast doubt on the validity of this interpretation by showing a probable inverse relation between the subjects' formal schooling and calendar age.

The data for higher-brain functioning presented here have been gained from two studies—a completed cross-sectional study (Study I) and a longitudinal study, initiated six years ago, which is still in progress (Study II). Also presented here are reliability and validity data from Study II.

Study I

Our data for Study I were obtained from production workers. Unusual care was exercised in drawing the samples for subgroups A and B. Subgroup A consisted of workers with calendar ages ranging from thirty-five to forty-five with a median age of forty; subgroup B consisted of workers doing identical work, but ranging in age from fifty-five to sixty-four with a median age of sixty. The mean age for the total sample is fifty, the standard deviation six years.

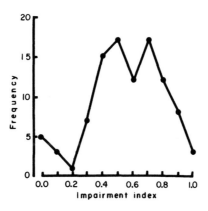

FIG. 1.

Fig. 1 shows the distribution of the Halstead index for the total sample regardless of age. The index can range from 0.0 to 1.0. In terms of criteria established independently of the present study, certain qualitative significances may be assigned to different values as follows:

> 0.0 to 0.3=normal functioning
> 0.4 to 0.5=borderline functioning
> 0.6 to 1.0=impaired functioning

In terms of adaptive brain power as measured by the battery of tests on which the index is based, a considerable percentage of the workers score in the impaired zone. In the four industries sampled in this study —and our conclusions must be restricted to this sample—very little of the potential creative brain power remains in workers with jobs requiring below average mental capacity. Does this brain power remain equally in the younger and older groups? No; relatively more of the younger workers score in the "unimpaired-functioning" zone. Are the tests too difficult for these workers? Normal children from twelve to fourteen with I.Q.'s of 100 characteristically score in the "unimpaired-functioning" zone. In one important sense, these are not intellectual tests at all—they simply reflect the neuropsychological status of those parts of the brain which contribute directly to the emergence of intellect. We shall not attempt to offer any satisfactory explanation of these findings, but state only that we regard them as entirely valid. Our collateral evidence indicates that there is con-

siderable incidence of head injury, neglected illness, and alcoholism
in this sample. There is also the possibility of high incidence of cerebrovascular disease in the group which scored "impaired functioning."
Independently of the psychological measurements, Dr. Bertha Klien
carried out searching ophthalmoscopic examinations on a double-
blind basis of the retinal vesicles of these subjects' eyes. Findings for
each person in the group were classified according to the Klien index:

> N=normal
> A=borderline unfavorable changes
> B=moderately severe changes
> C=severe changes
> D=advanced arteriopathology

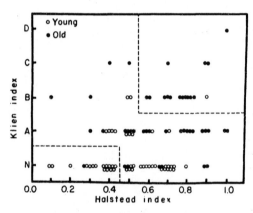

FIG. 2.

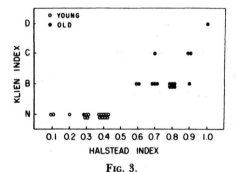

FIG. 3.

Comparison of the Halstead with the Klien index yields no significant correlation. A scattergram of the combined data gives a random distribution (Fig. 2). Why? The relation of retinal to cerebral vessels in cerebrovascular disease is, at present, uncertain, because of the difficulties of assessing with nonhistological methods the state of the cerebral vessels. A closer inspection of the data, however, raises an interesting possibility which may have implications for research design in this area.

Two groups, one with, the other without, early signs of cerebrovascular disease, can be identified in the scattergram shown in Fig. 3. (This is an operational definition for cerebrovascular disease, not a clinical diagnosis.) On this figure, the "unimpaired" range of the Halstead index has been extended to include 0.4, and the B, C, and D groups of Dr. Klien are considered together. Thus, an operationally normal individual would be defined as healthy if he had normal fundi and a Halstead index of less than 0.5. Conversely, a cerebrovascular suspect would have a fundus classification greater than A on the Klien index and a score·greater than 0.5 on the Halstead index. In the ninety-five workers tested, seventeen healthy subjects and sixteen cerebrovascular suspects (as operationally defined) were found. Should this proportion hold in further samples, it should be possible, with 625 subjects, to select 100 normal subjects and 100 cerebrovascular suspects for both diagnostic and therapeutic longitudinal studies. The goal is to identify the cerebrovascular suspects at an early stage of their unfavorable mental change before their ischemic attacks and/or strokes. Culling critical research samples from the total would also leave in ambiguous classifications a large number of individuals who could be observed longitudinally for incidence of spontaneous strokes or mental changes appropriate for age, occupation, and the like. This would help validate the operational criteria for prediction. We mention this possibility for rigorous research design in the hope that it might influence the direction of collaborative studies in this important area.

Various experts on vascular disease observe that the mental symptoms associated with cerebrovascular disease may progress to the point of severe mental deterioration without any associated stroke; conversely, stroke patients may be functioning at a high mental level until the time of the stroke. The U.S. Public Health Service estimated that in 1957 there were 453,840 deaths attributable to arteriosclerotic heart diseases (including coronary heart disease) and 188,040 deaths attributable to vascular lesions affecting the central nervous system (mainly strokes), but there is no breakdown for prevalence of or incidence of cerebrovascular disease characterized by symptoms of mental deterioration. This is an area where expert diagnosis is difficult until the mental changes are fairly well advanced.

Study II

Some years ago, in conjunction with Dr. Wright Adams, chairman of the Department of Medicine of the University of Chicago, and Dr. Emmet Bay, we began a longitudinal study by annual physical examination of several hundred top-level business executives. Each odd-numbered year of the past six years has included measurement by the Halstead index.

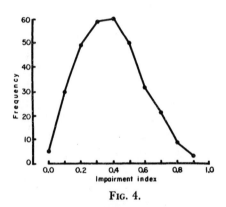

FIG. 4.

Fig. 4 shows the distribution of the Halstead index for a group of more than three hundred executives with a mean age of fifty at initial testing. Of this group, only about 20 per cent score in the "impaired-functioning" zone. It seems clear in terms of the samples compared here that by mean calendar-age fifty a higher residuum of creative brain power is found among executives than among production workers. Again, we shall not attempt to evaluate here the many factors which may contribute to this outcome. It may simply be that the executives take better care of themselves and have fewer head injuries from accidents. We are not sure that per-capita consumption of alcohol is less. Executive responsibility is undoubtedly taxing, possibly physiologically taxing, but it carries high personal satisfaction. Although our analyses are not yet complete, our findings suggest that the incidence of cerebrovascular disease may be considerably lower among the executives than it was among the production workers.

Here, again, the nature and adequacy of our population samples must be kept in mind. If we assume that approximately one in five of the executives is manifesting impaired higher-brain functioning with associated behavior alterations similar to those commonly observed in early senility, then we must look to the other end of the distribution and consider that many of these men are aging at a considerably slower rate than their occupational peers. These men stand out even more conspicuously against the backdrop of the total labor force of this country. They appear to be exceptions to the theory of the late Professor Thorndike of Columbia University that mental capacity declines after thirty at the rate of approximately 1 per cent a year. The mean age for the conspicuously healthy group is fifty-one, whereas the mean age of the impaired group is only fifty-two. The calendar obviously does not tell the whole story about the fate of creative brain power over time.

Are we justified in using the term "creative brain power"? We believe that we are. First, individuals who are creative members of society—professors, doctors, lawyers, ministers, government and military leaders—in the absence of neurological complications, score in the "unimpaired functioning" zone on the Halstead index. Even relatively severe psychiatric complications do not alter this. Second, we have some direct evidence that the Halstead index may have considerable validity in predicting the effectiveness of job performance in the upper levels of management.

DESIGN AND PROCEDURE FOR A
SPECIAL VALIDATION STUDY

A group of approximately one hundred top-level management personnel was given the Halstead tests prior to a special validity study. All scoring and interpretations were completed in writing by the authors without any direct contact with the subjects. A year later, the president of each participating company was interviewed in person or by letter to ascertain his willingness to supply us with confidential data on each of his executives without receiving our information in return.

The data requested were:

Please rate the following executives in your company on a three-point scale:

A=Outstanding in his work and personal effectiveness. Belongs in the inner circle. Merits upper levels of status and salary support.

B=Satisfactory in his work and personal effectiveness. Has probably surfaced maximally. Would support somewhat further with salary to hold but will not promote.

C=Marginally satisfactory in his work and personal effectiveness. Would not be reluctant to see move.

In spite of the apparent homogeneity of the testees, each president expressed the view that the scale as worded would apply to his men. Each supplied ratings on thirty-five men. The authors transcribed the ratings to a master work sheet opposite the serial case number assigned to each name; at this point, each man in the study became anonymous again. A laboratory assistant then removed the test scores for each man from a locked file. She was not told the purpose of the study, but was asked simply to call off the classification index (A, B, C) entered on our summary test-data sheet under each serial case number. These letters specify ranges of the Halstead index:

$$A=0, 1, 2, 3$$
$$B=4, 5$$
$$C=6, 7, 8, 9, 10$$

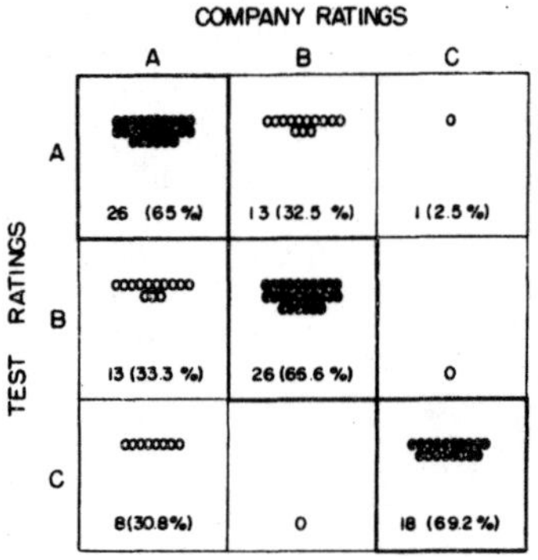

FIG. 5.

A 3×3 cell scattergram was plotted for each test prediction and each criterion rating (Fig. 5). Perfect agreement of test predictor ratings with company criterion ratings would have distributed all cases into the three diagonal cells heavily outlined from upper left to lower right. To a very encouraging extent, this tended to occur. For the forty test predictor ratings of A, twenty-six (65 per cent) of the company ratings agreed; for the thirty-nine test predictor ratings of B, twenty-six (66.6 per cent) of the company ratings agreed; for the twenty-six test predictor ratings of C, eighteen (69.2 per cent) of the company ratings agreed. The over-all agreement of the Halstead tests with the threefold company rating is 66.9 per cent. A chi-square value of 74.02 (P<.0005) indicates a very high degree of significance (nonindependence). It would require a correlation coefficient of .82 between predictor and criterion to predict this percentage of variance.

For purposes of this study, we shall assume that all company (or criterion) ratings are absolutely correct. Thus, all discrepancies must be attributed to faults in the test ratings. Although this may not be completely fair to the tests, they nevertheless do not perform too badly in this respect. Primarily the rating discrepancies appear to be boundary problems rather than confusion of extremes. Approximately one-third of the men that the Halstead tests rated A were rated B by the company; only one was rated C. Whether the company has simply failed to recognize the capacities of this group or whether the men somehow lack the will or skill to succeed can only be surmised. Of those the tests rated B, the company did not call one C, but did raise one-third to an A. It would be worthwhile to study this group to discern, wherever possible, what temperament and personality traits compensate for mediocre test capacities. Of those the tests rated C, the companies called no case B, but did rate eight of these men A. Here, again, it would be worthwhile to know whether these eight men have special attributes, experience, training, or counselling.

It is interesting to compress the threefold ratings into "satisfactory" and "unsatisfactory" with A and B "satisfactory" and C "unsatisfactory." Only nine cases out of 105 are mismatched in such a 2×2 table.

In view of the magnitude and nature of the variance successfully predicted by the Halstead battery, it seems safe to conclude that the tests are valid. They would appear to supply important predictor information concerning recruitment, assignment, and even retirement problems of key managerial personnel.

RELIABILITY OF
THE HALSTEAD TESTS

Sixty-one of the executives were retested after an interval of approximately one year. The agreement between the first and second testing is shown in Fig. 6.

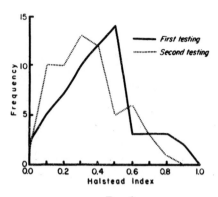

FIG. 6.

A rho of .84 (P<.005) was obtained between the two sets of scores. The mean of the differences between the two testings (.035) is not statistically significant. Thus, for prediction purposes a high degree of reliability is indicated for the Halstead tests. This is especially encouraging since we have not corrected the data for known discrepancies which could be attributed to changes in health (heart attacks, strokes, metabolic disturbances, and the like) during the year between testings.

It seems reasonable to conclude that the Halstead battery of neuropsychological tests, designed to reflect adequacy of higher-brain functioning, proves to be a valid and reliable predictor of upper-management effectiveness.

BIOLOGICAL AGE

Among the current searches for an index of biological age is one proposed recently by Sobel and Marmorston (1958). These authors suggest that the ratio of gel to fibers in connective tissue may be a reliable index to biological age. As a basis for this suggestion they point out:

> It is now definitely established that with aging the production of the precursors of the urinary ketosteroids and the androgens diminish markedly. On the other hand, the production of adrenal corticoids does not decrease as much. This disturbance in the function of the gonadal-adrenal systems would lead to the expectation that the progression of this alteration in the relative quantities of the anabolic–

anti-anabolic steroids might account for some of the loss of body protein which occurs with aging. Indeed it has been suggested that this process might advance aging itself.

This proposal is of particular interest in view of the embryological relations of connective tissue and a portion of the glial brain.

Our approach to the concept of biological age has been through behavior. From our testing of several hundred adults, we have noted that some individuals respond on the tests in a way similar to those who manifest early clinical signs of senility. Conversely, we have observed that some individuals in their sixties and seventies respond to critical parts of our tests in a manner characteristic of men in their twenties and thirties. By using a bonus- and penalty-point system and objective scoring, we now compute for each subject what we call his biological age. A comparison of the resulting ages computed in this manner for a group of more than three hundred top-level executives is shown with their calendar ages (Fig. 7).

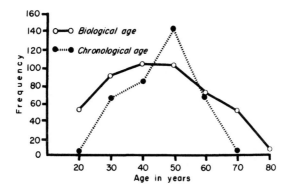

FIG. 7.

Can a man of fifty have a biological age of sixty-five? Or vice versa? Yes. Does this additional description of an individual have practical implication? The answer is tentative.

Using the same comparisons on the Klien index for the executives as for the production workers, it now appears possible to label some individuals strong cerebrovascular *suspects* well in advance of any manifest neurological signs, including so-called transient ischemic attacks. The data relevant to this are shown in figs. 8 and 9.

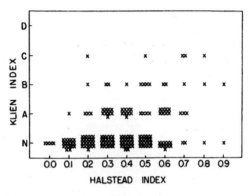

FIG. 8.

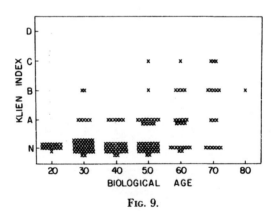

FIG. 9.

Whether anticoagulation or some other preventive therapy would influence the course of cerebrovascular disease in such individuals must await actual investigation.

In the meantime, if we are to succeed in identifying a true process of aging in the individual which can be relatively independent of his state of health, analytic studies along the lines suggested here must be carried out with appropriate scientific precision for several behavioral domains and organ systems. The neuropsychologist needs help from many quarters, but especially from neuropathology, neuroanatomy, and neurochemistry. How old is old? Perhaps one of man's four brains will someday supply an answer.

REFERENCES

Birren, J.E. (Ed.) *Handbook of aging and the individual: Psychological and biological aspects.* Chicago: The University of Chicago Press, 1959.

Chapman, L.F., Thetford, W.N., Berlin, L., Guthrie, T.C., & Wolff, H.G. Highest integrative functions in man during stress. *Res. Publ. Ass. nerv. ment. Dis.,* 1958, **36,** 491-534.

Halstead, W.C. *Brain and intelligence.* Chicago: The University of Chicago Press, 1947.

Jones, H.E., & Conrad, H.S. The growth and decline of intelligence: A study of a homogeneous group between the ages of ten and sixty. *Genet. Psychol. Monogr.,* 1933, **13,** 223-298.

Kløve, H. Relationship of differential electroencephalography patterns to distribution of Wechsler-Bellevue scores. *Neurology,* 1959, **9,** 871-876.

Lorge, I. Intelligence and learning in aging. In I.L. Webber (Ed.), *Aging: A current appraisal.* Gainesville: University of Florida Press, 1956. Pp. 51-62.

Reitan, R.M. Investigation of the validity of Halstead's measures of biological intelligence. *Arch. Neurol. Psychiat.,* 1955, **73,** 28-35.

Sobel, H., & Marmorston, J. Hormonal influences upon connective tissue changes of aging. *Recent Progr. Hormone Res.,* 1958, **14,** 457-481.

CHAPTER 9

Psychophysiological Techniques
in the Study of the Aged

BARRY M. SHMAVONIAN and
EWALD W. BUSSE

This paper falls into three sections: (1) already completed work using certain psychophysiological methods and giving a fairly detailed account of one experiment; (2) work in progress, the results of which, although not yet conclusive, might provide interesting leads; and (3) specific equipment and instrumentation which is described in the hope that it may be useful to other research workers.[1]

---

[1] All this work, unless otherwise stated, was done in the division of psychophysiologic research of the Department of Psychiatry at Duke University in conjunction with Drs. A.J. Silverman and S.I. Cohen. Material used here is liberally borrowed from joint publications (Cohen, Silverman, & Shmavonian, 1961; Shmavonian, Silverman, & Cohen, 1958; Silverman, Cohen, & Shmavonian, 1957).

C.N.S. ACTIVITY IN YOUNG AND AGED SUBJECTS

Many research studies representing various disciplines have suggested that aged persons show decreases in perceptual acuity; in the ability to perform tasks requiring sensory motor integration; in the efficiency of cognitive processes including memory, discrimination, decision-making, and attention span; in autonomic response capacity; and in the capacity to be conditioned (Barnes, Busse, & Friedman, 1956; Birren, 1955; Bortz, 1957; Botwinick, Brinley, & Robbin, 1958a; Botwinick, Brinley, & Robbin, 1958b; Bromley, 1957; Busse, Barnes, & Silverman, 1954; Busse, Barnes, & Silverman, 1956; Dennis, 1953; Fraser, 1950; Freeman, Pincus, Elmadjian, & Romonoff, 1955; Inglis, 1957; Korchin & Basowitz, 1956; Kirchner, 1958; Nelson & Gellhorn, 1957; Nelson & Gellhorn, 1958; Silverman, Busse, Barnes, Frost, & Thaler, 1957; Thaler, Frost, & Busse, 1953; Wilcox, 1956).

Deficiencies in performing complex intellectual and psychomotor tasks have been attributed in part to a decrease in perceptual acuity, which, in turn, has been assumed to be a function of, or related to, some change in the central nervous system with the aging process. It has never been fully clarified, however, whether the changes responsible for the decreased functioning are primarily changes in the sensory end organs, the afferent conducting pathways, the central integrating and transmission systems, or the efferent pathways. The aim of the experiment reported here was to observe differences in central nervous system reactivity levels between young and old subjects and to explore interrelations between central nervous system reactivity and perceptual responses.

The Experiment

Subjects were ten young males (ages twenty to twenty-four) and ten aged males (ages sixty to seventy). The former were third- and fourth-year students at Duke University, the latter from Duke University's Center for Aging where there was a great deal of physical and psychological information recorded on the subjects. The two groups were matched for I.Q., ranging from 115 to 130, and had no overt medical disease, sensory defect, or mental illness.

The subjects were led into the dimly lit experimental room where they were made comfortable on cots. Electrodes were placed on their feet for the galvanic skin response (GSR). The purpose of the electrodes was explained, and the subjects were reassured that they were not going to be shocked or made uncomfortable. The presence of speakers and microphones in the room was also explained, and the subjects were told this was an experiment to see how well they responded physiologically to external stimuli. They were asked to try not to go to sleep. It should be noted that the level of stimuli was high enough for sleeping to have been unlikely and that no subject did fall asleep during the experiment. The subjects were instructed, "You will hear various sounds and phrases over the loudspeaker. You are not expected to do anything. Just lie back, relax, and listen." The subject was then left alone, and there was a five-minute resting record. After this, a tape recorder connected to a loudspeaker in the subject's room was turned on. For the next fifty minutes, while the subject heard sentences and tones on the tape, continuous skin resistance records were taken. The experimental tape was divided into five periods which were run consecutively without any interruption. The sequence is presented in outline form in Table 1.

In Period 1, four clear, distinguishable sounds (S_1 1,000, S_2 250, S_3 500, and S_4 2,000 cps) were played at ten-second intervals and were repeated five times in the same sequence. In Period 2, two (noncharged or N-C) bland phrases were presented at twenty-second intervals three consecutive times in the same sequence. (N-C_1 was "books on the table" and N-C_2 "clouds in the sky.") The pattern of presentation was then reversed, and the expressions were presented three more times.

During Period 3, statements the investigators considered charged for a young college group (CY) and an elderly group (CO) were presented. These were systematically associated with the previously named tones and bland statements (Table 1). The four sounds were briefly presented immediately prior to each of the four types of phrases. The phrase, "books on the table," always preceded the statements directed at the young group, and the expression, "clouds in the sky," always preceded the phrases directed at the aged group. This series was presented in sequence eight times (a series of four expressions with their accompanying tones was presented eight times). In the last four presentations, the order of presentation was altered, but the time between stimulus presentation was not changed. The young and old statements which were paired in sequence were associated with similar areas for each group ("too young for sex" and "too old for sex").

The four tones that had been presented in Period 1 were repeated three times in Period 4. In Period 5, the two bland phrases were presented twice without tones. The tones and noncharged ex-

TABLE 1
EXPERIMENTAL DESIGN

Subject seated, electrodes placed, tape recording as follows:

Period I: tones

S_1	20 sec.	S_2	20 sec.	S_3	20 sec.	S_4	(repeated five times)
1000 cps		250 cps		500 cps		2000 cps	

Period II: phrases

NC^1 20 sec. NC^2

("Books on the table") 20 sec. ("Clouds in the sky")

(repeated three times, then reversed and repeated three times)

Period III: tones and phrases

S_1NC_1 20 sec. S_2CY_1 20 sec. S_3NC_2 20 sec. S_4CO_1
("Too young to know anything") ("Too old and careless")

S_1NC_1 20 sec. S_2CY_2 20 sec. S_3NC_2 20 sec. S_4CO_2
("Too young for sex") ("Too old for sex")

S_1NC_1 20 sec. S_2CY_3 20 sec. S_3NC_2 20 sec. S_4CO_3
("You might flunk out") ("An old failing body")

S_1NC_1 20 sec. S_2CY_4 20 sec. S_3NC_2 20 sec. S_4CO_4
("Not really an adult") ("Old and not wanted")

Order reversed:

S_3NC_2 20 sec. S_4CO_5 20 sec. S_1NC_1 20 sec. S_2CY_5
("Mind is getting weaker") ("Too smart for your own good")

S_3NC_2 20 sec. S_4CO_6 20 sec. S_1NC_1 20 sec. S_2CY_6
("No more respect") ("Respect your elder")

S_3NC_2 20 sec. S_4CO_7 20 sec. S_1NC_1 20 sec. S_2CY_7
("Old and afraid") ("Young and cocky")

S_3NC_2 20 sec. S_4CO_8 20 sec. S_1NC_1 20 sec. S_2CY_8
("No pleasures left") ("Study more and play less")

Period IV:

S_1 20 sec. S_2 20 sec. S_3 20 sec. S_4
(repeated three times)

Period V:

NC_1 20 sec. NC_2 20 sec. NC_2 20 sec. NC_1

Postexperimental interview aimed at ability to perceive and recall portions of experiment and associations to phrases, affect evaluation.

pressions were presented in periods 4 and 5 to determine whether any autonomic conditioning had occurred.

After the experiment and an introductory statement intended to reassure the subject and encourage him to talk about any thoughts, ideas, or feelings that he may have had during the experiment, the interviewer asked him to describe the experiment in detail. No attempts were made to explore the subject's associations at this point. Following this, his memory of the experiment was further evaluated by the interviewer who asked specific questions about the sequence of the experiment and the stimuli. The interview was constructed in such a way that the subject was given an opportunity to report spontaneously whatever he recalled. When the subject indicated that he was unwilling or unable to go on, the interviewer offered progressively informative cues in a systematic way. When the subject could not identify a portion of the experiment, it was described so that the investigator could determine whether the subject recognized it. After this, the subject was asked to list all the experimental expressions he could recall. The interviewer then handed the subject forty-eight index cards each with an expression on it. The eighteen expressions in the experiment were included among others with similar or strikingly different meanings.

The main instrument used was the GSR apparatus built by the personnel at the Wright Aero-Medical Laboratories. This is a particularly sensitive machine with variable settings for sensitivity, the highest of which will provide approximately one-mm. deflection per 12 ohms on the standard 50-mm. Grass polygraph oscillograph. Details of this instrument have been given by Silverman et al. (1959). By initially balancing the bridge, base resistance can be read directly. Changes in base resistance are compensated by the machine up to five steps in either direction of the zero point, eliminating much manual readjustment and consequent loss of data. If the deflections happen to surpass five steps in either direction, manual readjustment is necessary, and a new base resistance reading is taken. For many subjects, this manual recentering is rarely necessary, although for highly aroused subjects, one has to recenter fairly frequently. The three measures that we use with this equipment are: (1) base resistance, (2) the amplitude of GSR deflection to a specific stimulus (amplitude of the specific), and (3) the number of nonspecifics. This is a fairly new measure, made possible only by very sensitive GSR meters. However, in the early 1930's, Darrow (1927; 1936) made a reference to these nonspecific fluctuations and stated that perhaps they reflected activity of the ascending reticular activating system. Fig. 1 shows some of the relations among activation, amplitude of the specific, and number of nonspecifics. These relations have been worked out in some detail by Burch and Greiner (1958) and our present group. As the figure indicates, increased activation increases the size of specific which then decreases gradually in an inverted U curve. This phenomenon is

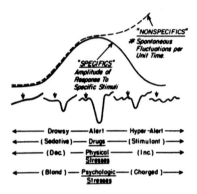

FIG. 1. Relations of activation, amplitude of the specific, and number of nonspecifics (Silverman et al., 1959, Fig. 1).

discussed in great detail by Furster (1958) and Malmo (1959). The number of nonspecifics, on the other hand, has a more S-shaped curve, for with increased activation there is an increase in the frequency of this number, presumably hitting an asymptote eventually. These two measures are obviously not mutually exclusive, since it is the increased frequency and activation of the nonspecifics which block the possible appearance of good-sized specifics.

Results

Although much speculation and some experimental findings suggest that latencies should differ in young and old subjects, they were not found to be different when analyzed for either the entire experiment or separate periods. During Period 3, in both young and old subjects, the latencies were slightly shorter to the charged than to the noncharged statements, but the differences were not significant. In all these cases, the latencies were measured from the onset of the stimulus to the beginning of the specific GSR response.

The implication of this finding is that there are apparently no sensory or sensory integrative differences between healthy, bright young and old subjects. Wherever such a difference appears behaviorally, it is probably a result of either motor in-coordination or disrupted conduction caused by lesions or circulatory difficulties. In this experiment we were using aged subjects who were above average in intelligence and in health; consequently, these findings should not be generalized; within our groups, however, they were very consistent.

The experimental design allowed comparison of any GSR conditioning to the neutral sentences or to all the sentences which preceded the charged sentences. It was hypothesized initially that there might be differential and selective conditioning between the young and old subjects. However, the results indicated no conditioning whatsoever in the young or the old subjects in either the critical third, fourth, or fifth period. There was no basis of comparison, therefore, between the groups. Since previous studies have shown the plausibility of GSR conditioning to verbal stimuli, its absence in the present experiment must have been primarily caused by the design's complexity which did not allow enough expectation of such stimuli's being followed by the charged material.

The Interrelations

The detailed relationships of the three GSR measures have been published elsewhere (Silverman et al., 1959). Up to a certain level of activation, the number of nonspecifics and the amplitude of the specific should relate very closely, whereas after this point the size of the specific starts decreasing again, while the number of nonspecifics continues to rise. In this experiment the subjects were not exposed to any great stress, and, from observation of the records, it is probably safe to assume that nobody was excited enough to pass the peak of the bell-shaped curve; the relationships, consequently, are high (Table 2). The first line of this table is not very meaningful, since it is a correlation between the total rank on the three measures and the individual measures, and obviously there is a heavy loading of the individual measures in the total rank. Inspection of the table, however, indicates that there is a close relation between amplitude of specific and the number of nonspecifics and a significant relation between the number of nonspecifics and base resistance, whereas the amplitude of specific and base resistance, although positive, does not achieve significant level. The absence of significant correlation in the latter relation is not critical, since the subjects were not greatly activated during the

TABLE 2
RANK ORDER CORRELATIONS
OF AROUSAL INDEXES

	Mean amplitude of specifics	*Number of non-specifics minus number of specifics*	*Base resist-ance*
Total on three measures	.804*	.881*	.718*
Mean amplitudes of specifics	—	.735*	.208
Number of non-specifics minus number of specifics	—	—	.393†

*= P < .01
†= P < .05

experiment, thus grouping the small base resistance changes. From other experiments it is apparent that these three measures are closely and consistently related. From our experience it is also apparent that the number of nonspecifics usually gives the best measure of activation. Number of nonspecifics can very easily be compared from day to day and from subject to subject, and electrode placement and other extraneous GSR problems are not so troublesome as they are in base resistance readings. Also, in monitoring the subject without specific stimulation, the nonspecifics are a much better index than the size of the specific since the latter depends entirely on external stimuli.

Comparison of Nonspecific Reactivity

On inspection of the records and reduced figures, it seemed that younger subjects were giving a higher number of nonspecifics than the aged. Although statistical analysis did not show this difference to be significant for the experiment as a whole, an interesting pattern emerged when the five periods were analyzed separately. In Period 1, when subjects were being exposed only to the tones, there was a significantly lower number of nonspecifics in the aged subjects than in the young. This significant difference disappeared from the second period on, although the old were consistently lower in number of nonspecifics than the young. It is tempting to speculate that the meaningless tones of Period 1 did not arouse the aged subjects and thus attribute the significant difference to the tones' arousing the younger subjects. The phrases of periods 2-5, however, did activate the aged subjects. The implications of this finding lie primarily in appropriate stimulation for the aged. It may be that during aging people gradually lose interest in the meaningless stimuli which bombard them every day of their lives and that this selective inattention gives an impression of a slowing central nervous system. When stimuli are given an appropriate meaning, however, the difference between the two groups disappears, and, in essence, the aged can react appropriately. An incidental, but possibly interesting, additional finding germane to this was that, when the sequence changed halfway through Period 3, the aged subjects showed an appreciable rise in activation whereas the young subjects showed none. It is difficult to interpret this finding except by saying that change, even from a temporary routine, seemed to alert the aged subjects more than it did the young subjects. Whether this is rigidity or apprehension about the unknown is hard to say at present.

Cognitive Correlates of GSR Activation

In the interview after the experimental period, the subjects were given forty-eight cards of phrases from which they were to choose the ones they remembered from the experiment. The number of correct selections was correlated with the GSR measures during Period 3 when the subjects were exposed to these phrases. Although all three measures correlated positively with the recognition scores, only the number of nonspecifics did so significantly—the subjects with the highest number of nonspecifics had the highest recognition scores. The range did not separate according to age group: the young subjects, on the average, had more nonspecifics and higher recognition scores, but there was a considerable overlap between the age groups. This correlation has important implications. Although at this stage it cannot be considered a measure of complex central functioning like memory, it certainly provides a good start for evaluating these central functions in an objective way without resorting to surgical or other impractical direct observations. Furthermore, it reinforces the authors' view that nonspecifics are a good measure of c.n.s. activity and that use of this particular measure in other studies would provide much information presently missed because of reliance on gross base resistance changes.

Response Specificity

When the pre- and poststimulation periods were compared for reactions to the charged and noncharged statements, the picture in Fig. 2 emerged. This figure reveals that in both the number of nonspecifics and the mean amplitude of the specifics the charged

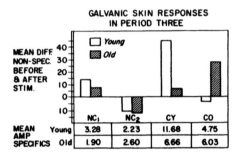

FIG. 2. Comparison of pre- and poststimulation for noncharged and charged statements (Silverman et al., 1959, Fig. 10).

sentences provoked a much larger difference of GSR activation between the pre- and poststimulation periods than the noncharged did. Furthermore, it is obvious that the young subjects responded more actively to the statements charged for the young and that the old subjects, to those charged for the old. These differences cannot be attributed to novel stimuli since none of the charged sentences was stated more than once. If novelty had been the only factor arousing the subjects, there would have been no differences between the groups for different statements.

CONCLUSIONS

This experiment revealed that, by using the new, high-sensitivity GSR apparatus, one can learn interesting information from nonspecifics which would have been difficult or impossible to get with the more traditional use of base resistance and amplitude of specific changes. The present attempt is not intended to prove one GSR measure superior to another, but rather to use the most appropriate measure for a given experiment. In long-term experiments base-line resistance would be a useful measure for comparing subjects; on the other hand, drying and placing the electrodes or repeating the experiment with the same subject creates well-known ambiguities in base resistance. In experiments like generalization studies where the experimenter is primarily interested in the immediate response to a given stimulus, the amplitude of nonspecifics is a useful measure. In experiments where one is interested in comparing the subject's activation level for one short period of time with his level at another, the number of nonspecifics seems to be the best measure.

Any generalizations about the findings of the above experiment are inappropriate at this point. We can summarize by saying that, although the superior aged subjects we used showed a lower initial level of activation, appropriate stimulation could raise this level so that differences between young and old disappear. Furthermore, this is not general hyperactivity, but a specific reaction to stimuli appropriate for different age groups.

VASOMOTOR CONDITIONING AND ITS
RELATION TO CATECHOL AMINES

In studies of the learning ability of aged subjects, interest has been concentrated mainly on cortical functioning as manifested in tasks ranging from simple motor skill to serial, complex learning. The performance of the aged subjects differs according to the complexity of the task, involvement of the subject, variety of instruction, and such factors as latencies and number of trials to master tasks. However, autonomic conditioning, an important domain of specific learning, has been neglected in the study of the aged, perhaps because the realm of autonomic conditioning in human subjects is uncertain at the present.

Since Pavlov's work, it has been assumed that autonomic conditioning in the laboratory is a *fait accompli* which the experimenter has only to demonstrate. The work of Hudgins (1933), Casson (1922), and Baker (1938) on pupillary conditioning was accepted uncritically. Not until Young's (1954) definitive studies of the same reflex was it demonstrated that pupillary conditioning is impossible in human subjects when the unconditioned stimulus is light and the reflex is pupillary constriction. Young's studies clearly indicated that using an unconditional stimulus appropriate to the given reflex does not necessarily result in conditioning. He did not investigate, however, what conditions might facilitate such conditioning. Likewise, Menzies' work (1937; 1941) on vasomotor conditioning was assumed true until, with better instrumentation and controls, Harwood (1953) and others found that vasomotor conditioning was not a result of warm and cold stimulation of bilateral vasomotor reflexes in the hands. In 1957, Shmavonian (1959), using a new photocrystal plethysmograph (discussed below), did not find vasomotor conditioning to hot and cold water although clear-cut conditioning was obtained with a general autonomic arouser such as electric shock. Opinion on this reflex is that conditioning is readily evoked by electric shock but not by constrictors and dilators at the periphery.

Aside from general interest in vasomotor and autonomic conditioning, the investigation in progress was stimulated by some of Kimble's recent, still unfinished work.[2] Using the eyelid response, he has noted that the conditioned and unconditioned response in the elderly is usually much smaller than in normal young adults. Furthermore, he found that, after several couplings of conditional and unconditional stimuli, the response to the unconditional stimulus disappears altogether—the subject no longer blinks in reaction to a puff of air which is coupled to a light. When the light is removed, however, and the puff of air comes alone, the response returns, indicating inhibitory influences of these stimuli when presented in pairs. Of course, the eyelid response is neither clearly autonomic nor completely involuntary. Botwinick and Kornetsky (1960) showed age differences in acquisition and extinction of GSR. The present study is concerned with a similar investigation and uses a measure which is more clearly autonomic than the eyelid response. Although vasomotor conditioning has been clearly demonstrated in the young, the age differences noted by Kimble in eyelid conditioning may also be found in vasomotor responses. Other relevant factors which should be studied are the latencies and general flexibility of peripheral vascular activity, inhibitory and facilitative influences, and the acquisition and extinction of vasomotor conditioning and its relation to other autonomic measures.

Changes from aging have been reported in the central nervous system in general and in the autonomic nervous system in particular. Cannon (1939; 1942) described how the preservation of stability is impaired and homeostasis maintained in a narrower range in the aged. Norris, Shock, and Yiengst (1953) have demonstrated a slower compensatory response in the systolic and diastolic blood pres-

[2] The findings were written in a personal communication (1960).

sure of older people when they are tilted from a horizontal to a vertical plane. Crawford (1924) found older subjects to decline distinctly in pulse-rate reaction after an atropine injection, and Schneiberg and Fineston (1952) found a significant depression of tolerance to intravenous glucose among older subjects. Experimental studies of animals have presented evidence of decline in the functioning of the autonomic nervous system. In older rats, Safford and Gellhorn (1945) found diminished excitability of the sympathetic adrenal system when measured by the blood-sugar reaction to anoxia. S.M. Friedman, Pinkey, and C.L. Friedman (1956) reported a decline in neuropituitary function.

Histopathologic studies have supported physiological evidence of autonomic nervous system changes with age. Kuntz (1937) found a progressive change in dendrites, reduction in chromidial substance, and deposition of melanotic pigment in autonomic ganglion cells all to be associated with age. The deposition of pigment, which Critchley (1942) believed the most important change, was least obvious in the hypothalamus. In an extensive study of structural alterations with aging, however, Andrew (1956) stated that the nuclei of the hypothalamus show perhaps the most impressive incidence of specific age changes seen anywhere in the nervous system. He found an increase in cellular size eight to ten times that of comparable cells in young people.

Nelson and Gellhorn (1957) demonstrated that age caused a statistically significant increase in the hypotensive action of mecholyl and suggested that the shifting action of mecholyl indicated a decrease in sympathetic hypothalamic excitability. They mentioned that the action, with increasing age, of mecholyl on the blood pressure might theoretically be attributed to the changed action of mecholyl on blood vessels as well as on any alteration in the sympathetic centers of the brain stem. In interpreting the changes with the mecholyl test in aged and young subjects, however, they felt that the changes were caused by the effect of age on central, rather than peripheral, autonomic or vascular structures. The hypothalamus was felt to be primarily involved for two reasons. First, the hypotensive action of mecholyl increases with age although hypertensive cases were eliminated and the mean blood pressures remained practically constant; it seemed improbable that the state and reactivity of such peripheral structures as blood vessels were greatly altered under these conditions. Second, numerous investigations have shown that alterations of internal environment, such as anoxia and hypoglycemia, primarily affect central, not peripheral, structures in the central nervous system; Himwich (1951) described the cerebral cortical and diencephalic structures as more sensitive than the medulla oblongata and spinal cord. The principle of a central gradient of reactivity seemed involved in the mecholyl test. It was also shown by Nakoa, Ballim, and Gellhorn (1956) that the action of mecholyl on blood pressure depends primarily on the baroreceptor reflexes. These reflexes are still present after elimination of the diencephalon, but their sensitivity lessens. Consequently, the hypotensive action of mecholyl is increased, and the secondary hypertensive phase is eliminated as the sensitivity of the sympathetic division of the hypothalamus lessens. Nelson and Gellhorn (1957) believe that such a loss of sensitivity is primarily involved in the changed reaction, caused by age, to the mecholyl test.

Gellhorn, Nakoa, and Redgate (1956) observed a diminution, with increasing age, of the reflex involving the parasympathetic division, and they attributed this to a diminishing reactivity ability of the parasympathetic areas of the hypothalamus. Theoretically, they felt that the reactivity of the peripheral blood vessels to noradrenaline may change with age, but, even if this were the case, it would not be of any consequence because their interpretation of the noradrenaline test as an indicator of central hypothalamic parasympathetic reactivity was based on a parasympathetic index using the ratio of the pulse's slowing to the blood pressure's rising. Their most striking finding was that sympathetic, as well as parasympathetic, reaction decreased with age.

A study of the urinary excretion of adrenaline and noradrenaline reported by Bergsman (1959) indicated that the adrenaline output of patients with senile dementia was much lower than that of healthy young subjects and that the differences between their respective means were highly significant. Excretion of noradrenaline, on the other hand, was significantly higher. The differences between patients with senile dementia and normal aged subjects were similar, although smaller. It was also reported that in insulin tests the excretion of adrenaline rose very slightly during the insulin period (90') and showed a small significant increase in the postinsulin period (90'-180'). In comparison to young control subjects, the rise in the ageds' percentage of adrenaline in the total amine content between the resting period (6 per cent) and the insulin period (28 per cent) in the aged was quite small. The total excretion of adrenaline was also lower for the mentally ill than for healthy aged subjects. Noradrenaline excretion did not change during the insulin test period. The data strongly suggested that sympathetic adrenal responsivity, as measured by the urinary levels of catechol amines, diminished in the aged subjects, particularly those with a clinical diagnosis of senile dementia.

In a duplication of the study in the first part of this paper, urine samples were obtained to explore differences in the endocrinological correlates of central nervous arousal during exposure to psychologically stressful situations. In this study, significantly higher resting levels of noradrenaline were observed among aged subjects than among young ones. Further, during psychologically stressful situations, the amount of change in noradrenaline appeared to be less among aged subjects, which suggested that there was less activation of peripheral sympathetic activity. In another study, the response of young and aged subjects following the administration of histamine and insulin (after an initial resting period) was examined. Older subjects showed less increase in noradrenaline levels after insulin than younger subjects, although older subjects' resting levels were significantly higher. Adrenaline levels were lower during the resting period and less responsive to the hypoglycemic stimuli.

This work raises questions about the relation of peripheral autonomic conditioned responses and central autonomic reactivity. Differences in vascular responses to drugs and other stimuli associated with peripheral vasomotor changes and different conditioning characteristics in young and aged subjects may be related to a change in the reactivity of the hypothalamus in the aged subject. This may be of consequence considering the lowered vascular status frequently reported in aged people.

Partial destruction of the hypothalamus or the mesencephalic reticular formation may destroy some autonomic conditioned reflexes, but the corresponding unconditioned reflexes persist as Chow (1954) and Hernandez-Peon, Brust-Carmona, Eckhaus, Lopez-Mendoza, and Alcoceruaron (1956) have shown. These subcortical structures are believed to play an important role in elaborating conditioned reflexes and behavior.

It is believed that the formation of conditioned reflexes involves, and is probably facilitated by, activation of the hypothalamic-cortical system. Most investigations point to the fact that conditioning is the result of an interaction between central excitatory processes in the midbrain and hypothalamus set up by conditioned and unconditioned stimuli. Without activation of mesencephalic and hypothalamic centers, conditioning will not occur, many students believe. Furthermore, it has been demonstrated that vasomotor conditioning depends on general autonomic arousal and not merely on changes produced in peripheral vessels by unconditional stimuli, such as warm and cold water, which the subject does not feel to be noxious.

Method and Approach

In our current studies, two groups, one of fifteen young, the other of fifteen old, subjects are matched for general intelligence, socioeconomic level, and health. The subjects are brought into the laboratory and asked to urinate. After drinking two cups of water, they rest for an hour, at the end of which pre-experimental urine samples are gathered, more water is given, the experiment is performed, and postexperimental urine samples are gathered.

The actual experiment involves placing the photocrystal plethysmograph, GSR electrodes, E.E.G. leads, and shock electrodes on the subjects. The experimenter superficially explains the measures that will be taken, then a shock level, at which the subjects feel pain without feeling inordinate discomfort, is established. A rough determination of auditory threshold is obtained, and conditional stimulus is set at 15 db. above this threshold to minimize startle responses. The subject is told that he will not receive shocks higher than the one already determined. He is asked to sit comfortably, not to move, and not to go to sleep; he is given a bland book to read during the experiment.

The interval between the conditional and unconditional stimuli (CS-US) is filled by a fifteen-second tone and a five-second shock which overlaps the last five seconds of the tone. Ten acquisition and ten extinction trials are given with a one- to four-minute interval between stimuli.

This procedure allows investigation of the phenomena observed by Kimble and comparison between the young and old subjects in acquisition and extinction rates; latencies; and relations of the blood flow, GSR, and E.E.G. Furthermore, catechol amines are being made as indicators of sympathetic adrenal responsivity.

After this experiment is completed, variations in the conditioning parameters will be studied, including variations in stimulus intensity and duration, CS-US interval, instructions, and emotional states aroused. Future studies will attempt to alter the state of central nervous system excitation, particularly that of the hypothalamus, by using pharmacological agents. We will study the effects of changes in the neurophysiological state of the organism on peripheral autonomic conditioning, sympathetic adrenal responsivity, and vasomotor reflex changes.

Instrumentation

From experience at the Duke University Psychophysiology Laboratory, we feel that a description of two instruments not commonly used might be helpful.

The photocrystal plethysmograph was developed by the Department of Psychology at the University of Washington and was first used and reported by Shmavonian (1959). It consists of a cadmium selenide photocrystal, clairex Clx103, embedded on one side of an aluminum ring approximately one-half inch wide and adjustable in diameter. On the opposite side of the ring a small source of light is embedded and aimed at the photocrystal. The photocrystal constitutes one arm of a Wheatstone bridge. Its resistance varies with the amount of light transmitted through the finger which, in turn, is modified by the increase and decrease of blood flowing between the light source and the photocrystal. Increased volume causes increased resistance to light. The voltage changes are amplified through a Grass DC amplifier and recorded on one of the Grass DC polygraph channels. The output of the photocrystal is reasonably high. With forty-five volts applied to the bridge, an output of over fifty microvolts was obtained with an average pulse.

The action of this recording system was checked against a hydraulic finger plethysmograph. The results clearly showed that the photocrystal plethysmograph gave much better tracings of continuous blood flow than the hydraulic system. Furthermore, the hydraulic system was extremely sensitive to slight finger and arm movements, whereas the photocrystal plethysmograph was relatively insensitive to these. Interference by muscular artifacts is clearly distinguishable in the record from changes in blood flow. This feature makes the plethysmograph valuable for conditioning work when there is reason to suspect that what is conditioned might be slight muscular tensions, not vasomotor activity. Furthermore, the pulse rate is superimposed on the fluctuations caused by blood flow, and this enables the experimenter to use both pulse rate and variations in blood flow from the same writeout channel. A sample record is shown in Fig. 3.

The E.E.G. analyzer was designed and perfected by Burch. It has many advantages over commercial analyzers, and it facilitates such studies as E.E.G. conditioning, changes in E.E.G. patterns during serial learning, and constant monitoring of activation from E.E.G. It is valuable in many other situations where an analyzer increases the efficiency of E.E.G. information and facilitates recording and com-

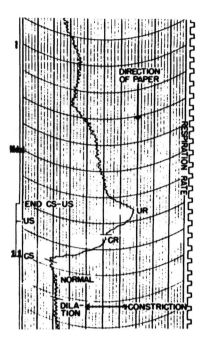

Fig. 3. Sample record of photocrystal plethysmograph (Shmavonian, 1959).

puting any changes. There is no lag between input and analysis, so that measurements of latencies can be made without difficulty. Also, in many E.E.G. studies, the experimenter had, in the past, to choose only good alpha subjects for experiments, since alpha breakdown can be traced visually only in the records of subjects with high alpha amplitude. The present analysis does not require such selection, and this in itself makes it highly desirable.

For period analysis of the E.E.G., each wave in the E.E.G. is treated as a unique event, and its duration or period is measured. No account is taken of the amplitude of each wave or any activity superimposed on it. The latter is handled by the complexity analysis section, which will be described. The electronic circuits for carrying out this period analysis are straightforward. Fig. 4A shows typical E.E.G. waves which are fed to the period analyzer. Figs. 4B and C indicate what happens to this wave as it goes through stages of the analyzer, which is sketched in block form beside the figures.

In Stage 1, the E.E.G. waves are clipped and amplified to give a series of rough, square waves. Stage 2 completes the squaring by having the E.E.G. waves from Stage 1 operate a high-speed relay, which switches direct current off and on. The result is a squared E.E.G. wave for each input wave. The dimension of duration has been kept, but amplitude has been lost, since all the squared E.E.G. waves are of equal amplitude, as shown in Fig. 4B.

This series of squared waves has both positive and negative polarity, but only the positive waves are sent to the next stage, where their duration is measured. The negative squared waves are used as a writeout signal. Fig. 4C shows the series of positive squared E.E.G. waves, which is analyzed in Stage 3.

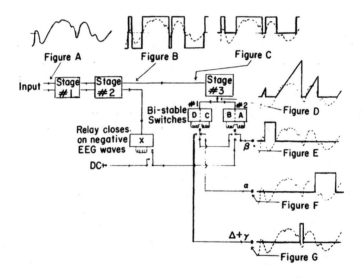

Fig. 4. Stages in E.E.G. waves fed to period analyzer.

Stage 3 is, in essence, a capacitor which is charged through a resistor. The positive squared waves from Stage 2 are applied across this resistor-capacitor combination, and, since all the squared waves are of equal amplitude, the voltage across the capacitor is proportional to the duration of the charging squared wave and thus to the duration of the E.E.G. wave. The output of Stage 3 is shown in Fig. 4D. The output of this stage is fed to two bi-stable electronic switches. These switches are normally in the A and C conditions, respectively, with the relay contacts they control resting in the positions shown. If the output voltage of the capacitor stage remains below an arbitrary critical value, both switches will remain in the A and C positions. This is the case for the first, short-duration E.E.G. wave of Fig. 4A. On the negative half of the E.E.G. wave immediately following this, Stage 2 sends a positive DC voltage to the point marked DC+ by closing the relay at point X. The output shown in Fig. 4E results. The critical value below which the switches do not operate is usually set so that beta waves, whose frequency is greater than twelve or thirteen cycles, activate this output channel.

If the output voltage of Stage 3 is greater than the critical value, but less than another, higher critical value, Switch 2 transfers to the B state, whereas Switch 1 remains in the C state. When the DC writeout signal is produced by Stage 2 on the following negative half of the E.E.G. wave, this signal appears in the channel marked *a*. This happens in the case of the third wave shown in Fig. 4A, and the corresponding output is shown in Fig. 4G. In the final case, the output voltage of Stage 3 is higher than both critical values, so both switches transfer, and an output appears at the terminals marked $\Delta + \gamma$. This corresponds to the second, long-duration wave in the diagram.

Thus the duration of each E.E.G. wave. is measured and produces a writeout signal which indicates that it falls into a certain range of durations. These ranges are adjustable between wide limits. We usually set the three output channels below 8 cps, 8 to 12.5 cps, and greater than 12.5 cps.

This analysis is capable of very fine frequency discrimination. For example, the original E.E.G. could be recorded on tape and played back several times. On the first playback, the middle channel might be set at 8 to 9 cycles; on the second, from 9 to 10 cycles; on the third from 10 to 11 cycles, and so on.

In the period analysis described, activity superimposed on a base wave was ignored, and the duration of the base wave was the only information obtained. Complexity analysis, performed simultaneously with period analysis, provides an index of superimposed activity. Although it tells nothing about amplitude, it does produce an output pulse every time superimposed activity occurs. Fig. 5 shows the same E.E.G. waves as Fig. 4. The three base waves have three waves superimposed on them. An output pulse results each time the sign of the slope changes from positive to negative; thus one pulse is produced for each base wave, plus one pulse each time there is superimposed activity.

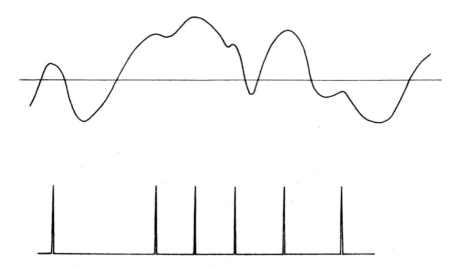

FIG. 5. Activity superimposed on base waves.

Fig. 6 illustrates how this complexity analysis is carried out. Fig. 6A shows the same series of input waves entering the complexity analyzer. Stage 1 amplifies them. Stage 2 differentiates the waves by passing them through a small condenser, producing the output shown

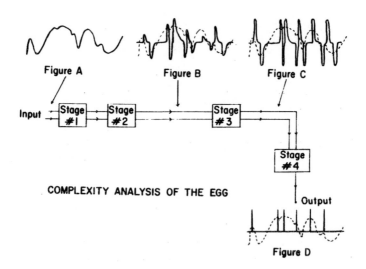

FIG. 6. Complexity analysis of the E.E.G.

in Fig. 6B. At this point we are producing an output for negative-to-positive, as well as positive-to-negative, slope changes.

The amplitude of this output varies with the frequency and amplitude of the superimposed activity. Since this output is not suitable for counting, Stage 3 further amplifies and clips all these output signals to the same amplitude. Stage 4 continues this process, producing a high-voltage, short-duration pulse for each positive-to-negative slope change. The negative-to-positive slope changes are thrown out, and the output wave is suitable for scaling.

The output of both the period analysis and complexity analysis sections are scaled before being written out. The scaling units use Dekatron rotary counting tubes. They produce one output pulse for every ten input pulses. In addition, the complexity and beta wave channels have a second scaling unit connected to the first, thus producing an output for every hundred inputs. When comparing the outputs of the channels over long intervals, this scaling feature saves an immense amount of counting.

REFERENCES

Andrew, W. Structural alterations with aging in the nervous system. *J. chronic Dis.,* 1956, **3,** 575-596.

Baker, L.E. The pupillary response condition to subliminal auditory stimuli. *Psychol. Monogr.,* 1938, **50,** No. 223.

Barnes, R.H., Busse, E.W., & Friedman, E.L. The psychological functioning of aged individuals with normal and abnormal electroencephalograms. II: A study of hospitalized individuals. *J. nerv. ment. Dis.,* 1956, **124,** 585-593.

Bergsman, M. The urinary excretion of adrenaline and noradrenaline in some mental diseases. *Acta Psychiat. Neurol. Scand., Suppl.,* 1959, **133,** 11-107.

Birren, J.E. Age changes in speed of simple responses and perception, their significance for complex behavior. In *Old age in the modern world.* Edinburgh: E. & S. Livingstone, 1955. Pp. 235-247.

Bortz, E.L. Growth and aging. *Amer. J. Psychiat.,* 1957, **114,** 114-118.

Botwinick, J., Brinley, J.F., & Robbin, J.S. The interaction effects of perceptual difficulty and stimulus exposure time on age differences in speed and accuracy of response. *Gerontologia,* 1958, **2,** 1-10. (a)

Botwinick, J., Brinley, J.F., & Robbin, J.S. The effect of motivation by electrical shocks on reaction time in relation to age. *Amer. J. Psychol.,* 1958, **71,** 408-411. (b)

Botwinick, J., & Kornetsky, C. Age differences in the acquisition and extinction of the GSR. *J. Geront.,* 1960, **15,** 83-84.

Bromley, D.B. Some effects of age on the quality of intellectual output. *J. Geront.,* 1957, **12,** 315-323.

Burch, N.R., & Greiner, T. Drugs and human fatigue: GSR parameters. *J. Psychol.*, 1958, **45**, 3-10.

Busse, E.W., Barnes, R.H., & Silverman, A.J. Studies in the process of aging. *Dis. nerv. Syst.*, 1954, **15**, 22-26.

Busse, E.W., Barnes, R.H., Friedman, E.L., & Kelty, E.J. The psychological functioning of aged individuals with normal and abnormal electro-encephalograms. I: A study of non-hospitalized patients. *J. nerv. ment. Dis.*, 1956, **124**, 135-144.

Cannon, W.B. Homeostasis in senescence. *J. Mt. Sinai Hosp., N.Y.*, 1939, **5**, 598-606.

Cannon, W.B. Aging of homeostatic mechanisms. In E.V. Cowdry (Ed.), *Problems of ageing*. Baltimore: Williams and Wilkins, 1942. Pp. 567-582.

Casson, H. The conditioned pupillary reaction. *J. exp. Psychol.*, 1922, **5**, 108-146.

Chow, K.L. Lack of behavioral effects following destruction of some thalamic association nuclei in monkey. *Arch. Neurol. Psychiat.*, 1954, **71**, 762-771.

Cohen, S.I., Silverman, A.J., & Shmavonian, B.M. The influence of psycho-dynamic factors on central nervous system functioning in young and aged subjects. *Psychosom. Med.*, 1961, **23**, 123-137.

Crawford, J.H. The influence of the vagus on the heart rate. *J. Pharmacol.*, 1924, **22**, 1-19.

Critchley, J.H. *Problems of ageing*. Baltimore: Williams and Wilkins, 1942.

Darrow, C.W. Sensory, secretory, and electrical changes in the skin following bodily excitation. *J. exp. Psychol.*, 1927, **10**, 197-226.

Darrow, C.W. The GSR and blood pressure or preparatory and facilitative function. *Psychol. Bull.*, 1936, **33**, 73-94.

Dennis, W. Age and behavior. Randolph Field Air Force Base, Texas: U.S. Air Force School of Aviation Medicine, 1953.

Fraser, D.C. Decay of immediate memory. *Nature*, 1950, **182**, 1163.

Freeman, H., Pincus, G., Elmadjian, F., & Romonoff, Louise. Adrenal responsivity in aged psychotic patients. *Geriatrics*, 1955, **10**, 72-77.

Friedman, S.M., Pinkey, J.A., & Friedman, C.L. Neurohypophyseal responsiveness in the normal and senescent rat. *J. Geront.*, 1956, **11**, 286-291.

Furster, J.M. Effects of stimulation of brain stem on tachistoscopic perception. *Science*, 1958, **127**, 150.

Gellhorn, E., Nakoa, H., & Redgate, E. The influence of lesions in the anterior and posterior hypothalamus on tonic and phasic autonomic reactions. *J. Physiol.*, 1956, **131**, 402-423.

Harwood, C.W. Vasomotor conditioning in human subjects. Unpublished doctoral dissertation, University of Washington, 1953.

Hernandez-Peon, R., Brust-Carmona, H., Eckhaus, E., Lopez-Mendoza, E., & Alcoceruaron, C. Functional role of brain stem reticular system in salivary conditioned response. *Fed. Proc., Baltimore*, 1956, **15**, 91. (Abstract)

Himwich, H.E. *Brain metabolism and cerebral disorders*. Baltimore: Williams and Wilkins, 1951.

Hudgins, C.O. Conditioning and the voluntary control of the pupillary light reflex. *J. gen. Psychol.*, 1933, **8**, 3-51.

Inglis, J. An experimental study of learning and "memory" functions in elderly psychiatric patients. *J. ment. Sci.*, 1957, **103**, 796-803.

Kirchner, W.R. Age differences in short term retention of rapidly changing information. *J. exp. Psychol.*, 1958, **55**, 352-358.

Korchin, S.J., & Basowitz, H. The judgment of ambiguous stimuli as an index of cognitive functioning in aging. *J. Pers.*, 1956, **25**, 81-95.

Kuntz, A. Histological variations in autonomic ganglia and ganglion cells associated with age and disease. *J. Psychol.*, 1937, **4**, 75-120.

Malmo, R.B. Activation: A neuropsychological dimension. *Psychol. Rev.*, 1959, **66**, 367-386.

Menzies, R. Conditioned vasomotor responses in human subjects. *J. Psychol.*, 1937, **4**, 75-120.

Menzies, R. Further studies of conditional vasomotor responses in human subjects. *J. exp. Psychol.*, 1941, **29**, 457-482.

Nakoa, H., Ballim, H.M., & Gellhorn, E. The role of the sino-aortic receptors in the action of adrenaline, noradrenaline, and acetylcholine on the cerebral cortex. *EEG clin. Neurosphysiol.*, 1956, **8**, 413-420.

Nelson, R., & Gellhorn, E. The action of autonomic drugs on normal persons and neuropsychiatric patients. *Psychosom. Med.*, 1957, **19**, 486-494.

Nelson, R., & Gellhorn, E. The influence of age and functional neuropsychiatric disorders on sympathetic and parasympathetic functions. *J. psychosom. Res.*, 1958, **3**, 12-16.

Norris, A.H., Shock, N.W., & Yiengst, M.J. Age changes in heart rate and blood pressure responses to tilting and standardized exercise. *Circulation*, 1953, **8**, 521-526.

Safford, H., & Gellhorn, E. Age and autonomic balance. *Proc. Soc. exp. Biol.*, 1945, **60**, 98-101.

Schneiberg, N.G., & Fineston, I. The effect of age on intravenous glucose tolerance test. *J. Geront.*, 1952, **7**, 54-62.

Shmavonian, B.M. Methodological study of vasomotor conditioning in human subjects. *J. comp. physiol. Psychol.*, 1959, **52**, 315-321.

Shmavonian, B.M., Silverman, A.J., & Cohen, S.I. CNS arousal in the elderly. *J. Geront.*, 1958, **13**, 443. (Abstract)

Silverman, A.J., Busse, E.W., Barnes, R.H., Frost, L.L., & Thaler, Margaret. Studies on the processes of aging. IV: Physiologic influences on psychic functioning in elderly people. *Geriatrics*, 1957, **8**, 370-376.

Silverman, A.J., Cohen, S.I., & Shmavonian, B.M. Investigation of psychophysiologic relationships with skin resistance measures. *J. psychosom. Res.*, 1959, **4**, 65-87.

Thaler, Margaret, Frost, L.L., & Busse, E.W. Studies on the processes of aging. VIII: Physiological and psychological correlates of aging. Paper presented to the American Psychological Association, Cleveland, 1953.

Young, F.A. An attempt to obtain pupillary conditioning with infrared photography. *J. exp. Psychol.*, 1954, **48**, 62-68.

Wilcox, H.H. Changes in nervous system with age. *Publ. Hlth Rep.*, 1956, **71**, 1179-1184.

CHAPTER 10

Assessing Biological Age

FRANCOIS BOURLIÈRE

It becomes more evident every day that both pathological and environmental factors play a major role in the rate of aging. Different people of the same chronological age give physiological and psychological performances that may vary widely, according to the health and the ecological factors of their lives. It is, therefore, of the utmost importance not only to analyze and describe carefully the physical, nutritional, and social conditions which make up the human environment, but also to measure as accurately as possible the biological age of many organs and tissues. In such a way, it will probably be possible some day to find significant correlations between ecological factors and physiological and psychological variables.

The purpose of this paper is to discuss the possibility of using a battery of physiological tests to measure as simply and accu-

184

rately as possible the biological age of some important functions. It is based mainly on the personal experience of the author and his co-workers when studying the ecology of human aging at the Centre de Gerontologie Claude-Bernard in Paris.

CRITERIA FOR BIOMETRIC AGE TESTS

The effect of age on various physiological functions has been extensively studied during the past fifteen years (Binet & Bourlière, 1955; Birren, 1959; Bourlière, 1958; Burger, 1957; Coppinger, 1955; Lansing, 1952; Shock, 1956). In most cases the effect is obvious, and a priori it looks easy to design a battery of functional tests which would give a reasonable estimate of biological age. In practice, the problem is more complicated. To be of practical use in estimating the biological ages of a large number of noninstitutionalized subjects, the tests must fulfill two conditions. First, the physiological functions they measure must vary continuously, appreciably, and, if possible, regularly, from the end of the growth period until advanced age. When there are different ways of showing variation with age for a given function, it is obvious that one must choose the test which shows the greatest variation among the age groups being studied. Second, the tests must be painless and technically as simple as possible, requiring minimum venous or arterial punctures or urinary catheterizations. Moreover, the whole examination must be completed in a few hours. Any technique involving prolonged or repeated stays in the laboratory must be avoided, especially in longitudinal studies.

In our experience, the best way to start such an investigation is with a careful medical check by a competent clinician. Such a procedure has many advantages for both the investigator and the patient. Any past major disease is recorded in the case history of the subject, and the routine examinations (electrocardiogram, fluoroscopic examination of the lungs, blood count, erythrocyte sedimentation rate, blood sugar and non-protein nitrogen), made at the same time as functional tests, give a good estimate of the subject's health. Moreover, the subject has the comforting feeling that the examinations he is undergoing are as important and useful for him as for the investigator. He will not feel like an experimental animal and will probably cooperate in the future. Thus we have been able to study people who otherwise would probably never have answered our appointment notices.

PHYSIOLOGICAL TESTS FOR
BIOLOGICAL AGE

Morphological and functional involution, which character-izes aging in higher vertebrates and man, is, broadly speaking, caused by two phenomena: (1) the decrease of the lean, oxidizing, proto-plasmic body mass, and (2) qualitative age changes in tissues and organs. Some simple methods assess these two age changes quantita-tively.

Estimation of the Active Body Mass

The most accurate way to estimate rapidly the amount of lean, oxidizing, protoplasmic body mass (active body mass) is prob-ably the technique recently devised by Anderson and Langham (1959) to measure the potassium concentration in the human body. Its prin-ciple is simple. About 98 per cent of the body potassium is intra-cellular; thus a change in the potassium concentration reflects a change in the ratio of protoplasmic mass to the mass of other body constituents containing little or no potassium (for example, skeleton or fat). Multiplication of the potassium concentration by the weight of the subject will, therefore, measure the amount of protoplasm in his body. In vivo, the measurement of the potassium content of the human body is now made possible by the use of natural potassium 40 and liquid scintillation gamma counters. This method is so easy that Anderson and Langham (1959) were able to study 4,000 people in fifteen days with a counting time of forty seconds for each. The re-sults of an analysis of their data for 1,590 people ranging in age from under one year to seventy-nine years are shown in Fig. 1. In people over twenty, there is a steady decrease with age of potassium con-centration throughout adult life. The standard deviation of the mean for the age groups up to sixty-eight years ranges from 1 to 4 per cent. The principal cause of variability is probably represented by indi-vidual differences in amounts of fat. Between ages twenty and sixty, the net loss in protoplasmic mass of males was about 18 per cent.

Another, but less precise, way to estimate the decrease in active body mass is the basal metabolic rate, which also diminishes regularly with age and correlates closely ($+0.95$) with potassium 40 determinations. The decrease in basal metabolic rate is mainly caused by the reduction of living protoplasm; if one computes the oxygen

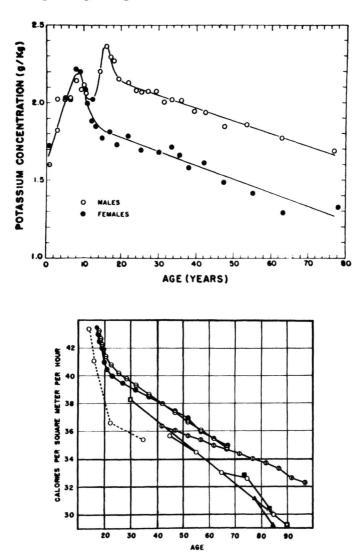

Fig. 1. The decline with age of the active body mass as shown by (top) the potassium 40 test (after Anderson & Langham, 1959) and (bottom) basal metabolic rate (after Shock, 1955).

uptake per unit of body water (the amount of extracellular fluid remaining constant with age), one finds that there is no age decrease whatsoever (Shock, 1955).

Estimation of the Inactive Body Mass

In vivo, it is much more difficult to estimate the metabolically inactive body mass (especially fat and connective tissue) than the lean body mass.

Comparing stature and body weight of each subject gives a rough estimate of the importance of fattening, but it is desirable to

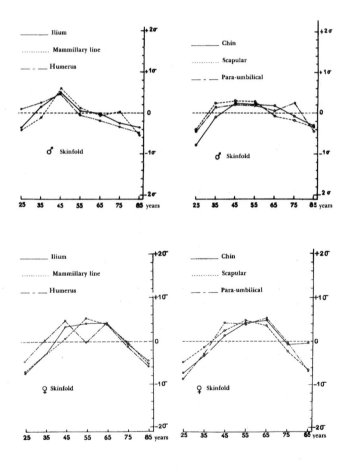

FIG. 2. Age variations of the inactive body mass as shown by the skin-fold method.

have more precise measurements. Two techniques—the roentgenogram and the skin-fold method—may be used for this purpose. In both cases, it is the subcutaneous fat layer which is studied. In the former, the amount of subcutaneous fat is determined by measuring fat-plus-skin shadow on soft-tissue X rays (Garn, 1957); in the latter, the estimate is made by measuring with calipers the thickness of a fold of skin held between the fingers. Although the X ray method is considered more precise, the extensive equipment needed limits it to the laboratory. The caliper method does not have this disadvantage. Moreover, the relation between the measurements made by these methods is sufficiently high (.88) to allow comparisons between results of both methods (Garn, 1956). In our inquiry, therefore, we used the Harpenden caliper (Tanner & Whitehouse, 1955) to measure seven body sites. The age variations we observed are shown in Fig. 2. The rate of decrease of subcutaneous fat deposits in older people is constant.

Ventilation

The functional tests of vital capacity and maximum breathing capacity are both easy to perform on a routine basis and give a clear picture of the influence of age on respiratory functions. Figs. 3 and 4 show the results from our sample of healthy subjects. In both tests, the decline is important and very regular, but the maximum breathing capacity declines more than the vital capacity. Furthermore, the second method, maximum breathing capacity, appears to be much

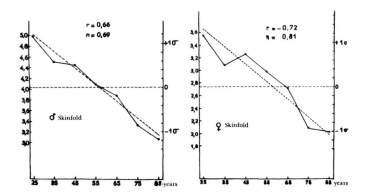

FIG. 3. Age variations of the vital capacity.

more sensitive than the first. We find a striking difference when comparing sedentary and active people of the same age (Fig. 4).

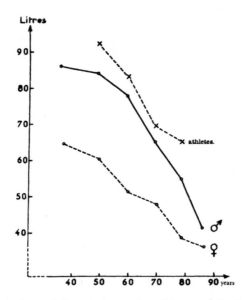

FIG. 4. Age variations of the maximum breathing capacity in sportsmen (top curve) compared with males and females of the general population.

Circulation

It has been shown that cardiac output decreases regularly with age in healthy people and that circulation time simultaneously increases. Unfortunately the techniques of such investigations are too complicated to use on a routine basis for aging studies; furthermore, the wide scatter of values within each age group greatly reduces the practicability of these techniques. Therefore, we restricted our circulatory investigations to blood pressure and pulse rate (both under basal conditions).

Fig. 5 summarizes our results. The systolic blood pressure increases regularly from twenty-five to eighty-five years; the diastolic blood pressure does the same, but more slowly. The pulse rate tends to decrease and is always lower in very active subjects than it is in sedentary ones.

It would be desirable to complete these measurements by some simple exercise tolerance test like the one devised by Master and Oppenheimer (1929), which allows the investigator to measure the maximum increase of blood pressure and heart rate after standard

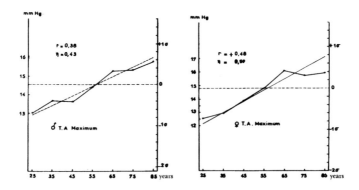

Fig. 5. Age variations of the systolic blood pressure.

exercise and the time necessary to return to basal values. Methods, such as running to exhaustion on a treadmill (Robinson, 1938), are far too hard and dangerous for people over fifty.

An estimate of the serum cholesterol and beta-lipoproteins is made for the blood of every subject with the very simple technique of Burstein and Samaille (1958) (Fig. 6).

Renal Excretion

The various clearance tests used in internal medicine show a regular decline with age of glomerular filtration rate and tubular excretory capacity (Shock, 1952); unfortunately, these tests cannot be easily performed on a routine basis on noninstitutionalized subjects.

Muscle Strength

Quantitative measures of the strength of various muscle groups show a maximum at twenty-five to thirty years, followed by a gradual decrement. The strength of the hand grip is the easiest to measure in practice, and we used the Smedley hand dynamometer, according to the procedure of Fisher and Birren (1947). The subject is asked to squeeze the dynamometer at three-second intervals, beginning with a squeeze of twenty-seven kilos for men and eighteen kilos for women, and increasing by three kilos the force exerted each time until

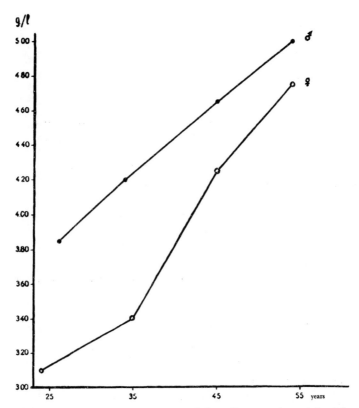

Fig. 6. Age variations in the serum and beta-lipoproteins of healthy men (top curve) and women (bottom curve) (after Burstein & Samaille, 1958).

the subject is unable to achieve the required increase. The score for one hand is the kilogram reading of the last try.

Endocrine Glands and Reproduction

Many tests may be used to evaluate the function of the endocrines, but few can be performed systematically on healthy subjects.

The measurement of neutral 17-ketosteroid excretion, used to indicate the amount of androgens elaborated by adrenal cortices and the interstitial cells of the testes, is by far the most useful, although all androgens do not give the reaction for 17-ketosteroids and certain nonandrogenic substances do give it. The decrease of 17-ketosteroid excretion with age in both men and women is very important and regular (Fig. 7), as shown by Pincus, Romonoff, and Carlo (1954) and other investigators. The only technical difficulty is persuading the subjects of the importance of returning an accurate, complete, daily urine output to the laboratory.

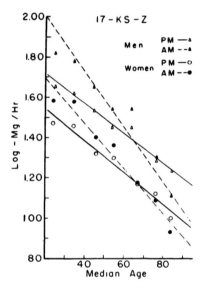

FIG. 7. Age variations in 17-ketosteroids of healthy men and women (after Pincus et al., 1954).

Urinary oestrogens also decrease with age in women, but unfortunately there is not as yet any reliable chemical method to estimate this decrease; bioassays are too expensive and time-consuming to be used in our case.

Chemical estimations must be completed by some basic data pertaining to the sexual and reproductive life of the subject: age at first menstruation, duration and regularity of the menstrual cycle, number of births and abortions, age of climacterics, and the like. In males, the periodicity of sexual intercourse is always recorded, and our data, on the whole, agree with the findings of other investigators (for instance, Newman & Nichols, 1960), showing that elderly people may continue sexual activity to an advanced age, given reasonably good health and partners who are healthy.

Sensory Functions

Basic research in sensory functions has been fairly extensive (Weiss, 1959), but relatively few tests can be performed in routine examinations.

For vision, the easiest measurement is the range of accommodation, which diminishes regularly from infancy to the age of fifty-five. There is, nevertheless, no further decrease after that age, and other tests must be used for older subjects. Critical flicker fusion declines with age in a linear and negative way to an advanced age (Fig. 8), but this measurement is difficult to make, and we had to give

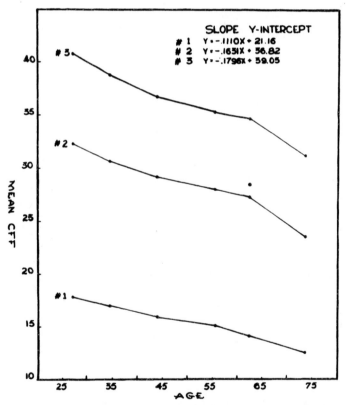

Fig. 8. Critical flicker frequency as a function of chronologic age for three levels of stimulus brightness (after Coppinger, 1955).

it up in our present inquiry. After many trials, we finally adopted a simple version of the dark adaptation test, measuring recovery time from a bright illumination of a given intensity and duration. Our results are summarized in Fig. 9, which shows a regular increase with age in the time necessary to discern dots and simple figures of a given brightness.

The rise of auditory thresholds with age is well known; above twenty or twenty-five years, there is a progressive loss of hearing which is relatively large at high frequencies and smaller at low. It would, therefore, be useful to include an audiogram in our examinations, but for practical reasons, we have been unable to do so at the present.

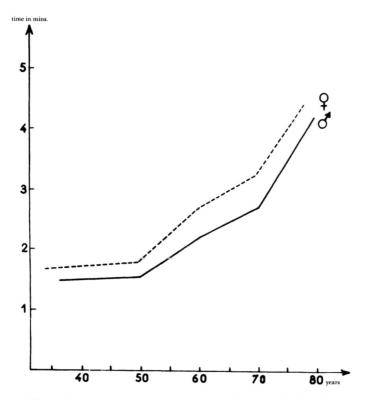

Fig. 9. Age variations in recovery time after a bright illumination of given intensity.

Central Nervous System

Age changes in cerebral blood flow and oxygen consumption have been found in men, but such determinations involve techniques which are far too complicated to be performed on noninstitutionalized subjects. There are also some age variations in the electroencephalogram and its reaction to hyperventilation and photic stimulation. They are so slight, however, that they are of little practical use for measuring age changes in the central nervous system of subjects in good health.

DISCUSSION

These physiological tests, the medical check, and the routine examinations usually take no longer than two or three hours for each subject. When leaving the laboratory, the subject is given a vessel (with necessary instructions) in which to collect a day's urine. This he does on the day preceding his second visit. During the second visit to the laboratory the psychological tests are administered, and standard anthropological measurements are made of standing height, sitting height, biacromial breadth, and bi-iliac breadth. The anthropological data and blood-grouping (ABO, MN, and Rh systems) help assess the racial and hereditary characteristics of the people examined and allow comparison of the sample studied with the population from which it is drawn. In our 1959 investigations, for instance, we were able to check whether the anthropometric measurements and the p, q, and r gene frequencies in our sample were similar to those of the French population as a whole. Basic data on habitat, sources of income, family life, work, social life, and hobbies are also collected on the second visit.

Although the morphological measurements and functional tests described here are far from a complete picture of the anatomical and physiological changes in the aging organism, they do, nevertheless, enable the investigator to make some objective comparisons between the rates of aging of people living in different environments. They should also help psychologists and sociologists to estimate more accurately the health of the subjects they study and, eventually, to find some correlations between biological and behavioral phenomena. These criteria of biological age should also enable physicians to judge less subjectively the effectiveness—or the ineffectiveness—of the drugs which are said to improve the health of older people.

REFERENCES

Anderson, E.C., & Langham, W.H. Average potassium concentration of the human body as a function of age. *Science*, 1959, **130**, 713-714.

Binet, L., & Bourlière, F. *Précis de gerontologie*. Paris: Masson, 1955.

Birren, J.E. (Ed.) *Handbook of aging and the individual: Psychological and biological aspects*. Chicago: The University of Chicago Press, 1959.

Bourlière, F. *Senescence et senilité*. Paris: Doin, 1958.

Burger, M. *Altern und krankheit*. (3rd ed.) Leipzig: Thieme, 1957.

Burstein, M., & Samaille, J. Dosage des B-lipoproteines sériques après précipitation sélective par l'héparine. *Presse med.*, 1958, **66**, 974-975.

Fisher, M.B., & Birren, J.E. Age and strength. *J. appl. Psychol.*, 1947, **31**, 490-497.

Garn, S.M. Comparison of pinch-caliper and X-ray measurements of skin plus subcutaneous fat. *Science*, 1956, **124**, 178-179.

Garn, S.M. Roentgenogrammetric determinations of body composition. *Hum. Biol.*, 1957, **29**, 337-353.

Lansing, A.I. (Ed.) *Cowdry's problems of ageing*. (3rd ed.) Baltimore: Williams and Wilkins, 1952.

Master, A.M., & Oppenheimer, E.T. A simple exercise tolerance test for circulatory efficiency with standard tables for normal individuals. *Amer. J. med. Sciences*, 1929, **177**, 223-243.

Newman, G., & Nichols, C.R. Sexual activities and attitudes in older persons. *J. Amer. med. Ass.*, 1960, **173**, 33-35.

Pincus, G., Romonoff, Louise, & Carlo, J. The excretion of urinary steroids by men and women of various ages. *J. Geront.*, 1954, **9**, 113-132.

Robinson, S. Experimental studies of physical fitness in relation to age. *Arbeitsphysiologie*, 1938, **10**, 251-323.

Shock, N.W. Age changes in renal function. In A.I. Lansing (Ed.), *Cowdry's problems of ageing*. (3rd ed.) Baltimore: Williams and Wilkins, 1952.

Shock, N.W. Metabolism and age. *J. chronic Dis.*, 1955, **2**, 687-703.

Shock, N.W. Physiological aspects of mental disorders in later life. In O.J. Kaplan (Ed.), *Mental disorders in later life*. Stanford: Stanford University Press, 1956. Pp. 47-97.

Tanner, J.M., & Whitehouse, R.H. The Harpenden caliper. *Amer. J. phys. Anthropol.*, 1955, **13**, 743-746.

Weiss, A.D. Sensory functions. In J.E. Birren (Ed.), *Handbook of aging and the individual: Psychological and biological aspects*. Chicago: The University of Chicago Press, 1959. Pp. 503-542.

SECTION III

Psychological
Environment

CHAPTER 11

Appraising Environment

MARIAN RADKE YARROW

There are many reasons for thinking that environment plays a significant role in human aging and the individual's adjustment to being old—perhaps more important than it plays in the preceding adult years and as important as its plays in the formative childhood years. Many of the normal changes in the physical and social environments of old age are drastic changes for which substitutions are impossible. The general situation which the individual has come to take for granted (his family, his job, the feeling of being needed, loved, or respected) may be severely altered. Also, the individual's control over these changes becomes more limited in old age than in earlier adulthood. The attitudes of the young toward the old, the stereotypes about the aged, and the institutional restrictions with regard to age place the elderly individual in a socially marginal position. With each new generation, new requirements in skills and tastes in industry, housekeeping, and community living intrude on habits and security built over a lifetime, putting the older person somewhat out of step with his surroundings. Thus, the reality may be that in old age environment is pushing the person hard while he is experiencing many uncertainties and changes.

Dynamically, the relation of a person to his environment in this period of life is unclear. Has the individual learned to insulate himself from environmental factors, or has he become more vulnerable to social forces as his own power to control them diminishes? Many observers of the aged, especially those coming to the attention of a psychiatrist or physician, have described a lack of concern about the social situation, a lessened influence of everyday social controls, and a dominance of self-concern. Such observations would seem to speak for relative independence of the aged from environmental influences. On the other hand, there are frequent psychiatric references to the older person's feelings of loss of identity as his meaningful roles and personal relationships are lost; the aged are criticized by the middle-aged and young for their oversensitivity to what is said and done around them. These observations suggest interdependence between the older person and his environment. The nature of the relationship between aging and environment will remain unsettled until environmental variables are investigated more systematically with greater conceptual clarity.

This paper is concerned with the scientific appraisal of environment, general systematic problems, and particularly problems in the context of gerontological research. It is pointed toward three research issues: (1) description and conceptualization of environmental variables, (2) formulation of questions concerning environmental influences on the aged, and (3) methodology for obtaining environmental data. We are not primarily concerned with the question of how much variance in old age is attributable to the effects of environment, but rather with how we can better determine relationships among environmental, biological-medical, psychological, and behavioral variables. We are concerned with how we can more adequately take into account the environments in which the individual functions. To a great extent, investigation is a function of what we know how to measure, and we are not yet facile in formulating problems of contextual influences or assessing contexts of behavior.

THE CONCEPT OF ENVIRONMENT

Environment as a scientific concept has not been regarded with reverence in psychology. Psychology generally has emphasized the person and developed concepts and methods for dealing with "person" problems. Much less systematic research has been directed to understanding the impact of environment in human development and functioning although there are certain psychological problems in which environment has been given a prominent place, such as research on child-rearing, worker performance, and institutional settings. In gerontological research, consideration of environmental factors derives, in the main, from applied problems and crises associated with age, such as problems of institutionalization, retirement policies, lowered capacities, and the like. When, in such critical circumstances, an effort has been made to take a systematic account of environment, it has contributed substantially to the understanding of individual behavior and the formulation of principles for the applied fields.

It is not only in gerontology, but in research generally, that environment is more often the practitioner's, rather than the theorist's, variable. Careful descriptions of the environments of adults are rare in the behavioral sciences. Descriptions are either at extremely gross levels, such as culture or class, or extremely limited levels, such as immediate stimulus conditions. A serious attempt to investigate environment as a problem of psychology involves various difficult theoretical and methodological issues: what is meant by environment? how does one distinguish the geographical, physical, and psychological environments? how does one distinguish between what is inside the person and what is outside? It is necessary to think of the environment as it exists independently of the person and as it is experienced by the person. When one is concerned with manipulating environment, as in treatment, enrichment, or setting up experiments with systematic variation in specific stimuli, one focuses on the external qualities which can be described independently of the person. When one is concerned with evaluating the impact of the environment on the person, however, one must be concerned with the experiential environment: Are the confines of the institution experienced as a prison by the patient, or do its closed doors mean security to him?

Problems of individual psychological environment and environmental determinants of behavior have been dealt with most specifically in Lewin's (1936) concept of the life space, a concept which

includes the objective features and the cognitive elements (the awareness and intentions of the individual). It was in the early work of
Lewin and his associates (Barker, Dembo, Tamara, & Lewin, 1941;
Lippitt, 1940) that environment, in the complex sense of multiple,
psychologically defined dimensions, came into experimental social
psychology. Although many problems of conceptualization and measurement remained unsolved in Lewin's unfinished system, Heider
and Chein, influenced by Lewin, have concerned themselves with some
of the issues of investigating environment in relation to behavior.
Heider (1959) deals with the basic problem of distinguishing between
inside and outside a person.

> When we talk about the person as opposed to the geographical
> environment we attribute a minimum to the outside entities, that is,
> we attribute to the outside only those properties which it shows in
> interactions with the widest possible range of other objects, regardless
> of whether they are persons or inorganic objects. When we confront the
> person with the geo-behavioral environment we attribute to the outside
> a great deal more, namely everything that persons have in common in
> the interactions with the environment. In a way, the average person is
> then attributed to the outside. In this way we can enter more and more
> on the accounts of the environment until the person shrinks to an
> undifferentiated point: it becomes the environment characteristic for
> one particular person at one particular moment.
> However, the geographical environment is still with us, and the
> problem arises now of relating this physicalistic environment to the
> different other "enriched" environments. And we have not given up
> entirely the attribution to the person. We have to characterize these
> environments by saying: this is the environment for this group, or for
> this person. And why do we still call it environment when it is in some
> way latched on to a particular person?
> These questions have to do with the problems of intention or repre-
> sentation which every cognitive psychology has to meet in some way.
> Something belonging to the inside part, the person, is described in terms
> of the outside part, the environment. The so-called intervening variables
> can be related to environmental variables in two different ways: causally,
> or through intentionality. In stimulus response theories the intervening
> variables are defined by the causal relation; in cognitive theories they
> are defined both by the causal relation and by the relation of intention
> or reference. When we think about mentalistic concepts we are apt to
> be so occupied with the difficulty of anchoring them in observables that
> we forget that they have also this feature of intentionality which places
> them somewhat apart from other scientific concepts (pp. 5-7).

Chein (1954) speaks directly about the decisions confronting
the researcher as he tries to describe and measure environment. He

presents a design for dealing with environment intermediately, between the objective environment and the surroundings as they are uniquely perceived by each person. He conceives of the environment psychologically, in terms of the conditions in it which initiate behavior and determine its feasibility and the presence or absence of goals, "noxiants," and the like, as these may be expected to influence the average person.

The general conceptual problems of environment remain nebulous and difficult, but an appreciation of their nature, existence, and implications should guide investigation away from a too superficial approach to problems of interaction between person and environment and a too easy dismissal of methodological issues in the study of the "outside" of the person.

ENVIRONMENTAL VARIABLES

The individual never functions in a single environment, but in many overlapping contexts. Except, perhaps, in the limiting case of extremely traumatic, compelling circumstances, the psychological environment of the individual must be viewed as a set of interdependent variables. Consider a problem in aging: The worker receives notification of his retirement. This event occurs in the context of supportive or nonsupportive family relations; good or bad economic resources; a social class placing definite values on leisure, achievement, youth, age, and so on; and—to varying extents—a fulfilling and successful past. To ask how the aging individual's functioning is modified by retirement is to ask a question involving all these factors. One should deal with the impact of the interacting dimensions, although the difficulties presented for theory development and research procedures are obviously many and not easily met.

The several contexts of retirement demonstrate still another characteristic which muddies research on environmental influences. The units in which environment is viewed vary tremendously. The referent may be historical events, the immediate physical structures, a single and momentary stimulus, a lifetime setting, or the current total milieu. Any generalizations about environment must be qualified by the specific units in which environment has been conceived and measured. How inclusively or in what units one should consider environmental factors in research will depend on the particular question and the particular behavior of the people being investigated.

Let us consider the questions of multiple, overlapping contexts and variable environmental units, specifically in problems of gerontological research. How have environmental variables been used in studies of aging? They often enter as gross classifications considered in the selection of research subjects. Social class, community or institutional residence, retirement status are the familiar categories in such instances; however, environment is here considered in order to control it or to ensure a representative sample. These gross classifications are also used as variables in descriptive and correlational designs. In such studies psychological and behavioral characteristics of the aged, as well as health and longevity data, are compared across these sociologically defined environmental settings. In other gerontological research, specific material surroundings (type of housing, economic resources, and the like) are related to the older person's functioning. Many studies of human aging and cognitive functioning, problem-solving, personality characteristics, and health are made without cognizance of the environmental settings in which the subjects live. Where environmental factors have been considered, few psychological concepts or unifying theories have guided the accumulation of data to contribute systematic additional knowledge concerning these influences in aging.

We hope to make some theoretic and methodologic progress by emphasizing the units in which environment can be studied relative to gerontological problems and by examining some conceptual and measurement problems posed by each of them. At least four units can be specified.

First are the general life situational factors. These include the familiar sociological classifications of the more-or-less stable features of the individual's environment—family status; educational and occupational levels; ethnic, racial, and religious background. (Some of these factors might be regarded as variables inside, rather than external to, the person, but to the extent that they represent certain predictable patterns of stimuli to which an individual has been exposed, they can be regarded as environmental variables.) In general, they are the individual's lifetime environments, which, more specifically, represent the goals, values, social pressures, possessions, surroundings, and behavior by which he has lived. A cumulative character and, in general, an irreversibility are significant properties of these environments. Some of these characteristics are held in common by groups identified by class, ethnic background, and so on; more are highly individualized patterns. Both may have significant bearing on aging and adjustments in old age.

Although the time extended variables are typically past variables, they also include the anticipated psychological impact of the future. The impact of Christmas Future on Scrooge was no less, and perhaps greater, than that of Christmas Past and Christmas Present. For the aged the dimensions of future environments may be particularly potent because of the expectations, uncertainties, and threats to security which they hold. Psychological research has given most of its attention to the past and present.

Another environmental unit concerns the specific environmental assaults which the individual has experienced prior to or in old age. These are the losses that are of symbolic value, such as declining status, the loss of love objects, or the displacements of new surroundings. There is also the physical assault of illness and failing capacities, which carry direct environmental consequences through the limitations they impose on available physical and social surroundings or through changed responses to the sick or incapacitated individual.

The total contemporaneous milieu in which the individual lives is a third environmental variable. The impact of institutionalization or retirement on the aged, general problems of work for the aging, the environment of the older person in the family and community are milieu problems. It should be possible to investigate the milieu problems analytically to specify their significant dimensions.

Often the most tangible environmental variables, which involve the fewest intervening assumptions about their effects on behavior, are the immediate and transitory situational stimuli, the fourth environmental view. These are the reinforcement given the subject in his performance of specific laboratory tasks, the rebuff from his children, the refusal on a job application, the experience in a golden age club.

It is apparent that general and momentary, past and present, environments are closely related. As the attitudes of a man's children toward him change for the better, the job refusal is likely to be seen in a different light. His lifelong cultural values regarding achievement are likely to influence his response to experimental motivation for the performance of laboratory tasks, and so on. Thus, there is much challenge for research in determining the relevance of the narrow and of the inclusive environmental variables for different functions and conditions among the aged.

In any unit of environmental variables, the point of view from which the measurements are made can vary. It can be (1) the observer measuring the features of physical and social environment as they exist externally to the person (income level, family cohesion, institutional residence); (2) the psychological observer in Chein's sense (1954), viewing the environment of the subject from the standpoint of one who presupposes individuals with wants and desires; or (3) the subject providing his own construction and experience of his environment. The differences among the three points of observation may or may not be large. The subject and the observer may view the environment in the same or very different physical or statistical terms. The psychological observer may be able to approximate very closely what is experienced by a particular individual behaving in a situation. The point of view from which data are gathered and analyzed should be specified in any research.

PROBLEMS OF MEASUREMENT

Depending on whether the research variables are background variables, broad present milieu variables, or immediate momentary circumstances, problems of assumptions and measurement arise.

Broad Background Variables

The cumulative environments of a lifetime, particularly of class and culture, show numerous, provocative associations with a variety of characteristics of the aged. Health patterns and mortality rate (von Mering & Wineger, 1959), electroencephalographic changes (Busse, Barnes, Friedman, & Kelty, 1956), and social adjustment (von Mering & Wineger, 1959) are among these characteristics. If we investigate to the point of finding associations such as these and stop there, we do not explain much. Furthermore, there are dangers in jumping from these descriptive associations to speculative explanations. Such jumps move toward gross oversimplification and often involve inferences concerning remote causal links between environment and aging phenomena. They may greatly exaggerate the direct role of environment in aging by ignoring biological factors associated with certain sociocultural groups, and they do not provide information about the interaction between these broadly defined environments and the aging characteristics. If cultural background is associated with longevity, what are the mechanisms by which the differential survival comes about? If normal brain waves are found less frequently in certain socioeconomic groups, are the differences accounted for by culturally linked biological factors or specific environmental stresses?

If old-age characteristics are distributed differently among subcultures in our population, we need to ask more direct, analytic questions about cultural contexts, describe them psychologically, and investigate the processes of influence. It would seem necessary to conceive of background variables psychologically, as conditions which determine the feasibility of particular behavior and present various goals, frustrations, and the like. The individual's religious, ethnic, and educational backgrounds define and summarize different learning environments to which he has been exposed, as well as certain material and social aspects of the settings in which he has lived. They define the characteristic daily experience; the individual's family, which influences him socially and which he, as its head, has developed; the attitudes he has toward time, people, health, illness, pain; his goals; the mores governing aspects of his interpersonal behavior. In these terms, social and cultural life history is part of the present psychological field of the aged person and may play a significant role in his functioning. It seems probable that settings defined by different cultural variables develop different strengths and vulnerabilities in the individual, some of which may be relevant in old age. Also, different cultures make certain environments more-or-less likely in old age.

Isolation, or fear of isolation, in old age has been found a frequent and severe problem. Close family ties during this age period give significant support. Class culture may also contribute significantly in many ways, the most simple and direct of which is the number of children per family (which varies by class and religion) and the likelihood of having children around during old age. Relations between parents and children during childhood and adolescence vary with class and culture in the parent-child status, types of control, severity of discipline, and closeness of family ties. These may lay foundations for different relationships between adult children and elderly parents.

Ill health, one of the predominant crises of old age, may also be viewed through cultural glasses. To the extent that cultural life-history differences have bred different attitudes toward health, responses to pain, beliefs about disease, and predestined causes of death, cultural backgrounds may have significant force in old age through identifiable and, to an extent, manipulable psychological processes. For example, Zborowski (1952) studied response to pain in three American subcultures, Italian, Jewish, and "Old American." A number of his observations suggest implications about how readily people of different origins withstand strains of illness in old age, how they use illness in manipulating their social environment, and what responses (sympathy, support, distrust) they evoke from others. Italian and Jewish groups, particularly immigrants, are described as very emotional in response to pain; they exaggerate their experiences. Among the Old Americans there was less emotional complaining and a tendency, in extreme pain, to withdraw and be alone. In contrast to Old Americans, Italian and Jewish patients willingly admitted that when they were in pain they complained a great deal, called for help, and expected sympathy and assistance, especially from their families. From these findings one might hypothesize that individuals from different cultural backgrounds come to old age with different vulnerabilities, resiliencies, and attitudes to physical illness, which create different interpersonal problems.

The different goal orientations of the lower, middle, and upper-middle socioeconomic groups will probably affect adjustment to retirement. One might predict that the middle-class person, with his orientation toward distant goals and delayed satisfaction, will find retirement more difficult than the lower-class person, who is oriented more toward immediate goals and satisfaction. However strongly this difference in values might operate in old age, one thinks immediately of its interaction with other differences which reinforce or cancel the advantages of one class over the other. How, for example, do differences in immediate versus future goal orientations interact with other class-linked characteristics, such as the presumably greater inner resources of the educated man or poorer health of the lower class? One quickly realizes the necessity for simultaneously considering several aspects of cultural environment.

Perhaps a word should be said about the relevance of global concepts of class, cultural, or ethnic membership, too. Indeed, it may be the aged person's identification with the destiny or model of a class that influences his functioning. (A good German farmer doesn't stop working just because he is old; a good Scot doesn't wear his troubles on his sleeve.) In this instance the sociological classification may be also a psychological variable with significance in old-age adjustment.

Earlier Events

Historical influences on the present are not always thought of in the general, cumulative situations of which we have spoken. In studying older adults, young adults, or children, many investigators have been interested in the effects of specific early experiences on later development or status. The experience may have been a discrete event no longer in effect at the time of investigation (institutionalization during childhood, failure in a job or as a parent, hospitalization in middle age) or an event which permanently changed the environment (divorce, emigration, loss of hearing). In studies of the aged attention to such earlier events might be fruitful.

Personality theory, which has stressed infant and early childhood experiences in understanding the young adult, has not tended to extend across the broad span of years from childhood to old age. On theoretical grounds this can be defended; there are dangers in an uncritical introduction of constructs of early development into research with the aged. There are dangers, too, in causal inferences for such remote associations because of the chances of overlay from events intervening between childhood and old age.

The earlier events of adult life and their consequences in old age should be given greater attention. In old age what are the consequences of the death of a spouse, emigration to a new culture, earlier fame and success? Here, as in the study of cultural backgrounds, explanation must be in terms of processes set in motion by the event and what it represents in the present environment of the individual. This is easy to see, for example, in the death of a spouse, which results in lack of a love object. Similarly, that less adequate adjustments to old age have been made by men who immigrated to the United States in adulthood than by a comparable group of aged native-born men (Yarrow, Blank, Quinn, Youmans, & Stein, 1961) may be understood by considering displacement of emigration. Immigrants are confronted in old age with the remoteness of their family and family identifications and the "foreignness" of their values and mores in many spheres. These supports, frustrations, and values probably characterize emigration in the psychological environment of the aged. Thus, conceptually, the situation of the elderly immigrant, the elderly parent brought to live with his children in a large city, and the elderly person moving to an old people's home bear some similarity to one another.

Adult illness is an earlier experience of certain significance as the individual grows older. How does illness or the expectation of illness reshape the physical and social environments of the aging individual, and how much is the new environment caused by illness or the expectation of illness imposed on him or initiated by him?

Obtaining data on earlier environments of the aged presents the usual problems of retrospective reconstruction. In using retrospective reports, the investigator must be clear in his purposes. The subject's report of his past as he evaluates it and as it appears to him now has its own validity. As a source of objective data (earlier economic circumstances, family difficulties, goals, frustrations, and achievements), the aged subject is particularly problematic. Several independ-

ent reports from observers and the aged subjects may be an avenue to
the remote data, and age peers and adult children may also be. Although memory must be reckoned with, consistency or supplementary
information in several reports may lead to reasonable inferences about
the psychological past. Even so, it is well to keep in mind that one is
using inferences removed several times.

Another problem that is hard to bypass in the use of retrospective data over a generation of time is the possibility of an altered
yardstick for measuring the past. It is difficult to remove oneself from
current perspectives and assume those which prevailed at the earlier
period. What is viewed as necessity now may have been luxury a half-
century ago; what is improper, ignorant, harsh, or conservative may be
judged differently or incorporated into different value systems. When
we are aware of trends from one generation to the next, we can attempt to correct present reports about the past, but the methodological
difficulty remains and is magnified by cultural change.

Present Milieu

Many questions of environmental influences concern the
present behavioral settings of the aged, such as retirement, institutionalization, living in three-generation families, living alone, and so
on. The independent variables of these questions are *sets* of interdependent factors. The conceptual problems and methods of measurement are, therefore, difficult. As first approximations to understanding
in this area, it has been useful to study these settings as undifferen-
tiated wholes and make comparisons between pre- and postretirement
groups, institutionalized and noninstitutionalized aged, and widowed
living alone and living in children's households, asking how people
in these settings differ in health, behavior, and attitudes. This approach, of course, side-steps analytical questions. Obviously the next
research step is milieu studies which do ask such questions. We need
to ask in what ways and how much the particular milieu supports,
deprives, challenges, or discourages the aged person. How and why
does the environment stimulate or fail to stimulate independent behavior of the aged? In what ways does it foster respect or disrespect,
exclusion or inclusion? How, and how frequently, does it reinforce
social interaction or punish deviant behavior?

Milieu studies require an analysis of the factors in the setting and variables selected for their theoretical relevance to the behavior under study. Furthermore, it is recognized that the milieu
does not act on a passive recipient. Although there is often little or

no check on the contribution of the person to his environment, this factor would be considered in the ideal design, and gerontology has many examples of these contributions. Some people become irritable and aggressive in the face of frustrations, deny signs of aging by much activity, meticulously guard against any situation which will test the failings they fear, or give themselves up to complete helplessness and dependence; these replies vary with social environment. We can arrive only at the average effects of a present milieu on aging until the subject is viewed as both response and stimulus in his environment.

Perhaps the broadest of what we may call "milieu problems" in aging is the social fact of being an old person. Murphy, Murphy, and Newcomb (1937) have said of childhood, "To be a given [chronological] age is to be in a certain sort of social situation; what is really a product of the stimulus situation must not be uncritically ascribed to the physiological growth curve" (p. 325). Social expectations and practices allow or restrain, praise or punish, different behaviors and provide or prevent certain opportunities for children of different ages. Deviance from adult standards of modesty and honesty that is tolerated in the three-year-old draws severe censure a few years later. At school age the induction into the society beyond the family brings five- and six-year-olds stimulation, requirements, and prohibitions unknown to their four-year-old siblings. Shifts in social norms as the child moves to adolescence are sometimes striking in their effect on his personal life.

Illustrations of age-determined environments in childhood can be easily multiplied, but are there similar ways in which chronological *old age* changes social situations? Obvious demonstrations come to mind—age-grading in seniority practices, hiring older workers, and compulsory retirement ages. Prevailing attitudes can create among the aged the feeling of belonging to a minority. Tuckman and Lorge (1953) indicate that the dominant stereotype of an old person stresses the negative, disagreeable, and ineffectual qualities of old age. Does this social climate have measurable effects? In research on racial and ethnic prejudice, it has been demonstrated that similar condemning and degrading stereotypes have their consequences—sometimes in self-depreciation, sometimes in behavior altered to conform to or strive against the stereotype, and sometimes in hostile feelings toward the majority. There may be analogous processes in the aged if they are a socially devalued group.

Accounts of characteristic psychological symptoms of the aged, such as exclusion of stimuli (Weinberg, 1956) and disengagement from the social surroundings (Cumming, Dean, Newell, & McCaffrey, 1960) may be reviewed with reference to the form in which aging and its social milieu support these reactions. If the aged tend to withdraw from interaction, what are the factors in the environment that foster withdrawal? If the aged show fewer interests and creative contributions, what learning opportunities does society offer to older people? Youth is pushed by expectation and institutional opportunities to learn, achieve, and find gratification in achievement. To what extent are similar incentives and opportunities offered the older adult?

I should like to follow the general social situation of old age further to its implications regarding biological and environmental research in aging and some suggestions for action research. In a discussion of the interaction between organism and environment (primarily concerned with child development), Anderson (1944) posed the question which might be reformulated slightly for old age: "What happens when an organism with increasing intrinsic limits moves chronologically into an environment of increasing constraints?" In general, biological and environmental constraints in old age reinforce one another. Decreased physical and physiological capacities and multiplied environmental constraints may result. These concurrent alterations in biological and environmental factors may reflect each other, and together they may determine the behavior and attitudes of the older person.

The problem which Anderson posed regarding the interaction between the child and his environment and which we have transposed to old age has certain similarities at the two age levels, but important differences should also be pointed out. The child lacks experience; by testing the environment, he learns the freedoms and constraints external to him and the limits and potentialities of his own capacities. Generally he is encouraged and socially supported in the testing. The aged person, on the other hand, has vast experience regarding his potentialities and those of the environment. As internal or external changes occur, a renewed testing process is needed, but it is difficult, because the testing leads, in many instances, to unlearning and, frequently, to such unpleasant or unacceptable learning as demonstration of inability to do something formerly done well. The experience of inability may seriously interfere with further exploration into new areas, such as learning new skills, developing other talents, and performing untried roles. Testing is also more difficult for the older person, because it receives little social encouragement and because there is little understanding of its importance. Our culture is relatively scientific about the social adjustments of children, but there is no parallel science for old age. I felt this very keenly as I observed an old, somewhat infirm man in the bustle of a suburban supermarket. The man was in a line approaching the checker's stand. His cart was piled high with groceries. As he fumbled his packages, got them onto the conveyor belt too slowly, and neglected to have his fruit weighed before arriving at the checkout counter, open impatience and superior amusement spread among the immediate observers. It was discomforting to watch and impossible to intervene; it must have been humiliating and angering to the man. The need for research, or plain education of adults, concerning human aging is apparent.

Parents have been steeped in laboratory and clinic findings on children's maturation stages and the dynamics of parent-child relations. Parents expect and demand different things from the two- and ten-year-old, because they are cognizant of the effects of rejection, separation, reward, and frustration on the child's behavior and personality. Similar indoctrination is lacking in the characteristics of and relations with the aged parent, worker, client, patient, and citizen. Gerontological research cannot as yet offer the facts and theories that are available on child development, but gathering scientific information for planned environmental change—through changed understanding and sympathy in the control figures or general social milieu—might reveal the degree to which variables of social adjustment make a difference in aging.

Twin needs for better studies of the settings and socialization problems of old age are (1) more detailed first-hand data on environments and (2) concepts for dealing with the data. To these issues we want to give our attention below, noting first, however, some measurement problems in which environment inadvertently enters into gerontological research.

An Unplanned Variable

Environment may invade studies in which it is not a planned variable. Thus, many studies of aging involve comparisons of young and old in which the investigator is interested in performance as an intrinsic function of aging. He may ignore, control, or match environmental factors. If he matches for social backgrounds, for example, he is faced with a problem. Shall he match by class status at the present or during youth? Some of the problems are illustrated in this description of an elderly subject in a National Institute of Mental Health human aging project. A man of seventy-eight spent his early childhood in east Poland. His early induction into his father's trade left little time for formal schooling, which consisted of a few years at Hebrew school. Fleeing poverty and religious discrimination, he arrived in the New York slums at eighteen. Years of lonely shifting from job to job followed. Finally he established a small business of his own. Now, at seventy-eight, he looks back on some thirty years in a prosperous business which left him well off financially when he retired eleven years ago. He and his wife live comfortably, travel, enjoy concerts and the theater, and take pride in their son's successful professional achievements. For aged subjects like this man what is an appropriately matched group in educational, social, and cultural terms?

Even where matching cultural backgrounds poses no problem, young and aged subjects may be living in circumstances which differ vitally in aspects relevant to laboratory performance. For the college freshman a laboratory learning problem is familiar ground, and his total college situation, in a sense, builds in the incentives for achievement on the task. What of conditions for the elderly man or woman whose general situation may lack incentive and to whose experience the laboratory tasks are wholly foreign?

Another situational factor that enters aging research is the relative youth, compared to their aged subjects, of many investigators. What situational influence this has on the subject is unknown. Exploration of investigators' feelings in the N.I.M.H. project on human aging (Birren, Butler, Greenhouse, Sokoloff, & Yarrow, in press) revealed conscious adjustments introduced by the age and status differences. A young psychologist in this project reported: "I had trouble with that guy, and by the time we were finished I was pretty mad. He kept trying to lord it over me and play the father role. It made me feel like being tough." With another subject and another young investigator this was observed: "Everybody called him Pop, so I did too. He seemed to like it. I felt he didn't really take me very seriously, like, 'Well, this is a nice kid; if he wants me to play tiddlywinks, I'll play along.'"

ENVIRONMENT AND
PSYCHOLOGICAL CONCEPTS

Thus far we have pointed to deficiencies rooted in inadequate conceptualization of the environment in gerontological research. Environments are handled in almost exclusively empirical terms. Thus there are studies of institutional effects, retirement, compulsory retirement codes, occupational settings, widowhood, independent living versus living in three-generation families, economic limitations, restricted environments because of perceptual and physical limitations, and so on. In a sense, environments are only labeled. Precise definitions of the discrete variables in these conditions are lacking, impairing measurement and precluding the possibilities of replication or comparison of studies.

By relating empirical conditions to psychological concepts, research could proceed with a more orderly approach to environmental influence. With variables conceptually ordered, questions could be formulated in the framework of psychological theory.

Environments may be said to have certain pervasive features which are manifested at many levels in various forms, but are consistent in quality, direction, and effect. An infant's environment may be pervasively characterized by warmth and tender, maternal care. A college freshman's environment may present overwhelming ego threats and stresses in his academic career, new friends, and absent family. It may be fruitful to examine the environments of the aging through pervasive features expected to influence functioning. In a sense, this reduces manifold environmental variables to more abstract common denominators—a step to be followed, however, by a sterner, analytic process.

Deprivation in the environment is one recognizable aspect of many social and medical problems of the aged. Psychological deprivation may be a significant quality of institutional life. Surely it marks living with economic limitations. It characterizes psychological isolation from the community and intimate family and physical isolation because of physical and perceptual failures that decrease access to the environment. Each speaks of a paucity and monotony of stimulation.

The increasing constraints which may pervade old age can reduce stimulation and, to this degree, do not differ from deprivations. Constraint itself, however, refers to barriers in the path of the individual. The degree of constraint experienced might characterize and simplify environments, making it possible to compare empirical conditions in which constraints play a part (medical problems, social policies, social expectations, individual age-related demands, and personality characteristics which evoke constraining response).

From the aged person's position, the degree of manipulability or inflexibility in the environment is both similar to and different from constraints. This is more a contest of powers—the possibility of the individual ability to intervene, make decisions, and change the environment. For all aged people this ability seems to diminish over earlier adulthood, especially for the institutionalized and those without sufficient income to be independent.

Environments might also be evaluated by the degree of trauma to which a person is subjected. We are thinking here of immediate trauma, such as disease, the death of friends, rejection by children, discovering one's limitations, learning that one's age is being judged critically by others. Indeed, the individual may be confronted with a number of simultaneous traumatic conditions, and deprivation might be the aftermath of these age-related traumata.

Change may be another pervasive environmental feature with potential significance in the adjustment of the aging. With change comes the related characteristic, unpredictability. Change and unpredictability may be viewed in cognitive terms as situations resulting in a lack of clarity for the aged person in the structure of his social world. Similarly, an environment characterized by frequent, unplanned, and drastic changes may require successive, drastic cognitive restructuring, for example, in terms of the aging person's dependence on and authority in his family, work, and community. Change and uncertainty in the environment may also be formulated in changing conditions of gratification. How do the environmental changes affect gratifying conditions for the older person? Does he find that different behaviors and attitudes are rewarded or punished now? Do the sources of his gratification or punishment become less predictable? In either formulation, hypotheses about disorganized, maladjusted behaviors in the aged suggest themselves as a function of conditions for change and unpredictability. These can be related to general psychological theory.

The environmental features described above have not been offered as mutually exclusive, precisely defined variables or as an exhaustive list, but as first approaches to assessments which go beyond purely empirical conditions.

A POSSIBLE APPROACH

It may not be sufficient or meaningful to deal with these broad features for all research problems. Each can be developed in discrete and more accurate, measurable elements or concepts. Such an approach is illustrated by deprivation in the environment of the aged.

Various stimulus deprivations have been studied in experimental and developmental psychology. Laboratory and clinical observations furnish data on behavioral disturbance and atypical development following extreme or prolonged deprivation. We are assuming that deprivations experienced in old age have similar consequences in disturbed functioning.

Environmental deprivations can be separated into relatively discrete categories: sensory deprivation, social deprivation (primary and secondary), intellectual deprivation, affectional and emotional deprivation.[1] Sensory stimulation in the environment is rarely analyzed unless there are major restrictions in sensory input. Environments of the aged, however, undoubtedly vary greatly in sensory stimulation. Deficiencies in social stimulation, common to many problems of the aged, take the form of few contacts—few in number, frequency, variety, or interaction. These deprivations occur at the primary level of face-to-face contact and at secondary levels of social events, community life, and world affairs. Spending time in a hospital with a serious illness often turns attention inward, causing a temporary social deprivation of the secondary type for a person of any age. Coming out of the hospital, a person must re-establish, for himself, how things are going. Illness and institutionalization may cause this kind of isolation for the aged. Intellectual deprivation may be defined as the lack of stimulating ideas, intellectual problems, and discoveries. Affectional deprivations may involve emotional blandness, neutrality, and monotony, as well as hostility and lack of love. Even the casual observer will easily spot these impoverishments in the lives of the aged. Social deprivations may stand out for the dean of women who retires to a remote country retreat, intellectual deprivation for the scientist whose failing perceptual faculties contribute to a withdrawal from activity, affectional deprivation for the elderly widow who has lost her family or whose children neglect her, or sensory deprivation in a custodial institution which offers little sense stimulation in amount or variety.

With a systematic conceptualization of variables along these lines, it should be possible to measure many essential environmental elements and make more precise comparisons of empirical conditions. Environments, thereby, are more open to research if they are pinned down without loss of complexity. The approach to deprivation could be followed in other dimensions, and the interaction of several dimen-

---

[1] In an analysis of maternal deprivation, Leon Yarrow (1961) offered an approach in which kinds of deprivation and stress in mother-infant relations were differentiated. Many of the ideas he presented have been useful in the present discussion.

sions in an environment could be studied. This definition of environmental variables in psychological terms brings the formulation of research problems closer to theoretical questions. Then, too, the selection of dependent variables (individual apathy, disengagement, chaotic functioning, and the like) can be more surely guided by theoretical considerations.

Only with variables clearly defined can problems be clearly formulated. When an investigator understands the variables he wishes to study, methods for obtaining the data and designs appropriate to the research question can be chosen and developed.

Data in existing studies of gerontological environment have been gathered largely through interviews, questionnaires, statistics, and clinical observations. Environmental designs are virtually nonexistent; there are few comparative studies; systematic observations are rarely done. This leaves several handicaps. We lack detailed, firsthand data on the natural environments of the aged. How do the aged live? We have few direct data on the responses of the elderly to environmental factors. For neither sets of these data have we adequate control or comparative data. How do people of other ages live and respond to environmental factors? The directives for research are clear: data from observation and experiment are needed to supplement the present resources.

As we arrive at reasonably standard environmental variables and concepts and more precise data, it should be possible to pursue questions more basic than those studied to date. Research need not be confined to correlations of gross environmental variables with other characteristics of the aged. Also, environmental variables can be taken more seriously in behaviorial-biological questions.

CONCLUSIONS

We have taken the position that environmental variables have a place in the science of human behavior, and that they need, and presently do not have, systematic definition and measurement. To pursue the topics of this paper, it has been necessary to give environment an exceedingly prominent role in behavior, at times, more than anyone, save a staunch environmentalist, would be willing to give.

The environments of cells and environments in physical and chemical terms have demonstrated consequences in the life of the organism. The environment of the human behaviors surrounding an individual has effects as well, but we are less adept at determining how it affects aging and how basic the effects it exerts are.

At this stage, it is probably inappropriate to argue whether organic or environmental factors are more fundamental in the behavior of the old person without specifying the locus of the question. It may be premature, too, to draw conclusions concerning the direction of influence in all instances of interdependence between biological and environmental conditions.

Usually one pretests one's research questions and design plans among colleagues who, by training and scientific disposition, are similar to oneself. Within this homogeneous group the framework and support for one's research activity are built. As a complement, not a substitute, to this procedure, would it not be fruitful in early (and late) research planning and practice to expose one's ideas to more worldly research perspectives and colleagues whose disciplines, interests, scientific points of view, methods, and designs differ materially from one's own? For example, to the investigator studying a particular internal course of biological aging, this might mean discussing his research with the investigator studying aging in terms of personality disorders or social processes; the reverse could also take place.

In this process the good social psychologist is not converted into an amateur psychiatrist; the clinician does not drop his problems and methods for those honored by the experimentalist. The result is rather that, by learning and respecting the research considerations which colleagues in other disciplines bring to bear on one's research, the investigator proceeds in his own research with deeper and broader knowledge. There should be a good gain in the loss of narrow, provincial research without concurrent loss of disciplinary and theoretical identities.

REFERENCES

Anderson, J.E. Freedom and constraint or potentiality and environment. *Psychol. Bull.*, 1944, **41**, 1-29.
Barker, R., Dembo, Tamara, & Lewin, K. Frustration and regression: An experiment with young children. (Studies in topological and vector psychology: II). *Univ. Iowa Stud. Child Welf.*, 1941, **18**, No. 1. (Ames, Iowa)
Birren, J.E., Butler, R., Greenhouse, S., Sokoloff, L., & Yarrow, Marian R. *Biological and behavioral aspects of human aging.* (In press)
Busse, E.W., Barnes, R.H., Friedman, E.L., & Kelty, E.J. Psychological functioning of aged individuals with normal and abnormal electro-

encephalograms. I: A study of non-hospitalized community volunteers. *J. nerv. ment. Dis.,* 1956, **124,** 135-141.

Chein, I. The environment as a determinant of behavior. *J. soc. Psychol.,* 1954, **39,** 115-126.

Cumming, Elaine, Dean, Lois, Newell, D.S., & McCaffrey, Isabel. Disengagement: A tentative theory of aging. *Sociometry,* 1960, **23,** 23-35.

Heider, F. On Lewin's methods and theory. *J. soc. Issues,* Suppl. Ser., 1959, No. 13, 3-13.

Lewin, K. *Principles of topological psychology.* New York and London: McGraw-Hill, 1936.

Lippitt, R. An experimental study of the effect of democratic and authoritarian group atmospheres. (Studies in topological and vector psychology: I). *Univ. Iowa Stud. Child Welf.,* 1940, **16,** No. 3, 45-195. (Ames, Iowa)

Mering, O. von, & Wineger, F.L., Social-cultural background of the aging individual. In J.E. Birren (Ed.), *Handbook of aging and the individual: Psychological and biological aspects.* Chicago: The University of Chicago Press, 1959. Pp. 279-335.

Murphy, G., Murphy, Lois, & Newcomb, T. *Experimental social psychology.* New York: Harper & Brothers, 1937.

Tuckman, J., & Lorge, I. "When aging begins" and stereotypes about aging. *J. Geront.,* 1953, **8,** 489-492.

Weinberg, J. Personal and social adjustment. In J.E. Anderson (Ed.), *Psychological aspects of aging.* Washington, D.C.: American Psychological Association, 1956. Pp. 17-21.

Yarrow, L. Maternal deprivation: Toward an empirical and conceptual reevaluation. *Psychol. Bull.,* 1961, **58,** 459-490.

Yarrow, Marian R., Blank, P., Quinn, Olive, Youmans, G., & Stein, Johanna. Social psychological characteristics of old age. In *Human aging: A biological and behavioral study.* Washington, D.C.: U.S. Government Printing Office, 1961.

Zborowski, M. Cultural components in response to pain. *J. Soc. Issues,* 1952, **8** (4), 16-30.

CHAPTER 12

*Environment and
Meaningful Activity*

JOHN E. ANDERSON

The problem of environment is important for older people, because there are so many of them with little or nothing to do. Approximately one million people pass their sixty-fifth birthday each year. Of these, the majority cease working; if they do not retire at sixty-five, they do so within the next five years. As a result, within any decade, millions of people move into a new status in society, freed from the demands of the work-oriented world in which they have lived all their lives. On the average, these people with time on their hands are likely, if they are male, to live fourteen additional years and, if female, seventeen additional years. In these years they must meet the challenges of living without the responsibility of working in a complex society. These people are predominantly producers who

223

have lived in an environment in which such responsibilities as working, rearing a family, and caring for themselves and their own households have been primary. For people above sixty-five, the first two of
these responsibilities have disappeared, and only the third is left.

A fundamental, practical question arises: How can we create
an environment, in the larger sense, or a whole series of environments,
in the smaller sense, in which these people can live happily and well?
It is becoming clear that the present environment is not adequate. As
time passes, questions of environmental facilities, opportunities, and
outlets will become even more apparent.

Not only is there this general question of the environment
for older people in the community; there is also the question of the
many specific environments which have been and are being established
for older people. There are facilities for the indigent elderly, apartments built by private operators, retirement communities supported
by agencies, institutions for sheltered care, day centers, golden age
clubs, and sheltered work opportunities for older people in the community. It is clear that the organization of the general environment
and various specific environments for older people is taking on great
practical significance.

Is the psychologist, with his interests in stimulation, organization of behavior, and adjustment of the person, able to contribute
to the solution of these problems? Can he develop the theory and
research that will reveal the basic relations and give information from
which a practical program can be developed? What do we know
about the environment of older people? What might we know? What
information can we give to people who are designing environments
for older people? What might we say about a more general program
for all older people? How might we design research to supply the
necessary information?

THE ENVIRONMENT

There are two fundamental approaches to the problem of
human beings and environment: the first asks what the human being
does to his environment, seeking to learn how the person projects himself on the external world; the second asks what the environment does
to the human being, seeking to know how the environment modifies
the person. Psychologists are interested in both problems, but more
attention has been given to the first. Recently, however, with the

problem of deprivation and emphasis on early training as an influence on later life, more attention has been directed to environment.

Historically, psychologists have been little concerned with milieu in its most general aspects, but have been very concerned with the effects of specific stimulation on the person. There is an immense literature based on the introduction of specific stimuli, usually under controlled conditions, in order to determine the modifications in behavior produced by single or repeated stimulation. There is considerable experimentation concerned with objects and the relations between objects and much study of the linguistic substitutes for objects and relations. Note, however, that much of this work is concerned with immediate, or, at most, briefly delayed, results of stimulation on behavior. For some years, the Gestalt psychologists have emphasized Gestalts, or configurations, which cover constellations (complexes of stimuli), usually organized in a moment. "Situation" is another term used, particularly by behaviorists, to refer to a constellation. More recently, the terms "climate," sometimes "social climate," and "atmosphere" have come into use, particularly in studies of children. Although these terms sometimes refer to a momentary situation, most commonly they cover over-all characteristics of the environment which extend in time. Thus we can speak of a school room or an institution as having a climate. In so doing, we usually refer to its typical characteristics, not to its occasional departures from them. In one sense, a climate is a repetition and summation of similar specific stimuli to the exclusion of others; in another sense, it is a current of common properties running through a variety of situations. From this terminology, it is clear that attention is going to combinations and larger features of the environment extended in time.

We finally come to the term "setting," a recent term widely used in gerontology to describe a constellation of physical and psychological characteristics which exists for an extended time and the effects of which may be measured. If we think of a setting in the continuity of time, distinct from stimuli or situations that exist momentarily, we can ask questions about its nature. A first question centers on the content. Settings can be graded by the quality and variety of stimulation they afford. Presumably some settings are more powerful than others in content, some more diverse in content. A second question concerns the time a setting operates; some operate for very short, others for very long, periods. The home, for example, operates over twenty-one years with the same people, whereas the school operates over sixteen years with major changes like the transition from one

level, teacher, and course to another. A third question is the change
in the content. Not only is there change in flow, but also in the level
and complexity of the material to which the individual is exposed.
The fourth question concerns the interaction among settings. From
early life, a person is in different settings at different times of day. In
some respects these interfere with one another, in some respects they
facilitate and support one another. We must think of a person as exposed to many settings, some of which have much, some little, in
common. Thus we can think of homogeneous and heterogeneous environments. Moreover, we can conceive an over-all relation, the general
atmosphere, among settings if they are congruent.

In this survey we have described aspects of the environment.
It should be clear that settings have climates composed of stimulation
which can be broken down into the specific stimuli, objects, relations,
verbal symbols, and so on which make up the situations. The effects of such stimulation when it is extended in time and involves
iteration are also important. More and more we see the human being
in flow concepts, such as those in information theory and stochastic
processes. For example, consider prohibition in an environment. Here,
whatever the responses to a specific "no" on a particular occasion, a
count can be made of the prohibitions and reinforcements over a
period of time for all situations in the environment. An atmosphere
may emerge in which there are 90 per cent prohibitions (no's) and
10 per cent reinforcements (yes's), which can be compared with another behavior in which there are 30 per cent prohibitions and 70
per cent reinforcements. Thus specific stimuli become summated into
an atmosphere by isolating the continuing characteristic methods of
control. From this point, it is only a step to experiments in which
atmospheres can be deliberately set up, or settings manipulated, to
reveal significant relations.

It should be clear that we are talking about a psychological
as well as a physical environment. In thinking about environments
for older people, attention is too often given the physical aspects, to
the exclusion of the psychological aspects. Objects and people may
be in the physical environment of a person of any age without
affecting him. In one sense, the psychological environment is narrower
than the physical, since the capacity of the human being's information
channels is limited and since, as a functioning organism, the human
being can act only as a unit, performing only one major action at a
time, as was demonstrated by Sherrington. The effectiveness of stimuli
in eliciting behavior depends on the behavior already under way and

the vigilance of the whole system. Some, but generally very few, stimuli and events are so powerful that they force selective regard, regardless of a person's age or condition. These generally have great intensity, such as a lightning flash, earthquake, accident, or the like. But it is not these unusual circumstances with which we deal. We deal with the principle that man is selective in his environment and that what he sees, hears, and feels is determined not only by objective stimuli, but also by the condition of his sense organs and his readiness to respond. The psychological environment is distinct from the physical environment in some respects, but overlaps it in others. In the sense that the organism does not react to all the potential stimuli about him, the psychological environment is narrower than the physical environment.

If, however, one examines what a person is doing, he quickly finds that in a particular physical environment the person may be reacting to past events or future possibilities rather than to present stimuli. People reach backward and forward in time and have a way of reacting to objects and people who are psychologically present although physically absent. This extension of the time dimension is important in behavior. It leads to major problems when we attempt to define the existing environment for a particular person at a particular time in a particular place.

The problem of the physical and the psychological environment has an analogue in practice. Here the problem is distinguishing between the physical and psychological availability of equipment. It is often assumed that the physical presence of facilities ensures their use, yet the question of whether they are used remains. If they are not used, can they be made psychologically available? In some institutions for older people, there are excellent facilities which are not used by the residents. In research, too, reports on facilities need to be supplemented by observations on their use.

THE OLDER PERSON

In considering the effects of environment on the aging, we must distinguish between the immediate environment and the effects of past experience. An older person is a complex structure of perceptive, motor, and intellective skills, symbols and knowledge, attitudes and values, and social skills and personal relations, which have been elaborated in lifelong contact with a series of environments. In some instances this environment has been homogeneous and restricted throughout development and maturity; in other instances it has been heterogeneous. The older person is, then, an enormous filing cabinet of experience, ready to respond to an appropriate stimulation. In this system there has been some loss, since storage is imperfect, and some gain, since wisdom emerges with experience. Note that it is the same person who goes through the experiences of a particular life. He is an independent unit with his own intake, output, and mechanism for storage. Since the same nervous system recorded all the experience, there is always continuity. This continuity reveals itself in certain expectancies and modes of behavior which characterize the person approaching the situations presented by aging.

Thus a person has an intrinsic continuity that is not in the environment. He moves from one environment to another in a physical and psychological sense. Usually changes are not drastic; under some conditions they may be. This gradual series of small transformations may, in time, become great. As he ages, he is faced with many oportunities among which he must choose. These have marked effects on later behavior, since they determine the environment the person will be exposed to at later periods. At some point in late adolescence or early adulthood, a person chooses a vocation, a choice which establishes a subsequent continuity, since it determines the experiences he will have, people he will meet, and activities he will carry on for the next forty or fifty years. Although this is obviously a major decision, one can point to many similar decisions at earlier ages. From this process, the interests and activities with which a person fills his waking time emerge. When we view his interests and activities, as single pursuits or a pattern of pursuits, it becomes clear that life is highly structured. In old age, however, particularly if the person retires, much of this structure breaks down. The person leaves his job, with all that it means to him as activity and in social relations, and must strike out anew (Friedman & Havighurst, 1954).

There are, of course, a number of theoretical possibilities about outcome. Assuming a pattern of rich activity and stimulation in early life, there is some possibility that it will be continued, because a person with such a history may, when older, seek a stimulating environment or because the expectancies he has created in others will crowd him and enrich his environment. There also is the possibility of a shift to a less stimulating environment or to one with almost no stimulation. Similarly, for the average person there is a possibility of continuing at the same level, moving to a richer environment, or moving to a less stimulating one. At first glance, the second possibility does not seem real, but some investigation of retirement communities in Florida suggests that there are environments which older people really find more stimulating than their earlier environments. For a person from an environment of little value and variety, there is some chance of continuing in the same environment or finding a better environment in old age. We can thus construct a sixfold table in which to consider the possibilities of two variables of three gradations each. Any consideration indicates the need of assessing the person as well as the environment.

It is also possible that the older person has a greater store of equipment with which to meet unfavorable environments than the younger person. First, he has survived many stresses. Second, he has his whole life to dwell on in revery, and, if he makes an effort to recall it, he is likely to have successful experiences on which to dwell. Some evidence in the literature on prison camps suggests a relation between the capacity to recall rich, varied experiences and the ability to withstand boredom.

Environmental Effects

Given any one of the environments we have discussed and the older people who are exposed to them, we face the problem of measuring the effects of environmental stimulation. Here we cannot use direct measurement, but must depend on either modifications in the behavior concurrently recorded or tests of skill, knowledge, or attitude given to people who have contrasting environments. With results of the latter type, we may still face the problem of breaking the variance in behavior and activity into its relations with such components as setting, age, sex, personality, companions, experience, methods of occupying himself, and social and familial relations. In this field of complex, overlapping forces, analysis of the relation of single factors to single outcomes is likely to result in generalizations which give some factors undue emphasis, produce artifacts about other factors, and omit important underlying factors.

The problem in which I am most interested is the relation between the stimulation available in the environment and the free use of time (Anderson, 1958; Anderson, 1959). My concern has been the use of time. If we consider the methods available for the study of environment, we can make a sharp distinction between those concerned with the introduction of specific stimuli or configurations of stimuli and those concerned with the measurement of the effects of climates, atmospheres, and settings. In the former we set up laboratory experiments, carefully isolating the phenomena to be studied; in the latter we observe behavior in natural situations, even though in some instances there may be some contrivance in the circumstances on which observations are to be made. Almost inevitably the use of the available techniques leads directly to some practical outcomes as well as generalizations about behavior. In fact, the techniques of observation have been of considerable value in industry (Mundel, 1950) and have had wide application in business and the design of equipment, furniture, housing, and so on.

The methods can be divided into several broad classes. There are check lists which depend on the subject's capacity to recall what he did the preceding day, week, or, perhaps, at any time. Analyses of such check lists have given interesting data on the development of activity and interest and offer a method for rapidly surveying a group of any age. But when we look at the reports of such studies, some of which have been summarized by Pressey and Kuhlen (1957), we find counts and averages that can be analyzed in various ways, but which tend, on the whole, to seem to give superficial information, since we cannot evaluate the depth of the person's concern with the activity or whether there were any outcomes. There is also the question whether expressed interest in or report of an activity is related to actual participation, since Chalfen (1956) found that older persons of comparable age and background from homes for the aged and recreation centers were similar in expressed interests, but those from recreation centers engaged in more activities.

A second method, used less frequently with children but more frequently with young and old adults, is the diary (Foote, 1961). Over a week, month, or longer, a person records his behavior on prepared forms marked for the time of day or writes a running account in which he records time. This technique presents some difficulty, since about one-quarter of the population is unable to read or write well enough to keep such a diary and many other people are very hesitant or fail to cooperate. Thus the sampling tends to be biased. Another difficulty arises, because the person selects what he reports since a complete report is out of the question. Without advance training, the ordinary person tends to keep a poor record, partly because items which seem important to the scientist seem unimportant to him. Records are best for concurrent factual events.

A third method uses observers placed in the environment who record the behavior for a definite period of time. By using successive observers, data can be obtained for the whole day or a number of days. The most successful attempts at this are those of Barker and Wright (1951; 1955), who found that observers could observe for short periods of time—a half-hour at most—and that the observations were more complete when there was questioning at the end of the period. In some observational techniques, precautions are taken to isolate the observer physically or psychologically from the situation, as in using one-way vision screens to minimize the effects of the observer on the situation. Some studies show, however, that in a short time people who are observed adapt to observers to such a degree that they neglect them, and a trained observer tends to become a piece of furniture in relation to the situation. In anthropological and community studies, observers may live as members of the community and obtain data as participants. Scientifically the problem is not whether there is error. In modern terminology we think errors exist in every observation and experiment in the biological and social sciences. The problem is to reduce error to a minimum by using several parallel observers, a technique which controls the bias and nullifies error in some fashion.

Obviously these methods can be used in combination or separately and can be extended to cover the most minute, as well as the most general, aspects of behavior. The modern scientist also has motion pictures and sound recording, which produce even more detailed and exact records. There is some question, however, whether the gain in information from a minute recording justifies the extra time and expense it incurs. Suppose that one laborious and detailed method gives 95 per cent of the available information, whereas a shorter, less detailed method gives 90 per cent. How do we balance the gain in information against the extra time and effort necessary for a 5 per-cent gain? What we need are methodological studies in which information is obtained from the same or similar people by various methods over comparable periods of time with some study of the proportion of information obtained in relation to the possible information. There is still the question of whether a skilled observer looking for specific behavior items would not gain better information than that obtained from detailed work over miles of film and records of minute events that must be coded in broad classes for later analysis and interpretation. Coding is a matter of course in the final analysis of the data. Why go to the effort of collecting complete data in order to code them broadly on an IBM card for later statistical purposes? Would it not be better to code in advance by using protocols from pilot studies?

There is a problem even more important than coding. This has been discussed in the methodological literature on child development for many years and emerges as a problem in the study of responses to environments. It relates to the size and nature of the unit of behavior in terms of the goal. We can count the steps a person takes in walking a city block and describe his movements in great detail, but from this we cannot tell whether he is on his way to the bank to cash a check before going on a long trip, on his way to buy a necktie, or killing time, because he is ten minutes early for an appointment. We either have to ask the person what he is doing or observe his behavior for a longer period, for here are three out of an infinite number of possible outcomes which can be distinguished only by purpose and each of which is part of a larger unit when that purpose is considered. Walking the block is a necessary, but somewhat irrelevant, bit of behavior in the outcome.

Barker and Wright (1951; 1955) solved this problem in accordance with Lewinian principles by defining an episode and setting up criteria which linked all behavior leading to a particular outcome. The next episode was considered to begin when the observed person shifted to another goal. Although this too often results in fractional behavior, it is an advance over microscopic recording. Larger units can be used. It is obvious that in research we cannot dodge coding and classification and that we must approach data with some theory of organization evolved from preliminary manipulation of actual data.

A further methodological difficulty in analyzing environments is short-term assessment compared with study over time. Although we have methods for making cross-section assessments, we could give some attention to the effect of environments over time. We can distinguish between the process of organizing behavior, technically called learning, and the content of behavior which becomes a permanent part of the person. Thus there is a separation between learning to read and the content of the reading done by the person or between learning to drive and the skill manifested on the road. Of these two approaches, it is the latter with which we are concerned when we view a person over time and consider what he can do in the society of which he is a member. A person becomes a bundle of skills, knowledge, and attitudes, all of which are neatly packaged, organized resources which become available to meet the demands of the external world. When we talk about personality and adjustment, we consider the manner in which these resources combine to make the total person.

What features of the environment keep behavior functioning? This is a question of theoretical and practical interest. As time passes, experiences crowd each other out, skills disappear through lack of use, and activities are extinguished. All these phenomena show gradients related to the lapse of time, but they have one common feature—for one reason or another, functional relations disappear in time. We can assume that any connection has its own length of life and that unless it is restimulated or re-established, it will disappear. This leads to an examination of the environment, which is found to be composed of many iterative stimuli and situations. In many environments, moreover, there is stability despite superficial appearances of change. How can we separate stability from stimuli which affect the person only momentarily? For example, in teaching reading in underdeveloped countries, UNESCO found it comparatively easy to build reading skill in some countries. After some years, however, the skills disappeared in spite of the effective teaching, because there was no reading material available in the environment with which to maintain the skill. The point is clear: to maintain literacy, you must not only teach people how to read, but you must also have reading material available continuously. In our society there are newspapers, books, magazines, letters, street signs, and so on to such a degree that, once a person has learned to read, he has great difficulty avoiding reading. In some studies of the community activities of young people, it is found that activity and interest patterns within groups diminish when leadership changes or even disappear completely when the leaders move or drop out. There is also evidence of substantial correlation between the behavior of mothers toward their young children and behavior toward the same children when they are older. Continuity of facilities, relations, and people as sources of iterated stimulation is involved.

To determine sources of some behavioral consistency, we must distinguish environments, analyze them for continuity and change, and look for successive contacts with objects, relations, and people which have an identity or great similarity over long periods. This view is in line with the flow concept of behavior. But caution must be taken, for some iterative stimulation in the environment is relevant, some irrelevant, to the problems studied. In large part, analysis of the environment over time involves separating the relevant from the irrelevant.

As examples of studies on older people which have been

concerned in one or another manner with the relation of environmental factors to activity patterns, we may mention a few and refer the reader to the longer analyses by Kleemeier (1959; 1961) and Chalfen (1956), who investigated homes for the aged and found the environments physically and psychologically restricting. By matching subgroups for occupation, economic identification, age, education, and religion, all of which were related to the amount of activity, and comparing the home with the recreation center, Chalfen concluded that the home was not so influential as the center in determining activity, emphasizing environmental opportunities.

To show the effect of sensory intake, Kleemeier and Justiss (1955) compared people with and without hearing aids who were matched for age and ability to walk and care for themselves. Those with the sensory deficiency were less active, particularly in listening activities, such as auditorium programs and radio. The groups were similar in television viewing.

The effect of institutional living on preoccupation with the past was shown by Fink (1957), who studied men over sixty living in county infirmaries with those living in the community. He found that those in the institutions were preoccupied with the past (68 per cent of the items), whereas those in the community were preoccupied with the future (51 per cent of the items). He also found the older members in each group more preoccupied with the past, but concluded that age did not account for all the differences. Activities, such as work and hobbies, gave old men perspectives that were future-oriented.

The effect of the image of self is shown by Tuckman and Lavell (1957). In a large institution, they found that the indigent aged who classified themselves "old" spent more time in sedentary activities or doing nothing than those who classified themselves "not old." They also were less likely to read, write letters, or the like.

Burgess (1954) showed that isolation is related to activity. He found that the residents of homes for the aged who were classified as leaders engaged in many more activities than those classified as isolates and that participation related to good adjustment. Kleemeier (1951) found that participation in the institutional work program was accompanied by higher personal adjustment scores.

The relation of the staff to institutional life is shown by Kandler and Hyde (1951), who, working in a mental hospital with a trained, sensitive staff, found a decreased social and general activity in a ward after a reduction in staff personnel.

The Environment as a Whole

In another paper (Anderson, 1944) I made an analysis of the manner in which we might approach the whole environment and its significance for the individual. In approaching such a problem we need dimensions under which we will subsume the mass of detail. There were, in my opinion, three dimensions which could be used to analyze the environment—resources, incentives, and constraints.

By resources we mean the content of the environment or the products of the group to which the person reacts. Included are all materials available in the culture—institutions, facilities, equipment, symbols, means of communication, and the like. People vary in their language, games, books, music, work, and so on, because of the content of the culture into which they were born.

Incentives are developed in group living to encourage people to respond to group purposes and values. From birth a person is surrounded by incentives, many of which are symbolic. Incentives grow from the intercourse among people and represent positive impulsion, as opposed to constraints, which act negatively.

Constraints are the limitations which surround a person and prevent him from realizing his potentialities. They include not only prohibitions that are explicitly verbalized, but also all interferences, deficiencies, and inadequacies that prevent the use of personal, material, and group resources.

In the constraints we find, perhaps, the most important dimension, since these cannot be detected without a detailed examination by direct observation of the relations among people, of the control system which operates in the environment. Any factor which tends to limit the full range of behavior and possibilities of exploration is a constraint. It may be a physical constraint, as in confinement; social, as with a taboo; or personal, as with an inferior feeling. Here we emphasize interaction of the organism and the environment. Any institution, contrasted with living in the community, is, in some sense, a constraining situation. And, as Kleemeier has pointed out in his discussion of settings, institutional life automatically sets up a system of constraints by virtue of the fact that schedules imposed by a staff have to be met, meals have to be served at certain hours, and sleep hours have to be maintained. An individual who is bedridden or limited in his capacity to move is constrained. Similarly, we can talk of psychological constraints which range from direct social restriction, which is embodied in law, to the various limitations which arise in the relation of staff to residents or in the leadership pattern of a group. It has also become apparent in various studies that a system of constraint may influence behavior even when a person is free. For example, rigid control may result in letting off steam when the controls are removed, producing difficulties in adjustment. Hence observations should be made over long periods. Thus we suggest taking a look at environments by recording events and behavior and then classifying what occurs in some dimensions, such as those proposed, to describe what is happening in the environment. From such protocols it is but a step to the control of settings in experimental studies in order to verify some of the relations discovered.

At first analysis, it seemed to me that these were distinct, unrelated dimensions. Although I now realize that incentive and constraint might be considered the ends of a continuum, it seems more helpful to think of them as independent continua. In any event, for purposes of analyzing an environment, they should be treated separately.

From the theoretical point of view, an environment, to be rich, must have substantial resources in it. The individual needs resources to work with and content to manipulate. Presumably, the greater resources, the more likely the person is to find satisfactory activity and relations. We live in a world in which we are surrounded by incentives. A catalogue of supportive devices in an environment would list the extent to which the environment facilitates adjustment and accomplishment; a catalogue of constraints would list the limits within which people can operate. Generalized ratings or summations with respect to these dimensions would permit comparison of environments and selection of contrasting ones for more detailed study of short- and long-term effects.

Stimulation

Assuming that some of the inactivity and quietness of older people in institutions and the community can be traced to environmental factors, we can ask whether there are any intrinsic psychological characteristics of either stimulation or activity that are involved. If we could locate such attributes, we could capitalize on them in our practical programs. To answer this question, I suggested (Anderson, 1958) that activities resembling work in complexity, power over time, and possibilities of identification and involvement might so function. I also pointed out the deficiencies of activities for essentially momentary entertainment. Presumably one outcome of restricted activity, as well as of a deprivation of sensory stimulation, is boredom, which, over time, may cause deterioration. The relation of sensory deprivation to boredom has lately received much emphasis in the literature (Heron, 1957). A significant book by Berlyne (1960) deals with arousal, curiosity, and the attributes of stimulation which keep the organism vigilant and active. Much of the following discussion is based on the material he presents that seemed appropriate to our problem.

Berlyne points out a dimension, which can be called vigilance, ranging from deep sleep to alert wakefulness. The awake animal in a complex environment continually scans that environment for stimuli which have potential danger or at least require adaptation on his part. Presumably, in an environment of routine stimulation that can be met by habitual responses, the organism functions at a low level and is less alert. The moment stimulation with certain attributes appears, however, the organism becomes aroused and is ready for action. Thus resources are mobilized to meet some types of stimuli.

This point of view differs from traditional theory, which emphasizes specific stimuli that reduce the needs of the organism, such as hunger, thirst, sex, and the like. But a living organism is concerned with more than basic biological needs since he lives in a complex, external environment of potential danger. In this environment there are many more stimuli competing for his attention than he can possibly react to at any particular time. He scans his environment, therefore, and, if appropriate stimuli appear, attends to them. Apparently there are mechanisms in the reticular formation concerned with arousal and blocking groups of stimuli which might interfere with adaptation. Thus high selectivity and mobilization of resources are outcomes of the continuous survey of the environment. When not directly concerned with biological needs, the organism explores his environment for sources of danger. When stimulation possesses certain qualities, the organism shifts from scanning to alertness and thus is ready for whatever happens.

Cannon (1939) developed a theory stating that the exciting emotions involved mobilizing the energy of the organism in threatening or doubtful situations. Berlyne (1960) points out, however, that such mobilization is characteristic not only of emotional excitement, but is also part of everyday living in a normal environment. It is an upward extension of wakefulness. Arousal states in the individual organism vary from time to time and from one organism to another. Berlyne then asks questions about the characteristics of stimuli that lead to alertness and mobilize a person. The four variables are novelty, uncertainty, conflict, and complexity. By novelty, he means any stimulation which is new and strange to the organism at the moment it is first perceived. By uncertainty, he refers to doubt about the outcome of the stimulation and confusion about what to do. By conflict, he refers to the interference among stimuli, each of which leads to a particular act, and the necessity of resolving the contradictory tendencies or choosing an alternative. By complexity, he refers to the demands made by the multiple stimuli for organization into a pattern. An object or environment with many varying elements is more complex than one with few elements of much the same type. Of course, there is some overlap among these attributes. Any novel situation is likely to contain some uncertainty, any uncertainty may lead to conflict, any complex situation is likely to lead to both uncertainty and conflict. It is obvious that experimentation might be undertaken on stimulation with and without these attributes, but there is another phase of the problem that deserves consideration.

A striking characteristic of the young child is his activity. Much of his energy goes to prowling the environment in search of new experiences and to reacting to the novel and uncertain. Hence, there is difficulty in separating the activity from the stimulation in a young child, since through his rambling the child creates novelty, uncertainty, conflicts, and complexity. In the young adult, who has been structured for twenty or more years, there is more directed, less exploratory activity; if exploratory activity is shown it tends to be confined to a few channels. The older person is highly structured, even compared with the young adult and particularly when compared with the child.

It has been questioned whether interest in the surroundings can be developed by increasing activity or whether activity can be increased by changing the surroundings. Here is a reciprocal relation in which stimulation affects activity and activity affects stimulation. But lurking in the background there is an even more basic question: Can full participation and continuing interest in life's activities and surroundings preserve the organism at a higher level of functioning for a longer time? Theoretically we are talking about active, curious people. In this framework, being a spectator is a superficial response which fails to energize the organism to the same degree as participation. Studies of children as observers and participants show much greater involvement when the child is a participant.

Basic to much of Berlyne's thinking is the assumption that

activity, novelty, uncertainty, conflict, and complexity are interrelated and that the spectator relation to environment presents a special case, rather than the primary kind of behavior. We may learn to be spectators by inhibiting participant responses. Thus it is possible that in adult social life a disjunction develops between activity and perception that does not exist in early development.

Aging has been discussed essentially as a process in which a person disengages himself from life because of progressive changes in sensory and motor capacities, diminished activity, changes in personal relations and the attitudes of others, and the breakup of friendships and associations through death and inactivity. Whatever the factors, evidence supports the view that there is a progressive withdrawal from life's concerns. The proposed question asks the degree to which these processes can be reversed. How can we work against individual disengagement and encourage continuing activity? There seem to be two major possibilities.

The first possibility involves establishing environments in which the older person will encounter novel, uncertain, conflicting, and complex stimulations. If we can control these aspects of stimulation, we can discover whether curiosity and activity are increased. In environments in which these attributes are varied, we could measure the activity and participation of older people by observational methods. We might even be able to maximize novelty while holding uncertainty, conflict, and complexity at moderate levels or work out any other combination and then study the outcomes for activity and participation. It might also be possible to work out combinations of attributes. To start such research, we might list the experiences to which older people are exposed, classify them to the extent that these attributes are present, and describe stimulation in psychological dimensions rather than in content.

The second possibility asks: How can the zest, energy, and activity with which the younger person approaches life be restored to an older person? This assumes that with growth we educate out many characteristics by which young people maintain an interest in their environment and fill their time. There is no doubt that the active three- or four-year-old child can convert almost any object into a plaything and secure much pleasure from it. In a striking way he possesses a capacity to generate stimulating activities which fill his time. Many people have pointed out that the excess energy revealed in play, the curiosity and manipulation which are part of play, and the skills developed in play are not only time-filling, but, from the long-term view, are of great utility in the organization of adaptive responses. Huizinga (1950) even goes as far as the theory that culture develops from play rather than from the reduction of biological needs. From this excess manipulation emerge interest and capacity to generate infinite behaviors, societies, and civilizations. Thus, in the evolution of culture, what people do in meeting basic drives is not so important as what they do above meeting basic drives. If we accept this, we must ask what society does to old people to train them out of their capacity to generate interest in and zest for living.

Experimentation in this area is more difficult than working with the attributes of stimulation, but a possibility is study of the manner in which increased participation leads to curiosity and more concern with the environment. Here we would not ask what attributes of stimulation produce increased concern, but how situations could be developed which would lead older persons to explore their environments. A basic assumption would be that the older people studied would be placed in settings with possibilities for exploration. Another possibility would be detailed histories of interests developed by old people, showing where they originated, where supportive stimulation came from, and how the activity was organized as a pursuit which occupied substantial time. What we want to know is how a momentary interest, perhaps even an imposed one, moves to autonomy in a person's interest until it begins to generate searching activity which result in skill and knowledge. Such an analysis would reveal phenomena peculiar to each activity—music as distinct from art, art as distinct from gardening—but nevertheless there should be enough common features to enable us to generalize about the conditions under which activities flourish and disappear. How much concern arises because of social pressures? At what stage does an activity become interiorized? When does it become a lasting part of a person's life pattern? We want to know how dedication arises. We can think of dedication existing not only in people working for a worthy cause or in scientific endeavor, but also as a widespread characteristic of people at all levels in society. Dedication leads to extensive exploration in and concern with an area. How can such patterns, which have self-generating characteristics, be established?

When we think in this fashion, it becomes apparent that in the relation of the person to his environment there comes a time when he ceases to be a passive recipient of stimulation and becomes an active searcher for it. Thus he changes his role and orientation in particular activities. Little attention has focused on the components of stimulation which will arouse interest in older people and even less on how older people might generate their own activities, thus becoming positively oriented toward their environment instead of merely accepting it. We are concerned with the dynamics of stimulation, arousal, alertness, and activity, rather than catalogues of activities, no matter how useful they may be in early research.

Settings and Control

When we view and attempt to classify the environments in which we find older people, we find great variety. One scheme divides them into living in the community and living in institutions.

Of the older people living in the community, some live as couples in single households, some live with children, and some live alone. Although it would be worthwhile to study the effect of these types of living on behavior, my belief is that most of the variance in behavior is produced not by these settings, but by the characteristics which the person brings to each setting from his own past and by other features, such as the available facilities and the social opportunities.

In many communities, day and recreation centers for older people are being established with facilities and programs for stimulating activity. Some offer formal training. In any event, these special environments deserve some experimental work and study, even though experimental control may be limited. At the moment, it is important to develop the practical methodology of these centers according to appropriately designed research.

Institutions for older persons vary immensely. There are general hospitals and mental hospitals which care for young and old patients. There are the special institutions for older people which range from facilities for apartment living with the person completely responsible for his own affairs much as adults at earlier ages are, through various living and rooming facilities with single or joint occupancy and meals taken out, to complete living within the walls of an institution, as in the nursing home in which the person is an invalid or semi-invalid and receives most of his care from other people. There are also public homes and homes under private religious, fraternal, and charitable auspices. Some homes for the aged present a complete range of facilities from efficiency apartments at one end, in which the person prepares his own meals and takes care of his own household routines, through an intermediate zone in which the individual lives in a room or apartment by himself but eats out and is furnished with some domestic service, to space in which infirmary care is given to semi-invalids and invalids. In addition to the wide variation in the physical characteristics and the auspices of institutional settings for older people, there is a very wide range in the programs of activity, education, therapy, and administration. In many localities there are also the so-called retirement communities in which older people live in single residences or apartments much as anyone would live in any other community. These communities provide special facilities, activities, and entertainment for older people and stress the fact that they are designed for them.

With such a wide variety of facilities in so many sections of the country and so much variation in management, there are difficulties in arriving at satisfactory classifications. But it should be possible, if funds and scientific interest are available, to select contrasting institutions, not so much in terms of formal characteristics, but in terms of psychological constructs, and make some comparisons between them in facilities and resources, stimulation patterns, incentives, constraints, modes of control, and so on and record the effects upon behavior. The independent variables would be found in the characteristics of the settings; the dependent variables, in both concurrent and long-term measures of behavior and adjustment of the residents. With data available about the people studied, controls could be placed on some background variables, and, for others, the variance could be analyzed by its sources.

It is but a step from this type of research to more deliberate control of the content and procedures of the settings with observations of the changes in behavior that appear as a result. Here the content of the setting is manipulated in order to locate significant relations.

CONCLUSION

In this paper we have raised a number of questions about research possibilities that would lead to better knowledge of the ways in which the environments of older people might be improved. The practical problems are not without theoretical significance, since we badly need some conceptualization of environment as a psychological manifold as well as a series of constructs which can be used to break the environment into meaningful continua on the basis of which research can be done. At present we are limited to cataloguing activities which have their source in stimulation and are not able to categorize them except in their superficial aspects.

Probably the most important developmental phenomenon relates to the manner in which a person organizes his energy so that he can be productive and obtain satisfaction from the interests and activities he undertakes. We know much about the effects of stimuli and situations in producing immediate behavior; we know much less about the manner in which the over-all environment, operating over time, facilitates the exploration of behavior possibilities.

At present there is a considerable shift in the thinking of psychologists about the origin of behavior. More and more we see the young organism as stimulus- and activity-oriented. Through searching the environment, he develops the interests and activities that permit effective organization of his life. For older persons who face a similar problem of organizing their free time, we may ask two questions: Through what attributes of stimulation may we set up personality-enhancing environments? Through what interests may we make the older person an active participant in living?

Summary

Since we are now engaged in creating environments for millions of older people in both the community and special institutions, questions about the relation between environments and meaningful activity have theoretical and practical implications.

A number of terms describe aspects of environment. For our purposes we are less interested in the immediate stimuli and short-term situations than we are in the climates, atmospheres, and settings which operate over a longer period.

The person with a lifetime of experience comes into the environments of old age as a complex structure of perceptive, motor, and intellective skills; of symbols and knowledge; of attitudes and value systems; of social skills and personal relations.

Difficulties arise in measuring the effects of environments on behavior. The check list, the diary, and the direct recording by observers in natural situations have advantages and disadvantages. A major problem concerns the units into which behavior is divided. Another concerns the separation of the relevant from the irrelevant iterative stimuli that make up the environment. Present literature indicates some success in isolating factors.

As a suggestion for a technique to study environments as wholes, it is proposed that such constructs as resources, incentives, and constraints be used and that summations be developed that will make it possible to determine their effects on behavior.

Another approach seeks information about the intrinsic characteristics of stimulation that keep organisms alert and active. Berlyne proposes novelty, uncertainty, conflict, and complexity as characteristics which promote vigilance. It is suggested that an analysis of existing environments be made for these attributes and that the effect of designed environments possessing these characteristics be analyzed. It is also suggested that we examine the possibilities of restoring to or creating in older people the curiosity and behavior that will enable them to develop their own interests and activities.

In the community older people live in a variety of environments. Data could be gathered about the effects of contrasting environments on behavior and personality. Such exploratory studies could be followed by studies in which settings are experimentally modified in order to measure the effects of environmental factors on behavior.

REFERENCES

Anderson, J.E. Freedom and constraint or potentiality and environment. *Psychol. Bull.*, 1944, **41,** 1-29.
Anderson, J.E. Psychological aspects of the use of free time. In Wilma Donahue, W.W. Hunter, Dorothy Coons, & Helen Maurice (Eds.), *Free time: Challenge to later maturity.* Ann Arbor: University of Michigan Press, 1958. Pp. 29-44.
Anderson, J.E. The use of time and energy. In J.E. Birren (Ed.), *Handbook of aging and the individual: Psychological and biological aspects.* Chicago: The University of Chicago Press, 1959. Pp. 769-796.
Barker, R.G., & Wright, H.F. *One boy's day: A specimen record of behavior.* New York: Harper and Brothers, 1951.
Barker, R. G., & Wright, H.F. *Midwest and its children.* Evanston, Ill.: Row, Peterson and Co., 1955.
Berlyne, P.E. *Conflict through arousal and curiosity.* New York: McGraw-Hill, 1960.
Burgess, E.W. Social relations, activities and personal adjustment. *Amer. J. Sociol.*, 1954, **59,** 352-360.
Cannon, W.B. *Wisdom of the body.* New York: W.W. Norton, 1939.
Chalfen, L. Leisure-time adjustment of the aged. II: Activities and interests and some factors influencing choice. *J. genet. Psychol.*, 1956, **88,** 261-276.
Fink, H.H. The relationship of time perspective to age, institutionalization, and activity. *J. Geront.*, 1957, **12,** 414-417.
Foote, N.H. Methods for study of meaning in the use of time. In R.W. Kleemeier (Ed.), *Aging and leisure: A research perspective into the*

meaningful use of time. New York: Oxford University Press, 1961. Pp. 155-176.

Friedman, E.A., & Havighurst, R.J. (Eds.) *The meaning of work and retirement.* Chicago: The University of Chicago Press, 1954.

Heron, W. The pathology of boredom. *Scient. Amer.,* 1957, **196,** 52-56.

Huizinga, J. *Homo ludens: A study of the play element in culture.* Boston: Beacon Press, 1950.

Kandler, H.M., & Hyde, R.W. A socialization activity index for a mental hospital. *The nursing World,* 1951, **125,** 343-345.

Kleemeier, R.W. The effect of a work program on adjustment attitudes in an aged population. *J. Geront.,* 1951, **6,** 373-379.

Kleemeier, R.W. Behavior and the organization of the bodily and the external environment. In J.E. Birren (Ed.), *Handbook of aging and the individual: Psychological and biological aspects.* Chicago: The University of Chicago Press, 1959. Pp. 400-451.

Kleemeier, R.W. The use and meaning of time in special settings: Retirement communities, homes for the aged, hospitals, and other settings. In R.W. Kleemeier (Ed.), *Aging and leisure: A research perspective into the meaningful use of time.* New York: Oxford University Press, 1961. Pp. 273-308.

Kleemeier, R.W., & Justiss, W.A. Adjustment to hearing loss and to hearing aids in old age. In I.L. Webber (Ed.), *Aging and retirement.* Gainesville: University of Florida Press, 1955. Pp. 34-48.

Mundel, M.D. *Motion and time study: Principles and practice.* Englewood Cliffs, N.J.: Prentice-Hall, Inc., 1950.

Pressey, S.L., & Kuhlen, R.G. *Psychological development through the life span.* New York: Harper and Brothers, 1957.

Tuckman, J., & Lavell, Martha. Self classification as old or not old. *Geriatrics,* 1957, **12,** 666-671.

CHAPTER 13

Sixty-five and Over

ROGER G. BARKER and
LOUISE S. BARKER

This paper reports a portion of the findings of a comprehensive ecological study of a Kansas and a Yorkshire town (Barker, R.G., 1960; Barker, R.G., & Barker, Louise S., 1961).[1] We are concerned with the old people of these towns and in particular with the degree and nature of their participation in the two community systems, breadth of their social relationships, and behavior of the old

[1] The collection and analysis of the data reported here were aided by a grant from the Carnegie Corporation of New York and by grants from the National Institute of Mental Health (M-1513). Opportunity to develop the theories in this paper was afforded the first author by a fellowship at the Center for Advanced Study in the Behavioral Sciences, Stanford University. A portion of the data has been published previously (Barker, R.G., & Barker, Louise S. Ecology of old people in Midwest, Kansas, and Yoredale, Yorkshire, *J. Geront.*, 1961, **16**(2), 144-149).

people in these towns. Some of the data are purely descriptive, some interpreted in the context of a particular theory of community functioning. The study exemplifies one approach to describing the ecological environment of behavior, a problem which must be solved if we are to deal effectively with the living conditions of old people.

We shall begin our paper with two simple observations. First, Yoredale has a flourishing Over 60 Club, whereas Midwest has no social organization for old people of any age. Second, the present investigators, who have deep roots in Midwest, coded their Midwest data by designating old age as sixty-five and over before they were introduced to Yoredale's sixty-year-olds. These two observations suggest that old age may have different meanings and age ranges in the towns. Our systematic data do not bear explicitly on this issue, but they support the suggestion sufficiently to emphasize the difficult technical problem of identifying the old people for research purposes. Our naïve assignment of the Midwest standard of old age, though not perfect, is probably as good a solution as could be found at the present; at any rate, old age in this paper begins at sixty-five in both Midwest and Yoredale.

Midwest is a county seat in eastern Kansas. Yoredale is a market town and the seat of a rural district council in North Yorkshire. Both towns are rural distribution centers, comparable in industry, governmental institutions, and nearness to cities. Midwest has a population of 715 and Yoredale 1,300. By careful selection, we aimed to eliminate community differences with which we are not concerned. The data were gathered from September, 1954, through August, 1955.

METHODS

The methods and concepts we have used are, in some ways, unique, so they will have to be described.

Behavior Settings

The unit by which we have described the community behavior systems of Midwest and Yoredale is the "behavior setting," the description of which is adapted from a previous study (Barker & Wright, 1955). When a mother writes, "There is a baseball game in progress on the playground across the street," she does not refer to any individual behavior, but to the behavior of the children en masse. The same is true of a newspaper item which reports, "The annual fete held in the St. Ambrose Church garden was a great success." These are

behavior settings. Behavior settings are highly visible behavior phenomena; laymen mention them in conversation and writing as frequently as they mention individual people. The ten behavior settings
of Midwest and Yoredale in which the old people of the towns spend
the greatest time, with the number of hours they spend annually in
each setting, are listed in Table 1.

TABLE 1
BEHAVIOR SETTINGS MOST HEAVILY POPULATED
BY OLD PEOPLE

Midwest		Yoredale	
Behavior setting	Occupancy time	Behavior setting	Occupancy time
Streets and side-walks	12,000	Streets and side-walks	33,000
Poole's Grocery	3,994	Market day	5,720
Kane's Grocery & Feed Store	3,966	Webber Bakery & Kitchen	2,480
The Midwest Weekly office	3,420	Maynard, Milk Re-tailer & Dairy	1,424
Murray's Grocery Store	3,312	Dale's Cafe	1,300
Cabell Department Store	2,963	Harbor & Lawson, Gen. Draper	1,100
Beattie's Shoe Re-pair Shop	2,790	Red Lion Pub & Dining Room	1,000
Graham's Lumber Yard	2,440	Kings Arms Pub & Dining Room	1,000
French & French Attorneys & Abstract Co.	2,440	Three Tuns Pub & Dining Room	1,000
Pearson Diary Farm	2,190	Pied Bull Pub	1,000

Note — All these names are fictitious.

Such behavior settings as these are entities with features and
boundaries as precisely identifiable as organisms, mountain ranges, or
gas jets. Of special relevance in the present connection, however, are
these characteristics of settings: (1) the ongoing patterns of extra-
individual behavior whose identity and function are independent of

the participation of particular people; (2) the circumjacent physical objects like walls, doors, fences, chairs, dishes, typewriters, ad infinitum, arranged in a characteristic spatial pattern at a particular temporal and physical locus; (3) the homeostatic nature of the systems which normally persist, often for years, at a relatively stable level.

A behavior setting is a behavior entity, but its laws of operation are not the laws of individual psychology. In the functioning of the Pearl Café in Midwest, for example, the availability and price of food, the season, the temperature, the size, lighting, and ventilation of the building, the state laws concerning hygienic practices, the customers, and the employees are all involved. We only begin to understand how these incommensurate phenomena are combined into the reliable entity so well known to Midwest residents.

Most of what we know about behavior settings is simple description, with any conceptualization close to the surface of the settings. Some of the behavior settings of one town are essentially duplicates of other towns. Groups of such similar settings are called "varieties of settings." Midwest has nine, Yoredale eleven, settings comprising the variety "restaurants and taverns." In this research we have handled only nonfamily behavior settings (settings outside the home).

Measures of Participation

The basic data we used to discover the nature and degree of participation by the old people in the behavior settings of the towns are territorial range, occupancy and exposure times, and depth of penetration of behavior settings.

Territorial range refers to the number of behavior settings a person or group of people inhabits in any capacity during a year. Data will show that the 162 old people of Midwest have a territorial range of 462. This means that one or more Midwest resident over sixty-five was observed in 462 of Midwest's behavior settings during the year of the study. It is sometimes convenient to express the territorial range as a percentage of the total settings in the town. We call this the "territorial index." The concepts of territorial range and territorial index are applicable to any designated characteristic of behavior settings—the territorial range of music in Midwest would refer to the number of behavior settings in which music, however defined, occurred.

Occupancy time is the number of hours a person or the members of an identified class of people spend in a behavior setting or territorial range of settings during a year. Examples have been given in Table 1. Here is another example: Old people in Midwest spend 89,050 hours a year in the 462 behavior settings of their territorial range. This is the occupancy time of Midwest by its aged; it is 9.5 per cent of the total occupancy time of all Midwest behavior settings by people of all ages. Occupancy time, divided by the number of people in the class under consideration, indicates the average time each class member inhabits the settings in its territorial range. For the old people of Midwest, the average occupancy time is 550 hours a year. This is the mean amount of time the Midwest aged spend in the town's behavior settings.

The residents of Midwest and of Yoredale not only inhabit settings for different amounts of time, but they participate in them in different capacities and with different degrees of involvement and responsibility. Six degrees of the latter have been defined and are represented as zones of increasing centrality. The more central the zone, the deeper the penetration and the greater the involvement and responsibility of its occupants in the functioning of the setting. These zones of penetration follow (adapted from Barker & Wright, 1955).

Zone 1—*Onlooker:* This is the most peripheral behavior setting zone. People in it are inhabitants of the behavior setting, but they take no active part in the behavior pattern. They are onlookers; they are tolerated but not welcomed; they have no power. They are the infant who accompanies his mother to Kane's Grocery, loafers at the post office, a child waiting in Lewis Stern's dental office while her friend has a tooth filled.

Zone 2—*Audience or invited guest:* The inhabitants of this zone have a definite place and are welcome, but they have little power in the setting; at most, they can applaud or express disapproval. These are the spectators at a ball game, those in the church congregation who are not members of the church, the mothers invited to the Cub Scouts' Christmas party.

Zone 3—*Member or customer:* Occupants of Zone 3 have great potential power, but usually little immediate power. They are the voting members and the paying customers who ultimately make or break the setting—the member at Rotary Club meeting, subscriber to *The Midwest Weekly*, pupil in the first-grade academic activities.

Zone 4—*Active functionary:* The inhabitants of this zone have an active part in the operation of the setting, but they do not lead it. Included here are the store clerk, church deacon, organization secretary. The people in this zone have direct power over a limited part of the setting.

Zone 5—*Joint leaders:* People who enter Zone 5 lead the setting with others. They have immediate authority over the whole setting, but their power is shared. They are Mr. and Mrs. Cabell, who jointly own and operate the Cabell Department Store; the president of the high school drama club and the sponsoring teacher, who share responsibility for the high school drama club meeting.

Zone 6—*Single leader:* Zone 6 is the most central zone. Here are all the people who serve as single leaders of behavior settings. These single leaders may have helpers or subordinate leaders from Zone 4. People in Zone 6 have immediate authority over the whole setting: the teacher in second-grade academic activities, the scout master at a Boy Scout troop meeting; the band leader at the summer band concert.

Behavior settings outside the territorial range of a person or class of people are sometimes identified as Zone 0. Behavior settings in penetration Zone 0 are, therefore, settings which the person or class of people does not inhabit.

The penetration rating we have used is maximal depth of penetration. This refers to the most central zone of a setting that any individual or any member of a designated class is observed to inhabit. For example, no Midwest citizen over sixty-five was observed to penetrate the behavior setting Kane's Grocery to a degree greater than Zone 3. All old people in Kane's Grocery were customers or onlookers (loafers) or accompanied other shoppers; none was employed as a clerk, bookkeeper, manager, or the like. The rating of the Midwest aged for penetration of Kane's Grocery is, therefore, three. On the other hand, the editor of *The Midwest Weekly* was a man in his seventies, so in this case the Midwest aged received a penetration rating of six for the setting *The Midwest Weekly.*

The standing behavior patterns of behavior settings have many discernible features. We have rated them on the following thirteen variables, called "action patterns": art, business, education, government, nutrition, orientation, personal appearance, philanthropy, professional leadership, physical health, recreation, religion, and social interaction. The names give a general notion of the variables; they are defined with precision in Barker and Wright

(1955). The ratings, ranging from zero to fourteen, indicate the degree to which the behavior described by a variable occurs in a setting. The ratings of the behavior setting Presbyterian worship service are art 6, business 0, education 3, government 1, nutrition 0, orientation 1, personal appearance 2, philanthropy 3, professional leadership 1, physical health 0, recreation 1, religion 8, and social interaction 6.

Action pattern ratings of six and above have special significance, for in this range an action pattern is so prominent a feature of the total behavior pattern of a setting that it is commonly seen as one of its major purposes. We have called these prominent action patterns. Examples of behavior settings with prominent ratings on the action pattern recreation are high school boys' basketball game, circus, and town band concert.

The degree to which an action pattern occurs in a setting is indicated by the rating just described. When all the behavior settings of a particular territorial range are considered, action pattern exposure time is the measure used. This is the average number of hours a year the inhabitants of a territorial range occupy behavior settings with the action pattern in question. For example, Midwest's 715 inhabitants occupy behavior settings where recreation is prominent for 135,138 hours during a year. The average exposure of Midwest's inhabitants to this action pattern is, therefore, 189 hours a year.

Exposure times can be determined for any degree of action pattern occurrence. In this paper exposure times are reported for action patterns that are prominent in behavior settings and of all degrees of occurrence in behavior settings (action pattern rated one and above). When the former are reported, they are identified as the exposure times of prominent action patterns; when the latter are reported, they are identified simply as action pattern exposure times. Action pattern exposure times include, of course, exposure to prominent action patterns.

RESULTS

Before presenting data on the special problems of the aged, some general information about Midwest and Yoredale is essential.

General Ecology of Midwest and Yoredale

Midwest's population is smaller than Yoredale's (715 versus 1,300), and it is smaller at each age level. Yoredale is larger in behavior settings (579 versus 494); less diversified in varieties of settings (77 versus 87); has fewer large (77 versus 98) and more small (122 versus 69) behavior settings; Midwest's citizens occupy the town's behavior settings more hours (1,313 versus 1,195, average) a year than Yoredale's (Table 2).

TABLE 2
GENERAL ECOLOGICAL DATA

	Midwest	*Yoredale*
Total population:	715	1,300
Infant population (1:11 and under)	24	41
Preschool population (2:0-5:11)	50	81
Younger school population		
(6:0-8:9)	28	72
Older school population (9:0-11:11)	26	51
Adolescent population (12:0-17:11)	50	107
Adult population (18:0-64:11)	375	770
Aged population (65 and over)	162	178
Number of behavior settings	579	494
Varieties of behavior settings	77	87
Behavior setting occupancy time:		
Small (under 56 hours)	122	69
Medium (56-6,929 hours)	380	329
Large (over 6,929 hours)	77	98
Behavior setting occupancy time	1,313	1,195

Note — 1:11 stands for one year, eleven months, and so on.

The community's exposure to action patterns and prominent action patterns is reported in Fig. 1. Action patterns are placed on the abscissa of the graph in order of their exposure times in Midwest. It will be seen that the average exposure to the action pattern social interaction is over 1,100 hours a year in both Midwest and Yoredale; it exceeds all other action patterns in exposure time. At the lower end of the list, exposure to religion is fewer than 200 hours a year in both towns.

The curves representing action pattern exposure times in Midwest and Yoredale are, in general, parallel; the product-moment correlation between exposure times in the towns is .94; it is .98 for prominent action patterns. The exposure time to prominent action patterns in each of the towns, however, differs considerably from exposure to action patterns on all rating levels in the same town. The correlation between the two exposure times is .46 in Midwest and .44 in Yoredale. It is clear that action pattern exposure time and exposure to prominent action patterns have little in common, even though the former includes the latter. This is not unexpected, since exposure to some prominent action patterns contributes less than 2 per cent of the total action pattern exposure time. This is true, for example, of philanthropy; the behavior "giving to good causes" frequently occurs as a minor part of the total behavior pattern of a setting like church worship service, where it is rated less than six. Philanthropy seldom occurs—and then only for short durations—as the dominant feature of a behavior setting. One of the rare instances is the Red Cross fund drive, where philanthropy is rated more than six.

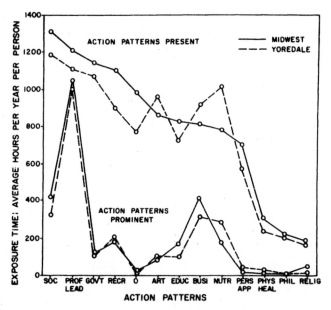

FIG. 1. Exposure of total population to action patterns.

The data of Fig. 1 reveal important differences between the towns. Midwest citizens are exposed to ten of the thirteen action patterns for longer times than Yoredale citizens. The excess of the exposure in Midwest varies from 214 hours a person a year for orientation to twenty-three hours a person a year for religion. The three action patterns to which exposure is greater in Yoredale are nutrition (235 hours excess), business (111 hours excess), and art (100 hours excess). Community differences in exposure to prominent action patterns are much smaller. Exposure is greater in Midwest to seven action patterns, and it is greater in Yoredale to six action patterns.

Here, then, is background information about the populations of Midwest and Yoredale, and about the number, variety, size, and action pattern characteristics of their behavior settings. These data define in general terms the nature of the public, nonfamily habitat areas of the towns; they describe some of the environmental conditions the towns provided for old people.

In very general terms, this background information indicates that Midwest has fewer inhabitants and more behavior settings than Yoredale, that it is, therefore, less densely populated; and that Midwest's citizens are exposed to its public behavior areas and the action patterns they contain for longer times. The background information shows, too, that exposure to different action patterns varies greatly in both towns, the greatest exposure time being more than six times that of the smallest exposure time. The relative amounts of time, however, to which Midwest and Yoredale citizens are exposed to these action patterns is remarkably similar.

Territorial Range of the Aged

The territorial range of each age group is given in Fig. 2. According to these data, the old people of Midwest have a larger territorial range than those of Yoredale (this difference between the towns is not peculiar to the old inhabitants; Midwest's territorial ranges are larger than Yoredale's at all age levels); the relative excess of the territorial ranges in Midwest decreases from infancy to adulthood and increases again in old age; the territorial ranges of the old people of Yoredale and Midwest are almost the same as the territorial ranges of the adolescents of the towns; and the old people of Midwest and Yoredale stand in almost identical relations to other age groups with respect to territorial range. These statements hold for territorial indexes, too (the percentage of the towns' behavior settings in the various territorial ranges).

In interpreting these data, it is essential to bear in mind that the smaller territorial ranges of Yoredale age groups occur in spite of greater populations at each age. Yoredale's smaller territorial ranges are not, therefore, a consequence of having fewer people than Midwest to inhabit the town's settings. Midwest's 162 old people in-

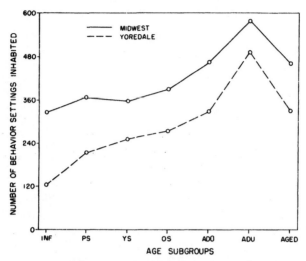

FIG. 2. Territorial ranges of age subgroups.

habit a greater number and percentage of Midwest's 579 settings than Yoredale's 178 old citizens inhabit of Yoredale's 494 settings. In spite of the greater population, Yoredale's old people live in a more limited range of the town, both absolutely and relatively, than Midwest's old people (67 per cent or 332 of Yoredale's settings versus 80 per cent or 462 of Midwest's).

Penetration of Behavior Settings by the Aged

Data regarding depth of penetration of aged citizens into the behavior settings of Midwest and Yoredale are shown in Table 3, where the number and percentage of settings penetrated to each zone are given. These data show that the old people of Midwest penetrate the town's behavior settings to peripheral levels (zones 1 and 2) and performance levels (zones 4, 5, and 6) more frequently than the old people of Yoredale. This is true both in absolute numbers of settings and percentage of settings. Yoredale's old people, on the other hand, are more frequently noninhabitants of the town's behavior settings (Zone 0), as already noted, and penetrate to Zone 3 (the level of members) more frequently than Midwest's old people.

These town differences are not peculiar to the old people. In Fig. 3, data on penetration to zones 4, 5, and 6 (performers) are provided for all age groups. This figure shows that at every age

TABLE 3
PENETRATION OF BEHAVIOR SETTINGS BY THE AGED

Maximal penetration zone	*Midwest*		*Yoredale*	
	Number of settings	Percentage of settings	Number of settings	Percentage of settings
0(Stranger)	117	20	162	33
1(Onlooker)	65	11	1	0+
2(Guest)	80	14	41	8
3(Member)	176	30	212	43
4(Functionary)	64	11	44	9
5(Joint leaders)	49	8	27	5
6(Single leader)	28	5	7	1

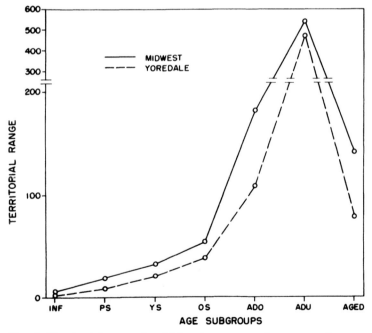

Fig. 3. Territorial ranges in which subgroup members are performers.

Midwest citizens are more frequently performers than Yoredale citizens. Fig. 3 shows, too, that in both towns aged citizens are performers in slightly fewer behavior settings than adolescents are.

Age Segregation

Behavior settings differ not only in the degree to which they are inhabited and penetrated, but also in the characteristics of the people who inhabit and penetrate them. Some settings are inhabited only by males, others only by females. Here we are concerned with segregation of behavior settings on the basis of age.

Data on the degree to which the old people of Midwest and Yoredale associate with other age groups in the behavior settings they inhabit are given in Fig. 4. According to these data, all age groups are present in more behavior settings of the territorial range of Midwest old people than of Yoredale old people. This is true at every age level. In general, age segregation is less frequent in Midwest than in Yoredale. The position of old people among other age groups with respect to degree of segregation is equivalent in the two towns.

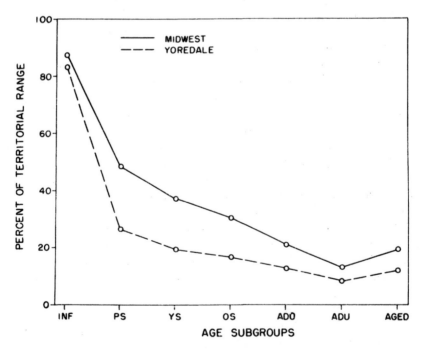

FIG. 4. Percentage of territorial ranges in which all ages are inhabitants.

Occupancy Time in Old Age

Behavior setting occupancy time is the number of hours a class of people inhabits the behavior settings of a town or territorial range in a town. We have already reported that the mean occupancy time of the total population of Midwest is greater than that of the total population of Yoredale; the two occupancy times are 1,313 and 1,195 hours a year a resident, respectively; thus Yoredale's occupancy time is 91 per cent of Midwest's.

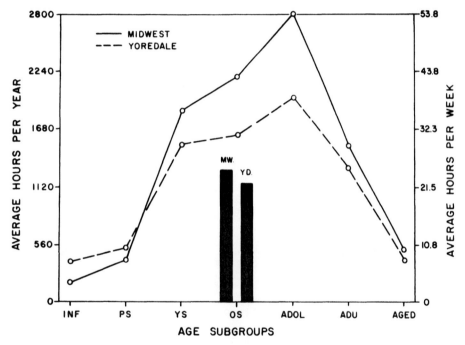

Fig. 5. Occupancy times of total populations (bars) and of age subgroups (lines).

The mean occupancy times of the total population of the towns and of all age groups are plotted in Fig. 5. These data show that the aged citizens of Midwest occupy the behavior settings in their territorial range for 550 hours a year, on the average, and that for the old people of Yoredale the occupancy time is 415 hours. The lower occupancy time of Yoredale's old people is in accord with that of the whole population; the deficit, however, is greater. The occupancy time of Yoredale old people is 75 per cent as great as that of Midwest old people, instead of 91 per cent when all citizens are included. Yoredale old people differ from Midwest old people more than Yoredale differs from Midwest as far as occupancy of behavior settings is concerned. In the towns there is a similar discrepancy. The mean occupancy time of the old people of Midwest is 42 per cent as great as that of the whole population, whereas the mean occupancy time of Yoredale old people is 35 per cent as great as that of the whole population. Yoredale old people differ from the town as a whole more than Midwest old people differ from Midwest as a whole. The behavior setting occupancy time of the old people in both towns is on the level of preschool children.

Action Pattern Exposure Time

The exposure times of the aged of Midwest and Yoredale to the thirteen action patterns are shown in Fig. 6. These data show that there is great similarity between the towns in the degree to which their old people are exposed to action patterns. The correlation between action pattern exposure times in the two towns is .96; it is .93 for prominent action patterns. The data of Fig. 6 show, too, that the old people of Midwest are exposed to most action patterns for a

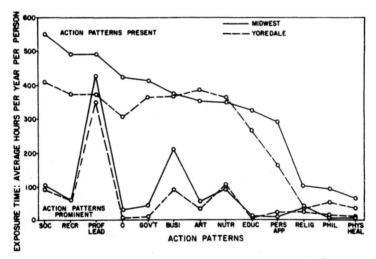

FIG. 6. Exposure of aged populations to action patterns.

greater length of time than Yoredale old people. On only one action pattern, nutrition, is the exposure time in Yoredale greater at both rating levels; in the case of art, personal appearance, and physical health the Yoredale aged have greater exposure at one rating level.

In these respects, the old people of Midwest and Yoredale mirror the towns. The parallels are evident in Fig. 7, where the exposure times of the aged citizens and of all inhabitants are presented. The correlations between the action pattern exposure times of the

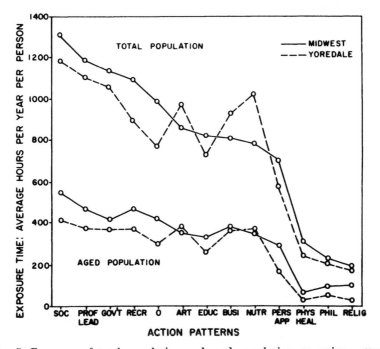

Fig. 7. Exposure of total population and aged populations to action patterns.

aged and of the total population are .96 and .99 for Midwest and Yoredale respectively; they are .98 for both towns in the case of prominent action patterns.

Data too extensive to be presented here show that the exposure times of action patterns are lowest in early childhood and old age. The general picture is essentially the same as that which holds for behavior setting occupancy times (Fig. 5). The situation of the old people of Midwest and Yoredale can, in these respects, be described as regressive, for there is a difference between adulthood and old age of the sort that exists between adulthood and childhood. We shall call this phenomenon "environmental regression."

Environmental regression occurs with territorial range and behavior setting penetration. In these cases, regression to about the level of adolescents occurs in old age, whereas occupancy of behavior settings and exposure to action patterns regress to preschool age levels. It appears that the old people of both Midwest and Yoredale maintain their contacts and positions in behavior settings on a higher level than they maintain their occupancy of the settings and exposure to action patterns.

This is not the whole story which our data tell about action pattern exposure time. Further analysis shows that there are some differences between the old people of Midwest and Yoredale that are not manifestations of general community differences. If environmental regression were uniform for all action patterns, exposure to every action pattern in old age would be 42 per cent of the community's exposure time in Midwest, and it would be 35 per cent in Yoredale. These are the expected exposure times, because the old people of Midwest and Yoredale occupy behavior settings 42 per cent and 35 per cent as long as the average resident. We have computed the exposure times expected in old age if exposure to all action patterns were in complete harmony with exposure in the community, and we have compared these expected exposure times with the actual exposure times in old age. The ratios of actual to expected exposure times are given in Table 4 in per-cent terms:

$$\frac{\text{actual exposure time}}{\text{expected exposure time}} \times 100.$$

These percentages, called "selection ratios" in the discussion, indicate relative deviation in old age from the community norms of action pattern exposure. Where the selection ratio is greater than 100, there is relative overselection for the action pattern in old age; where the ratio is less than 100, there is relative underselection. In the former case, regression in action pattern exposure times is less than regression in occupancy of behavior settings; in the latter case, it is more.

The data in Table 4 tell a number of things about selection of action patterns in old age.

1. There are great deviations from expected exposure times in both towns, ranging from less than twenty per cent of the ex-

TABLE 4
ACTION PATTERN EXPOSURE TIMES OF THE AGED EXPRESSED AS PERCENTAGES OF EXPECTED EXPOSURE TIMES

Midwest		*Yoredale*	
Action pattern	Percentage	Action pattern	Percentage
Action pattern rating 1+			
Religion	122	Recreation	122
Business	110	Business	117
Nutrition	106	Art	115
Orientation	103	Orientation	115
Recreation	103	Education	106
Social interaction	100	Nutrition	102
Art	98	Social interaction	101
Personal appearance	98	Government	99
Philanthropy	95	Professional leader-	
Professional leader-		ship	98
ship	94	Personal appearance	81
Education	93	Philanthropy	73
Government	87	Religion	60
Physical health	46	Physical health	46
Action pattern rating 6+			
Orientation	273	Religion	267
Art	174	Orientation	147
Religion	173	Art	122
Philanthropy	170	Personal appearance	106
Nutrition	129	Nutrition	102
Business	121	Professional leader-	
Personal appearance	108	ship	99
Professional leader-		Recreation	82
ship	98	Business	82
Government	84	Social interaction	76
Recreation	76	Philanthropy	60
Social interaction	57	Physical health	27
Physical health	33	Government	24
Education	18	Education	5

pected exposure time to more than two and one-half times the expected exposure time.

2. Deviations from expected values are less for action patterns than for prominent action patterns.

3. The rank order correlations between the towns in the selection ratios of Table 3 are .30 for action patterns and .67 for prominent action patterns.

4. When action patterns on all rating levels are considered
   (a) the old people of both Midwest and Yoredale are exposed to a slightly greater degree than expected to business (selection ratio above 109);
   (b) they are exposed to physical health less than expected (selection ratio below forty-seven);
   (c) Midwest old people are exposed to religion more than expected (selection ratio 122) and Yoredale old people are exposed to religion less than expected (selection ratio sixty).

5. When prominent action patterns are considered
   (a) the old people of both towns are exposed to a greater degree than expected to religion, orientation, and art (selection ratios above 121);
   (b) they are exposed to a lesser degree than expected to government, education, physical health, social interaction, and recreation (selection ratios below eighty-five);
   (c) Midwest old people have higher selection ratios than those of Yoredale for orientation, philanthropy, government, art, and business (Midwest selection ratios exceed Yoredale selection ratios by more than thirty-eight points); the old people of Midwest have a lower selection ratio for religion (Midwest selection ratio lower by ninety-four points).

In summarizing these findings, we find that either through choice or necessity the old people of both Midwest and Yoredale over-inhabit behavior settings where religion, orientation, and art are prominent and where business occurs, and they underinhabit settings where education, physical health, government, social interaction, and recreation are prominent. The greatest discrepancy between the towns is religion. Yoredale old people greatly overinhabit behavior settings where religion is prominent, and they underinhabit settings where religion occurs; Midwest old people overinhabit religious settings at both rating levels.

These data say nothing about the actual level of exposure times for the aged of Midwest and Yoredale, which have already been reported. The present data measure action pattern exposure relative to expected exposure (the exposure which would occur if average citizens had the behavior setting occupancy times of old people). Selection ratios above and below 100 indicate deviations from these theoretical norms in the territorial ranges of old people.

We found no evidence that the selection processes occur this way in other age groups. For example, the rank order correlations between the selection ratios for old people and for adolescents are –.62 in Midwest and –.32 in Yoredale for action patterns, and they are –.05 in Midwest and –.10 in Yoredale for prominent action patterns. The selection ratios are characteristic of the old people, and for a few action patterns the selection ratios are unique to the old people of one town. This is one of the few ways we have been able to discover in which the environmental situations of the old people of Midwest and Yoredale fail to reflect general community differences which also appear at most other age levels. It must be emphasized, however, that these processes operate in a narrow range. After all, they do not disturb the correlations of .93 to .99 between action pattern exposure times in old age and in the communities as a whole. But, even these correlations, based as they are on a wide range of exposure times, leave some freedom for different aging processes.

THEORY OF BEHAVIOR SETTINGS

Behavior settings were useful units for describing the environments of the old people of Midwest and Yoredale. This is not the end of their usefulness. The dynamic properties of behavior settings appear to clarify some community differences we discovered.

Behavior settings are complicated entities with dynamic properties we are only beginning to understand. Our work in Midwest and Yoredale, however, led us to a theory about one dynamic property of settings which appears relevant in the present connection. This theory has three major parts.

The first part states that a behavior setting is a homeostatic system with controls that maintain the setting intact at a relatively stable functional level when operating under varying conditions. The stability of a behavior setting comes from its multiple independent controls. Some of these sources of stability reside in the setting itself; some involve input and feedback circuits which couple the setting with external conditions; other control loops link the setting with its inhabitants and other internal components. We regret that it is not possible to give evidence for this conception of behavior settings here; it will have to be taken as a postulate, but we are sure many have personally experienced the strength of a setting's control mechanisms when they have tried to change the functioning of one of them, such as a college class. The inertia one encounters is frequently irresistible.

The second part of the theory is that the setting and the people who inhabit it stand in the relation of thing to medium, respectively. We use the terms "thing" and "medium" in the way Heider defined them (Heider, 1959). Things are entities which are internally constrained. They have internal forces that impose patterns on their own internal components and on external entities that are coupled with them. A chair is a thing with respect to its legs, its back, its arms, and with respect to people who sit in it; its form is impressed on them. A sentence is a thing with respect to the words that compose it and the meaning a reader gets from it. The components of a thing have little freedom; an increase in their freedom leads to their destruction. Things are not docile.

A medium, on the other hand, is externally constrained; its freedom is not limited by its own internal arrangements, but by external forces that play on it. The parts of a chair when it is dismantled and the words of a sentence as they occur in a dictionary have the qualities of a medium. An appropriate external force may impose a wide range of forms on them: the parts of the chair become a bed or rose trellis; the words of the sentence express another idea. A medium is docile.

Different thing-medium relations are common in nature. According to Heider's analysis, the possibility of perception from a distance depends on it. Molecules of the air are media to a vibrating tuning fork, which is a thing in relation to them. It is because of this relation that the molecules can transmit the wave pattern imposed on them by the fork. Small entities are frequently the component media of circumjacent entities that have the relation of things to them. When a jet of gas issues under pressure from a small opening of a container, the molecules of the gas are the media of the jet. The jet is the superordinate thing—it constrains, according to the laws of gaseous jets, the behavior of the molecules, which still, however, behave according to molecular laws (of thermal agitation, for example).

In this and every case where a system is made of an entity and its component media, the characteristics and laws of the interior elements, the media, differ from those of the entity, the thing, yet the two are closely coupled. The laws of molecules are not the laws of gas jets. Such facts as these present science with the fundamental problem of how to account for and incorporate, in a single system of understanding, phenomena as disparate as molecules and gas jets, words and sentences, bats and crickets, people and behavior settings.

We have by no means solved this problem. What we now propose does not bridge the conceptual gap between molecules and gas jets, words and ideas, people and behavior settings, but it does suggest one way in which elements on one level of a system enter, in a derivable way yet according to their own laws, the structure and processes of superordinate entities which also continue to operate according to their own laws. This involves putting together behavior settings and the ideas of thing and medium, but it applies generally to any homeostatic system and its component media.

According to Heider, a medium is always a manifold of elements; quality of a medium is a property of the manifold, not the separate elements. A single element of such a manifold has properties of a thing to a high degree; a single molecule, a single word, a single cricket player have limited medium-quality. Multiple independent elements are essential. Other things being equal, the number of parts of a set of entities is directly related to the medium potentialities of the set. A baby's single word provides him with a poor medium for expressing his much-more-than-single ideas and desires; 270 words at two years are a better verbal medium; with a 1,000-word vocabulary more can be said better, and so on. There are many ways in which the medium-quality of a medium is reduced; one of them is a reduction of elements in the medium manifold.

The third part of the theory states that for every homeostatic level of a thing with internal media there is an optimal number of elements in its internal medium manifold. Every setting has an optimal number of inhabitants for its functional level. The setting baseball game calls for twenty participants, eighteen players and two officials; in Midwest the setting first-grade academic activities is believed to do best with twenty-three inhabitants, twenty-two pupils and one teacher. However—and this is crucial—the homeostatic mechanisms of a behavior setting maintain the setting intact and the functional level essentially unchanged when the medium-quality of its component manifold is reduced below the optimal level in the number of its inhabitants. This can occur, of course, only within limits, but, to the degree that it does occur, certain consequences follow the inhabitants who remain in the medium manifold: the strength of the forces acting on the individual inhabitants increases, and the range in the direction of the forces acting on the individual inhabitants increases.

There is nothing mysterious about this simple arithmetic: as long as the homeostatic controls maintain the functional level of the setting, the same strength and pattern of forces is distributed among fewer persons. Accordingly, these people are pressed more strongly in more directions.

We shall now consider our findings about the old people of Midwest and Yoredale in the light of this theory and certain ecological facts about the towns. Here is the argument:

People are component media of behavior settings.

Behavior settings are homeostatic systems with optimal media requirements at each homeostatic level.

Within a limited range, homeostatic mechanisms maintain the functional level of a setting when the inhabitants fall below the optimum number.

Midwest and Yoredale settings are equivalent in the above respects, but Midwest settings are more frequently below the optimal level in number of inhabitants than Yoredale settings, therefore the inhabitants of Midwest settings, compared with those in Yoredale settings, are pressed by stronger forces in more directions.

The manifestations of these predictions take many forms, and we have not collected data on the aged of Midwest and Yoredale relevant to all of them. The ones on which we do have information are marked by an asterisk. The more obvious manifestations follow. Because of the strong forces acting on them, residents of Midwest, in comparison with those of Yoredale, (1) participate in more settings * (2) more intensively (3) for longer periods of time * in (4) more difficult tasks and (5) more responsible positions.* (6) They experience greater insecurity and (7) more frequent success and (8) failure. Because of the varied directions of the forces, residents of Midwest, in comparison with those of Yoredale, (9) engage in more varied activities * on (10) lower maximal levels of performance. Reduction below the optimal number of people who make up the component medium of the behavior settings has consequences for the behavior settings, too. Because of the stronger forces acting on the inhabitants, particularly at the boundaries, the behavior settings of Midwest, in comparison with those of Yoredale, are less selective about their inhabitants. Furthermore, a greater number of Midwest inhabitants is essential to the functioning of the setting.

Two characteristics of Midwest and Yoredale operate to increase the magnitude of the theory's crucial variables and increase the probability of the predicted consequences. First, there is evidence that the average homeostatic level of Yoredale's settings is not equal to that of Midwest's, as the theory assumes, but is, in fact, lower. To the degree that this is true, the pressure on Yoredale citizens is further reduced below that already derived from the relative overpopulation of the Yoredale settings. The evidence for the lower homeostatic level of Yoredale's behavior settings comes from the greater centralization of institutional control in England and the weaker local autonomy of behavior settings in Yoredale. In fact, 45 per cent of Yoredale's settings have limited local control of their plans and policies. This is true, for example, of the banks, the cooperative store, the milk collection depot, and the railroad station. Thirty-three per cent of Midwest's settings are similarly limited in local authority. It seems tenable that among otherwise equivalent behavior settings those which have complete autonomy over their affairs must carry a greater load of functions and responsibilities, and thus have a higher homeostatic level than those which are not locally autonomous.

The second relevant characteristic of the towns in the present connection is the difference in the meaning of old age. We judge that this itself may be a consequence of differences in behavior setting pressures, which, when made formal, enter as independent, salient features of the community situation. In Midwest there are many more graduations and matriculations than in Yoredale, but none from adulthood to old age; there is no welcoming Over 60 Club and retirement banquet. Most Midwest citizens drift into retirement, whereas it is formally acknowledged in Yoredale. This more frequent designation of old age as a special period of life with a definite beginning serves, in effect, to increase the unsuitability of Yoredale old people for many behavior settings. The reduced pressure for participation, therefore, is even less effective than the same pressure would be in Midwest. Undoubtedly part of the greater regression in participation in behavior settings in Yoredale resides herein.

Other ideological differences in the towns are probably the

source of some of the Midwest-Yoredale differences peculiar to the aged of the towns, but the importance of these unique differences relative to the over-all community differences is small in the present case, suggesting that differing ideologies may be of minor significance in determining the place of age groups and other population subgroups in a community system.

Here, then, is a theory of community functioning to account for the major findings of our research. According to it, Midwest citizens are under greater pressure than Yoredale citizens to participate widely and deeply in the behavior settings of the town, and this difference in pressure is exhibited with special clarity when it operates upon deviant groups that are, in varying degrees, unsuited to the demands of behavior settings (the selective screens of the community). This, as we see it, is the source of the wider, deeper environment of Midwest old people and young people, too, and of the lesser regression of old people in Midwest from the community norms.

The pressures from the homeostatically maintained forces of Midwest's relatively undermanned behavior settings are not only more manifest in their impact on some kinds of people than on others, but they are more evident in connection with some behavior than with other behavior. Our findings indicate, as seems reasonable, that measures based on presence or absence (territorial range and penetration) are less sensitive to these forces than measures of duration (behavior setting, occupancy times, and action pattern exposure times).

According to the theory, Midwest old people are not different from Yoredale old people in their motives, abilities, and basic ideologies and under the lesser pressures of Yoredale would behave as Yoredale old people behave. We heard reports in Yoredale of the war years when Yoredale behavior settings were undermanned. Judging by the reminiscences, the transformation of life in the town was impressive in precisely the directions we would predict; in particular, old people came out of retirement and participated with evident gusto and effectiveness in maintaining old and manning new settings.

We shall end this report with some concrete data. The lists below contain the behavior setting varieties in which Midwest and Yoredale old people were performers (entered behavior settings to zones 4, 5, and 6) during the survey year. The number of behavior settings in the three categories of the varieties are given, too. These lists may convey some impression of the different duties and opportunities the environments of Midwest and Yoredale present to their aged citizens.

Varieties of behavior settings in which old people are performers follow.

In Midwest, but not in Yoredale
Barbers and beauticians
Educational groups, academic
Educational groups, music
Elections (polling places)
Fire station
Food sales
Government and school offices
Hardware and home furnishers
Hotels and rooming houses
Insurance agents
Laundries
Libraries
Motor vehicles, sales and service
Newspapers and printers
Parties
Streets and sidewalks
Watch repair and jewelry shops
Volunteer work groups
(Total behavior settings: 36)

In Yoredale, but not in Midwest
Athletic contests, outdoors
Restaurants and pubs
(Total behavior settings: 4)

In both communities
Athletic contests, indoors
Builders, repairers, and suppliers
Courts
Dairy barns
Dinners and banquets
Drug and department stores
Fairs, circuses, and carnivals
Fund and membership drives
Food and feed distributors
Funerals
Meetings, executive
Meetings, organization business
Meetings, social (cultural)
Meetings, social (recreational)
Outings
Plays, concerts, and programs
Recognition programs
Religious services and classes
(Total behavior settings:
Midwest, 92; Yoredale, 67)

REFERENCES

Barker, R.G. Ecology and motivation. In M.R. Jones (Ed.), *Nebraska symposium on motivation, 1960*. Lincoln: University of Nebraska Press, 1960. Pp. 1-49.

Barker, R.G., & Barker, Louise S. Behavior units for the comparative study of culture. In B. Kaplan (Ed.), *Studying personality across culture*. Evanston, Ill.: Row, Peterson & Co., 1961. Pp. 457-476.

Barker, R.G., & Wright, H.F. *Midwest and its children*. Evanston, Ill.: Row, Peterson & Co., 1955.

Heider, F. On perception, event structure and the psychological environment; selected papers. *Psychol. Issues,* 1959, **3,** 1-123.

CHAPTER 14

Expectations of Supervisors
Concerning Older Workers

ALASTAIR HERON and
SHEILA M. CHOWN

It will be readily agreed that a major determinant of
the psychological environment at work is found in the attitudes of one's
supervisors and fellow workers. Such attitudes are general, specific, and
clearly complex in their effect on relations among particular people
or between a person and the working group of which he is a member—
whether in a position of authority or otherwise. Here we are concerned with the expectations arising from the attitudes toward older
employees held by industrial supervisors. These are regarded as a
climate of opinion which must affect the status, well-being, and prospects of the older worker. No attempt has been made to probe the
undoubtedly complex origins of individual differences in expectations
which were anticipated and encountered. The new material presented
here was obtained during a survey of the aging in manufacturing

273

industry, carried out by the authors and their colleagues in 1958.[1]

Twenty-one firms were approached, and twenty of these agreed to participate in the survey. Each firm was drawn from a different subclass in nine of the thirteen manufacturing orders of the industrial tables according to the 1951 British Census. Of these twenty firms, seven were in industries over-represented on Merseyside, compared with England and Wales; the remaining thirteen industries were typical. This was a deliberate compromise between the conflicting needs for local involvement and wider generalization of the findings. Among them the twenty firms employed approximately twenty-five thousand people, paid hourly, of whom about two-thirds were men. Fifteen employed between four hundred and one thousand, three between one thousand and two thousand, and two over two thousand. In this connection, it should be noted that although only 6 per cent of the manufacturing establishments in England and Wales employ more than four hundred people, half the working population of the manufacturing industry is found in this minority of larger establishments. The industries represented were chemicals, rubber, food, light sheet metal, electrical equipment, paper and printing, and clothing. The percentage of male shop-floor workers over forty years of age proved to be 47.7, slightly below the national average of fifty. In seven firms, more than half the men were over forty, one firm having 70 per cent above this age; at the other extreme, there was a firm with only 32 per cent over forty. When the figures were further broken down into age groups, it was found that some firms had a great many men over fifty-five, whereas others had a preponderance in the forty to fifty-four age group. No firm had less than 11 per cent of men over fifty-five.

PROCEDURE

In each firm, permission was obtained to interview all managers (those in charge of a complete section of the factory) in whose departments a substantial majority of male workers was employed. Since time could not be spared to interview all the foremen (senior first-line supervisors), we selected the one in each department who happened to have the greatest variety of semiskilled jobs under his control. This selection procedure resulted in 101 pairs of interviews

[1] Material forming part of this paper has been drawn from a White Memorandum of the Medical Research Council, in course of publication by H.M. Stationery Office, London. It is reprinted with the permission of the Controller of Her Britannic Majesty's Stationery Office.

with departmental managers and one of their foremen. The results to be quoted are based on these 101 pairs.

At both manager and foreman levels the topics covered included preferred age for taking on new men, jobs considered suitable and unsuitable for older men, changes with age in efficiency, attitudes, and personality; labor turnover, timekeeping and absence, and opinions about retirement age. For foremen questions were added on learning and training; for managers, on age limits for promotion. Thus on one hand, we were trying to get at perceptions and opinions about firms' policy and practice on age questions and, on the other hand, at changes in shop-floor workers as perceived by their supervisors.

To reduce interviewer bias, fixed, open-ended questions were used in a given order, each supplemented by a predetermined range of follow-up questions.

RESULTS

The results will be summarized under the main topics already mentioned.

Efficiency

The inquiry into changes in work performance with age led, first and foremost, to statements about slowing up, mentioned by between one-third and one-half of the managers and foremen. For this, the age of onset was given at points ranging from forty-six to fifty-five by foremen and from fifty-one to sixty-five by managers. Only one-eighth said outright that efficiency decreased over forty; nearly half preferred to stress that in their view efficiency increased throughout the thirties and forties. Foremen more frequently than managers pointed out that older men compensated by putting more effort into their work or that they developed knacks through long experience.

Our pilot study, in which we had interviewed men on the shop floor, provided a comparison under this heading. In that study we saw approximately seventy men in each of three age groups, twenty-five to thirty-nine, forty to fifty-four, and fifty-five to seventy. Only in the fifty-five to seventy group did many men say that they had noticed themselves becoming slower or that their health was worse.

Physical Health

To managers and foremen in the main survey, the slowing down was, to some extent, seen as physical in origin. Between one-quarter and one-third pointed out, as the chief physical change, that men moved about more slowly as they got older. Another quarter mentioned that men became tired more quickly or that a general deterioration in health occurred. These broad answers were more frequent than mention of specific ills such as failing eyesight, chest trouble, or stomach ulcers, each of which was selected by a few managers and foremen (more often by managers in the case of the last two).

Learning and Training

Changes seen in men on the job are reflected to some extent in the changes in learning reported by foremen. About two-fifths mentioned slowness in learning, especially after forty years of age. The more cautious pointed out, however, that these older men were often more dependable, probably because of family ties and a desire for security, and might eventually do as well as a younger man who happened to be less strongly motivated. Similar answers were obtained when we asked managers and foremen for opinions about the best age at which to hire men for semiskilled work. The very young were not favored, being regarded as irresponsible and unsettled. About half preferred those with domestic responsibilities, one-third actually specifying the thirty-one to forty age group. Adaptability and trainability were mentioned by one-quarter, the optimum age range for these qualities being regarded as fifteen to thirty-five years.

Promotion

Managers were asked only about promotions to the foreman level, and whether there was in practice—as distinct from policy—an age bar. Half the managers said that there was no upper age limit for promotion, one-quarter said that there was an age limit above fifty, one-sixth mentioned ages between forty-one and fifty, and only a few fixed a limit at forty or below. Later, details of actual promotion ages for all their present foremen were obtained from eighteen of the firms. It was found that, of the 547 men involved, only two in seven had reached their foreman status later than the age of forty-five, only one in ten after fifty. The average age of promotion to foreman was, in fact, forty. Thus, whereas three-quarters of the foremen had gained promotion between the ages of thirty and fifty, three-quarters of the managers said that there was no upper age limit to promotion or gave an age over fifty. Reasons given for an age bar included a "general preference for younger men," "difficulties encountered with a pension scheme," "lack of ability," "lack of adaptability," or that a man is "not worth promotion if he has not gained it before a specified age."

Attitudes and Personality

Changes in work performance certainly accompany other changes with age, notably in attitudes and personality. A few of these changes have been mentioned in answers to questions about learning and hiring new men. A majority of managers and foremen saw most of these other changes as favorable. Nearly half thought that men in their forties needed less supervision, because they were responsible, reliable, and settled in their jobs. One-third said that men in their forties and fifties were more conscientious and less likely to skimp the job and waste time. These age groups were felt to be more interested in their work by one-quarter of their managers and foremen.

Several other improvements with age were mentioned, each by a number of supervisors. They are all rather similar, though expressed in different terms. Older people were described as more philosophical and detached in contrast with the young, who were felt to be always wanting something. Older people were said to like being trusted, to be loyal and cooperative, more tolerant, more reasonable, less impulsive, and less hotheaded and argumentative. It is interesting to note that in our shop-floor sample both the twenty-five to thirty-nine and forty to fifty-four age groups mentioned changes for the better in their own personalities, whereas only the twenty-five to thirty-nine group mentioned increased skill and experience at their job. On the other hand, a few managers and foremen considered that the older men were more awkward to handle because of their "I know it all" attitude. A few others mentioned a lack of adaptability or confidence, with a consequent tendency to avoid taking responsibility. Of course, men's natures do not all alter in the same way. Supervisors have different personalities, too, so that a man will react in one way to one person and in another way to another, but there is no doubt that the majority of supervisors found older men much easier to supervise than they found younger men. If we could sum up their remarks under one heading, it would be that older men work with a supervisor for the common aim of getting the job done, but younger men work more for themselves. This is consistent with the supervisors' subjective impressions about labor turnover, absence, and bad timekeeping. Two-thirds of the supervisors thought these indexes were better among older men, and only one in one hundred was prepared to describe them as worse. Between one-third and one-half thought that older men had fewer accidents. They explained this by saying that older men are less slapdash and know the dangers better than the younger ones, who rush into things without thinking (another possibility—not mentioned—is that older men may be moved away from work that is considered dangerous).

These impressions may be compared with factual information obtained from firms where reliable records were available. Labor turnover was indeed lower among older men. During 1957, 29 per cent of the twenty-five to thirty-nine age group left seventeen of the firms, whereas only 11 per cent of the forty to fifty-four and 10 per cent of the fifty-five to sixty-nine age groups did so. Within no age group were losses made good by replacements, the net figures being down by 18 per cent for the twenty-five to thirty-nine age group, 5 per cent for the forty to fifty-four, and 8 per cent for the fifty-five to sixty-nine age group. It has to be remembered that the 10 per-cent labor turnover in the fifty-five to sixty-nine age group includes retirements, so that one would naturally expect a larger discrepancy between turnover and intake here. Men between forty and fifty-four were the most nearly replaced age group, whereas only forty-eight men over fifty-five were hired in all seventeen firms. Actual figures for absence by age group of absentee were collected from twelve firms whose records were kept in sufficient detail to make this possible. The total for all twelve firms clearly showed that the average frequency of absence during 1957 decreased with age. Average length of absence, on the other hand, increased with age, from 8.5 days in the twenty-five to thirty-nine age group to 14.8 days in the fifty-five to sixty-nine group. These trends, however, were not present in all twelve firms: in two the largest number of absences was among the forty to fifty-four age group, whereas length of absence in five firms was lowest in this age group. Such individual differences among firms partly explain why no opinion obtained from supervisors is unanimous.

A question designed to elicit the extent to which interest in trade-union activities might alter with age was not very productive. About one-quarter of the managers and foremen did not know, and a roughly equal number said they had noticed no change.

Suitable Work for Older Men

It has been established by previous research that on work which is paced the average age is lower than on work which is not paced. This leads one to ask what happens to men who get too old for a particular paced job. This question could best be answered by studying men formerly engaged in paced work, but meanwhile one wonders what work is considered suitable for older men, at what ages they tend to be transferred from unsuitable work, and what, in the opinion of supervisors, constitutes unsuitable work. It was found that the most usual reason for transfers, given by one-quarter of the managers and foremen, was that the old job was too strenuous physically, involving lifting, awkward movement, or heavy manual work. Managers most often gave fifty-one to fifty-five as the age when this occurred, but foremen put it over fifty-five. A small number, about one-tenth, mentioned pacing or speed, and again over fifty was the age. An equal number referred to fineness and concentration, and about one in seven mentioned unfavorable conditions, including hazards.

Approximately half the managers and foremen said that in their departments it was not usual to have to transfer men from jobs because the jobs had become too much for them. There would seem to be alternative explanations for this: either most older men can continue to do all the jobs—in some cases more slowly, in others without showing clear signs of distress—or transfer was taking place unrecognized in the general course of rearrangement. By asking, "Are there *no* jobs which are unsuitable for older men?" an attempt was made to find out which was the case, but it produced very few answers.

As one might expect, when we asked about jobs to which men were transferred, we were usually given the complementary picture. About one-fifth of the supervisors mentioned less strenuous work, lighter work, or work with less strain; only one in twenty referred to work which was not paced. One-seventh mentioned such things as good hours, no night work, no hazards such as climbing, and more responsible jobs. Similarly, when we asked about work especially suitable for older men, lighter work was most often mentioned (by one-third), but work in which experience could be brought to bear was referred to by one in twelve and unpaced work by one in twelve. A list of all the jobs mentioned as suitable for older men who were transferred contains a high proportion of sweeping, cleaning, or other unskilled jobs, though there were some where specialized knowledge could be used. The jobs considered suitable for old newcomers were, without exception, very simple.

Each manager and foreman was asked whether he had ever tried to modify jobs or working conditions to make them more suitable for older men. Although it was not uncommon for general improvements to be mentioned in reply to this question, no respondent claimed to have had the needs of older men especially in mind.

Retirement

For the individual worker retirement is both an economic and psychological problem. In this investigation we were mainly concerned with the psychological aspects, in particular a fixed retirement age.

When asked, "Do you think that all men should be retired at the same age or should the age vary?" one in eight managers and foremen favored the fixed policy; in only one case were the manager and foreman in the same department.

Three-fifths of those preferring a fixed policy chose sixty as the best age; two-fifths, sixty-five. Their reasons fell almost entirely into three categories. They thought that "men were entitled to some leisure after a lifetime's work"; "if everyone retired at the same age, ill feeling was prevented, and everybody knew how they were placed"; "by the chosen age most people were tiring and not as fit as they once were."

The great majority of those interviewed preferred the idea of a flexible retirement age, and their reasons were usually based on the undoubted fact that workers of any given chronological age vary enormously in their capabilities, health, and attitude to work. Thus, about half thought that an individual's health ought to be the deciding factor, and an equal proportion mentioned individual differences in abilities. (Managers were more likely to mention individual differences than foremen were.) Between one-third and one-half said that retirement ought to be voluntary, depending on the man's choice and self-assessment. Approximately one-fifth pointed out that many men are so wrapped up in their work that they feel unwanted and finished when they have to give it up. (This belief was mentioned more often by foremen than managers.) One important point mentioned by one-sixth of the managers and by nearly one-third of the foremen was the need for an adequate pension. This colored their views on the desirability of a flexible retirement age, since it is obviously not sensible to ask an active, healthy man to retire with money insufficient to live on. About one in eleven suggested gradual retirement or getting another job as one way of meeting these needs. Data from the pilot study have some relevance here. One-third of a random sample of 225 men from the shop floor expressed a preference for a fixed retirement age, and the most popular ages were sixty-five and sixty, in that order. The reasons for choosing the fixed policy corresponded well with those given by managers and supervisors in the main survey, except that, among the men who had not been promoted at all, the additional item "promotion blocking" appeared. One-third of those choosing a fixed age stressed the need for an adequate pension.

Where a preference for flexible retirement ages was expressed, shop-floor workers again gave the same reasons as managers and foremen, but in a different order. A smaller proportion of workers mentioned fitness and ability, and more of them mentioned the idea that men need their work as an interest, feeling lost if deprived of it. These differences are in line with those already found between managers and foremen, suggesting that among people of different status there is a real difference in perception of the satisfaction men on the shop floor gain from work.

Opinions in Relation to Chronological Age

It has often been said that, as one becomes older, middle age recedes, always remaining about ten years beyond one's actual age. Since there might be a similar effect with the term "older man," provision was made for the way the actual age of the men being interviewed was related to the age at which they regarded the term an appropriate description of others. The topic was introduced by saying, "We have talked about 'older men' a good deal in the past few minutes. What age do you think of when 'older' is mentioned?" Most men of all ages regarded the fifties as the beginning of "older"; few in their thirties, however, suggested an age later than the fifties, whereas few in their sixties suggested any age earlier than the fifties. The answers of those in their own forties and fifties spread more widely, from the forties to the sixties. Simply stated, the younger the person interviewed, the younger his image of an "older man" was likely to be. There was no significant difference between managers and supervisors, thus occupational status apparently did not affect opinion on this point. This was, however, the one topic on which significant differences in reaction to the interviewer were found. The oldest and youngest interviewers (male and female, respectively) were consistently given higher estimates than the other two (also one man and one woman). We are at a loss to account for this difference, but since it is consistent for all ages, it served to widen the range of ages recorded.

These findings suggest that the age of the person speaking might have an important bearing on all his comments about changes in older men and age-related topics such as retirement. For this reason, all our results were analyzed according to the chronological age of the interviewee, and one significant difference was found: among foremen, in answer to the question about changes in work performance, more older foremen mentioned the value of the added experience and skill of older men. When all unfavorable changes in performance were taken together, it could clearly be seen that they decreased in number as the age of our interviewees increased. The difference is not unexpected, but it does underline the point that the fate of older men in a plant may, to some extent, depend on the age of the supervisory staff.

DISCUSSION

What, then, are the supervisors' expectations concerning men in the second half of their working lives?

By far the most outstanding expectation of supervisors is that men will tend to become slower at the job once they have passed the age of fifty, and some feel that this physical and mental slowing down is accompanied by a general deterioration in health. The spontaneous mention of "slowing up" is consistent with laboratory studies (Welford, 1958), examination of performance records (Bowers, 1952), supervisors' evaluations (Smith, 1953), and measured output for a man-hour (U.S. Bureau of Labor Statistics, 1956). All the industrial studies cited show the fall in performance to be relatively small, even after the age of fifty-five which is specifically referred to in the 1956 report.

We find that recognition of "slowing up," however, is usually accompanied by a good deal of tolerance on the part of supervisors. For one thing, they seem to appreciate that older men often put more effort into their work and that the skill acquired from experience helps compensate for some loss of speed. Even when extra effort and skill are no longer sufficient to disguise slowing, there is little need for the supervisor or the worker to worry about falling production for a long time, except on rapidly paced jobs. In one way we consider this tolerance unfortunate, for by the time everyone recognizes that a job change will have to be made, the firm often thinks it too late to make training the man for another job worthwhile.

Expectations about the behavior and attitudes of older workers seem to be very favorable. The man thirty, forty, or older is regarded as more reliable, reasonable, conscientious, and interested in his work than the younger man. Foremen and managers are quick to mention these personality qualities which must make their supervision easier. Managers and foremen also believe older men to be better time-keepers and have better attendance records and to show less turnover; these beliefs were substantiated by such records as were available in the firms we visited. Our findings on these matters reinforce much widely scattered previous evidence. (A particularly comparable example is to be found in *The Employment of Elderly Workers* [Industrial Welfare Society, 1950], in which a majority of 376 firms was reported to have used many of the same favorable adjectives.) It seems more than likely that these good points do a great deal to offset the effects on supervisory attitudes of decreased speed and physical deterioration.

Questioned about the meaning of the term "older man," managers and foremen revealed age differences among themselves, with the older ones more likely to give a higher age. The majority of managers and foremen, however, applied the term to those in or over their fifties, coincident with the age when slowdown became noticeable to them. As far as work performance was concerned, it seemed that older supervisors gave fewer unfavorable comments. Here is a hint that, if the average age of supervisors were lowered, attitudes toward older workers might become less favorable. Much here may depend on the type of work involved, the method of collecting data, and the age range of the shop-floor workers under discussion. According to Peterson (1954), the age of supervisors did not appear to affect the rating they gave to workers over sixty on over-all performance, and Kirchner and Dunnette (1954) found no significant age difference in the mean attitude score of supervisors toward older workers. (In this study, however, there were only twenty-seven supervisors of whom only eight were under forty.) Among the seventy shop-floor employees the older ones had a more favorable attitude to their older fellow workers.

We now come to the question of transfer. Here the supervisors' first reaction was often denial of job transfers. Most supervisors seem to expect their men, unless on very heavy physical work or hazardous work, to be able to carry on until retirement age. They regard the transfers which do occur as special cases, usually caused by illness or disability. Further discussion of jobs suitable for older men, however, revealed that job changes did take place. In some cases these were informal team changes and, therefore, were not regarded by the supervisor as transfers. Where completely different jobs were involved, the changes usually involved loss of both status and pay. The fact that supervisors avoided downgrading transfers, if they could, showed that they recognized this as a problem, but by the time they came to deal with it, the opportunity for achieving a more satisfactory solution had usually passed.

Managers and foremen appear to recognize that there are big individual differences in the ability of men beyond the normal retiring age to carry on their jobs. This was the reason given by the majority of supervisors for preferring flexible retirement policies. They certainly did not expect all shop-floor workers to wish to retire at any given age, and the majority of shop-floor workers seen in the pilot study agreed, preferring a flexible policy. This accords with the attitudes of industrial workers in California, reported by Crook and Heinstein (1958), where over half the workers were prepared to give an age for retirement only with qualifications, although the California group seemed readier to agree with fixed retirement as a policy than their British counterparts.

We have found supervisors benevolent but unimaginative on the question of the older worker and his problems. This might seem a harsh judgment if we neglected to note that supervisory attitudes are inevitably circumscribed—certainly in expression if not in formation—by the views and actions of top management. For example, one may express the conviction that the well-being of the semiskilled industrial worker beyond the age of sixty can best be promoted through action taken by industry itself to minimize the strains imposed on these men during the previous ten to fifteen years, but action of this kind can be initiated and sustained only by top management, which still needs to be convinced that it is necessary to find out what these strains are. Those responsible for job analysis are, at present, seldom, if ever, encouraged to carry out their work with an eye to discovering the causes of difficulty for older men. Stimulation of such an awareness by management could lead to genuine job modification in the interests of the older operator. As things are at present, jobs are modified only in an informal way, by altering the type of work handed out to each worker by the foreman. The idea of job modification is not new; during World War II, many industrial jobs were redesigned to make them suitable for women operatives. Similar work has, of course, been done in industrial rehabilitation in many firms.

Much more experimentation with methods of training and retraining, not only for the middle-aged and older worker, is required on the part of industry. Here we see the other side of the coin; although job analysis and work study are well-established, the special needs of the older worker are still neglected, and systematic training of the semiskilled remains in its infancy. As the attention of top management is drawn to the general need for training and retraining, the opportunity to ensure training methods appropriate to each major age group must not be lost. It is at such a point of potential progress that the supervisors' unimaginative outlook, however benevolent, may prove a serious obstacle. If they start with the assumption that it is not worth trying to train workers over forty because they are slowing down, training will have to start with the supervisors. It can be seen, therefore, that the climate of attitude is of considerable importance at all levels in industry as far as the well-being and prospects of the worker over forty are concerned. The problem will have to be simultaneously attacked at all levels if success is to be ensured.

REFERENCES

Bowers, W.H. An appraisal of worker characteristics as related to age. *J. appl. Psychol.,* 1952, **36,** 296-300.

Crook, G.H., & Heinstein, M. The older worker in industry. Berkeley: University of California Institute of Industrial Relations, 1958.

Industrial Welfare Society. *The employment of elderly workers.* London: Author, 1950.

Kirchner, W.K., & Dunnette, M.D. Attitudes toward older workers. *Personnel Psychol.,* 1954, **7,** 257-265.

Peterson, R.L. Effectiveness of older workers in a sample of American firms. In *Old age in the modern world.* Edinburgh: E. & S. Livingstone, 1954. Pp. 316-320.

Smith, M.W. Older worker's efficiency in jobs of various types. *Personnel J.,* 1953, **32,** 19-23.

U.S. Bureau of Labor Statistics. Job performance and age: A study of measurement. U.S. Bur. Lab. Stat. Bull., 1956, No. 1203. Washington, D.C.: U.S. Government Printing Office.

Welford, A.T. *Ageing and human skill.* London: Oxford University Press, 1958.

PART TWO

Successful Aging

INTRODUCTION

RICHARD H. WILLIAMS

Part Two continues with a level of analysis similar to the level in Section III of Part One. It is concerned with social personality and the immediate social worlds, or psychological environments, of older people. The emphasis here, however, is less on the ecological characteristics of these environments and more on the ways in which older people cope with immediate systems of behavior in which they participate directly.

The theory of action is useful as an analytical frame of reference in understanding the details of the structure and dynamics of the various parts of society. It is concerned with the development of social personality and the tendency of people to conform to moral behavior patterns in social control and social motivation. Conversely, it is also concerned with the genesis and development of deviant behavior, particularly with strains which have a cumulative tendency to produce deviance. One of the most important structural aspects of a social system is its framework of positions, without which it would be impossible to orient oneself to the behavior of others. There are many specific frameworks in organizations, and in addition there are some more general ones, the most important of which are age, sex, and social class.

A particularly important question is the extent to which shifts in social position change the individual's ability to meet such basic needs as wealth, power, recognition of achievement, and emotional satisfaction. When we look at the factual evidence already available, mostly from surveys, it becomes apparent, for example, that retirement is not a single major variable which necessarily involves a traumatic shift in social position. The consequences of a general shift in position with age must be viewed in function of a series of such factors as health (especially social and psychological health), personality, and fit between the preferred style of life and the realities of the individual's social life space. These factors cluster and are cumulative in their effects. They can and do produce a truly anomic, disorganized group among some aged who have a cumulative tendency to deviate toward withdrawal and extreme dependency. Fortunately this group appears to be small, but it creates a disproportionate drain on the energies of others, so that, unfortunately, it presents a real problem.

The theory of action is also very useful in the few studies of the aging process which study individual cases intensively over a period of time. The individual can be seen in the context of his social life space or his social system. His orientation to interaction in the system can be determined by special instruments and by his responses over time to indirect questions. Changes in his life space toward constriction or expansion become clear. His value system and satisfaction with life can be fairly accurately estimated, and insights into the dynamics of his personality can be gained. Thus it is possible to obtain a more systematic understanding of the structure and dynamics of aging. This approach can be strengthened by obtaining similar data from the various parts of the social world surrounding the individual who is the focus of study.

All the chapters in this part study variants of this general approach. They address themselves to various aspects of successful aging. By using the concepts of internalization and reciprocity of social roles, Tréanton (Chapter 15) bridges the gap which too frequently exists between sociological and psychological approaches. Through scale construction Havighurst (Chapter 16) tackles the problem of satisfaction directly. Reichard, who participated in the Berkeley seminar, delineated five personality types—the mature, the rocking-chair group, the armored, the angry men, and the self-haters.[1] She indicated that both adjustment and satisfaction may vary by personality type. Neugarten (Chapter 17) faces the very difficult problem of changes with age which may occur in the more covert aspects of personality dynamics. She presents preliminary evidence on probable significant changes in such matters as view of the external world, stance toward the world (active to passive mastery), available ego energy, and preoccupation with the problems of inner life. Williams (Chapter 18) suggests an approach in terms of the dynamics, energy transactions, and general stability of the individual social system.

All these approaches give new perspectives to aging. The theory of disengagement, referred to frequently in this section, is a notable example. All the chapters suggest that in modern society there is a normal process of growing old successfully which is probably more widespread than much of the literature on social gerontology would indicate. This view in no way minimizes the problems of older people, many of which are cumulative in character, but it should give new hope for the achievement of greater congruence between old age and mental health.

[1] Dr. Reichard's material was published separately in Reichard, Suzanne, Livson, Florine, & Petersen, P.G. *Aging and personality: A study of eighty-seven older men.* New York: John Wiley & Sons, 1962.

CHAPTER 15

The Concept of
Adjustment in Old Age

JEAN-RENÉ TRÉANTON

The word "adjustment," frequently used in geron-
tology, is rather confusing. Although this concept was most popular
between 1935 and 1945 (Cottrell, 1942; Shaffer, 1936; Young, 1940), it
has roots in the nineteenth-century intellectual tradition. In the
Darwinian school of thought, adjustment refers to the process of meeting a threatening environment successfully. At that biological level, it
designates that the organism has triumphed over any danger, fatigue,
or disease.

The responsive human organism is exposed to numerous
stimuli during its life. Its responses become reinforced, eliminated, or
elaborated in such a way that gradually a more complicated system of
responses to new, progressively more complicated stimuli is built up.
When this process deteriorates (with age, for instance), adjustment

decreases and may end in the radical incompatibility of the organism and its surroundings. This way of understanding the relations between the organism and the external world is inherited from the behaviorist school of psychology and is notably discussed in Kimball Young's book (1940).

Is this approach useful in understanding processes of old age? We may raise the question when we consider the caution and, sometimes, the obscurity of authors who use it in research or discussion. "Adjustment is usually indicated negatively as the degree of maladjustment. We may assume that the amount of tension, anxiety and frustration generated by the attempt to discover and play a given role is an index of the individual's adjustment to such a role" (Cottrell, 1942, p. 617). "In popular psychology, this much used term means anything from the passive toleration of the morally intolerable to the earning of a large income . . . ," states Cattell (1950, p. 262). Trying for a meaningful concept, he continues, "Adjustment describes the goodness of the internal arrangements by which an adaptation is maintained. . . . Until mental energy and goodness of adaptation can be measured, it is thus not possible to measure, except in theory, the goodness of adjustment" (Cattell, 1950, p. 263).

Without being absolute, one might say that it is necessary to rely on clinical (nonquantitative) methods in psychology to detect the symptoms of exhaustion, anxiety, nervousness, tension, and frustration which are generally considered the most typical symptoms of nonadjustment. When Cavan, Burgess, Havighurst, and Goldhamer (1949) utilize this dimension in the five criteria of general adjustment, they measure it through the observation of a person with psychiatric or psychological training.

It is certainly easier to get precise measurements of satisfaction. In fact, if not in theory, some research identifies adjustment with satisfaction or happiness. For instance, Havighurst and Albrecht state, "The terms *happiness* and *good adjustment* will be used interchangeably . . . , even though they do not have exactly the same meanings. Justification for this lies in the fact that the personal adjustment of older people depends largely upon their present happiness, much more than it does for younger people" (1953, p. 52). Reichard (1962) takes the position that feelings of inner satisfaction are a better index of adjustment to aging than actual role performance is.

Although these definitions do not coincide in detail, they agree on at least one point: the study of adjustment bears on the individual's state of mind, inner feelings, and subjective psychological reactions. The attitude inventory used by Havighurst and Albrecht (1953) is designed to measure the individual's feelings of happiness, usefulness, and satisfaction with his activities, health, and economic status.

PERSONAL AND SOCIETAL ADJUSTMENT

It does not follow, of course, that the above research neglects the outer world. Pollak (1948), as well as Cavan et al. (1949), makes an explicit distinction between personal and societal (social) adjustment. Societal adjustment "is always concerned with changes in existing conditions, while individual adjustment is largely limited to changes in responses to existing conditions although within a narrow sphere the individual may also try to change those conditions" (Pollak, 1948, p. 41). From this, we may isolate three elements: (1) the dichotomy between individual (personal) and societal adjustment, (2) the concept of individual adjustment as a response to a given situation, and (3) the recognition that "within a narrow sphere" societal adjustment may become a personal concern.

It is characteristic of most of the books which have a definition of social adjustment not to pay much attention to it. For instance, Cavan et al. state: "Social adjustment, or the adaptation of society or one of its institutions to social change, is the process of revising social standards and procedures in order to increase the social efficiency and to facilitate the personal adjustment of its members" (1949, p. 11). Yet they focus almost exclusively on individual adjustment. This may be explained by the fact that their approach (1) is fundamentally normative and action-centered (one of the aims of gerontology is making old people happier) and (2) gives foremost importance to psychological and personality problems without submitting a consistent, clear conception of personality, a task which is indeed difficult (Blum, 1953; Hall & Lindzey, 1958).

A PSYCHOSOCIOLOGICAL APPROACH

If one defines the study of personal adjustment as psychological, relevant to social psychology rather than pure psychology, and the study of social adjustment as sociological, which has rarely been done, there is still room for a psychosociological approach. The expression is less frequent in American than in European sociology, but there are some notable instances of American use, for example:

We might designate as social psychology the study of personality, which seeks to explain individual action not only by considering the psychological properties of the person but also by giving systematic attention to sociocultural forces in the individual's action situation. We might designate as psychosociology efforts to explain the functioning and change of social systems which not only consider properties of social systems but give systematic consideration to general personality theory or to the modal personalities of the system's participants and their psychological adjustment to the social forces impinging on them (Inkeles, 1959, p. 274).

The difference is not simply a difference of vocabulary, but of outlook. The psychosociologist—from this point, we will say, "the sociologist," for simplicity's sake—is interested in gerontology as far as he is concerned with the place and role of old people in the structure and functioning of large or small social systems.

A Non-Value-Judgmental Approach in Gerontology

This sociological approach should remain descriptive and explanatory, at least in its first phase. We will ask, what problems are raised by the presence of old people in a middle-class family? what disruptions and adaptations in the family's roles and social relations are caused by their presence? how do these changes affect the relation of the family to larger social systems like the community, nation, and so on? These are descriptions, not value judgments. In this approach, the happiness of all or some of the family's members, because the system functions well, is only a derivative datum, not a primary one. It might even be completely left out of the picture, especially if the emphasis is on the third question.

Later, when we have accumulated enough data on the functioning of all social systems and subsystems in which old people participate, we may address ourselves to the fundamental question: From the viewpoint of gerontology, what is the best social system at the level of family or community or nation or so on? This question may be still more difficult to answer than "What is the good life?"

CONDITIONS FOR INTERNATIONAL COMPARISON

I am personally convinced that the sociological and the psychosociological approaches are prerequisites to any international comparison of old people. It would be pointless to compare the levels of individual adjustment of the aged through the traditional techniques of social psychology without first analyzing the social systems in which the adjustments are taking place. On the other hand, the skills of the psychologist are needed from the beginning in order to study and compare the personality types and characteristics which are the fundamental components of social systems and subsystems. The concept of "modal personality type" (Inkeles, 1959; Inkeles & Levinson, 1954) is very important from this point of view.

Role

If I have taken the family as an example of the social level at which the integration of the psychological and sociological approaches may prove fruitful for research, it is because at precisely that level the personality types of the participants are clearly fundamental variables in the functioning of the social system (defined as a relatively enduring system of action shared by all family members). The concept of role, which has been growing more popular in the past ten years, is essential to the coordination of psychological and sociological analysis.

Role has something in common with adjustment. For a long time, role had a vague meaning. "Frequently in the literature, the concept is used without any attempt on the part of the writer to define or delimit the concept, the assumption being that both writer and reader will achieve an immediate compatible consensus" (Neiman & Hughes, 1951, p. 149). This statement is now more than ten years old, and since 1951 the concept has been deepened and clarified.

As for the use of role in age categories, the ambitious program of research outlined by Cottrell as early as 1942 is still far from being accomplished. This program still retains most of its value. The purpose of this paper is not to check off the solved and unsolved questions, but only to call attention to some aspects of the role concept and its usefulness in gerontology.

Two characteristics of Cottrell's concept of role may be contrasted with subsequent refinements. First, he still seems to follow a behaviorist approach in some respects when, for instance, he defines role as "an internally consistent series of conditioned responses by one member of a social situation which represents the stimulus pattern for a similarly internally consistent series of conditioned responses of the other(s) in that situation" (1942, p. 617). Is it only a question of vocabulary? No, for he tends to consider role too much as something external—a stimulus or an element of the situation—to which the individual has to adjust. It is very significant that today the tendency is to speak of internalization, or assumption of role rather than adjustment to role. Second, he does not utilize the idea of reciprocal role. When the individual perceives his role, he must first locate the position and the reciprocal roles of the others. The enactment or expectation of the reciprocal role is thus fundamental to the elaboration of the individual's role. There is a strong, interdependent relation between the two concepts (Maucorps & Bassoul, 1960).

The Roles of Older People

Some recent research on aging has developed methods to analyze the connection between roles and reciprocal roles, for instance, between the younger and older generations' roles in the family (Neugarten & Gutmann, 1958; Neugarten & Gutmann, 1959). Research in the following directions might be rewarding. It may be that the "desocialization" process of the aged—their difficulty in fitting themselves into the social environment and in assuming corresponding roles—is caused by a growing decline in social perception; the aged may no longer perceive the reciprocal roles or expectations of others, however clear they may be. This is a modified formulation of the "clarity criterion" proposed by Cottrell. Also, an older person can no longer accept a frustrating role as a temporary, though necessary, step toward a more rewarding role. In the chain of roles, the expectation of future roles has an important influence on the feelings which accompany the present role and, perhaps, on its actual performance. This relates to the statement of Havighurst and Albrecht (1953, quoted above) on the importance, for the older person's adjustment, of present happiness as opposed to future expectations. This hypothesis should also be taken into account when studying bureaucratic careers (Tréanton, 1960) and the adjustment of old people to them.

As long as these connections of roles may be understood only in the perspective of the total system of relations, they probably offer the best field for close interdisciplinary cooperation between psychologists and sociologists interested in old age.

REFERENCES

Blum, G.S. *Psychoanalytic theories of personality*. New York: McGraw-Hill, 1953.
Cattell, R.B. *Personality*. New York: McGraw-Hill, 1950.
Cavan, Ruth S., Burgess, E.W., Havighurst, R.J., & Goldhamer, H. *Personal adjustment in old age*. Chicago: Science Research Associates, 1949.
Cottrell, L.S., Jr. The adjustment of the individual to his age and sex roles. *Amer. sociol. Rev.*, 1942, **7**, 617-620. (Abstract)

Hall, C.S., & Lindzey, G. *Theories of personality.* New York: John Wiley & Sons, 1958.

Havighurst, R.J., & Albrecht, Ruth. *Older people.* New York: Longmans Green, 1953.

Inkeles, A. Personality and social structure. In R.K. Merton, L. Broom, & L. S. Cottrell, Jr. (Eds.), *Sociology today.* New York: Basic Books, 1959. Pp. 249-276.

Inkeles, A., & Levinson, D.J. National character: The study of modal personality and sociocultural systems. In G. Lindzey (Ed.), *Handbook of social psychology.* Vol. 2. Cambridge, Mass.: Addison-Wesley, 1954. Pp. 977-1020.

Maucorps, P.H., & Bassoul, R. *Empathies et connaissance d'autrui.* Paris: Centre Nationale de la Recherche Scientifique, 1960.

Neiman, L.J., & Hughes, J.W. The problem of the concept of role—a re-survey of the literature. *Soc. Forces,* 1951, **30,** 141-149.

Neugarten, Bernice L., & Gutmann, D.L. Age-sex roles and personality in middle age: A thematic apperception study. *Psychol. Monogr.,* 1958, **72,** No. 17.

Neugarten, Bernice L., & Gutmann, D.L. The views of middle-aged parents toward intergenerational relations within the family. Paper presented at the annual meeting of the American Psychological Association, Cincinnati, 1959.

Pollak, O. *Social adjustment in old age.* New York: Social Science Research Council, 1948.

Reichard, Suzanne, Livson, Florine, & Petersen, P.G. *Aging and personality: A study of eighty-seven older men.* New York: John Wiley & Sons, 1962.

Shaffer, L.F. *The psychology of adjustment.* Boston: Houghton-Mifflin, 1936.

Tréanton, J.R. Le concept de carrière. *Rev. Franc. social.,* 1960, **1,** 73-80.

Young, K. *Personality and problems of adjustment.* New York: Appleton-Century-Crofts, 1940.

CHAPTER 16

Successful Aging

ROBERT J. HAVIGHURST

The practical purpose of gerontology is to help people live better in their later years. However, we do not have general agreement on what good living in the later years is. We agree on some of the determining conditions of good living, such as health, economic security, presence of friends and family, but there is disagreement on actual signs of good living in the feelings and behavior of a person as he grows older. Some believe that good living in old age consists of maintaining activity and involvement, as in middle age. Others believe that good living for elderly people is just the opposite—a retirement to the rocking chair and decrease of activity as the years pass by. Thus the definition of successful aging may appear to require a value judgment on which people are bound to disagree. This is true if the definition of successful aging is based on such behavior as social and civic activity and family affairs. Still, there is a fair degree of consensus concerning what appropriate behavior for older people is, and, therefore, it should be possible to develop an instrument to measure the social acceptability of people's behavior and, consequently, the degree of their success in aging.

A measure of successful aging was attempted by Havighurst and Albrecht (1953) on the basis of a study of public opinion concerning the activities of older people. Based on this study, a social approval scale was developed which could be applied to any person's life as he reached later maturity. Another, perhaps better, way of measuring successful aging does not require a social or individual value judgment concerning the behavior of older people. This consists of finding out how older people feel about their present and past. If they are happy and satisfied with their lives, they are said to be aging successfully.

Thus there are two general approaches to the definition and measurement of successful aging. It seems useful to keep these two approaches clear and separate. At the same time, it is important to recognize the fact that the two aspects of successful aging are interrelated, though it would not be true to say that they are inner and outer aspects of the same thing. The measures of the inner, subjective entity correlate highly with measures of the outer, behavioral entity, but not higher than .5 or .6, which allows for various behaviors which do not correlate highly enough among themselves to be fairly highly correlated with the inner entity of satisfaction.

PREVIOUS DEFINITIONS

An Inner, Subjective Entity

A good example of measurement of successful aging using the inner definition is Kutner's morale scale, which was derived from the Elmira study conducted by the Department of Anthropology and Sociology of Cornell University. Kutner, Fanshel, Togo, and Langner (1956) say, "Morale refers to a mental state or a set of dispositions, while adjustment refers to behaviors that stem from these dispositions. Hence, we may assume that an attitude or evaluation scale of morale measures life adjustment" (p. 48). The morale scale employed by Kutner et al. follows.

1. How often do you feel there's just no point in living?

2. Things just keep getting worse and worse for me as I get older.

3. How much do you regret the chances you missed during your life to do a better job of living?

4. All in all, how much unhappiness would you say you find in life today?

5. On the whole, how satisfied would you say you are with your way of life today?

6. How much do you plan ahead the things you will be doing next week or the week after—would you say you make many plans, a few plans, or almost none?

7. As you get older, would you say things seem to be better or worse than you thought they would be?

Social Competence

The measurement of successful aging using the outer definition is illustrated by Havighurst and Albrecht (1953) in the Prairie City study and by Havighurst (1957) in the Kansas City study. Here success was defined as competent behavior in the common social roles of worker, parent, spouse, homemaker, citizen, friend, association member, and church member. A set of rating scales was created to measure a person's performance against the societal norms in these areas. Another measure of the outer type is the activity score on the schedule entitled "Your Activities and Attitudes," developed by Cavan, Burgess, Havighurst, and Goldhamer (1949), which sums up a person's participation in various activities.

Eclectic Measures

Recognizing that the inner and outer aspects of successful aging are closely related, though not in a strict one-to-one relationship, many researchers have used methods of measurement which combine the two aspects in one procedure. For example, a widely used measure is the Chicago attitude inventory, first described by Cavan et al. (1949), somewhat revised by Havighurst and Albrecht (1953), and adapted for use with middle-aged people by Havighurst (1957). In this instrument, a person is asked about his satisfaction with his economic situation, work, family, friends, home, health, associations or clubs, and his happiness and feeling of usefulness. His score is thus a combination of his attitudes about his activities in several areas and his inner feelings of happiness independent of his outer behavior. The parts of this

instrument dealing with happiness and feelings of usefulness correlate
.84 and .76 with the total attitude score and have been used as a short
form of the inventory at times. These two subsections, therefore,
represent a use of the inner definition.

Another eclectic measure is the Cavan adjustment-rating
scale developed by Cavan et al. (1949) and modified by Havighurst
(1957) for use with middle-aged people. This is a rating based on
a personal interview, and it takes into account association with family, friends, formal and informal groups, feelings of importance and
satisfaction, and emotional stability.

Coefficients of correlation between four instruments of various types are given for the Prairie City study (Havighurst & Albrecht,
1953) in Table 1. The lowest coefficient is .58, and the highest is .78,
which is about the range that will be found in the studies which use
instruments of these types.

TABLE 1
INTERCORRELATIONS OF VARIOUS INSTRUMENTS FOR
THE MEASUREMENT OF SUCCESSFUL AGING

**Product-moment correlation coefficients from the Prairie City
study by Havighurst and Albrecht (1953)**

Instrument	A	B	C	D	E
A. Attitude inventory					
B. Cavan adjustment rating	.73				
C. Role activity score (social competence)	.58	.71			
D. Total activities score	.78	.67	.66		
E. Socioeconomic status	.13	.23	.47	.27	
Age (male)	−.20	−.05	−.22	−.38	−.07
Age (female)	−.07	−.21	−.22	−.17	.00

**Product-moment correlation coefficients from the Kansas City
study by Havighurst (1957)**

Instrument	X	A	B
X. Life satisfaction rating			
A. Life satisfaction, Index A	.58		
B. Life satisfaction, Index B	.71	.73	
C. Socioeconomic status	.39	.36	.41
Age	−.97	−.10	−.07

Validity

All the measures which have been discussed have a surface validity, for their content obviously is related to one or another definition of successful aging. Some researchers simply accept this fact as sufficient. For example, Kutner assumes that his morale scale measures life adjustment and lets it go at that; others have been content to follow his lead. Some researchers, like Havighurst (1951), have sought an acceptable criterion of adjustment or successful aging to test the validity of their instruments. Havighurst has used a form of rating by experienced judges as the criterion against which to validate self-report measures such as the Chicago attitude inventory, for self-report instruments are vulnerable to conscious and unconscious psychological defenses and should be validated against a more objective measure.

Another aspect of validity is related to defining successful aging. If the inner definition is used and measures of happiness and satisfaction are developed, these should be validated against a criterion of successful aging which is also inner and does not depend on the social and economic activities of a person. Only in this way can circularity be avoided in evaluating the effectiveness of social policies aimed to increase the involvement of older people in social and economic activities. The current study attempts to avoid circularity by defining successful aging in inner terms and, rating people on this basis, attempts to validate the self-report instrument against this criterion.

SCALING TECHNIQUES

In developing attitude scales for the measurement of successful aging, the model has frequently been the Guttman scale. The essential characteristic of a Guttman scale is that all people who answer a given question positively will have higher scores than those who answer it negatively. The items on the scale, therefore, are ranked in order of difficulty, and they have the same rank for all, or nearly all, respondents.

A successful Guttman scale measures only one dimension and gives a series of scores which rank the respondents reliably on this dimension. If there are several dimensions in the entity being studied (in this case, successful aging), there should be as many Guttman scales as there are dimensions. I believe that the limited efficiency of the Guttman scales that have been created for the study of morale or adjustment to aging does not justify the restriction of research instruments to these scales at present. A somewhat broader, looser use of attitude items seems to be desirable, although the time will probably come when a set of Guttman scales will be developed that are useful in social gerontology.

The difficulty with the present Guttman scales is illustrated by the scale developed in the Elmira study and adapted by Kutner et al. First, by creating only one scale, the researchers limited themselves to treating adjustment to aging or successful aging as one-dimensional in the attitude area, although this seems unlikely to be true.

Perhaps the difficulty the users of the Kutner scale have had in getting all the items to scale properly is related to the restriction to one dimension. Thus Kutner et al. (1956) report that Item 6 had to be scored differently in their study than it had been scored in the original Elmira study. "This difference in the performance of the scale in the two studies serves to illustrate the point that a scale that meets scaling criteria when used with one population will not necessarily meet the same criteria when used with another population" (Kutner et al., 1956, p. 303). The difference is probably caused by the fact that the scale was used on two quite different populations, one native-born and rural, the other foreign-born and urban. With such different populations, the meanings of key words in the items may shift, changing the positions of the items on the scale.

An even greater effect of this sort is seen in the adaptation of the Kutner scale made by Morrison and Kristjanson (1958) for use in South Dakota. They found that the item Kutner ranked fifth, "On the whole, how satisfied would you say you are with your way of life today?" ranked third on their adaptation of the scale, with 78 per cent of the respondents saying, "Very satisfied," compared to 38 per cent of Kutner's respondents. On the other hand, Kutner's third ranked sixth for the South Dakota group, and finally they threw out this item, because it did not scale well with their other items. Thus, a Guttman scale for one population is not for another. Nevertheless, in the judgment of the writer the separate items of the Kutner scale are good for the measurement of successful aging, and the two items mentioned above are used in the instruments of the present study.

Another shortcoming in attitude scales of the Guttman type is that often the scale is not fully used. The Kutner scale, for example, has seven steps and should lend itself well to correlation analysis.

Kutner, however, combined the scores into three levels, high, medium, and low, and used a chi-square analysis with them. Morrison and Kristjanson divided their scores into only two levels and used a chi-square analysis. It hardly seems worthwhile to create a Guttman scale of seven or eight steps if it is going to be used as a two- or three-step scale.

At present it is more useful to develop inclusive attitude scales with enough items to permit correlation analysis and to use these scales in this way, with the expectation that when more is known about the number of dimensions that should be considered in the study of successful aging, Guttman scales for each dimension will be created of sufficient length for accurate computation of correlation coefficients and for testing differences between means.

The Life Satisfaction Scales

Dr. Bernice Neugarten and I, with our students, have been working on defining and measuring successful aging on the basis of the work that has been discussed above. It was decided to define successful aging in inner terms as inner feelings of happiness and satisfaction with one's present and past life. The basic definition of successful aging was "a person is aging successfully if he feels satisfied with his present and past life." The problem then was to break satisfaction into a number of components sufficient to represent its complexity and to find ways of measuring these components. The concepts were devised and applied to a sample of people from fifty to eighty in the Kansas City study of adult life.

The research group began by examining the measures of adjustment and morale that had been used by other investigators and looking for distinguishable components of inner satisfaction and happiness. At the same time a researcher on the field staff of the Kansas City study was holding intensive interviews with a small number of people and rating them on morale. After intensive interviews, Dr. Lois Dean, a psychologist, first ranked ten people on morale and then submitted her disciplined intuitive judgment to interviewing by other staff members, on the basis of which several elements of morale were described (Cumming, Dean, & Newell, 1959).

Eventually a combination of these procedures produced an operational definition of life satisfaction in five components: (1) zest versus apathy, (2) resolution and fortitude, (3) goodness of fit between desired and achieved goals, (4) positive self-concept, and (5) mood tone. Each component can be rated on a five-point scale (see Appendix C), and the ratings can be added to get a life satisfaction rating with a range of scores from five to twenty-five.

Based on four lengthy interviews over a period of three years, two judges rated each person in the Kansas City sample. The two ratings were averaged to secure a more reliable score. Even without the averaging the reliability was high, for the correlation coefficient between the two judges for 187 cases was .78. Of 885 paired judgments, 94 per cent showed exact agreement or agreement within one step on a five-step scale. In all, ten judges did the ratings, and all but one maintained a high level of agreement with the others. The over-all scores ranged from eight to twenty-five, with a mean of 17.8 and a standard deviation of 4.6.

TABLE 2
INTERCORRELATIONS OF THE COMPONENTS
OF LIFE SATISFACTION

	Resolution	Goodness of fit	Self-concept	Mood tone
Zest	.67	.56	.79	.84
Resolution		.70	.83	.48
Goodness of fit			.73	.57
Self-concept				.82

Note—This table was previously published in Neugarten, Havighurst, and Tobin. (1961, p. 139).

Correlations among the five components of the life satisfaction ratings are shown in Table 2. Although the five components are positively interrelated, the correlations are low enough to suggest that more than one dimension is involved. Without submitting these correlation coefficients to a factor analysis, it appears that zest, mood tone, and possibly self-concept form a cluster, with the probability of one or two other factors. At any rate, it appears useful to proceed on the inference that life satisfaction is more than a one-dimensional entity.

For the present, the life satisfaction rating is being used as a criterion for successful aging, against which other possible measures and correlates can be tested. Meanwhile, a clinical psychologist is interviewing and rating eighty people in Kansas City on the life satisfaction scales as a further check on the validity of the ratings made by judges, who read interviews, but did not actually see or speak to the respondents.

Indexes A and B

To get a simpler, more generally usable procedure for measuring life satisfaction, work has been done with two forms of self-report instruments.

One instrument, the life satisfaction Index A, is an attitude scale of twenty items selected from existing scales or invented to get four or five items representing each of the five components. This instrument contains three of the Kutner morale scale items and several items from the happiness scale of the Chicago attitude inventory. At first this index contained twenty-five items, but five were dropped after an item analysis which compared responses on each item with the total score on the rating scale. The first correlation coefficient between the rating scale and Index A was .52. After dropping five items, the correlation coefficient rose to .58. For ninety cases the mean score on this index is 12.4 and the standard deviation 4.4.

The other instrument, life satisfaction Index B, is a combination of six open-ended questions and six check list items which are scored on a three-point scale, from zero to two. Four of the twelve items are from Kutner's morale scale, and others come from various sources. At first there were nineteen items in this instrument, but seven of them were discarded on the basis of an item analysis against the total score on the rating scale. The first correlation coefficient of the nineteen-item instrument with the rating scale was .59, and this was raised to .71 for the twelve-item instrument after discarding seven items on the basis of the item analysis. For ninety-two cases the mean score on Index B is 15.1 and the standard deviation 4.7.

The two self-report instruments are presented here with the scoring key indicated for Index B (see appendixes A, B, and C). Their correlations with the rating scale should be cross-validated with another sample, for these may be fortuitously high because of the elimination of items which did not contribute to the correlation in this sample.

The coefficient of correlation between A and B is .73 for ninety cases, indicating a substantial communality between them. The combined score of A and B has a correlation of .62 with the rating scale, a mean score of 27.6, and a standard deviation of 6.7.

These three procedures for measuring life satisfaction all depend on an inner definition of successful aging. They can be used, therefore, to study the effects of social and economic conditions on people and the relations between various ways of life and life satisfaction, without the circularity of the earlier measures, in which social conditions or ways of life were reflected in the instruments used to measure success. The validity of these instruments, however, depends on the definition which has been made of successful aging in constructing them.

THEORIES OF SUCCESSFUL AGING

Since there is a possibility of individual and social choice among conditions of life for older people, it is useful to have a theory of successful aging. Guided by such a theory, a person may make choices for himself about such things as age of retirement, where to live, what to do in his free time, and how to relate to his family in the belief that he can live more happily through making wise choices. Similarly, a society can make choices, guided by a theory of successful aging, about social policies and practices concerning social security, age of retirement, public housing, and health services for older people. In order to make wise choices, it is necessary either to have a satisfactory working theory of successful aging or to be able to test rival theories. Since there are rival theories, it is useful to test them and to find out how well they work for various people and societies.

To test a theory of successful aging requires a definition of successful aging [1] and a method of measuring it. The preceding part of this paper has attempted to give these. A definition of successful aging and a method of measuring it will be useful only if they do not beg the question. That is, the definition of successful aging and the method of measuring it must not assume that one of the rival theories is correct. The definition of successful aging as satisfaction with present and past life seems to avoid this difficulty, for it does not favor either of the two broad rival theories of successful aging, the activity theory and the disengagement theory. The activity theory states that

---

[1] It is important to make a distinction between a theory of the process of aging, and a theory of successful aging. In the former one is concerned only with generalizations about the processes which go on in the body, personality, and social environment as a person ages. One does not take into consideration the questions of happiness or success. The disengagement theory should be regarded primarily as a theory of process of aging, although it also has clear implications for a theory of successful aging.

successful aging means the maintenance, as far and as long as possible, of the activities and attitudes of middle age. The disengagement theory defines successful aging as the acceptance of and desire for disengagement from active life.

The activity theory is favored by most of the practical workers in gerontology. They believe that people should maintain the activities and attitudes of middle age as long as possible and then find substitutes for the activities which they must give up—for work when they are forced to retire, for clubs and associations, for friends and loved ones whom they lose by death.

However, as Henry and Cumming (1959) have pointed out, "Our conceptions predispose us to use the middle-age status as a model of desirable social and personal development, and hence to see any deviation from this model as negative and undesirable. This may perhaps result in a failure to conceive of old age as a potential developmental stage in its own right, having features qualitatively different from middle age" (p. 383).

The disengagement theory is based on the observation that as people grow older they generally curtail the activities of middle age. As stated by Cumming and McCaffrey (1960):

> This theory starts from the common-sense observation that in America, the old person is less involved in the life around him than he was when he was younger and proceeds without making assumptions about the desirability of this fact. *Aging in the modal person is thought of in this theory as a mutual withdrawal or disengagement which takes place between the aging person and others in the social systems to which he belongs.* He may withdraw more markedly from some classes of people and remain relatively close to others. This withdrawal may be accompanied from the outset by increased preoccupation with himself. When the aging process is complete, the equilibrium which existed in middle life between the individual and his society has given way to a new equilibrium characterized by a greater distance and an altered type of relationship. In a previous report, we have presented data which suggest that one of the early stages of disengagement occurs when the aging individual withdraws emotional investment from the environment. We have thought of the inner process as being an ego change in which object cathexis is reduced; this results in an appearance of self-centeredness, and an orientation to others which betrays less sense of mutual obligation. This is accompanied by a somewhat freer and more expressive manner. The fully disengaged person can be thought of as having transferred much of his cathexis to his own inner life; his memories, his fantasies, his image of himself as someone who *was* something, and *did* accomplish things.

There is no doubt that disengagement does take place with aging, but proponents of the activity theory regard this as a result of society's withdrawal from the aging person against his will and desire. However, the disengagement theory stated by Cumming, Dean, Newell, and McCaffrey (1960) regards disengagement as a natural process which the aging person accepts and desires. They speak of disengagement as being "primarily intrinsic, and secondarily responsive."

On her eightieth birthday, Lady Astor, for example, is supposed to have said, "Years ago, I thought old age would be dreadful, because I would not be able to do all the things I would want to do. Now I find there is nothing I want to do." A seventy-four-year-old woman in the Kansas City study, when asked what were the best things about being her age, said, "The change—over a period of several years—freedom from petty conventions, children, husband. A sense of relief from petty fears about jobs, finances, social position, new clothes. Freedom to accept or decline invitations and appointments without strain on my husband's business, or hurting my children, or the Victorian standards of my parents." Yet she expressed some of her ambivalence about disengagement when she answered the question about the worst thing about being her age: "The realization that for better or for worse, the job is done, and there is no chance to make any more contributions to your generation."

Cumming et al. (1960) have stated and tested three hypotheses about the process of disengagement:

1. Rate of interaction and variety of interaction will lessen with age.
2. Changes in amount, and variety, of interaction will be accompanied by concomitant changes in perception of the size of the life space.
3. A change in the quality of interaction will accompany decrease in the social life space, from absorption with others to absorption with self, and from evaluative to carefree.

Tests of the Theories

Unless the process of disengagement is so thoroughly intrinsic that there is no stopping or delaying it, there is a considerable margin of social and individual choice between activity and disengagement, and within this area it would be useful to test the two theories to find out how they are related to life satisfaction.

I believe that life satisfaction will be positively related to activity for some people and to disengagement for others. A person with an active, achieving, and outward-directed way of life style will be best satisfied to continue this into old age with only slight diminution. Other people with a passive, dependent, home-centered way of life will be best satisfied with disengagement. Cumming and McCaffrey (1960) suggest this when they say that there may be "important non-modal groups of the die-with-your-boots-on school. We do not yet know who they are except that there is evidence that academics do not disengage, in the sense that we are using it here, to the same degree that, for example, skilled workmen or clerical workers do."

Reichard, Livson, and Petersen (1962) in a study of working-class men found three types of successful agers, one active, one passive, and one mature, who almost certainly would be differentiated if their activity-disengagement processes were studied.

It is important to add that disengagement is not the same as passive, dependent living. Disengagement refers primarily to the weakening of the bonds that tie the individual to his social environment. It may result in rocking-chair inaction, but it may also result in a carefree attitude combined with assertiveness and activity as exemplified by the seventy-four-year-old woman previously described.

Conclusions

This discussion of theories of successful aging supports the view that social gerontology needs good measures of successful aging, which, in turn, needs operational definitions. Some progress is being made in this direction through separating inner satisfaction with life from the outer behavior which is related to it as a means rather than an end. Inner satisfaction can be usefully defined and measured as a criterion of successful aging.

APPENDIX A

Life Satisfaction Index A—
Attitude Inventory [2]

Here are some statements about life in general that people feel different ways about. Would you read each statement on the list and if you agree with it, put a check mark in the space under "AGREE." If you do not agree with a statement, put a check mark in the space under "DISAGREE." If you are not sure one way or the other, put a check mark in the space under "?." Please be sure to answer every question on the list.

	AGREE	DISAGREE	?
1. As I grow older, things seem better than I thought they would be.	1._____	_____	_____
2. I have gotten more of the breaks in life than most of the people I know.	2._____	_____	_____
3. This is the dreariest time of my life.	3._____	_____	_____
4. I am just as happy as when I was younger.	4._____	_____	_____
5. My life could be happier than it is now.	5._____	_____	_____
6. These are the best years of my life.	6._____	_____	_____
7. Most of the things I do are boring or monotonous.	7._____	_____	_____
8. I expect some interesting and pleasant things to happen to me in the future.	8._____	_____	_____
9. The things I do are as interesting to me as they ever were.	9._____	_____	_____

[2] Appendix A was previously published in Neugarten, Havighurst, and Tobin, 1961, p. 141.

10. I feel old and somewhat tired.　　10.＿＿＿＿ ＿＿＿＿ ＿＿＿＿

11. I feel my age, but it does not bother me.　　11.＿＿＿＿ ＿＿＿＿ ＿＿＿＿

12. As I look back on my life, I am fairly well satisfied.　　12.＿＿＿＿ ＿＿＿＿ ＿＿＿＿

13. I would not change my past life even if I could.　　13.＿＿＿＿ ＿＿＿＿ ＿＿＿＿

14. Compared to other people my age, I've made a lot of foolish decisions in my life.　　14.＿＿＿＿ ＿＿＿＿ ＿＿＿＿

15. Compared to other people my age, I make a good appearance.　　15.＿＿＿＿ ＿＿＿＿ ＿＿＿＿

16. I have made plans for things I'll be doing a month or a year from now.　　16.＿＿＿＿ ＿＿＿＿ ＿＿＿＿

17. When I think back over my life, I didn't get most of the important things I wanted.　　17.＿＿＿＿ ＿＿＿＿ ＿＿＿＿

18. Compared to other people, I get down in the dumps too often.　　18.＿＿＿＿ ＿＿＿＿ ＿＿＿＿

19. I've gotten pretty much what I expected out of life.　　19.＿＿＿＿ ＿＿＿＿ ＿＿＿＿

20. In spite of what some people say, the lot of the average man is getting worse, not better.　　20.＿＿＿＿ ＿＿＿＿ ＿＿＿＿

APPENDIX B

Life Satisfaction Index B—
Questionnaire with Scoring Key [3]

Would you please comment freely in answer to the following questions?

1. What are the best things about being the age you are now?

    2 _____
    1 Positive answer
    0 Nothing good about it

2. What do you think you will be doing five years from now? How do you expect things will be different from the way they are now, in your life?

    2 Better or no change
    1 Contingent—depends
    0 Worse

3. What is the most important thing in your life right now?

    2 Anything outside self, or pleasant interpretation of future.
    1 "Hanging on." Keeping my health, or job.
    0 Getting out of difficulty, or "nothing now," or reference to past.

4. How happy would you say you are right now, compared with the earlier periods in your life?

    2 This is the happiest time. All have been happy. Hard to make a choice.
    1 Some decrease in recent years.
    0 Earlier periods were better. This is a bad time.

[3] Appendix B was previously published in Neugarten, Havighurst, and Tobin, 1961, pp. 141-142.

5. Do you ever worry about your ability to do what people expect of you—to meet demands that people make on you?

    2 No

    1 Qualified yes or no

    0 Yes

6. If you could do anything you pleased, in what part of _____ would you most like to live?

    2 Present location

    1 _____

    0 Any other location

7. How often do you find yourself feeling lonely?

    2 Never

    2 Hardly ever

    1 Sometimes

    0 Fairly often

    0 Very often

8. How often do you feel there is no point in living?

    2 Never

    2 Hardly ever

    1 Sometimes

    0 Fairly often

    0 Very often

9. Do you wish you could see more of your close friends than you do, or would you like more time to yourself?

    0 Wish could see more

    0 More time to self

    2 Okay as is

10. How much unhappiness would you say you find in your life today?

    0 A good deal

    1 Some

    2 Almost none

11. As you get older, would you say things seem to be better or worse than you thought they would be?

    2 Better

    0 Worse

    1 About what expected

12. How satisfied would you say you are with your way of life?

    2 Very satisfied

    1 Fairly satisfied

    0 Not very satisfied

Resolution and Fortitude

Here we are concerned with the extent to which the respondent accepts personal responsibility for his life, the opposite of feeling resigned, or of merely condoning or passively accepting that which life has brought him. The extent to which the respondent accepts his life as meaningful and inevitable, and is relatively unafraid of death. This is Erikson's "integrity."

This is not to be confused with autonomy or the extent to which the respondent's life has been self-propelled or characterized by initiative. The respondent may not have been a person of high initiative, but yet he may accept resolutely and relatively positively that which life has been for him. He may feel it was a series of hard knocks, but that he has stood up under them (this would be a high rating).

There are two types of low ratings, the highly intropunitive, where the respondent blames himself overly much; and the extrapunitive, where the respondent blames others or the world in general for whatever failures or disappointments he has experienced.

5 (high):   Try and try again attitude. Bloody but unbowed. Fights back; withstanding, not giving up. Active personal responsibility—takes the bad and good and makes the most of it. Wouldn't change the past.

4:   Can take life as it comes. "I have no complaint on the way life has treated me." Assumes responsibility readily. "If you look for the good side of life, you'll find it." "Your activities, your outlook on life, determine your age." Does not mind talking about difficulties in life, but does not dwell on them either. "You have to give up some things."

3:   Says, "I've had my ups and downs; sometimes on top, sometimes on the bottom." Shows a trace of extrapunitiveness or intropunitiveness concerning his difficulties in life.

2:   Feels he hasn't done better because he hasn't gotten the breaks. Feels great difference in life now than at age forty-five; the change has been for the worse. "I've worked hard but never got anywhere."

1:   Talks of hard knocks which he has not mastered (extrapunitive). Feels helpless. Blames self a great deal (intropunitive). Overwhelmed by life.

Goodness of Fit

Here we are concerned with the extent to which the respond-dent feels he has achieved his goals in life, whatever those goals might be; feels he has succeeded in accomplishing what *he* regards as important.

High ratings would go, for instance, to the man who says, "I've managed to keep out of jail" just as to the man who says, "I managed to send all my kids through college."

Low ratings would go to the respondent who feels he's missed most of his opportunities or who says, "I've never been suited to my work" or "I always wanted to be a doctor, but never could get there." Also to the respondent who wants most to be "loved," but instead feels merely "approved." Expressions of regret for lack of education are not counted in this connection.

5 (high): Feels he has accomplished what he wanted to do. He has achieved or is achieving his own personal goals.

4: Regrets "somewhat" the chances missed during life. "Maybe I could have made more of certain opportunities." Nevertheless, feels that he has been fairly successful in accomplishing what he wanted to do in life.

3: Has a fifty-fifty record of opportunities taken and opportunities missed. Would have done some little things differently, if he had life to live over. Might have gotten more education.

2: Has regrets about major opportunities missed but feels good about accomplishment in one area (may be avocation).

1: Feels he has missed most opportunities in life.

Positive Self-Concept

Here we are concerned with the respondent's concept of self —physical and psychological attributes.

High ratings would go to the respondent who is concerned with grooming and appearance; who thinks of himself as wise, mellow (and thus is comfortable in giving advice to others); who feels proud of his accomplishments; who feels he deserves whatever good breaks he has had; who feels he is important to someone else.

Low ratings to the respondent who feels "old," weak, sick, incompetent; who feels himself a burden to others; who speaks disparagingly of himself or old people.

5 (high): Feels at his best. "I do better work now than ever before." "There was never any better time." Thinks of self as wise, mellow; physically able or attractive; feels important to others. Feels he has the right to indulge himself.

4: Feels more fortunate than the average. Is sure that he can meet the exigencies of life. "When I retire, I'll just substitute other activities." Compensates well for any difficulty of health. Feels worthy of being indulged. "Things I want to do, I can do, but I'll not overexert myself." Feels in control of self in relation to the situation.

3:   Sees self as competent in at least one area, for example, work; but has doubts about self in other areas. Acknowledges loss of youthful vigor, but accepts it in a realistic way. Feels relatively unimportant, but doesn't mind. Feels he takes, but also gives. Senses a general, but not extreme, loss of status as he grows older. Reports health better than average.

2:   Feels that other people look down on him. Tends to speak disparagingly of older people. Is defensive about what the years are doing to him.

1:   Feels old. Feels worthless; in the way. Makes self-disparaging remarks. "I'm endured by others."

Mood Tone

High ratings for the respondent who expresses happy, optimistic attitudes and mood; who uses spontaneous positively toned affective terms for people and things; who takes pleasure from life and expresses it.

Low ratings for depression, "feel blue and lonely"; for feelings of bitterness; for frequent irritability and anger.

(Here we consider not only the respondent's verbal attitudes in the interview; but make inferences from all we know of his interpersonal relationships, how others react to him, and so on.)

5 (high):   "This is the best time of my life." Is nearly always cheerful, optimistic. Cheerfulness may seem unrealistic to an observer, but the respondent shows no sign of "putting up a bold front."

4:   Gets pleasure out of life, knows it and shows it. There is enough restraint to seem appropriate to a younger person. Practically always has a positive affect. Optimistic.

3:   Seems to move along on an even temperamental keel. Any depressions are neutralized by positive mood swings. Generally neutral-to-positive affect. May show some irritability.

2:   Wants things quiet and peaceful. General neutral-to-negative affect. Some depression.

1:   Pessimistic, complaining, bitter. Complains of being lonely. Feels "blue" a good deal of the time. May get angry when in contact with people.

APPENDIX C

Scale for Rating
Life Satisfaction

Zest versus Apathy

To be rated here are enthusiasm of response, and degree of ego-involvement—in any of various activities, persons, or ideas, whether or not these be activities which involve him with other people, are "good" or "socially approved" or "status-giving" or "self-improving." Thus the person who "just loves to sit home and knit" rates as high as the person who "loves to get out and meet people."

Physical energy is *not* to be involved in this rating.

A low rating is given for listlessness and apathy; for being "bored with most things"; for "I have to force myself to do things"; also for meaningless (and unenjoyed) hyperactivity.

5 (high): Speaks of several activities with enthusiasm. Feels that "now" is the best time of life. Loves to do things, even sitting at home. Takes up new activities; makes new friends readily, seeks self-improvement. Shows zest in several areas of life.

4: Shows zest, but in a limited fashion—limited to one or two special interests, or limited to certain periods of time. May show disappointment or anger when things go wrong, if they keep him from active enjoyment of life. Plans ahead, even though in small time units.

3: Has a bland approach to life. Does things, but does not seem to get much pleasure out of them. Seeks relaxation in the passive sense. Has a limited degree of involvement in things. May be quite detached (aloof) from many activities.

2: Thinks life is monotonous for most part. May complain of fatigue. Feels bored with many things. If active, finds little meaning or enjoyment in the activity.

1:    Lives on the basis of routine. Doesn't think anything worth
      doing.

REFERENCES

Cavan, Ruth S., Burgess, E.W., Havighurst, R.J., & Goldhamer, H. *Personal adjustment in old age.* Chicago: Science Research Associates, 1949.

Cumming, Elaine, Dean, Lois R., & Newell, D.S. What is morale? A case history of a validity problem. *Hum. Organiz.,* 1959, **17** (2), 3-8.

Cumming, Elaine, Dean, Lois R., Newell, D.S., & McCaffrey, Isabel. Disengagement—a tentative theory of aging. *Sociometry,* 1960, **23,** 23-35.

Cumming, Elaine, & McCaffrey, Isabel. Some conditions associated with morale among the aging. Paper presented at the annual meeting of the American Psychopathological Association, New York, 1960.

Havighurst, R.J. Validity of the Chicago attitude inventory as a measure of personal adjustment in old age. *J. abnorm. soc. Psychol.,* 1951, **46,** 24-29.

Havighurst, R.J. The social competence of middle-aged people. *Genet. Psychol. Monogr.,* 1957, **56,** 297-375.

Havighurst, R.J., & Albrecht, Ruth. *Older people.* New York: Longmans Green, 1953.

Henry, W.E., & Cumming, Elaine. Personality development in adulthood and old age. *J. proj. Tech.,* 1959, **23** (4), 383-390.

Kutner, B., Fanshel, D., Togo, Alice M., & Langner, T. S. *Five hundred over sixty.* New York: Russell Sage Foundation, 1956.

Morrison, D.E., & Kristjanson, G.A. Personal adjustment among older persons. *Agric. Exp. Sta. tech. Bull.,* 1958, **21.** (South Dakota State College of Agriculture and Mechanic Arts, Brookings, S.D.)

Neugarten, Bernice, Havighurst, R.J., & Tobin, S. The measurement of life satisfaction. *Gerontology,* 1961, **16,** 134-143.

Reichard, Suzanne, Livson, Florine, & Petersen, P.G. *Aging and personality: A study of eighty-seven older men.* New York: John Wiley & Sons, 1962.

CHAPTER 17

Personality and
the Aging Process

BERNICE L. NEUGARTEN

Knowledge of personality changes that occur during the middle and later years is scanty. There have been relatively few empirical studies from which findings can be generalized. More important, there is not yet available a systematic body of theory on the aging personality as a framework within which isolated and fragmentary findings can be related. Existing personality theories, developed primarily for ordering observations of child and adolescent personality, appear insufficient and inappropriate for describing the changes that occur as a person moves from young adulthood to old age.

Against this background, a number of studies of personality processes from age forty to seventy have been carried out with the larger research undertakings that have come to be known as the Kansas

321

City studies of adult life.[1] Although these studies are still in progress, the findings are beginning to form a consistent pattern now and point to a theory that can be tested by other investigators.

SAMPLING

A major problem in studies of personality differences with age is sampling. Most reports have been based on groups of institutionalized old people, psychiatric patients, or volunteer samples. The studies in this paper share one important characteristic: they all deal with subjects drawn from two large samples of adults residing in the Midwestern metropolitan area, Kansas City. The groups constituted random samples of people, age forty to seventy-one, drawn by modified area-probability techniques, but stratified by age, sex, and socioeconomic level. The first sample was drawn in 1953; the second, in 1955. (A group of ambulatory old people, age seventy to eighty-five, have recently been added to our study groups.) Altogether, in the course of the Kansas City studies of adult life, varying amounts of information have been gathered on over one thousand people forty and over, all living in their own homes and participating in the activities characteristic of functioning members of the community. They were volunteers only in the sense that, after being approached and, to varying degrees, persuaded, by a member of our field staff, they agreed to be interviewed.

All the studies in this paper were based on subsamples drawn from this pool. Each study, furthermore, involved a relatively large group of subjects—in each instance, more than one hundred. Although all these studies have been primarily concerned with age as the major variable, it should be made clear that the data are all cross-sectional, not longitudinal. Thus inferences drawn regarding changes with age are, strictly speaking, statements based on observed differences among age groups.

[1] These studies have been carried out under the auspices of the Committee on Human Development of the University of Chicago. The first set of investigations, supported by a grant from the Carnegie Foundation, was conducted by a research committee of which Robert J. Havighurst was chairman. The second set, financed by Grant 3M-9082 from the National Institute of Mental Health, is under the supervision of William E. Henry (principal investigator), Robert J. Havighurst, and Bernice L. Neugarten. The study director is Elaine Cumming; the field director, Lois R. Dean.

SOCIAL COMPETENCE AND
LIFE SATISFACTION

In these Kansas City studies there are three different lines of investigation that bear on personality functioning. The first may be called the "social personality." Here attention has been focused on gross patterns of social interaction and competence, thus on relatively overt, public behavior. The second is the area that measures what, for lack of a better term, has often been called "adjustment" or "successful aging" and individual happiness or satisfaction with life. The third line of investigation, the one with which the present report is primarily concerned, relates to the more covert, less readily observed aspects of personality dynamics. These three aspects of behavior are, of course, inextricably woven into everyone's life, yet they may be investigated separately. Indeed, these studies have produced rather different findings about the significance of chronological age in each of these areas.

When the investigator's attention was focused on social aspects of behavior or competence, the findings showed neither significant nor consistent age changes from forty to sixty-five. In more exact terms, chronological age has not proved a meaningful variable in the variance in scores. Thus, Havighurst rated the performance of 240 men and women from varying social levels in roles of worker, parent, spouse, homemaker, user of leisure time, friend, citizen, club and association member, and church member. If a person were not penalized for the absence of one or more roles (the widow, for instance, by definition is no longer filling the role of spouse, so she was rated on eight, rather than nine, roles), then the quality of role performance did not vary appreciably over the age range from forty to sixty-five (Havighurst, 1957).

It is not until people reach their mid-sixties, on the average, that gross patterns of social interaction show marked changes. This is demonstrated in the study by Cumming, Dean, Newell, and McCaffrey (1960) in which various measures of social interaction were utilized: hours of a typical day spent with other persons; total interactions with different kinds of people over one month; number of social roles the person fills. Here, with a sample of more than two hundred people from fifty through eighty-five, grouped in five-year age intervals, there were relatively consistent changes over this wide age range as age increased. At the same time, the most marked changes in score pattern appeared around sixty-five (Cumming et al., 1960). As far as our measures of social interaction are concerned, then, it appears that the period from the forties to the mid-sixties may be viewed as a plateau, relative to the periods that precede and follow. Systematic changes related to chronological age are not evident.

It should be pointed out that the behaviors described here are relatively gross. To say that a man continues to perform well on his job or that a woman continues to interact with the same number of people when she is sixty as when she was forty is not to deny that there may be measurable changes occurring in quality and mode of social interaction. More refined observations might be expected to produce different findings regarding changes with age in this area of behavior.

In the second area of investigation, adjustment and/or life satisfaction, the Kansas City studies showed no consistent relations with age, even, perhaps, to the age of eighty-five. For instance, Peck and Berkowitz rated over-all adjustment for a sample of 120 persons, age forty to sixty-four, from all social levels and found no relation to chronological age (Peck & Berkowitz, 1959). Similarly, Havighurst and Neugarten, using four rounds of interviews over a period of two years, rated more than two hundred people from fifty to eighty-five on five components of life satisfaction (zest for life; mood tone; sense of resolution or fortitude; consistency between desired and achieved life goals; and degree to which the self is positively regarded). No correlation was found between these ratings and chronological age (Havighurst, *supra*). It appears, therefore, that age is not a significant variable, not only in the twenty-five years prior to sixty-five, but probably in the seventies and eighties as well. (Relative to life satisfaction at the older ages, this finding must be interpreted with caution, since the seventy- and eighty-year-old subjects did not suffer from major illness or economic deprivation, thus constituting a select group of survivors.)

AGE-RELATED CHANGES IN PERSONALITY

Turning now to studies that deal with the more covert, inner aspects of personality, the picture is different as regards chronological age. Here, when the investigator was concerned with such issues as the perception of the self vis-à-vis the external environment, handling of impulse life, or nature of ego boundaries, the findings lead to the conclusion that there are significant and consistent age differences after forty.

These differences are not always readily discernible, however, as even some of our own investigations have produced varying results on this point. The variation has been caused, to some extent, by using different theoretical approaches and sets of personality variables; to perhaps greater extent, by the particular type of data used; and by whether an inductive or deductive approach was taken. Because the studies illustrate different points regarding method, they are described separately.

In one investigation (Gruen, 1958), an adaptation of Erikson's theory of ego development through life was used. Conceiving Erikson's eight so-called nuclear stages of ego development as independent personality dimensions, Gruen devised rating scales for them (trust versus distrust; autonomy versus shame; initiative versus guilt; industry versus inferiority; ego identity versus role diffusion; intimacy versus ego isolation; generativeness versus ego stagnation; and ego integrity versus despair) and rated 108 men and women from forty to sixty-four, of varying social classes, on the basis of interview data. The interviews contained open-ended questions about work, retirement, plans for the future, use of leisure time, health, attitude toward aging, spouse and children, religion, friends, expression of emotional states and evaluation of life. Ratings were based on the whole interview protocol, not on particular questions. An analysis of variance showed no consistent variance attributable to age.

In another study, Peck and Berkowitz (1959) used the same interview data with responses to six TAT (Thematic Apperception Test) cards for a sample of 120 men and women from forty to sixty-four. Ratings were made on seven personality variables derived from a developmental theory formulated by Peck (1956). This theory proposes that particular adaptive capacities in the personality become salient one after another as the adult attempts to resolve the psychological crises that accompany events of the middle and older years, such as widowhood or retirement. The variables are entitled flexibility of cathection, mental flexibility, ego transcendence, body transcendence, body satisfaction, and sexual integration. As in Gruen's study, statistical analysis of the ratings on these variables showed no consistent age differences.

Problems of Method

These two studies are at variance with others of our studies of personality as far as they show no significant change with age from forty to sixty-five. The discrepancy is probably related to differences of method. The next studies to be described were based on projective data analyzed blind for age, whereas the two studies just cited were based on interview data that could not be disguised for age.

The point about method is not merely that projective data and interview data may yield different orders of information about the same personality nor that research of this kind is always improved to the extent that the investigator's biases can be controlled, as they are when the data are blinded for age. The point is rather that the invesigator's bias is particularly difficult to control in studying the relatively unfamiliar area of developmental differences in adulthood, as compared to studying developmental differences in childhood or adolescence. The researcher operates under special difficulties in making evaluative judgments from interview data. Not only is the adult subject more practiced than the child in controlling the information he reveals in an interview, but the investigator himself has difficulty in avoiding a shifting frame of reference in making his judgments. The same datum of behavior, when it appears in a seventy-year-old, is often differently regarded from when it appears in a forty-year-old. (As we have witnessed many times in our training sessions, a frequent thought process in the judge seems to be, "That's quite good—for a seventy-year-old!") Nor is such a bias consistent from datum to datum on the same subject.

Ensuring that the same units of measurements have been applied to all members of a sample is a problem common to all rating methods; it is a more likely source of error in handling the behavior of forty-, fifty-, and sixty-year-olds than that of two-, four-, and six-year-olds. This is because developmental psychologists have become relatively sophisticated about the characteristic behavior of children at various developmental points. Furthermore, in studies of childhood and adolescence, there are clearer concepts of what constitutes an appropriate normative population. In dealing with adults, such concepts are less clear. Are forty-year-olds and seventy-year-olds to be regarded as a single population? If not, what developmental points can be used to establish appropriate normative groupings? Such problems as these have proven to be major ones. They will be overcome only when more research has been done on normal adults and when more developmental bench marks become available. Controlling for age bias and maintaining constant points of reference is also largely avoided when responses to specific interview questions constitute the data for analysis. Such data can usually be treated in straightforward fashion, and a set of categories initially independent of age can be established.

The problem lies, therefore, not with the interview method, but with making evaluations of interview data.

For the reasons implied in these comments, most of our studies of age differences in personality have been based on projective data. It has proved difficult to blind interview data for age, but relatively easy to detach, for instance, the TAT protocol from the rest of the interview and analyze it blind for age.[2]

The first of these projective studies on Kansas City subjects was one that has been reported by Neugarten and Gutmann (1958). Responses of 131 working-class and middle-class men and women aged forty to seventy to a specially drawn type of TAT picture were analyzed. Although this study was first undertaken as an investigation of age-sex roles, it became apparent that the data reflected consistent personality differences related to age. The individual's covert investment in his roles, sources of gratification, and preferred modes of action seemed to differ markedly between forty-year-olds and sixty-year-olds. There were, for instance, different views of the nature of the external world. Forty-year-olds seemed to see themselves possessing energy congruent with the opportunities perceived in the outer world. The environment was seen to reward boldness and risk-taking —a person gets from the world what he gives to it. For older respondents the outer world was complex and a bit dangerous. It was not to be reformed according to personal wishes; instead, one conformed and accommodated oneself to its demands. To the older respondent, the individual no longer manipulated the object world forcefully, but was, instead, a rather passive object manipulated by the environment.

This study also gave evidence that, with increasing age, the ego qualities of the personality that regulate impulses and adapt to environmental demands seem to contract. With increased age, the ego seemed not only in a position of lessened mastery relative to the outer world, but also the ego seemed less in contact with and less effective in controlling and channeling impulse.

With increasing age the data suggested, "Ego functions are turned inward, as it were, and while rational thought processes are still important in the personality, thought is less relevant to action" (Neugarten & Gutmann, 1958, p. 23).

The same study suggested important differences between

[2] Our analyses have been primarily of Thematic Apperception Test data, although we have available also sentence-completion and Draw-a-Person data for some groups. Preliminary analyses of these projective data corroborate the over-all finding of consistent differences related to age.

men and women as they age. For instance, men seem to become more receptive to their own affiliative, nurturant, and sensual promptings, whereas women seem to become more responsive toward, and less guilty about, their own aggressive, egocentric impulses. Although sex differences cannot be elaborated in the present paper, the fact should be mentioned that such differences have appeared in most of these studies. Social class has also proven to be an important variable.

Studies of Ego Functions

To follow some of the leads from the study just mentioned, several subsequent investigations of ego functions were undertaken. In one study (Gutmann, Henry, & Neugarten, 1959) the stories told by 144 men to four standard TAT cards were analyzed. Here the individual stories, rather than individual men, were treated as the units for analysis. Stories that were similar in central focus and structure were grouped together to form categories, and the categories were then ranked on a continuum from active to passive mastery. That is, stories that reflected an energetic, motoric, or alloplastic approach to the environment were placed at the active end of the continuum; stories that reflected a passive, autoplastic attitude—where the hero was resigned, deferential, or constricted in the face of environmental pressures—were ranked at the passive end of the continuum. The percentage of stories in each category was computed for each age group, and from these percentages the psychological issues that are most prominent at each age were inferred. For instance, the most frequent stories given by men in the forty to forty-nine age group stressed virility and resistance to coercion. Intrusive energies were ascribed to the hero figures, passive and dependent wishes were denied, problems were thrashed out in combat with the environment.

Stories told by fifty-year-olds were frequently those in which passive and deferential rather than rebellious or defiant heroes were projected, although there was also a high percentage of stories reflecting striving and active mastery. Thus, both relations to the environment were given prominence—as if fifty-year-old men are conflicted more than the other age groups. They begin to favor short-range, sensual, and affiliative rewards over long-range achievement goals, yet they seem reluctant to retreat from the struggle.

In the stories of the sixty-year-olds, the conflicts seem to have been resolved. The most frequent stories were those in which the heroes conform, abase themselves, and are meek, friendly, and mild. Aggression was ascribed only to the external world, and parental figures or impersonal institutional demands are important in the outcomes.

In contrast to the study just described, Rosen and Neugarten (1960) took a deductive approach in studying changes with age in the ego processes. Following the indication that ego functions seem to diminish in effectiveness with increased age, the investigators proceeded on certain formulations developed by ego psychologists (particularly Hartmann, 1951; Lustman, 1957; Rapaport, 1951) relating to the concept of ego energy. A research design was established for testing the hypothesis that during the middle and later years there is a decrease in the energy available to the ego for responding to, or maintaining former investment in, outer world events.

On the postulation that they would provide gross estimates of available ego energy, four dimensions of ego function were selected for study, and methods for measuring them by TAT data were delineated. These dimensions and the corresponding TAT measures were ability to integrate wide ranges of stimuli (measured by introducing nonpictorial characters into TAT stories); readiness to perceive or handle complicated, challenging, or conflict-filled situations (measured by introducing conflict, controversy, choice, or decision into the stories); tendency toward vigorous, assertive activity (measured by the activity-energy level ascribed to story characters); and tendency to perceive or to be concerned with emotions as these play a part in life situations (measured by the degree to which affect states are seen as playing a role in the story productions).

The sample was 144 men and women from forty to seventy-one, divided into eighteen equal cells on the bases of age, sex, and social class. The TAT stories were scored blind, then a three-way analysis of variance was carried out. Results indicated that on all four measures only the factor of age was significant in accounting for variance. Scores decreased from age group to age group in the predicted direction.

Dr. Gutmann has proceeded to investigate further the indication that problems with inner life increase as aging progresses. Using TAT data for 145 men aged forty to seventy-one and working inductively from the data, he made a formulation about each man's personality for major concerns and preoccupations, especially in the unconscious drive (impulse life); ego defenses (coping mechanisms) elaborated in response to such preoccupations; and success or failure of these coping mechanisms as indicated by the form of the TAT stories, the accuracy of interpreting the stimuli, the flexibility or rigidity of approach, the themes, and the expression of affect and energy (Gutmann, 1959). Five major personality types were established. When the data were decoded, the five types were distributed by age, and the differences in the distribution proved to be statistically significant.

We cannot define the types here, but the data indicate the older men fall off markedly in active participation with the outer world, shifting their attention to intrapsychic events. Whereas the forty-year-old man tends to ignore the inner life and strives to dominate the outer world, older respondents seem to deploy their energy inward in the attempt to master the psychic life. They also seem to have resolved autonomy-dependency problems, which preoccupied the younger men, with solutions in the direction of passivity and deference. There is an age shift from reliance on ego to reliance on superego elements of the personality—in solving issues and problems there is more concern with abstract rules and authority than with working out rational, adaptive solutions, an increased frequency of distorted and inappropriate interpretations, and other evidence of ineffective ego controls.

The findings from this study confirm and elaborate those from the earlier ones. To recapitulate, in males there are age-related differences from forty to seventy that indicate a shift from active to passive mastery in dealing with the outer world, greater preoccupation with impulse life, less efficient modes of coping with impulse life, greater emphasis on conformity and constriction, and greater dependency on superego functions in handling problems from within and without.

In a similar analysis of TAT data for women aged forty to seventy-one, five major personality types were also delineated, although the most salient psychological issues for women are not identical with those for men (Gutmann, 1960). The typology for women is based on the extent to which issues and personal conflicts are externalized and projected onto the outside world, effectiveness of ego controls over impulse, extent of intropunitiveness or extrapunitiveness, and balance between maternal and altruistic, versus domineering and retentive, motivations (the latter are usually revealed by stories dealing with children or young people interacting with older people).

When the five types were arrayed along a continuum from good to defective ego control and from maternal and altruistic orientation to egocentric and retentive orientation and when the protocols were decoded for age, there was a clear relationship between personality type and chronological age for women aged fifty to seventy. The women aged forty to fifty, however, were distributed over all five types. The meaning of this finding is not yet clear and awaits further analyses of other data on the women. It is apparent, however, that, although men's and women's personalities change differently with age, there are significant age changes in both sexes.

We are now at that point where we have demonstrated significant age differences in the period from forty to sixty-five in the more covert and private motivational and attitudinal aspects of personality. Now we are moving to the study of the relations between these personality measures and other types of information on the same individuals. Although generalizations are still premature, our first attempts in this direction are yielding meaningful findings. To illustrate, it appears that there is a positive relation between personality type as delineated by Gutmann on the basis of the TAT and life satisfaction, with those men who are high on active-mastery being those who are also high on life satisfaction. Similarly, there seems to be a positive relation between ego energy, as delineated by Rosen on the basis of the TAT, and the individual's outlook on the future, as reflected in responses to interview questions. If meaningful relationships such as these continue to appear, they will provide some valid measure for these personality assessments. At the same time, they will constitute further evidence that inductive approaches to the study of personality change in adulthood are fruitful.

SUMMARY AND IMPLICATIONS

In summary, these studies have demonstrated significant age differences in the period from forty to sixty-five in the covert, motivational, and attitudinal aspects of personality. These changes have been (1) in mode of relating to the environment and handling impulses, with a movement of energy from an outer-world to inner-world orientation and from active to passive mastery; (2) in the degree of effectiveness of ego functions; and (3) in the amount of energy available to the ego. These functions are obviously interrelated and may only constitute different reflections of increased constriction and turning inward as a person grows old. That these processes occur in the years from forty to sixty-five is the point to be stressed, since in these years gross measures of social competence show no age changes.

These findings are, it should be repeated, based on cross-sectional data, and it remains to be demonstrated that they represent developmental changes. If the latter can be demonstrated, however, the implication is that we have evidence that corroborates the theory of disengagement, formulated by Cumming and Henry (Cumming et al., 1960; Henry & Cumming, 1959), "A theory of aging in which a disengaging process which may be primarily intrinsic, and secondarily responsive, leads to a disengaged state. The individual is pictured as participating with others in his social systems in a process of mutual withdrawal, rather than being deserted by others in the structure" (Cumming et al., 1960, p. 34).

Data from the Kansas City studies about patterns of social interaction show no marked differences and thus do not directly reflect disengagement until the mid-sixties. The data summarized here, however, indicate that personality changes consonant with the disengagement theory are measurable as early as the forties. With due regard for the facts that the aspects of social interaction thus far measured are very broad and that the measurements have been relatively gross, the differences in the timing of age changes are nevertheless impressive. The suggestion is that changes occur within the individual long before they are manifested in his social interactions. If this difference is borne out when more refined measures of social interaction become available, it would be justifiable to infer that disengagement does have intrinsic as well as responsive components.

The aspects of personality measured here lie closer, perhaps, to biological than to social determinants of behavior. It is true that we lack data for assessing the interrelations between biological, psychological, and social factors in the aging process and that any attempt to categorize behavior or its determinants is, at best, only a heuristic device. At the same time, no theory of aging can be attempted without giving at least some consideration to possible interactions between such classes of factors. Accordingly, we are suggesting here that, just as biological maturation is primary for the development of an adequately functioning ego in the early years of life, it may be that biological factors again take precedence in maintaining the ego functions of the aging individual. Decreased efficiency in these personality functions may be closely related to decreased efficiency in biological functions. In this connection, other investigators have pointed out that until at least the mid-sixties the average person maintains social competence in the face of considerable biological change (Havighurst, 1957). The present studies indicate a somewhat parallel phenomenon—that people maintain social competence in the face of considerable personality change.

To proceed further in these speculations, it is possible, just as it is with biological changes, that only when personality changes go beyond a certain threshold are the visible patterns of social functioning affected. Or, in different terms, the biological organism shows unmistakable signs of aging during the period from forty to sixty-five; so does the psychological organism, but within a considerable range the changes seem to remain relatively independent of social performance and personal satisfaction with life. Only when there is gross biological malfunction or illness is the independence between biological and social functions destroyed. The same may be true of the personality processes studied here. Only when there is marked distortion or gross breakdown of ego functions will there be a visible effect on everyday behavior.

REFERENCES

Cumming, Elaine, Dean, Lois R., Newell, D.S., & McCaffrey, Isabel. Disengagement—a tentative theory of aging. *Sociometry*, 1960, **23**, 23-35.

Gruen, W. An experimental application of Erikson's theory of ego development. Unpublished memorandum on file with the Committee on Human Development, University of Chicago, 1958.

Gutmann, D.L. Personality change with age in males. Unpublished research report on file with the Committee on Human Development, University of Chicago, 1959.

Gutmann, D.L. Personality change with age in females. Unpublished memorandum on file with the Committee on Human Development, University of Chicago, 1960.

Gutmann, D.L., Henry, W.E., & Neugarten, Bernice L. Personality development in middle-aged men. Paper read at the annual meeting of the American Psychological Association, Cincinnati, 1959.

Hartmann, H. Ego psychology and the problem of adaptation. In D. Rapaport (Ed.), *Organization and pathology of thought*. New York: Columbia University Press, 1951. Pp. 362-396.

Havighurst, R.J. The social competence of middle-aged people. *Genet. Psychol. Monogr.*, 1957, **56**, 297-375.

Henry, W.E., & Cumming, Elaine. Personality development in adulthood and old age. *J. proj. Tech.*, 1959, **23**, 383-390.

Lustman, S. Psychic energy and mechanisms of defense. In Ruth S. Eissler, Anna Freud, H. Hartmann, & G. Kris (Eds.), *The psychoanalytic study of the child*. Vol. 12. New York: International Universities Press, 1957. Pp. 151-165.

Neugarten, Bernice L., & Gutmann, D.L. Age-sex roles and personality in middle age: A thematic apperception study. *Psychol. Monogr.*, 1958, **72**, No. 17.

Peck, R.F. Psychological developments in the second half of life. In J.E. Anderson (Ed.), *Psychological aspects of aging.* Washington, D.C.: American Psychological Association, 1956. Pp. 42-53.

Peck, R.F., & Berkowitz, H. Personality and adjustment in middle age. Unpublished memorandum on file with the Committee on Human Development, University of Chicago, 1959.

Rapaport, D. Toward a theory of thinking. In D. Rapaport (Ed.), *Organization and pathology of thought.* New York: Columbia University Press, 1951. Pp. 689-730.

Rosen, Jacqueline L., & Neugarten, Bernice L. Ego functions in the middle and later years: A thematic apperception study of normal adults. *J. Geront.*, 1960, **15**, 62-67.

CHAPTER 18

Styles of Life and
Successful Aging

RICHARD H. WILLIAMS

The Kansas City study of adult life is central to two previous chapters, Chapter 16 by Havighurst and Chapter 17 by Neugarten. It has produced a rich body of data which can be analyzed in a variety of ways. The present focus is on an intensive study of the data on twenty older people in an attempt to delineate their various styles of life and to make some global judgments about the success of these older subjects. The writer has not interviewed or even seen any of the subjects, so, in a sense, this effort is a test of the usefulness of the data for intensive case study in contrast to the purposes of more formal analyses. We are still in a preliminary stage in the social and psychological research of aging, a stage in which case studies on natural history and phenomenological levels are potentially useful.

In studying these cases, a definition of successful aging has been developed, which, in turn, involves a type of analysis not yet undertaken by any of the staff of the Kansas City study. It has not yet been sufficiently operationalized to be readily used by other analysts, but it is reasonable to suppose that it can be or at least that the effort to do so would be worthwhile.

DEFINITION

Selection of Cases

The member of the Kansas City field team in charge of interviewing, who herself had done some intensive interviewing, was asked to select ten cases. The intent was to get as full a range of life situations as possible. On completion of these ten cases, it was apparent that the range was not adequate in family structure, and four cases were added to give a better spread in this respect. From the special panel of people in their seventies, six cases were selected, three men and three women, two of whom lived alone, two with another person, and two with his or her spouse.

In a technical sense the cases are not a sample from the Kansas City study. No statements can be made at this time about the relative frequency of the various styles of life. In the future it will be possible to run through all the cases, determine how representative the twenty cases are, and add cases as needed. It must also be emphasized that the panels from which these cases were drawn exclude people near the top or the bottom of the socioeconomic scale, people who are institutionalized, and people who have gross medical pathology. These points are especially important in relation to the rankings of successful aging. None of the persons in this series reaches the limit of unsuccessful aging, so it would be more proper to speak of degrees of success.

Some Concepts and Measures

From the beginning of the present Kansas City study, there has been a strong interest in the social life space of the respondents and their modes of interaction in it (Williams, 1960; Williams & Loeb, 1956). Certain scores and indexes have been developed in this framework. A life space score indicates the number of people with whom the respondent interacts in a week; the intensity of interaction is given an index from one to five, and a count is made of the roles which he performs. In relation to a major theory which will be developed in this study, a particularly interesting measure is the perceived life space. This indicates whether the person perceives his life space as smaller or larger than it was when he was forty-five years old.

The orientation of the respondent to interaction in his life space is classified by a combination of variables central to the theory of action developed by Talcott Parsons (1958, p. 130). This classification is described by Cumming, Dean, Newell, and McCaffrey (1960) as follows:

1. A diffuse-affective set toward interaction carries the expectation of potentially unlimited mutual obligation and affection, and the anticipated relational reward is unconditional acceptance, or *love*. The nuclear family is the ideal type.
2. A diffuse-neutral set toward interaction carries an expectation of potentially unlimited mutual obligation, but no expectation of mutual affection. The ideal type occurs in such goal-directed collectivity as a union, a charitable organization, or a fraternal order. The anticipated relational reward is *esteem*, and the tone is moral and evaluative.
3. The specific-affective set toward interaction carries the expectation of short-run gratification. The anticipated relational reward is *responsiveness* in the immediate situation. It occurs in any interaction undertaken purely for recreation; it can be called a hedonistic set.
4. The specific-neutral set toward interaction carries the expectation of adequate mutual performance toward a goal apart from the interaction itself; no emotional gratification is involved. The ideal type is work and the contractual world. The anticipated relational reward is *approval* (pp. 32-33).

There has also been strong interest in morale and life satisfaction. These matters are discussed in some detail by Havighurst in Chapter 16, *supra* (see also Cumming, Dean, & Newell, 1958). For the cases in the present study, a morale index from zero to four is available (it will be discussed more fully in the following analysis) as is an alienation score. The score ranges from seven to twenty-one, the low side indicating conformity; the high, alienation. For the panel of fifty- to seventy-year-olds an F score reflecting either liberal or authoritarian tendencies and a rating of psychological types, as discussed by Neugarten in Chapter 17, *supra,* and by Henry and Cumming (1959), are available.

Social Systems of Individual Actors

Sociologists and social psychologists have handled large populations, communities, large organizations, and small groups, either artificial or natural, such as the family. It is sometimes thought that psychologists, or at least some psychologists, deal with "the individual," but the sociopsychological world can be sliced in a different way, yielding the abstraction, "the social system of the individual actor." A given actor, such as a respondent in the panel, can be taken as the focal point and questioned about the dimensions and structure of his social life space, modes of interaction in it, attitudinal set toward it, satisfaction or dissatisfaction he derives from it, and degree of its stability over time. This system should not be looked on or analyzed as a group qua group. Each actor in this system has his own social system. Ideally, data should be gathered from various points of the system and not solely from the individual actor, but they should be gathered with the point of view of the original actor as the focus. The researcher should get such data through interviews with significant others, direct observation, or instruments. This procedure had not yet been followed in the Kansas City study at the time this analysis was made, but the data have subsequently been gathered. This type of data should greatly enrich our understanding of the aging of individual social systems.

Theories of Aging

One qualification and two supplementary points which have relevance for the present analysis will be suggested as theories of aging. The activity theory is not properly a theory in the same sense as the disengagement theory. When Dr. Elaine Cumming was developing the disengagement theory, she originally called the activity theory "the latent theory," because it represents a latent or implicit point of view in the writings of many applied social gerontologists. It is a view about kinds of intervention for the aging rather than a scientific theory about the aging process. The disengagement theory is a theory in this latter sense.

Cassetta, Newell, and Parlagreco (1960) have indicated that the disengagement has three facets—physical, social, and emotional. Significant questions can be asked about varying rates of disengagement for all three, especially about the equilibruim or disequilibrium among them. Furthermore there can be equilibrium or disequilibrium at both high and low over-all levels of engagement. As the author has indicated (Williams, 1960, p. 268), disengagement can, in turn, be related to the concept of differentiation as developed by Parsons (1955). The actor disengages from parts of his individual social system, the system thereby becomes "de-differentiated," and the total life space of the system moves toward constriction. Such a shift is congruent with changes in ego functioning described by Neugarten in Chapter 17, *supra*. This problem of differentiation of the social system of the individual actor is undoubtedly crucial at both ends of the life cycle and has much to do with success in life and success in aging.

A Definition of Successful Aging

The definition of successful aging developed in this analysis is a combination of two judgments made about the social systems of the individual subjects studied.

The first judgment concerns the exchange of action-specific energy between the individual and parts of his social system. How much work (output) does he contribute to the system, and how much work (input) of others does it take to keep him going? If there is a balance on account or a plus value on the output side, the individual is said to be autonomous, but, if it takes more energy than he gives the system to maintain him, he is said to be dependent. At one end of this continuum, one can readily distinguish highly dependent people (people who are unable to maintain themselves as organisms without a great deal of help from others or people who are an emotional drain on others) and at the other end highly autonomous (independent) people. It is difficult, however, to make precise measurements along this continuum, because we do not have any single scale for measuring units of action-specific energy or work. Also, the situation represented at any point along such a scale can have various possible contents. For example, a completely autonomous person in all spheres of action would be a hermit who raises his own food, makes his own clothes, has built his own dwelling, and so on, but his balance on account with the social system is zero—he doesn't take anything from it, but he doesn't give anything to it.

Autonomy-dependency can be related to any one of four basic needs of human social behavior:

1. *Wealth,* since to act always requires some command over scarce means. People can be economically autonomous or dependent.

2. *Power,* the ability to make decisions and influence others. Some people are almost completely dependent on others for all decisions, thus are virtually unable to exercise influence, whereas others literally command their social systems.

3. *Success,* the recognition of accomplishments, prestige on which some people are highly dependent. They need con-

stant evaluation from others and are highly sensitive to praise
and blame. Others are more autonomous in this respect.

4. *Affective response* is inordinately required by some people;
they are emotionally dependent. Here, too, one can think of
action-specific energy and how much emotional response one
takes from and gives to others. Again the hermit comes out
zero unless he abandoned his family somewhere.

Relatively greater weight is given to the fourth aspect of dependency
in the present analysis, although the suggested perspective may add
something to understanding all four types. Also, it is useful to distinguish dependency which is conditional to the actor and over which
he has no control (for example, mass unemployment) from dependency in which he is more actively involved (emotional dependency is the type case).

The other judgment pertains to the probable future of the
system: will it persist, change to a different system, or collapse? In
short, is it persistent or precarious? There are four combinations of
these judgments:

autonomous-persistent	successful aging
autonomous-precarious	potentially unsuccessful aging
dependent-persistent	successfully unsuccessful aging
dependent-precarious	unsuccessful aging

Cases can be ranked in each of the four categories (in this instance from
one to twenty) with each successive category starting with a higher
number. The extreme case of unsuccessful aging lies outside the
four categories and is represented by becoming a public charge, being
committed to an institution, or committing suicide. The relationship
can be diagrammed as follows:

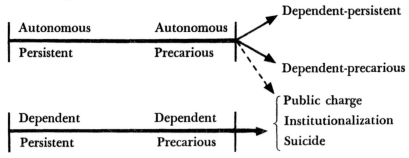

This approach does not deny the value of the approach
described by Havighurst. It is independent of it and intended to

supplement it. The judgments here have been made without regard to the happiness of the subjects or the degree of satisfaction they are getting out of life. The relationship between autonomous-persistent and life satisfaction is problematical, a meaningful and interesting question.

The autonomy-dependency of the social system of an individual actor is a complex matter to judge. The input-output balance is a matter of action energy and certainly not exclusively—or even primarily—a matter of physical energy. Thus an invalid who requires extensive nursing care, but provides emotional satisfaction to the others in his primary network, would be more autonomous than a physically vigorous person who is neurotogenic for the significant others.

The probability of the subject's death is not taken into account in these judgments, nor is the death of one or more of the significant people around him. For example, it could be known that the subject will die in a certain time, and he might still have an autonomous-persistent social system. If he were highly dependent on his wife, however, and it were known that she would die shortly, his system would definitely be more precarious than it would otherwise be. The health of the subject as such is not a factor in these judgments; only the way he uses his health in his transactions with the others in his system is important. The same consideration applies to the subject's financial security. All the subjects in this series are relatively autonomous financially, and all but one are likely to remain so, but they differ significantly in degree of over-all autonomy. In short, the judgment pertains to the actor's social system and not to his systems of health or economy.

Of the two judgments, the persistent-precarious is somewhat harder to make because of its predictive nature. It should be particularly emphasized that the persistence or precariousness is of the social system of the individual actor, with the actor as the focus, not a judgment about the social system within which the actor lives (for example, it is not a judgment about the entire family or community), although this latter consideration must be taken into account in making the judgment.

This definition of successful aging meets a basic requirement indicated by Havighurst. It is independent of any theory of aging, but it can well be used to explore certain aspects of a theory, as will be done below. A person, for example, can be autonomous and engaged or autonomous and disengaged, dependent and engaged or dependent and disengaged. Also, in terms of direction of change or of intervention in therapy, for some people a shift toward autonomy would come with increased activity and involvement, whereas for others it would come with increased disengagement.

THE CASES

The cases have been grouped according to the main focus of the respondents' style of life. One group of seven cases is clearly focused on the world of work, whether the respondent is still working or has retired. A smaller group—two, but probably a relatively larger group in the entire panel—is absorbed in family and has a strong familistic value system. In a group of five the way of life is dominated by living alone; in a group of six the respondent is primarily part of an elderly couple. The groups have been given names to suggest the theme of the respondents' way of life in their later years. This latter device is admittedly more literary than systematic, but it may have some use in this early speculative and phenomenological stage of the analysis.

This classification of cases was made independently of the judgment rating of successful aging on the autonomy-dependency and persistence-precariousness continua. Certain relations will, however, appear between the two types of relations, which will be analyzed later. The order of presentation of cases in each class does take the success dimension into consideration to emphasize the point that successful aging can occur in several ways of life. It is also used to bring out certain marked contrasts in styles of aging.

In the interests of time and space some cases are described more fully than others to give some indication of the kinds of analyses needed to get the basic configuration and to make the kind of judgment which is central to this approach. With these unusually rich data, each case could be analyzed in considerable detail, according to the following outline:

1. Brief description of the person, setting, and background variables.
2. Life history (much more data on some cases than on others, but there will be equally extensive data on over half the subjects before the study is terminated).
3. Structure and range of the social network.

4. Interaction style and direction: is the subject disengaging?
5. Sources of support.
6. Summary of attitudinal set, orientation to action, values, and life themes.
7. The judgment and reasons for it.

This outline has been approximated, with some variations, in most of the cases.

All ages given are for the beginning of the series of interviews. In the case of the original panel (seventy and under), the series began in 1956. This group was interviewed over approximately three and a half years with a variation of three or four months either way. Some of the cases run through early 1960. For the additional panel (in the seventies) the cases run from mid- or late 1958 up to early 1960, about a year and a half.

The World of Work

The Protestant Ethic and Problems of Retirement. A seventy-year-old man lives in a comfortable home with his wife. They have adopted children, and there are grandchildren, but none of the children or grandchildren is part of the immediate household. The man was born in another Midwestern city, but has lived in Kansas City for fifty-two years. He owns a small business and so did his father. He is Protestant but a not very active member of his church. He was graduated from high school. On the Warner index of social class (ISC) his rating is forty-two, which puts him somewhere near the bottom of the upper-middle class.

It is apparent that this man was born and grew up in an urban middle-class environment. He has been married for most of his adult life. By the age of forty-five he was a moderately successful businessman and club member who enjoyed playing golf and poker with his cronies at the club. His wife's mother lived with them for thirty-five years and took care of the children while his wife played a good deal of golf. He thinks of thirty-five to fifty-five, when business was good, as the best years of his life. The depression hit him fairly hard, but he managed to weather the storm.

When he was first interviewed, he had just sold the business, but had started another one more-or-less in relation with his son and so still considered himself an active businessman. Six months later we found that he had left this business, having lost money on it. In the meantime he had tried still another business with his son, but

had also lost money, and he now is working as an assistant superintendent of a small company—or so he claims. His occupational
status seems rather vague. He admits that things are going badly and
he is not feeling so well. He joined the church (his wife seemed to be
behind this). During the interview his wife was complaining in the
background that he didn't work around the house, he didn't visit,
and so on. He states, however, that he plans to work as long as he
can and might go into another business. He takes an all-or-nothing
attitude on retirement and expects to be working five years hence,
although he is shocked to find how hard it is to get a job and regrets
having sold his business.

A similar picture, only perhaps a little more so, is seen about
six months later. Four months after that, he admits that he is not
working and is dreaming of a mail-order business. He has vague plans
about visiting the West Coast and seems rather confused about
whether he is working. His son seems to be doing well as a sales
manager, but he is ambivalent about the son. He blames himself for
the way he raised him and says that he undoubtedly spoiled him. At
one point he had blocked his son's marriage. He thinks it would be
much better for his wife and himself if he had an office away from
home. Six months later he says he is working around the house, for
"I haven't had much work lately." He is again discussing going into
business with his son. He has stopped going to church. If he suddenly
came into money (in response to a specific question about this), he
would get his son into his own business. Six months after this, he
indicates that it was his father who got him into business; he still feels
that it was a mistake to have sold it. He still wants to get back into
business and admits that he is depressed by retirement.

Here is the case of a man who inadvertently retired himself
by selling his business and then gradually moved into a rather anomic
kind of life. His life space suddenly became constricted. He mentions
two friends, but does not seem to interact with them on any regular
basis. At one point he mentioned a friend who had moved away, but
his wife chimed in to say that this was her friend. The effort to become
involved in church was abortive. He had never been active in church
organizations, did not become so, and soon stopped going to church
altogether. He was going through a process of disengagement, but
finding it painful. He was becoming more dependent on his wife
without giving her much in return. His old pleasures, golf and poker,
had lost their flavor for him. His orientation to action is specific-
neutral and diffuse-affective, but his diffuse-affective orientation be-

comes dependent in the absence of a meaningful network for specific-neutral relationships.

His value system is the middle-class, secular version of the Protestant ethic. However, there is some evidence that this ethic was not wholly assimilated. He admits that breaks are important in business and that he had them. He also regrets that he did not make much more money than he actually did and that he did not save enough, wasting it on things like poker. (It was interesting to note, after having analyzed this case, that it is the only one in the series of twenty which has a personality-type rating of "ego-defect.")

This man is in reasonably good health, as far as the evidence goes, and is not in any immediate danger of being financially impoverished in spite of his business losses. His wife and son can probably meet his emotional needs on a minimal level, but he certainly will not contribute much to their well-being.

This case has been classified as dependent-persistent and ranked as number eighteen, toward the bottom of the series on this success scale.

Work, Work, Work. This man is fifty-two, fairly tall and well-built, and works at various semiskilled jobs. He was first married about twenty years ago and divorced two years later. He was married again ten years later and still lives with his second wife. They have no children. They live in a moderately comfortable apartment in a congested residential area. The apartment is full of parakeets. His wife works as a superintendent in a manufacturing concern. His ISC is eighty, which places him somewhat above average in the upper-lower class. He was born in a medium-sized city, but his father was a farmer and he probably has some rural experience in his background. He has lived in Kansas City for most of his adult life.

At the time of the first interview, he had a semiskilled job and was very proud of his ability to work a long day six days a week. His wife, about nine years younger than he, also worked, earning about the same amount as he. On his day off he just loafs. He does very little reading, sometimes listens to the radio, and very occasionally visits friends. His wife works on his day off. He belongs to no clubs. He mentions two friends with whom he gets together only occasionally. He has a sister, whom he sees very regularly in his home city, a few hours' drive away.

A year later, he had changed jobs and was no longer working weekends. He could go to see his sister in the nearby city more frequently. He still has only a few casual friends. He sees his mother a few times a year. He has no retirement plans and plans to keep on working indefinitely. Five years from now he projects that he will be working if he is still alive.

Four months later he had changed jobs again and was working at night. This paid more money. Again, he has no really close friends. About a year later he had moved and was buying a house. Both he and his wife were working and in good health. He is tempted to drink occasionally. His wife does not approve of that, and he is sure his mother wouldn't either, but he gives in anyway. Obviously, however, this drinking has not got to the point where it interferes with his work.

About a year after that he is still in much the same situation. In that interview, however, we learn some interesting things about his general background and way of life. He considers work with trucks or driving trucks to be his life work (although he had not actually been driving trucks in recent years), and he would continue to work along these lines as long as his health keeps up. He states that he never could afford to say "to heck with it" and get depressed. He thinks of his mother as someone who has always been good and kind to him, but feels that he is more like his father (who left his mother when he was very young) because his mother was quiet and he is not. He remembers his father's being good to him although he was very stern and had a quick temper. His description of his wife is particularly interesting. He mentions her in response to a question about someone in his present life whom he most admires and wants to resemble. "She's average. Just like most women. She's a good saver, a good housekeeper. She's fairly good to me." His own behavior toward her is "sometimes good, sometimes not so good—we do have our disagreements." His perception of how she acts and feels toward him is "the same way—sometimes good, sometimes bad or not so good—oh, don't misunderstand me, we get along fairly good." When asked if he thought about her when he was tempted to do something, he replied, "No, no—well, if I want to get a jug—I know she's against that so why ask her? I just go right ahead and get one." He does not feel that he could resemble her in any way. "There's no one in the world that can be like her. She's been a boss so long that she thinks no one can boss her." When asked whether it matters how she feels about him, he replies "No, not at all," then laughs and adds, "we are used to each other—it doesn't matter too much—not a whole lot—it wouldn't do any good—even if I did."

This man is in good health and not in any immediate danger

of losing his income. His wife, who is younger than he, is also not in danger of losing her income. He and his wife seem to provide each other with the minimal emotional satisfaction which they require.

This man's value system is clearly one of accepting the inevitability of work. He has never had any great ambition to get ahead. His orientation to action is specific neutral-*specific* affective, which is somewhat atypical; his relation to the parakeets is a good example of the specific-affective. Besides his acceptance of the inevitability of work, he is somewhat alienated in his value system, and his F score of eleven is high for this group.

This case has been classified as autonomous-precarious. His system is in no immediate danger of collapse. His emotional input-output is about balanced with those of his wife and sister. He is in no immediate danger of loss of income, nor is his wife, who could support him if necessary. He lives in a small network and, in the immediate future, will not have to cope with disengagement. I have ranked him eleven, as the least precarious of the autonomous-precarious group. There are, however, elements of long-range precariousness. Should anything happen to his wife or sister, he might be sufficiently thrown out of emotional balance to turn to heavier drinking. And when, ultimately, he has to stop working, he will suddenly be disengaged and thrown considerably off balance.

The Working Grandmother. This sixty-five-year-old widow lives in a household with her daughter, son-in-law, and two grandchildren. She was married early in life, divorced about five years later, remarried several years after that, and had been widowed for nearly ten years at the time of the first interview. Her husband had a small business, and she had worked with him. Subsequent to his death she went to work full-time, and at the time of the interview period she was manager of a department in a company dealing with legal matters. She had a high school education. Her father owned and managed a theater, and she had helped her father in this business in her late teens. Her ISC is fifty-eight, which puts her toward the top of the lower-middle class.

In this instance the daily round gives an excellent picture of the structure of her social network and interaction style. She gets up early, goes downtown for breakfast, which she eats alone and considers the best time of her day. She works all day, eats lunch alone, supervises her employees, but does not have any close ties with them. She occasionally eats dinner with the family if she gets home on time; frequently, however, she works late. She works Saturday mornings and sometimes Saturday afternoons. If she is not working Saturday afternoon, she shops. She reads in her room at night and does not particularly care for television. On Sunday mornings she is at home with the family and states, rather significantly, that she enjoys "being with the family whether they are here or not—listening to them coming and going."

Secondary relationships (functionally specific, neutral, and universal) are very important to her, and she has a large number of them, especially through her work. Friendships are not particularly important. Her son is an official with an airline and provides her with an airline pass. She visits him in a Southern city at least once a year and visits two sisters in California once a year. These are her closest relationships. She does have a hobby, photography, and occasionally does some developing and printing with her grandson over the weekend. Otherwise her interactions with the members of the household are minimal.

She plans to work as long as her health will permit and has no thoughts or plans about retirement. If she were not working, she thinks, vaguely, that she might travel more and spend more time on her photography. This pattern persisted throughout the three years of the interview period, although near the end she admitted she was slowing down a bit. Her health appears good, she is financially solvent, and she seems, on a level of minimal interaction, to get and give emotional satisfaction within the household.

She has a conformist (non-alienated) value system, her F score of seven is fairly liberal, and her personality type is active mastery (1). This woman has been classified as autonomous-precarious, with a rank of fourteen in this series. Her pattern of work appears an elaborate defense against over-involvement with her family. She will probably have to stop working within three or four years. She might have the financial and physical resources to travel for a while and maintain a social system alternately alone and with relatives, but this pattern could not last long, and it, too, would be an autonomous-precarious system. She is likely to find herself living with her family full-time within four or five years, becoming something of a drain on their action system. Then her system would be dependent-persistent. It is doubtful she will ever become dependent-precarious.

The Retired Working Girl. This seventy-five-year-old woman is single and lives in a household which includes her brother about half the time. She is a graduate of high school and a retired secretary. Her father was a semiprofessional man in the commercial world.

She has an ISC of fifty-seven, which places her toward the top of the lower-middle class. The house in which she lives was left to her by a relative for as long as she actually lives in it. Should she die or move, the house is willed to charity. There appear to be elements of spite and jealousy in this arrangement for she does not like the house, but feels she is forced to live in it.

She belongs to two patriotic groups, although she is somewhat bored with one of them and thinks it might be better if there were some men in it. She uses it occasionally for bridge tournaments. She has a small circle of friends, including a bridge group, and plays bridge fairly frequently. She has two nieces living in Kansas City, one of whom calls her on the phone almost every day and treats her as if she were her mother.

She seems to be financially solvent, although one of the recurrent themes of several interviews is her deep regret that she sold some property in the South. She has had periods of bad health in the past. During the period of the interviews she had a spastic colon for a while, but her health seemed to be generally improving.

Her brother's wife is in an institution out of the city, and he spends about half his time away from Kansas City visiting the wife. During those periods she is not exactly lonely, but is very anxious and looks forward to her brother's return. She mentions specific periods of anxiety at night and a need to check all the doors and windows. She has a recurrent dream in which she is on a train, but has lost her baggage or a shoe—or her brother.

This woman has been classified as autonomous-precarious, with a rank of thirteen, in about the middle of the precarious group. Toward the end of the interviews, her brother had stayed away for a longer period than usual, and she was not sure when he would return. She manifested considerable anxiety. Should her brother stay away for a variety of probable reasons, she would probably develop a very dependent relationship with her niece and would fall into the dependent-persistent category. It is doubtful that she will ever become the dependent-precarious type.

Forced Inactivity. This seventy-four-year-old man lives in a household with his wife. Until very recently he had had a responsible skilled-labor position. Because of a heart attack he was placed on the inactive, but—at his own insistence—not on the retired list.

Since his heart attack he sits all day, rarely reading or engaging in any other activity. During the winter he watches television at night. He is rabidly interested in baseball, and his friends take him to baseball games on Sunday whenever they are played.

Until the time of his forced retirement he lived very much in a male-oriented society. He enjoyed his work thoroughly and went to frequent parties with male co-workers. He belonged to and was very active in his union. He also belonged to two lodges although he was less active in them. He has one stepdaughter, but his relation to her appears rather remote, like a distant cousin. His wife he describes as having been a pretty little thing and a good wife; she's a good cook. He also admits that she has had a hard time of it since he has been sick. Before he was sick, he was often away in the evening with union affairs or parties with his boy friends. When asked whether he considered his marriage a happy one, he replied, "Heck, I'm always happy—there's no point in bickering."

His disengagement from male society was not a sudden one. He stopped going to parties with his boy friends ten years previously, when he felt his health getting bad. He also stopped drinking beer at that time, but he had expected to work for several more years (even at the age of seventy-four). His heart condition improved somewhat during the period of the interviews, and he gave a little thought to returning to work, although he remained inactive. He appears to be financially solvent with his disability (and ultimately his retirement) pension.

This man has been classified dependent-persistent, with a rank of seventeen on the success continuum in this series. He clearly takes more from his wife than he contributes to her. This same sort of balance seems to exist with the few friends that he still has. His stepdaughter is in a neutral position. His wife was present at one interview, but did not participate in it; the interviewer commented that she seemed bad tempered. She did participate in the background in some other interviews and commented at one point, "We never got no good breaks." There seem to be minimal elements of instability in the system, however, and it will probably continue as long as this man's health permits him to live.

Mr. Average Man, Slightly Overworked. This fifty-five-year-old man lives in a household with his wife. He has one stepson who lived with him for a while at the beginning of the interview period, but left, returned, and then left again to get married. He is engaged in maintenance and repair work, the nature of which is so exacting that he works six days a week (seven in the summer) with occasional days off and a brief paid vacation each year. He has an ISC of eighty, which places him toward the top of the upper-lower class.

He has a few friends and some relatives, including a father, in the area, with whom he interacts as much as time will permit. He will face mandatory retirement at the age of sixty-five.

He has been classified as autonomous-precarious, largely because of the relationship which he has with his wife and others. It would be expected that, on retirement, he will fall into a relatively dependent relationship with them and would then be classified as dependent-persistent. He has, however, been ranked twelfth, or the next to the least precarious of the precarious group.

From Retirement to a New Career. In October, 1956, we find this fifty-nine-year-old man as a postal transportation clerk and part-time preacher. He lives with his wife, and they have no children. They have a charming two-story frame house in a middle-class neighborhood. His ISC is sixty-eight, which places him in the lower-middle class. His father was a teacher and postmaster in a small town.

He served in both world wars, holding a commission in World War II. As a boy he had wanted to be a preacher, but was unsettled when he got out of the Army after World War I and decided to take a civil service exam to get a secure job. He has been at this work, routine in content but irregular in hours, as a postal clerk on a railroad ever since—"a hard monotonous grind"— except for the wartime interruption. At the time of the first interview, however, he is within one month of retirement and has begun to get into the ministry, although he was not yet ordained. The following spring he has retired and is doing full-time church work, studying to be ordained by a correspondence course. At this point his wife looks rather ill, gray, anemic, and dispirited. The respondent, on the other hand, looks better than ever. He indicates that he is "not dependent on his wife's being well or not." His mother-in-law, who had spent winters with them for a number of years, has died. He is proud of his high marks in the correspondence course. He has attracted forty new church members, and the board of trustees has raised his pay, so things are going well except that "her being ill has been inconvenient." He has been asked to speak at various organizations and make memorial addresses.

He has a few distant relatives whom he scarcely, if ever, sees. He says hello and occasionally chats, but not visits, with the neighbors. He does not go around with his church members, because, as he rationalizes it, one must be careful about jealousy and rivalry. He considers his present way of life much more productive and satisfying than his former one and expects it to continue indefinitely.

In late summer his wife appears somewhat better. After careful thought, he mentions some four hundred and fifty friends, none of them close. A year later he has a new church. He has also been to summer school in another city. He has been a leader in a postal clerks' convention and is very proud of this. He says he feels some physical letdown and has a little stomach trouble, but neither of these things seems to bother him particularly. His wife, who was present at this interview, points out that he cannot handle young children. He considers the best years of his life to be the past three, since his retirement.

The following summer he is still very active in the ministry. He says the sermon tires him, and he ends up wet with perspiration after delivering it. However, he prefers the age he is, sixty-one. He has a sister living in the city and talks with her occasionally when he feels depressed, but most of the time he describes his mood as jubilant.

His father was, and still is, the most admired person in his life. His father now lives nearby, and he visits him every day. He says his father taught school and ran a post office, greatly influencing the people he taught. In several interviews he describes his father as having a great sense of humor and being very bright. The respondent was never able to live up to this pattern and drank and gambled in his early adulthood, just after he was back from the war. His fantasies include traveling, war experiences, money, being in prison, and "all sorts of silly thoughts."

His health is reasonably good, he is financially secure with a pension plus his salary as a minister, and he derives a great deal of satisfaction from his work in the ministry.

This case is especially difficult to classify. There is no doubt about his autonomy. He gets somewhat more from his wife than he gives to her, which is minimal, but he puts a great deal of energy into his ministerial activities without demanding much in return. It is possible that he will continue in this fashion and be successful in the ministry for a number of years. It is also possible that he will eventually be able to disengage himself from ministerial activities and retire a second time with sufficient inner resources to keep himself going on an autonomous basis—a number of ministers in their eighties are like this. If the probable occurrence of this pattern were high, he would certainly be classed as autonomous-persistent and ranked among the first three on the success rating. The interviews, however, give the distinct impression that he is wearing himself out with his ministerial activities and will have to give them up in a relatively short period of time, probably five years, and almost definitely by the time he is seventy. If this happens, it is likely that he will go into a mild depression and be dependent on a somewhat worn-out wife and, perhaps, his sister—his father would most probably be dead by that time. The probability of this development seems distinctly greater than the probability of the other. If this judgment is correct, the precariousness is certainly overwhelming. He has, therefore, been classified autonomous-precarious and ranked fifteen in this series, or the most precarious of the precarious group. It is probable that he will move into the dependent-persistent group temporarily and that he may, in turn, move from there to the dependent-precarious with possibilities of institutionalization.

Familism

Into Retirement and Becoming a Widower. At the beginning of the interview period Mr. X is seventy-one years old, a fire-insurance underwriter, who lives with his wife in a large and beautiful home. The surrounding grounds are well-kept, and gardening is one of his hobbies. He has lived in Kansas City for more than thirty-three years at two different periods. He and his wife have two sons and one daughter, and there are seven grandchildren, three boys and four girls, ranging from ten years to eighteen months. His ISC is forty-six, placing him in the upper-middle class. His father was a railroad engineer. The interior of the house suggests warmth and gracious living. The children also live in Kansas City, and he very much enjoys living right where he is, near his friends, his church, and his children. He is Catholic.

He works a full, long day and likes his evenings at home with his wife. Their evening activities are varied. He is concerned about his wife's health and insists that she stay in bed until 8 A.M. and take a nap in the afternoon. He has various activities on the weekend; usually one of the grandchildren comes over on Saturday. Religion means a great deal to him, and on Sundays he goes to Mass and spends an hour at a shrine.

The following spring, his wife looks rather ill. They were planning a trip to visit their daughter, who is a nun. He also wants to travel in the Northwest so that he will have visited every state in the Union. He goes bowling with his grandsons. It has become too much for his wife to have big family dinners, so the daughters-in-law have taken over. He has a number of friends and knows twelve of his neighbors well. He plans to retire the first of the following year, take a good rest, and go down to the gulf; then he may dabble in real estate or travel. He indicates that life has been fine, that he has a wonderful wife, and that her health is very important to him. His wife, who was present at this interview, says that he ought to be thinking of his own health more. In December of that year he greeted the interviewer heartily and was looking forward to retirement on January 1.

His wife died by the end of that year. They had been able to take the trip to the gulf in the early part of the year and had visited the daughter, who by then had become a mother superior. They were very proud of her. His wife was taken ill in the spring and was diagnosed as having a terminal illness. The children want him to come and live with them, but he has not made up his mind. He wants to carry on and help the children all he can. He says he is very lonely without his wife, but he can work things out for himself. He agrees with the statement that women do not like retired husbands around the house and states that he enjoys baby-sitting with his grandsons.

By the following summer he has decided to stay on in his home and not to live with his children. He does usually eat dinner at his sons' homes. One gets the impression that he is still very much alive and has a wide variety of interests. His value system centers on his religion, and he is moderately conservative.

His health is reasonably good, he is financially secure, and he derives tremendous emotional satisfaction from his family and obviously gives emotional satisfaction to them. He has been classified autonomous-persistent and second in rank on the success continuum for fairly obvious reasons. There was probably sufficient evidence in the first two interviews to classify him in this way. His strong anchorage in religion, family, cultural interests, and gardening, and his rather evident creativity in living should be sufficient to sustain him for as long as his health permits. It is interesting, of course, that we actually have a case for which such a prediction could be made and which did survive the crises of retirement and widowhood.

Solidly Familistic. This is the case of a fifty-eight-year-old woman living with her husband in a comfortable but not elegant home surrounded by a large yard and beautiful garden. Her husband is a skilled worker of foreign background who speaks somewhat broken English. They are Catholic. They have two daughters and one son, all living in Kansas City; one of the daughters lives across the street.

There are five grandchildren. Her father was a cabinetmaker. Her ISC is seventy-six, placing her in the upper-lower class.

She likes her neighbors, who often come to look at the garden. She and her husband both work in the garden and make frequent tours of it when he is home. She likes the children in the neighborhood because they are good and "do not bother the flowers." Of her husband, she says that he "works and doesn't talk to no one." She has some concerns about what will happen when he retires, but does not seem particularly anxious in this respect. She has four or five close friends and many acquaintances, tending to draw the line on intimacy with friends; her family is much more important. She seems to be especially successful in the role of mother to her married children. Her sons-in-law seem as fond of her as are her own daughters.

Her health is reasonably good, and she is not preoccupied with health problems. The family is financially solvent. She obviously gets a great deal of emotional satisfaction from and gives emotional satisfaction to her family, which very much includes the grown children and grandchildren.

She has a medium alienation score and is moderately religious and conservative. Her personality type has been indicated as passive-mastery (2). She has been classified as autonomous-persistent with a rank of four.

Living Alone

Loneliness. This seventy-four-year-old man is a retired machine worker living entirely alone in a cluttered, gloomy apartment in a low-rent housing project. He has two sons and two daughters and ten grandchildren, but he does not know their ages, because he is not in touch with them. He stopped work when he was sixty because it got too heavy for him and lived on his savings from sixty to sixty-five. Now he lives on Social Security and a pension. When he was forty-five years old, he was vice-president and chief instructor in an auto mechanic school and made an excellent income.

He gets out very little. He does walk around occasionally, enjoys cutting the grass, and is acquainted with his neighbors, whom he likes to help out, particularly with their cars. He is Catholic and goes to church regularly. He occasionally visits his stepchildren who live in Kansas City. He claims that he likes visiting, but adds, "I am old now, and people are not interested." He also says, "I like to hunt and fish, but there's no place to go." He admits that he is lonely.

His parents were Methodist, but he became a Catholic. He describes both his wives as fine, good Catholics and both marriages as perfect. The children are doing all right, but he rarely sees them.

He clearly fits one stereotype of the "plight of older people" and expresses this explicitly. For example, he says, "When one is younger, one doesn't realize how lonely old people are—not enough people care about old people, because they don't believe in God enough." If it were not for television, he would have no pleasure at all.

He left home when he was fourteen, when his mother died, and worked his way through school studying "steam." He was forty-eight when his first wife died, and he married again at fifty-two. His second wife died when he was seventy-one. His father lived to be ninety-eight years old and died when the respondent was forty-eight. His father had been a veterinarian, and the respondent had frequently helped him with money in his later years. He thinks of his father as a wonderful man.

For a time a girl who looked like his daughter lived in his apartment with him. He prayed that she would convert to Catholicism and he gave her money and clothes, but she was "kind of wild." He has great admiration for a number of Catholic figures. His health is reasonably good, and he does not seem especially preoccupied with it. He recovered from two hernia operations with little difficulty and has minor complaints about having to take pills. He has grown accustomed to his low income. He gets few satisfactions from life, but prominent among them is helping other people, such as the neighbors. He is lonely and somewhat unhappy, but not depressed in the clinical sense. He has reconciled himself to his way of life.

He has been classified as autonomous-persistent with a rank of eight. He is a particularly good example of the fact that people do not have to be satisfied, active, or living in a network of close relationships in order to age sucessfully, according to the definition of successful aging in this analysis.

The Isolate. This fifty-nine-year-old man lives entirely alone. He is a self-employed salesman of small objects—in short, a peddler. He is one of the cases intensively interviewed by a senior staff member, and her description of him is particularly apt:

> He is also quite alone in the world, the most isolated, except for highly specific work contacts, of any of the intensively interviewed panel members. His mother died twenty years ago, his father four years ago. He has no brothers and sisters, and he never married, leaving him, when his father died, with only one significant relative, a lady cousin—who,

however, died between the first and second waves of our study. He has no close friends and seemed to be on friendly, interactive terms with only one person outside of work—a neighbor, who, however, has now moved away. It appears, indeed, that Mr. S's only diffuse interactions (and even these are relatively nonobligatory) are with the interviewers from our study. We have, I think, roughly tripled his life space.

He does not like living in Kansas City, especially because of the traffic, and frequently mentions that, while crossing the street, his father was killed by a hit-and-run driver. He grew up in a smaller city nearby and regrets that the family moved from there to Kansas City, where his father and he owned and operated a number of small grocery stores until they were forced out by the chain stores. He is an alert and intelligent person with a remarkable memory and can give the exact addresses of all the places that his father and he worked. He says that all he does is work. He has no time for television. He does listen to the radio, but the programs are getting worse. On the second interview, however, he says a male cousin had given him a television set. He didn't think he would like it, but it does cheer him up and pass the time. This same male cousin takes him out to dinner on Christmas and other holidays. He recognizes that he has not measured up to what he should have been in life, but has no profound regrets and is in no sense bitter.

When asked, at one point, what was the best thing that had recently happened to him, he said that it was being in the hospital when he had a prostate operation. For a time he got a great deal of attention and was gleefully all alone in a room, being waited on hand and foot.

His health is fair, and his financial position is somewhat shaky. He clearly enjoys anyone's taking the trouble to do something for him (as when he was waited on in the hospital). He is mildly religious and goes to church occasionally, but does so less and less. This is not a disengagement process, for he was never very much engaged. The people closest to him in his network simply dropped off by death or moved away.

He has the highest possible alienation score and a high F score. His personality type is passive-mastery. He has been classified dependent-precarious and given a rank of twenty in this series; in other words, he is the least successful ager. It is probable that within a relatively brief time he will be a public charge in one way or another, perhaps in an institution, and he will probably enjoy this situation.

Living Alone and Liking It. This seventy-five-year-old widow lives entirely alone. Her husband was a doctor and died in 1925. For forty years she had been a registered nurse. She got interested in nursing while visiting relatives in England, the period of her life which she considers to have been her happiest and which she never has forgotten. Her father had a merchandise and grocery store. She has an ISC of sixty-nine, placing her toward the top of the lower-middle class. She continued nursing after her husband's death, nursing a sick sister-in-law until she died in 1942; she then did night nursing until she was about fifty-five. She somewhat regrets having given nursing up and misses it. In fact, her "widowhood" seems to be caused more by retirement from her nursing career than by the death of her husband.

She has no children. She has two sisters and a brother, but all of them live out of town. She sees them once a year and writes frequently. She has one very close friend who has a car, and they go shopping together. There are six close friends in all, and she considers them very important. She knows ten neighbors casually and has lived in the neighborhood thirty-three years. One of the neighbors is a close friend. She talked enthusiastically of recently taking her first airplane ride to visit a sister.

At one time in her life, she got confused mentally because of "a nervous condition during the menopause," which came very early, at the age of forty. She talks about this very freely, however, and has had no difficulty since. She is in good health and financially secure. At the fifth interview, she had followed her plan of becoming more active in church. She gets a great deal of emotional satisfaction from her friendships, and the Gestalt one gets is clearly of a person who gives as much as, or more than, she takes in these friendships. Her value system is typical for her age and class. She has been classified as autonomous-persistent and given the rank of three in the series.

The Grieving Widower. When first interviewed, this seventy-eight-year-old man had very recently been widowed. He had taken a roomer into the house, with whom he interacts minimally. At this time he was keeping busy with his pets. He had worked at two different semiskilled, but well-paid jobs and retired a number of years ago with considerable savings. His ISC is fifty-seven or in the lower-middle class.

At the very early age of eighteen, he became a bartender in a bar owned by his brother. Another brother also worked in the bar. The two brothers were seriously addicted to alcohol and died, hospitalized with delirium tremens, in their early thirties. He, on the other hand, boasts of the fact that he has never tasted liquor in his life. At various times he was also in the trucking business and did fairly well at that, although most of his money seems to have been made as a bartender.

His whole life seems to have been wrapped up with that of his wife, although they were apparently somewhat different in temperament, because he preferred to stay home and she liked "to go." He lived in the same house all his life. When he was forty-eight years old, he and his wife adopted a son. The son had done reasonably well although he did create difficulty for a time. The respondent's wife was Catholic, whereas he is a Presbyterian who never goes to church. The boy was raised in the Catholic faith, but he left the church, and that broke his mother's heart. The respondent, however, describes him as a good boy and does maintain a close relationship with him and the two grandchildren.

During the first interview it was extremely apparent that he was in a period of deep grief. His wife and he had done everything together. He feels very much cut off from his wife, but not from his job (in contrast to the preceding case, in which the respondent felt cut off from her nursing career, but not from her husband). As time progresses, he still expresses his great loss, but is adapting to the situation. His mode of life has changed somewhat in that he has had to sell his pets and was offered a high price for the home in which he had lived all his life. He bought another place and plans to live with his son when he gets it fixed up, ultimately giving it to his son. He will have separate quarters in the house. He is in good health, financially secure, and enjoys doing things for other people.

Later he bought a car and is seeing a number of friends. He "tried lady friends a few times" on advice of some of his friends, but some of them were no pleasure, and others wanted money—a couple of them even asked for new cars—so he gave that up. He does enjoy playing with his grandchildren. He recognizes that he sits by himself in the house too much, but is not particularly worried by this.

He thinks of his father as a good, honest man who drank too much. In addition to his two brothers, he had a sister who died from drinking. His mother was a wonderful and well-liked woman, but she was epileptic.

Here is a man with a marked history of alcoholism and epilepsy in his family, who led a very wife-centered life and who had recently been widowed. Yet he is very much intact. He relates well to his adopted son and his own and his son's family, but does not intrude or make demands on their lives. He is concerned with what he can do for them.

He has been classified as autonomous-persistent and given a rank of seven in this series. This case again illustrates the fact that the judgment on successful aging made here is certainly not dependent on happiness or satisfaction with the present mode of life.

The Late Bloomer. This sixty-two-year-old single woman lives with a teacher and the teacher's brother. She is a teacher of physical therapy and an aide for handicapped children. She has an ISC of fifty-four, which would place her in about the middle of the middle class.

This respondent's life history is particularly significant in making an analysis in relation to aging. She describes herself as a sickly child who was in and out of school and could not complete her education. At one period in her young adult life, she had a "nervous breakdown." Her mother died when the subject was in her thirties, and she spent eleven years at home taking care of her father. They lived in a small town.

When the respondent was forty-nine, her father died. She found it very distressing to break up housekeeping. She moved to Kansas City and got her first and only full-time job as an untrained physical therapist and helper in a school for children suffering from cerebral palsy. For the first year she felt rather insecure in her job and lonely in a big city, but from then on she literally began to bloom. She enjoys her work, but she looks forward even more to retiring, which she must do at sixty-five. She thinks that her present age is the best time in life and that she would not want to be any younger than fifty.

She has minimal interaction with the other members of the household and, in fact, tries to keep certain aspects of her life secret from them. She has a few fairly close friends, but her network is focused on her colleagues at work and the children. She has a sister living in Chicago, who has two married children in Denver. She has toyed a bit with the idea of living with her sister after retirement, but she much prefers the idea of living with her nieces and their families in Denver. During the interview period, her sister died, and then she definitely planned to go to Denver. She is looking forward to this life, and apparently her relation to the nieces and their families is a very solid one, for they look forward to having her come. Denver will definitely be "a place I can call home."

She now considers her health excellent. With some investments and a trust fund from her parents, she is financially secure. She derives great satisfaction from helping other people.

It can be said of this woman that she was a rather unsuccessful "lifer," but a highly successful ager. Literally, she was born to be old. Probably she will fulfill the aunt and great-aunt role quite successfully. She has been classified as autonomous-persistent with the rank of one.

Elderly Couples

We Just Go Blandly On. At the beginning of the interview period, a childless woman of sixty-eight was living with her husband, a skilled worker. Her ISC is sixty-two or somewhere in the lower-middle class. She grew up on a farm near a small town in Missouri. She had two years of college and had planned to be a domestic-science teacher at one point, something she rather vaguely regrets not having done. She was married in 1913 and has apparently lived much the same sort of life for the past forty-three years. She is afflicted with asthma, but the couple had recently moved to a small, new home which is air-conditioned, and her asthma seems to have abated. She does not drive a car and has never worked outside her home, stating that her husband is opposed to that. Her husband likes gardening. He belongs to the Masons, but doesn't participate actively. Visiting with friends is curtailed by her asthma. She has not been active in church for the past few years. (The interviewer commented at one point that she talked about these matters as she would talk about the laundry.) She belongs to three clubs, but is not very active in them. Until recently she took an interest in a little study club, and she mentions four friends, all of whom are members of this club. She has an eighty-three-year-old sister and a seventy-six-year-old brother who are still living on the farm.

Her daily round of activities is quite routine. She does much reading. She finds company a little too upsetting and resists being too intimate with the neighbors. Her husband does not expect to retire in the near future, but she anticipates no problems with retirement— "there's always plenty to do around home." She expects life to be about the same five years hence.

In the interviews in the next two years (around her seventieth birthday), she talks about nice summer trips that she and her husband had taken. Her asthma bothers her less. She claims that she is never lonely. She was more active just before she was forty-five, but then she began to get attacks of asthma. The greater activity was more gardening. The daily round on the third interview was just what it had been three years previously.

In her youth she had an aunt who was an excellent cook, and this got her interested in food and food preparation. In describing her mother, she says, "Mother was born in Germany and was just a few weeks old when she was brought to this country. Her mother died either on the boat or shortly after arriving here. She had just one sister. My mother had a very nice voice and could have been a good singer. She did things well, but nothing outstanding." When asked about people she dislikes, she says that she forms "general dislikes of, say, movie actresses—like Ingrid Bergman. She's so unconventional and unpredictable. Did you read the story? Before she was really rid of Rossellini, she had this other Swedish doctor on the string. After she was oh, so in love with Rossellini. You wonder what she thinks about, if she does."

This woman had never been extremely involved with anything and became even more disengaged after forty-five. Her health seems to be improving, and she is not especially preoccupied with it. There is no evidence that she uses her asthmatic condition for demanding emotional or other help from her husband. The couple is financially solvent. She does her homemaking willingly and takes considerable pride in it.

This case has been classified autonomous-persistent and ranked as number five in the series.

Successful Widowhood. This sixty-nine-year-old lady was widowed in 1945 and lives with a somewhat younger sister in a small house. Her husband owned a plumbing shop and was seriously ill for some time prior to his death. Her father was a railroad stationmaster in a small town. The sister's grandchildren come every year and stay a week. The woman is somewhere in the lower-middle class.

She likes the neighborhood. There are three teachers living on one side and two sisters on the other. The three teachers are fairly good friends, the two sisters are not (in fact, they are considered filthy and queer). She watches television with one of the teachers next door and does much sewing. She goes to the theater every Tuesday night with the teachers. She loves to travel and every year takes a bus trip with tours paid in advance. She belongs to no organization and has never been a joiner.

She had fallen and broken her pelvic bone at the time of the second interview and was proud to have been in bed only six weeks. Things had not changed in any significant way the following year, although her sister had bought a car, and she enjoys that. She has stopped the daytime television routine and seems to interact somewhat less with the teachers next door. The broken pelvic bone slows her down somewhat, but she doesn't seem to mind it a bit. Six months later she indicated that her sister and she visit her sister's son, a psychologist at a university in a nearby city, more frequently now that they have a car.

She does not want to engage in anything that's going to affect anyone else very much. Her sister and she are definitely a couple.

She has conformist attitudes and a relatively high F score. She copes with health problems very well and is in a sound financial position, for she owns her home and has business property as an investment. She obviously enjoys keeping house for her sister.

She has been classified autonomous-persistent with a rank of six.

The Dreamy Home Companion. This fifty-two-year-old woman, a high school graduate, assists her husband, who is a professional man. They have no children. Her ISC is fifty-two, which puts her toward the bottom of the upper-middle class.

She is very much wrapped up in her life as it is. She belongs to a "Unity" church and is very active in the Unity movement. She was hostess for a Sunday school junior department, but she loves to stay home and indicates that, as one gets older, there is not so much need for social life. She has one sister and two aunts in Kansas City and some cousins on the West Coast. She feels close to some nieces, but they do not live in Kansas City. She rarely sees her mother. Her parents were divorced, and she was raised by her grandmother. She does not visit with the neighbors, but she interacts freely and frequently with the many people who come into her husband's office. She is vaguely bothered by the idea of retirement. There is indication that her husband had a psychiatric illness at one time, an area of her life about which she does not want to talk.

She is not particularly concerned with health and is in good financial position. It seems fairly clear that she gives more to her marriage than she gets from it. On special occasions she is happy to help others.

This case has been classified autonomous-persistent, with a rank of ten. She is closest to the autonomous-precarious group of this particular series, for there is a slight element of precariousness in her relation with her husband. If, however, they were disturbed for any reason, such as an illness on his part or death, she would probably find sufficient satisfaction to go autonomously on by plunging even further into the Unity movement.

The "Clutched" One. This sixty-one-year-old woman lives with her husband, who is a skilled worker. They are somewhere at the bottom of the lower-middle class. Her father was a bookkeeper. She had a high school education. The house is adequate, but has a small, drab, old-fashioned living room. She has lived in Kansas City for fifty years and will probably stay right where she is, although she "does not like the colored situation."

On the first interview, the interviewer gained the distinct impression that this woman was an unwilling subject. Shortly thereafter, however, she had an intensive interview with a senior staff member. As a result, we get a much better impression of what she is like. Also, it is interesting that after this interview she was much freer in the regular interviews. The senior staff member says of her:

> She strikes me as a "clutched" personality—taut and overcontrolled— and it is this quality about her, I think, that gave the first interviewer the idea that she is an unwilling panel member. This is clearly not the case; she is an eminently willing panel member who badly wants to express herself on a subjective level and who seeks a way out of the emotional clutch she is in. Something is suffocating her, choking off large areas of self-expression—and I think that something is a Puritan sense of duty that she resents but can't kick over. I think she is suffering from a severe case of galloping hedonism, strongly repressed. The "do-it-yourself" theme was too much protested, as were references to the horrors of "overindulgence." I think this woman is having difficulty disengaging from family obligations (son and daughter-in-law), not because she needs the sense of usefulness that she derives from them so much as she needs the function these obligations perform in distracting her from her inner conflicts and the hostility these conflicts generate.

She has a good deal of resentment about her parents, makes unfavorable judgments of her mother, and feels that she was not properly guided when she was young. She wanted more education, but didn't know what kind or how to get it.

Her son and daughter-in-law live in the East, and there are two grandchildren. One of them was visiting her at the time of the first interview. There is a good deal of evidence throughout the interviews that the respondent is still trying to guide and play an important part in her son's life, a situation which the son and daughter-in-law are both resisting. At one time they lost a baby, but the respondent was not asked to come East. She seemed to resent their failure to ask her.

She and her husband participate in bridge groups and have a moderately large circle of friends. She is fairly active in the church and belongs to two clubs, participating in one of them.

In response to the question whether life is made for pleasure, she says no, one must earn pleasure after discharging all his responsibilities. "We are put here for a purpose—I often wonder what mine is."

In 1959 she is getting somewhat bored with the card-playing group, but says she will keep on anyway. She would prefer less circulation in groups and seems to be getting into more of it because she simply cannot say no.

She and her husband spend a great deal of time remodeling parts of the house on Saturdays. She is moderately conformist and has a moderately high F score. She is not particularly preoccupied with matters of health, and the financial situation appears fairly sound. She does, however, appear to use her patterns of social interaction to satisfy her own rather demanding needs, even though this is kept under fairly good control on the surface. For this reason in particular, she has been classified dependent-persistent, with a rank order of sixteen. One feels less sure about this classification and ranking, however, than about any other case. She may well be much more autonomous than she appears to be on the surface, and this, of course, would not only change her classification but would also make a considerable difference in her rank order.

The Disengaged Couple. This seventy-seven-year-old woman lives with her husband in an attractive, small home in the suburbs. Her husband was a traveling missionary for many years, and after that they made candy at home, but had given that up several years before. Their ISC is forty-five, placing them somewhere toward the bottom of the upper-middle class.

They had tried living in California for a while, but returned to Kansas City, mainly because a married daughter lives in the area. They do not go to church much any more. They used to know everybody at church, but, after they returned from California, this was no longer the case. The daughter occasionally comes to take them for a drive. The subject speaks very highly of her husband and says he has been fine in retirement, although he has a little heart trouble. She is very proud of her two sons, who live in the East; one of them has done well in the entertainment field. They try to plan trips to see their sons once a year. She mentions five friends with considerable warmth, but does not use them in relation to personal problems. Her husband is the one she would turn to. She is very conscious of losing friends by death and sees them only erratically. She does not seem deeply troubled by this, however.

At the age of seventy-eight, she is in excellent health, mowing the lawn and gardening. The couple is in good financial condition. She obviously contributes much to the life of her husband and children without overinvolvement.

She has been classified as autonomous-persistent, in the rank of eight.

I Am Myself, and I Look Integrated—But . . . . This sixty-eight-year-old man lives with his wife. At the time of the first interview, he was still employed in a fairly important white-collar job, but was a retired civil servant by the time of the second interview. His father was a farmer. The subject had some college education and started a career of teaching, but gave that up to go into civil service. He has an ISC of fifty-four, which puts him toward the bottom of the upper-middle class.

This is a particularly interesting case; there is a great amount of data, including intensive interviews by a senior staff member, impressions by another senior member of the research staff and another professional member of the staff, a special TAT analysis, and other materials not contained in all the other cases. It is interesting because somewhat different impressions are gained from the different kinds of data and because it illustrates a number of methodological problems.

On the surface this man appears to be, in the words of one of the staff members, "an impressive figure of a man with a spare, Grant Wood look about him, and a manner that conveys a high level of alertness and vitality." He is highly verbal and in most of the interviews conveys a picture of solid, middle-class integrity. In a few of the interviews there are notations about a "vague femininity." In the TAT analysis it is stated: "I think this guy is—since his retirement —quite bothered by unconscious desires to act out, to be childish, to give up earnest endeavor and responsibility." One of the members of the professional staff who saw him states:

> If forced to describe him in a few words, I would say, "Egocentric (if not narcissistic), disengaged, sadistic, and dependent." There is obvious tension between Mr. and Mrs. My hypothesis is that there was less before he retired. He likes to stay home, puttering about his roses, reading magazines devoted to sentimentality, etc., and he wants his wife there with him. She, on the other hand, has been having a ball since the children left home. She admits to "going all the time," and he complains about it. She says, "I need a husband-sitter." What she really

wants, and says so, is for her husband to get a job, so that she can have the car to go and come as she pleases without him complaining about it all the time. He claims he is not well enough to work, and she says "nonsense."

The senior member of the staff says he "seems to me a narcissistic man who enjoys being interviewed. He is interested in the subject of himself, whether it is about his kinship system or some other aspect of his life. There is tension between him and his wife." The other staff members, whose impressions were somewhat contrary to this, did, however, indicate that his activity in rose-growing, his primary hobby, was done less for love of roses than for proving to himself that he could grow all possible varieties.

After weighing and sorting all the data, it was noted that in particular he worries about his health more than his actual physical condition would seem to warrant and uses the health problems in a demanding way. His relations with his children do seem to be quite narcissistic. He is unable to get very close to anyone or to give much of himself. In general, he has become something of a parasite in his interaction network. He has, therefore, been classified dependent-persistent, with a rank of nineteen in this series of twenty.

ANALYSIS AND CONCLUSIONS

The array of cases, classified and ranked, is indicated in Table 1.

Three further steps are necessary before any very significant conclusions can be expected from this type of analysis. More cases should be added, and a check should be made on various aspects of the representativeness of the panels from which they were drawn. Data from others in the social systems of the respondents should be analyzed. Finally, the analysis should be much more definitely refined and operationalized, so that it can be used by others and its reliability can be checked. There are, however, a few suggestive findings.

After the individual cases had been analyzed, classified, and ranked, a check was made to see whether any relations could be discovered with numerical scores on ratings that had already been made.

Life space scores were put in rank order. The rank order correlation with the success rating used here is −.2421. This figure is not statistically significant, but it is interesting that it does go in a negative direction and that it indicates this judgment of success is not

TABLE 1
THE CASES

	Persistent	Precarious
Autonomous	1. The Late Bloomer 2. Into Retirement and Becoming a Widower 3. Living Alone and Liking It 4. Solidly Familistic 5. We Just Go Blandly On 6. Successful Widowhood 7. The Grieving Widower 8. The Disengaged Couple 9. Loneliness 10. The Dreamy Home Companion	11. Work, Work, Work 12. Mr. Average Man, Slightly Over-worked 13. The Retired Working Girl 14. The Working Grandmother 15. From Retirement to a New Career
Dependent	16. The "Clutched" One 17. Forced Inactivity 18. The Protestant Ethic and Problems of Retirement 19. I Am Myself, and I Look Intergrated—But	20. The Isolate

based on large or small life spaces. The success rankings were grouped into high (seven cases), medium (seven cases), and low (six cases). The average interaction index for the highs is 1.7; the mediums, 2.4; and the lows, 2.5. These differences are not statistically significant, but again it is interesting to note that the highs are relatively low interactors. Inspection indicates no relationship with role count or orientation to interaction, although the seven highs had seven out of the eight possible combinations of orientation—they are all different in this rather significant respect. The average alienation score is 11 for the highs, 11 for the mediums, and 10.5 for the lows. Obviously, they are not being ranked on whether they share "nice" values. F scores are not available for the six people in the seventies, so they were not run

TABLE 2
SUCCESSFUL AGING AND PERCEIVED LIFE SPACE

| | Perceived life space | | | |
Success	High	Medium	Low	Totals
High	0	0	7	7
Medium	4	3	0	7
Low	1	1	4	6
Totals	5	4	11	20

$$\chi^2 = 14.65 \qquad P < .01$$

TABLE 3
SUCCESSFUL AGING AND PERCEIVED LIFE SPACE

| | Perceived life space | | |
Success	High and medium	Low	Totals
High	0	7	7
Medium	7	0	7
Low	2	4	6
Totals	9	11	20

$$\chi^2 = 16.25 \qquad df = 2 \qquad P < .001$$

with the success rankings, but it is probable that no relationship would be found.

One theoretically important measure, perceived life space, did prove to be statistically significant, as indicated in tables 2 and 3. This statistical significance has to be viewed with some caution because of the small numbers. The four low lows disturb a straight-line interpretation. (Two of these four, however, are within one point of the medium perceived life space score; they do not perceive their life spaces as having shrunk very much since the age of forty-five.) It is interesting that the first nine of the ten people classed autonomous-persistent all have low perceived life spaces. These figures certainly suggest a relation between successful aging, as defined here, and low perceived life space, which, in turn, suggests a relation with disengagement.

There are two relations which seem to emerge between a person's life style and successful aging.

Both of the "familistic" cases are in the autonomous-persistent category, and both happen to be Catholic. This situation is not surprising, but with only two cases we certainly cannot prove anything.

All the autonomous-precarious cases are, or have been, heavily involved in the world of work. The two "world of work" cases which are not in this category are in the dependent-persistent category, into which, one predicts, several of the autonomous-precarious people will ultimately fall. All of the autonomous-precarious men are still working, whereas one of the women is working and one is retired. But it should be emphasized that these people were so classed because of their heavy and primary involvement in the world of work. Several of the people in the other categories are working or have retired from their paid emloyment, but they have other facets of life which are more characteristic of their style. Certainly this relation should not be taken to suggest that leaving the world of work is the major crisis of aging for people in general or for employed men—and it should not be used as an argument for or against fixed retirement. It does suggest that heavy or almost exclusive involvement in the world of work does add to the precariousness of the actor's social system in his later years.

There is a need to refine the classification of life styles, but this must await the additional cases. And there is a need to push the analysis in other directions, particularly toward the relation of autonomy-dependency and equilibrium at different levels of disengagement and, in turn, personality type.

There is one important relation to sex which emerges. Seven of the ten autonomous-persistent cases are women. There is only one dependent woman in this series, and of all the cases one feels least sure about her degree of dependency or autonomy. These facts conform with other findings of the Kansas City study that show men and women to age differently, the differences appearing markedly in the seventies and eighties, and men, in general, to age less successfully than women.

Thus, this mode of analysis and this definition of successful aging may be useful in the exploration of two major developments in the Kansas City study, the disengagement theory and the differences between men and women in aging. It is hoped that with the additional suggested steps it may also contribute to other aspects of the sociology and psychology of aging.

REFERENCES

Cassetta, Rhondda, Newell, D.S., & Parlagreco, Mary Lou. Morale changes in women during aging. Paper presented at the annual meetings of the Midwest Sociological Society, St. Louis, 1960.

Cumming, Elaine, Dean, Lois, Newell, D.S., & McCaffrey, Isabel. Disengagement—a tentative theory of aging. *Sociometry,* 1960, **23,** 23-35.

Cumming, Elaine, Dean, Lois R., & Newell, D.S. What is morale? A case history of a validity problem. *Hum. Organiz.,* 1958, **17,** 3-8.

Henry, W.E., & Cumming, Elaine. Personality development in adulthood and old age. *J. proj. Tech.,* 1959, **23,** 383-390.

Parsons, T. *The social system.* Glencoe, Ill.: The Free Press, 1958.

Parsons, T., & Bales, R.F. *Family, socialization, and interaction process.* Glencoe, Ill.: The Free Press, 1955.

Williams, R.H. Changing status, roles and relationships. In C. Tibbitts (Ed.), *Handbook of social gerontology: Societal aspects of aging.* Chicago: The University of Chicago Press, 1960. Pp. 261-297.

Williams, R.H. & Loeb, M.B. The adult social life space and successful aging. Paper presented at the annual meeting of the Gerontological Society, Chicago, 1956.

PART THREE

Psychopathology of Aging

INTRODUCTION

WILMA DONAHUE

In all highly developed countries, an increase in mental illness is found, and the prevalence among older people is far higher than that among younger age groups. The increase in the number of people becoming mentally ill may be only an apparent one because the developed countries have the means which are lacking in less developed countries to find the cases and hospitalize them. Perhaps more important than incidence to the study of mental illness is the fact that the patterns and etiologies of mental illness are shifting in ways which reflect the social consequences of urbanization and the demands and hazards of an industrial economy. Biologic susceptibility to severe mental breakdown is probably not different for people of varied cultures, but the presence, nature, and timing of psychological and social stresses are different. The social and geographic distance imposed on old people living in highly urbanized areas forces a high degree of social isolation on many of them. Consequent loneliness is further aggravated by the almost inevitable loss of the spouse (especially

375

among women) and other affectional figures. And peculiar to contemporary society are those stresses brought about by the loss, on retirement, of economic roles, the downgrading of status, and the absence of satisfactory substitutes.

These new demands occur at a period in life when changes resulting in loss of physical and psychic energy and the ability to manage are already underway. In addition, with each passing year there is increased susceptibility to pathologic changes which further burden the organism in its attempts to meet the exigencies of daily living. That a larger number of older than of younger people become mentally ill seems a natural consequence of these factors. The problem lies in determining the nature and etiologies of the illnesses, the potentials, and the means of prevention, intervention, and rehabilitation. At present there are no complete and unquestioned measures for diag-, nostic classification and no agreement on implications for future development or current techniques to mitigate the consequences for affected individuals, their families, and society at large. At this point, then, we are seeking more definitive answers to the various aspects of these problems. The papers in Part Three of this volume report some of the directions in which research is seeking to provide deeper understanding, more general agreement, and new approaches in resolving problems which appear to be assuming increasingly ominous proportions as we accept the responsibility of making better social provisions for the psychopathologies of the aged.

THE PROBLEM

Although there is little reason to postulate a dichotomy between the psychopathologies of youth and those of age, old age is characterized by a number of relatively distinct diagnostic entities which can be differentiated from each other by clinical criteria. The validity of these differentiations can be confirmed by the outcomes of the diagnosed cases. In spite of these conclusions, however, no substantial agreement on a system of diagnosing and classifying mental illness exists now. In Chapter 19 Janzarik indicates the differences that are revealed when representatives of different countries assemble to discover what each can contribute to the solution of common problems. Psychopathology is an area where, in the absence of adequate research, differences in interest and emphasis still obscure agreement on the definition of terms. Not only representatives of different countries speak in different diagnostic and classificatory terms; representatives of different schools within a single country also disagree.

Diagnostic categories are set up because they represent a variation among symptoms which may have a common cause. Diagnosis and classification are just one step in the study of the etiology of disease; similarly, epidemiology does not define cause, but it does pave the way for a definition of causes. Obviously, general agreement among scientists on the definition of old-age disorders would be of great value. In discussion, Dr. Roth recommended that a small international group be convened to bring about this agreement. He illustrated the need by pointing out that the rate of admission for a certain old-age disorder is twenty times greater in England than in New York. It is not known, however, whether there is a real disparity in the incidence of the disease, whether the disparity is in the nosology employed, or whether the disparity is a chance factor. The most probable reason is a difference in the terminology applied to the same pattern of symptoms.

The differences between clinical entities are being investigated by pathological, chemical, neurophysiological, psychological, and other means. It would be convenient to depend on findings at autopsy to give a clearer understanding of behavior manifestations observed and recorded before death, but the correspondence demonstrated thus far has been found limited. In the seminar discussion, Dr. J. A. N. Corsellis reported on his study of the clinical records and post-mortem examinations of 300 patients who died in an English hospital. In about 75 per cent of the cases, there was a correlation between the types of pathological changes expected in various diagnostic categories, but, in the other 25 per cent, diagnostic categories based on recorded history and post-mortem findings failed to correspond.

Functional disorders, more frequently recognized and stressed in younger people, also contribute to the mental illnesses of old age. In fact, careful diagnosis has indicated that as many as 50 per cent of mentally ill aged are suffering from functional disorders, especially those of a depressive nature. If untreated, many of these may develop organic changes, so that mixed types of mental illness are not uncommon.

The term "psychic dynamics" suggests emphasis on process; practical circumstances often require diagnosis at a particular time—when overt manifestations of disorder must be recognized and acted on—in order to encourage classification in identifiable, discrete terms. Prognosis is then derived from diagnosis. There is pragmatic justification for this approach, for it facilitates the handling of social provisions for the care of the mentally ill, but it has the disastrous conse-

quence of promoting familiarity with concepts which clearly demand
drastic revision.

At present, an older person may not have his mental health
evaluated and properly treated until he arrives at a public institution
for the mentally ill—perhaps after a long wait. In other cases, deterioration in conduct or difficulties associated with physical illness may
force intervention and emergency admission. In the latter situation it
is not unusual, at least in America, for the patient to reach the mental
hospital by way of the admitting service of a general hospital. Here
facilities are frequently taxed to the limit (Simon & Neal, Chapter
21), and a decision concerning disposal of the patient must take precedence over detailed study. Experience indicates that in the case of older
patients the old catch-all "probable senile brain disease," provides
a more convenient justification for referral to a mental hospital than
the more exact "mentally disturbed; diagnosis postponed." It is significant that more errors in diagnosis—a significant proportion of
errors—have been noted when such an assumption is included in the
diagnosis (Post, Chapter 24). Any casual acceptance of a diagnosis of
organic brain disorder can have disastrous consequences for the patient. Frequently this classifies him among those for whom custodial
care is appropriate. After that, the opportunities for therapeutic
treatment and rehabilitation may be minimal.

We lack data concerning the frequency with which correction
or improvement of physical disability may be associated with decrease
or disappearance of mental confusion or other evidence of mental
illness, although Janzarik and Kay and Roth have contributed pertinent observations. Similarly, other kinds of physical impairment,
especially deafness, are recognized as contributing to manifestations of
mental disorder. Evidence supports a conclusion that correction of
physical disorders or disabilities should logically precede any final
assessment or even any tentative diagnosis of the degree of mental
impairment. If an individual was an accepted member of the social
community before his illness, should his return to the community be
jeopardized by calling special attention to a concurrent mental disturbance? Obviously the answer should be yes only if such attention
implies therapeutic treatment for both mental and physical disorders.
Too often psychopathological diagnosis seems to imply delayed ac-
knowledgement of an untreated condition which might improve with
appropriate therapy. But the therapeutic possibilities will not be
explored. The dynamics of mental illness are neglected once a classification has been entered in the record.

MEETING THE PROBLEM

Custodial institutional care is the traditional way in which society provides for those whose mental illness requires social intervention. A large proportion of such care is devoted to the schizophrenics, who may require protection at a relatively early age but who live to swell the number of those sixty-five and over who may spend all their later years in institutions for the mentally ill. Schizophrenia is a problem of mental illness that persists in old age, and it is relevant to the prevalence of psychopathology in older populations, but certainly irrelevant to the development of mental difficulties in later life unless we accept the redefinition of terms suggested by Kay and Roth (Chapter 20). The distinction has been emphasized in some studies of the psychopathologies of the aged by limiting investigation to those who are first admitted after the age of sixty-four (Simon & Neal, Chapter 21).

Custodial care meets the needs only of those whose disorders have been demonstrated to be associated with irreversible destructive changes where remission of symptoms cannot be anticipated and where deterioration has progressed to advanced stages. It is not appropriate for anyone whose impairment is minor or a matter of conjecture based largely on the evidence of an organic impairment combined with mental illness. Increasingly it is recognized that functional mental disorder may first be manifested very late in life (Kay & Roth; Post). Mental confusion, especially when accompanied by physical illness, toxic conditions, or malnutrition, may be contributing an unknown proportion to statistics concerning first admissions of the aged to mental hospitals. Not statistics concerning admissions but diagnoses —delayed and well-founded diagnoses—are the only legitimate grounds for decision and prognosis. It is tragic that the opportunity for adequate diagnosis may be denied to some people because institutions which are essentially custodial may be the only ones available to receive them in the limited time permitted for disposal of their "cases."

Lieberman and Lakin (Chapter 22) indicate that even under the best of circumstances institutionalization may be a traumatic experience. Illness and other disruptive developments occurring at the time of admission may aggravate difficulties. Such observations suggest that attention should be given to the psychological and social consequences of our present provisions for care of the mentally ill and to the opportunities for prevention, therapy, and rehabilitation.

SECTION I

Diagnosis and Classification

CHAPTER 19

Diagnostic and Nosological
Aspects of Mental Disorder
in Old Age

WERNER JANZARIK

PROBLEMS OF PSYCHIATRIC DIAGNOSIS

The diagnoses by which psychiatry tries to find a classification system similar to nosological systems of other medical branches are continually changing. The psychiatric diagnostic schemes of the past 150 years have seldom remained valid for more than a few decades. They were often applicable only within a particular school and seldom beyond a certain linguistic frontier.

The world-wide accord that appeared to be forming in Kraepelin's time proved to be illusory. Since then we do have a psychiatric terminology understood everywhere, but the same terms are often used to describe totally different facts. Some of those apparently certain diagnoses simulate a knowledge which in fact does not yet exist. The medical examiner who is convinced that he has found an

383

objectively correct diagnosis tends to overlook the fact that his own diagnosis is often correct only under certain assumptions and that another medical examiner will find a different diagnosis for the same psychopathological phenomena under different assumptions. Nowhere are the difficulties of diagnosis greater and the basic doubts respecting psychiatric nosology more evident than in dealing with the mental disorders of old age.

Every attempt to form a diagnostic classification must remain superficial if an explanation of the assumptions is not given beforehand. These assumptions and the derived diagnostic classification then lead to application of diagnostic distinctions in any individual case. The scientific tradition which influenced each examiner is decisive for his diagnostic convictions. The conceptions put forward here are based on German psychiatry. Their nosological base corresponds to the classification developed by Schneider (1959) on the basis of Kraepelin's work. Their psychopathological base corresponds to the so-called phenomenological research methods founded by K. Jaspers and expanded by Gruhle, Mayer-Gross, K. Schneider, and others. The present diagnoses are largely temporary, and we must note that they tend to be based on different principles within various linguistic frontiers. We would be mistaken in the belief that there is already an internationally accepted psychiatry in the sense that general medicine is now to a great extent international. Nevertheless, diagnosis is necessary, and a uniform diagnostic system is an aim, distant to be sure, but at least theoretically within reach.

The unique position of psychiatry among the medical branches explains the dependence of psychiatric diagnoses on so many differing assumptions and therefore their merely relative validity. Psychiatry, like the other branches of medicine, tries to recognize and heal illnesses by such somatological (biological) methods as serological or histological diagnosis of a general paralysis, electroencephalographic diagnosis of epilepsy, and application of somatic treatments. However, these somatological methods—the real medical foundation—alone fail to meet the demands of psychiatry. The abnormal kinds of experience and behavior which are for psychiatry much more important than physical disorders can be dealt with only by psychological means. Psychiatry has a philosophical as well as a biological basis and is, as we would say in German, not only a *Naturwissenschaft,* but also a *Geisteswissenschaft.* Psychiatry therefore occupies a special position among the branches of medicine. Psychiatric diagnosis must be somatologically oriented and must have generally valid biological foundations before it can attain generally valid results. When, owing to a lack of somatic findings (for example, in dealing with the so-called endogenous psychoses), basically psychological methods are applied, diagnosis loses its accuracy, because we do not have a single psychology, but schools of psychology which vary with philosophical background. The psychological schools and their origins in behaviorism, dialectical materialism, psychoanalysis, existential philosophy, association-psychology, act-psychology, or structure-psychology influence basically the way of diagnosing and the value which is set on diagnosis.

DIAGNOSTIC CLASSIFICATION IN ITS PSYCHOPATHOLOGICAL ASPECTS

In distinguishing among psychic disorders of the higher age groups, we shall have to depend mainly on the psychological aspects; in many cases, nothing can be said about the physical foundations of mental disorders. The author agrees in general and in many particulars with the classification of Schneider (1959), whose work is now available in English. We distinguish between (1) abnormal variations of psychic life and (2) psychotic abnormalities (a) with a somatic basis and (b) without known somatic basis. The diagnostic distinctions to be applied to the special conditions of old age require a more precise explanation and differentiation.

First, by "abnormal variations of psychic life" we understand those deviations from the normal state which are not caused by an illness in the medical meaning of the word, that is, which are caused by neither an acute or chronic organic process and its consequences nor a defective structure. The abnormal variations of psychic life include the constitutional lack of intelligence, abnormal (psychopathic) personality, abnormal reaction to experiences, atypical mental developments (*fehlentwicklungen*), and atypical mental attitudes (*fehlhaltungen*). These atypical mental developments and attitudes are often referred to as neuroses, but it is desirable to avoid the term "neurosis" for diagnostic purposes because it depends on supposition, has too many meanings, and is not exact. The term "neurosis" is a perfect example of the dependence of a diagnosis obtained by psychological means on previous decisions which lie beyond the limits of medical science. It depends essentially on these previous decisions whether the emphasis in neurotic disorders is placed more on pathogenic formations or on constitutional predispositions and whether deep impressions in early childhood, present conflicts, certain impulses, or guiding values play the more important role. The term "neurosis" can give no idea of the personality and fate of the neurotic in question nor of the various sources of his atypical mental attitude.

We do not speak of the abnormal variations of psychic life nor of neurotic abnormalities as illnesses, in spite of the customary use of the term "illness" to cover all mental disorders which lead to seriously abnormal behavior or to grave impairment of the patient's well-being. Such a use is dangerous in that each diagnostician is completely free to draw distinctions between illness and health according to the degree of psychological abnormality. Even if we describe as pathological only mental abnormalities that are based on pathological organic processes, the distinctions which can be drawn between illness and health by means of pathological anatomical and pathophysiological research are still not always exact, but they are much more reliable and more generally valid than those formed by psychological means. Nevertheless, it is still unsatisfactory that the pathological basis of many mental disturbances is assumed and not confirmed and that, on the other hand, the medical meaning of illness sometimes fails to include grave mental abnormalities. For example, a serious obsession neurosis is not regarded as an illness in the medical meaning of the word although it might defy any kind of therapy and cast its shadow over a whole life. Certainly, physical factors play an important role in many abnormal variations of psychic life without the mental abnormalities being primarily an expression of a pathological organic process. The beginning and fixation of an atypical mental attitude in old age is often influenced by chronic illness, organic defects, a general loss of vitality, and a decrease of efficiency due to some physical cause. On the other hand, atypical mental attitudes can acquire an organic basis and thereby develop into an illness in the strict medical meaning of the word. When addicts reach old age, their atypical mental attitudes are often shoved into the background by the consequent organic defects.

Somatically caused deteriorations and psychoses are diagnosed both somatologically and psychologically. The physical findings are more important for diagnosis than the psychopathological features; a general paralysis confirmed by serological means remains a general paralysis whether the physical changes cause a simple dementia, an expansive or depressive syndrome, or even symptoms that are usually found only in endogenous psychoses. Within psychiatry, a medical diagnosis in the strict sense of the word is possible only when dealing with physically caused psychoses and deteriorations, because only here are definite—that is, somatic—findings available. The psychological aspect of an illness already proved to be organic is nonspecific and, as has been known since Bonhoeffer (1910), has many different diagnostic meanings. In dealing with acute stages, a disturbance of consciousness is most obvious. In somatically based psychoses, these disturbances of consciousness take the form, not only of deviations from the normal clarity and breadth of consciousness, but often of a deterioration of the order and arrangement of the field of consciousness and its continuance in the course of time as well. The disturbance of consciousness forms the core of many exogenous syndromes. The psychopathological manifestations ranging from a hardly noticeable clouding of consciousness to severe confusional or delirious psychoses implies, however, nothing definite about the somatically effective noxae in spite of many affinities between certain defects and certain syndromes.

Compared to the syndromes centering around a disturbance of consciousness, somatically based psychoses are far more infrequent, but also more remarkable. They appear to occur more frequently in old age than during the prime of life and claim special theoretical interest. These psychoses, effecting no proven clouding of consciousness, are characterized by hallucinatory or delusional-hallucinatory symptoms or affective disorders, especially depressive or manic disturbances. Therefore, they are not far removed from endogenous psychoses.

On the one hand, we have to deal with acute, somatically based psychoses and, on the other, we are confronted with chronic deterioration characterized by personality deterioration and intellectual dementia. In this respect, we have to deal with relatively uniform manifestations, although they might be hidden under exacerbation. These deteriorations, whose first symptoms appear during the years of health, form the core of the psychiatry of old age because of their numerical superiority. Nevertheless, as far as diagnosis is concerned, they, as well as the other psychopathological syndromes already discussed, are less remarkable than the endogenous psychoses that appear less frequently in old age and whose diagnostic frame we will now outline.

In speaking of endogenous psychoses, we understand chiefly a certain type of psychotic syndrome. The further conception of these psychoses as primarily caused by endogenous predispositions is controversial and in any case not binding on the whole lot of observations, which, from a psychopathological point of view, are referred to as endogenous. The special problems of these psychoses result from the fact that no somatic abnormality that might be regarded as the substratum of psychopathological abnormalities has yet been established in spite of the nonspecific findings of numerous investigations. The frequently detectable inheritability of the illness; the senseless invasion of the psychotic episodes; the qualitative innovation of psychopathological symptoms; the unusual successes of somatic therapy, which has transformed the atmosphere of mental hospitals in an almost revolutionary way, all point to the probability that even the endogenous psychoses are caused by pathological somatic processes or malfunctions and are therefore diseases in the medical sense of the word. We do not thereby state anything with regard to the genesis or nature of abnormality presumed to exist on the somatological level. A multidimensional approach could best deal with these complicated circumstances. Especially in the psychiatry of old age, we have to consider the highly complex structure of the various clinical pictures. Here we may recall Mayer-Gross and his associates (Mayer-Gross, Slater, & Roth, 1960), whose basic phenomenological notion was supplemented by multidimensional points of view and whose ideas are especially helpful in diagnosis (Roth, 1955; Roth, 1957; Roth, 1959).

As to diagnosis of endogenous psychoses, possible only psychopathologically, we commonly distinguish between the thymopathic (cyclothymic, manic-depressive, affective) and the schizophrenic groups. The prototypes, on the one hand, are characterized by recurring depressive and manic phases which thereafter lead back to the starting point without lasting injurious effect; on the other hand, schizophrenic psychoses result in a defective condition either progressively or in sudden outbursts. Considering first the characteristic types, we shall outline the symptoms that influence the diagnosis.

In manic-depressive psychoses, the depressive phases prevail. Most cases are without manic episodes at all. With regard to endogenous depression, it is typical that the extent and duration of the emotional disorders appear to be much more severe than the normal fluctuation of mood and that these feelings are experienced in a characteristic physical way. Anxiety, sadness, and the loss of feeling are described in close relation to tightness; pressure; pain; restlessness; and emptiness of the body, chest, throat, or head. Many patients suffer from inhibition and stiffness, whereas others experience a painful excitability. At the beginning or at the fading away of a phase and in a less severe case, the patient feels a little better in the afternoon, and his condition will sometimes become unobtrusive or even hypomanic as the day progresses. The patient will only be able to sleep during the first hours of the night, if at all. Soon after midnight he awakes for the rest of the night and waits, frightened, for the challenges of the next day. Except for contentless and "vital depressions" [1] without characteristic features, the three themes of hypochondria, impoverishment, and guilt are in the foreground. The contents may reach delusional extent in their inflexibility and limitlessness, especially in those patients suffering from psychotic anxiety. The inclination to suicide is notable even in those patients who, because of their ethics and religious ties, would never normally consider suicide. After recovery, the patient understands neither the contents and experiences of the past phase nor his own delusional convictions.

In the rarely occurring manic phases, the patient's behavior is characterized by motor releases; by a cheerful, insolent discord; by the impulses to move and to develop his own possibilities; by emotional excess; by volatile and disconnected thinking and talking; by belief in his own physical and mental vigor and efficiency; and by an uncritical presumptuousness and lack of scruples. A dynamic expansion includes these and other peculiarities of mania, which can be compared with that dynamic reduction typical of depressive manifestations. The occasionally occurring irritation and aggression in manic patients can usually be regarded as the reaction to a frustrated exhibitionist impulse.

Compared with the manic-depressive syndrome, typical schizophrenic symptoms appear to be stranger, less regular, and more clearly differentiated from the normal variations of psychic life. Delusional perceptions—the experience of influences in the realm of feeling, striving, volition and thought—are typical of the psychosis' beginning. Later, the psychosis is characterized by the experience of influences playing on the body, mostly in the sexual sphere and most often connected with an elaborate delusion. As to the other (sensory) hallucinations, hearing voices produced by audible thoughts is most typical. These voices talk about the patient, insult him, give him orders, and comment on his doings. Especially during the destructive phase of the illness, expression and thought disorders are of primary importance. They are less important with regard to diagnosis, but nevertheless very instructive to the experienced observer. They include mannerisms and eccentricities, unusual word formation, and a decay of thought

---

[1] Mayer-Gross (Mayer-Gross, Slater, & Roth, 1960) writes, "By this term attention is drawn to the deeper stratum of the personality involved in the endogenous depression, a stratum closely connected with the somatic concomitants of the affect" (p. 205).

processes leading to complete destruction of speech. If the florid schizophrenic psychoses are characterized by an unsteadiness of emotions
and intentions, the destructive state is chiefly marked by a loss of mental dynamics. In the course of an active illness, the dynamic emptying
can be displaced by later psychotic invasions.

Diagnosis and, with it, the nosology of endogenous psychoses
would not be so difficult if we had to deal only with the typical cyclothymias and schizophrenias. Against the background of clearly manic-
depressive and schizophrenic psychoses, it is not generally too difficult
to describe reactive discords, constitutionally abnormal moods, paranoid reactions and developments, abnormal mental attitudes, and
somatically based psychoses against a clearly manic-depressive and
schizophrenic psychosis. The limits of the two endogenous groups can
be fixed without great difficulty by means of typical cases; atypical observations, however, occur remarkably often. Diagnostic difficulties develop from, among others, the fact that manic-depressive cases sometimes lead to permanent psychic changes. Numerous depressions start
uncharacteristically as reactive bad moods or in connection with
somatic injuries and develop only later, after a vitalization of the depressive moods, into a cyclothymic depression. Between the cyclothymic and schizophrenic psychoses are many shades, rather frequently
within manic states. Again and again we can observe psychoses resulting
from intoxications, encephalitises, and other organic illnesses which
cannot be distinguished from schizophrenia. With old age, these diagnostic difficulties increase. They should not be hidden by a schematic
way of thinking, but should be evaluated according to their importance, since we can best improve our present rather superficial knowledge by analyzing those cases which remain inexplicable by traditional
diagnostic means.

ABNORMAL VARIATIONS OF
PSYCHIC LIFE IN OLD AGE

The survey of old-age mental disorders which follows cannot
go into detail and therefore can indicate only the diagnostic difficulties and the nosological considerations inspired by them. Personal
experience collected in a mental hospital and in activities with the
West German public health service form the basis for this survey.
Practical knowledge concerning old-age clinics, psychology, and psychopathology cannot be described in detail within the limits of this necessarily short survey. It has already been extensively published and

instead of referring to the numerous publications, we will mention only reference works by Bronisch (1958; 1959), Kaplan (1956), Ruffin (1960), and Schulte and Harlfinger (1956), which serve as an introduction to the more detailed literature.

As stated before, abnormal variations of psychic life are not illnesses in the medical sense, although they can lead to grave disturbances of well-being and behavior. We do not deal here with diagnostic differentiations in the strictest sense, but with the various types of abnormal behavior which must be defined. The specific conditions of old age complicate the situation, since with increasing age the consequences of organic damage—for example, arteriosclerotic cerebral processes—become greater relative to the entire pathogenic complex. In multidimensional diagnosis, the definition of what part each aspect plays in each individual clinical picture is more important than the fixing of the limits between abnormal psychic variations on the one hand and organic illnesses on the other.

First we shall explore the modifications in old age of those striking symptoms which already existed during the earlier years as predisposing factors or which developed as a consequence of certain experiences. Abnormal personalities are in the foreground. These may change greatly with age, toward either mitigation and compensation or a focusing on and aggravation of existing peculiarities. The nature of these old-age modifications seems to depend essentially on the relation between the abnormal personality features and the fixation, narrowing, stiffening, and loss of vitality and tension potentials which usually occur in old age. Stiffness, obstinacy, pedantry, suspicion, and egocentrism become worse, while emotional lability, lack of stability, the tendency to short-circuit reactions, and frequently also the fanaticism and the querulous tendencies of earlier years are mitigated by the stabilization and decrease of impulsive drives during the aging process. In dealing with the more-or-less aggravated lack of pure intellectual powers, we should not expect a decompensation if an adaptation to life's tasks had been accomplished. On the other hand, a combination of intellectual inferiority and a pre-existing insufficiency of general functional capacity, now critically aggravated, is serious. For these imbecilic patients, permanent hospital treatment which might have been avoided in younger years may now become necessary because of the senile processes and the human isolation occurring at the same time. The abnormal mental attitudes which originated during earlier periods and were maintained until old age are closely connected with abnormal personalities, since they, too, develop from predispositions and abnormal psychic features, even though they depend on the effects of experiences. It is of great interest to follow the old-age alteration of lifelong abnormal mental attitudes: mitigation, or occasionally a complete release, of addictions and their complications by cerebral damage caused by the addictions; modifications of criminal habits; old-age forms of sexual perversion; and the increasing loss of liberty of some obsessional personalities, leading to complete torpidity. From a merely diagnostic point of view, these striking pre-existent characteristics do not present problems.

These abnormal patterns of experience and behavior which develop along new lines with age might raise the questions of whether we are confronted with endogenous psychoses and what is the part played by organic factors in each case. It is important to gain a clear picture of the internal and external situation forming the background of the abnormalities. These cases occur more frequently toward the fiftieth year and during the fifties than in the sixties, which is the period of life investigated in this paper. A clear external situation must not lead us to simplify the internal situation according to certain preconceptions. We must take into consideration the individual's personal values developed during his life, as well as some of the general developmental tendencies of old-age value orientation, in order to comprehend the crises of advanced age and in order not to mistakenly diagnose them as endogenous, especially depressive, psychoses. At the beginning of old age, abnormal mental attitudes and reactions often develop as reactions to the destruction of life goals, the loss of influence, the onset of human isolation, the endangering of economic security, and other grave losses. In old and especially very old age, we often find remarkably simple, usually concrete, causes of mental decompensation. Sometimes, very old people remain surprisingly undisturbed when confronted with, for example, the death of a member of the family, complete isolation, impoverishment, or increasing neglect, whereas a slight somatic disturbance, such as a forced rearrangement of the household or a forced change of residence, may cause a serious attempt at suicide.

In reactive ill humor and depressive mental attitudes (particularly of a hypochondriac nature), we can draw from the history facts important in distinguishing these from endogenous depressions. Positive psychopathological criteria are not available. The physically delimited cyclothymic depressions are a pattern from which other depressive discord states deviate more or less in their more dysphoric coloring, in their less important share in the physical sphere, and in further variations. An unsolved nosological problem is that there are various depressions with endogenous as well as reactive (or "neurotic") features which range between unquestionably endogenous depressions and, on the other hand, certain reactively caused discords. These intermediate cases cannot be classified correctly under either the first or the second designation. We can consider the specific observations as endoreactive dysthymias (Weitbrecht, 1952) without thereby anticipating a later nosological system.

Distinguishing paranoid and querulous developments from schizophrenic psychoses in extremely suspicious old patients and resistant backbiters can be difficult. These developments usually represent a sharpening of pre-existing, but hitherto hidden, features and tendencies. Among other predisposing conditions, we should like to mention partial and complete deafness as the basis of paranoid developments and chronic alcoholism as the basis of extreme jealousy. Whereas querulous people often become milder and more conciliatory with age, there are other patients who begin only in advanced age to fight officials and courts, displaying thereby a paranoid sullenness. Among these we find a surprising number of former criminals. In differential diagnosis of schizophrenia, only a few cases are unexplained, for the schizophrenic symptoms really do differ from abnormal mental attitudes of a paranoid nature if a strict standard is applied. This is not the case with limitation of endogenous depressions.

Somatically Based Psychoses and
Deterioration Syndromes

In diagnosing acute and chronic psychic disorders which have a somatic basis, the somatological and psychopathological aspects are so closely connected that discussing them separately is justified only by didactic considerations. Somatic findings, which will be discussed first, would allow for the most reliable classification of the psychic disorders so arranged if these findings really were always at hand and if the proven somatic symptoms always explained sufficiently the psychopathological symptoms observed at the same time. Very often, however, both these conditions are absent. The differential diagnosis between mental disorders that can be attributed to senile and arteriosclerotic cerebral processes, which are the most important illnesses for old-age psychiatry, depends significantly on the progress of the illness; the nature and extent of the organic processes can usually be discovered only indirectly by considering the subjective complaints, the neurological symptoms, and the psychopathological picture. Often, there is a great difference between the clinical findings and the later anatomical findings. Similar difficulties arise when forming a judgment about other organic processes. Nevertheless, these difficulties should not keep us from pursuing a somatological diagnosis as far as possible. It is important to know whether a dementia is caused by a senile and/or presenile brain atrophy or by a general paralysis; whether we are confronted with an arteriosclerosis of the cerebral vessels or with a brain tumor; whether the delirious confusional states of aged patients are caused by bronchial pneumonia, by inanition through chronic malnutrition, by the misuse of alcohol or soporifics, or by other acute or chronic intoxications.

In old age the somatic disorders forming the basis of the psychopathological symptoms are often very complex. This situation appears especially in acute psychoses and in exacerbations of chronic deterioration syndromes. In most of the specific observations, somatic methods of examination—the roentgenological techniques being among the most important—indicate damage that must have existed for years and that by itself cannot explain the decompensation. Instances are cerebral atrophies with a senile and arteriosclerotic basis resulting from encephalitis, chronic misuse of alcohol or other noxae, cerebral damage during early childhood, deformity of the brain, and traumatic cerebral damage. The acute and possibly permanent decompensations can be started by a simple febrile infection—even by pneumonia—by the stress of an operation and anaesthesia, by a temporary cardiac insufficiency, or by other stresses on old patients already weakened in this way but who had nevertheless functioned efficiently. Psychic factors often seem to be of great importance in the pathogenic complex, although it is necessary to consider whether these might not also be the result of somatic malfunctions, especially when a disturbance of circulation must be considered. With age, a cerebral blood insufficiency and the resultant lack of oxygen is apparently an important pathogenetic factor. Even with those psychoses which, from a psychopathological point of view, must be related to senile brain atrophy, treatment of the heart and circulation may cause surprising improvement. This applies also to confusional states that arise from mental stresses.

Since somatological diagnosis is hindered by the fact that the somatic findings are often difficult to get and, even when available, are complex and nonspecific as to their relation to the psychic symptoms, the weakness of psychopathological diagnosis is caused by the ambiguity of the findings. With the help of psychopathological symptoms surrounding disturbances of consciousness, personality deterioration, and dementia, the specific type of somatically based psychosis is easily recognized. Specific diagnosis assumes, however, that clinical data and the physical findings will also be included. We cannot enter here into particulars on the various psychopathological syndromes and the diagnostic differentiations. Only those difficulties will be mentioned which may arise in distinguishing this entire group of illnesses from psychic symptoms of another genesis.

We have already mentioned the relationship between abnormal mental variations and somatically based psychoses. We shall state here in addition that it is not only old-age deterioration which aggravates pre-existent symptoms. For instance, the chronically dysphoric and sometimes even the hyperthymic discord states of some older patients may be an expression of organic deterioration independent of predisposing factors. Apparently pseudodemented behavior is often nothing more than a demonstration of organically based helplessness and is therefore comparable to a pseudodementia which may superimpose itself on a serious cerebral injury.

Differential diagnosis in the endogenous manifestations is the chief consideration with those psychoses which initially appear in old age. If these psychoses are of the purely endogenous type, we must be careful in accepting a diagnosis of somatically based psychosis even if the somatic findings are weighty. Even if the endogenous symptoms appeared at the same time as the somatic disorders—for instance, an intoxication—the problem remains as to whether we are not confronted with an endogenous psychosis that was merely released by a somatic illness. Considering the frequency of this finding in old patients, the proof of cerebral atrophy does not immediately justify the interpretation of an endogenous syndrome as a somatically based psychosis.

With a combination of endogenous and organic symptoms, the diagnosis orients itself with the progress of the illness. Endogenous psychoses that arose during earlier years will certainly not become somatically based psychoses when organic changes occur in old age. In these cases, the specific conditions of old age have only pathoplastic importance. For instance, a cyclothymic depression, formerly occurring in phases, may take on a chronic, constant character; the sadness may gain a more dysphoric character; and the contents of the delusion may gain nihilistic features. In dealing with illnesses that occurred first in old age and where endogenous and organic features intersect, it is often not possible to decide whether we are confronted with an accidental combination, with an endogenous psychosis caused by organic changes, or with an atypical, somatically based psychosis. Important clues may be had if similar psychoses occur within the same family. Special consideration should be paid to psychoses which start as merely endogenous psychoses and which then gain more organic features—endogenous depressions developing finally to an arteriosclerotic dementia or schizophrenic psychoses finally growing to senile dementia. Observations of this kind remind one of the endogenous syndromes commonly occurring at the beginning of a general paralysis. Their nosological interpretation depends entirely on the standpoint of the individual investigator.

The Endogenous Psychoses

The increasing frequency of endogenous syndromes in patients of the higher age groups corresponds to the increasing number of old people in the population of highly civilized countries. Nevertheless, the diagnosis endogenous psychosis is still used reluctantly when applied to patients who became psychotic for the first time between sixty and eighty years of age. Although it is admitted that these late illnesses are somehow similar to cyclothymias and schizophrenic psychoses of younger patients, there remains a greater readiness to regard them as senile or arteriosclerotic psychoses. Especially as regards the late schizophrenic psychoses, there are prejudices that have their roots in the period when schizophrenic psychoses—restricted, of course, to the younger patients—were still referred to as dementia praecox. By regarding them as involutional psychoses, the observations in question will be classified terminologically, but their nosological position will still remain unexplained. In the perspective of the previous diagnostic considerations, the occurrence of primary cyclothymic and schizophrenic illnesses in old age is implicitly assumed, and some statements have even been made as to their limitations. Because the endogenous old-age psychoses are especially disputed, their phenomenological aspect will have to be considered more intensely than that of the other old-age disorders. As an explanation, we shall first give the history of a cyclothymic patient and then of a schizophrenic psychosis.

A woman, aged eighty-two, who has been remarkably active physically and mentally, complains of headache, loss of appetite, constipation, and sleeplessness. She is failing in energy and activity, becoming increasingly less impulsive, then agitated, and she alarms her family by wishing to be dead since nothing can be done about her state. At the time of her admission to the hospital, this state has persisted for one year. In spite of her old age and hypertension, the patient still proves to be physically healthy. Complaining, and with a sad expression on her face, she reports headache and tormenting pressure on her chest. She is, she says, sad, yet unable to cry, and feels so excited that she is unable to relax. The patient, who is in well-ordered familial and economic circumstances, regards her own sadness as unreasonable. She is convinced that she will never get well again and admits that she is thinking of suicide.

The initial doubts as to the diagnosis of an endogenous psychosis can easily be rejected, since it was discovered that three of the patient's eight children had suffered from clearly cyclothymic phases in their younger years. During the course of the initially applied pharmacotherapy and accompanied by descending blood pressure, the agitated state of the patient becomes complicated by states of organic confusion. In spite of her old age, ECT is finally administered, and this effects a remission of the depressive psychosis.

Apart from the temporary organic confusion mentioned, this history could just as well apply to an illness of a younger patient. A far-reaching agreement that this was an endogenous psychosis could be achieved, although it was not entirely typical. One who is convinced that, within the limits of endogenous depression, nosologically independent subclassifications can be found could describe several of these. In doing so, one must consider not only special psychopathological variations—caused by anxiety and agitation, depersonalization, nihilistic delusions, paranoid contents, and so on—but also heredity, age of the patient at onset of the illness, and the course of the illness. By considering all thymopathic psychoses as a nosological unity, one will recognize various types which overlap one another and whose distinctions are possibly caused by the meeting of a predisposed release of basic mood and impulse with personal predispositions of various kinds. It is hardly necessary to add that, within the older age groups, complicating organic factors may cause additional modifications of the various types of thymopathic psychoses.

We have already explained the difficulties of distinguishing endogenous depressions from reactive ill humor and somatically based psychoses. These difficulties have to be expected more frequently in old-age psychoses than in those of younger patients. In what follows, we shall make some supplementary observations on manic psychoses of old age. These old-age manias do not always represent a cyclothymic phase. Real cyclothymic manias apparently occur even less frequently in old age than in younger years. To be distinguished from these are the maniform states of ill humor which are organically based, which most commonly occur in hyperthymic personalities or in alcoholics and which tend to become chronic. Some old-age manias may be a maniform schizophrenia. Here we can get no evidence from observing the progress of the illness. Especially within the thymopathic core group, within the strictly manic-depressive psychoses, we relatively often find atypical forms overlapping schizophrenic symptoms (Kinkelin, 1954). Manic-depressive psychoses at the climax of life can develop a schizophrenic course with age and may even lead to a defective state. The nosological problems stressed here will be dealt with later. First, we shall discuss the schizophrenic psychoses of old age, once again starting from an example.

> A former bookkeeper, female, aged seventy-five, hitherto apparently normal, becomes desultory in thinking, suspicious, and irritable. She is convinced that she is being persecuted and runs around at night, listening at the walls in the apartment of her relatives, where she as a refugee had been lovingly received. In the hospital, the patient appears shy and distressed. Displaying a tense expression on her face she listens to "voices" and "telephone conversations" about herself. She is disturbed by disgusting smells and sees animals, people, and silent scenes in their entire reality. She feels hypnotized, her thoughts are repressed, she is convinced that people talk about her. The old lady receives chlorpromazine treatment and thereafter is completely all right, energetic, and as interested as she was before the onset of her mental illness. But this remission lasts only a few months. Again she becomes timid, helpless, tormented. People look at her strangely, she is influenced by "chlorpromazine rays" and "ether waves." During the night, she is "pumped" by a male member of the "air-waves group," and this disconnects her thoughts. She hears voices giving her orders, forbidding her to eat, and expressing what she was going to think. Since the twice-attained therapeutic effect lasts only a short time, now, aged seventy-six, she must be hospitalized. She is clearly oriented, but at the same time completely turned away from her surroundings, often tense and irritable, talking with and scolding her "voices," from which she tries to flee in ill-planned escapes. Aged eighty, the patient remains influenced by her hallucinations. She needs constant supervision because of her refusal to eat and her suicidal tendencies.

Schizophrenics often become quieter and the psychotic symptoms become more uniform and are put in the background after an illness that has remained for decades, whereas psychoses appearing first in old age often show a special number of symptoms and are most tempestuous. Müller (1959) is the most recent author to deal with the modifications of old-age psychoses. Our own researches (Janzarik, 1957) refer to primary onsets after the sixtieth year. There we found that, among these late-appearing illnesses, the creeping paranoid psychoses which have few symptoms and which appear frequently between the fortieth and sixtieth year again occur more rarely. After the sixtieth year, paranoid-hallucinatory psychoses are more predominant and are similar to psychoses of younger years in their many forms and agitation. Except for acute episodes which quickly fade away, these late illnesses are characterized by the tendency to end as chronic hallucinations although they may start as completely delusional. In old age, the precipitating factors play a far more important role than in schizophrenias of younger years. Especially events which even in age force a thoroughly new orientation, for example, the death of husband or wife, seem to be pathogenetically relevant.

In addition to observations that permit a clear diagnosis, as in the case cited, there are others which cannot yet be classified. We meet with diagnostic difficulties when schizophrenic symptoms and organic features overlap or when schizophrenic psychoses merge with those of the thymopathic group. For instance, we may meet psychoses in old alcoholics that can equally well be regarded as alcoholic hallucinoses or as paranoid schizophrenias with particularly distinct hallucinations. A persecutory delusion, which in younger years would simply be called schizophrenic, may with age begin a course which finally ends as organic dementia. The transitions to thymopathic psychoses are especially frequent and varied in form. Along with increasing anxiety and agitation, depressive states can develop into a schizophrenic picture; schizophrenic symptoms may correspond to vital depressive ill humor or high spirits. During the course of some old-age psychoses, sometimes the schizophrenic and sometimes the cyclothymic aspects prevail.

We must ask whether the difficulties of outlining the endogenous psychoses of old age are sufficiently explained by the imperfection of diagnostic methods and whether transitions in various directions do not belong to the nature of these psychoses. The nosology of endogenous psychoses is still not definitely clarified. Perhaps we start from the wrong basis if we regard them on the same level as well-defined illnesses and expect to be able to outline a schizophrenia, a cyclothymic depression, or a mania just as precisely as, for instance, a general paralysis. If we regard endogenous psychoses as basically disturbances of psychic dynamics, as changes occurring primarily in the sphere of emotion and intent which only from this point affect the personality (Janzarik, 1959), we must from the beginning count on overlapping of the symptoms regarded as typical. The differentiations among endogenous psychoses are not to be sought in the single symptoms, but in the disturbances which, as the bases of these psychoses, must be presumed to be on the emotional and intentional level. The question of whether disturbances of this kind always presume predispositions remains. Experience with old-age psychoses causes one to ask whether the psychopathological syndromes which we regard as endogenous psychoses might not be prepared for by organic damage, perhaps even independently of hereditary predispositions. Finally, it is notable that schizophrenic and thymopathic old-age psychoses often overlap each other. The idea of a unit psychosis, developed by Romantic psychiatry and saved from being forgotten by the works of Llopis (1954; 1960 with references to earlier works of the author) and Ey (1952) might be applicable to some of these psychoses. In principle, all diagnostic difficulties must serve as a test of our nosological knowledge and thereby finally contribute to widening our knowledge.

REFERENCES

Bonhoeffer, K. *Die symptomatischen psychosen im gefolge von akuten infektionen und inneren erkrankungen.* Leipzig and Vienna: Deuticke, 1910.

Bronisch, F.W. Psychopathologie des höheren lebensalters. *Schweiz. Arch. Neurol. Psychiat.*, 1958, **81,** 105-123.

Bronisch, F.W. Die endogenen psychosen des höheren lebensalters. *Schweiz. Arch. Neurol. Psychiat.*, 1959, **83,** 69-77.

Ey, H. *Études psychiatriques I.* (2nd ed.) Paris: Desclée de Brouwer, 1952.

Janzarik, W. Zur problematik schizophrener psychosen im höheren lebensalter. *Nervenarzt*, 1957, **28,** 535-542.

Janzarik, W. *Dynamische grundkonstellationen in endogenen psychosen.* Berlin, Göttingen, and Heidelberg: Springer, 1959.

Kaplan, O.J. (Ed.) *Mental disorders in later life.* (2nd ed.) Stanford: Stanford University Press, 1956.

Kinkelin, M. Verlauf und prognose des manisch-depressiven irreseins. *Schweiz. Arch. Neurol. Psychiat.*, 1954, **73,** 100-146.

Llopis, B. La psicosis unica. *Arch. de Neurobiologia*, 1954, **17,** 141-163.

Llopis, B. Das allen psychosen gemeinsame axialsyndrom. *Fortschr. Neurol. Psychiat.*, 1960, **28,** 106-129.

Mayer-Gross, W., Slater, E., & Roth, M. *Clinical psychiatry.* (2nd ed.) London: Cassell, 1960.

Müller, C. *Über das senium der schizophrenen.* Basel and New York: Karger, 1959.

Roth, M. The natural history of mental disorder in old age. *J. ment. Sci.*, 1955, **101,** 281-301.

Roth, M. Interaction of genetic and environmental factors in the causation of schizophrenia. In D. Richter (Ed.), *Schizophrenia, somatic aspects.* London, New York, and Paris: Pergamon Press, 1957. Pp. 15-31.

Roth, M. The phenomenology of depressive states. *Canad. psychiat. Ass. J.*, spec. suppl., 1959, **4,** 32-53.

Ruffin, H. Das altern und die psychiatrie des seniums. In H.W. Gruhle, R. Jung, W. Mayer-Gross, & M. Müller (Eds.), *Psychiatrie der gegenwart.* Vol. 2. Berlin, Göttingen, and Heidelberg: Springer, 1960. Pp. 1088-1160.

Schneider, K. *Clinical psychopathology.* Trans by M.W. Hamilton. New York and London: Grune and Stratton, 1959.

Schulte, W., & Harlfinger, H. Seelisches altern als lebensproblem. *Forschr. Neurol. Psychiat.,* 1956, **24,** 341-368.

Weitbrecht, H.J. Zur typologie depressiver psychosen. *Fortschr. Neurol. Psychiat.,* 1952, **20,** 247-269.

CHAPTER 20

Schizophrenias of Old Age

D.W.K. KAY and
MARTIN ROTH

The paraphrenias (schizophrenias of old age) raise
a number of problems common to many other disorders in psychiatry,
and their solution might therefore advance knowledge in a number
of directions.[1] The relationship of paraphrenic, paranoid, and schizophrenic illness has long been disputed, and no present view commands
general acceptance. It seems that these controversies often turn on un-

[1] Dr. Kay wishes to acknowledge his indebtedness to the Mental Health Research
Fund for enabling him to carry out his study in Sweden during 1956-1958, to Prof.
Torsten Sjögren, head of the Psychiatric Clinic at the Karolinska Hospital, Stock-
holm, and to Dr. Carl-Henry Alström for their constant help and encouragement.
We are indebted to our colleagues on the consultant staff of Graylingwell Hospital,
Chichester, for their willing cooperation. We also thank the Foundations' Fund for
Research in Psychiatry and the Research Committee of the Newcastle Regional
Hospital Board, who have supported our investigations into the problems of mental
disorder in old age.

acknowledged assumptions about whether clinical, prognostic, genetic, or all of these criteria, were to be employed in deciding the issue.

In a descriptive sense the term "paraphrenia" has been applied by continental and English authors to a condition, usually arising in the fourth or fifth decade of life, in which paranoid delusions and hallucinations are prominent, but the affective, volitional, and intellectual aspects of the personality remain fairly well-preserved despite a chronic course. It is customarily distinguished from paranoid schizophrenia on the grounds that typically schizophrenic symptoms are absent. It is also considered distinct from paranoia, where the delusions are very well systematized and hallucinations do not occur. Yet when the later course of the illness is taken into account, many of these distinctions fail, since W. Mayer found (1921) that after a few years more than half the patients with paraphrenia do exhibit typical schizophrenic symptoms and Kolle (1931) found nearly all of a group of patients with paranoia to have primary delusions, which are widely regarded as pathognomonic of schizophrenia. Kolle's studies also showed genetic affinities between paranoia and schizophrenia, for typical cases of schizophrenia were six times as common as in the average population (though less common than among the relatives of schizophrenics) among the children of paraphrenics and three times as common among the sibs of paraphrenics. The result has been that chronic delusional states with or without hallucinosis are now regarded by many authorities as mild forms of schizophrenia attenuated and modified by certain constitutional features. In the American classification, however, paranoia is classified among the paranoid states which are regarded as "reactions," schizophrenia including the paranoid form being specifically excluded here.

The term "paranoid reactions" is widely used to cover a group of conditions, mostly of short duration, but sometimes chronic, which arise in adverse circumstances and are characterized by paranoid and referential ideas, often with hallucinations but without the nuclear symptoms of schizophrenia. The personality is often oversensitive, prone to suspiciousness, or otherwise abnormal. These reactions have been observed during imprisonment, adolescence, and the period of involution, among aliens, refugees, and the deaf and disfigured, and in compensation cases, *folies à deux*, infections, and intoxications. In some of these conditions family studies have also shown some increase over the expected occurrence of schizophrenia among relatives.

When paranoid delusions commence in old age, they are generally believed to be caused by senile or arteriosclerotic changes in the brain. Yet, as the above account shows, the etiology of paranoid psychoses is complex. In the paranoid reactions and the chronic delusional states, genetic and other more general constitutional factors interact with exogenous ones to produce the mental illness, and even in schizophrenia itself the studies on twins by Slater (1953) and on social factors by Hollingshead and Redlich (1953) and by Hare (1956) have focused attention on the contribution made by the environment.

In this study, "late paraphrenia" is used as a suitable descriptive term, without prejudice as to etiology, for all cases with a paranoid symptom-complex in which signs of organic dementia or sustained confusion were absent and in which the condition was judged, from the content of the delusional and hallucinatory symptoms, not to be caused by a primary affective disorder. Provided that these criteria were satisfied, no case showing a paranoid psychosis was excluded. In the result, cases were found to have more-or-less well-marked schizophrenic symptoms, and a small proportion exhibited no hallucinations. The material was studied as one group in order to see what related factors emerged as the most significant and consistent. If this proved possible, different varieties would be identified and their etiology studied. Special importance was attached to following the cases up to determine the mortality rate and the incidence of cerebral disease.

In the course of these studies, we became aware that many patients were solitary, eccentric, isolated, and difficult individuals and that these characteristics were long-standing, not imposed by a recent illness. They, therefore, presented a particularly favorable opportunity for investigating the phenomenon that has been rather crudely called "social isolation." In addition to schizophrenia, where a failure of social communication was first suggested as a factor in causation by Faris and Dunham (1939), the mental disorders of migrants, minority groups, the deaf, and people who attempt and commit suicide have been frequently attributed in part to a social predicament of this nature. An etiological role has been attributed to social isolation in these diverse settings largely on the strength of statistical associations elicited in epidemiological research. The network of cause and effect is difficult, if not impossible, to disentangle in these inquiries. The essential complement to them is detailed investigation of small groups of cases, for until confirmation has been adduced from studying life histories of actual patients with mental illness, the role of social isolation as a cause of psychiatric disorder must remain conjectural. This investigation has, therefore, sought to define consistencies in a group of intensively studied cases. To exclude as far as possible the likelihood that a systematic error was being introduced by the fact that findings were based on patients already in the hospital or some other irrelevant contingency, the findings have been compared with a set of control cases, aged sixty or more, who have affective and organic psychoses and who were admitted to the hospital during the same periods.

The main questions we set out to investigate in the late paraphrenias were the extent to which social isolation or difficulty in social communication was peculiar to this group of old-age mental disorders, the role isolation and difficulty could have played in causation, the relationship they bore to genetic, psychological, social, and organic factors, and what part they could have played in postponing the breakdown until old age—an answer which would be highly desirable for the study of all schizophrenic disorders.

SUBJECTS

Although the subjects came from two sources, the diagnostic criteria in each instance were those described above.

From 1951 to 1955 patients aged sixty and over who were admitted to Graylingwell Hospital, Chichester, were examined by one or both of the authors and allocated to various diagnostic groups (Roth, 1955). During this time forty-two patients, thirty-nine women and three men, were diagnosed to have late paraphrenia. All but six of these patients have been followed up for at least five years, and it has also been possible to get detailed social and family histories for the majority and information about the circumstances in which the illness developed for the remainder.

The records of all patients aged sixty and over who were admitted to the Psychiatric Hospital, Stockholm, from 1931 to 1937 were examined, and as a result fifty-seven patients, forty-eight women and nine men, were diagnosed as suffering from paraphrenia with the onset late in life. As part of a clinical and genetic study, these cases were all followed until death or June, 1956, and in addition a family investigation was made into the incidence of psychosis among the relatives. Information was obtained from members of the families and from the parish registers, which are exceptionally complete in Sweden. Since the Psychiatric Hospital was a teaching hospital, the case records were unusually complete in such items as previous illness, personality, and social and domestic circumstances, information which is sometimes lacking in mental-hospital records.

TABLE 1
AGE AND SEX DISTRIBUTION OF PARAPHRENIC CASES

Age bracket	Graylingwell (1951-1955)			Stockholm (1931-1937)			Total
	M	F	Both	M	F	Both	Both
60-64	1	9*	10*	1	20	21	31*
65-74	0	17	17	6	20	26	43
75 and over	2	13	15	2	8	10	25
All ages	3	39	42	9	48	57	99

*One female aged fifty-nine

In both hospitals cases with paraphrenia formed about 10 per cent of all admissions over sixty. The age and sex distributions are shown in Table 1. The mean age was about seventy years, and women predominated in excess of the population imbalance. Only seven cases had been previously admitted to a mental hospital, but in every case except one this took place after the age of sixty. The duration of illness varied from a few weeks to twenty years, but in the majority symptoms had been present for less than two years, and in no case was the onset before the age of fifty-five.

CLINICAL PICTURE

Background of the Illness

The social setting of the illness appears, as will emerge from the data, linked in a number of ways with the fact that the large majority were women over half of whom were unmarried. The sex distribution is strikingly different from both the population figures standardized for age (according to which twenty-one males and thirty-six females, instead of only nine males and forty-eight females, might have been expected in the Stockholm cases) and the incidence of schizophrenia in early life, where the majority of cases is male. The predominance of the unmarried in both sexes is also greatly in excess of expectation. Compared to the eleven that might have been expected according to population figures, there were thirty-six unmarried patients in Stockholm and only eight married patients instead of twenty-seven expected (thirteen, instead of nineteen expected, were widowed or divorced). At Graylingwell, although the predominance of unmarried patients was not so marked, seventeen of the thirty-nine women were single, eleven were married, and eleven were widowed.

A third point is that in both series over 40 per cent of the patients were living alone, some in private houses or flats, others in rooms in lodgings or hotels. Far more often patients with paraphrenia were living alone at the time they fell ill than were people with affective disorders (12 per cent living alone) or organic psychoses (16 per cent).

TABLE 2

NUMBER OF SINGLE AND WIDOWED WOMEN LIVING ALONE

Living status	Affective disorder			Paraphrenia		
	Single	Widowed	Total	Single	Widowed	Total
Stockholm*						
Alone	2	5	7	16	3	19
Not alone	12	15	27	15	5	20
Total	14	20	34	31	8	39
Graylingwell†						
Alone	16	10	26	10	8	18
Not alone	37	41	78	7	3	10
Total	53	51	104‡	17	11	28

*$\chi^2 = 6.258$, df = 1, P = < 0.02 > 0.01
†$\chi^2 = > 12$, df = 1, P = < 0.01
‡Five cases were excluded, because the situation was not known.

It is, of course, possible to live alone yet be in close touch with relatives, friends, or neighbors. Careful inquiry showed, however, that all except two, possibly three, of the Graylingwell paraphrenics who were living alone were isolated in a social, if not in an actual, sense, whereas only five of the twenty-six patients with affective disorders who were living alone were isolated. It is true that in five of the latter cases the information was insufficient to allow a definite conclusion, but over half were certainly in close or regular touch with other people, and some were in daily employment, ran boarding houses, or frequently visited relatives. Among the paraphrenics only one was working; another was in regular contact with a sibling. Table 3 shows the frequency of isolation among all the single and widowed women.

TABLE 3

SOCIAL ISOLATION AMONG SINGLE AND WIDOWED WOMEN*

Graylingwell patients	*Affective disorder*			*Paraphrenia*		
	Single	Widowed	Total	Single	Widowed	Total
Isolated	3	3	6	9	6	15
Not isolated	50	48	98	8	5	13
Total	53	51	104†	17	11	28

*$\chi^2 = > 12$, df $= 1$, P $= < 0.01$
†Five cases excluded because the situation was not known.

Of the eleven married women, one had lived in isolation since her husband's admission to a mental hospital many years previously, and another lived with an aging, taciturn man in an isolated rural cottage. In two cases the husbands shared some of the patients' delusions, so that in at least four instances the husband was a remote, ineffectual, or submissive partner. Another patient had remarried shortly before her psychotic breakdown. Four of these five patients were childless, and the children of the fifth were living in a different part of the country. In Stockholm there were insufficient data to make a comparison of the frequency of social isolation in the different groups, but, if admission to hospital through the agency of the police or another authority demonstrates lack of contact with relatives, then, as Table 4 shows, this was much more common among unmarried and widowed paraphrenics than among the affective and organic groups. Whether the patients in social isolation were the victims of accidental circumstances or their own lifelong personality peculiarities will be discussed at a later stage.

Although a few of the patients with paraphrenia were relatively well off and all social classes were represented among them, some account must be taken of the fact that, whereas nearly all had at

TABLE 4
MODE OF ADMISSION TO HOSPITAL AMONG MARRIED AND
WIDOWED PATIENTS IN STOCKHOLM*

Mode of admission	Affective	Organic	Paraphrenic	All groups
Police, and so on	2	11	18	31
Other methods†	49	39	31	119
Total	51	50	49	150

*χ^2 = 16.53, df = 2, P = < 0.01
† Admitted at own request, through petition by relatives, by transfer
from a general hospital, and so on

one time been regularly employed, many were currently living in straitened or insecure circumstances on small state pensions or national assistance. Although such social consequences are no doubt the lot of many aged, we believe that these consequences and the general decline in health and vigor associated with senescence fell with special severity on this group of paraphrenics, as it consisted predominantly of women, unmarried people, and people without close family or personal attachments.

General physical health did not seem to differ from the norm for a general population of similar age. Exceptionally good vigorous health was noted in several cases, and serious physical disease was uncommon, a fact which is clearly in accord with the practically normal life span of the Stockholm cases. Special attention was given to the occurrence of sensory impairment and central nervous system disease of the focal type. Visual defect, found in 15 per cent of cases (in about half these cases the defects were severe) was not more frequent than in the control groups of comparable age and seems to have played only an occasional part in promoting ideas of persecution, as it did in the case of a totally blind woman of eighty-four who lived in a home where, from time to time, she displayed noisy and abusive behavior, accusing the staff of stealing her possessions.

At Graylingwell some impairment of hearing was found in about 40 per cent of the cases, to a marked degree in about 15 per cent. In Stockholm, where probably only the more severe cases were recorded, the incidence was 16 per cent, whereas among the patients with affective disorders, who were an average of three years younger, the frequency was only 7 per cent. An even larger difference was found at Graylingwell, where seventy-four out of ninety-one affective and organic cases were considered to have normal hearing and good sight for their age, whereas only twenty out of forty-one paraphrenics were neither blind nor deaf in some degree. Although the assessments were made by rough methods and some milder cases may have been overlooked among the affective and organic cases, the differences are large enough to direct attention to them. The presence of a visual or hearing defect did not, as a rule, greatly modify the symptomatology. Visual hallucinations were very prominent in some blind patients, and hallucinations characterized by loud sounds, singing, and music were common in the deaf. In several cases, hallucinosis was confined to the deaf ear, and sometimes head noises (tinnitus) seemed to provide a physical basis for the hallucinations.

Focal cerebral disease was seldom found, no doubt because of the criteria by which organic psychiatric syndromes were excluded. Some evidence of cerebral disease or injury was obtained on admission in eight cases (8 per cent), but in very few of these, as will be described below, did it seem to have any bearing on the later course of the illness. The time of origin of the organic condition was usually very far from that of the paraphrenic psychosis. Five patients showed pyramidal signs: one had a congenital weak, deformed hand and suffered from petit mal attacks, one was hemiplegic from a childhood head injury, a third suffered from hemiparesis with an expressive dysphasia, thought to have followed a skull fracture eight years previously, another had a facial paresis with transient lameness, attributed to "a small hemorrhage" which had occurred twenty-eight years previously, and the fifth stated he had had "several small (cerebral) hemorrhages," over the previous ten years although no neurological evidence of them was found. In addition, two patients had coarse tremors of the senile type, and there was a patient who had developed epileptiform fits soon after the onset of the psychosis. Three of these patients, all over seventy, exhibited impairment of memory and orientation, but these impairments were not continuously observable or not severe enough to warrant exclusion from the series. Moreover, the paraphrenic symptoms were usually typical. We conclude that paraphrenia arises occasionally in the presence of focal brain damage, which acts, however, not as a true precipitating factor, but (if its presence is not entirely fortuitous) by increasing susceptibility to the psychosis among predisposed individuals.

Precipitating Events

Hitherto we have considered some general characteristics of the group and have concluded that being female, unmarried, isolated, or deaf is probably a significant factor and, because of that, economic and social insecurity and such normal age-specific changes as failure of eyesight and general health, though neither more severe nor frequent than expected, are likely to cause greater handicaps than in the general population of similar age. But nearly one-quarter of the cases were not unmarried, childless, living alone, or deaf. We thought, therefore, that it might be profitable to estimate the frequency of such traumatic events as bereavements, acute illnesses, quarrels, and domestic upheavals that could be dated accurately and related in time to the onset of illness. We find that traumatic events of this kind which may have played a part in initiating the psychosis are relatively infrequent. In Stockholm, where a comparison was made between the affective and paraphrenic groups, no precipitation could be found in three-quarters of the paraphrenic patients, whereas only 39 per cent of affectives were apparently entirely endogenous. The fact that in 25 per cent of paraphrenics some event was uncovered does not, of course, mean that in every case it was causally connected with the psychosis; the figure is a maximal estimate, and some traumas apparently associated with the onset of illness may have been fortuitous.

Among the forty-two Graylingwell cases, acute physical illnesses or operations were rare, but eye operations precipitated the onset of psychoses of long duration in two cases. More common were disturbances affecting the balance and regularity of domestic life; three patients fell ill soon after the marriage of a child, another after a second marriage at the age of sixty-four. Bereavement per se did not seem to be important, since only once did the psychosis follow the death of a husband, and then in the form of paranoid accusations about the will. In Stockholm cases it also appeared to be the upheaval of domestic life after the loss of a spouse, particularly the necessity of moving to new surroundings, that was connected with the beginning of the psychosis. In a few cases, however, the death of a favorite child ushered in a period of mourning after which the paranoid illness developed. Of all events, only bereavement was relatively more common (33 per cent) among cases where none of the factors discussed earlier, such as isolation, existed. Thus, although family ties were relatively few, where they did exist, their disruption may have been an important factor leading to the illness.

Duration of Illness and
Symptoms at Admission

In affective disorder the duration is usually a matter of months, whereas senile psychosis comes on insidiously over two or more years. Among paraphrenics the duration usually falls in between these two extremes with very wide variations of a few weeks to many years. In about 15 per cent of paraphrenic cases, the time of onset could not be decided, owing, as a rule, not to lack of information but to the gradual evolution of a personality disorder that could not be sharply distinguished from illness. Another feature of such cases was the absence of hallucinations, so that the cases form a relatively distinct subgroup which is described separately below.

In the remainder of the cases the descriptions of the duration and development of the illness seem to depend more on the extent of the witnesses' knowledge of the patient than on important differences in symptomatology. Unavoidable contact with other people, as in marriage or family living, powerful emotional ("affect-laden") responses such as anger or panic, and early occurrence of hallucinations all tend to bring on early admission to a hospital.

When there are no witnesses living in the house or in close touch, the first signs of something wrong are likely to be interpreted as a change in personality happening over a period of months—sometimes longer—and manifested in increasing quarrelsomeness or unprovoked abuse of those living near. Oddities in speech, appearance, or other aspects of behavior are noticed. The patient may seclude himself, refuse callers, break off contact with tradesmen, and wander outside or move about the house at night, talking, laughing, or crying out. Hospitalization finally takes place when obvious self-neglect, assaults, attempted suicide, or repeated baseless complaints to the authorities force some action.

Among patients who are more integrated socially and about whose illness more details are known, florid hallucinatory states are generally found to have occurred early and were often the first indubitable psychotic symptoms, prompting admission to hospital a few months—sometimes weeks or days—after their appearance. In fewer than one-fifth of the cases, hallucinations are altogether absent, and then the illness usually develops gradually over a period of one or more years. When hallucinations occur, the prehallucinatory phase varies considerably in duration. There may be a period of weeks or months during which the patient is dejected, irritable, suspicious, and sleeps poorly, culminating in the development of ideas of reference immediately before the outbreak of hallucinations. Occasionally this phase may last, with fluctuations, for several years during which there are ill-defined complaints of fatigue, weakness, and loss of weight and sleep; the patient may visit the doctor frequently because of nervousness, indigestion, or vague pains. Character traits such as bad temper, hypochondria, and suspiciousness are likely to come to the fore.

To what extent do patients with late paraphrenia show the disorders of thought, affect, and volition characteristic of schizophrenia? How are the symptoms modified by age? Can paranoid reactions be identified? Or are the cases composed mainly of paranoid depressions and organic states, as Fish (1960) maintains in his study of senile paranoid psychoses?

Primary affective disorders, many of them with prominent paranoid symptoms, have been carefully excluded from this material. A few cases that seem to correspond to the "suspicious (*argwöhnische*) depressives" of Leonhard (1959) have been included, however, since follow-up study has shown that in time the paranoid-hallucinatory symptoms tend to dominate the picture increasingly. The depression, moreover, which the patients always attribute to incessant, unjust persecution, does not seem to be the primary disorder and is, at times, overshadowed by anger or fear. Eventually the mood becomes shallow or even euphoric. We believe, therefore, that these cases fall into the paranoid, rather than the affective, group of illnesses.

Organic states with a history of increasing suspiciousness and forgetfulness with subsequent ideas of being robbed are, of course, very common, but all cases showing unequivocal mental symptoms of organic deterioration on admission have been excluded by our criteria, and follow-up study has shown that our paraphrenics have survived, on the average, about five times as long as organic groups with dementia. The life expectancy of the mentally afflicted is, in fact, almost normal. Considering the patients' age, neither somatic disease nor physical signs of cerebral disease are particularly common, so the role of organic deterioration in late paraphrenia appears to be confined, in the majority of cases, to the mental and physical effects of normal age-specific processes.

Many typically schizophrenic symptoms, including paranoid delusions, which are often closely linked to hallucinatory experiences, occur. For example, a woman patient suddenly accuses a man who has never shown the slightest interest in her of interfering with her at night or of actually entering her bed, or believes a person whose voice is heard uttering threats to be intent on committing murder. The delusions may be more-or-less systematized and fantastic. They are usually persecutory, but also erotic, hypochondriacal, or grandiose (in that order of frequency) with varied combinations and tend to be restricted to those in the patient's daily contact, house, room, bed, or body.

In 28 per cent of the Stockholm and Graylingwell cases, feelings of mental or physical influence were found. Patients feel drugged, hypnotized, or as if their thoughts have been read and their minds and bodies worked on by rays, machines, or electricity; they complain that they are being spied upon and can get no privacy in thought or act. Catatonic stupor is rare, but unpredictable behavior may occur in connection with auditory hallucinations.

Hallucinations in clear consciousness are frequent and obtrusive. Auditory hallucinations occur in three-quarters of the cases. They consist of threatening, accusing, commanding, or cajoling voices, jeering commentaries, screams, shouts for help, obscene words and songs, music, loud bangs, rappings, shots, or explosions. "Messages" are received from a distance and acted upon. The thoughts are repeated aloud. God, spirits, distant or deceased relatives, or, most often, jealous, hostile neighbors are held responsible.

Hallucinosis is often more disturbing at night, particularly in aged patients, and accounts of men, boys, or animals seen or felt to enter the bedroom through the walls are characteristic. In other cases intruders are spied on the roof, faces appear on the ceiling, or famous people pass outside. Bad smells, fumes, the stench of rotting corpses, poisoned food, electric feelings, or vibrations in the perineum or abdomen are all common. Patients say their body is being cut or stabbed, their "backbone split in two." These experiences form, as a rule, a very conspicuous part of the paranoid beliefs, and in some cases they wax and wane in a conspicuous manner, behavior being correspondingly very disturbed or almost normal.

Incoherence of talk, even neologisms, occur, but are unusual except in cases of long duration. The patients are generally lucid, but verbosity, circumstantiality, or irrelevance are found in some 30 per cent of cases, and might be put down to senile deterioration except for the fact that they persist unchanged over many years.

Considering that all these phenomena occur in clear consciousness, they have a veritable schizophrenic quality. When they are accentuated at night, an element of diminished awareness may be postulated, but even so they are later remembered, elaborated, and acted upon with total lack of insight. Memory is generally surprisingly well-preserved. Disorientation, if present, rarely amounts to more than uncertainties about the date of the month or the name of the hospital, and absurd ideas about great age and misidentifications of people (when not caused by visual defects) are unusual or part of the patient's delusional system although nine patients, seven of whom were over seventy, had disturbances of both memory and orientation, which, though not severe, were more prominent than the disturbances of the other patients. The outcome of these cases is described below.

Finally, whereas affective changes of the gross kind seen in hebephrenic deterioration and catatonic withdrawal do not occur, some emotional dullness, mild incongruity, or euphoria is common in cases that have lasted any length of time. In the earlier stages, the emotional responses are congruous and consist of fear, anger, depression, or occasionally excitement. Compared with manic-depressive psychosis, the mood, even when depression is prominent, is much more variable, often with rapid changes, and schizophrenic features soon become evident although retardation and self-accusations are rare. Clearly the affective changes are much more akin to those of schizophrenia than to those of affective disorder.

LATER COURSE OF THE ILLNESS

In the Graylingwell cases only one lasting recovery is known, and only four of the twenty-four patients ascertained to be alive after five years were out of the hospital. Of the six patients who were discharged and are so far untraced, only one was considered to be well at the time of last contact, which varied from a few months to three years after admission. Of the fourteen deaths, only two took place after discharge, and neither of these patients had recovered mentally. A similar state of affairs was found in Stockholm. Although more patients were discharged under supervision, about half their remaining life was spent in mental hospitals or similar institutions, so that fifty-seven people spent a combined total of nearly six hundred years in the hospital.

With ECT (electroconvulsive therapy) or tranquilizing drugs (which appeared valuable in disturbed cases), temporary remission occurred spontaneously in about one-quarter of cases treated at Graylingwell; sometimes it lasted for several months. In half the cases, however, hospitalization was uninterrupted for at least five years or until death. Twelve out of the forty-two patients received full courses of ECT, and of these seven improved and were discharged; the remainder did not improve and were not discharged. Five were re-admitted within a year and again discharged after ECT, and three out of four patients were sent home after a third admission. Follow-up letters have shown, however, that only one patient has remained well, after moving from an isolated rural cottage of her daughter's home to another part of the country. The small number of patients considered suitable for ECT and the poor response to it are further evidence that a primary affective disorder was not in question.

The clinical changes that occur with time are the same as those seen in schizophrenia and reported after follow-up in a high proportion of cases of paraphrenia commencing before senescence (Mayer, 1921). Affective blunting or incongruity appears or becomes more conspicuous, and some patients, especially the deaf, become mute, incoherent, and inaccessible. In about one-quarter of the cases, marked fluctuations in behavior continue for years, coinciding with episodes of hallucinatory activity and quiescence. During their more disturbed spells, patients are abusive and hostile, or preoccupied, withdrawn, and negativistic. This picture is indistinguishable from that seen in chronic schizophrenics. Nevertheless, pronounced deterioration of intellect, personality, and habits is not usual, and many patients remain clean and tidy, and generally conduct themselves well. Sometimes after years the illness apparently becomes "burnt out," leaving residual defects in a way entirely comparable to schizophrenia, since the patient does not gain insight and regards the previous beliefs, though he no longer expresses them, as real experiences.

As age advances, memory tends to fail in some cases, especially on such matters as length of time spent in the hospital, and episodes of disorientation may occur for which a physical cause may or may not be found. In the latter case, the episodes are usually associated with an exacerbation of other symptoms. About 21 per cent of cases eventually develop features suggestive of senile dementia or focal signs of cerebral disease.

We shall first describe the outcome of those eight cases in which the patient showed evidence of cerebral damage on admission. Four of these patients from Stockholm were found to have survived for periods ranging from six months to nineteen years. None of them developed further neurological signs, nor did organic psychiatric symptoms supervene. Only in one case was death attributed to cerebral thrombosis (and cancer of the pancreas), but no fresh neurological signs were described.[2] The patient with epilepsy died within six months from macrocytic anemia, but the psychosis had lasted for at least eight years. Of the four Graylingwell patients, two have died: the patient with congenital monoplegia from a coronary occlusion, soon after admission; the patient with dysphasia and signs of an acute cerebral accident, after four years. This patient had developed an unequivocal organic psychiatric picture, the only one of these cases to do so. Two patients are still living, neurologically unchanged: the patient with hemiplegia since childhood shows a markedly deteriorated memory after five years (at the age of ninety-one, however), the patient with senile tremor is considerably improved mentally and fit to be discharged to a geriatric unit after eight years. We conclude from the follow-up that there is little evidence of cerebral disease of a progressive kind in these cases, except in the one instance, and that the presence of the organic condition was either wholly fortuitous or, as previously suggested, served merely to increase vulnerability to the mental illness in some unexplained way.

There remain eight patients in whom signs of cerebrovascular disease or seizures possibly caused by this arose later in the illness, sometimes very shortly before death. Organic psychiatric symptoms appeared in six, usually after the appearance of focal signs. Of the four Graylingwell patients, two are still living, one without evidence of organic mental symptoms. The remaining six patients survived for a mean duration of five years after admission (one to sixteen years), but after the advent of organic disease seldom for more than two years. Previous to this, the duration of the psychosis was over four years in four cases (in two cases over ten years). From these observations, we conclude that cerebrovascular disease sufficiently advanced to affect brain function is unlikely to have existed at the onset of the paraphrenic illness in more than five cases at the most, a figure that includes the patient with dysphasia whose psychosis had existed for several years prior to admission. Thus, whereas the total incidence of cases with focal cerebral disease is 16 per cent (including the cases with evidence for this on admission to hospital), the proportion in which the organic disease may, with some probability, be thought to have brought on the psychosis is much smaller (about 5 per cent).

[2] Because of the certified cause of death, this case is included with the eight cases who later developed signs of cerebrovascular disease in the course of their illness.

Turning to how often symptoms of senile dementia appeared later in the illness, we find it necessary to rely almost entirely on the descriptive evidence available in the hospital and institutional records. Only one patient was seen personally at follow-up. The diagnosis may be difficult, for objective signs are absent in this condition, psychological tests were not carried out, and autopsy reports are not much assistance. A pathological degree of mental change may have to be distinguished from subterminal confusion states and ordinary age changes, which may be difficult with patients in their eighth or ninth decade. In addition, allowance has to be made for the effects of deafness and blindness and such symptoms of the psychosis as hallucinosis or blunting of affect that may contribute to a state of secondary dementia, mimicking true organic dementia. In Stockholm, seven patients (12 per cent) eventually developed mental symptoms difficult to distinguish from those of organic senile dementia. There were three other cases about whom there was much more doubt. The time lapse between the development of organic psychiatric symptoms and admission to hospital was long, however, for in no case did the organic symptoms appear within the first five years after admission; in two cases they appeared between five and ten years later and in the remainder only after ten years. In Stockholm seven patients developed senile change and five focal cerebral signs after admission (21 per cent). At Graylingwell, where the follow-up has been of shorter duration, indications of dementia in the absence of focal cerebral signs or seizures have appeared in only one patient, now seventy-five, after a very long illness.

Finally we shall consider the outcome in those nine cases where the patients had equivocal organic psychiatric symptoms on admission. Did follow-up show that they were suffering from gross progressive cerebral disease? With two, possibly three, exceptions (included above), the answer is probably "no." Despite their advanced age, six patients survived for more than five years. The quasiorganic picture can be accounted for by a severe psychotic disturbance colored by age-specific changes of normal variation.

Systematic examination of the certified causes of death of all the Stockholm cases showed that only 10 per cent were attributed to cerebral hemorrhage and allied causes, a figure that corresponded exactly with the frequency of deaths from these causes in Stockholm's population of seventy years and over. In other respects, too, the causes of death corresponded with those found among the aged population.

SURVIVAL AND MORTALITY

Evidence that these cases as a group are distinct from the organic psychoses is provided independently of the clinical picture by the long period of survival and the relatively low rate of mortality. In the Stockholm cases the length of survival was almost normal compared to a life expectancy of only one-quarter of the normal in a series of senile and arteriosclerotic patients followed up during the same period. Two-thirds of the paraphrenics were still living after five years and about one-half after ten years, whereas four-fifths of the organic cases were dead after five years.

TABLE 5

MORTALITY RATE AMONG PARAPHRENIC
AND ORGANIC CASES

(Percentage dead after two, five, and ten years)

	Paraphrenia		*Organic psychosis*	
	Graylingwell (*N* =42)	Stockholm (*N* =57)	Graylingwell (*N* =98)	Stockholm (*N* =81)
Two years	14	11	80	63
Five years	32	35	—	81
Ten years	—	51	—	96

At Graylingwell the rate of mortality was very similar and was far less than that found by Roth (1955) in two organic groups he investigated at that hospital. In Table 5 the mortality rates of the paraphrenic and organic groups at the two hospitals are compared.

CLINICAL VARIETIES

Clinical varieties may be distinguished by differences in symptomatology or etiology. Thus, in symptomatology the cases might be grouped according to the presence or absence of hallucinations or marked affective coloring (the "affect-laden paraphrenia" of Leonhard, 1959) or according to the quality of the delusions. Such methods of classification would seem, however, to have only descriptive value. The following three groups, based mainly on the Graylingwell cases, are tentatively put forward on grounds of possible differences in etiology. But since etiology in paraphrenia is certainly complex, these may well be differences of degree, not of kind, and it is doubtful whether any sharp boundaries exist among the three groups described here.

The first group consists of abnormal personalities with paranoid psychoses and no hallucinosis. When all cases without hallucinosis (20 per cent) were provisionally separated from the rest, it was found that they had certain other features in common: long-standing abnormalities of personality that interfered with human relationships; advanced age, often over 75, on admission; physical stigmata, including sensory defects, associated with aging; delusions almost exclusively confined to ideas of theft, ill-treatment, or poisoning by those in everyday contact with the patient.

The onset of the psychosis in these patients is hard to date, for relatives tend to regard it as a caricature of the usual personality. Here we may be seeing long-standing paranoid or other abnormal modes of reaction becoming accentuated in response to the mental, physical, and social changes that accompany aging.

The second group consists of paraphrenias arising under unusual circumstances or after prolonged isolation. In above 25 per cent of cases, the delusional ideas were partially intelligible, in light of the patient's actual circumstances. For example, a single, solitary woman who suffered a unilateral facial paralysis and an epithelioma of the lip following burns from X-ray treatment for hirsuties had long been very sensitive about her appearance. For about four years she had had ideas of reference and then began to believe that she was being tormented by the other guests in her lodgings. They had "got hold of her mind in some way." After an operation on her lip, she left the hospital but was still seclusive and reticent.

A married woman who became psychotic after sharing a house for some years with two psychotic tenants and a husband who also suffered from an induced psychosis, though of the milder form, was free of symptoms in the hospital but relapsed three times after returning to the same environment. In a third case, a housekeeper living alone with an elderly man developed a persecuted, hallucinated state that had obvious links with the social and sexual conflicts she felt about her situation. The remaining patients in this group were mostly single women living isolated lives, whose paranoid ideas concerned eviction and burglary and mirrored understandable anxieties. In a few cases serious physical disease or blindness modified or dominated the clinical picture.

For most of these patients, no future outside an institution could be envisaged, and, though a few did gradually improve, only one patient, for whom satisfactory arrangements could be made, eventually made a lasting recovery. In the remaining cases the illness pursued a progressive and chronic course unaffected by environmental circumstances. Moreover, such schizophrenic symptoms as ideas of influence and affective incongruity were present, and schizoid traits in the premorbid personality were relatively common. Situational factors are, therefore, not adequate causes of the illness, nor do they suffice to explain why it is chronic. Clearly we are not dealing with paranoid reactions in the sense of potentially reversible responses to adversity, and the distinction from the mainly endogenous paraphrenias (described in the paragraphs below) is a relative one.

The third group consists mainly of endogenous paraphrenias. The bulk of the cases, at least 55 per cent, fall into this group. External stresses are absent or, if present, seem to have little bearing on the delusions, which are systematized and fantastic in varying degrees. Further subdivision is unwarranted in the present state of knowledge, but the group contains five women showing very marked schizophrenic features after psychoses of long duration. There are also five or six patients (15 per cent) with a marked depressed mood, but the scope of the paranoid symptoms, the later development of bizarre or erotic delusions, and persistent auditory hallucinations confirmed that the illness was a paranoid one.

Inherited predisposition is probably relatively important in this group, since three of the patients had psychotic sibs. But deafness, which occurred in nearly 50 per cent of these cases, aging, and social isolation may have provided the specific stresses that caused the illness to become manifest.

The subdivision into these three groups is tentative, and it has been suggested mainly to facilitate further inquiry into etiological factors. The common features linking the three groups are frequency of the premorbid abnormalities of personality (to be described below); social isolation because of social, psychological, physical, or accidental factors; and the chronic, inveterate nature of the illness. The distinction is most clear between the first and the remaining two groups in that in the former the illness appears to grow insensibly from the premorbid abnormalities of personality without the sharp, step-like change that had occurred so often at some stage in cases belonging to the second and third groups. This distinction is underlined by the absence in all the cases of the first group of hallucinations as well as other features generally regarded as characteristic of schizophrenia. The course of events in the first group therefore exhibits many features of abnormal "development," as distinct from the disease "process" manifest in the second and third groups. After the illness has been in progress for a number of years, however, these distinctions become somewhat blurred, and it may well be that the differences among the three groups are of a quantitative, rather than a qualitative, kind.

PREDISPOSITION AND ENVIRONMENT

The question of predisposition is of major importance. Of the etiological factors so far identified—lack of close ties, situational stress, deafness—none is specific; they occur in many people, most of whom never fall ill. Evidently only certain people are vulnerable. This vulnerability may be caused by either a major gene's causing mental illness (manifestation of which is delayed until late in life) or deviating personality characteristics, such as eccentricity, which may be attributed to a major gene, but more probably arise from complex inherited and environmental factors, of a kind that interact to produce different types of temperament and body build. The evidence for monohybrid inheritance is discussed below. In eccentric individuals, sufficiently adverse circumstances may precipitate an overt mental disorder, which presents the features of the premorbid personality in caricature. We have observed this sequence of events in Group 1 of the clinical varieties referred to above.

Personality and Body Build

Regarding body build, it is of interest that the pyknic type was uncommon, in contrast to its frequent occurrence among the affective groups. Cycloid character traits were also conspicuously absent, and there is, therefore, no support for the idea that the presence of a manic-depressive diathesis is one of the factors that tend to postpone the onset of paranoid illness until late life, as Kolle suggested (1931).

In both series of cases, the personality traits found were predominantly paranoid and schizoid (jealousy, suspiciousness, arrogance, egocentricity, emotional coldness, extreme solitariness) in 45 per cent and 33 per cent were described as explosive, sensitive, or members of minority religious sects. In Stockholm six of the nine males were solitary, homosexual, criminal, or vagrant, and two were alcoholic.

Compared with the affective groups, both sexes were more often narrow, quarrelsome, religious, suspicious, unsociable, coldhearted, and less often kind, thoughtful, affectionate, sociable, even-tempered, nervous, worried, or dependent. Brief sketches of the personalities, however, give a better picture than a list of traits.

The personalities of all the patients in Group 1 were very abnormal, and the psychotic symptoms appeared to caricature long-standing traits. The following two cases are taken from the Grayling-well group, where four of the eight cases were over eighty and only two under seventy. Sight, hearing, or both were severely defective in six. The first case is that of a single woman of eighty-seven who had art training, but had never been employed. She had been gay, charming, and sociable, but shallow, egocentric, and supercilious. She had never had any love affairs and had made no friends, though she had many acquaintances. For thirty years she lived with her sister and had never kept her sister company in the evenings, always ate meals out, never did any housework or cooking, never knit, sewed, or went to the movies or theater. Her only interests were Christian Science literature and meetings. Admission to the hospital was arranged because of the emergence, over two months, of paranoid ideas, centering on her sister. During the previous year, this patient had shown some deterioration in memory, habits, sight, and hearing, but considering her delusions, had been sufficiently mentally integrated to act energetically and appropriately, visiting her lawyer on several occasions to change her will. She was found to be correctly oriented. Four years later she was still alive, expressing bizarre delusions of persecution and grandiose ideas, but still keeping clean in her personal hygiene.

The second case is that of a single woman, age eighty-two, who had worked successfully as a school teacher and, later, as a film-scenario writer. She had been engaged once, late in life. Usually pleasant to meet and talk with, courageous and energetic, she was very difficult if annoyed or frustrated in any way, becoming willful, mischief-making, prejudiced against doctors, and, later in life, suspicious. After the death of a brother, she lived alone with a collection of animals. A niece summarized her as a "hopeless crank, tiresome, eccentric, and prone to violent rages." The illness came on insidiously. For some years before admission, she had lived alone in sordid conditions, accusing first one, then another, person of ill treating her, stealing her money, and poisoning her food. She was disposed to wander and gave vent to outbursts of rage when attempts were made to restrain her. Yet she was found to have a fair memory and to be correctly oriented, despite being almost blind and very deaf. She died after two and a half years, shortly after having a "stroke." At the autopsy the main findings were atheroma of the major cerebral arteries and renal arteriosclerosis (the brain was hardened uncut, and the report is not yet available).

In Group 2 the personalities were less eccentric, and abnormalities were hinted at rather than described in full-blooded terms. In one case, a woman whose character was eulogized by her husband (who suffered from *folie à deux*) was said by a nephew to have "always seemed queer and not quite normal." She suffered from asthma and hypertension and for long periods had been confined to her house, which she shared with her husband and with two psychotic tenants who lived on the floor above. After several years of this situation, she began to seal the doors and windows to keep out "poisonous fumes" and to believe that she was being hypnotized by one of her psychotic neighbors.

Isolation was, however, the most common form of stress in this group. The patients were women, and they were all either unmarried or widowed when they became ill. The psychosis featured ideas of eviction or robbery, sometimes with erotic elements. Three cases may be cited briefly. A seventy-four-year-old widow had seriously attempted suicide nine years after the death of her husband, and later she developed a paranoid psychosis with very vivid auditory hallucinations. She had been a capable woman of pleasant, even temperament, who had married a man twenty years her senior; the couple had no children. To the time of marriage she had been a strict Baptist, but afterward had adhered to many different religious sects, which she always abandoned after a short time. During her married life, she and her husband had never settled anywhere, but had continually moved their home from one town to another.

Another patient in Group 2 was seventy-nine and had lived alone since the death of her husband and her only son about ten years previously. She had always been very correct, prim, Victorian, and conversant with medical folklore and fallacious theories about the causation of illness. Admission to the hospital took place after she was found, dressed in a nightgown, wandering in the road and looking for imaginary men, who, she believed, were constantly entering her house at night to torment her and steal her food, furniture, and keys. A third patient, aged seventy-two, was cheerful and friendly, but touchy, terrified of hospitals, obstinate, willful, very independent, and ultraconservative in her attitude to modern conveniences. She lived in a cottage with oil lamps and stoves and gradually became a recluse, although she was regularly visited by a half sister once a year. In her illness she heard the voice of a brother from Australia and believed that her half sister was stealing her money and persecuting her.

In Group 3 good and bad traits also often coexisted in a patient, but environmental conditions were relatively favorable. The patients differed from those in Group 1 in that their illnesses were much more sharply defined from their previous personalities and sometimes arose without any premonition. When young, a twice-married woman of sixty-five had been cheerful, lively, talkative, well-dressed. She liked going out and was a competent housewife, but had no community interests whatever and never made real friends. At the age of sixty-four, a year after her second marriage, she suddenly complained that the spirits of her deceased relatives were following her and threatening to murder her.

A single woman of eighty-three, living with a sister, was strong-willed, independent, energetic, versatile, capable, kind, and fond of children. She had a sense of humor and was never moody or overanxious. But she belonged to a religious sect, the Brides of Christ, and led a life regulated by its principles, which absolutely forbade marriage and sexual intercourse. Six weeks before admission she began to believe that the child living in the upstairs flat was being tortured and calling to her for help; she rapidly built an elaborate delusional system in which this child became her adopted son. Other patients described her as "jealous," "stubborn and headstrong," "took violent dislikes to people," "erratic and impulsive and very obstinate," "never made friends, dictatorial, very sensitive, imaginative, sulky, with narrow interests."

A seventy-eight-year-old spinster was "very domineering, independent, active, tactless, particular, and precise, a perfect lady, but with a vicarious interest in sex." This patient was living in lodgings as a paying guest. The first symptom of illness that anyone noticed was that she would come downstairs half-dressed, "to show off her figure." Later she developed a belief that men entered her bed at night and that she was having syphilis injected into her eyes by the landlady.

On the whole the personalities in Group 2 were more normal than those in the other groups. In both the Graylingwell and Stockholm cases there was, however, evidence of psychosexual abnormality. In addition to the large proportion of unmarried patients, those who had married often did so late in life, had few children, sometimes violently disliked their stepchildren, or were frigid, very jealous of their husbands, or cold and unloving mothers.

The general conclusions were that personality abnormalities were present in a large number of the patients and were probably related to the frequent failure to marry, low fertility, and social isolation, as well as the actual psychosis.

Personality Factors Related to
Marriage and Isolation

Are the abnormal, stressful social circumstances which many paraphrenics experience accidental, or do they reflect a primary anomaly of personality? Such circumstances may arise from causes over which a person has no control, or they may be self-created, brought about wholly or in part by a person's temperamental peculiarities. Of the factors already discussed, deafness and physical illness which render communication difficult are probably unrelated to the personality. On the other hand social isolation might well be caused mainly by personal eccentricity. The detailed case histories which suggest that for many patients isolation was the preferred mode of existence or was brought about by their difficult behavior make this a likely explanation. For years some patients had deliberately avoided any close relationships. Others, through the tolerance and sense of responsibility shown by a relative, had escaped total isolation, yet had fallen ill.

In order to test further the hypothesis that a primary personality disorder was one cause of isolation in paraphrenic patients, the social histories of a group of unmarried women who were admitted to Graylingwell Hospital when sixty or over and who were suffering from affective and organic psychoses were examined to determine the frequency of such traits as explosive temper, awkwardness in human relations, egocentricity, or extreme independence which could have accounted to some extent for their failure to marry. Single people are known to form a high proportion of those admitted to mental hospitals in old age, and we wished to estimate the frequency of "isolating" personality traits and actual isolation among elderly unmarried patients in general. The records showed that of fifty-five patients, about half showed such traits, but they were far less frequent among the married or widowed. Therefore, although personality factors of this kind may well be associated with failure to marry and perhaps with falling ill, they are evidently not peculiar to paraphrenics. The second question, the frequency of isolation among these difficult unmarried female patients with affective or organic psychoses, was also answered definitely. Taking isolation to mean that a patient was living alone, in a lodginghouse or hotel where she had not taken root, was not working, and was not in close or regular touch with a relative or friend, it was found that six, possibly nine, of the seventeen unmarried paraphrenic patients (35 to 50 per cent), but only one, possibly two, (about 7 per cent) of the patients with other conditions, were isolated. A similar difference between patients with paraphrenia and those with affective disorder was found among widows. Hence the oddities of personality which are probably related to the unmarried state of many paraphrenic patients do not wholly explain their isolation.

It is quite likely that important qualitative differences in personality with a closer bearing on the risk of social isolation may have existed but were not brought to light by our crude methods of assessment. Be this as it may, as far as the present analysis goes, the poverty of human contacts suffered by our paraphrenic patients is only partly explained by inherent personality traits, and further reasons for their isolation have to be sought.

The role of deafness, which was observed frequently at an early stage of our studies, clearly called for investigation. It was found in 41 per cent (seven out of seventeen cases) of unmarried paraphrenics, but in only three (11 per cent) of the twenty-seven patients with abnormal personalities who did not suffer from paraphrenia. Deafness was also more frequent among widowed paraphrenics (four out of ten were severely deaf), and it seems very unlikely that such a severe degree of deafness was overlooked in the other group, where a hearing defect was noted in only three out of fifty-four cases. Thus deafness probably played some part in determining the temperamental difficulties which resulted in isolation for the group of unmarried paraphrenics, but not for the others. The role of other contributory factors was suggested by the finding that several extremely difficult patients had succeeded in avoiding isolation, having been tolerated at home over many years by close relatives. On an average, did the paraphrenics have fewer relatives than the other groups?

After excluding patients under sixty-five, it was found that paraphrenics at Graylingwell and Stockholm had fewer surviving sibs than patients with affective disorder who were of a similar mean age (Table 6). Nearly one-third of all the women paraphrenics had no living sibs, and the average number for each patient was fewer (1.7) than for the affectives (2.2), only 17 per cent of whom were without sibs. Of the patients with abnormal personalities but without para-

TABLE 6
LIVING SIBS OF WOMEN PATIENTS*

	Affective disorder			Paraphrenia		
	Graylingwell	Stockholm	Total	Graylingwell	Stockholm	Total
With sibs	72	22	94	25	31	56
Without sibs	14	5	19	10	16	26
Totals	86	27	113†	35	47	82‡
Mean ages			70.91			70.49

*$\chi^2 = 5.938$, df = 1, P = < .02 > .01.
†Four patients whose ages were unknown and the group from sixty to sixty-four were omitted.
‡Four cases excluded because age was not known.

phrenia (whose mean age was about one year older than that of the paraphrenics), only 11 per cent had no surviving sibs, and the average number of sibs for each patient was 2.4. Surviving sibs did protect these affective and organic cases from the risk of isolation, for nearly half of them were living with sisters.

When the matter of sibs was being investigated, an interesting and unexpected finding came to light. It has an obvious bearing on the likelihood of having living sibs and may help explain the difference between the two groups as far as isolation goes. Of the thirty-nine Graylingwell paraphrenics, fourteen were the youngest children in their families, the position of nine was unknown, and only three were the oldest; among 129 affectives, nineteen were the youngest, forty-four the oldest, and the position of thirteen was unknown. In Stockholm these peculiarities were not observed, but the discrepancy may be attributed to several social characteristics of nineteenth century Sweden, such as the comparatively high rate of infant and child mortality, frequent half and step-siblings, and the common custom of boarding a child out. These would all tend to obscure the possible effects of position in the family.

In view of these findings, it was also thought worthwhile to make a count of living children among the married patients; the results are shown in Table 8. The Graylingwell paraphrenics had an average of one living child compared with an average of two living

TABLE 7
POSITION OF PATIENTS IN FAMILY*

Graylingwell	Affective	Paraphrenic	Both groups
Eldest	44	3	47
Youngest	19	14	33
Intermediate	66	12	78
Total	129†	29‡	158

*$\chi^2 = 17.05$, df = 2, P = < .01.
†Excludes thirteen whose positions were not known and three only children.
‡Excludes nine whose positions were not known and one only child.

children among affectives. Among the paraphrenics who were still married, 45 per cent had no living children, compared with 32 per cent in the other groups. In Stockholm the same differences were noted; married paraphrenics were childless in 33 per cent of cases, and the group had an average of 1.5 children. Only 12 per cent of the affectives were childless, and the group had an average of two chil-

TABLE 8
LIVING CHILDREN OF MARRIED AND WIDOWED WOMEN*

	Affective disorder			Paraphrenia		
	Graylingwell	Stockholm	Total	Graylingwell	Stockholm	Total
With children	63	41	104	12	11	23
Without children	24	6	30	10	6	16
Totals	87*	47	134†	22	17	39

*$\chi^2 = 5.374$, df = 1, P = < 0.05 > 0.02.
†Excluded are three patients about whose children nothing is known.

dren. In this case, since the difference is caused by the lower fertility of paraphrenics, personality defects may be thought to act indirectly, by tending to cause postponement of marriage until late in life and to restrict the size of families in other ways. In any case, here is one more factor decided early in life that impairs the chances of avoiding isolation and desolation in senescence.

In deciding whether an individual is forced into isolation in old age, positive personality qualities—capacity for warmth and ease in human relations, for giving and evoking affection—may be even more important than the negative attributes which have been stressed in the present context. The correlative aspects of personality traits already given point to a definite difference between those who develop paraphrenia and those who develop affective disorder. There is one objective finding which confirms this view and underlines the importance of long-standing personality defects in deciding the isolation of paraphrenics. In the Stockholm group, over one-quarter of the women had had illegitimate children, but only two married the fathers; among the patients with affective disorder, the much smaller number with illegitimate children legitimized their union almost without exception. This is a striking illustration of the differences in the affective lives and personal adjustments of paraphrenic and affective cases about fifty years before their breakdowns. But the original hypothesis that isolation was a consequence of personality defects requires modification, since unrelated intrinsic factors—deafness, fewer surviving siblings, smaller families, and fewer surviving children—clearly made a substantial contribution.

Heredity

In reviewing the literature of schizophrenia, Strömgren (1938) found the risk of schizophrenics' siblings' developing schizophrenia to be 6-12 per cent, whereas Kallmann (1956) reported the risk among their children to be 10-22 per cent. In the present study, the corresponding risks were found to be much lower. Only one case of a sib with an untreated paranoid illness beginning in middle age was found at Graylingwell, although some of the six relatives that the patients' histories report "mentally ill with unknown conditions" may have suffered from schizophrenia. In Stockholm, where the investigation was very thorough, the combined risk among sibs and children was only 3.4 ± 1.2 per cent (Kay, 1959). These findings make it unlikely that precisely the same hereditary factors operate in both schizophrenia and late paraphrenia.

There were, however, eight additional cases (three from Stockholm and five from Graylingwell) where a parent or sib had developed a paranoid illness late in life (after the standard "risk period" of twenty to fifty years old). Three of these were treated in mental hospitals and showed characteristic late paraphrenia. The existence of these eight cases among the relatives of ninety-nine patients may be compared to an incidence of only two cases of affective disorder among the families of over two hundred patients with affective disorder. Schultz (1930) also found a rather high risk (6 per cent) of senile persecution mania among the sibs of a group of patients suffering from senile psychoses with paranoid coloring, although the risk for schizophrenia proper was only 1.7 per cent among the combined sibs and children. Paranoid or schizoid psychopathy was also more common among the relatives in our paraphrenic group, whereas depressive psychoses were rare.

We conclude, therefore, that in late paraphrenia there is some hereditary predisposition to mental illness. But the observed risks among relatives are difficult to reconcile with any simple monogenic mode of inheritance. We are inclined to favor a multifactorial hypothesis, which has the advantage of allowing ample scope for the operation of environmental and other exogenous factors which we believe important. Furthermore, the high incidence of personality deviations would accord most readily with such a theory. Consideration is given to these matters below.

DISCUSSION

The Contribution of
Organic Cerebral Degeneration

All classification systems in psychiatry have serious shortcomings which are inevitable at the present stage of development and knowledge. The weakness of the Kraepelinian system, which forms the basis of most classifications, is that it is based on two principles. According to one, mental disorders are divided into "organic" and "functional" categories on the basis of certain psychological symptoms and signs; according to the other, division into the same two categories depends on the presence or absence of cerebral or somatic structural disease. This dual system leads to ambiguities which deserve careful analysis. Where neurasthenic, depressive, or manic symptoms, for example, develop in close association with some infective illness such as influenza, it is customary to regard the mental disturbance as symptomatic: the chronic paranoid psychoses of epileptics are called epileptic psychoses, those of alcoholics and drug addicts, toxic psychoses, and so on. Some important considerations are overlooked when Kraepelinian nomenclature is employed. Thus, if knowledge of the associated organic factor had been withheld, diagnoses which differentiate these conditions from functional depressive, manic, and schizophrenic illnesses would have been impossible in many cases.

The close resemblance between these organic psychoses and schizo-phrenic illness has been recently illustrated in a particularly cogent manner by the discovery that many chronic amphetamine addicts are mistaken for schizophrenics. Three out of seven cases seen within the past three years at our clinic had previously been given deep insulin coma therapy, and one of the three had had a prefrontal leucotomy carried out at a university psychiatric clinic (Beamish & Kiloh, 1960).

Past attempts have been made to accommodate such facts within the theory that those who responded to organic disease with functional symptoms of this nature were genetically predisposed to do so. The schizophrenia-like psychoses of epileptics, alcoholics, and drug addicts were, in other words, attributed to a coexistence of two phenomena, epilepsy or addiction on one hand and the constitutional predisposition peculiar to schizophrenics on the other. Genetic studies by Slater and Beard (1959) in epilepsy, by Benedetti (1952) in alcoholic hallucinosis, and clinical investigations into amphetamine psychoses by Connell (1958) and others have made such simple theories un-tenable. Although such functional syndromes in the setting of cerebral or metabolic disease are relatively uncommon, recent observations have shown that their relevance for the functional group of mental dis-orders is indubitable and that they may have an important bearing on etiological problems in this field.

Among the mental disorders of the aged, the dual system of classification has led to particular difficulties. Here we are most prone to encounter depressive psychoses after an attack of pneumonia, manic episodes after surgical operations, paranoid disorders with or without physical illness in old people with mild memory defects, or any one of these syndromes in patients with peripheral and retinal arteriosclerosis or perhaps hypertension and a mild cerebrovascular accident some years previously.

Such common associations have led to regarding most of these diseases—of whatever kind—as essentially organic in etiology when they have begun after the age of sixty-five, although the specific psychiatric manifestations of cerebral disease may be absent. That some degree of real overlap exists between functional and organic psychoses in senescence, as at all ages, is not in question. But this overlap, together with the fact that senile and arteriosclerotic change will be a relatively common finding in any group of old people after long periods of observation, has tended to perpetuate the view that cerebral disease has an ubiquitous etiological role in old age mental disorder. Recent follow-up and neuropathological studies have made such views untenable. First, Roth and Morrissey (1952) showed that there were striking differences between paraphrenic and organic groups of cases in the mortality rate. The present study, on different material and from two separate sources, has amply confirmed this earlier work. After two years and five years the rate of mortality was, respectively, only 12 per cent and 34 per cent among the paraphrenics with substantial agreement in the two series, compared with a rate of 63 per cent and 81 per cent in the organic cases collected from the Stockholm records. At Graylingwell the rate in this group was still higher, 80 per cent after two years (Roth, 1955). After ten years half the Stockholm paraphrenics were still alive whereas nearly all the organic cases had died. The size of these differences seems to exclude organic cerebral disease of the kind found in the organic dementias as a major factor in late paraphrenia, but does not entirely controvert the view that early or mild degrees of cerebral change may be responsible.

This argument, as well as the objection that the organic cases are an older group, is met by a comparison of the actual length of survival with the mean life expectancy for a group of comparable age and sex in the Stockholm population. Among paraphrenics the period of survival was almost normal; among organic cases it was only one-quarter as long as that of the standard population. Yet despite this long survival, it is probable that some contribution is in fact made by cerebral disease. This follows from the existence of those few cases, about 5 per cent, that exhibited somatic signs of cerebral disease in connection with the onset of the psychosis or within a space of three or four years, and prima facie from the eventual appearance of cerebrovascular or presumptive senile change in 21 per cent of cases in the Stockholm series. That paranoid symptoms and organic changes often coexist is apparent from the frequency of paranoid coloring in those old age psychoses that are clearly of organic origin. But the contribution is probably small. The figure of 21 per cent is in all probability far too high an estimate of the importance of cerebral damage as a causative factor for two reasons.

First, evidence of senile change did not appear until at least five years and, in the majority of cases, not until ten or more years after admission. The picture then was often indistinguishable from that of secondary dementia, a condition known to occur in chronic mental illness after prolonged institutionalization, accentuated in this instance by deafness and the effects of normal age-specific mental changes (most of the patients were in their eighties by then). Second, in a systematic examination of the brains of groups of patients who died in a mental hospital, Corsellis (personal communication, 1960) found that the frequency of gross cerebral lesions was significantly higher in the diagnostic groups where the mean interval between admission to hospital and death was less than five years. These were the groups of senile and arteriosclerotic psychoses and a group showing features of both these conditions. For example, the incidence of gross cerebral vascular change was 48 per cent; of cerebral atrophy, 42 per cent. Among Corsellis' groups with a diagnosis of functional psychosis (affective, schizophrenic, and paranoid) whose mean age of onset was well before the senium and, as was the case among our paraphrenics, whose period of hospitalization was long, gross vascular lesions were found at autopsy in 15 per cent of the patients, and cerebral atrophy in 16 per cent. The incidence of such lesions increased with age in both the functional and organic groups, but the difference between the groups remained consistent at all ages and, according to Corsellis, the incidence found among the former may provisionally be taken to represent the expectancy of the normal population. It is not very surprising, therefore, that among the paraphrenics, whose mean age at death was over seventy-five, clinical signs of cerebrovascular disease or senile mental change should have eventually appeared in 21 per cent of cases.

Hence, when allowance has been made for the normal hazards of growing old, the only patients in whom we can be reasonably certain that organic factors have played a part in causation are the 5 per cent in whom neurological signs appeared about the time or within a few years of the beginning of the illness. It is of interest, however, that in most of these with neurological signs at the onset, organic psychiatric features were completely lacking. We have here a counterpart of those schizophreniform psychoses of earlier life in which the psychological characteristics of cerebral disease are absent or minimal despite an organic etiological basis in dextroamphetamine intoxication, alcoholism, or epilepsy. It is just possible that cerebral changes have an etiological significance that extends beyond the 5 per cent of the paraphrenic cases already mentioned. Although the 21 per cent of cases who exhibit senile or arteriosclerotic changes after many years of observation represent little, if any, excess over normal risk of cerebral degeneration at this age, we cannot exclude the possibility that in a group of susceptible personalities such changes contribute to the disease process. In other words, whereas normal cerebral degeneration might never bring the patient under psychiatric care, in the case of a schizoid personality the result might be a paraphrenic illness, which is usually an imperative cause for admission to a hospital. Any such degenerative cerebral changes must have an entirely different qualitative character or be of an entirely different order of subtlety from those active in the senile and arteriosclerotic psychoses proper. Otherwise, it is not possible to account for the gross discrepancy in life expectancy between the two groups, for the paraphrenic group appears to enjoy a normal life span.

Are Late Paraphrenias a Homogeneous Clinical Group?

There was considerable variation in such factors as the prominence or absence of severe environmental stresses, premorbid personality defects, and deafness, so that the material lends itself at first sight to a number of subdivisions. Of forty-two patients at Graylingwell, for example, there were ten female patients in whom the illness had arisen in a particularly abnormal environmental setting; this had colored the content of the delusions and hallucinations in an easily understood manner (Group 2). Eight of these cases had lived alone for a very long period, but only one was deaf. In a second group of twenty-four patients, delusions of a much more bizarre character were present, and these were far less clearly intelligible in terms of the environmental stress endured by the patient. Serious adversity had been less often experienced by these patients, and only eight had been living alone, but eleven were deaf. This group included six patients in whom a very marked depressive coloring was present in the early phase of the illness. These cases certainly deserve special mention in that a temporary response to ECT was usually obtained, and, although the paranoid delusions and hallucinations eventually became the predominant features of the illness, the prognosis for discharge from the hospital and subsequent survival in the community were relatively good. There were also five women in whom the presence of symptoms generally associated with schizophrenia in early life was the outstanding feature. Three of these were the only cases we studied whose illness had been of very long duration. They were in their late seventies or eighties, but the illness had probably commenced twenty years earlier. Four showed a marked incoherence of thought and speech, and one patient was deaf and inaccessible in addition. Another patient showed stupor of the catatonic type. All these cases were regarded as mainly endogenous paraphrenias.

The points of similarity between patients are, however, far more impressive than the differences. In all, the condition was dominated by similar delusions and hallucinations and followed a chronic course. Examples of suspicious, hostile, arrogant, eccentric, or extremely solitary personalities were found in each. Moreover, although there was a certain amount of variation in the type of exogenous factor that had contributed to the illness, it was clear that most of these exogenous factors had tended to undermine adjustment in a similar way, and they had acted in an additive fashion in the many cases in which several factors coexisted: the unmarried state; few surviving sibs; few children; infrequent social contacts owing to circumstances, personality difficulties, or both; deafness and infirmity. These factors produce very similar adverse effects.

There is a group of eight patients at Graylingwell which, in the light of observations to date, seems to be more distinct from the rest of the material than any other group which can be tentatively created on descriptive grounds. In these cases the differentiation between the over-all behavior disturbances characteristic of personality and those which are the result of illness seem to merge with one another. These are lifelong paranoid personalities whose histories show them to have become increasingly embroiled in conflicts with those in their environments. They are often described by their relatives as "not ill but exaggeratedly themselves" and "I always expected this to happen." It is of some interest that an independent, objectively definable feature characterizes all these patients: no patient in this group had hallucinations. However, in the light of the progress of these cases, the description of paranoid reaction as a potentially reversible response to vicissitudes by oversensitive or suspicious personalities would hardly be accurate. In many of the remaining cases, there are important common basic personality features—the frequency of social isolation and deafness, and the progressive course and inveterate nature of the illness. For research purposes these cases earn some independent consideration, but it is doubtful whether they presently deserve a nosological status wholly apart from the paraphrenias of late life. In effect we are saying that we are unable to draw any hard and fast distinction between the paranoid reactions and the paranoid schizophrenias of old age.

Even if the small subgroup of eight cases discussed above is regarded as similar to the paranoid reactions described by Kretschmer (1927) under the heading of *"sensitive Beziehungswahn,"* the question, "Can the paraphrenias of late life be legitimately classed with the schizophrenias?" still must be raised about the greater part of the material. Also it has to be remembered that all researchers would not accept the paranoid reactions of early life as wholly distinct from schizophrenia and irrelevant for the etiological problems of this disorder.

It seems to us that the diagnosis of schizophrenia must be based on an operational definition which incorporates all those symptoms and signs which, according to general consensus, constitute the primary or process features of the condition. As the etiological basis of the condition is unknown, it seems illogical to apply etiological criteria, as is done by excluding from the schizophrenias cases which follow some psychological stress or even a physical illness. As far as is known, when symptoms of process type are present, cases precipitated in this manner do not behave any differently in their pattern of outcome from the general run of schizophrenic cases. Again, although genetic studies have proven valuable research tools, it is unwise, with our present knowledge, to separate a group from the schizophrenias on the basis of genetic findings alone. It is important to attempt to differentiate schizophrenic cases with more-or-less favorable prognoses, but prognostic criteria, since they can be effectively applied only *post factum* in the individual case, must clearly play a secondary role in the diagnosis of schizophrenia. Nor should we assume at this stage of our knowledge that any real dividing line separates cases with good and bad prognoses.

If the grouping of schizophrenic cases must be decided, as we believe, by the presence or absence of the primary symptoms of schizophrenia, the main group of the paraphrenic cases we have studied with their ideas of influence, paranoid delusions, hallucinations in clear consciousness, oddities, and, at times, incongruity of affect must be regarded as schizophrenic. Any identified etiological factors may reasonably be assumed to have a certain relevance for problems of etiology among all schizophrenias.

Genetic Factors

From studies of twins and other genetic investigations, the etiological factors for which there is most conclusive evidence are the genetic ones. It is not implied that these are the only factors, but their important contribution seems undeniable in the light of the findings of Kallmann, Feingold, and Bondy (1951), Slater (1953), and others. It has been shown that paraphrenias are not genetically uniform with the schizophrenias in early life. If a period of risk similar to that generally employed in genetic investigation into schizophrenia is used as a basis for calculation, the morbid risk for schizophrenia among the immediate relatives of paraphrenics does not differ to a significant extent from that of the population at large though it is somewhat greater. We are dealing, therefore, with a group in whom the genetic loading for schizophrenic illness proper is relatively small. On the other hand, there were six families (if collateral relatives are included) with more than one secondary case of schizophrenia, and eight instances of secondary cases with late developing paranoid psychoses similar to that in the propositi. That the psychoses arose entirely through the effects of a similarly adverse environment appears highly improbable; some genetic contribution to causation is, therefore, likely.

The available data are insufficient to justify an attempt at a precise definition of the mode of inheritance. A crucial question is the homogeneity of the material. Does it consist of a clinically indistinguishable mixture of mainly endogenous and exogenous cases? A mixture of this kind has been suggested to account for the low morbidity among relatives of patients with affective disorders of late onset (Kay, 1960; Stenstedt, 1959), and the same question has been raised for schizophrenia itself. Our argument that there are exogenous causes of schizophrenia is quite compatible with this hypothesis. But certain features of the illness suggest that the hereditary loading is more evenly spread; these are the frequency of premorbid personality deviations and the coloring they lend to the clinical picture and the apparently close interdependence and interaction of all causal factors —such long standing social difficulties as isolation, deafness, previous personality pattern, and precipitating stresses—in the evolution of the disorder. Susceptibility to breakdown as reflected in personality deficiencies and degree of environmental stress shows considerable quantitative variation, and to some extent these factors appear to be inversely correlated with one another. Moreover, we have a number of distinct constitutional, social, psychological, and organic factors in varying combinations, but they probably act additively to produce an essentially similar phenomenon. If this is the situation, then, taken with the very low morbidity risk for mental illness among the relatives, it suggests the effects of polygenes more than the specific monohybrid inheritance often considered to underlie schizophrenia. We need to know much more about the frequency and nature of abnormal personality traits among the relatives of schizophrenics, paraphrenics, and control groups.

Social Isolation and Paraphrenia

Is social isolation of the paraphrenic patient before illness a cause of his ultimate breakdown or do isolation and the mental illness which develops in late life both express some common factor, perhaps a lifelong personality anomaly, determined by constitutional factors? An almost identical question has been asked about many psychiatric disorders. Thus, some sixty years ago, Durkheim's (1951) classical studies of suicide led him to conclude that its incidence varied inversely with the degree of social cohesion in the community. Wherever ties from beliefs, aspirations, and activities shared with, or practiced in common by, the social group were weakened, the chances of suicide were adversely affected. Investigating suicide in London, Sainsbury (1955) was able to show that the suicide rate in different boroughs varied in a pattern which Durkheim might have predicted. There were significant correlations between suicide rate and indexes of social isolation, social disorganization, and social mobility within the boroughs; some of the highest rates had been registered in Chelsea, Hampstead, and St. Marylebone, where material adversity was uncommon. Such predominantly working-class boroughs as Stepney, Limehouse, and Bethnal Green, where a relatively high degree of social cohesion prevailed, had low suicide rates. Sainsbury was inclined to attribute a causal role to isolation in relation to suicide, and the weight of evidence certainly favored this view. The extent to which suicide rate changes as a result of the tendency of those who are mentally ill and potentially suicidal to drift into areas where they can lead an anonymous existence free from social ties and responsibilities has yet to receive adequate investigation.

Findings in certain other areas where this question has been raised call for a systematic inquiry to disentangle the network of cause and effect. It has been known for some time that immigrants have a relatively high incidence of mental disorder, as reflected by hospital admission (Malzberg & Lee, 1956), yet Ødegaard (1932; 1953; 1959) has adduced much evidence favoring the view that this high incidence comes from the fact that those with abnormal personalities in whom there is a high risk of psychotic breakdown are especially prone to migrate. He has also assembled data showing that the high incidence of mental disorder among those who fail to marry and those who work in certain occupations may be attributed to a process of social selection rather than to any ill effects exerted by loneliness and isolation. Those with deviant personalities fail in the competition for spouses and occupations and are also especially liable to become psychotic. In other words, it seems that the social failure of those predisposed to become mentally ill tends to lead to isolation and not that the isolation engenders mental illness.

A similar controversy has been in progress about the other social factors in the causation of schizophrenia. In their classical survey of first admission rates to a mental hospital, Faris and Dunham (1939) discovered that a disproportionately large number of schizophrenics in different parts of Chicago not only belonged to the lowest social class, but also came from either the central lodginghouse areas of the city or its "hobohemia," where social cohesion was minimal. (Mental disorder in old age and delinquency showed similar distributions.) Once again, opinions have differed as to whether this could be a cause and/or effect of schizophrenic illness. The work of Hollingshead and Redlich (1953) has shown that a disproportionately large number of schizophrenics under treatment came from the lowest social classes, whereas the upper classes contributed less than the expected number of schizophrenics. In further studies (Hollingshead & Redlich, 1954; Hollingshead & Redlich, 1958) they examined and rejected the possibility that this was caused by a downward social drift of schizophrenics who had been demoted to unskilled jobs because of the incompetence caused by their disease. On the other hand, Morrison (1959) found that the fathers of schizophrenics were a representative sample of the normal population as far as occupation was concerned, suggesting that drift had occurred. In a study of mental health in Bristol, Hare (1956), however, was able to provide partial confirmation for the findings of Faris and Dunham. He concluded that schizophrenics were in social seclusion largely because they had severed their social ties after their illness began to undermine their social adjustments although isolation in about one-third of the cases had resulted from accidental circumstances rather than social failure.

The essential complement to statistical studies of this kind is detailed investigation of individual cases in which such social stresses as isolation are suspected to operate. At first sight, it seems unlikely that mental disorders that appear for the first time in old age can be partly attributable to lifelong personality defects which have always created social difficulties for the individual, although the findings suggest that this constitutes a large part of the explanation. Approximately half the personalities were hostile, suspicious, hard, arrogant, shy, solitary, or extremely eccentric; the incidence of some such abnormal personalities was significantly higher here than among the control groups. There are two particularly good examples that illustrate the way in which these people segregate themselves rather than become isolated by accident or force of circumstance. The first is the contrasting behavior of paraphrenic and affective women following illegitimate pregnancies. The second example is the fact that adherence to minority religious groups was relatively common among the paranoid cases and far more rare in the affective groups.

These findings, therefore, lend some support to the views of Ødegaard (1953; 1959) that the unmarried state reflects rather than causes the paraphrenic's abnormal personality and subsequent illness. One may also suspect that the isolation of such individuals may be self-created and that they, not chance, decided that they should bear few children. Indeed, clinical experience teaches that attempts to analyze the isolation of such individuals meet with little success. One can, in fact, ask whether these individuals could have remained socially active until late life if circumstances had forced them into close associations with other people or whether their immunity from open breakdown until senescence may not owe something to their successfully keeping social contacts at arm's length. However, even if the most extreme interpretation is placed on the available facts, not all the factors tending toward seclusion can be considered self-created. It was not through personal choice that they were so often the youngest child and so often left with few surviving siblings in old age, nor could frequent deafness have been conditioned by their anomalies of personality.

It would seem, therefore, that the isolation in which so many of our patients were found had been fashioned by multiple factors. The relative importance of these factors cannot be precisely determined, but the personality oddities of many patients stand out and probably made a large contribution. We have suggested the possibility that, far from being a cause, the solitary and eccentric ways of these patients may have been the defensive, self-protective responses of people poorly equipped for emotional relationships. On the other hand, having formed few friendships in early life, their social assets must have depreciated at a more rapid rate than those of most people. An attitude of determined and aggressive independence which helps to make the individual socially viable in early life might also contribute to making his integration impossible in old age. Although isolation initially may have been the schizoid's special need and preference, it probably became a cause of increased isolation because of its steady and cumulative erosion of the patient's resources for adjustment in late life.

This view is partially confirmed by the fact that in some cases breakdown finally occurs at about the same time that extraneous influences (the death of relatives, the progress of deafness, the advent of physical infirmity) begin to drive the patients into deeper isolation. Personality is only one factor in the situation. In most of the cases, severe anomalies of personality were present, but a few patients in Group 2 appeared to be relatively normal people for whom an aggregation of unusually intense extraneous influences had enforced isolation. In other cases, a situation between these two extremes emerged, for environmental and physical handicaps of moderate severity were associated with premorbid personalities and not particularly severe peculiarities. The conclusion emerges that the theory of isolation and lack of social communication as causes of schizophrenia (Faris & Dunham, 1939) is an oversimplification when applied to the paraphrenias of the aged. Segregation often results from lifelong personality traits which are extended preludes intimately related to psychotic breakdowns in senescence. To a small extent these patients are victims of circumstance, and to this extent isolation would appear to be a cause of paraphrenic illness. To a greater extent, as far as the present data are concerned, isolation is merely a consequence of personality anomalies that also portend a schizophrenia in late life.

The Findings and Etiological Theories
of Schizophrenia

It is held by many workers that schizophrenia is a condition determined by specific genes whose manifestation may be influenced, though only within rather narrow limits, by environmental factors. Sharp differences in the incidence of the condition in different social classes have recently been clearly demonstrated, but the significance of these findings is far from clear and the view that they reflect an environmental factor in the causation of schizophrenia has certainly not won general acceptance. In late paraphrenia we appear to have a very different situation as far as etiology is concerned. Genetic factors play some part, but are less important, and it seems unlikely that they are of the specific monohybrid kind postulated for schizophrenia. The prominence of environmental, physical, and exogenous factors, the varying combinations in which they are found, the additive fashion in which personality deviation and environmental stress interact to create ill effects, suggest a disorder of multifactorial etiology. The hereditary basis of such a condition is also likely to be multifactorial, that is, polygenic. In the predisposed personalities of paraphrenics, we are probably dealing with extreme deviations of temperament and character, rather than any rare and specific constitution.

One possible way to reconcile these facts is to conclude that the constellation of symptoms called schizophrenia has different causes in early and late life and that the environmental factors and sensory deprivation identified as causal agents in paraphrenia are irrelevant to theories about the etiology of schizophrenia before the age of sixty. This formulation would be cogent except for the fact that close examination of the present evidence on the causation of schizophrenia shows some interesting parallels with the situation described here in late paraphrenia.

Recent investigations tend to suggest that even in the cases where schizophrenic symptoms occur in the absence of organic disease genetic factors are not only insufficient, but perhaps not always necessary, causes of the illness. Thus Rosenthal's (1959) examination of Slater's material has revealed that, in the families of identical twins where only one twin was schizophrenic, the genetic loading with schizophrenia is extremely low, whereas it is very high in the families of concordant twins. He suggested that there may be two etiologically distinct types of schizophrenia, one caused by genetic, the other by environmental, factors. The evidence from this line of investigation does not altogether point in one direction, for in a similar study Luxenburger (1939) registered an opposite finding. Further studies on twins will be necessary to decide the issue, but if some allowance is made for the evidence about the roles of social class and social isolation, the view that the causes of schizophrenia cover a spectrum ranging from the predominantly genetic at one extreme to the predominantly exogenous and environmental at the other seems reasonable and cogent. Perhaps Kolle's (1931) genetic studies of paranoid psychopaths among the relatives of patients with paranoia are relevant in this context. This etiological scheme would accord more with multifactorial than with monohybrid genetic causes.

We only mean to suggest here that, because neither the theory of simple dominance or simple recessivity adequately accounts for all the family data in schizophrenia, more attention should now be given to the role of polygenes. *Ad hoc* hypotheses of "inhibition of manifestation" and "genetic modifiers" have been introduced to make the data fit the theoretical requirements of Mendelian ratios; but, although these hypotheses involve polygenic interaction, the main research in this field still concerns the mode of inheritance of the major gene which is assumed to underlie schizophrenic illness. The predisposition to illness, however, may be a graded characteristic depending on quantitative variation. That schizophrenic illness presents itself as a steplike, "all-or-none" phenomenon is not a conclusive argument against this view, since threshold effects may be involved; but disputed borderline cases—*formes frustes* and psychopathic paranoid and schizoid personalities—are not rare, and they form a link between the normal and the indubitably abnormal. In three common psychiatric conditions—the subcultural variety of mental defect (Roberts, 1950), obsessional neurosis (Rüdin, 1953), and epilepsy (Harvald, 1951)—inheritance has been shown to be probably multifactorial, and in each of these conditions environmental or other exogenous factors are certainly important. On the other hand, those mental abnormalities attributed without doubt to major genes are rare and much less influenced by external factors. We urgently need, therefore, to develop psychometric, physiological, or biochemical methods for identifying predisposition to schizophrenia in the same way that intelligence is revealed by mental testing and subclinical epilepsy by the E.E.G. When these methods are developed, we may find that schizophrenia and its latent forms, which are presently attributed to heterozygosity or inhibition of manifestation, are really caused by an accumulation of polygenes with additive action and graded effect.

Genetic factors are probably more important in causing schizophrenia in early life than in old age, whereas the reverse is probably true of environmental factors. In the light of the above discussion, however, the differences may well be quantitative rather than qualitative. Also, if the kinship of late paraphrenia and the schizophrenias is accepted, the difference in incidence by social class in the latter and the isolation in which many schizophrenics live are unlikely to be wholly caused by moves down the social scale or by some bias in selecting cases. To some extent, adverse social circumstances are likely to prove causes as well as consequences of schizophrenic breakdown in earlier life, although their contribution will probably be less important here than in the late paraphrenias.

SUMMARY

A clinical follow-up and genetic study has been made on ninety-nine patients of sixty and over (with a mean age of about seventy) suffering from late paraphrenia. The patients consist of two groups, one from the Psychiatric Hospital in Stockholm (1931-1940), the other from Graylingwell Hospital, Chichester, United Kingdom (1951-1955). The control group comprises patients of similar age who had affective and organic disorders and who were admitted to the hospitals during the same periods as the paraphrenics. The paraphrenic patients at both hospitals show the same characteristics, which are summarized here.

Females predominate by about seven to one, significantly in excess of expectation. In both sexes there are significantly more unmarried patients; married patients are less common here than in the general population of similar age. Fertility among the married patients is low.

Examining the background of the illness shows that more paraphrenics were living alone when they fell ill than were patients with affective disorder. This appears to have been caused by several factors: the frequency of the unmarried state, the low fertility among the paraphrenics, the infrequency of surviving sibs.

Of those living alone, many more patients with paraphrenia than with affective disorder were socially isolated. Three factors seem to be responsible: deafness, abnormalities of personality, and few surviving relatives. Deafness was found to some degree in 40 per cent of the Graylingwell paraphrenics and to a severe degree in 15 per cent of all cases, with a much lower incidence for the other groups. Personality traits among paraphrenics and affectives also differed markedly. Among the former they were commonly of the paranoid-schizoid type, and they contributed substantially to the failure to marry, social isolation, and probably to the development of the psychosis itself. But factors unconnected with the personality, such as absence of relatives, played some part in deciding whether isolation did occur.

Except in one subgroup (referred to below) the clinical picture is remarkably uniform and characterized by the presence of many schizophrenia-like disorders of thought, mood, and volition, by relatively good preservation of formal intellect, personality, and memory, and by conspicuous hallucinations. In about 20 per cent of the Graylingwell cases, hallucinosis was entirely absent, and the illness appeared to represent a caricature of deviating personality traits of long standing; perhaps these cases may be regarded as paranoid reactions to the physical and social consequences of growing old. But to a greater or lesser extent, exogenous factors (deafness, isolation) or personality attributes are always present, and it is doubtful whether any clear demarcation between groups of cases really exists. At this stage, therefore, it seems far more profitable to treat the late paraphrenias as a whole.

An inherited predisposition to late paraphrenia must be postulated, but this is likely to be of lesser degree than in schizophrenia occurring early in life. The mode of inheritance is probably multi-factorial.

A pathological degree of cerebral degeneration is probably not related to the onset of psychosis in more than 5 per cent of cases, but some contribution by normal age-specific mental changes cannot be ruled out in cases where there are gross, long-standing abnormalities of personality.

The course of the illness tends to be chronic, and changes of the schizophrenic type usually become more prominent. Sometimes, however, a "burnt out" state with residual defects is seen, or else the illness merges after many years into a state difficult to distinguish from that of senile dementia (12 per cent). The life span is only slightly shortened by the illness.

It is concluded that late paraphrenia has to be regarded as the mode of manifestation of schizophrenia in old age. The etiological factors identified in late paraphrenia are, therefore, likely to have some relevance for the problem of causation of schizophrenia itself. The social isolation in which many paraphrenics live is to some extent the result of self-segregation by people for whom social contact and communication are difficult or stressful but the evidence suggests that isolation must be attributed to some extent to such accidental factors as deafness, position in family, or lack of surviving relations. The cumulative effects of such factors may account for the final breakdown in old age. At younger ages also, the onset of schizophrenia is sometimes likely to result from isolation and not be merely a cause of it. Perhaps the findings also bear on the general relation of social isolation to mental illness.[3]

REFERENCES

Beamish, R., & Kiloh, L.G. Psychoses due to amphetamine consumption. *J. ment. Sci.*, 1960, **106,** 337-343.

Benedetti, G. *The alcohol hallucinoses.* Stuttgart: Thieme and Grune, 1952.

Connell, P.H. Amphetamine psychosis. *Maudsley Monograph*, 1958, No. 5. (Institute of Psychiatry, London)

Durkheim, É. *Suicide.* Trans. by J.A. Spaulding & G. Simpson. Glencoe, Ill.: The Free Press, 1951.

Faris, R.E.L., & Dunham, H.W. *Mental disorders in urban areas.* Chicago: The University of Chicago Press, 1939.

Fish, F. Senile schizophrenia. *J. ment. Sci.*, 1960, **106,** 938-946.

[3] The tables and part of this paper have previously been published (Kay & Roth, Environmental and heredity factors in the schizophrenias of old age ["late paraphrenia"] and their bearing on the general problem of causation in schizophrenia. *J. ment. Sci.*, 1961, **107,** 649-686).

Hare, E.H. Mental illness and social conditions in Bristol. *J. ment. Sci.,* 1956, **102,** 349-357.

Harvald, B. On genetic prognosis of epilepsy. *Acta Psychiat. Neurol. Scand.,* 1951, **26,** 339-352.

Hollinsghead, A.B., & Redlich, F.C. Social stratification and psychiatric disorders. *Amer. sociol. Rev.,* 1953, **18,** 163-169.

Hollingshead, A.B., & Redlich, F.C. Schizophrenia and social structure. *Amer. J. Psychiat.,* 1954, **110,** 695-701.

Hollingshead, A.B., & Redlich, F.C. *Social class and mental illness.* New York: John Wiley & Sons, 1958.

Kallmann, F.J. Genetic aspects of mental disorders in later life. In O.J. Kaplan (Ed.), *Mental disorders in later life.* (2nd ed.) London: Oxford University Press, 1956. Pp. 26-46.

Kallmann, F.J., Feingold, Lissy, & Bondy, Eva. Comparative adaptational, social and psychometric data on life histories of senescent twin pairs. *Amer. J. hum. Genet.,* 1951, **3,** 65-73.

Kay, D.W.K. Observations on the natural history and genetics of old age psychoses: A Stockholm survey, 1931-1937. *Proc. roy. Soc. Med.,* 1959, **52,** 791-794. (Abridged)

Kay, D.W.K. The natural history and genetics of affective and paranoid disorders in the elderly. Unpublished doctoral thesis, Oxford University, 1960.

Kolle, K. *Primary paranoia.* Leipzig: Thieme, 1931.

Kretschmer, E. *Der sensitive beziehungswahn.* Berlin: Springer, 1927.

Leonhard, K. Classification of schizophrenias. In *Congress report, international congress of psychiatry, Zurich, 1957.* Vol. 4. Zurich: Orell Füssli Arts Graphiques S.A., 1959. Pp. 214-216.

Luxenburger, H. *Handbook of genetic biology of man.* Berlin: Springer, 1939.

Malzberg, B., & Lee, E.S. *Migration and mental disease.* New York: Social Science Research Council, 1956.

Mayer, W. On paraphrenic psychoses. *Z. Neurol. Psychiat.,* 1921, **71,** 187-206.

Morrison, S.L. Principles and methods of epidemiological research and their application to psychiatric illness. *J. ment. Sci.,* 1959, **105,** 999-1011.

Ødegaard, Ø. Emigration and insanity: Study of mental 'disease among Norwegian born population of Minnesota. *Acta Psychiat. Neur.,* Suppl. 4, 1932, **7,** 1-206.

Ødegaard, Ø. Marriage and mental health. *Acta Psychiat. Neurol. Scand.,* Suppl. 80, 1953, **28,** 153-161.

Ødegaard, Ø. The epidemiology of schizophrenia in Norway. In *Congress Report, International Congress of Psychiatry, Zurich, 1957.* Vol. 3. Zurich: Orell Füssli Arts Graphiques S.A., 1959. Pp. 49-52.

Roberts, J.A.F. Génétique de l'oligophrénie. (l). In *Rapports, Congrès international de psychiatrie, Paris, 1950.* Paris: Hermann, 1950. Pp. 115-117.

Rosenthal, D. Schizophrenia in monozygotic twins. *J. nerv. ment. Dis.,* 1959, **129,** 1-10.

Roth, M. The natural history of mental disorders in old age. *J. ment. Sci.,* 1955, **101,** 281-301.

Roth, M., & Morrissey, J.D. Problems in the diagnosis and classification of mental disorder in old age. *J. ment. Sci.*, 1952, **98**, 66-80.

Rüdin, E. On the problem of compulsive disease with special reference to its hereditary relations. *Arch. Psychiat. Nervenkr.*, 1953, **191**, 14-54.

Sainsbury, P. Suicide in London. *Maudsley Monograph*, 1955. No. 1. (Institute of Psychiatry, London)

Schultz, B. Über die hereditaren beziehungen paranoid gefärbter alterpsychosen. *Z. Neurol. Psychiat.*, 1930, **129**, 147-190.

Slater, E. Psychotic and neurotic illnesses in twins. *Medical Research Council Special Report Series*, 1953, Nc. 278. (London: H.M. Stationery Office)

Slater, E., & Beard, A. *Psychoses with epilepsy: Problems of classification.* London: Institute of Psychiatry, 1959.

Stenstedt, Å. Involutional melancholia. *Acta Psychiat. Neurol. Scand.*, Suppl. 127, 1959, **34.**

Strömgren, E. *Beiträge zur psychiatrischen erblehre.* Copenhagen: Munksgaard, 1938.

CHAPTER 21

*Patterns of
Geriatric Mental Illness*

ALEXANDER SIMON and
MIRON W. NEAL

Eight per cent of the United States population is over sixty-five, yet 26 per cent of the new patients admitted to mental hospitals are over sixty-five, and the proportion of older people in the population is steadily expanding. The problems of geriatric mental illness, therefore, demand increasing medical and social attention.[1] Although only 1.0 per cent of the people who are sixty-five and over are in public mental hospitals, they nevertheless increasingly tax the limits of our state institutions and our county and community budgets (U.S. Department of Health, Education, & Welfare, 1960). On June 30, 1958, California had 11,388 patients of sixty-five and over—31 per cent of the total population (Department of Mental Hygiene, 1960) in its state hospitals for the mentally ill.

[1] This research is supported by the U.S. Public Health Service, National Institute of Mental Health Grant 3M-9145.

449

Staffs of mental hospitals sometimes state that not all older patients are admitted because of mental illness alone, but because the local communities are reluctant to provide adequate facilities for care. A survey of geriatric patients admitted in June, 1950, to California mental hospitals, estimates that 55 per cent of them could have been cared for outside a mental hospital had suitable facilities existed. Of these patients, 35 per cent were not considered psychotic, and another 20 per cent had psychotic symptoms so mild that they did not require mental-hospital care (Governor's Conference, 1950). Such reports have been taken to mean that older people are abandoned by their families and communities, but the facts to substantiate such conclusions have never been adequately presented. A study of Connecticut's three mental hospitals (Shindell & Cornfield, 1956) showed, however, that at the time of the survey only 6.5 per cent of the hospitalized patients could be cared for in nonhospital facilities for chronic patients. It was concluded that the so-called senile patients who can be cared for outside mental hospitals have not substantially contributed to mental-hospital overcrowding. Goldfarb (1961b) has reported a three-year study (1956-1959) of 2,200 people over sixty-four who were new admissions to New York City old-age homes, nursing homes, or state hospitals. The study, based on direct psychiatric, medical, and psychologic examinations, indicates that a large portion of these people resembles each other in their psychiatric, medical, and social needs for help. The data do not indicate "overuse and abuse of psychiatric hospitals through the unwarranted admission and retention of aged patients" (Goldfarb, 1961a, p. 260).

The problem of evaluating such reports depends on a critical definition of who is considered suitable for admission to the various institutions. Which old people are mentally ill? For what illnesses are some hospitalized, and which might respond to preventive measures or to prompt, early treatment? What is the role of physical illness in the development of the psychologic problem or in the precipitation of a crisis that leads to psychiatric hospitalization? How many aged people truly need treatment in a psychiatric institution, at what point in their illnesses, and for how long?

The stereotype of the aged mentally ill patient is one who suffers from intellectual deterioration and behavioral disturbances associated with chronic, irreversible structural changes in the brain. This structural damage is usually ascribed to a cerebral circulatory disorder or to a so-called senile brain disease. This stereotype was challenged by Roth (1955) in his report of 450 patients of sixty or over who were admitted to a British mental hospital. Almost half the patients had functional disorders (affective psychoses and paraphrenia) without evidence of the psychologic disturbances related to organic brain disease that are seen in senile psychosis and arteriosclerotic psychosis (about 40 per cent) and in acute confusion (about 10 per cent).

In contrast, the distribution of diagnoses reported for various United States mental-hospital patients of sixty and over has varied greatly. For example, 91 per cent of twenty-six thousand new admissions to New York mental hospitals from 1943 to 1948 had chronic brain diseases, and only 9 per cent had other disorders (Malzberg, 1958). In 1956, of the 2,690 new admissions to California state mental hospitals, 75 per cent of the patients who were sixty and over had diagnoses of chronic brain diseases and 25 per cent had other mental disorders without organic brain disorder like depressive, schizophrenic, paranoid, and psychoneurotic reactions, and alcohol addiction (Department of Mental Hygiene, 1957, p. 37).

It is often difficult, if not impossible, to relate the clinical picture of the patient at the time of diagnosis to the neuroanatomic changes that may be found at autopsy. The differences in the distribution of diagnostic categories of the studies just cited may represent varied diagnostic and clinical judgments, or they may represent the difficulties of diagnosis at different stages of the illness.

In an effort to learn how the demonstrable neuropathologic changes found at autopsy correlate with the clinical diagnoses, we have summarized the findings in a recent neuropathologic study of 505 cases (Simon & Malamud, 1953) and have cited a few pertinent data from the literature. The pathoanatomic findings in 505 consecutive autopsies of the patients in several large mental hospitals who at death had the clinical diagnosis of either psychosis with cerebral arteriosclerosis or senile (including presenile) psychosis were surveyed by standard techniques.

In senile brain disease there were nonspecific degeneration and dropping out of nerve cells, with specific senile plaques and neurofibrillary changes of Alzheimer's. In cases of Alzheimer's disease, presenile dementia, the above changes were widespread and intense, with onset of the disease established before the age of sixty-five. Not just vascular disease, but focal destructive lesions as well, was the basis for cerebral arteriosclerosis; macroscopic infarcts characterized atherosclerosis. Miliary foci of perivascular gliosis, often associated with old or recent hemorrhages, characterized arteriolar sclerosis. In either condition the lesions may have been old or recent.

In the miscellaneous disorders, two other presenile disorders were differentiated. Pick's disease had a characteristic pattern of focal atrophies with argyrophilic changes in definite areas, limited to the frontal, temporal, and parietal lobes. In unclassified organic brain disease, diffuse cortical atrophy was associated with a spongy tissue degeneration of neurones, but there were no argyrophilic changes of either Alzheimer's or Pick's disease.

At autopsy, 61 per cent of the 505 cases showed some evidence of significant changes of the type labeled senile brain disease: 34 per cent showed only senile changes, 7 per cent Alzheimer's, and 20 per cent a mixed senile and arteriosclerotic picture. Of the 505 cases, 24 per cent showed significant arteriosclerotic brain disease without evidence of associated senile changes. Another 11 per cent included such organic brain disease as Pick's disease, toxic encephalopathy, chronic Wernicke's encephalopathy, and brain tumors. Only 4 per cent showed no cerebral pathology.

On the basis of the assumption that the neuropathologic changes just described are closely related to the psychologic and behavioral manifestations of these patients, it is evident that psychiatrists diagnosed the chronic brain disorder correctly in almost all cases; in diagnosing the types, however, they were less accurate. In comparing the neuropathologic findings with the clinical diagnoses, the most frequent error (in 210 cases, or 41 per cent) was the diagnosis of cerebral arteriosclerosis when the autopsy findings primarily showed senile brain disease or a mixed senile and arteriosclerotic picture.

Only eleven of the 505 cases were pathologically diagnosed to have toxic encephalopathy. This small number may not accurately reflect the actual incidence of such acute brain disease and may be the result of limited techniques for pathologic diagnosis. The mortality rates of geriatric patients in their first month of hospitalization imply a higher frequency of acute brain syndromes, at least as a terminal manifestation. For example, in a twenty-seven-month period, of 540 male patients sixty and over who entered a New York state hospital for the first time, 23 per cent of the group died within the first month, and 35 per cent within three months (Whittier & Korenyi, 1961). In a few cases (4 per cent), no cerebral pathology could be demonstrated. A review of their clinical records pointed, in some cases, to a paranoid state or an affective psychosis; in others the clinical data were too meager for a diagnosis.

In the series of 505 cases, the severity of the clinically assessed intellectual deterioration was closely related to the severity of the senile and arteriosclerotic neuropathologic lesions. To be sure, this group of patients constituted a select sample. They were so severely ill that they were diagnosed as suffering from a psychosis caused by senile or arteriosclerotic brain changes. They were ill enough, too, to be admitted to a mental hospital.

Studies by Gellerstedt (1933), Rothschild (1956) and others, though often cited to indicate a lack of correlation between the severity of pathologic changes and of psychopathologic disturbance, do not wholly support such a conclusion. Rothschild has emphasized that the organic brain changes observed at the autopsies of patients who had been diagnosed as suffering from senile and arteriosclerotic psychoses must be considered with personal and social elements as causal factors; the ability of individuals to withstand cerebral damage varies greatly, and the same damage that produces a psychosis in one may not do so in another. He repeatedly emphasized the role of social and situational stresses and even unfavorable personality traits, which in some cases distinguish the socially acceptable from the psychotic senile or arteriosclerotic older person.

Gellerstedt (1933) has reported on autopsies of fifty patients sixty-five and older who died in Munich general hospitals. He considered the senile plaques so often found in senile brains a measure of the degree of physiologic senile involution and not a basis for dementia, since their frequency did not always parallel the mental disturbances. His conclusion is limited in that these so-called normal elderly patients had not been psychiatrically examined before death.

Thus, in the community there may be aged persons with evidence of neuropathologic change related to senility or cerebral arteriosclerosis who show few if any signs of intellectual impairment up to or near the time of death.

Since 1959 the staff of the Geriatric Research Project, Langley Porter Neuropsychiatric Institute, have studied the psychiatric and other medical factors and the psychologic and social characteristics of patients sixty and older admitted in 1959 to the psychiatric receiving wards of San Francisco General Hospital, a large municipal hospital. The purposes are to clarify factors contributing to the high admission rates of elderly patients to mental hospitals, to improve the understanding of the clinical manifestations of various geriatric mental illnesses, and to determine the relative importance of medical, psychologic, and social factors in the development of geriatric mental illness.

THE STUDY

To focus on the problems of age-linked mental illness in a particular urban area, the study group of 534 patients was limited to patients who had been residents of San Francisco for at least one year and who had not been hospitalized in a psychiatric ward before the age of sixty. Excluded from this group were 235 patients of sixty and over who were admitted during 1959 but who did not meet the requirement of San Francisco residence, had histories of psychiatric hospitalization before sixty, were still on mental-hospital rolls, and had histories of criminal arrests before reaching sixty.

The patients of the study group were examined by project psychiatrists, psychologists, and social scientists who worked independently from the hospital's medical staff, but all information in the hospital records was utilized. Historical information was gathered by interviews with patients and from such collateral sources as family members, friends, landlords, social agencies, and police.

As Pollack, Person, Kramer, and Goldstein (1959) have pointed out, an analysis of hospital admissions must take into account many factors besides illness. Particularly in the older groups, both admissions and dispositions will be affected by available alternative facilities for care; by the medical, social, and economic climate of the community from which the patients come; by hospital policies of admission and treatment; by the amount of hospital funds, staff time, and space for each patient; and by the attitudes of the patient and the community toward aging, mental illness, and psychiatric hospitals. Perhaps of greatest importance is the point in the patient's career at which his illness is evaluated. These considerations may be as significant as the variations in diagnostic standards in explaining the differences in reports of admission rates of disease types.

The Setting

To judge properly the results of our study, it is necessary to know the general background of these patients and the circumstances in which they were studied. In 1960 the city of San Francisco had a relatively high population of people sixty-five or over: 93,608 (12.6 per cent) in its total population of 740,316. This percentage was 8.8 for the state of California and 9.2 for the nation as a whole (U.S. Bureau of the Census, 1960). Facilities for the chronically ill, especially those with gross intellectual impairment or behavioral disturbance, are limited.

The city's chronic-illness and domiciliary-care institution has a waiting period of several months for patients who require nursing care; it does not accept people with serious behavioral disturbances. In general, the domiciliary facilities operated by voluntary agencies accept only the ambulatory aged. The cost of nursing care in private facilities is high and beyond the economic ability of almost all the people in our sample. Psychiatric outpatient treatment centers have long waiting lists, and few psychiatrists have specific interests in treating older people.

In California about 25 per cent of those sixty-five and over live in one-person households (Department of Public Health, 1959). In the hospital sample about twice as many (47 per cent) lived either alone (45 per cent) or with people not related to them (2 per cent); the parallel proportion for San Francisco as a whole is not known. An estimated 55 per cent of those sixty-five and over have no income other than Social Security pensions or public welfare support.[2] Many of these people depend largely on public or voluntary outpatient clinics for medical care. In short, for the nonambulatory physically ill and for the mentally ill who cannot afford private care, little stands between the home and the municipal hospital except the support and tolerance of family members, where available, neighbors, or landlords.

Yet there is little evidence for the current statements that many older people are abandoned to public institutions by families unwilling to assume responsibility for them (Shanas, 1960). For both the patients and their families, psychiatric hospitalization often carries a stigma. Usually they regard it as a step to be taken reluctantly—a last resort after every other possibility has been exhausted. This attitude contrasts sharply with that of the community from which the patients of Roth's study came: the psychiatric hospital was viewed favorably as a well-run center for treatment, and the patients moved freely in and out of the hospital.[3]

Even so, in San Francisco older people are sent to state mental hospitals at a rate twice that for California as a whole and over four times that for Los Angeles, the state's other major urban area (Blain, 1961). The high rate reflects the influence of several factors: a greater population of older people, the city's lack of domiciliary and nursing-care facilities for low-income groups, and the policies of the municipal general hospital.

[2] United Community Fund of San Francisco, personal communication, 1960.
[3] M. Roth, personal communication, 1959.

From an inquiry among the local psychiatric facilities, we have estimated that, for at least 95 per cent of the San Franciscans sixty and over who are hospitalized on psychiatric wards, the point of entry is the receiving wards of San Francisco General Hospital. The receiving wards are small and overcrowded. They sometimes carry more than double their capacity. The limited number of medical, nursing, and social-service personnel often cannot give sufficient time to individual cases. The shortage of space forces a policy of attempting to empty the receiving wards of patients by discharge or transfer to another facility within five days. The hospital has a small psychiatric treatment unit whose strict eligibility requirements and maximum stay of ninety days tend to restrict its use largely to young patients with hopeful prognoses.

In the majority of cases, therefore, the psychiatric patient—whether admitted by the hospital staff for observation or brought to the psychiatric ward on a commitment petition—is committed by court order to a state hospital within three to five days after admission.

The group of 534 patients constituted all admissions to the psychiatric receiving wards who were residents of San Francisco, sixty and over, and who had not entered a psychiatric ward before they were sixty. No information could be obtained on four of the 534. Of the remaining 530, there were 250 men and 280 women. By decades, the age distribution of the group was sixty to sixty-nine 32 per cent, seventy to seventy-nine 41 per cent, and over eighty 27 per cent. The oldest patient was ninety-nine. In the first decade, the men outnumbered the women by almost three to two, and they had a slight majority in the middle decade. In the oldest decade there were almost twice as many women as men.

By and large the group came from the lower economic strata of the community. No data on income were recorded in 104 cases. Of the remaining 433 persons, 73 per cent had annual incomes under $2,000; 54 per cent, under $1,500. For 69 per cent the main source of income was Social Security ($119 maximum for a wage earner) or public welfare ($95 maximum). Only 20 per cent of the sample had been graduated from high school, and only 5 per cent had one or more years in college. An analysis of the patients' occupations (or those of their husbands' in the cases of wives or widows) indicates that even as middle-aged adults, 83 per cent had stood in either the low-middle or low class economically.

At the time of admission, 27 per cent of the men were married, compared with 18 per cent of the women, but 54 per cent of the women were widowed, compared with 20 per cent of the men. For 25 per cent of the study group, the customary dwelling unit was a hotel or rooming house, 57 per cent lived in their own house or apartment, 15 per cent had been placed in institutions more than a month before their admission to the psychiatric ward, and 3 per cent were unknown. Up to at least a month before hospital entry, 45 per cent customarily lived alone, 36 per cent lived with a spouse or other family member, 2 per cent with people who were not related to them, 15 per cent had already been living in some institution, and 2 per cent were unknown. The proportions of men and women living with a family member are identical (35 per cent), but more men (26 per cent) than women (17 per cent) lived with their spouses with or without children in the household—a reflection of the greater number of widows than widowers.

An analysis in 390 consecutive cases of the type of care under which the patients were living just before admission shows that 25 per cent were transferred to the psychiatric wards from institutions (13 per cent from general hospitals and 12 per cent from nursing or old people's homes), 31 per cent were already receiving extensive daily care from family or friends at home, 40 per cent were living alone without regular daily assistance, 2 per cent came from jail, and information on 4 per cent was unknown.

In the course of hospitalization, 445 patients (84 per cent of the group) underwent legal commitment proceedings, and 81 per cent of these (67 per cent of the group) were transferred by court order to a state mental hospital. Of the 445 considered for commitment, 61 per cent had been brought to the psychiatric wards after petitions for commitment had already been filed. No patients were transferred to state hospitals as voluntary admissions.

CLINICAL DIAGNOSTIC CATEGORIES

Chronic Brain Disorder

The patients had a history of gradual intellectual and personality disorganization extending from months to several years; they also had disturbances in comprehension, memory, and orientation. Such disturbances in affect as emotional instability, irritability, anxiety, apathy, and hallucinations or delusions were observed in many cases. The chronic brain disorders were subdivided as follows.

Senile brain disease. With onset after sixty-five (before sixty-five, presenile dementia), the patient had a history of gradual and progressive inability to deal with day-to-day life situations. This was associated with clinical evidence of intellectual deterioration (of months to years in duration) and without history or neurologic evidence of one or more cerebrovascular accidents or evidence of chronic alcoholic, syphilitic, or other brain disease.

Arteriosclerotic brain disease. The patient's intellectual deterioration, of months to years in duration, was associated with focal neurologic signs and symptoms as observed in the case history or clinical findings or both, and secondary to one or more cerebrovascular accidents (probably atherosclerotic in origin). Included were patients with histories of fluctuating course or one or more seizures associated with severe hypertension (probably with cerebral arteriolar changes) or both.

Chronic alcoholic brain disease. The patient had a history of excessive alcohol indulgence over many years and evidence of intellectual deterioration (with or without a Korsakoff-like syndrome) of months to years in duration. Because of the definite history of excessive alcoholism, the intellectual deterioration was attributed to neuropathologic changes secondary to alcoholism rather than to senile disease (the clinical differentiation is often difficult).

Chronic brain syndromes. Some patients had widely varying conditions, of months to years in duration, caused by trauma, convulsive disorder, idiopathic Parkinsonism, central nervous system syphilis, and chronic brain disease of undetermined origin.

Acute Brain Disorder

Acute brain disorder is usually of abrupt onset seldom coming more than one month before the patient's admission. It is characterized by fluctuating disturbance in consciousness, varying from mild confusion to stupor and coma; impairment of intellectual functions, principally memory disturbance and disorientation; in some cases, illusions, delusions, and hallucinations; pathological emotional states like fear, apprehension, emotional lability, irritability, or apathy; and a physiologic disturbance the onset of which was associated with the psychiatric upset.

This symptom complex may be completely reversible if the underlying physiologic disturbance can be corrected, or it may indicate a terminal state (as in uremia, certain malignancies, cardiac failure, or the sequelae of a cerebrovascular accident). It may also be superimposed on a long-term chronic brain syndrome which is revealed if the manifestations of the acute brain disorder clear up. This last group includes patients with only transient episodes of noisy, restless, and disturbed behavior during a senile or arteriosclerotic psychosis if the episodes are associated with a physiologic disturbance like cardiac failure or cerebrovascular accident.

These are unusually broad diagnostic categories of acute brain disorder, and they subsume many of the acute psychiatric disturbances that are sometimes thought to be part of the course of geriatric mental illnesses asociated with chronic structural and physiologic changes in the brain. Certainly it is illogical to state that transient acute brain disorders do not occur during a chronic brain disorder. Because of the underlying mental illness, such patients often tend to neglect their health, seldom seek medical attention, suffer from malnutrition and vitamin deficiency and are, therefore, prone to acute physiologic disturbance. There are several physiologic disturbances associated with acute brain disordrers.

1. *Cerebrovascular.* An acute brain disturbance may abruptly develop after an apoplectic attack; it is generally associated with either a temporary or permanent occlusion of a cerebral artery or cerebral hemorrhage.

2. *Malnutrition.* Often there was evidence or history of deficient food intake in the period immediately before the acute onset of such symptoms as debility, dehydration, peripheral edema, pellagroid skin changes, glossitis, or cheilitis.

3. *Cardiac failure.* The patient displayed such signs as cyanosis, increased venous pressure, pulmonary congestion, hepatomegaly, dependent edema, orthopnea, or cardiac arrhythmia.

4. *Alcohol.* For the patient with a history of prolonged and excessive alcoholic indulgence before the abrupt appearance of symptoms the symptoms might resemble those of delirium tremens or be a state of apathy, perplexity, and clouded consciousness without evidence of illusions, delusions, or hallucinations. It might persist for several days after acute intoxication. A chronic brain disorder like Korsakoff's syndrome might persist. There were no cases of acute alcoholic hallucinosis in this series.

5. *Drugs and toxins.* An abrupt impairment of consciousness resulted from the ingestion of such drugs as barbiturates or from toxicity caused by an overdosage of digitalis.

6. *Head trauma.* Some patients had histories of head trauma suf-

ficiently severe to produce immediate unconsciousness or evidence, on physical examination, of head trauma followed by a clinical picture of acute brain syndrome.

7. *Surgery*. The precipitating factor was a major surgical procedure followed within a few days by the clinical manifestations of acute brain syndrome.

8. *Pulmonary disease*. Pneumonia, viral pneumonitis, advanced emphysema, and tuberculosis which seriously interfered with pulmonary function, often febrile, were physiologic disturbances associated with the acute brain syndrome.

Affective Disorders

Affective disorders constituted depressive reactions (manic-depressive, involutional, neurotic, reactive, or psychotic), whether or not recurrent. If the depressed patient had attempted suicide by poison or drugs, thus causing an acute brain disorder, the primary diagnosis was acute brain disorder, the secondary one depressive reaction.

Paranoid Disorders

Paranoid disorders can be subdivided into paranoid states characterized by a well-organized system of paranoid delusions with or without hallucinations and with little or no evidence of intellectual impairment associated with organic brain disease, psychotic paranoid reactions associated with disturbance in intellectual function related to chronic brain disease, and acute brain syndromes in patients with paranoid or schizophrenic personality patterns of many years' duration.

Problem Drinkers

Any person who drank so much that it interfered with his social and economic adjustment was diagnosed as a problem drinker. If at admission the patient was in a state of alcohol intoxication, the primary diagnosis was problem drinking; if he manifested an acute brain disorder, that was the primary diagnosis, and problem drinking became the secondary diagnosis.

Other Types

Miscellaneous disorders without organic brain disease, such as personality disorders or situational maladjustments, were classified "other." Sometimes the diagnosis was undetermined because of lack of information, too short a hospital stay, and the like.

PROBLEMS OF MULTIPLE DIAGNOSIS

The primary diagnosis was the clinical condition which precipitated the patient's admission to the psychiatric ward of the hospital. Examples are the increasingly severe symptoms associated with a chronic brain disorder like senile or arteriosclerotic psychosis, an acute brain disorder because of alcohol as the primary diagnosis with long-term problem drinking as the secondary diagnosis, or an acute brain disorder as the primary diagnosis with a long-term chronic arteriosclerotic or senile brain disorder the secondary diagnosis, and so on.

Secondary and tertiary diagnoses were based on duration. For example, a sixty-five-year-old man who had been a problem drinker for twenty years attempted suicide by swallowing a large dose of barbiturates after a depression of four months. He was admitted to the hospital in a coma. The primary diagnosis was acute brain syndrome, the secondary one depression, and the tertiary one problem drinking. A triple diagnosis common to problem drinkers is a primary diagnosis of acute brain syndrome (clouded, confused state) of a few days' duration, a secondary diagnosis of chronic brain disorder (chronic alcoholic encephalopathy) of a few months' to several years' duration, and a tertiary diagnosis of prolonged problem drinking.

To illustrate, an example of a case which required multiple diagnostic categories follows.

A white man of seventy-two was admitted to the psychiatric ward after he had abruptly lost consciousness and fallen to the street. On awakening a few minutes later, he spoke incoherently and was grossly disoriented, confused, argumentative, and resistive to assistance. In the hospital his condition cleared rapidly, and by the second day he was a physically vigorous, highly intelligent, literate man, although still somewhat dazed and mentally sluggish. There were no other signs of intellectual impairment. On the whole, he appeared five years younger than his given age. By the fourth day he was, his close friends said, "back to his old self." In the physical and neurologic examinations, a blood pressure of 160/110 and a bilateral inguinal hernia were found. His performance on the WAIS verbal subtests indicated an I.Q. of over 120.

Although the patient had long been treated for essential hypertension, the present episode was the first evidence of cerebral disease. Since his retirement at sixty-five from his position as a sales clerk, he had worked part time as a watchman. Divorced, he lived in a hotel room. He actively participated in a religious group. His obsessive-compulsive reaction patterns were strong, but never disabling, his intellectual pursuits somewhat esoteric, but absorbing.

At his own request he was discharged from the hospital with the recommendation that he seek outpatient care under his health plan. The primary diagnosis was acute brain syndrome associated with cerebral arteriosclerosis.

During the next six months he was readmitted to the psychiatric ward four times and was committed to a mental hospital twice. Four days after his first discharge, he was readmitted because he attempted suicide. Because of his obvious depression, he was committed to a state hospital from which he was discharged in six weeks, after his depression had quickly lifted. A month later he was returned to the psychiatric ward on transfer from another hospital because of his agitation and confusion for two nights after a bilateral hernia repair under spinal anesthesia. He recognized staff personnel on the psychiatric ward, but for the first time he was suspicious, vaguely referring to plots. Commitment to a state hospital was recommended. By his fifth day at the hospital he had recovered sufficiently to convince the judge to discharge him. Twice in the next two months he was readmitted to the psychiatric ward: once he became acutely confused during argument with a neighbor; the other time he roused his neighbors at night with shouts that someone was trying to kill him. During both readmissions his moderate confusion partially cleared. The first time he was discharged against medical advice; the second time he admitted that he had been fasting as penance for about a week, and he was again committed to a state hospital.

In the six-month interval the patient had aged grossly in physical appearance and mental performance. Stooped, thin, mildly tremulous, he was easily irritated, and his memory was impaired. He would become confused under relatively minor emotional stress.

After three weeks in the state hospital, he demanded a rehearing, and, although he had some residual impairment of his intellectual functions, he had again improved enough to be considered legally competent, and the court discharged him to his own care. Thereafter, he could not be located.

A progressive organic brain disease was evident in this patient. Four of his five admissions had been prompted by acute, self-limited, confusional episodes. The first admission followed a small cerebral infarct; the second, an attempt at suicide during a state of depression as he faced aging and potential loss of his intellectual skills; the third, surgery; the fourth, during intense emotional involvement; and the fifth, after a brief, self-induced dietary deficiency. At different periods the patient displayed acute confusional states, depression, transient paranoid delusions and ideas of reference, and, after the onset of his illness, a deterioration of his intellectual functions.

Despite evidence of some chronic organic brain disease in this case, the acute episodes should not be dismissed as only part of a chronic brain process, nor would a unitary diagnosis of "chronic brain syndrome—improved" after each episode fit the whole clinical picture. The chronic process undoubtedly impaired the patient's psychobiologic reserve and ability to compensate for the disturbance of homeostasis. The episodes, however, were apparently precipitated by a combination of psychologic, interpersonal, and physiologic insults. Each episode may have exacerbated and advanced the chronic process, yet it is useful to view each episode as an entity, primarily an acute process—potentially reversible to some degree—superimposed on a chronic process which is probably progressive.

DISTRIBUTION BY DIAGNOSIS

Of the study group of 530 patients, only 143 (27 per cent) were admitted for symptoms or behavior primarily associated with chronic brain disease. Of these, senile brain disease was the most common form of chronic illness (14 per cent of the 530 patients), followed by cerebral arteriosclerosis (8 per cent), a group of miscellaneous disorders (3 per cent), and chronic alcoholic encephalopathy (2 per cent).

In the majority (55 per cent) of the patients, acute brain syndrome was the primary diagnosis, based on disturbances of behavior or psychologic function associated with recent physical disease. In 9 per cent of the 530 patients a primary diagnosis was affective disorder, in 4 per cent schizoid disorder, in 2 per cent problem drinking without any evidence of organic brain disease, and in 3 per cent miscellaneous psychogenic disorders.

The acute brain disorders were of relatively equal frequency in all age groups, but the chronic organic disorders became more frequent with increasing age; the depressions, paranoid disorders, and problem drinking were concentrated in the youngest group (sixty to seventy). Men consistently showed more acute brain disorder at all ages than did women.

A comparison of the diagnoses of all 765 patients sixty and over who were admitted in 1959 indicates that the 235 patients who were excluded from the study group (largely because of hospitalization before the age of sixty) had a far higher proportion of psychogenic disorders than did the 530 in the study group, none of whom had entered psychiatric wards before the age of sixty. Of the 235 patients excluded, 48 per cent were diagnosed by the hospital staff as suffering primarily from depression, paranoid disorder, problem drinking, or miscellaneous functional disorders, compared with only 18 per cent of the study group in these diagnostic categories. In contrast, organic brain disease, either acute or chronic, accounted for 82 per cent of the study group but only 41 per cent of the excluded group. In 11 per cent of the cases the diagnosis was undetermined.

Chronic Brain Disorders

Of the 530 patients, 316 (60 per cent) were diagnosed as having chronic senile or arteriosclerotic brain disease as one aspect of their clinical picture. Of these 316 cases, a combination of senile and arteriosclerotic symptoms was noted in sixty-nine cases (22 per cent). In 102 (32 per cent), only chronic arteriosclerotic symptoms were noted, and in 145 (46 per cent), only chronic senile symptoms were noted. This distribution agrees closely with that of the clinical-neuro-pathologic study (Simon & Malamud, 1953). In 167 of the 316 cases, the chronic senile or arteriosclerotic process had a superimposed acute brain disorder. Behavioral disturbance associated with acute brain disorder precipitated the patient's admission to the hospital. In 115 cases the chronic disorder was a primary diagnosis. In general, a steady deterioration of behavior and intellectual functions, sometimes associated with incontinence, brought these patients to the hospital. In the remaining thirty-four cases the chronic brain disorder, usually mild, was present, but the symptoms for which the patient was admitted were primarily those of a superimposed depression, paranoid reaction, drinking problem, or severe personality disorder. The duration of the chronic senile or arteriosclerotic process varied from one to ten or more years.

The twenty-six patients who had miscellaneous chronic brain disorders included those with disorders attributed to exogenous trauma, syphilis, epilepsy, birth injury, and cases of unknown etiology. In twelve of the twenty-six cases, acute brain syndrome, often associated with problem drinking, was superimposed on the chronic brain disorder.

Alcoholism

In 107 patients (20 per cent) excessive drinking had constituted a problem, usually for many years. The extent of alcoholism in the community in people sixty and over is unknown, but surely not one of every five such people is a problem drinker. In some instances, the patient's excessive drinking was revealed during the study, but alcoholism was not the main reason for the patient's admission in all cases. About twice as many men as women were problem drinkers—seventy-two men (28 per cent of the men in the sample) against thirty-five women (12 per cent of the women in the sample). With both men and women the proportion of people with an alcoholic problem decreased with advancing years. In the entire sample of sixty- to sixty-four-year-old people, twenty-one men (49 per cent) and thirteen women (42 per cent) were alcoholics, but only two men over eighty and relatively few women over seventy were alcoholics.

The 107 alcoholics could be divided into five groups: those without any associated organic brain disease (fourteen), those with chronic alcoholic brain disease without an acute brain disorder (ten), those with an acute brain syndrome superimposed on chronic alcoholic brain disease (twenty-nine), those with an acute brain disorder without evidence of chronic brain disease (thirty-nine), and those with an associated senile or arteriosclerotic brain disorder (fifteen, seven of them with an acute brain syndrome).

Of the alcoholics, thirty-nine (36 per cent) had some evidence of chronic alcoholic brain disease. Of the seventy-five (70 per cent) who were admitted with an acute brain syndrome, usually associated with a recent drinking bout and malnutrition, twenty-nine had evidence of chronic alcoholic brain disease, and forty-six did not. In general, there were two acute confusional states: one resembled delirium tremens with hallucinations, delusions, and disturbance in intellectual function; the other was a dull, clouded amnestic state without delusions or hallucinations, a state which persisted for a few days after the effects of the acute alcoholic intoxication had passed. There were no cases of alcoholic hallucinosis (auditory hallucinations without disturbance in intellectual function).

The fact that problem drinking accompanied evidence of senile brain disease in seven patients and of cerebral arteriosclerosis in eight indicates the difficulty of diagnosis. Clinically, it is impossible to differentiate in such patients the proportionate roles of alcoholism and senile or arteriosclerotic brain disease in the development of the chronic brain disease.

Alcoholism is a serious problem, and this group of geriatric patients must be considered in any preventive public health measures directed at alcoholism. To be sure, this is a select sample, since the hospital and psychiatric receiving ward policy is to admit only those alcoholics who are overtly psychotic or who request admission so they can be committed to a mental hospital for care and treatment.

There were three common drinking patterns. First, there was a pattern of problem drinking since early adult life with no history of psychiatric hospitalization, although the patient may have had a history of arrests or medical hospitalization; most of this group had evidence of chronic alcoholic brain disease. Another pattern was heavy social drinking as an adult. The drinking did not seriously interfere with occupational adjustment. After the age of sixty or after retirement, drinking increased or tolerance for alcohol decreased, leading to behavioral disturbance that precipitated admission to a psychiatric hospital. A third pattern of drinking, usually that of the female abstainer or light social drinker, was discovering the delights of muscatel or port after sixty.

Acute Brain Syndromes

Of the study group, 287 patients (55 per cent) had the primary diagnosis of acute brain disorder. The incidence was relatively the same for all age groups, though significantly higher in men than in women (60 per cent of the men contrasted with 48 per cent of the women). The acute brain syndromes resulted from a variety of causes: malnutrition (24 per cent), cerebral hypoxia associated with cardiac insufficiency (21 per cent), alcohol (15 per cent), cerebrovascular accidents (11 per cent), and ingestion of drugs and toxins, including patients who attempted suicide thereby and were hospitalized in a state of impaired consciousness superimposed on an underlying depressive disorder (7 per cent). The common types of physiologic disorder connected with acute brain disorder—febrile pulmonary disease (4 per cent), cerebral trauma (3 per cent), renal insufficiency (2 per cent), postoperative deliria (2 per cent), and diabetic acidosis (1 per cent)—were relatively few in our series. Perhaps such conditions are promptly diagnosed by physicians outside the hospital or in the admitting room, and the patients are sent to a medical rather than a psychiatric ward. In addition, 6 per cent of the patients had such diverse physiologic disturbances as carcinoma, convulsive disorder, or disseminated lupus erythematosis; in 4 per cent of the cases the associated physiologic disturbance could not be identified.

The acute disorder was superimposed on an underlying chronic brain disorder in 218 of the 287 cases with a primary diagnosis of acute brain syndrome. In the other sixty-nine cases, depression was present in fifteen, alcoholism in thirty-one, no diagnosis other than acute brain syndrome in twenty, and other diagnoses in three.

Affective Disorders

Of the 530 patients, sixty-nine (13 per cent) had affective disorders. They were diagnosed as depressive disorder (manic-depressive, involutional, psychotic, or neurotic) either alone or combined with another diagnosis. Forty-six of these patients were without evidence of acute or chronic organic brain disease. Of the other twenty-three patients, seven had an associated chronic brain disease (senile, arteriosclerotic, or alcoholic), and sixteen were admitted primarily because of an acute brain disorder, attributed in the majority of cases to ingestion of drugs or poisons in attempted suicide. The depressive disorders without concomitant chronic brain disease occurred before seventy-five, whether or not they were associated with problem drinking or a personality disorder. In the seven patients with the combined diagnosis of depressive disorder and chronic brain disorder, the intellectual disturbance was mild.

The proportion of patients with affective disorders (13 per cent of the total sample) is certainly much smaller than that reported by Roth (1955). In all probability such factors as selection, methods of admission, social class, and availability of treatment facilities other than a mental hospital are of importance in explaining the difference.

Paranoid Disorders

The diagnoses of the thirty patients with paranoid disorders can be divided into three subgroups: (1) paranoid states without associated evidence of disturbance in intellectual function related to organic brain disease, (2) psychotic paranoid reactions associated with such a disturbance, and (3) acute brain syndrome reactions in people with schizoid or paranoid personality patterns.

There were almost three times as many females (twenty-two) as males (eight) in the paranoid group, two-thirds of them (nineteen) between sixty and sixty-nine. About half lived alone (sixteen), and nearly half with others (fourteen). There were thirteen widows and one widower. Six patients were single, six married, three separated or divorced, and one of unknown marital status. Although most of the patients had long been suspicious and withdrawn, frank delusions had not developed until after the age of fifty. Behavior related to the paranoid delusional system consisted of complaints to the police about

people's following or threatening them, a wife's accusing her husband
of infidelity, or neighbors' complaints about the filthy condition of the
patient's room or apartment. Such behavior usually precipitated the
hospitalization.

Of the seventeen patients (twelve females, five males) diagnosed as suffering from paranoid states without evidence of organic
brain disease, almost all had fairly poor vision, and three had impaired hearing. The clinical picture was generally characterized by
delusions of persecution (police, neighbors, Communists, spouse's infidelity) and occasionally by hallucinations. Personal deterioration was
seen in increasingly slovenly personal habits and a tendency to lose
interest in food or adopt dietary fads, which resulted in malnutrition.
Paranoid states in the aged occurred most often in the youngest group
(sixty to sixty-nine) and mostly in single or widowed females.

Of the six patients diagnosed as having paranoid disturbances
associated with a chronic brain disorder because of either senile or
arteriosclerotic brain disease, three were in their seventies and three
in their eighties. At least five of the six had had overt paranoid delusional ideas for seven or more years. Their paranoid symptoms had
brought them to the attention of authorities, who were requested to
arrange hospital care. During the course of psychiatric and psychologic
examinations, significant decreases in the level of intellectual functions
were noted. The duration of the symptoms ascribed to a chronic
brain disease was estimated at several years and judged gradual in
development. Of the six patients, five had moderately impaired vision
and hearing.

An acute brain syndrome was superimposed on long-term
paranoid personality reaction patterns in seven patients, of whom
three lived alone and four with others. Visual and auditory problems
were moderately severe. A female patient of sixty-five who lived with
her alcoholic husband and who was a problem drinker herself had an
acute brain syndrome, apparently the result of her alcoholism. A widow
of sixty-five had moved often during the past three years because she
felt persecuted by a priest and the police. She ate poorly, and an acute
confusional state had developed. In a sixty-seven-year-old widow congestive failure and an acute brain syndrome had developed; she had
had a stroke two years before admission and a hip fracture with
surgical reduction five months before.

In summary, this group of paranoid patients was mostly
women between sixty and sixty-nine, widowed for many years or single.
They came to the attention of the police, family, or neighbors and

were referred to the hospital primarily because of their paranoid delusions.

In paranoid patients with chronic brain disease, it remains to be seen whether the resulting intellectual deterioration is progressive, and, if it is, how the rate of deterioration compares with that of patients with chronic brain disease without paranoid manifestations. As a rule such manifestations occur in people over seventy, when senile and arteriosclerotic brain changes are more common. The acute brain syndromes in this group occurred in the late sixties and seventies, usually precipitated by a vitamin deficiency associated with malnutrition or by congestive heart failure.

SUMMARY

A study of the admissions to a psychiatric receiving ward of a metropolitan general hospital has been carried out to define and evaluate the mentally ill geriatric population, the types of illnesses leading to hospitalization, and the social, psychological, and medical factors involved. The admissions and dispositions of these patients are affected by the alternative facilities available for care; by the hospital policies of admission and treatment; by the attitudes of patients and the community toward aging, mental illness, and psychiatric hospitalization; and by the manner of dealing with critical situations.

In this specific community, the majority of elderly patients studied were committed to state mental hospitals, but none was abandoned to public institutions by families evading their responsibilities. In general the patients came from the lower economic strata—either lower-middle or lower class groups—and had very limited incomes. Most of them lived in their own houses or apartments, but a sizable number lived in hotels or rooming houses or came to the psychiatric ward from other medical facilities. Almost half of the total lived alone.

In general many patients suffered individually from several conditions. In such cases, the diagnosis consisted of the primary diagnosis—the clinical condition that induced the patient's admission—and the secondary and tertiary conditions, which were usually long-term conditions.

In slightly more than half the patients, an acute brain syndrome was the primary condition that resulted in the patient's hospitalization. The acute brain syndrome was often superimposed on an underlying chronic brain disease ascribed to senile, arteriosclerotic, or alcoholic brain disorders. For the most part, the acute

brain syndrome resulted from such causes as malnutrition, cerebral
hypoxia associated with cardiac insufficiency, alcoholism, or cerebrovascular accidents.

In about one-fourth of the group, the primary diagnosis was
chronic brain disease; in one-fifth alcoholism constituted a problem,
although often it was not the primary cause for admission; about one-
eighth suffered from affective disorders, the majority of them without
evidence of chronic brain disease.

REFERENCES

Blain, D. Commitment of aged persons to state hospitals. Circular letter,
    Jan. 3, 1961, No. 2298, with attachment. (Dept. of Mental Hygiene,
    Sacramento, California)

Department of Mental Hygiene. California statistical report for year ending
    June 30, 1956. Sacramento: Author, 1957.

Department of Mental Hygiene. California statistical report, biennium ending
    June 30, 1958. Sacramento: Author, 1960.

Department of Public Health. *California's older people—their health prob-
    lems.* Berkeley: Author, 1959.

Gellerstedt, N. *Zur kenntnis der hirnveränderungen bei der normalen alter-
    involution.* Uppsala: Almquist & Wiksells Boktryckeri A.B., 1933.

Goldfarb, A.I. Current trends in the management of the psychiatrically ill
    aged. In P.H. Hoch & J. Zubin (Eds.), *Psychopathology of aging.*
    New York: Grune & Stratton, 1961, Pp. 248-265. (a)

Goldfarb, A.I. Summarization of survey findings from the office of consultant
    on services for the aged. In *The autumn years.* Annual report
    (legislative document), 1961, No. 79. (Joint Legislative Committee
    on Problems of the Aging, New York) (b)

Governor's Conference on Care and Treatment of Senile Patients. Report
    from California department of mental hygiene, Sept. 8, 1950.
    (Sacramento, Calif.)

Malzberg, B. *Cohort studies of mental disease in New York state, 1943-1949.*
    New York: National Association for Mental Health, 1958.

Pollack, E.S., Person, P.H., Jr., Kramer, M., & Goldstein, H. Patterns of
    retention, release and death of first admissions to state mental
    hospitals. *Publ. Hlth Monogr.*, 1959, **58**, 1-52.

Roth, M. The natural history of mental disorder in old age. *J. ment. Sci.*,
    1955, **101**, 281-301.

Rothschild, D. Senile psychoses and psychoses with cerebral arteriosclerosis.
    In O.J. Kaplan (Ed.), *Mental disorders in later life.* (2nd ed.)
    Stanford: Stanford University Press, 1956. Pp. 289-331.

Shanas, Ethel. Family responsibility and the health of older people. *J. Geront.*,
    1960, **15**, 408-411.

Shindell, S., & Cornfield, Elizabeth. Aged in Connecticut state mental hos-
    pitals. *J. Amer. med. Ass.*, 1956, **160**, 1121-1125.

Simon, A., & Malamud, N. The inadequacy of clinical diagnosis in geriatric psychoses. Paper presented at Gerontological Society, San Francisco, 1953.

U.S. Bureau of the Census, 1960. *Population characteristics: Final reports.* Vol. 1, chapters A and B. Washington, D.C.: U.S. Government Printing Office, 1961.

U.S. Department of Health, Education, & Welfare. Patients in mental institutions 1957. *Public Hlth Serv. Pub.,* Part II, 1960, No. 715. (U.S. Government Printing Office, Washington, D.C.)

Whittier, J.R., & Korenyi, C. Selected biological, medical and psychiatric characteristics of male patients aged 60 and over upon admission to state hospital for the first time. In J. Wortis (Ed.), *Recent advances in biological psychiatry, 3.* New York: Grune & Stratton, 1961. Pp. 93-95.

SECTION II

*Psychological
Processes and Variables*

CHAPTER 22

*On Becoming
an Institutionalized Aged Person*

MORTON A. LIEBERMAN and
MARTIN LAKIN

This investigation explores the psychological processes of an aged person's transition from relative autonomy in the community to residence in an old age home.[1] We wished to determine the effect of impending institutionalization on the older person's view of himself and others. We wanted to know how he construed the institutional setting prior to entering it and what modifications in self-percept he found necessary in making the transition to institutional life.[2] We were interested in the meaning that institutionalization has for a person and in the kinds of ego maneuvers he found necessary to make this crucial step a palatable one.

[1] We wish to thank Ben Grossman, director, and the staff of the Drexel Home for the Aged for their cooperation in carrying out this study.
[2] The study was supported by a research grant (M-2379) from the National Institutes of Public Health, Public Health Service.

Considerable research has been done on the aged who are already in institutions, and virtually all investigators in this area have stressed the important situational factors like loss of income, job, and self-esteem which precede institutionalization. Psychotherapeutic work with institutionalized aged (Goldfarb, 1953; Goldfarb, 1956; Hollender, 1952) has been the basis for conclusions regarding affective and intellective disturbances among the aged. A Rorschach study of institutionalized aged (Davidson & Kruglov, 1952) listed the attributes of their impaired level of over-all adjustment. Laverty (1950) concluded, on the basis of her comparison of the relative adjustments of institutionalized aged with those living at home in a more-or-less conventional community pattern, that institutionalization accelerates mental and physical deterioration. Replacement therapies have sought to introduce worklike recreation into the institutional setting on the assumption that such activities would help sustain the self-image of a person of consequence (Lakin & Dray, 1958; Weil, 1953).

More general views of the psychological status of the aged emphasize the psychological and physical limitations of this group. Banham (1951), Pollack (1948), and Gitelson (1940) considered the impairments of aging in detail. Banham emphasized the potential utility of certain psychological limitations (like reduced emotional responsiveness) for the aged person in the face of disruptive interpersonal stimuli. Gitelson viewed psychological deficit in the aged as the product of interaction between developmental and environmental factors.

These studies indicate the need for investigation of the nonpsychiatrically ill aged prior to institutionalization. The factors of psychiatric disturbance and institutionalization may affect personality and performance so adversely that they severely limit the ability to generalize on conclusions about already hospitalized or institutionalized elderly people.

Birren (1958) regards adjustment to institutionalization as a deep and pervasive process for the individual. Meerloo (1953), citing cases in which aged individuals were able to resist the psychological implications of difficult circumstances until they had to move, considers that for the aged the prospect of change from a familiar surrounding becomes a symbol of approaching death. Meerloo also argues that the sexual drives (libido) of the aged are still active, though denied normal channels for expression. Newman and Nichols (1960) studied sexual activity among the noninstitutionalized normal aged and found that sexual activity is actually maintained longer and with greater frequency than had been thought.

The transition from conventional autonomous or semi-autonomous living to living in a home for the aged—no matter how benevolent—probably arouses ambivalent feelings in the applicant. On one hand, he may feel that this is the only solution for him, and he may even look forward to the protective social environment it promises. On the other hand, there may be feelings of anger, rejection, dread, and an even further lowering of his already damaged self-esteem. It is clear that such inferences, based on institutional populations or on psychiatric samples, will not provide appropriate data for the evaluation of this problem. It is necessary to study the individuals in this transition in order to understand their interpretations of it.

THE STUDY

This study is a descriptive study. The central question it sets out to study is how the individual who has made a decision to enter a home for the aged views himself in relation to the institution. How does he experience the change from life in the community to institutional life? Specifically, the investigation focused on expectations about interpersonal experiences, conceptions of self, comparisons between male and female responses about anticipated institutionalization, characteristics of the transition period, and modifications in self-concept and interpersonal expectations following institutionalization.

The data presented in this study were collected over six months. Twenty-two subjects (nine men and thirteen women) were seen during this period. Two classes of people were studied: those whose entrance to the institution was imminent, and those who had recently (within a two-week period) been placed on the home's waiting list to wait up to one year for admission. Those entering immediately had been on the waiting list for a period ranging from several months to one year. All candidates admitted to the home or placed on the home's waiting list during a six-month period were included in the study population. The average age of the female subjects was seventy-seven, ranging from sixty-four to eighty-nine; the average age of the male subjects was seventy-nine, ranging from sixty-one to ninety. These figures approximate the general admission ages for the institution. The majority of the population was widows or widowers, with the death of the spouse ranging from three to forty-eight years prior to admission. The men in the population tended to be widowed more recently than the women had been. None of the men studied was single; almost half the women were. Most of the men had been employed in small businesses; a few had been skilled workers. The women who had worked had been employed in needle trades or white-collar jobs. Since half the population was foreign-born, no reliable information is available on their level of education by American standards.

The admissions policy of the home for the aged is geared to relieve various social, psychological, economic, and medical problems for the applicant. The institution classifies its population as ambulatory (needing no special physical care), semiambulatory (needing some special physical care), and bedridden. Only one of the subjects was sufficiently disabled to be listed as semiambulatory. Although one-quarter and one-fifth of the subjects had medical and economic problems, respectively, the most frequent problem (approximately 80 per cent) was psychological. Included were such concerns as "fear of being alone," "wish for congregate living," or "feelings of inability to care for self."

The study was conducted with the cooperation of the Drexel Home for the Aged, which is affiliated with the Jewish Federation of Chicago. All admissions are voluntary, and psychiatric and medical screening is routine. The home's services, currently administered to approximately two hundred and twenty-five residents, include medical care, physical and occupational therapy, and religious, social, and educational programs.

The data of the study were the subjects' responses to a specially constructed series of TAT-type cards. The writers' experience was that interviewing seemed to make the subject feel threatened about admission and to elicit relatively conscious resistance when the institution became the focus. A comparison of the TAT and interview data on the same subjects suggests that the projective instrument overcame this resistance.

The series of drawings depicted a range of situations considered characteristic of the transition to institutional living. Where the institution was involved, the details were closely patterned after its actual physical plant. Figures were drawn to suggest ambiguous attitudes, although age differentiations were made clear. The original drawings were in charcoal. They were photographed and enlarged to 11×14 cards. The series was constructed to provide alternate forms for male and female subjects. The situations depicted and the hypothesized stimulus demand follow.

1. An aged person packing a suitcase as several people depicting younger adults and children stand in the foreground and background—separation and/or rejection.
2. An aged person walking down the path into a building clearly signified as an old-age institution—personal entry into the institution.
3. A group of aged men and women in a large room showing a typical formal institutional setting—group situation.
4. An aged person entering a room clearly marked as the office of an institutional director who is drawn as a middle-aged man—relationships to an authority figure.
5. Four aged people, two men and two women, sitting around a dining-room table in an institutional setting—intimate group relations.
6. An aged person in a wheel chair being pushed by another aged person of the same sex with a hospital aide in background—reaction to the feelings of incapacitation and dependency.
7. Two aged people of the same sex sitting in a bedroom drawn to represent a typical room in the institution—interpersonal relationships.
8. An aged man and woman sitting on a park bench outside the institution—heterosexual relationships.

Instructions to the subjects followed those established for TAT administration. Most of the subjects were interviewed and tested in their own homes after a social worker had contacted them. Several were seen during a preliminary visit to the home. For evaluation of postinstitutionalization processes, it was possible to retest seven of the subjects in the home.

Clinical impressions gleaned from inspection of the TAT protocols were tested by a more controlled method. Two rating systems were developed. The first categorized response aspects specific to each card; these included dimensions of place, person, interpersonal and personal anticipations, major identifications, and feeling tone. The marginal entries in Table 1 give the categories for the set of cards. The second system categorized self-concepts. Table 2 shows the areas of self-concept covered by this system.

TABLE 1
RATINGS OF TAT CARDS
(Percentages of response categories)

TAT Card	Category	Total	Male	Female	Preinstitutionalization	Postinstitutionalization
1	a) Setting					
	Noninstitution*	66	88	44	84	67
	Institution	19	0	33	17	17
	Other	14	11	16	0	17
	b) Identification of hero					
	Like self	75	66	83	84	67
	Unlike self	9	11	8	0	17
	No information	14	22	8	17	17
	c) Stimulus demand					
	Denial	38	44	33	33	33
	Recognition	61	55	66	67	50
	No information	0	0	0	0	17
	d) Source of action					
	Self	66	66	66	100	50
	Not self	19	11	17	0	33
	No information	19	22	17	0	17
	e) Reason for action					
	Guilt	9	12	0	17	0
	Independence	38	12	50	50	17

Rejection	9	12	0	0	17
Weakness in others	5	6	0	0	17
Other	19	18	8	17	33
No information	24	36	41	17	17
f) Emotional tone*					
Depressed	38	66	17	50	50
Hopeful	52	22	75	33	33
Other	5	0	8	0	0
No information	5	11	0	17	17
2 a) Hero					
Like self	75	66	83	67	84
Unlike self	24	33	17	33	17
b) Expectation					
Relief from loneliness	40	32	66	67	33
Resignation about death	14	8	22	0	17
Physical survival	23	48	8	17	50
Other	14	16	14	17	0
c) Degree of hope					
Hopeful	25	22	35	33	33
Ambivalent	40	33	35	50	50
Not hopeful	26	33	14	17	17
No information	7	11	0	0	0

TABLE 1 (Cont.)

TAT Card	Category	Total	Male	Female	Preinstitutionalization	Postinstitutionalization
3	**a) Setting**					
	Institution	66	77	58	50	84
	Noninstitution	24	22	25	50	17
	No information	9	0	17	0	0
	b) Interaction					
	Yes	71	88	58	84	50
	Minimal	28	11	42	17	50
	c) Nature of inter-action*					
	Angry-competitive	38	22	50	33	33
	Helpful-giving	19	33	8	33	50
	Passive-resigned	14	0	25	0	0
	Other	19	33	8	33	17
	No information	9	11	8	0	0
	d) Hero†					
	Same sex	47	66	33	50	67
	Opposite sex	24	0	42	17	17
	No information	28	33	25	33	17
	e) Action of hero					
	Ascendance	33	22	42	33	84
	Submissive	14	11	17	17	17

Mixed	14	11	17	17	0
No information	38	55	25	33	0
f) Expectation†					
Support	28	44	17	17	50
Rejection	24	0	42	17	33
Ambivalence	9	11	8	17	17
No information	38	44	33	50	0
g) Type of interaction					
Friendly	33	44	25	33	50
Attack	24	11	33	0	17
Ambivalent	5	11	0	0	17
No information	38	33	25	67	17
4 a) Setting					
Institution	87	77	100	84	84
Noninstitution	11	22	0	17	17
b) Identification of people					
As authority	87	77	100	84	84
As equals	11	22	0	17	17
c) Action of authority*					
Disinterested, un-giving	34	66	9	33	17
Helpful, giving	44	11	72	33	67
Punishing	6	0	9	0	33
No information	15	22	9	33	33

TABLE 1 (Cont.)

TAT Card	Category	Total	Male	Female	Preinstitutionalization	Postinstitutionalization
4 (cont.)	**d) Feeling of hero†**					
	Helped	39	11	63	17	50
	Not helped	25	33	18	33	33
	Mixed	25	33	18	0	0
	No information	10	22	0	50	17
	e) Action of hero					
	Active	29	33	27	17	33
	Passive	44	22	63	33	0
	No information	25	44	9	50	67
	f) Mechanism used by hero					
	Plaintive	38	44	36	50	50
	Assertive	24	22	27	17	17
	Other	14	0	27	17	33
	No information	19	33	9	17	0
5	**a) Setting**					
	Institution	56	66	50	33	50
	Noninstitution	38	33	42	50	50
	No information	5	0	8	17	0
	b) Identifications					
	Home residents	56	66	50	33	50
	Family	33	33	33	50	33
	No information	4	0	17	17	17

c) Age					
All old	70	85	58	50	84
Mixed	20	0	33	33	17
No information	10	15	8	17	0
d) Hero					
No hero	35	37	33	17	50
Hero	35	37	33	33	33
No information	30	25	33	50	17
e) Action of hero					
Active, assertive	24	33	17	17	33
Passive	19	33	8	33	0
No information	56	33	75	50	67
f) Feeling of hero					
Pleasant	27	44	17	17	17
Unpleasant	18	0	33	67	17
Angry	9	22	0	0	17
No information	45	33	49	17	50
g) Expectation					
Help, support	9	0	17	0	33
No help	27	44	16	33	0
Intimacy	18	22	16	33	33
Reject, hostility	23	11	32	17	0
Other	5	0	8	0	17
No information	18	22	16	17	17

TABLE 1 (Cont.)

TAT Card	Category	Total	Male	Female	Preinstitutionalization	Postinstitutionalization
5 (cont.)	**h) Major theme†**					
	Social pleasure	28	0	48	33	50
	Survival	33	62	16	33	0
	Other	9	0	16	0	0
	No information	28	36	24	33	50
6	**a) Setting**					
	Institution	94	88	100	84	50
	Noninstitution	6	11	0	17	50
	b) Hero					
	Being pushed	75	88	66	100	67
	No information	25	11	34	0	33
	c) Nature of impairment					
	Permanent	52	66	42	67	84
	Temporary	14	11	17	17	0
	No information	33	22	42	17	17
7	**a) Setting**					
	Institution	75	77	75	67	67
	Noninstitution	9	11	8	0	17
	No information	14	11	17	33	17

b) Amount of interaction					
Intense	33	22	42	50	17
Moderate	24	33	17	17	33
Superficial	38	44	33	33	50
No information	5	0	8		
c) Relationship					
Passive, dependent	19	22	33	0	0
Supportive	52	44	58	67	67
Competitive	19	11	25	0	17
No information	9	22	0	33	17
d) Expectation‡					
Warmth, support, sympathy	33	11	50	67	33
Nothing	28	66	0	17	17
Rejection, anger	14	11	17	0	17
Other	24	11	33	17	33
a) Setting					
Institution	47	33	58	33	84
Noninstitution	28	33	25	33	17
No information	24	33	17	33	0
b) Age of characters					
Retained	80	88	75	84	100
Reduced	9	0	17	17	0
No information	9	11	8	0	0

8

TABLE 1 (Cont.)

TAT Card	Category	Total	Male	Female	Preinstitutionalization	Postinstitutionalization
8 (cont.)	c) Orientation to time					
	Growth	44	42	44	50	17
	Momentary	38	22	50	33	67
	No information	19	33	8	17	17
	d) Expectation					
	Love	28	33	25	33	0
	Companionship	28	0	50	17	84
	Listener	28	44	17	50	17
	Other	9	11	8	0	0
	No information	5	11	0	0	0
	e) Amount of investment					
	High	47	33	58	50	0
	Moderate	9	11	8	0	50
	Low	42	55	33	50	50

* = 05 level of significance
† = .10 level of significance
‡ = .01 level of significanee

TABLE 2
SELF-CONCEPT DESCRIPTIONS

Descriptive category	Frequency of descriptive words	
	Male	Female
Self as rejected	10	13
Loss of power		
*a. Physical	25	4
†b. Interpersonal	37	17
*c. Total	62	21
Needing external supplies	24	14
Preserved power		
a. Sexual	4	5
b. Interpersonal	2	12
c. Mental	1	4
*d. Total	7	21
Self as angry	14	11
Self as hopeless		
a. Interpersonal loss	16	10
b. Feeling	5	14
c. Total	21	24
Self as fearful	10	6
Self as guilty	2	4
*Self as express positive feelings	10	33

*= .001 level of significance
†= .01 level of significance

For the specific category ratings, the series of TAT protocols was rated card by card rather than person by person in order to establish the central tendencies of the group in the dimensions being studied. It was felt that this method would minimize the tendency to respond to unique personality characteristics. The only information about the respondent that was given to the rater was the sex of the subject. Raters independently rated a selection of the cards, and a comparison yielded substantial agreement with the original rating. The majority of the discrepancies in the ratings appeared where quantitative judgment of degree was involved. Some examples of these dimensions were such items as degree of hope, degree of feelings of being helped, and so on. Disagreement was rare when only a categorical judgment was necessary.

To analyze the data relevant to self-concept, the rating procedure identified the main character for each story. All phrases or words describing the main character were culled from the stories by a rater who had no previous contact with the data. From 294 statements this procedure produced approximately ninety adjectives which were organized in a few descriptive categories. Two independent raters then sorted the 294 adjectives into the nine categories. Seventy-seven per cent of the time the raters agreed on which of the nine categories an adjective should be placed in.

RESULTS

The TAT cards presented to the subjects depicted two general categories of interpersonal relationships. Cards 3, 5, 6, 7, and 8 depict situations where the relationship is between peers. Cards 1 and 4 depict scenes in which the central relationship is between aged and younger persons. Card 2 shows a solitary, aged individual.

Interpersonal Relations

We first studied the series of cards that depict peer relationships; the most striking qualitative aspect of these cards is the lack of gratification expected in a relationship with another human being. The authors were impressed by the lack of satisfaction that one person expected from another and by the absence of any engagement in the relationship. The following stories are selected to illustrate this point.

Subject 1, male, age eighty-six, TAT Card 3:

[Long deliberation.] Well, these are old people in a home. They are not doing nothing. They are talking. One man looks like he's praying or looking at something. This fellow looks like he's telling something to the other one. [Probe.] I don't know what he's saying. It's a hard thing for me to know. They look like they are home people. They are sitting down. [Probe about feeling.] They are comfortable; having a chat with one another. [Probe about past.] That I couldn't say. I couldn't know what to guess. [Probe about future.] They're getting old. That might be the end of it [laughs]. Oh, we'll all go some time.

Subject 2, male, age ninety, TAT Card 7:

They're discussing something. They are very old—older than me. They're discussing, but I don't know what. Politics, or about indigestion. They feel in good health. [Probe.] I don't know, my imagination isn't good any more. They look to be content to me. I suppose they are in one room—there are two beds. [Probe.] Well, they are not angry looking. Each room has a window. Look to be content, dressed clean. [Probe.] I told you, what can happen? They go to sleep when their time comes.

Subject 20, female, age seventy, TAT Card 5:

I imagine this is in the home. It is some Friday night meal. He looks as if he's making a prayer. They all have pious expressions on their face. Well, I think they all have their individual thoughts. Their thoughts are all withdrawn. [Probe.] Well, I think, as I said before, it looks like some kind of religious holiday, and he's praying before they indulge in food. [Probe.] Nothing particular that I can see. [Probe.] It's all within their hearts. They have feelings of sadness and gladness. It's in their hearts. No one is given their lives to live over. Time goes quickly.

These stories are typical. The projected interaction may be compared to descriptions of children's parallel play, in which the degree of interaction and interpersonal satisfaction stems from the generalized presence of another person rather than from anything specific that the other person can give. Although the situations portrayed in the stories are interpersonal, the degree of contact between the people seems to signify that very little specific gratification can be obtained from another person.

The lack of anticipated gratification in interpersonal relations seemed to contrast markedly with the subjects' avowed desire for congregate living as a motive for seeking admission to the home. Ratings of the hero's motives in Card 2 show that the dominant motive for entering the home was relief from loneliness (Table 1). If one accepts the thesis that the motives attributed to the main characters are less open to conscious manipulation than the verbal reports are, it appears that the subjects need an interpersonal situation to alleviate the seemingly painful experience of loneliness. It also appears, however, that contact with others for relief of loneliness does not necessarily involve specific expectations of gratification from the other person; it appears that just the presence of a "generalized other person" is sufficient to provide some relief.

In attempting to understand the character of these interpersonal relationships, the investigators considered several different

possibilities. One was that the lack of expected interpersonal gratification was not specific to the particular age or transitional situation.
We asked whether the low level of interpersonal expectation might
not be a product of long-standing patterns of poor relations with
others. Unfortunately the case histories did not allow a careful check
of this hypothesis. The data did indicate, however, that, in a formal
sense at least, the majority had had long interpersonal relationships
with spouses, children, and others. Thus, the investigators did not
think that a previously low level of interpersonal relationships was
sufficient to account for the current phenomena.

Because the past levels of interpersonal relationships were
not an adequate explanation of the current findings, we turned to the
contemporary level of the subjects' functioning. At first we wondered
whether this degree of interpersonal gratification (simply being with
others) was all that the subjects could accept. Impoverishment of the
ego and the possible regressive phenomena noted in the object relationships might account for this type of interpersonal relation. Such a
hypothesis seemed to fit many responses. It became apparent, however,
that the parallel-play phenomenon does not take precedence in all
relationships for all subjects. In fact, it was rare that any one subject
described this type of interpersonal relation throughout the series of
cards. Because there were TAT situations in which the aged person
could portray an interpersonal relationship in which there was specific
gratification, a hypothesis that relied solely on the effects of impoverished egos was not adequate. It seemed, rather, that, when the
subject told a story in which little or no specific gratification came
from the interpersonal relationship, he was saying, in essence, that he
could not hope to get anything from someone else. The dampening
of interpersonal expectation seemed related to a basic ego defense—a
restriction of hope. In broader terms, it seemed that these people were
more concerned with the conservative, protective aspects of life than
with the possibility of gratification. It seems likely that such a position
would be intensified during the transition which was taking place at
the time of testing. The experience of being cast aside by society and
family may be the context into which all relationships are cast. Card 1,
in which the aged individual was portrayed as packing, uniformly
elicited a great deal of anxiety and, in many cases, despair.

Now we may consider the responses where the interpersonal
relations and anticipated gratifications were of a different order. In
these cases specific gratification from a social relationship was anticipated when the relationship was described as if the people interacting

were not aged. The following responses illustrate the different levels of involvement noted.

Subject 12, male, age eighty-two, TAT Card 3:

Well, they're conversing, the old cronies, talking politics. I don't know, discussing, an old lady and three cronies. He is counting with his fingers, counting his chips. Maybe he's playing poker. I'm joking. [Probe.] Well, they are more settled than this guy that walked in there. They are all pointing and talking to one another. They're a more friendly bunch; been there a year or maybe five years. They are used to the place. [Probe.] I can't give you an answer. Maybe they got friendly and kibitz. Maybe he's telling jokes; don't you think so? Maybe he's figuring something. Do you ask questions of all the guys that come in here?

Subject 7, female, age eighty-five, TAT Card 3:

Couldn't tell you who they are. [Probe.] Is it supposed to be in the home? [Probe.] Could be. Oh, just conversing, getting together to meet people; being friendly. They look like they're contented and happy. [Probe.] I could no more answer that question. To me it's absurd. No, I can't say. I wouldn't know what to say. They seemed to be friendly and discussing things in a sociable way.

Several things are worth noting in these two responses. By suggesting that the respondents are acting "as if" they were not old, we do not intend to imply that a distortion of the stimulus in terms of age, setting, and so on has necessarily taken place. Both subjects identify the setting as an institution and see the people as old. The "as if" hypothesis refers to the type of relationship. The first story gives a flavor of "the boys in the back room"—a mode of relating that was most likely characteristic of times past. The second subject acts as if the people are old, and the story is notable for its lack of interpersonal engagement.

Another illustration can be found in the responses to Card 5, which depicts an intimate group.

Subject 12, male, age eighty-two, TAT Card 5:

It's a religious home for one thing. They are ready to . . . [two words lost]. They are finishing up eating. They feel very well. [Probe.] Could be anything. Could be a girl home from college. He's [the center figure] saying a blessing. This man [the one on the right] looks very religious. Some religious service brought them together. It's a family. I might be saying all the wrong things. I don't know. They might be arguing like lots of families do. The one that gets the last word in wins the fight.

Subject 4, male, age ninety, TAT Card 5:

I suppose they are in an old-age home eating lunch or breakfast or something. They are thinking about digesting the food. These are hard questions to answer. They are not smiling I see. Well, the old men are grouchy anyway, maybe saying a blessing or prayers or something. It's all nice and clean. I say they're not smiling, I don't know why. [Probe.] Well, they may say their prayers before the meal. I cannot tell you, I'm not a mind reader. I'm afraid I'll take the fifth amendment. You have to be a psychologist to tell you what they think.

These two stories may again illustrate the differences we have in mind. In the first, the key message is that the potential of interpersonal gratification remains and that the respondent is engaged in an interpersonal relationship, albeit a conflicting one. The second story illustrates without interpersonal engagement a focus around food. TAT Card 5 depicts men and women. Here the women subjects focused around engaging in relationships "as if" they were in a family. Generally the male subjects did not see this card as a family scene and focused predominantly on survival.

Card 7, which depicts a relationship between people of the same sex, and Card 8, which depicts a relationship between people of both sexes, illustrate the same general point. On Card 7, when the women cast the scene to portray two housewives outside the institutional setting or, more frequently, as a mother and daughter relationship, interpersonal engagement was noted. Several subjects described the mother-daughter theme in an undisguised form, but generally it was cast as a relationship between a less experienced and a more experienced person or between housewives.

Subject 15, female, age sixty-seven, TAT Card 7:

They are arguing about something. This one [on the right] looks happy, but this one looks down in the mouth. Well, she's telling her something; I can't explain it. [Probe.] I don't know if they are in a home. Yes, there are two beds there, one here and one here. Well, on [sic] this one she is pretty happy and this one isn't. She is telling her something. I think they are both roommates. Well, maybe everything will come out all right. I think this one will talk to the other, and the other will see it her way.

Subject 19, female, age eighty-five, TAT Card 7:

You've got some more? I can't see. They're doing something with their hands. It seems to be two women sitting and talking. Well, they have a conversation about something. [Probe.] They might talk about something. They might talk about cooking and baking. They seem to feel all right; they've got smiles on their face. Oh, they're watching a little man; a little boy. See? [Points to a small object on the bureau.] They might have gone over and gotten the boy and then taken him home. Maybe they took him to school. Maybe he's this woman's boy. Well, they got home, and I don't know what they did at home. They took the little boy home.

For men the scene was rarely cast in the "as if" mode. This is a typical story of the men's lack of engagement.

Subject 2, male, age seventy-nine, TAT Card 7:

These people are in a home. Waiting from dinner to supper. In the meantime they are talking. They're just talking to pass time. [Probe.] I don't know what they talk about. What happened twenty-five or fifty years ago. Well, they just come to home and wait for death.

Generally the relationship the men portrayed on this card was transient, with the death motif appearing frequently.

Card 8 exhibited the same general point. Both the men and women portrayed interpersonal relationships on this card but on very different levels. For most women it was a case of "as if" they were in an adolescent mode with a great deal of sexual flirtation. For some of the men it had the character of nurturance, with a maternal figure. The examples presented are all from TAT cards 3, 5, 7, and 8, cards in which the people were all aged. Here, the relationship in the stories between the "as if" mode and engagement has few exceptions. Engagement in an interpersonal relationship does not necessarily imply satisfaction from the other person, but it does signify involvement. This may be exemplified by the men's responses to Card 3. On this card the general theme of "the boys in the back room" is followed by many subjects; for most, however, it is a threatening, anxious stimulus. The stories portray interpersonal engagement by kibitzing, arguing, and the like and emphasize competitive elements. On Card 3 it seems that the reward of the interpersonal relation for most of the men is the potential for establishing an identity in the group.

In summary, two major themes dominate the interpersonal anticipations. During the transition from community to institution, the aged people in our sample appear to expect little gratification from any other aged people in the institution. It seems as if merely being with another person relieves the sense of loneliness. Becoming involved with other aged people seems feasible only if the people act as if they were engaged in roles characteristic of a previous time. For some people this can be accomplished only by a distortion of the stimulus to make it correspond to the past or to a noninstitutional setting. For others, actual distortion of the age or setting does not seem to be necessary, but a similar psychological process, the postulation of the situation "as if" it were another, is undergone.

Heterosexual Intimacy

The responses to Card 8, which depicts interaction between an elderly male and female, had three unique characteristics—the unanimity of happy responses, the quality of the imagery, and the projection of the relationship into the future (Table 1).

As mentioned previously, the typical responses to the cards had the quality of displeasure or uncertainty. Only on Card 8 did the responses indicate playful flights into personal fantasy. Entertaining the idea that this relationship could have a future and that time was not confined to the immediate present or the past contrasts markedly to the responses to the other cards. Considered together, these three qualities indicate a high hope for potential gratification and a relatively major investment in the stimulus provided by Card 8. Here are two examples.

Subject 10, female, age sixty-four, TAT Card 8:

Maybe they are flirting, huh? He looks like a nice elderly man. She is older too. They are sitting in a park talking about their past lives. Neither one of them is sad. They both are very contented. Well, they are old and probably been through their lives and now are going to make the best of it. They are in a home, but they make the best of it. I don't think they knew each other before. They made their acquaintance in the home. Well they get acquainted in the home, and they go for coffee and things.

Subject 16, male, age seventy-nine, TAT Card 8:

This one is different. I don't know if this is the mother or sweetheart. He's enjoying himself in the fresh air, and they expect everything to be all right from now on. They all feel happy—the last two people. The old man is calling the woman. You can tell the way he holds his head. He is calling a lady to him. The way it looks to me, there'll be a marriage or something. Something turned up, and everybody is happy hereafter.

The responses to this stimulus ranged from a relatively asexual need for nurturance (most male subjects) to more overt responses indicating expectations of physical gratification (the majority of female subjects). Some of the men saw the woman as a social worker, interviewer, or mother image. Here nurturance was the need that could be gratified in this relationship. In general, there was less overt reference to sexuality by the men. On the other hand, many of the women's responses had a quality of adolescent flirtation and more direct sexual implications.

Little is known about the sexual feelings and attitudes of older adults. A recent investigation of noninstitutionalized aged (Newman & Nichols, 1960) suggests considerable sexual activity in the seventies, eighties, and nineties, given reasonably good health and the availability of a socially sanctioned partner who is also in reasonably good health. The study also suggests that even when these two conditions are not met, sexual interests and feelings can still be high.

In attempting to evaluate the results of the subjects' responses to this card, the authors raised the following question: Why should a group which characteristically expects so little gratification express so different an expectation when presented with a stimulus depicting a heterosexual relationship? Two conditions relative to becoming institutionalized are suggested for understanding this result. First, entering an institution intensifies loss of status, a useful role in society, and so on. It is likely that the fantasy of sexual interaction is the only area where institutional candidates can still maintain an image in which they see themselves capable of engaging in a real interpersonal exchange. In sexuality they can feel that part of their past self still lives. In all likelihood, a second condition that heightens the enthusiasm in response to this card is the stimulus offered by the individual's impending entrance to the home. Congregate living, presumably with more access to relationships with the opposite sex, may be seen as one of the distinctly positive aspects of institutionalization. Easier access to heterosexual companionship is perhaps the one nonprotective aspect which the older person sees as partial compensation for the losses incurred in institutional living.

Some differences in the character of male and female responses have already been noted. The categories marked by an asterisk in Table 1 indicate significant differences in the responses of male and female subjects. A series of chi-square analyses was carried out, and nine categories were found to be significant. (This is above the number of categories that could be expected to be significant by chance alone.) Table 2 presents the different descriptive words or phrases used by men and women to describe the "hero." A series of binomial tests indicated several significant differences between the men and women in frequency of usage of particular categories.

In general, the men had less hope that life in the institution would be satisfactory. This was most graphically shown in the responses to Card 1. The frequent reference to death throughout the series of cards again suggests the relatively higher degree of hopelessness among the men. A second major distinction was the relative continuity or discontinuity of self-concept during the transition from life outside the institution to life inside the institution. Once institutionalized, the men's self-images were disrupted, again suggesting that self-concept is an important area for the men and that the self-concept which tends to organize around entering the home was not sufficient to meet the new situation of life in the home. A third major difference is exhibited in the situations on the TAT cards where engagement and potential gratification could be accomplished by the "as if" relationship. The men responded to and were more actively engaged on cards 3 and 4, the women on cards 5 and 7. A fourth difference was the more frequent indication of intense dependency and conflict over this dependency for the men than for the women. This dependency was most apparent in the men's frequent references to food and by some mèn's casting the heterosexual relationship (Card 8) as a nurturant one.

In reviewing these differences, the following issue seems to be basic: for the men, the trauma of becoming institutionalized centers around damage done to the self-concept of a potent individual who has some role in relation to others. This trauma plays itself out in the intense but ambivalent dependency seen in the male subjects; the wish to be taken care of conflicts with the retained ego image.

Men perceive their entering the institution as necessary for their physical survival. The most characteristic role attributed to the aged men on the TAT cards is that of a sick person (Table 2, Column 2a). This theme is also shown in the men's responses to Card 6, in which they invariably identify with the invalid. The invalid role appears to serve two major functions for the men. It resolves the conflict between dependency and the ego ideal, and it provides a way of organizing their self-concept to give some meaning to their identity.

In making the transition from autonomous life in the community to life in a home for the aged, the basic issue for the men is one of maintaining and re-establishing a coherent and acceptable self-image. The characters of the men's responses to cards 3 and 4 are expressions of this. On Card 3 several men were engaged in an interactive process, the central theme being the establishment of an identity based on past competency. On Card 4, depicting the authority relation, a number of the responses distorted the scene to make it an equalitarian relation or a relation between an employer and employee. Thus we see in these two situations a fantasy attempt to establish an interpersonal situation on the basis of an "as if" relation with a noninstitutionalized person and to utilize this transposition to establish an identity based on past competency.

In reviewing these findings, especially the intense dependency found among the men, the authors speculated about whether the differences between the male and female subjects could largely be attributed to the possibility that the males were less adequate than the females in their ability to cope with the stress of transition. There is no direct evidence on this point, but there are several indirect indications that the male subjects are not a less adequate group. Structural aspects—organization, length, and coherence—of the TAT responses indicate no major differences between the male and female subjects. A review of the subjects' case histories failed to reveal major differences between the sexes in the adequacy of their past interpersonal relationships.

For the women the basic trauma of entering an institution seems to center around rejection by their children and the implication of rejection by society. Their self-concept is that of an unwanted, lonely person. To demonstrate that they can be attractive and liked by another human being is to recoup this loss. This may explain the higher level of sexual fantasy on the part of the females. This is not limited to the responses to Card 8. In Card 3, for example, the general tendency of the females was to view the group in hostile interaction, but the hostility was seen as taking place among the males while the females on the card sat on the sidelines and waited. It seemed that they were describing a competitive struggle for their attention and favor.

The transition from life in the community to life in an institution appears to be an easier step for the females. They feel less discontinuity about their roles and less conflict over accepting the implied dependency of their new status. Most important, there is more hope that the task of demonstrating that they are wanted can be fulfilled within the institution. For the females, institutionalization did not imply a loss of past potency (Table 2).

The men show little hope that the institutional setting can provide relief by allowing a role that is continuous with their previous image of potency. Being sick, although useful during the transition period, is not adequate once in the institution.

Impacts of Institutionalization

What were the actual effects of institutionalization on the subjects' concepts of themselves and their expectations about others? This report has focused on the conceptions the individual builds up in relation to the institution he is about to enter and the shifts in self-concept that such a transition may effect. But what happens to these people after they have experienced life in the institution?

Using the TAT, subjects were retested from three to five months after their entrance into the institution. Unfortunately, during the period of the study, the number of subjects who had been in the home for three to five months was small—seven in all, three men and four women. (One of the female subjects did not complete the series of cards and is not considered in this analysis.) The same researcher administered the test. Because of the small number of subjects, the following points should be considered very tentative.

The analysis of the TAT's was conducted in a manner similar to that used for the earlier series. The judges were not informed that these responses were from a different series of TAT responses. Table 1 presents a comparison of the first and second ratings for the six subjects. It should be noted that some of the apparent shifts result from a movement from a particular category to a no-information category.

The postinstitutionalization stories indicated a lessened investment in the outside world and a shift to more active dealing with the other residents, who are now the important world. Concomitant with this was an expression of lessened adequacy and power in coping with the outside world. The stories for Card 1 most clearly express this lessened potency in dealing with the noninstitutional world. In the preinstitutionalization stories, entering the home was viewed by many of the subjects as a self-generated act; in the postinstitutionalization stories, it was an act imposed by others.

The shift in emphasis to people in the home was accompanied by a more clear-cut view of hostile and competitive interpersonal relationships. This view of interpersonal relations did not appear to be accompanied by increased anxiety. Rather, the heroes in the stories were seen as having more pleasurable than unpleasurable feelings in their competition. Expressions of anger were more frequent. It seems that the feeling of inadequacy in dealing with the external world and the shifting of involvement to the institutional world stimulated hostility and competition. It is as if the individual felt that there was something worth fighting about with the others in the institution. The evidence is unclear as to the focus of this increased competitiveness. It appears to revolve around the establishment of some identity in the institutional world.

A second major change from the pre- to the postinstitutionalization records centered around the responses to the heterosexual relationship card, Card 8. The postinstitutionalization stories characteristically viewed this as a transitory relation, showing a shift from feelings of sexual love and intense nurturance found in the preinstitutionalization stories. Why this change should have taken place is not wholly clear. The responses suggest an attitude of guilt and some hints that the source of the guilt may be the institution rather than the other aged individuals. Because of the small number of subjects, however, it is difficult to evaluate this evidence. It may be that the anticipated eroticism and extreme nurturance characteristic of the preinstitutionalization records must be modified after confrontation with institutional attitudes and/or the competitive interrelationships found in congregate living.

The last major shift from the pre- to postinstitutionalization records involves only the male subjects. In accepting institutionalization, the males find it important to picture themselves as sick, needing care and shelter. The postinstitutionalization responses indicate increased confusion about why they are in the institution and about their identities as institutionalized individuals. Concern about one's survival during the process of admission to the home serves as a focus for defining "who I am" to oneself and others. This issue, however, loses its importance after admission, and the individual may again face the problem of defining himself. It might be added that the institution does not support the "sick" role; activity and socializing are the values of a progressive home for the aged. Sometimes three to five months may not be long enough for an individual to begin to form a new concept of self; it is possible that further shift in self-image may occur later.

The Transition

The subjects could be divided into two groups on the basis of time of entry into the institution—the immediate-entrance group (those entering the home less than one week from the date of testing) and the waiting-list group (those who had been accepted for entrance within the past two weeks but would have to wait up to a year before an opening became available). In order to explore some characteristics of the transitional period, the groups' TAT responses were compared. We wondered whether the imminent entrance affected an individual's view of himself and what he expected from the institution. Chi-square analyses of the rated TAT responses did not support this hypothesis or reveal any difference between these two groups.

SUMMARY

This study explored aged individuals' views of themselves and their social environments during and after transition from autonomous life in the community to residence in a home for the aged. A special TAT was constructed to portray incidents involved in the aged individuals' transition to an institution and typical interpersonal situations within the institution. The series of eight TAT cards was administered to twenty-two subjects prior to their admission and readministered to seven subjects after three to five months' residence in the institution.

The authors' clinical impressions from the TAT protocols provided the basic data. Two rating procedures based on the TAT responses were used to supplement the clinical impressions. These data were augmented by case histories and an interview administered in conjunction with the TAT.

The results suggested that application to a home for the aged resulted in a shift in the way an individual perceives himself and was usually unrelated to any specific physical or economic crisis. Institutionalization was viewed as a conservation step by the prospective resident. This was expressed by an inabilty to survive without institutionalization and a need for protection from the future, when something "might" happen. The men tended to perceive this more in physical terms; the women, more in fear of isolation.

The personal meaning which institutionalization had was dependent on the sex of the individual. For the male it was a severe blow to an already shaky self-concept as an adequate, potent person; for the female it symbolized being unwanted and rejected. The sexes shared the interpersonal task of conservation and repair of their self-images.

The expectation that relationships with other human beings can provide specific gratification was minimal. It was suggested that this lack of expectation serves as a necessary protective device for the individual during this transition. Active engagement with and specific gratification from others could be accomplished only through a special type of interpersonal mechanism—becoming involved with other aged individuals as if they were engaged in a mode of interaction or role relation characteristic of a younger group.

Heterosexual relationships did not fit the typical pattern. It was the only area where potential growth and a future could be imagined and where the purely conservational aspects of institutionalization did not predominate.

Life in the institution resulted in several characteristic shifts. Among the most important were a further decrease in the person's feeling of power to cope with the outside world concomitant with a greater investment in the institutional world, a lessened interest in and an increased guilt over heterosexual relationships, and a more diffuse and precarious self-image for the men.

REFERENCES

Banham, K.M. Senescence and the emotions: A genetic theory. *J. genet. Psychol.,* 1951, **78,** 175-183.

Birren, J.E. Aging and psychological adjustment. *Rev. educ. Res.,* 1958, **28,** 476-490.

Davidson, Helen H., & Kruglov, Lorraine. Personality characteristics of the institutionalized aged. *J. consult. Psychol.,* 1952, **15,** 5-12.

Gitelson, M. The emotional problems of elderly people. *Geriatrics,* 1940. **3,** 135-150.

Goldfarb, A.I. Recommendations for psychiatric care in a home for the aged. *J. Geront.,* 1953, **8,** 343-347.

Goldfarb, A.I. Psychotherapy of the aged. *Psychoanal. Rev.,* 1956, **43,** 68-81.

Hollender, M.H. Individualizing the aged. *Soc. Casework,* 1952, **33,** 337-342.

Lakin, M., & Dray, M. Psychological aspects of activity for the aged. *Amer. J. occupat. Ther.,* 1958, **12,** 172-176.

Laverty, Ruth. Nonresident aid-community versus institutional care for older people. *J. Geront.,* 1950, **5,** 370-374.

Meerloo, J.A.M. Contribution of psychoanalysis to the problem of the aged. In M. Heiman (Ed.), *Psychoanalysis and social work.* New York: International Universities Press, 1953. Pp. 321-336.

Newman, G., & Nichols, C.R. Sexual activities and attitudes in older persons. *J. Amer. med. Ass.,* 1960, **173** (4), 33-35.

Pollack, O. Social adjustment in old age: A research planning report. *Soc. Sci. Research Council Bull.,* 1948, No. 59. (New York)

Weil, J. Life in the home for older persons. *Geriatrics,* 1953, **8,** 459-462.

CHAPTER 23

The Influence of
Age on Schizophrenia

CHRISTIAN MULLER

Today we are aware that there is no phase of human life in which both constructive and destructive processes are not operating. All too often gerontology is taken to represent only the negative, the deficient, the faulty, or the deteriorating in the elderly person. Particularly in psychiatry we have concerned ourselves for several decades with exhaustive studies of the manifold impairments of memory and other intellectual functions which culminate in senile dementia. If human senescence were describable solely as a gradual decline, aging would always be experienced as something negative. As implied in the opening sentence, however, we are of the opinion that senescence, in both subjective experience and psychopathological research, has both positive and negative aspects.

504

POSITIVE AND NEGATIVE ASPECTS

There is no need to deal here with the phenomena of senile dementia or the perplexing problem, emphasized by Malamud (1951), that no comprehensible correlation can be demonstrated between histopathologic brain changes and psychopathological findings. Hallervorden (1958), the well-known pathologist, has maintained that what we see in senile dementia and Alzheimer's disease is merely a pathological accentuation of physiological processes in the sense of colloidalchemical changes.

Bronisch (1958) emphasized how dubious is any attempt to apply a systematic psychopathological nomenclature to the senescent disorders. Only a few symptoms and behavior forms are ascribable to a specific illness. What strikes us in symptomatology is the shift in emphasis from the qualitative to the quantative. The limits of the normal are not fixed. According to Bronisch, an absolute psychopathology which strives at abstractions from the sociological, ethnological, or, in short, one which endeavors to make abstractions from the total relatedness of the individual to his environment is not feasible. By this he means that abnormal psychic developments in advanced age assume their form from the over-all alterations, brought about by decades of living combined with diverse physical ailments and social and domestic crises, in the individual's world. Primarily Bronisch regards the emergence of depressive and paranoid states in senescence as abnormal. Under certain circumstances, actual sensual stimuli are delusionally construed.

Existential anxiety and the consciousness of the finiteness of life, which were discussed by Schultz (1939), enlarge to become delusions of being robbed, impoverished, and persecuted. As both Stern (1955) and Stoll (1954a) have emphasized, it is part of the characteristic change of the aging person that he moves from extra- to introversion. This introversion can be regarded as a parallel to the retrospective tendency of the elderly. Fixation at an earlier phase of life and an inability to form new adjustments can proceed to psychological disturbances in old age, which bear a certain similarity to the neuroses seen in earlier phases of life. It is not surprising that these psychological disturbances manifest themselves as hypochondria, mistrust, envy, jealousy, and egocentricity. Then, too, the sense of time is different in aging people. According to Stern (1955), the majority of old people whom he investigated assert that time passes more slowly for them than it formerly did.

But this tendency toward introspection, toward reduction to essentials, toward preoccupation with the self, also carries with it richly positive potentialities. We would be less inclined to regard solely the destructive sides of senescence if we were to listen attentively to the people who have concerned themselves in an affirmative sense with their own aging. Consider the neurologist Monakow (1939), who, in his "Panegyrismus des natürlichen Greisenalters," records his observations of himself. Only in age was the fullness of the psychobiologic orchestra vouchsafed him; the inessential dropped away, and concentration on the essential heightened. Old memories evoked a subdued ecstasy which no longer overwhelmed him as before. Minkowski (1950; 1951), a European psychiatrist, has also given his attention to age and has risen to the defense of the love of recounting and loquacity that belongs to old age. He talks of *radotage senile*, by which he means senile logorrhea. For him this means the old person's need to turn back the pages of his own history and reinfuse them with life. In like manner, these quotations reveal how inseparable the positive is from the negative. La Rochefoucauld says, "En vieillissant on devient plus fou et plus sage" ("In age one grows madder and wiser"). Marie Ebner-von Eschenbach states, "Das Alter versteinert oder verklärt ("Age rigidifies or it transfigures"). Old age takes its contours from lifelong attitudes toward conflict and environment. Schindler (1953) has strikingly indicated the inherent relation between psychopathologic phenomena and the premorbid personality and environment. In favorable instances the economy of effort and the retrenchment and narrowing of inessential contacts can result in heightened concentration on the essential and the true wisdom of age. The more diversified the previous interests, the more nearly intact the personality remains. The unremitting effort hitherto required to master the world and the continuous compensations exacted in the struggle for life are reduced with age. The trauma of dislocation—for example, a change in domestic setting—will be the more catastrophic the closer the dependence on such things as family settings has been throughout life. The more devotedly a person has been cared for by his marriage partner, the more disastrous the social consequences of his senile dementia are apt to be. In brief, the whole matter can be summed up in one sentence: "On vieillit comme on a vécu" ("One grows old as one has lived") (Ajuriaguerra, Hecaen, & Guiguen, 1954).

Of course it is also possible to regard these psychological

and psychopathological changes in the analytic sense, as alterations in the economy of instincts. Repond (1954), for example, believes that occasionally increased aggressiveness in old people is related to a lessening of libido. He emphasizes, as do other authors, that in old age a reactivation of castration anxiety can lead to pathological developments. The problem of anxiety can, perhaps, be summarized by saying that senescence can bring about intensification, as well as an abatement, on various levels. The re-emergence and intensification of the anxiety which lies at the root of numerous pathological phenomena can be attributed to the impinging necessity of coming to grips with death; to the inevitable lessening of the person's feeling of personal worth, ensuing from inability to work; and finally to the loss, which looms ever larger, of important affective contacts. For a person who once was vital and dominating, the subjective awareness of dwindling strength in both physical and mental spheres can be a deeply traumatic experience. On the other hand, previously present anxiety can diminish or disappear, because libidinal conflicts tend to lose their urgency, and frustrations become more tolerable. And so a way can be cleared for that cheerfulness and serenity of age which has its roots in the blunting of affective life, which is organically determined, and in a true detachment from material things.

AGING IN SCHIZOPHRENICS

A number of years ago I undertook follow-up studies of a large number of compulsive-obsessive neurotics and was able to establish a marked influence of age upon the compulsions (Muller, 1953). The attributes of age which we have been discussing could be discerned to subdue or intensify the compulsive phenomena. Almost without exception these patients reported that with advancing age their compulsions had become much easier to bear, although they had not completely disappeared. The affective "thorn" had been removed. Here age had had a marked ameliorative influence.

Starting with the assumption that chronic schizophrenics can likewise undergo a change under the influence of bodily and psychic aging processes, follow-up studies were undertaken in 1957 (Muller, 1959) of about one hundred schizophrenics over sixty-five. Bleuler (1911), in his volume on schizophrenics, mentioned that occasionally in chronically excited, hallucinating schizophrenics a calming down can be observed in old age. In addition, he was of the opinion that actual psycho-organic changes determined by age (such as failing memory) occurred less frequently in schizophrenics than in the average population. This hypothesis has apparently been corroborated in recent years by Riemer (1950) and Bychowsky (1952), who found no psychopathological evidence of organic brain change in the old schizophrenics whom they studied. Riemer went as far as to conjecture that the elderly schizophrenic, hospitalized for years, has been protected from senile dementia because he has been spared the stress of modern life throughout large stretches of his life. Chronic, hospitalized schizophrenia and senile dementia were, in his view, mutually exclusive diseases. This hypothesis was not confirmed by my investigations. Among 101 old schizophrenics who had been hospitalized for many years, there were ten cases of severe organic dementia and twenty-two with a clearly marked organic psychosyndrome which had not as yet progressed to complete disorientation with such associated physical symptoms as incontinence. Barucci (1955a; 1955b), who has made a similar study of a large number of schizophrenics in Italy, arrived at similar conclusions. Differences in percentages are largely explainable as difficulties in differentiating the concept of senile dementia from milder forms of psycho-organic disorders.

What effect does age, either with or without associated psycho-organic disturbance, have on the symptomatology of schizophrenia; for instance, on the delusional component? In general it can be said that in roughly one-half of the cases investigated, senescence—the diverse expressions of involution—did not appear to have the slightest influence on the form or content of the schizophrenic psychosis. In the other half of these patients, however, a marked change was found, in either the direction of disappearance or expansion and consolidation of the delusion.

A further question of interest and importance for the theory of schizophrenia is whether only age and its psychodynamic effects, as opposed to the organic brain change, were decisive in altering the schizophrenic symptomatology. Our material yielded no clear answer here. I found fourteen cases where a psycho-organic syndrome developed simultaneously with an increase in schizophrenic symptomatology, whereas thirteen cases were accompanied by a simultaneous improvement in schizophrenic psychosis, primarily in lessened feelings of excitement, improved social adaptation, and affective contact. But such changes are also found in patients without psycho-organic syndromes in whom age could be assumed to be the only operative factor. It is, therefore, clear that the question cannot be answered by making an artificial separation of the organically determined change and the change in personality brought by age itself. This will become more evident when we turn to an individual case.

An example is the famous patient Aloise, a schizophrenic artist who has found her way into the literature through Steck (no date). Her pictures were exhibited at the International Psychiatric Congress in Zurich in 1957. For many decades she has been the inmate of a mental hospital for the chronically ill. The pictures she formerly painted were the unequivocal expression of her fight for femininity and the instinctual side of life. She painted erotically charged scenes in vibrant red tones, with a crassness of expression which is peculiar to the schizophrenic. Now that she is over seventy, such religious themes as Christmas and the Holy Virgin make their appearance in her painting. The brazen decolletés of the ubiquitous rosy-breasted, voluptuous females have been transformed to flowers which form an incidental decorative feature of the pictures. Here we can certainly speak of the spiritual and sublimating influence of age. It is noteworthy, however, that this patient lives in her delusional world, completely dissociated and inaccessible to communication, so that she is unable to give expression to any conscious experience of age.

With other less deteriorated patients, the effect of senescence on the schizophrenic delusion can be clearly observed. Whereas the content and prevailing themes remain unchanged, the subjective attitude of the patient towards his delusion can undergo appreciable change. Sometimes there is shrinkage; for example, a patient who formerly maintained he was king of all Europe now contents himself with being king of little Switzerland.

To sum up, I found five different possible modifications in the way the delusion was experienced in old schizophrenics:

1. Liquidation through suppression, retrenchment, and minimizing.
2. Shift of delusional content by a restructuring of the milieu.
3. Conversion of a productive delusion serving defense functions into one of nihilistic, depressive configuration.
4. Disappearance of the delusion, coincident with a psycho-organically induced regression and increased occupation with oral problems.
5. Expansion and fantastic generalization of the delusional themes.

When we survey the total material gleaned from these 101 patients and ask ourselves what characterizes those who improved from those who worsened with age, it can be said that a worsening of schizophrenic symptomatology manifested itself in reinforced regressive tendencies, increased encapsulation, and expansion of pre-existent delusions, whereas improvement was primarily marked by the general abatement of affectivity, equalizing of the personality, relaxation of defensive attitudes, tendencies toward sublimation, peaceful resignation, and better accommodation to the milieu. In those cases in which we could establish a true senile dementia, there was evidence of a slow decline in amnestic functions, indifference toward external irritations, and, very rarely, an acute confusional state of either manic or agitated-depressive type. The problem which Roth (1959) investigated in his study of diagnostic and etiologic aspects of confusional states in the aged scarcely appeared within the compass of our patient group. This fact could be regarded as lending support to Riemer's (1950) hypothesis which accords importance to the protected condition of the schizophrenic, whose prolonged hospitalization removes him from exposure to traumatic external stimuli.

SUMMARY

Thus the light and shadow of senescence and the sequences of age are also reflected in what we see in chronic schizophrenia. Even when we consider the changes conditioned by age on purely biological grounds—such as a disturbance in the adrenal system or adrenopause—and set up our pharmacotherapeutic measures to parallel them, we cannot help being impressed by the ambiguity of the effects: on one hand, improvement and subjective relief through subdued, blunted emotional tension; on the other, a disturbing state of depression, nihilism, and hypochondria evoked by the same conditions. Further significant indications for future research can be anticipated from a precise and accurate understanding of the premorbid personality, the major emphasis being on biographical development. Even in this specialized, restricted field, with the requisite warnings against inadmissible simplifications and exclusions in view, this area of psychodynamc research is of fundamental importance.

REFERENCES

Ajuriaguerra, J. de, Hecaen, H., & Guiguen, Y. Troubles mentaux de la sénilité. *Encyclopédie médico-chirurgienne.* Vol. 2, *s.v.* "Psychiatrie," Paris: Encyclopédie Médico-Chirurgienne, 1954. Pp. 1-11.

Barucci, M. La vecchiaia degli schizofrenici. *Riv. Patal. nerv. ment.*, 1955, **76**, 257-284. (a)

Barucci, M. La vecchiaia degli schizofrenici (reperti necropscopici). *Rass. Studi psichiat.*, 1955, **44**, 341-349. (b)

Bleuler, E. Dementia praecox. In J. Aschaffenburg (Ed.), *Handbuch d. psychiatrie.* Leipzig and Vienna: Deutike, 1911.

Bronisch, F.W. Neurologie und psychiatrie des höheren lebensalters. *Zbl. ges. Neurol. Psychiat.*, 1958, **144**, 5-6.

Bychowsky, G. Schizophrenia in the period of involution. *Dis. nerv. Syst.*, 1952, **13**, 150-153.

Hallervorden, J. Neurologie und psychiatrie des höheren lebensalters. *Zbl. ges. Neurol. Psychiat.*, 1958, **144**, 1-2.

Malamud, W. Problems of aging: Psychopathological aspects. In *Conference on problems of aging, trans. 12th conference.* New York: Josiah Macy Foundation, 1951. Pp. 140-175.

Minkowski, E. Problèmes d'adaptation au cours de la vieillesse. *Sem. hôp. Paris,* 1950, **26**, 2294-2295.

Minkowski, E. Aspects psychologiques de la vieillesse. *Evolut. Psychiat.*, 1951, **1**, 49-72.

Monakow, C. von. Panegyrismus des natürlichen greisenalters. *Schweiz. Arch. Neurol. Psychiat.*, 1939, **43**, 105-129.

Muller, C. Vorläufige mitteilung zur langen katamnese der zwangskranken. *Nervenarzt,* 1953, **24**, 112-115.

Muller, C. *Über das senium der schizophrenen.* Basel: Karger, 1959.

Repond, A. Psychologie, psychopathologie, et hygiène mentale de la senescence et de la vieillesse. *Schweiz. Arch. Neurol. Psychiat.*, 1954, **73**, 406-422.

Riemer, M.D. A study of the mental status of schizophrenics hospitalized for over 25 years into their senium. *Psychiat. Quart.*, 1950, **24**, 309-313.

Roth, M. Some diagnostic and aetiological aspects of confusional state in the elderly. *Gerontologia,* 1959, **1**, 83-99.

Schindler, R. Die psychischen factoren der senilen dekompensation. *Wien. Z. Nervenheilk,* 1953, **6**, 185-204.

Schultz, J.H. Das endgültigkeitsproblem in der psychologie des rücksbildungs-alters. *Z. ges. Neurol. Psychiat.*, 1939, **167**, 117-126.

Steck, H. L'art psychopathologique. Unpublished manuscript, no date.

Stern, E. *Der mensch in der zweiten lebenshälfte.* Zurich: Rascher, 1955.

Stoll, W.A. Wert und unwert psychischer altersveränderungen. *Schweiz. med. Wschr.*, 1954, **84**, 922-923. (a)

Stoll, W.A. *Seelisches krank- und gesundsein im alter: Geisteskraft und geistesstörung im alter.* Zurich: Orell Füssli, 1954. (b)

SECTION III

*Coping with
the Psychopathologies
of the Aged*

CHAPTER 24

*The Follow-Up Method in
the Management of
Aged Psychiatric Patients*

FELIX POST

Most reports on the treatment of psychiatric illness describe the immediate effects of various physical and pharmacological therapies. Clearly, it is highly desirable to bring an attack of mental disturbance to an end, but almost always the story does not close here. The mere fact that a person has suffered from a psychiatric illness, as well as the type of treatment used, may have profound effects on the patient's future physical and mental health. A young person will have to reckon with a tendency for further breakdowns, from which he may or may not recover; after the acute disturbance has subsided, the first attack may be followed by lifelong neurotic or psychotic invalidism. In old people a mental illness may herald cerebral deterioration and early death; in their case even more than that of young people, therefore, assessment of the long-term results of

515

treatment may be more instructive than reporting short-term effects.

In an older group the clinician is frequently faced with patients showing a perplexing mixture of many symptoms—disorientation, disturbed awareness, memory difficulties, depression, elation, anxiety, beliefs in or experiences of persecution, phobias, obsessions, and even hysterical conversions. Before embarking on the treatment of the most outstanding and troublesome symptom—the removal of depression—by electroconvulsive therapy (ECT) or the control of schizophrenic symptoms by psychotropic drugs, the psychiatrist should attempt to place the patient in a diagnostic group on the assumption that diagnosis allows predictions about the patient's future. To cite the most common problem, with a patient who shows a mixture of disorientation, memory disturbance, depression, and anxiety, the clinician will try to determine whether the diagnosis is psychosis because of cerebral disorder or agitated melancholia. Treatment with ECT may well produce immediate improvement in either case, but the further outlook for the patient may be very different, depending on the presence or absence of pathological changes in the brain. It must be admitted that in treating patients who are severely disturbed mentally and, consequently, in considerable physical danger, an undue preoccupation with diagnostic problems may be bad practice, but the importance of diagnosis when attempting the scientific assessment of a therapy can be illustrated with one example.

In a study of the efficacy of a vitamin preparation (Krawiecki, Couper, & Walton, 1957), the Wechsler memory scale was administered on four occasions to what were described as senile psychotic patients. At the beginning of the experiment all the patients, as well as the control group, clinically manifested a memory defect presumed to be associated with cerebral changes; improvement of memory function was found to have occurred to a significant extent in patients receiving the active preparation. At the end of the experiment, however, not only some of the subjects, but also some of the members of the control group had shown very striking rises in their scores on the memory scale. In some instances these had been so large that it was suggested that these patients might not have been brain damaged after all or possibly were damaged to a slighter extent than those patients who had shown little or no change on successive retesting. One of the authors (Walton, 1958) therefore considered it necessary to study the original cases for two more years in order to be more certain of the diagnoses and then to relate these diagnoses to the memory scale changes. In this way Walton hoped to more precisely evaluate the diagnostic and predictive accuracy of the memory scale with regard to senile dementia.

The follow-up findings showed that for both the experimental and control groups there were large differences between the first and final memory scores of the patients who had been either considered to have suffered from an affective disturbance at follow-up or discharged as recovered. Those finally diagnosed as organically ill made much less progress on successive retestings. Walton concluded that scores obtained at repeated retestings appeared to have considerable predictive and diagnostic importance.

It is argued that the value of the work, which started as a therapeutic experiment, lies in its diagnostic and prognostic implications. Walton and Black (1957) confirmed the earlier finding (Inglis, Shapiro, & Post, 1956) that memory impairment of the type reported by clinicians in elderly psychiatric patients was not always a useful indicator of the presence or absence of cerebral deterioration. In the course of the vitamin investigation, Walton (1958) also confirmed that his modified word-learning test was a promising measure for identifying patients with diffuse cerebral disorders. However, any conclusions which he and his fellow authors had drawn in the first study (Krawiecki et al., 1957) concerning the efficacy of a vitamin preparation on improving memory are clearly invalid, because in retrospect memory impairment was found to have occurred on a physical basis only in some cases; in others it may have been caused by the lack of mental stimulation that surrounds long-term hospital patients. Perusal of Walton's tables also shows that in twenty of the forty-eight patients who were successfully followed up, the diagnoses had been changed during the two years; this had been done though patients had been in the hospital for at least one year, but mostly for longer periods, up to fifty years. It is difficult to avoid the conclusion that so many changes of diagnosis in two years for patients under long-term care indicates that the first diagnosis had been the result of routine labeling, whereas the second diagnoses were the outcome of more intensive and individual study.

We reaffirm that two steps have to be taken if the treatment and management of our patients are to be carried out along rational lines: first, patients should be placed in a diagnostic group after full clinical assessment and, second, the treatment given over the next few years should be evaluated. Below we will critically review the role of follow-up studies in testing the validity of diagnostic assessments for treatment purposes and in evaluating the long-term results of therapy.

FOLLOW-UP STUDIES OF
DIAGNOSTIC ASSESSMENTS

The Usefulness of Diagnosis

When we speak of diagnosis in old-age psychiatry, we are not primarily concerned with affixing descriptive labels, but with making predictive statements; diagnoses are thus made only as a preliminary to casting prognoses. It has been alleged that in the past there was a tendency to neglect diagnosis in our age group because many physicians thought that, whatever the clinical picture at the beginning of the illness, it was only prodromal to the early emergence of senile dementia. It was pointed out on a previous occasion (Post, 1956) that informed psychiatrists have at no time used the label "senile psychosis" indiscriminately, but that they have always been guided in their clinical work by the awareness that many patients of all ages break down and then recover, especially if they suffered affective illnesses. When attempting to assess the outcome of mental breakdown in old age (Post, 1951), it was taken for granted that by perusing case records of patients who had spent only short periods in a mental observation unit it would be possible to differentiate patients suffering from schizophrenia or affective psychoses from those exhibiting mental symptoms associated with cerebral pathology (that is, suffering largely from arteriosclerotic and senile dementia). This rough-and-ready way of making differential diagnoses appeared, for the most part, to have been successful, as a follow-up of the patients' records over the next three and one-half years showed that 54 per cent of the patients with the favorable diagnostic label "functional" were again discharged from hospital, and only 26 per cent had died; in the case of patients diagnosed "cerebral organic" 60 per cent had died, and only 23 per cent had left hospital.

For two to three years Roth and Morrissey (1952) followed the progress of 150 patients over sixty who were admitted to a mental hospital during one year. They stressed the frequency of affective illnesses, which accounted for 54 per cent of cases; 8 per cent were diagnosed as late schizophrenics or paraphrenics, and the remainder were suffering from organic mental disorders of old age, mainly senile dementia, arteriosclerotic dementia, and acute confusional states occurring independently of another disorder. They showed that these diagnostic groupings had prognostic significance for the patient's duration of life and chances for discharge from the mental hospital.

Roth (1955) confirmed these impressions by extending his case material to 450 subjects, demonstrating that five diagnostic groupings could be sharply differentiated from each other, not only on grounds of the histories and clinical states, but also in outcome.

It may be objected that these follow-up studies deal only with early prognosis and that long-term observation would show an increasingly large number of patients who developed cerebral-organic disturbances. Also, making diagnoses and casting prognoses in old-age psychiatry may merely be academic exercises, because diagnostic groupings may not be stable when viewed over a period of time. Long-term follow-up studies are clearly necessary. It would be especially interesting to confirm or refute the possibility that the acute delirious reactions of old age, provided the patient survives them mentally intact, may or may not always herald the later manifestation of dementia. No long-term, follow-up study concerning patients like these appears to have been published since Avery (1945) studied seventeen patients who had first manifested mental changes in the form of acute confusional states while under medical care; they made complete recoveries from their physical and mental illnesses, but eight of them later suffered from a typical dementia and died, and only four were still known to be living without any serious senile changes. Kay (1959) has suggested that schizophrenics whose illness began after they were fifty-nine tend to show mental deterioration and that it is often difficult to decide whether the deterioration is of a schizophrenic or an organic type.

Only the affective syndrome has been studied well, and we now have three different investigations into the long-term course of this disorder. Though these investigations were carried out by different workers with different populations of patients, their results agree. First, we have the studies from a mental hospital in England, taking practically all the cases from a rural, small-town area (Kay, Roth, & Hopkins, 1955). The subjects of this study were 189 patients over sixty admitted to the hospital over a period of eighteen months and exhibting a manic or depressive symptom complex. Only fourteen patients showed an affective syndrome in a setting of senile or arteriosclerotic dementia. Personal examination had been possible in only one-third of cases; the follow-up period, ranging from nine to twenty-seven months (the average was twenty and one-half months), was relatively short. Of the 175 patients with uncomplicated affective disorders, only four developed cerebral-organic symptoms, probably all arteriosclerotic in origin. Furthermore, Roth argued that if affective disorders were frequent prodromes of old-age dementias, signs of neurological disorder or intellectual decline should be found more frequently in patients who developed their first affective symptoms late in life (after the age of sixty, compared with those who had suffered affective illnesses from an early age). He found that this was not the case.

In the second study Kay (1959) traced all 236 patients with certain old-age psychoses who had been admitted to a Stockholm psychiatric hospital during 1931-1937. Follow-up information was obtained from relatives, hospital records, and other official sources; as all but seventeen patients had died, this follow-up was almost complete. Ninety-seven patients had been diagnosed as suffering from affective psychoses, and Kay found that cerebral arteriosclerotic changes, leading to obvious symptoms or clearly acting as causes of death, had occurred in only 10 to 12 per cent of cases.

Thirdly, there is the London study (Post, 1961) of 100 depressed patients over sixty all of whom had been under personal care and most of whom had been re-examined during, or at the end of, a follow-up period of six years; the span of observation was extended to eight years by a postal follow-up. On admission to the hospital, 12 per cent had shown signs of cerebral arteriosclerosis in addition to an affective syndrome, and another 7 per cent had exhibited senile and other cerebral changes. Of the remaining patients, only another 7 per cent showed evidence of mental deterioration over the subsequent eight years, and this was hardly surprising, as some of them had been well into their seventies on admission. At first hand it seemed more disquieting that 18 per cent developed, *de novo*, focal signs or symptoms of the central nervous system disorders, presumably because of cerebral arteriosclerosis. However, this was not found to be significantly higher than might be expected in any other sample of the elderly population, for example, those which were reported, on the basis of surveys by repeated house-to-house canvassing in certain areas of the United States, by Collins, Trantham, and Lehmann (1955). In addition, the proportion of deaths associated with focal lesions of the c.n.s. was no higher in the study by Post than that found in post-mortem examinations of a representative sample in Norway (Cohen, 1955) or that in the figures reported for England and Wales by the registrar general.

Thus these three investigations agree that there is no unduly high incidence of late senile or arteriosclerotic brain changes in depressed elderly patients. In treatment and long-term management, we need not, therefore, be unduly concerned about the risks of cerebral complications. In passing, it may be mentioned that two investigations (Kay et al., 1955; Kay, Norris, & Post, 1956) found that on admission there was more often evidence of arteriosclerotic disorders in depressed patients than in the general elderly population. The recent physical health of patients with affective disorders was also poorer, and it is suggested that cerebral arteriosclerosis, with other physical diseases, is a frequent precipitating factor of affective illness in old age; both investigators found that general physical ill health, rather than cerebral arteriosclerosis, was responsible for the relatively high death rates of old people who have passed through depressive episodes.

The prognostic investigations so far reviewed have all been retrospective studies and are, therefore, open to the criticism that some of the information obtained at the follow-up stage may have contaminated the original diagnosis, thus affecting predictions of outcome. With this objection in view, we carried out two anterospective studies in which prognostic statements were made either explicitly or implicitly, in the form of treatment recommendations.

In one of these investigations (Kay et al., 1956), we assessed all patients over sixty ($N = 229$) admitted to an observation unit and placed them in one of three diagnostic categories: (1) functional psychoses, (2) organic dementias or confusional states, (3) organic psychoses with some functional symptomatology (depressive or paranoid admixtures). In each case we predicted either early death or survival beyond one year and whether early discharge from psychiatric inpatient care (social recovery) was going to occur. In making these predictions, we had in mind a number of assumptions which were based largely on diagnosis; for example, a favorable prognosis (survival and early discharge) was given to functional patients, and a poor one to organics, especially when they were devoid of functional admixtures. We also took note of the patient's physical health and degree of social integration at the time of admission. Patients were followed up by mail twelve months later, and the statistical analysis of our results showed that although we failed to predict exactly how many months patients would survive or stay in the hospital, we were successful in selecting 85 per cent of the patients who survived the first year following admission, as well as 71 per cent of those who made social recoveries during this period. In addition, we were able to work out a number of prognostic indicators and to confirm that the psychiatric diagnosis is a reliable indicator of the eventual outcome of the illness. Social recovery within one year occurred in twenty-one of thirty-one patients originally diagnosed "functional." It occurred only thirteen times among the 107 patients with simple dementia; thirty-five of the seventy-nine patients with organic psychoses complicated by some functional symptoms could be discharged from psychiatric inpatient care. Decisions concerning the future treatment or care of these patients were not in our hands, and our diagnostic and prognostic opinions remained unknown to the psychiatrists who made the treatment decisions.

In an earlier investigation (Norris & Post, 1954), the diagnostician had also been responsible for arranging treatment. This study was carried out in the course of routine psychiatric work in the outpatient department of the Maudsley Hospital. Subjects of the investigation were 192 patients, all over sixty, who were seen over a period of two years. As one might expect in the case of outpatient referrals, few patients were severely disturbed, and there were no old people in delirious states. Following assessments taking from forty-five to seventy-five minutes, patients were placed in one of three broad diagnostic groups, and, mainly according to the diagnostic category, one of three kinds of treatment recommendations was likely to be made. The first diagnostic group was composed of patients showing apparently irreversible personality disorganization because of degenerative brain changes; these were people with one of the dementias of old age. With them the usual recommendation was either continued family care under the family doctors or terminal institutional treatment (thirty-six of forty-six cases). The second group was made up of old people with long-term illnesses—neuroses, psychopathic difficulties, long-term schizophrenic disorders, and so on. These patients were usually brought to the clinic because some recent social problem had produced difficulties of management; as a rule, only social advice was given, and it was recommended that the patient stay in the community without special psychiatric treatment (twenty-six of thirty-three cases). The third group was diagnosed as suffering from recent functional psychoses, mostly mild, or moderately severe affective disorders. The most frequent recommendation here (eighty-five of 109 cases) was either admission to a hospital or frequent attendance at an outpatient clinic for some specific treatment, in many cases, ECT.

In all but fourteen cases the patients' course over the subsequent twelve to eighteen months was successfully followed, mainly by correspondence with their relatives, doctors, or hospitals. To test the validity of the advice given at consultations and, indirectly, the usefulness of the diagnostic categories on which it was based, each case was scored "recommendation successful" or "recommendation unsuccessful." Recommendation failures were all patients who had been recommended for active treatment but who had remained in the hospital continuously during the follow-up period or subjects who were admitted to a hospital or institution although supervision by the general practitioner had been advised. Unexpected deaths—unexpected in the sense that they were intimately associated with a psychiatric illness whose nature or severity had not been correctly assessed like suicide in a patient sent home or a fatal cerebral thrombosis in a person diagnosed as suffering from a recurrent depressive psychosis—were also scored "recommendation failed." We found that recommendations had been successful in 83 per cent of the patients diagnosed as having affective disorders, 70 per cent of the patients with long-term personality disorders, and 67 per cent of the patients found to be suffering from old-age dementias. Statistical evaluation of these, as well as a number of other findings, showed that, although there were many cases in which errors of diagnosis and recommendation were made, our three categories contained useful prognostic pointers in that they helped the consultant make many correct suggestions concerning treatment and management.

The Usefulness of Diagnostic Aids

We have demonstrated that careful diagnostic assessment of elderly patients will lead to reasonably reliable predictions regarding further duration of life and the chances of discharge from hospital care. Apart from helping the psychiatrist in making his pronouncements to the patient's friends, it is useful at the administrative level to be able to allocate the notoriously inadequate facilities for active psychiatric treatment to those elderly patients who are likely to respond. Clinical assessment, however, will have to be as full as that of younger patients. In order to differentiate organic from functional, or long-term from recent, disorders, the full history is essential. It is necessary to discover the way in which a patient's illness fits into his life story: does it represent the repetition of a previous pattern, or can it be demonstrated to be the terminal phase of a long-term development or decline? Full physical examination and a thorough assessment of the mental state are equally necessary; a comprehensive picture of the patient's psychopathology, at least in the descriptive sense of the term, should be obtained, and some forms of examination of so-called memory functions are diagnostically useful but time consuming. In practice, however, it may be impracticable to obtain an adequate history, and emotional disturbance may interfere with the assessment of the patient's mental and intellectual status. Thus we naturally wonder, especially when attempting to differentiate organic from functional disorders, whether we may not get help from special tests and investigations. We may even hope that some of these will be more sensitive than clinical procedures, allowing us to discover cerebral disorder before clinical symptoms have appeared. A considerable number of investigations have been published showing that physiological tests, especially those involving electroencephalography and estimations of oxygen utilization, are able to diagnose or exclude cerebral dysfunction in agreement with the judgments of the clinician. The same can be said of an even larger number of psychological tests; the usefulness of these procedures, however, is limited by the obvious snag that they cannot be applied where they are most needed—in the case of uncooperative patients with severe behavior disturbances, perplexity, confusion, refusal to speak—and where clinical differentiation may be impossible. Nevertheless there are, no doubt, situations where full clinical assessment of cooperative patients is impracticable and where tests may be usefully applied as screening procedures.

There also remains the possibility that physiological or psychological tests, being finer instruments than routine clinical examination, may yield more reliable predictions of the patient's future. This question can be decided only by follow-up studies in which predictions made on the basis of tests can be measured against the clinician's prognoses.

In the physiological area, the predictive value of the electro-encephalogram was examined by Pampiglione and Post (1958). Eighty-nine patients over sixty, who had been referred for E.E.G. examinations were followed up two years later by personal examination (thirty-one cases), reports from doctors and hospitals (twenty-seven cases), or by correspondence with their families (twenty-nine cases). Without knowledge of the E.E.G. findings and before the follow-up of patients was begun, the clinician, on clinical grounds, placed each case into one of the following categories, according to the suspected presence of cerebral pathology. Patients were called "definitely organic" (thirty-two cases) if they had clear histories of convulsions, strokes, or intellectual decline or in the presence of definite dementia or definite abnormal c.n.s. signs. Patients of this sort had been referred for E.E.G. examinations to assess the degree of brain damage or to establish the presence or absence of neoplasms. On the other hand, there were patients (twenty-three cases) with histories of fainting, dubious intellectual impairment, or perplexity who were labeled "unlikely organic" by the clinician, who wished to exclude the possibility of cerebral pathology more definitely by negative E.E.G. findings. Between these two groups there were thirty patients who were classed "doubtfully organic" because of dubious intellectual impairment and/or histories or neurological findings suggestive, but in no way conclusive, of the presence of brain damage. The electrophysiologists rated the results of the E.E.G. examination, which included overbreathing, photic stimulation, and recordings during quinal-barbital induced sleep, according to very precise criteria as "abnormal," "? abnormal," "? normal," and "normal."

There was a fair measure of agreement between the clinician's judgment and the electrophysiologist's findings: among the thirty-two patients classed on clinical grounds as "unlikely organic," only two had definitely abnormal, and seven "? abnormal," E.E.G. reports. Patients classed by the clinician as "doubtfully organic" had slightly more abnormal than normal E.E.G.'s. After follow-up, patients were graded according to the presence or absence of organic or functional psychiatric symptoms, according to whether they were at home or in a hospital, or according to cerebral or extracerebral causes of death. In general, there was a highly significant degree of accord between both the original clinical and E.E.G. gradings and the outcome after two years, but it had to be noted that the agreement between E.E.G. gradings and the outcomes was less than that between the clinical gradings and the outcomes; in other words, predictions based on clinical judgment were more reliable than those based on E.E.G. examination, and, furthermore, accord with outcome varied considerably with different E.E.G. gradings. As for clinical diagnoses, the agreement of the definitely organic grading with an outcome confirming the presence of cerebral disorder and the agreement of unlikely organic grading with a noncerebral outcome were both very highly significant, but, in the patients classed "doubtfully organic," the clinician was proved wrong by noncerebral outcome in a significant majority of cases. It was in this "doubtfully organic" group that the clinician needed the E.E.G. physician's help. We found that of the thirty-four patients in this group, there were only five in whom the dubious cerebral-organic features had become definite on follow-up. In four of them it was true that the E.E.G. had been definitely abnormal, but there were ten other patients in this clinically doubtful group who had definitely abnormal E.E.G.'s, but failed to develop clinical signs of brain damage during the two-year follow-up period. The possibility was considered that the presence of an abnormal

E.E.G., though not necessarily related to the development of future cerebral changes, might indicate a poor prognosis because of some underlying constitutional abnormality; this, however, was not the case, as many patients with E.E.G. abnormalities were free from symptoms two years later or, at any rate, were fit enough to live in their own homes. We came to the conclusion that clinical assessment had led to more reliable prognostications than E.E.G. examination, notwithstanding their value in special situations like diagnosing and locating neoplasms or differentially diagnosing the presenile dementias.

Turning to follow-up studies of psychological tests, Walton (1958) had found scores on the Wechsler memory scale and his modified word-learning test better predictors of outcome than clinical diagnoses. We suggested in the first section of this paper that these original diagnoses had not been well-founded.

Hopkins and Post (1955) have examined the value of some of Goldstein's tests of abstract and concrete behavior in arriving at differential diagnoses of elderly psychiatric patients. Briefly, we found that most patients, many of whom were elderly and some of whom were a young control group, were unable to assume the abstract attitude; in addition to brain damage, we suggested that low intelligence, age over sixty-eight years, and depression were factors in producing a concrete attitude. We found that the value of these tests in diagnosing the presence of cerebral disorder was very limited. Of more interest in the present context is that all the patients were followed up and rated according to outcome. Only one of the fifteen patients originally classified as free from cerebral pathology had developed evidence of brain changes; follow-up confirmed the original diagnosis of definitely psycho-organic in all but four of the sixteen patients; only two of eighteen patients classified as showing early dementia had come to show definite evidence of this disorder. Reclassifying the patients in the light of their later histories did not alter the relation between clinical judgment and test performance. Thus, the fact that so many of the patients were concrete in their attitudes did not have any prognostic significance, nor did it indicate that they were suffering from any clinically significant cerebral disorder.

More recently, Inglis, Colwell, and Post (1960), investigated the predictive power of an adaptation of the Bender Visual Motor Gestalt Test which had been shown (Shapiro, Post, Löfving, & Inglis, 1956) to differentiate significantly between functional and organic groups of elderly patients. As this test discriminated at a higher level of significance than many other measures which we had employed, it was studied more fully, and a more objective scoring system was evolved (Shapiro, Field, & Post, 1957). By summing the deviations from a right angle of each of the eight angles of two designs, we got an angles-measure score which differentiated the original criterion groups at the same high level of significance as the more subjective scoring method used earlier. In the more recent investigation we followed up, after two years, fifty-nine patients whom Field (1958) had tested and scored by their angles-measure scores. Twenty-one patients had been clinically diagnosed as organic and thirty-eight as functional. One of the investigators, a psychiatric social worker, obtained information from the patients and their friends, and the two other workers scored her reports independently on scales describing general adjustment, the presence or absence of psychiatric disabilities, and cognitive, and/or personality changes. These independent ratings were found to agree at an acceptable level of significance. Also the original clinical diagnosis correlated significantly with the various scores of adjustment at the time of the follow-up in that functional patients were found to have remained much better-adjusted to life, to have shown fewer psychiatric symptoms and intellectual and personality changes, and to have had a lower death rate. All this contrasted with the follow-up findings concerning those who had been clinically diagnosed as suffering from psychiatric illnesses secondary to cerebral changes at the time of testing. The Modified Bender Gestalt Test was again found to discriminate successfully between groups of organic and functional patients, but we were disappointed that the test lacked any predictive significance whatever for most of the follow-up items of adjustment. We also found that the test could not be used to predict either a malignant or relatively benign course in patients with organic psychoses and that it would not be useful in indicating the amount of future disability in the case of functional psychiatric disorders.

In concluding this section, we have to admit that none of the physiological and psychological tests so far employed is a better predictor of future health than clinical diagnosis.

TREATMENT-ORIENTED
FOLLOW-UP STUDIES

The studies so far reviewed may be criticized because they lack the human touch; we seem to have been too preoccupied with whether a patient died, developed signs of cerebral pathology, or remained in the same diagnostic category. However, these studies were valuable and necessary, for they made our therapeutic approach to aged mental patients more rational and scientific. In some of these studies we also began to rate the patients' follow-up status, not only in diagnostic categories, but also in different grades of adjustment or disability. We will now turn to studies which were more definitely geared to assessing progress and outcome in relation to treatment, and in this connection we shall discuss the shortcomings of the follow-up method as it has been practiced.

The first study owed its inception to recent trends in administrative psychiatry in Britain, which stress the role of community against the care of the hospital in treating mental patients (Colwell & Post, 1959). We were concerned to find out how much further help has to be given to elderly psychiatric patients after their discharge from inpatient treatment. We started our inquiry with the 130 patients who had been discharged during 1955 from the geriatric unit of the hospital, to which hopeless patients who need only nursing care are not usually admitted. All the same, about 25 per cent were suffering from organic psychoses of old age, 50 per cent were suffering from psychotic depressive reactions, 15 per cent had affective disorders of neurotic intensity, and about 10 per cent were so-called paraphrenics. The organic patients had largely been treated by occupational therapy and by giving attention to their general health and social problems. The depressed had been given psychotherapeutic guidance and, in most cases, ECT. Attention was given to family relationships, which was our only therapeutic approach to the paraphrenics at that time. Patients stayed in the unit for an average of about one hundred days, and they were followed up twenty-four months after discharge, in most cases with a personal meeting with the psychiatric social worker or psychiatrist. Though patients had remained in hospital until it was thought that they had received the maximum benefit from treatment, we found that only 15 per cent had made complete and lasting recoveries, 22 per cent recovered but had suffered early recurrence of symptoms, 24 per cent continued to show mild symptoms, and 39 per cent had remained continuously disabled by more severe disorders. The results of treatment were, of course, most disappointing in patients with mental symptoms from cerebral deterioration, but failure to recover completely from affective disorders and the high frequency of early recurrences of these disorders also emerged very clearly. Thus, our follow-up demonstrated that psychiatric illness in old age presented a continuity problem and that the great majority of patients in this age group would need further help. In fact, only 29 per cent of the patients went without further psychiatric attention; 20 per cent received further outpatient treatment, 31 per cent had further out- and inpatient treatment, and 20 per cent had further inpatient treatment. We estimated that one-third of the patients had been ill again without receiving any psychiatric treatment. During these times they had been in special need of community care and attention, especially from their family doctors, but also from social workers and agencies. We were disturbed to find that too many months might pass before these community workers referred patients back to a specialist for treatment. This study also confirmed our suspicion that preoccupations with diagnosis and the possible development of cerebral disorders may have diverted attention from some more important research problems of old-age psychiatry which were posed by the persistent nature of most conditions.

In another study (Post, 1961) 100 depressed patients over sixty were followed up for six years, and the surviving patients were re-examined by the psychiatrist under whose care they had been originally treated. Their situation was also evaluated by a psychiatric social worker. The original treatment had consisted of participation in a ward socializing program; a few patients were given planned psychotherapy, and for one-third special social casework was undertaken. At that time (1949-1951) we usually delayed ECT in the case of elderly patients until the ward program had been given a trial for four to six weeks. All the same, fifty-seven patients finally received this form of therapy. On discharge twenty-two patients were regarded as completely well, and sixty-five had some residual symptoms, although it was hoped that they were moving toward full recovery. Only one patient had died when in the hospital, and another twelve had not improved at all or had got worse.

Once again, the follow-up experience was chastening. We mentioned earlier that the risk of developing senile or arteriosclerotic brain changes was no higher in these depressed patients than in the general elderly population, but that they had shown a higher death rate from extracerebral disease (only one patient committed suicide). Review of the progress of our patients, however, revealed that only 25 per cent had recovered from all psychiatric symptoms; 28 per cent lost their affective disorder, but had continued to exhibit mainly hypochondriacal, anxious, or obsessional—so-called neurotic—symptoms, which had probably been present before they had become prone to affective illnesses. Forty-seven per cent of patients did not recover;

18 per cent had remained psychotic in the sense that they were never free from depression and delusional ideas or experiences. Twenty-nine per cent showed what seemed to be a personality change: in contrast to their previous adjustment, these patients became persistently miserable and morose and were suffering from hypochondriacal, anxious, and perhaps self-belittling feelings without any delusional elaborations or sleep or behavior disturbances. Moreover, there was a strong tendency toward further suffering and severe affective breakdowns. Only 7 per cent of the patients in this group failed to become more seriously ill, whereas among patients making good recoveries almost one-half remained free from recurrences. To a great extent, we failed to correlate the outcome of the illness with our patients' previous personalities, health, or illnesses. Depressed patients with definite dementia and clear evidence of arteriosclerotic brain damage did badly; patients who made the fullest recoveries tended to have been significantly more extroverted than the rest. The possibility of a relation between favorable outcome and a family history of no affective disorders and no severe affective illness before the age of fifty failed to reach statistically significant levels. In particular, we found no relationship between further progress and the type of treatment given: ECT did not affect ultimate outcome.

It was, therefore, of special interest to discover whether external circumstances in our patients' lives might have affected their mental health. The psychiatric social worker and the psychiatrist rated patients on whether they had deteriorated in their personal relationships, decreased their responsibilities, and failed to maintain their general and leisure interests in the course of the follow-up period. We also obtained more objective ratings by adding up numerical scores which had been given for changes during this period in housing, income, employment, number of people in the same household, and number of contacts outside the family. Combining the impressionistic with the more objective ratings (which agreed very well), we were able to distribute patients over a number of social-outcome groups. The top group contained people with well-maintained social adjustments and the bottom group patients with severely deteriorated social adjustments. Social outcome was found to correlate significantly with clinical outcome: in other words, patients who had been mentally ill during much of the follow-up period had also deteriorated in their social adjustments, whereas patients who had maintained their social position had either remained well or had recovered soon after suffering further breakdowns.

Unfortunately, we are unable to answer the questions which naturally follow from these observations: did our patients remain well, or did they become mental invalids because their social circumstances remained favorable or deteriorated? Or, had decline or improvement and social adjustment been caused by worsened or improved mental health? As far as our information went, it suggested that social changes for the better or the worse had been the results, rather than causes, of changes in mental health. But as our data were obtained mainly at the end of the follow-up period, our interpretations were made retrospectively. In fact this and all the previously discussed follow-up studies failed in one important respect: they took account of the subject's constitutional make-up, the symptomatology of his illness, and the treatment administered, but, apart from recording subsequent physical illness, no allowances were made in any of these studies for the patients' further life experiences—whether they were widowed or had lost their friends, incomes, homes, and so on.

By now the limitations of the follow-up method will be clear. Following up patients may be informative in administrative psychiatry where diagnostic labeling will help determine the patients' treatment and care; it has also been useful in confirming the value of a definite diagnosis before beginning treatment. But the follow-up method has failed to help us in what has turned out to be the main problem of old-age psychiatry—the long-term treatment, management, and care of our patients. It is suggested that in this area we shall make progress only if we begin to note and evaluate the events in the patients' lives for some time after they have received treatment. A method which follows patients from their original treatment up to some arbitrary date has to be replaced by a method which follows through. This means that patients will be followed through a span of their lives and that observations will be made not only at the end of, but also throughout, the period. In this way it should become much easier to unravel the cause and effect relationship which we suspect to exist between the fluctuations of our patients' health and fortunes.

The follow-through method was used in a therapeutic experiment with persistently confused old people suffering from arteriosclerotic or senile dementias (Cosin, Mort, Westropp, & Williams, 1958). A number of social, occupational, and combined therapeutic techniques were administered, each for four weeks, to small groups of patients. Ratings of behavior and the performance on a number of simple tests were assessed at the beginning and end of each treatment period, as well as at the end of the two weeks between treatments after the patients had been left to their own resources. Treatments continued over six months in some cases, over twelve months in others. In terms of their over-all progress, the patients thus treated did no better than an untreated control group, but the serial scores obtained in the course of this follow-through study showed very clearly and consistently that patients improved toward the end of each treatment period, only to fall back during the fortnights without treatment. By using the follow-through method we discovered that persistently confused old people responded equally well to a variety of social and occupational techniques, but that in patients with established dementia continuous and unceasing stimulation would be required to keep them at a higher level of functioning; in other words, treatment was likely to be palliative and supportive only. We recognized that our treatments might prove curative if applied to patients with early mental deterioration, but, when we tried to bring such early cases into treatment, we failed, and we discovered that patients tended to be referred for special treatment only at a time when their dementia was well-advanced.

FOLLOW-THROUGH INVESTIGATIONS

Post (1959) has discussed some causes for the delay in discovering old-age dementia, expressing the opinion that the fault did not lie with relatives or family doctors, as even experts were unable to discover early dementia and were often wrong in suspecting early mental deterioration in their clinical work. Making use of Cattell's (1943) concepts of "fluid" and "crystallized" abilities, an explanation was suggested for the apparently sudden appearance of clear-cut, relatively severe dementias: in pathological aging there might be a steep decline of fluid ability (the ability to handle new concepts). The patient's friends either do not notice this or gloss over it because old people rarely need to use their fluid abilities and bad memory is accepted as a normal accompaniment of old age. Ultimately crystallized ability deteriorates as well, and, when the old person begins failing to handle everyday routine matters, advice is sought, and severe, total, and largely irreversible dementia is easily confirmed.

It appears possible that cases of early dementia might be discovered by administering to old people every few months tests designed to measure different types of mental ability and by finding out whether the rate of decline in some abilities was steeper in deteriorating subjects than in normally aging subjects. Mass testing of old people in order to discover those in danger of becoming demented may appear a rather Utopian suggestion, but we should remember that a few years ago the suggestion of any program for treating mental senility would have sounded equally absurd. We have begun some preliminary studies. The Wechsler-Bellevue Intelligence Scale has been standardized for healthy elderly people, but no retest data are available yet. Our plan is to get such data for several testings in the course of one year, and we shall try to collect serial measurements from normal old people, patients with organic old-age psychoses, and functional psychiatric patients, some of whom are receiving ECT and some of whom are not. It is planned to obtain the same kind of data for two measures of memory functioning—Inglis' paired associate learning test (Inglis, 1957) and the Walton-Black modified word-learning test (1957). In this way we hope to obtain information concerning the rates of decline in several cognitive areas for normal as well as mentally ill old people. If consistent patterns of differential rates of decline are found, this may lead to using these or similar instruments to discover dementia at a stage at which it could still be treated.

Of more immediate practical value is another follow-through investigation concerning elderly patients with symptoms of persecution. When these symptoms are part of an affective illness, paranoid symptoms tend to disappear with the mood disorder; otherwise they usually persist and produce severe incapacity. Theoretically, paranoid symptoms in the elderly are held to be the result of either a late schizophrenic development sometimes called paraphrenia, or a slow deteriorating process of arteriosclerotic or senile origin, which usually occurs in people with suspicious, sensitive, or quarrelsome characters. There is no need to quote from the extensive literature ascribing to chlorpromazine and other psychotropic drugs beneficial effects on schizophrenic symptoms, especially paranoid ones. In our clinical work we have also found gratifying responses in the various paranoid disorders of elderly people. Sometimes symptoms recurred when patients discontinued the drugs, but, on resuming treatment, the symptoms were again controlled, and we felt that the stage for a more methodical investigation had been reached. The study has been planned not only to test the efficiency of the drug (Trifluoperazine in this case) by alternating it with a placebo, but also to try and find out whether varying responses to this treatment may not help to differentiate old-age paranoid illnesses. There is, for instance, a slight chance that late schizophrenics showing primary Bleulerian symptoms may respond less well to drugs than old people showing a character change or dementia with florid symptoms of persecution, including hallucinations but without passivity feelings, thought withdrawal, or other signs of dissolution of the ego boundaries. Patients will be studied over several years by re-examining them and seeing their friends every three months. In this way it should be possible to map each patient's progress in relation to drug dosage, physical health, and events in his social environment. We hope to gain valid information concerning the treatment of what has hitherto been one of the most intractable disorders of old age and to elucidate the theoretically important subject of late schizophrenia.

CONCLUSIONS

At the outset we emphasized that treatment of psychiatric disorders, especially those occurring in old age, should not be undertaken without considering long-term results and effects. In treating patients, we attempt to stimulate and encourage the natural processes of recovery; we try to compensate for deficiencies, and we may influence or even suppress trends which we fear will lead the patient further into his illness. In order to do this, we have to find out more about the condition from which the patient is suffering. We have to discover the nature of harmful trends, defects, and any mechanisms which might lead to readjustment under favorable circumstances. To put it briefly, we need to make some diagnostic and prognostic assessment.

We have shown how follow-up studies have been used to confirm the validity of diagnostic categories. Some evidence has been produced to show that elderly patients do not usually change from one reaction type to another and especially that people with depressive illnesses do not develop cerebral deterioration any more frequently than the elderly population in general.

We demonstrated that there were not yet physiological or psychological tests which could be used to predict future cerebral deterioration more reliably than diagnostic evaluations by careful clinicians. It has also become clear, however, that the future of even those psychiatric patients who were unlikely to develop cerebral pathology was far from rosy and that in a large majority of cases functional disorders tended to become chronic or recurred frequently. Treatment of mental ill health in old age will thus have to be continuous, and, in gauging the value of different ways of management, the follow-up method has been shown inadequate, as it failed to take account of the patient's life between his first attendance and an arbitrarily determined follow-up date.

A method by which patients are followed-through over a number of years has been suggested, and an investigation of this type, concerning the treatment of paranoid patients with a psychotropic drug, has been briefly described. The need for applying current methods in treating patients with early senile or arteriosclerotic changes—the most important illnesses of old age—has been demonstrated, and the difficulties of finding such patients have been stressed. We saw that follow-up studies have shown that by the time patients reach the psychiatrist differentiating between functional and organic mental disorders is not difficult. In the future, therefore, instead of asking whether a patient is becoming demented, we shall be concerned with discovering the speed at which deterioration in any area of mental ability is progressing. It is hoped that psychometric follow-through studies of normal and psychologically ill old people will furnish us with norms of deterioration rates and that these will be used to select people during the early stages of senile deterioration so that they can be successfully treated for this tragic and degrading disorder.

REFERENCES

Avery, L.W. Common factors precipitating mental symptoms in the aged. *Arch. Neurol. Psychiat.*, 1945, **54**, 312-314.

Cattell, R.B. The measurement of adult intelligence. *Psychol. Bull.*, 1943, **40**, 153-193.

Cohen, M.M. Cerebrovascular accidents. *Amer. med. Ass. Arch. Pathol.*, 1955, **60**, 296-307.

Collins, S.D., Trantham, K.S., & Lehmann, J.L. Sickness experience in selected areas of the United States. *Publ. Hlth Monogr.*, 1955, No. 25. (U.S. Department of Health, Education, and Welfare, Washington, D.C.)

Colwell, Catherine, & Post, F. Community needs of elderly psychiatric patients. *Brit. med. J.*, 1959, **2**, 214-217.

Cosin, L.Z., Mort, Margaret, Westropp, Celia, & Williams, Moyra. Experimental treatment of persistent senile confusion. *Int. J. soc. Psychiat.*, 1958, **4**, 24-42.

Field, J. An experimental investigation of the copying of designs by elderly psychiatric patients. Unpublished doctoral thesis, London, 1958.

Hopkins, Barbara, & Post, F. The significance of abstract and concrete behavior in elderly psychiatric patients and control subjects. *J. ment. Sci.*, 1955, **101**, 841-850.

Inglis, J. An experimental study of learning and "memory function" in elderly psychiatric patients. *J. ment. Sci.,* 1957, **103,** 796-803.

Inglis, J., Colwell, Catherine, & Post, F. An evaluation of the predictive power of a test known to differentiate between elderly "functional" and "organic" psychiatric patients. *J. ment. Sci.,* 1960, **106,** 1486-1492.

Inglis, J., Shapiro, M.B., & Post, F. "Memory function" in psychiatric patients over sixty, the role of memory in tests discriminating between "functional" and "organic" groups. *J. ment. Sci.,* 1956, **102,** 589-598.

Kay, D.W.K. Observations on the natural history and genetics of old age psychoses: A Stockholm survey, 1931-1937. *Proc. roy. Soc. Med.,* 1959, **52,** 791-794. (Abridged)

Kay, D.W.K., Roth, M., & Hopkins, Barbara. Affective disorders arising in the senium. I. Their association with cerebral degeneration. *J. ment. Sci.,* 1955, **101,** 302-316.

Kay, D.W.K., Norris, Vera, & Post, F. Prognosis in psychiatric disorders of the elderly. *J. ment. Sci.,* 1956, **102,** 129-140.

Krawiecki, J.A., Couper, L., & Walton, D. The efficacy of parentrovite in the treatment of a group of senile psychotics. *J. ment. Sci.,* 1957, **103,** 601-605.

Norris, Vera, & Post, F. Treatment of elderly psychiatric patients: Use of a diagnostic classification. *Brit. med. J.,* 1954, **1,** 675-679.

Pampiglione, G., & Post, F. The value of electroencephalographic examination in psychiatric disorders. *Geriatrics,* 1958, **13,** 725-732.

Post, F. The outcomes of mental breakdowns in old age. *Brit. med. J.,* 1951. **1,** 436-440.

Post, F. Some research problems in old age psychiatry. *Proc. royal Soc. Med.,* 1956, **49,** 240-243.

Post, F. Early treatment of persistent senile confusion. *Geront. clin.,* 1959, **1,** 114-121.

Post, F. The significance of affective symptoms in old age. Unpublished, London, 1961.

Roth, M. The natural history of mental disorders in old age. *J. ment. Sci.,* 1955, **101,** 281-301.

Roth, M., & Morrissey, J.D. Problems in the diagnoses and classification of mental disorder in old age. *J. ment. Sci.,* 1952, **98,** 66-80.

Shapiro, M.B., Post, F., Löfving, Barbro, & Inglis, J. Memory function in psychiatric patients over 60: Some methodological and diagnostic implications. *J. ment. Sci.,* 1956, **102,** 233-246.

Shapiro, M.B., Field, J., & Post, F. An inquiry into the determinants of a differentiation between elderly "organic" and "non-organic" psychiatric patients on the Bender Gestalt test. *J. ment. Sci.,* 1957, **103,** 364-374.

Walton, D. The diagnostic and predictive accuracy of the modified word learning test in psychiatric patients over 65. *J. ment. Sci.,* 1958, **104,** 1111-1122.

Walton, D., & Black, D.A. The validity of a psychological test of brain damage. *Brit. J. Med. Psychol.,* 1957, **30,** 270-279.

CHAPTER 25

*Community and Hospital Care
of the Mentally Ill*

PETER SAINSBURY

The emphasis in treatment of the mentally ill has been shifting in recent years from hospital to community care. The Worthing experiment, a domiciliary and day hospital service started by Dr. Carse in 1957 (Carse, Panton, & Watt, 1958) and recently extended to the Chichester area, is one of a number of schemes that represent this change. Its object, to quote Dr. Carse, was "to discover whether the provision of large-scale psychiatric treatment on an out-patient basis can materially affect the great annual increase of admissions to the mental hospital" (p. 39).

There is no doubt that the Worthing experiment has been outstandingly successful in achieving what it set out to do. Compared with the admissions in the year prior to the introduction of the community service (Carse, 1959), admissions to Graylingwell from the experimental area were reduced by 56 per cent in the first year of the experiment and by 62 per cent in the second year. This experiment, then, has shown that admissions to a mental hospital can be

537

reduced by a community psychiatric service. It has not, however, shown the comparative therapeutic values of the community and the traditional types of treatment; the benefits or burdens this type of service has brought to the community, particularly to the families of the patients who are treated at home; and which clinical and social considerations favor community care, which hospital care.

The medical staffs at Graylingwell and the Old Manor, Salisbury, and the Medical Research Council's Clinical Psychiatry Research Unit have, therefore, cooperated in an investigation to evaluate two aims of the community care program in Chichester. The first aim was to study the clinical, social, and environmental factors which determine whether a mentally ill patient is treated at home or in a hospital. For example, whether two clinically similar patients with a depressive illness of moderate severity are treated at home or in a hospital is likely to be determined by such factors as whether they are living alone, the type of job they have, or their family responsibilities. Our second aim was to study how caring for a mentally ill person at home affected his family and household.

The relation of clinical and social factors to disposal was explored in a preliminary study in which Dr. Morrissey, the consultant in charge of the Chichester area, and I compared the admissions from Chichester to Graylingwell in 1957 with those in 1958, the year in which the community service was introduced (Morrissey & Sainsbury, 1959). We found that there was a significantly greater reduction in certain vital social and clinical groups in 1958; male admissions, for example, decreased more than female and married people more than single. Similarly, neurotics, patients living near the hospital, patients of higher social class, and patients with affective psychoses or histories of mental disorder showed significantly greater reductions in 1958 admission rates.

We thought these findings justified a more detailed investigation. In our present study, therefore, Dr. Grad and I predicted certain factors likely to favor treatment at home and others likely to favor treatment by hospitalization. We planned to assess and compare these in two areas which resemble one another closely except that in one, Chichester, there is a domiciliary service, whereas in the other, Salisbury, there is the more usual and conservative policy for admission to the mental hospital.

Our method was to arrange for the clinical data on every new patient in both areas to be systematically recorded on a prepared item sheet which is completed by the psychiatrist at his initial interview with the patient. The clinical details recorded are family and history, duration of illness, the principal symptoms, diagnosis, treatment, and disposal. In the Chichester area the psychiatrist also records his clinical and social reasons for admitting or not admitting the patient.

In addition to the item sheet, a detailed social schedule is completed by the psychiatric social workers after a visit to the home of every new patient. They record data on social and familial factors believed to determine disposal: the patient's mode of living and composition of his household (this includes the age of members of the household, their relationship to the patient, and the number of people in the home), his social and economic status, the employment situation, housing, locality, family health, cooperation from friends and neighbors, attitude of household members toward the patient and his admission, and the effects of specified symptoms and their duration on the household.

In order to study our other aim, the effects on the family of caring for a mentally ill member, the psychiatric social workers also recorded the effects on the employment of household members, domestic routine, schooling, social and leisure activities, the family's income, the mental and physical health of household members, and relations with neighbors. In this way each family member's (informant's) appraisal of the advantages and disadvantages to his family of admission or domiciliary care is tabulated or rated.

This research is in its early stages, and so far only two pilot studies have been completed. Their purpose was to measure the reliability of the two questionnaires and to learn whether the doctors' item sheets and the social workers' schedules help in discerning the differences we seek and expect.

To assess the reliability of the item sheet, two psychiatrists independently completed it for ninety patients, and their agreements were recorded. The extent to which agreement on diagnosis is determined by agreement on symptoms, duration of the illness, history of illness, and so on has been calculated by Dr. Kreitman. He found that agreement on broad diagnostic categories was 79 per cent, organic illness 85 per cent, psychoses 71 per cent, neuroses 51.7 per cent, and all other conditions 33.3 per cent. Agreement on diagnosis was significantly related to the level of agreement on previous illness, although it was not related to agreement on symptoms.

The second pilot study was undertaken by Dr. Grad, Mrs. Collins, and Mrs. Stamp, who visited the households of sixty patients.

They visited in pairs, but completed separate schedules for each interview. The percentage of agreement on the seventy-two items in the schedule was assessed and showed agreement rate of at least 85 per cent on sixty-three items. With the information from the pilot study, unreliable questions were redefined or omitted from the schedule that is being used for the major inquiry.

The findings also indicate that interesting material is likely to emerge on factors determining disposal of patients and on the effects of caring for a mentally ill person at home. For example, the studies confirmed the preliminary findings that admission was related to household size, age, and diagnosis and also indicated a trend relating the patient's social class and financial status to admission to the hospital.

Our tentative conclusions from a preliminary analysis of the problems that these sixty patients were causing their families at the time of referral were that in 36 per cent of the families social activities had been restricted, in 25 per cent the job of a family member had been affected, and in 40 per cent there were some problems of management (in 20 per cent these were severe problems). The health of the family member was affected psychologically in 32 per cent and physically in 36 per cent; the health of other family members was affected in 44 per cent of households (severely in 20 per cent). These figures were higher in the families of those patients whom it was decided to admit. Following admission, however, the effects on the families of the inpatient group were numerically fewer than those on the families of the patients who remained at home.

Only when we have collected all the clinical and social data of patients on referral in both districts will it be possible to analyze and compare the findings in the two services and to begin a follow-up study to compare each outcome by clinical categories and type of treatment. We hope to assess outcome through the changes in the patient's clinical symptoms, the effects reported by his family, or his altered social and economic position.

REFERENCES

Carse, J. *The Worthing experiment: A report.* Chichester: Graylingwell Hospital, 1959.

Carse, J., Panton, Nydia E., & Watt, A. A district mental health service: The Worthing experiment. *Lancet,* 1958, **1,** 39-41.

Morrissey, J., & Sainsbury, P. Observations on the Chichester and district mental health service. *Proc. roy. Soc. Med.,* 1959, **52,** 1061-1063.

CHAPTER 26

Rehabilitation of
Long-Term Aged Patients

WILMA DONAHUE

The greatest threats of old age are long-term chronic illness, disability, and mental illness with consequent institutionalization and loss of independent status. The need is for programs of prevention and, when necessary, rehabilitation to relieve society of the burden of large numbers of dependent people and to ensure the aging of a continuing measure of self-reliance in normal community life.

Medical procedures for the rehabilitation of physical function are more advanced and accepted than are socioenvironmental therapies for the maintenance and restoration of personality function. To date, most experiments of the socioenvironmental type have been carried out in mental hospitals, but the principles found in these long-term institutions are probably equally applicable to hospitals serving the chronically ill aged.

541

Conceptualization of psychological and social aging has been needed to stimulate and assist the designing of psychosocial therapeutic programs for elderly people in institutional settings. Recently several theories relevant to planning effective treatment of ill older people have been proposed. The theories, however, are not in agreement. Some support the assumption that adjustment in old age will be promoted by continuing activity; others imply that good adjustment of the aged is tantamount to being able to give up customary activity roles and accept a continuously lower level of social participation and activity. Obviously the nature of programs to improve the personal and social functioning of the older person will vary, depending on which theory of social aging is accepted.

Data in support of the various theories are not yet conclusive. John Anderson (1960) makes a strong case for the necessity of the human organism to occupy time and space with interrelated activities without special reference to content. He points out that by nature the human being is active rather than passive and must be regarded as an energy system. He says:

> If we regard the living system as an energy system and ask questions about the relation of activity to the well-being of the system, particularly in the light of its capacity for self-maintenance and self-repair, provided input is kept up, it follows that use and activity are beneficial to the person and that the normal healthy person is essentially energetic and active. When the person becomes ill, or has inadequate nutrition, his activity level drops in order to conserve his resources. Non-activity and non-use in the long run result in deterioration (p. 771).

Exponents of the activity theory point to Heron's (1957) work on boredom, showing that confinement in an unchanging, restricting environment quickly resulted in deterioration of behavior and appearance of abnormal sensations and mental states. Hebb (1955) observed similar results in animals kept under conditions of minimal stimulation. Anderson (1959) points out that there is a "psychological tonus," similar to physiological tonus, which depends on the presence of arousal stimuli; if this tonus is lowered, mental activity is adversely affected.

In Chapter 9 of this volume, Shmavonian and Busse present some new data which lend credence from another modality to the activity hypothesis. Using the GSR (galvanic skin response) technique, they compared the nonspecific reactivity of young and old subjects. In periods when only meaningless tones were presented as stimuli, the aged showed a significantly lower number of nonspecifics (increase in amplitude of GSR unrelated to a specific stimulus, a new measure made possible by extremely sensitive GSR meters) than younger subjects. When meaningful stimuli (sentences) were used, the difference disappeared. It is suggested that the young subjects were generally more aroused and thus reacted to the nonspecific stimuli, whereas the old people were not aroused, and the tones failed to elicit a psychogalvanic reflex. The authors speculate that:

> It may well be that during aging people gradually lose interest in the meaningless stimuli which bombard them every day of their lives and that this selective inattention gives an impression of a slowing central nervous system. When stimuli are given an appropriate meaning, however, the difference between the two age groups disappears and, in essence, the aged can react appropriately.

For those acquainted with the monotony of institutional life in the average long-term hospital, it is easy to speculate that the personality deterioration so often seen in patients is, in large part, a response to the lack of meaningful stimulation and activity.

The need for continued activity as a means to good adjustment in old age is also supported by those who have sought to explain social aging according to role theory (Albrecht, 1951; Blau, 1956; Havighurst, 1957; Henry, 1956; Phillips, 1957). According to the concepts of role theory, the well-adjusted older person is one who has learned a number of socially approved roles earlier in life and then continues to enact at least some of them during later maturity. It has been suggested (Albrecht, 1951) that social aspects of senility may be prevented if suitable roles are available to older people. Havighurst (1957) enumerated such key roles for older people as citizen, worker, spouse, homemaker, parent, friend, and church and association member. He has found that role competency is positively related to the degree of ego-involvement and socioeconomic status and that role performance scores among a population of normal older adults from various occupations do not decline significantly with age.

If enactment of learned roles congruent with social expectancies is important to personal adjustment, it would appear that most institutional settings fail to provide the environment in which patients can find a social role. Instead, the individual is expected to find satisfaction in the patient role—a regressed state of dependency and passivity—and isolation from the world outside the hospital.

Another theory for social aging has been proposed by Cumming and Henry (1961). To some extent it opposes the activity theory and would, therefore, seem to dictate quite different goals for a treatment program. It postulates that a progressive disengagement from life is a natural response to growing older. Cumming and Henry (1961) state the theory as follows:

> In our theory, aging is an inevitable mutual withdrawal or disengagement, resulting in decreased interaction between the aging person and others in the social systems he belongs to. The process may be initiated by the individual or by others in the situation. The aging person may withdraw more markedly from some classes of people while remaining relatively close to others. His withdrawal may be accompanied from the outset by an increased preoccupation with himself; certain institutions in society may make this withdrawal easy for him. When the aging process is complete, the equilibrium which existed in middle life between the individual and his society has given way to a new equilibrium characterized by a greater distance and an altered type of relationship (p. 14).

They do not place a value judgment on the disengagement process, but do indicate that all signs of disengagement—object cathexis, lessened amount and variety of interaction, and so forth—occur with age. At the same time, however, they find that there is a slight rise in satisfaction and morale. By implication, at least, disengagement would seem to be one key to adjustment in old age. Cumming and Henry speculate that it may be the process by which people become ready to accept death.

With these theories of social aging as a background, some aspects of a demonstration-research project on the care and rehabilitation of chronically ill aged people will be reported here, and, although the project was not designed to test specific hypotheses, some interpretation of results in reference to these concepts will be attempted.

BACKGROUND AND DESIGN

Traditional stereotypes of the hopelessness of old age and the futility of putting money into treating people whose lives will not last very long have interfered with community and professional acceptance of responsibility for applying new knowledge and techniques. Further, newer information has not been disseminated yet, and the number of people trained to apply the new skills is inadequate. For these and other reasons, there is need for repeated demonstration and study to illustrate what modern science and clinical techniques can do to ameliorate the physical and mental ills of older people and, in so doing, improve the social health of the community while decreasing the financial burden placed on it.

With the assistance of a grant from the United States Office of Vocational Rehabilitation and the National Institutes of Health, The University of Michigan's Division of Gerontology and Medical School have undertaken such a study-demonstration in the tax supported medical-care facilities of three counties in Michigan. The primary purposes of the project were to survey the health and rehabilitation potential of the older patients being cared for in these facilities; to demonstrate the nature of medical and socioenvironmental programs which will help reinstate the physical and personal independence of the patients, reduce the effects of institutionalization, return the patients to the community, and establish permanent community-hospital relationships for serving the patients; and to train the hospital personnel so that they can carry on the programs after the close of the demonstration.

In order to discuss the rehabilitation of patients in a meaningful way, it is necessary to give a brief description of the county medical-care facilities in Michigan. There are thirty-nine such facilities which provide care for approximately 4,100 patients, 3,100 of whom are sixty-five and over (Winter, 1960). These facilities are the traditional public solution for the care of the indigent, incapacitated, and others unable to care for themselves. Typically, one-fourth of the patients are confined to bed, and almost another quarter are chairbound. Almost one-third are mentally confused, and a few are psychotic. In no more than three of these facilities has any attempt been made to provide more than custodial care. Physicians are usually retained on a part-time basis and make ward rounds once or twice a week. Nursing care is under the supervision of a registered nurse, but otherwise the nursing staff is made up of aides and a few licensed practical nurses. Except for treating patients who become acutely ill, medical specialists and therapists are used only rarely. Social activities are left almost entirely to the chance visits of community groups looking for captive audiences. All in all, these facilities present a picture of a dreary, passive, isolated environment where old people are offered meager medical and nursing regimens and where psychosocial rehabilitation is even less in evidence.

In this context the University of Michigan project was begun by selecting medical-care facilities matched for such characteristics as age, sex ratio, length of average stay, and nature of chronic illnesses and disabilities of patients and for such institutional variables as number of beds, cost, staffing patterns, and medical services. One of the three institutions was used for a control; the other two, Jackson and Washtenaw, were experimental units. Later the control also became an experimental hospital.

The Study Population

There are two population groups in each hospital, the demonstration population, made up of all the patients forty-four and over available for testing at the outset of the program, and the research population, composed of the patients from the demonstration group who were available for a second test assessment at the close of the experimental program. At Jackson there were forty patients in the demonstration group and twenty-nine in the research population; at Washtenaw the corresponding figures were thirty-five and twenty-two.

The project was limited to patients forty-five and older. However, only two patients of the seventy-five in the demonstration population from both hospitals were under fifty; fifty-eight were over sixty. The median age of the demonstration population at Jackson was seventy-three, at Washtenaw seventy-six (Table 1).

Procedure

The design of the demonstration study has been reported at some length (Donahue, 1960; Donahue & Rae, 1960), therefore only a summary will be included here.

The first phase of the study was the assessment of the physical, functional, psychosocial, and vocational status and potential of patients forty-five and over in all three hospitals. On the basis of the data, an evaluation of the potential of each patient was made, and a prescription for medical treatment and psychosocial therapy was determined. The second phase of the project consisted of an experimental program which provided socioenvironmental and medical treatment according to the assessed needs of the patients. In approximately nine months, a second assessment similar to the first one was made in all three hospitals to determine whether the program had resulted in measurable changes. After the third facility had served as a control for the other two, it became the third experimental hospital for the study. After a demonstration period equivalent to that in the other two hospitals, a final assessment of the patients will be made. Thus before and after data using the third hospital as its own control will be available for comparison.

Data

A group of specialists made the medical evaluation, which included a general physical; a functional evaluation; a neurological appraisal; and ophthalmological, dental, and speech examinations. Laboratory studies, which were done by a mobile team of technicians from The University of Michigan Hospital, included a hematocrit, blood sugar and glucose tolerance, serology, stool and urine; chest X rays were also made (Bloomer, 1960; Brandt, 1960; Brandt & Tupper, 1960; Currier, 1960; Di Napoli, Kingery, & Gibbons, 1960; Smith, Brandt, & Currier, 1960).

The psychological and social data were collected by personal interview, the Chicago attitudes scale (Cavan, Burgess, Havighurst, & Goldhamer, 1949), a patient schedule specially designed for the project, and the morale scale used by Kutner, Fanshel, Togo, and Langner (1956). Intelligence was tested with the WAIS, and some projective tests were administered in selected cases. A sociometric test was used to measure changes in social interaction (Donahue, Hunter, Coons, & Maurice, 1960). Other records included nurses' ratings of the patients' improvement and the patients' participation rating of various activities.

THE REHABILITATION PROGRAM

Discussion of the demonstration program will be restricted to the parts concerned with psychosocial rehabilitation, although, of course, it is related to the medical and physical restorative programs, and neither part would have been complete without the other.

The first step in the experimental program was to establish a more therapeutic milieu in the hospital. Swartz (1957) has given a useful classification of the components of this milieu, and the following report of the rehabilitation program is organized according to these components.

Organization and Activities

Relatively little could be done to change the actual system of organization within the hospital because of limitations in staff number and training and lack of funds to add needed personnel. To offset this, the demonstration team became, as far as possible, a functional part of the hospital staff, adding new skills, sharing the work of patient care, and expediting communication among the study team, staff, and patients. The hospital staff was formally trained in a week-long intensive program in rehabilitation care and treatment. During the program informal training took place continually through demonstrations of procedures and conscious efforts to communicate the goals of the program and the needs of the patients.

The investigators are inclined to agree with von Mering and King (1957), who point out that, no matter what type of therapy is employed, patients get better if people work with them. Some programs, however, lend themselves more readily to the achievement of therapeutic goals. The objectives which must be met if a mental hospital is to have a therapeutic milieu have been outlined by Swartz (1957):

> These goals are designed to (1) provide the patient with experiences that minimize his distortions of reality, (2) facilitate realistic and meaningful communications with others, (3) facilitate participation with others so that he derives greater satisfaction and security therefrom, (4) reduce his anxiety and increase his comfort, (5) increase his self-esteem, (6) provide him with insight into the causes and manifestations of his illness, (7) mobilize his initiative and motivate him to realize his potentialities for creativity and productiveness (p. 131).

We believe that the same goals with, perhaps, some shift in emphasis are equally applicable to long-term medical facilities for the care of the aged.

In order to realize these goals in the experimental hospitals, four specific therapeutic programs were instituted: (1) a sheltered workshop, (2) craft training, (3) social-recreational activities, and (4) friendly visiting. These activities were selected because we were interested in learning how much, if any, occupational potential these old people had and because they afforded opportunities to bring members of the local community into the therapeutic program.

The study was not designed to determine which therapy was most useful in bringing about the desired changes in patients, but we observed that each activity seemed to serve a different function and to represent different values for the patients. In the sheltered workshop they saw themselves in the role of worker, especially when the local employer who was supplying the contracts was pleased with their work and granted them pay increases. In the craft program, although they could earn money, the component of being employed seemed to be absent except in the instance of a patient who went into the business of making rugs to order. The role of creator was predominant for this activity. The social-recreational programs gave sanction to types of personal expression usually suppressed in the close living arrangements of the county hospital, and, because extramural activities were included, they broke the isolation—often of several years' duration—of the patient from the community. Finally, the visiting program provided each patient with his own special friend. The visitor was trained to be interested, friendly, understanding, and hopeful with "his" patient and to treat him as a unique individual with the right to personal strivings. This program seemed to fulfill still another of the therapeutic needs of the patient, the opportunity to enact the role of friend.

Setting

It was not possible to improve the physical environment of the patients. The hospitals afford practically no privacy for the patients; some live in large wards, and none lives in groups of less than four. The Jackson hospital in particular was seriously overcrowded, and the activities and physical restorative treatments had to be provided in halls, using portable equipment. The overcrowding was reflected in more bickering—sometimes physical fighting—among the Jackson patients than among the more spaciously housed Washtenaw patients. The difference in patient interaction was also apparent in the sociometric data.

Relations with the Nonhospital World

Von Mering and King (1957) observe that when a person is confined in an institution for a long time, his feeling of "lostness" is compounded and that preoccupation with self becomes more certain the longer he remains exclusively confined with his fellow patients. Kay and Roth (Chapter 20, *supra*) have shown that social isolation, fostered by such factors as deafness, position in a family, and lack of surviving relatives, appears to be causally related to mental illness, especially paraphrenia, in some elderly people.

To overcome some of the isolation from the community, volunteers were trained to serve as aides in the craft, workshop, and recreational programs. At Jackson, where no hospital auxiliary existed, one was established as a permanent service group for the hospital.

Other resources of the community were utilized, especially as a part of the discharge program. The Social Welfare Department supplied a social worker who attempted to find the special living arrangements needed by each patient to be discharged. The vocational counselors reviewed the potentials of patients recommended for employment. The local Goodwill Industries and Salvation Army provided some work for discharged patients, and the local golden age clubs and other groups for older people made special efforts to include them in their activities.

SOME RESULTS

At this time, it is possible to report on the most obvious accomplishments in the two hospitals and to give some data which show directional changes in the hospital groups. The before data, collected at the first assessment of the patients, and the after data, collected at the close of the active rehabilitation phase of the program, can be compared on some measures to show what change took place.

It is difficult to obtain measures which will show significant changes among a group of people whose problems are so profound and complex and whose personal and social resources are so limited. With only an occasional exception, the group is characterized by poverty, poor health, permanent physical damage, social isolation, low occupational level, and limited education (Table 1). In short, most of the patients have their origins in the lower social class and their motivations, wishes, aspirations, and values need to be interpreted with reference to the social norms of this class. Unfortunately, knowledge of these norms is largely lacking, as it is for the elderly of all other classes.

The meaning of rehabilitation, moreover, may vary greatly from one patient to another. For one, restoration of function and independence may be a desirable goal; for another it may mean only that he is to be placed in another situation, one much more stressful than that of being a handicapped hospital patient. Partial restoration of function which makes hospitalization unnecessary may result in the patient's returning to the community neither disabled nor fully functional. Such ambiguities in role have been found (Barker, Wright, Meyerson, & Gonick, 1953) to result in stress, frustration, and maladjustment. Fox (1959) questions whether the goals for rehabilitation of the aged are the same as those for younger people. He asks whether it is realistic to expect to restore the elderly person and reintegrate him in a social structure where he is expected to contribute to his own welfare and that of society. Would it be better to attempt to integrate the rehabilitated elderly person at a lower level of social involvement? Presumably this would imply less personal responsibility for his own welfare.

TABLE 1
SOCIAL CHARACTERISTICS AND MEDICAL DIAGNOSES

Item	Research population		Demonstration population	
	Jackson (N=29)	Washtenaw (N=22)	Jackson (N = 40)	Washtenaw (N=35)
Median age	75	74	73	76
Sex				
Male	20	11	27	18
Female	9	11	13	17
Marital status				
Married	3	0	4	1
Single	11	5	16	10
Other	15	17	20	24
Education				
None or no information	4	2	6	4
8 grades or less	13	10	20	15
Above 8 grades	12	10	14	16
Have living children	12	11	16	15
Previous occupation				
Professional	0	2	0	2
Clerical	2	2	2	4
Service	5	6	8	8
Agriculture	5	3	6	6
Skilled	5	2	7	3
Semi- and unskilled	12	7	14	10
Unemployed	—	0	3	2
Months in hospital				
11 or under	10	9	13	15
12 or 23	6	2	10	2
24 and over	13	11	17	18
Major diagnoses*				
Neurological	20	16	30	27
Musculo-skeletal	5	6	8	10
Special senses	8	4	9	7
Cardiovascular	6	2	8	2
Endocrine	1	1	1	1
Pulmonary	1	0	1	0
Other	1	1	2	1

*Multiple diagnoses have been included.

Patient Reaction

We can select case studies which show that for a significant number of people there were dramatic gains. The project is sprinkled with instances of restoring to physical health hopeless, bedridden patients who had given up the struggle for health and normal living; they ultimately returned to their own homes in the community. There are other equally dramatic instances where no amount of medical treatment, psychological motivation, and social therapy—given in a "total-push" program—was able to bring about observable or measurable change. In the face of high costs and limited professional services, one question that must be answered is whether the patients who will respond to therapy can be differentiated from those who will not, thus making prediction possible.

The day nurses, who knew the patients best, made independent rating of each patient on eleven items of possible change (Table 2). The ratings made by the nurses (six at Jackson, nine at Washtenaw) were pooled to get an improvement index in each of the rated areas. Using an improvement index of .40 and above as probably indicating significant observable change, slightly less than 30 per cent of the demonstration population at Washtenaw was judged, on the basis of the nurses' ratings, to have improved. At Jackson, the proportions for the demonstration population are 63 per cent for men and 100 per cent for women. The proportion of the research populations which improved was the same as for the demonstration group except that at Washtenaw slightly more than one-half of the women improved.

The apparent difference in the number improved in the two institutions may be attributed, in part, to the fact that, on an average, the Washtenaw patients were sicker and had less potential for improvement. A more important factor, however, may be the nursing staff itself. At Jackson, the staff morale was very high, and the nurses were eager to take an active part in all aspects of the rehabilitation program. On the other hand, the Washtenaw nurses were under poor supervision and were generally unenthusiastic about their work. Most took no interest in the new rehabilitation services. Thus in the first instance there was probably a positive halo effect; in the latter there was almost certainly a negative one.

At both hospitals greater improvement was judged to have taken place in the categories related to psychological behavior—participation in hospital life, cooperativeness, sociability, and morale—than in those more clearly related to health—appetite, complaints about health,

TABLE 2
DISTRIBUTION OF NURSE EVALUATION PATIENT IMPROVEMENT

A. Demonstration population

Improvement index	Jackson (N=40)				Washtenaw (N=35)			
	Males		Females		Males		Females	
	Number	Percentage	Number	Percentage	Number	Percentage	Number	Percentage
Below .00	1	3.7	—	—	6	33.3	4	23.5
.00 - .19	2	7.4	—	—	3	16.7	5	29.5
.20 - .39	7	25.9	—	—	4	22.2	3	17.6
.40 - .59	5	18.5	4	30.8	2	11.1	1	5.9
.60 - .79	10	37.1	5	38.4	1	5.6	3	17.6
.80 - .99	2	7.4	4	30.8	2	11.1	1	5.9
Total	27	100.0	13	100.0	18	100.0	17	100.0

B. Research population

Improvement index	Jackson (N=29)				Washtenaw (N=22)			
	Males		Females		Males		Females	
	Number	Percentage	Number	Percentage	Number	Percentage	Number	Percentage
Below .00	1	5.0	—	—	4	36.3	2	27.3
.00 - .19	1	5.0	—	—	2	18.2	3	22.7
.20 - .39	5	25.0	—	—	3	27.3	1	18.2
.40 - .59	2	10.0	2	22.2	0	—	1	4.5
.60 - .79	9	45.0	4	44.5	1	9.1	3	18.2
.80 - .99	2	10.0	3	33.3	1	9.1	1	9.1
Total	20	100.0	9	100.0	11	100.0	11	100.0

and so on (Table 3). Men at the Jackson hospital, on an average, showed less change in all categories than did the women; there was no essential difference in the amount of improvement between the men and women at Washtenaw.

TABLE 3
NURSE EVALUATION PATIENT IMPROVEMENT INDEX

	Research population			
	Average improvement index			
	Jackson (N=29)		Washtenaw (N=22)	
Index of change	Males	Females	Males	Females
Appetite	.24	.28	.29	.22
Complaints about health	.40	.55	.21	.20
Requests for medicine	.31	.43	.15	.22
Nursing care required	.33	.56	.21	.18
Endurance in tasks	.57	.85	.05	.15
Morale	.70	.96	.33	.35
Sociability	.70	.83	.21	.29
Cooperativeness	.70	.89	.23	.29
Participation in hospital life	.74	.91	.36	.38
General appearance	.42	.63	.22	.26
Amount of self-care	.42	.69	.16	.17

Sociometric Studies

The purpose of the sociometric studies was to determine whether there were changes in the social responsiveness of the group. It was assumed that if opportunities for interaction were increased and the life space within which the patients functioned were expanded in extent and complexity, the dynamics of the group would be materially changed. A further assumption was that such changes would be in the direction of a higher degree of socialization on the part of the subjects. Results have affirmed these assumptions.

The sociometric test consisted of two questions: (1) Among the patients, whom do you like to visit with most? (2) Among the patients, who is it that makes you the maddest? Patients were encouraged to make as many choices as they wished.

TABLE 4

CHOICES AND REJECTIONS OF PATIENTS BEFORE AND AFTER
PARTICIPATION IN ACTIVITY PROGRAMS

(Research populations)

Choices and rejections	Jackson County Hospital (N=29)			Washtenaw County Hospital (N=22)		
			Tests of significance			Tests of significance
	Test I	Test II	Probability	Test I	Test II	Probability
Choices						
Number of choices	7	20	—*	17	47	$P < .01^4$†
Number who made one or more choices	6	12	$.11^1$	10	20	$.002^1$†
Number who remained unchosen	23	17	$.07^1$	11	5	$.11^1$
Number who chose each other	—	4	$.12^2$	4	20	$P < .01^3$†
Rejections						
Number of rejections	6	16	—*	4	2	—*
Number who rejected one or more	5	12	$.07^1$	2	2	1.00^1
Number who were rejected by one or more	4	10	$.11^1$	2	2	1.00^1
Number who rejected each other	—	2	$.50^2$	—	—	1.00^1

[1] Test for correlated proportions. See McNemar, Q. *Psychological statistics*, (2nd ed.) New York: John Wiley & Sons, 1955. Pp. 56–57.

[2] Fisher's exact test. See Fisher, R. A. *Statistical methods for research workers*. Edinburgh: Oliver and Boyd, Ltd., 1946. Pp. 96–97.

[3] χ^2 test.

[4] t test for difference between correlated means. McNemar, *op. cit.* P. 108.

*A test of significance was not computed because of the lack of a normal distribution in the number of choices and/or rejections made.

†Significant at .01 level.

In both hospitals changes occurred in the expected direction (Table 4). At Washtenaw hospital they were statistically significant in three out of four categories: the total number of choices made, the number of patients who made one or more choices, and the number who chose each other. There were increases in group expansiveness (indicated by the number of choices made by the group), in group integration (indicated by the number of isolates), and in group cohesion (indicated by the number of mutual pairs of choices).

The number of rejections increased among the patients at the Jackson hospital, whereas they decreased at the Washtenaw hospital. In neither instance were the differences statistically significant. The introduction of the rehabilitation program served to release considerable aggression at the Jackson hospital (especially among females). It may be hypothesized that the negative expansiveness of the group changed for reasons similar to those resulting in positive reactions and that any change was preferable to the patients' tendency toward withdrawal, isolation, and unresponsiveness. Perhaps, then, the positive and negative responses could be combined without reference to sign, making the expansiveness of the Jackson group about equal to that of the Washtenaw group at the time of the second testing. Although one may argue that the adjustment of the Washtenaw patients is more desirable, the problem personalities at Jackson nevertheless entered group activities without disruption of goals, and, according to the nurses, they improved in cooperativeness and morale.

The sociometric data show changes not only in group structure, but also in the status of the individual patients. Patients who were obscure at the beginning of the program emerged as high-status people in both hospitals; a few suffered declines in social status. Although the sociometric data do not give clues about the causes of changes in group structure and status relationships of individual patients, they do correspond to the changes expected from improved physical status and function and the patients' participation in a program of varied activities. For example, the sheltered workshop enjoyed considerable prestige, thus people who became leaders in the workshop enjoyed improved social status. It may be concluded that patient participation in rehabilitation activities produced a more highly structured and socialized hospital community and afforded the patients an opportunity to take roles which improved their status, positive expansiveness, and close relationships—all characteristics associated with good personal adjustment.

The Chicago Attitude Scale of Adjustment

The Chicago attitude scale (Cavan et al., 1949) was designed to indicate whether adjustment of older people is good, average, or poor in eight categories—health, friends, work, money, religion, usefulness, happiness, and family. Scores are computed for each category, and the sum of six is used as a measure of general adjustment level.

The hospital populations showed low-average adjustment (Table 5) on the basis of the norms established for a normal noninstitutionalized population. When the attitude scores made by the patients at the time of the first testing period (I) are compared with those made at the close of the active rehabilitation period nine months later (II), it is found that a few of the patients in each hospital improved in adjustment, a few worsened, and most remained in the same range with a slight shift toward better adjustment (Table 5).

TABLE 5

ATTITUDE SCALE

DISTRIBUTION OF SCORES FOR THE TWO HOSPITAL
RESEARCH POPULATIONS FOR RATINGS AT TWO TIMES

Adjustment rating	*Attitude score*	*Jackson (N = 29)*		*Washtenaw (N = 22)*		*Both (N = 51)*	
		I	II	I	II	I	II
Good	6						
	5	1	1		3	1	4
Average	4	4	11	3	4	7	15
	3	11	10	9	7	20	17
	2	12	4	6	3	18	7
Poor	1	1	2	4	5	5	7
	0		1				1

When the scores made in the separate attitude categories at the first and second testing are compared, they show that most improvement took place in the areas where it would have been expected that the rehabilitation program would have the greatest impact—work, money, usefulness, and family (Table 6). One exception is health. The medical team judged that the general level of health and physical function was improved in a significant number of patients, yet the change was not reflected in the attitudes of the patients toward their health. Even though improved, most still suffered from one or more major chronic conditions, which perhaps accounted for the patients' unchanged health attitudes.

TABLE 6
ATTITUDE SCALE:
AVERAGE ADJUSTMENT SCORES

Adjustment Category	Jackson (N=29)		Washtenaw (N=22)		Both	
	Test I	Test II	Test I	Test II	Test I	Test II
Health	3.6	3.8	2.8	3.0	3.2	3.4
Friends	3.2	3.2	3.1	3.3	3.2	3.3
Work	2.5	3.3	2.3	2.7	2.4	3.0
Money	2.9	3.4	2.6	3.1	2.8	3.3
Religion	4.4	4.6	5.0	5.1	4.7	4.9
Usefulness	2.6	3.0	2.4	2.8	2.5	2.9
Happiness	2.7	2.7	1.8	2.1	2.3	2.4
Family	3.7	4.2	3.9	4.4	3.8	4.3

Both hospital groups made the highest scores in the category of religion. This was true for both the first and second testings. The investigators believe that the patients tended to give the expected conventional answers rather than their true attitudes. The case histories of most of the patients showed little evidence of a positive attitude toward religion in their earlier years or of more than minimal religious participation in their later years.

Two Selected Groups

When the average scores made on the attitude scale at the first testing were plotted against those made at the second testing, two clear-cut groups appeared. One was a group of patients who scored lowest in the group at both the first and second testing (the "low group"). The other was a group that scored relatively low—but higher than the first group—at the first testing and scored the highest in the study population on the second testing (the "high group"). When other data for the members of these two groups are compared, some fairly consistent differences appear (Table 7).

On the average, the scores of the low group in both hospitals

TABLE 7

COMPARISON OF TWO GROUPS SELECTED ON BASIS
OF ATTITUDE SCALE SCORES

	Jackson Hospital		*Washtenaw*	
	Low group (N=5)	High group (N=5)	Low group (N=5)	High group (N=6)
Percentage of males	100	60	60	66
Average age	69	74	72	70
Age range	54-88	62-82	59-77	56-84
Average number of months in hospital	76	32	22	26
Range of months in hospital	4-208	6-57	8-59	6-53
Range of years of education	8-10	0-10	7-12	5-12
Range in I.Q.	83-107*	82-102*	65-113*	77-108*
Improvement index†	.37	.62	.01	.68
Level of participation‡	1.2	3.0	1.6	2.4
Attitude scale (I)	2.6	3.3	1.7	3.8
Attitude scale (II)	1.9	4.5	1.4	4.8
Morale scale (I)	1.4	2.4	1.6	3.5
Morale scale (II)	1.0	4.2	1.0	4.5
Health self-rating (I)§	2.4	2.6	1.6	2.0
Health self-rating (II)	1.2	2.8	1.4	2.5

*Intelligence scores not available on all members of the group.

†Average of nurses' evaluation improvement scale.

‡Rated according to number of times participated when well enough to take part. Levels of participation were assigned the following scores: high 3, medium 2, low 1.

§Self-rating of health was assigned the following scores: poor 1, fair 2, or good 3.

were worse on the second testing than on the first. This was true not only in the attitude scale which was used to differentiate them from the group as a whole, but also for the morale scale and the self-rating of health status. The high groups in both institutions showed the reverse trend. Selected because there was improvement in their attitude-scale scores on the second testing, they showed the same directional trend on the morale scale and health rating. In short, the patients who were very poorly adjusted at the first testing, as measured by the attitude scale, moved in the direction of even poorer adjustment in spite of a more therapeutic milieu and a total-push rehabilitation program. On the other hand, patients who were average in adjustment at the beginning of the project moved in the direction of better adjustment during the same period under the same regimen. Any improvement was reflected in the evaluation of patient improvement made by the nurses; those in the low group showed considerably less or no improvement during the project, whereas the high group showed marked improvement in both hospitals.

The social and psychological data do not explain differences in the two groups' response to the total-push rehabilitation program. Table 7 shows that sex, age, length of stay in the hospital, and educational level are not determining factors. Probably intelligence is not a determining factor either, although ratings were not available for all patients. Level of participation, which was higher for the high groups, is not necessarily responsible for their achievement of better adjustment. If the two groups are compared in respect to medical diagnoses, there is still no essential difference.

Levels of Rehabilitation

The ultimate measures of the practical success of a demonstration program such as ours are how many patients were rehabilitated and at what functional level they stabilized. Since institutionalization is costly in our society and since it fosters dependency and promotes personality deterioration, the best outcome is to have patients restored to a level where they can take their place as independent, self-supporting citizens of the community.

Of the seventy-five patients who were members of the combined Jackson-Washtenaw demonstration population, nearly three-quarters achieved higher levels of independence and self-sufficiency (Table 8). Fourteen per cent were improved to the point that they could maintain themselves completely and be considered for employment. Another 30 per cent were made capable of living in the community with only minimal supervision and assistance and of undertaking some work, if it was available, on a limited scale.

TABLE 8

PLACEMENT PLANS FOR REHABILITATED PATIENTS AT CLOSE OF DEMONSTRATION PROJECT

Type of placement	*Number of patients recommended for discharge*	
	Jackson (Total $N=40$)	Washtenaw (Total $N=35$)
Own home or independent quarters	7	3
Boarding home with meals and housekeeping provided	5	1
Foster home with family-type supervision	5	11
Nursing home offering personal care	7	12
Nursing home offering skilled nursing care	4	2
Total	28	29

Impact on the Hospitals
and the Community

Both hospitals have enlarged their staffs in order to continue all the specific therapeutic programs instituted during the demonstration. The nursing staff is being upgraded by the addition of more trained personnel. The Washtenaw Hospital Medical Service has been brought under the aegis of The University of Michigan Hospital, which now provides the services of a medical director and two residents. The Jackson community voted on a bond issue to build a new county facility which will be located in the city and will provide a rehabilitation outpatient clinic, sheltered workshop, and other services to the community as a whole, thus ensuring reduction of the hospital patients' isolation.

Another important gain for the community was the demonstration that rehabilitative care of patients need be no more costly than custodial care. Results of the patient-discharge program are presently available only for the Jackson hospital. In this institution, 20 per cent of the original study population were discharged to non-nursing, lower-cost settings. Of those discharged, the net saving to the county averaged $3.50 a day for each patient. This figure represents the mean daily difference between post- and predischarge costs of these patients to the county. Although it is too early to know how many of the discharged patients might be readmitted during the first year after discharge, a conservative projection based on experience to date would indicate this figure to be less than one-third. If this holds and if the discharge, a conservative projection based on experience to date would mean a saving of approximately sixty cents a day for each bed in the hospital or $1,100 a year for each patient discharged. Although the cost of providing the appropriate physical and psychosocial restorative services would just about match this figure, better service can be provided, and more patients can be cared for at no extra cost to the community.

DISCUSSION

Results of the study may be evaluated with reference to the theories of social aging previously discussed.

Most of the patients could be rated as already extensively disengaged from the social system of their community at the outset of the project. In part, the disengagement is the result of illness's having forced them into the hospital; in part, it is society's rejection of indigent people who are objects of public charity. Also, if disengagement is the natural process of aging, the elderly patients in the group would, on this basis alone, already have achieved a new inner equilibrium requiring a lower level of social involvement.

We find support for the assumption that disengagement is natural when our findings are judged against the criteria of disengagement proposed by Cumming and her associates (Cumming, Dean, Newell, & McCaffery, 1960). For example, we found that the rate and variety of interaction with the community are negligible or entirely lacking—many of the patients have not been away from the hospital for years although they are ambulatory and able to make the effort. Their life space is no larger than the confines of the hospital yard; for some it is restricted to the hospital building itself, and for a few it is no greater than the hospital bed in which they lie day after day. Obviously all these patients must be experiencing a marked reduction in amount and kind of interaction in comparison to the middle years of their lives.

Further, although we have no indication about the extent of self-absorption the patients had in their earlier lives, we do know that most are greatly preoccupied with themselves. To a question about the three wishes they would most like to have granted, many of the patients gave answers which showed interests restricted to themselves: "I'd like to get well," "I'd like to be able to leave this place," "I'd like to be the way I used to be," "I'd like to be able to work," "I'd like a better mattress on my bed" were typical self-directed wishes. If, as Cumming et al. (1960) suggest, disengagement and an equilibrium which is realistic in the social circumstances are natural to and desired by older people, the patients in the study should have high morale and have been well-adjusted. This is not the case, however; measures indicate that the group as a whole has poor morale—only one person at the outset, and only three at the close, of the rehabilitation phase achieved a rating of good adjustment.

Inasmuch as the rehabilitation program was conceived in terms of the activity theory, it sought to provide opportunities for the patients to engage intensively in a variety of activities, to establish and express personal relationships, to take clear-cut roles similar to those of younger and noninstitutionalized people, and to expand the perception of their life space to include the economic and social lives of the community. In short, every effort was made to re-engage the patients by restoring function and providing channels through which re-engagement could take place. Results show that for most of the patients a higher level of interaction was achieved and that responsiveness to others in the environment increased. Morale tended to improve, and it improved more for those who participated more. Also, adjustment improved in the categories of usefulness, money, family, and work, all of which imply satisfactions associated with the goals of middle life.

On the basis of objective measures, we do not know whether life satisfaction is greater at the lower level of disengagement or whether it is greater after the patient achieved a higher equilibrium of involvement. If interview material and case histories are analyzed, however, we find much satisfaction expressed by those patients who improved functionally, who returned to the community, or who had an expanded life space and roles whose expectancies they knew, though they were still confined to the hospital.

In conclusion, it appears that we need definitive studies to determine the best theoretical construct on which to base practical programs of rehabilitation and goals for a therapeutic milieu. We need to know whether it is a disservice to re-engage aged, chronically ill patients into the more complex social structure if, as Cumming suggests, the ultimate task of disengagement is to strike an equilibrium where the individual can prepare for death. Should rehabilitation stop short of re-engagement and merely strive to keep the individual comfortable while he prepares for death? Obviously the answer would have profound implications for the future care and treatment of the aged.

REFERENCES

Albrecht, Ruth. Social roles in the prevention of senility. *J. Geront.*, 1951, **6,** 380-386.
Anderson, J. The use of time and energy. In J.E. Birren (Ed.), *Handbook of aging and the individual: Psychological and biological aspects.* Chicago: The University of Chicago Press, 1959. Pp. 769-796. (© 1959 by The University of Chicago)
Barker, R.G., Wright, Beatrice A., Meyerson, L., & Gonick, Mollie R. Adjustment to physical handicap and illness: A survey of social psychology of physique and disability. *Social Sci. Res. Council Bull.*, 1953, No. 55 (rev.). (New York)
Blau, Zena S. Changes in status and age identification. *Amer. sociol. Rev.*, 1956, **21,** 198-203.
Bloomer, H.H. Communication problems among aged county hospital patients. *Geriatrics*, 1960, **15,** 291-295.
Brandt, R.L. Decreased carbohydrate tolerance in elderly patients. *Geriatrics,* 1960, **15,** 315-325.
Brandt, R.L., & Tupper, C.J. Medical appraisal of elderly county hospital patients. *Geriatrics*, 1960, **15,** 233-253.
Cavan, Ruth S., Burgess, E.W., Havighurst, R.J., & Goldhamer, H. *Personal adjustment in old age.* Chicago: Science Research Associates, 1949.
Cumming, Elaine, Dean, Lois R., Newell, D.S., & McCaffery, Isabel. Disengagement—a tentative theory of aging. *Sociometry*, 1960, **23,** 23-35.
Cumming, Elaine, & Henry, W.E. *Growing old: A view in depth of the social and psychological processes in aging.* New York: Basic Books, 1961.
Currier, R.D. Neurologic findings in county hospital patients. *Geriatrics,* 1960, **15,** 254-263.
Di Napoli, A., Kingery, R.H., & Gibbons, P. Dental conditions of county hospital patients. *Geriatrics*, 1960, **15,** 306-314.
Donahue, Wilma. Social gerontology: A frame of reference for a study in the rehabilitation of the aged. In *Le vieillissement de fonctions psychologiques et psychophysiologiques.* Paris, France: Colloques Internationaux du Centre National de la Recherche Scientifique, XCVI, 1960. Pp. 303-322.
Donahue, Wilma, Hunter, W.W., Coons, Dorothy, & Maurice, Helen. Rehabilitation of geriatric patients in county hospitals. *Geriatrics,* 1960, **15,** 263-274.

Donahue, Wilma, & Rae, J.W., Jr. Design for a study of geriatric rehabilitation. *Geriatrics,* 1960, **15,** 229-232.

Fox, J.H. Sociological factors in the rehabilitation of the aging. *Newsletter (Geront. Soc.),* 1959, **6** (3), 38-41.

Havighurst, R.J. The social competence of middle-aged people. *Genet. Psychol. Monogr.,* 1957, **56,** 297-373.

Hebb, D.O. The mammal and his environment, *Amer. J. Psychiat.,* 1955, **111,** 826-831.

Henry, W.E. Affective complexity and role perceptions: Some suggestions for a conceptual framework for the study of adult personality. In J.E. Anderson (Ed.), *Psychological aspects of aging.* Washington, D.C.: American Psychological Association, 1956. Pp. 30-41.

Heron, W. The pathology of boredom. *Sci. Amer.,* 1957, **196,** 52-56.

Kutner, B., Fanshel, D., Togo, Alice M., & Langner, T.S. *Five hundred over sixty: A community survey of aging.* New York: Russell Sage Foundation, 1956.

Mering, O. von, & King, S.H. *Remotivating the mental patient.* New York: Russell Sage Foundation, 1957.

Phillips, B.S. A role theory approach to adjustments in old age. *Amer. sociol. Rev.,* 1957, **22,** 212-217.

Smith, E.M., Brandt, R.L., & Currier, R.D. Medical care needs and rehabilitation potential. *Geriatrics,* 1960, **15,** 296-305.

Swartz, M.S. What is a therapeutic milieu? In M. Greenblatt, D.J. Levinson, & R.H. Williams (Eds.), *The patient and the mental hospital.* Glencoe, Ill.: The Free Press, 1957. Pp. 130-144.

Winter, Kenton E. Michigan survey of geriatric nursing facilities. *Geriatrics,* 1960, **15,** 275-290.

PART FOUR

*Summary and
Conclusions*

CHAPTER 27

Implications for Future Research

RICHARD H. WILLIAMS

Aging is a complex process which tends to involve decrements, especially on the psychophysiological level, but which may also produce increments in understanding and maturation of the personality. Does the brain age? In the case of man, do the brain systems (brain stem, limbic stem, and neocortical system) age, and, if they do, do they age at different rates? More research, particularly on such lesser-known levels of the brain as the limbic system, is needed before a reasonably definitive answer can be given to these questions. There are suggestions that it may be possible to develop a global indicator of the level of functioning of these systems acting in unison. If so, it might be possible to predict dangers, such as strokes, and take preventive measures.

That speed of performance varies with age is well-documented in relation to both simple motor response and associative processes. The evidence is sufficiently convincing to imply some general process, yet the exact nature of this process remains to be discovered. Some psychological functions appear to vary little with chronological age in the later years, and there is suggestive evidence that for them style of life may be more important than the number of years lived. Studies of behavioral functioning as such are rewarding in that they are beginning to show uniformities and produce testable hypotheses. They should be pursued even though it may not yet be possible to refine these uniformities into an explanation on the neurophysiological level.

The study of change in psychological functioning with age is further complicated by changes in social systems. For example, in a society which, over time, has placed increasing demands on its members to perform certain complex tasks, differences between generations may appear as psychological deficits in cross-sectional studies. Analysis of the fit between social requirements and psychological capacity, however, is one of the most promising avenues of research. Given the current knowledge about slowing with age and changes in short-term storage, it should be well within our capabilities to develop optimal pacing and reduction in overloads in the later years. Insofar as there are decrements of psychological functioning with age, the supports and deprivations in the environment take on added significance for total functioning and well-being.

Degrees of penetration into, and engagement with, the social system are proving to be highly important variables in relation to fit between personality and culture. In turn the degree of fit is crucial to success or breakdown during the process of aging. How much does personality change with age? This question is also difficult to answer. The evidence suggests that changes do occur, but only beyond a certain threshold do they manifest themselves in patterns of social functioning.

Studies of extreme behavioral breakdown in the form of geriatric mental disorders should do much to illuminate the crises that, to some degree, are always present in aging. Here again we are not very far in basic understanding, but important beginnings have been made. Classification systems are being improved, and some progress is being made in differentiating the etiological contribution of biological, life-history, and situational factors. It is heartening, too, that applicable knowledge is being produced even though only approximate answers are available about etiology. Much has been learned about rehabilitation, the achievement of optimal social functioning with the available psychological and biological resources.

A most promising line of research is focusing on the whole action complex of individual people over a period of time. Such studies would throw light on the validity of diagnostic assessments. They would also be important in learning to detect early danger signs such as decline in ability to handle new situations. We need to move toward studies of life expectancy for various kinds of breakdowns, especially the mental disorders. Such research would make it possible to identify populations at risk. It would lead, in turn, to better understanding of why they are at risk and hence to better formulation of ways to prevent breakdown.

Do people age successfully by a gradual process of disengagement from some of their social demands and transactions, or do they age successfully by actively seeking modes of involvement? It seems clear that people must fill their life space meaningfully if psychological functioning is to be adequate. But the size of the individual social system, the degree of engagement with it, and how populated it is with roles and activities vary within the normal range and move differently in different pathologies.

The theory of disengagement was first developed as a theory of the aging process, rather than as a theory of successful aging, although it may well have implications for the latter. It is a reasonable hypothesis that mature people will disengage in a mature way in their eighties and find further self-realization in their disengagement. Less mature people are likely to disengage defensively by withdrawal or denial in their early seventies or even in their sixties. Still less mature people may remain engaged, but in an angry or self-hating fashion. In favoring disengagement or engagement, the societal context is also important. It is this contact which is the major focus of Volume II.

From an analysis of this volume emerges a definition of age which should prove valuable for future research. The age of any given population group is its life expectancy in reverse. It is old if its life expectancy is short, young if it is long. This is not an empty play on words. It points to the importance of viability—biological viability and the viability of the psychological and action systems—in relation to aging. A group of patients with terminal cancer is very old, regardless of chronological age. Given two people of the same health and chronological age, the person with a cramped personality and blocked action system which have only slim chances for persistence without serious breakdown is older than a mature person with a viably persistent system. The study of aging is thus the study of permanence and change in living organisms, with particular attention to that phase of the life cycle in which there is greater probability of change associated with decreased viability. It is the study of the organism's distance from death or psychosocial breakdown. In a simplified manner, it can be viewed as a four-fold table (Table 1).

TABLE 1

1	Biologically far Psychosocially far	2	Biologically near Psychosocially far
3	Biologically far Psychosocially near	4	Biologically near Psychosocially near

Note—"Near" and "far" refer to distance from death or breakdown.

In its applied phase, gerontology is concerned with ways to increase the viability of the organism and thus increase the distance from death or breakdown. Boxes 1-4 in this table may be thought of as a continuum of successful aging.

SUBJECT INDEX

Volume I

NAME INDEX

Volume I